SHRUBS
AND
CLIMBERS

SHRUBS
— AND —
CLIMBERS

A COMPLETE GUIDE TO SUCCESSFUL PLANTING AND GROWING

RICHARD BIRD

Photography by Jonathan Buckley

LORENZ BOOKS

First published in 1999 by Lorenz Books

© Anness Publishing Limited 1999

Lorenz Books is an imprint of
Anness Publishing Limited
Hermes House
88-89 Blackfriars Road
London SE1 8HA

This edition distributed in Canada by
Raincoast Books, 8680 Cambie Street
Vancouver, British Columbia V6P 6M9

ISBN 1 85967 983 8

A CIP catalogue record for this book is available from the British Library

Publisher: Joanna Lorenz
Senior Editor: Caroline Davison
Editors: Deborah Savage, Alison Bolus
Designer: Ian Sandom
Production Controller: Sarah Tucker
Photographer: Jonathan Buckley

Previously published in two separate volumes, *Sensational Shrubs* and
Glorious Climbers

Printed in Hong Kong/China

1 3 5 7 9 10 8 6 4 2

Half title page: *Salvia officinalis* 'Icterina'.
Frontispiece: Honeysuckle.
Title page: *Rosa* 'Zéphirine Drouhin', *Clematis* 'Lady Betty
Balfour' and *Vitis coignetiae*.
Above: *Pyracantha* hedge.
Opposite (top left): *Choisya ternata*.
Opposite (bottom left): *Rosa* 'Iceberg'.
Opposite (top right): *Campsis radicans*.
Opposite (bottom right): *Rhododendron*.

CONTENTS

INTRODUCTION   6

GARDENING TECHNIQUES   14

PLANTING AND MAINTENANCE   16

PRUNING   40

PROPAGATION   56

SHRUBS   66

DESIGNING A BORDER   68

CHOOSING SHRUBS   76

SHRUBS FOR ALL SEASONS   110

CLIMBERS   128

TYPES OF CLIMBERS   130

TRAINING CLIMBERS   148

SHRUBS LIST   178

CLIMBERS LIST   182

INDEX   186

ACKNOWLEDGEMENTS   192

INTRODUCTION

Shrubs and climbers are two of the most important groups of plants in any garden. For the casual gardener, they are highly attractive as well as relatively easy to care for, while for the keen gardener, who is perhaps a little more ambitious, they can prove the structural mainstay of the garden design and provide experience in a wide range of useful gardening techniques.

The most successful gardens are those that provide visual interest throughout the year. Although few plants can look stunning all the time, one of the advantages of some shrubs and climbers is that the flowers may be followed by attractive berries in autumn. Many shrubs and climbers are also evergreen, of course, which means that even once the flowers have faded you still have a

Above: *This lilac,* Syringa × henryi, *makes an attractive deciduous shrub with small pink flowers that are very fragrant.*

Above: *Jasmine (*Jasminum*), a climber, can always be relied on to provide a rich, sweet scent in the garden.*

leafy background against which to plant autumn- and winter-flowering bulbs and perennials.

One tends to think of shrubs and climbers in terms of the colour of their flowers – and the contribution these colours can make to your overall planting scheme. However, it is important to remember that the foliage of shrubs and climbers can also bring plenty of colour to the garden, often throughout the year. The colour range includes an infinite variety of greens as well as rich golds, subtle silvers, vivid purples and variegation of all kinds.

In the spring, the flower colours of shrubs and climbers are bright and fresh-looking, including a host of pinks and yellows, while in the autumn they have their final fling with a burst of glorious reds, golds and browns. As well as providing foliage colour and structure all year round, evergreen shrubs – and climbers, too, for that matter – can be invaluable when used as screens or grown as hedges. It should not be forgotten that, as with the flowers, the foliage may be cut and used for indoor decoration, especially in the winter.

Above: *The white flowers of mock orange* (Philadelphus coronarius) *have a wonderfully heady scent, reminiscent of oranges.*

Above: *The Chinese jasmine* (Trachelospermum jasminoides) *is a handsome evergreen climber with very fragrant white flowers.*

Although flower colour is the predominant reason for choosing most plants, the wide variety of shapes and leaf textures is of equal importance. Shrubs, for example, can be round and squat, tall and thin, open like fountains or run flat along the ground. Each of these forms and shapes has its place in the design of the garden. Although it may be the colour of the leaves or the brief flowering period that has the impact, the shape is generally more important. As a silhouette, a tall thin shape seen in the background can be very effective, acting as a focal point and drawing the eye into the distance. This design device can be used to make a garden seem larger than it actually is. Similarly, a fountain of branches can make a very striking feature. Shrubs with an attractive arching form include the white-flowered *Exochorda* × *macrantha* 'The Bride' and *Spiraea nipponica* 'Snowmound', also with white flowers. Another interesting shape is the evergreen *Mahonia media* 'Charity' which has spikes of scented yellow flowers and large leaves made up of spiny leaflets.

While evergreen shrubs provide effective all-year-round focal points, particularly in the rather less colourful winter months, it is important to remember that other shrubs, too, can have an equally dramatic appearance. For example, the skeletal outline of the branches of many

Above: Euonymus fortunei *'Emerald 'n' Gold' is an evergreen shrub whose variegated leaves have a pink tinge in winter.*

Above: *The flowering climbing* Hydrangea anomala *subsp.* petiolaris *is one of the few climbers that do well in shade, particularly on cool walls.*

deciduous shrubs can look just as beautiful as evergreens against a winter sky or when covered with frost.

Some shrubs can be grown as hedges and used to create barriers, both to keep people and animals from trespassing, and also to provide an element of privacy from the world outside. Hedges have numerous other functions. For example, they make excellent windbreaks, being more effective than a solid boundary, such as a wall, which can create a wind pocket at its base. They also act as a backdrop to the other plants in the border, often contributing much to the overall impact of the colour scheme. Hedges may also create useful screens and dividers within the garden itself, breaking the area down into smaller units. If you are lucky enough to have a large garden, there is nothing more intriguing than wandering from one garden "room" to the next and discovering different designs and colour schemes. In addition, shrubs that are grown as hedges are perfect for screening off ugly utility buildings, such as garages and sheds, or perhaps areas where dustbins (trash cans), oil tanks or washing lines are kept.

Shrubs can also be used to make up the whole of, or just a part of, a border. Unlike herbaceous plants and annuals, they are a constant feature of the border and can be used

Above: *The calico bush (*Kalmia latifolia*) is a magnificent rhododendron-like evergreen with large clusters of cup-shaped flowers.*

Above: *The attractive leaves of the evergreen Oregon grape (*Mahonia aquifolium*) turn wine-red in the winter.*

to provide a permanent planting structure. The various shapes provided by shrubs come into their own here because different shrubs must fit in with and enhance their neighbours in the bed to create a pleasing arrangement. Shrubs can be planted in groups of contrasting varieties, or in a group of one variety for massed effect. Used as a single specimen, they make good focal points, perhaps at the end of a path or in a lawn.

As well as looking good in the border or as specimens in the lawn, shrubs can also be used successfully in containers. They require much more attention than they would get in the open ground, mainly because they need

Above: *The Japanese hydrangea vine* (Schizophragma hydrangeoides) *is a deciduous climber that attaches to its support by means of aerial roots. The deep green leaves are silvery beneath. The flat flowerheads of creamy flowers are surrounded by lemon-coloured bracts in summer.*

constant watering, but the effort is definitely well worth it, especially if you only have a paved patio or a small balcony in which to garden. Remember that shape is very important when you choose a shrub for planting in a pot because it is usually seen in isolation.

Climbers can also be used as trailing plants and grown down a wall while smaller climbers may hang down from baskets. Why not use climbers, such as clematis, as scrambling plants and allow them to grow over bushes or low trees or simply let them spread across the ground, smothering the weeds as they go? Ivy, with its dense evergreen foliage, is an excellent ground-covering climber. You can also grow climbers up permanent structures such as wooden or metal tripods or use annual varieties in conjunction with temporary structures, such as a wigwam (teepee) of canes or pea-sticks.

Above: *Berberis are mainly grown for their rounded to cup-shaped, usually yellow, flowers. Some varieties are evergreen; the deciduous ones have attractive coloured foliage in autumn.*

Above: *The Etruscan honeysuckle (*Lonicera etrusca*) is a twining, woody-stemmed climber. The pink buds open as fragrant, pale yellow flowers which turn a deeper yellow with age.*

Shrubs and climbers are not difficult to grow. Indeed, in many ways they are amongst the easiest of garden plants to cultivate. The pruning of shrubs and climbers is often considered to be the most difficult aspect of their cultivation but like everything else in gardening it is simply a matter of experience and practice. You cannot be expected to know instinctively how to prune; it is something that must be learnt. Fortunately, it is not difficult and will soon become as easy as slicing bread.

If you are really put off by the thought of pruning, then you can always choose shrubs and climbers that need little or no pruning.

The propagation of shrubs and climbers is not an essential garden task. You can always simply buy your plants from the local garden centre. However, for many people, propagation is one of the most enjoyable aspects of gardening. It is truly magical to take a small seed or piece of stem and turn it into a fully-grown, flourishing plant. Propagation is not difficult; it simply needs a bit of practice.

There are literally thousands of spectacular shrubs and climbers to choose from. In many ways, the choosing is sometimes more daunting than the actual "doing". However, planning and creating a garden is both exciting and rewarding, and whether you thumb through books and catalogues looking for your favourite plants or visit local gardens and nurseries so that you can make a selection from those you see, you will gain a great deal of pleasure when the plants are in your own garden and growing well. After all, pleasure and enjoyment are what gardening is really all about.

Left: *The yew* (Taxus baccata*) is one of the best hedging and topiary plants, its dark green, needle-like leaves forming a dense, impenetrable thicket. It copes well with wind, pollution and drought, and makes a good boundary hedge. The flowers are barely visible, and are followed by small, cup-shaped, red berries. The leaves are highly poisonous. It grows in any good well-drained soil in sun or deep shade. Shown here is one of the Aurea Group.*

Right: Daphne *is a genus of evergreen, semi-evergreen and deciduous shrubs that are largely grown for their tubular flowers. These are usually beautifully scented. This* Daphne × burkwoodii *'Somerset' is a semi-evergreen, upright-growing shrub that produces thick clusters of highly fragrant white and pink flowers in late spring. Occasionally, there is a second burst of flowers in the autumn. Another species,* D. odora, *has fragrant flowers in mid-winter to early spring. Some species of daphne are also grown for their foliage or fruits although the seeds are poisonous.*

GARDENING TECHNIQUES

All the techniques needed to grow shrubs and climbers successfully are simple and often require no more than a little common sense. In this section of the book, as well as explaining how to grow shrubs and climbers, there are detailed instructions on preparing the soil ready for planting, weeding and mulching, and watering and feeding. There is also guidance on specific techniques for shrubs and climbers, including staking shrubs and providing support for climbers. Learning comes with practice, so use this section as a helpful starting point. However, to really know and understand your plants and garden, you will have to go outside and get your hands dirty!

Left: Ampelopsis glandulosa *var.* brevipedunculata *'Elegans' is a vigorous climber grown for its attractive foliage.*

PLANTING AND MAINTENANCE

Soil Preparation

One of the most important of all gardening techniques is soil preparation. It is the foundation of all future growth and success. Since both climbers and shrubs are likely to stay in the same position for many years, it is essential to prepare the ground well before planting. Inadequate attention to preparation at the outset is difficult to remedy once the plant has put down roots and become established.

REMOVING THE WEEDS

The first stage is to rid the ground of weeds. Annual weeds are a minor nuisance and, over a period, they will slowly be eliminated as their seed store in the ground is reduced. The real problem is persistent perennial weeds. If only one piece of these remains, it will soon regrow, and will be impossible to eradicate once the roots become entwined in those of the shrub or climber. In soft, friable soils, these weeds can be removed by hand as the ground is dug over. However, in heavier soils, the only reliable way is to use a chemical weedkiller. Modern herbicides are safe to use as long as the instructions on the packet are rigorously followed.

CONDITIONING THE SOIL

It is important to improve the condition of the soil before you start to plant. Digging is vital, as it breaks up the soil, allowing moisture and air to enter. As you dig the soil, incorporate well-rotted organic material to provide nutrients for the plants' growth. This will also improve drainage in heavy soils, creating a more crumbly consistency, while in light, free-draining soils it will increase retention of water and nutrients.

The best organic material is garden compost, which takes time to prepare: garden waste matter (with woody stems cut into small pieces, or left to rot down first) is piled up together with fruit and vegetable peelings from the kitchen, and left to break down naturally. Well-rotted manure and other proprietary soil conditioners can also be used. If possible, you should prepare an area of at least 1 m (3 ft) in diameter, so that the roots of the shrub or climber can spread out into good soil as they grow.

Above: *Climbers will grow vigorously in good, fertile soil. Here, ivy is being trained around a shape to create topiary.*

Left: *Soil preparation may seem tedious, but it will help to ensure a magnificent display of flowers, as in this* Escallonia *'Gwendolyn Anley'*

MAKING A NEW BED IN A LAWN

1 Choose the site of the bed and mark out its shape. This can be done with a hosepipe (garden hose), moving it around until you have the shape you want. Then dig around it with a spade, lawn edger or hoe.

2 For a circular bed, place a post in the centre of the proposed circle and tie a piece of string to it. Attach a sharp stick or tool at the radius (half the diameter) of the circle and, with the string pulled taut, scribe a circle around the central post. An alternative is to tie a bottle filled with sand to the string and allow the sand to trickle out as you move the bottle round the circle.

3 If the grass contains pernicious and persistent weeds, remove them before digging. The only sure way is to kill them with a herbicide. If the surrounding grass is full of such weeds, these should also be killed or they will soon encroach on the bed.

4 With many lawn grasses, it will not be necessary to use herbicide; simply skim off the surface grass and dig out any roots that remain.

5 Dig the soil, removing any weeds and stones. If possible, double dig the soil, breaking up the lower spit (spade's depth) but not bringing this soil to the surface.

6 Mix plenty of organic material into both layers of the soil, but especially the bottom layer, to encourage the roots to grow deeply.

7 If possible, leave the bed to weather for a few months after digging; then remove any residual weeds that have appeared. When you are ready to plant, add some well-rotted compost or ready-prepared soil conditioner to the soil and lightly fork it in. The weather should have broken the soil down to a certain extent, but the rain will also have compacted it. Lightly fork it over to loosen the soil, break down any lumps and work in any soil conditioner.

8 Rake the soil level, to give it its final tilth, but with a channel round the edge to allow you to trim the edge of the lawn.

Planting Shrubs

There is nothing difficult about planting a shrub, except possibly making the decision as to where to plant it. One thing that must always be borne in mind is that shrubs *do* grow, and it is a common mistake to underestimate by how much. The result is that shrubs are often planted too close together and then the gardener is faced with the heart-rending decision as to which to dig out so that the others can continue to grow. Avoid this by finding out how big the plant will grow and allowing for this when planting. This means there will be gaps between the shrubs for the first few years but these can be temporarily filled with herbaceous perennials and annuals.

PLANTING CARE

If you are planting more than one shrub at a time, stand them all, still in their pots, on the bed in the places where you wish to plant them, so that you can check that they will all fit in and that the arrangement is a good one. Make any adjustments before you begin to plant, as it does the shrubs no good to be dug up and replanted several times because you have put them in the wrong place.

The actual planting is not a difficult process but looking after the plant once it is planted is important. Water it well until it becomes established. If the site is a windy one, protect either the whole bed or individual shrubs with windbreak netting, until they are firmly established. In really hot weather, light shading will help relieve stress on the plant as its new roots struggle to get enough moisture to supply the rapidly transpiring leaves.

Other aspects to consider in positioning shrubs are discussed elsewhere in the book.

PLANTING TIMES

The recommended time for planting shrubs is at any time between autumn and early spring provided that the weather allows you to do so. Planting should not take place if the weather is too wet or too cold or if the ground is waterlogged or frozen.

However this advice is basically for bare-rooted plants – that is, those dug up from nursery beds. Although container-grown plants are easier to establish if planted at the same time, it is possible to plant out at any time of the year as long as the rootball is not disturbed. If planting takes place in the summer, then avoid doing it during very hot or dry weather. The plants will need constant watering and protection from the effects of drying winds and strong sun.

1 Before you start planting, check that the plant has been watered. If not, give it a thorough soaking, preferably at least an hour before planting.

2 If the soil has not been recently prepared, fork it over, removing any weeds. Add a slow-release fertilizer, such as bonemeal, wearing rubber or vinyl gloves if required, and fork this in.

3 Dig the hole, preferably much wider than the rootball of the shrub. Place the plant, still in its pot, in the hole and check that the hole is deep enough by placing a stick or cane across the hole: the top of the pot should align with the top of the soil. Adjust the depth of the hole accordingly.

4 Remove the plant from its pot, being careful not to disturb the rootball. If it is in a plastic bag, cut the bag away rather than trying to pull it off. Place the shrub in the hole and pull the earth back around it. Firm the soil down well around the plant with the heel of your boot and water well.

5 Finally, mulch all around the shrub, covering the soil with 7.5–10 cm (3–4 in) of bark or similar material. This will not only help to preserve the moisture but will also help to prevent weeds from germinating.

Right: *White frothy mounds of flowers are produced by* Spiraea 'Arguta' *during the spring. Since it produces its flowers before many other shrubs come into leaf, it can be planted towards the back of the border where it will show up while in flower but then merge into the background for the rest of the year when it is not so striking.*

Planting Climbers

There are so many different types of climbers that you are bound to be able to choose one that is suitable for any place in the garden. As always, though, the trick is to match up the plant and the planting position correctly.

CHOOSING A POSITION

Probably the most important thing to remember about planting a climber is that it is essential to pause and consider whether you are planting it in the right place. Once planted, with the roots spreading and the stems attached to their supports, it is very difficult to move a climber successfully. Once it has grown to its full size, if you realise that you have got the site wrong, you will have a choice of living with your mistake or scrapping the plant and starting all over again with another one. So, think carefully about the position of any climber you plan to introduce.

As well as considering how the climber looks in its intended position, there is a practical consideration. If you are planting against a wall or fence, the plant should be set a distance away, as the ground immediately adjacent to such structures is usually very dry. Similarly, if a pole or post has been concreted in or simply surrounded with rammed earth, it is best for the roots of your climber to be planted a short distance out and the stems led to the support with canes or sticks.

Most plants should be planted at the same depth as they were in their pot or in the nursery bed (usually indicated by the soil line on the stem). The main exception is clematis, which should be planted 5 cm (2 in) deeper, so that the base of the stems is covered.

Mulching around the climber helps to preserve moisture and to keep the weeds down. A variety of methods can be used for mulching; any of them will be of benefit at this stage in helping the climber to establish itself quickly.

PLANTING TIMES

Traditionally, climbers were planted, when the weather allowed, between mid-autumn and mid-spring, but most climbers are now sold as container-grown plants and these can be planted at any time of the year, as long as the weather is not too extreme. Bare-rooted climbers have the best chance of survival if planted at the traditional time. Avoid planting any climber when the weather is very hot and dry, or when there are drying winds. In winter, avoid times when the ground is waterlogged or frozen.

1 Dig over the proposed site for the climber, loosening the soil and removing any weeds that have grown since the ground was prepared. If the ground has not recently been prepared, work some well-rotted organic material into the soil to improve soil texture and fertility.

2 Before planting, add a general or specialist shrub fertilizer to the soil at the dosage recommended on the packet. Work the fertilizer into the soil around the planting area with a fork. A slow-release organic fertilizer, such as bonemeal, is best.

3 Water the plant in the pot. Dig a hole that is much wider than the rootball of the plant. Place the soil evenly around the hole, so that it can easily be worked in around the plant. The hole should be away from any compacted soil, near a support and at least 30 cm (12 in) away from a wall or fence. Before removing the plant from its pot, stand it in the hole, to make certain that the depth and width are correct.

4 Place a cane or stick across the hole; the top of the rootball should be at the same level. Dig deeper or add soil to the bottom of the hole, as necessary, to bring it up to the correct height. Remove the plant from the pot, being careful that none of the soil falls away from the rootball. If the plant is in a polythene (plastic) container rather than a pot, cut the bag away rather than pulling it off. Holding the plant steady, pull in the soil from around the hole, filling in around the rootball. Firm as you go, with your hands, and then finally firm down all around the plant with your foot, making certain that there are no cavities or large air pockets.

5 Train the stems of the climber up individual canes to their main support. Tie the stems in with string or plastic ties. Even twining plants or plants with tendrils will need this initial help. Spread them out, so that they ultimately cover the whole of their support. Water the plant in well.

6 Put a layer of mulch around the plant, to help preserve the moisture and prevent weed growth.

Right: *The delicate bells of* Clematis viticella *hang suspended in mid-air.*

Weeding and Mulching

Keeping your garden weed-free will improve the health and appearance of all your plants. While strong, vigorous plants are able to grow in grass without much difficulty, your shrubs and climbers will benefit from being regularly weeded and protected with a suitable mulch.

WEEDING

Long grass appearing through the lower branches of a bush or growing up through a climber makes the plant look untidy and is difficult to remove. In addition, once the pervasive roots of perennial weeds become entwined among the roots of a plant, they are very difficult to remove. It is therefore essential to prevent weeds from establishing themselves, or at least to remove them as soon as they appear.

Young shrubs in particular do not like competition from weeds. From a health point of view, weeds not only remove vital nutrients and moisture from the soil but, if the shrubs are small, weeds can smother them, preventing light from reaching the foliage. Another disadvantage of allowing weeds to grow under established bushes is that they also provide a constant nuisance by seeding into the surrounding beds and borders.

Prepare the soil thoroughly before planting, so that every piece of perennial weed is either removed by hand or killed off with a herbicide. Once the climber or shrub is planted, weed around it regularly with a hand-fork or hoe, but be careful not to dig too deeply or you may disturb shallow roots lying just below the surface.

USING WEEDKILLER

Unless it is really necessary, it is best to avoid using chemical weedkillers around shrubs. It is so easy to damage or kill the shrub by mistake because most weedkillers will kill or damage whatever they come in contact with. Always follow the instructions on the packet carefully, and keep aside a special watering can to prevent harmful residues killing any of your other plants.

1 Treat deep-rooted weeds like ground elder and bindweed with a translocated weedkiller based on glyphosate, which is moved by the plant to all parts. Use a gel formulation to paint on the weed if watering on the weedkiller is likely to damage plants nearby.

2 If it is possible to water on the weedkiller with a watering can, use a piece of board to shield those plants you don't want to be affected with the weedkiller. If the weeds are not deep-rooted, you could use a contact killer, although it is preferable to use a hoe to remove the weeds if possible.

1 Removing weeds by hand is one of the surest ways of catching them all. Some people find this process tedious but, if carried out regularly, it need not be so. In fact, it is an opportunity to stop and examine the bushes at close quarters, not only to look for problems but to appreciate the plants. Use a small hand-fork but take care not to disturb the roots of established plants.

2 Another method of removing weeds by hand is by hoeing. This is quick and simple, and best carried out in hot weather so that any weeds hoed up quickly die. A large hoe can be used but, for more control in confined areas, a small onion hoe is better.

MULCHING

Mulching has many benefits in the garden: the main one is that it cuts down on the amount of time required for watering and weeding, as it holds the moisture in and makes it difficult for weeds to get through. It will not prevent perennial weeds that are already established from coming up, but it will prevent seed in the soil from germinating. Never mulch over the top of perennial weeds and always ensure that the soil is moist before you mulch, watering the ground if needed. A wide range of mulches can be used. Organic ones are best because they slowly decompose into the soil, adding to its structure and fertility, so benefiting the plant in the longer term as well.

1 Here, the potentilla is surrounded by bare earth. This provides an attractive finish as long as it is weed-free and dug over from time to time, to refresh the surface. But to save on labour in your garden, it is best to add a mulch.

2 Grass clippings make a cheap and effective mulch. Never apply them too thickly – 5 cm (2 in) is the maximum depth – or the heat they produce as they decompose may harm the stems of the plant. Never use mowings from grass that has gone to seed or the mulch could provide the reverse of its intended effect!

3 Chipped or composted bark is a very good mulch. It should be stored for several months to let it release any resin and start to decompose. Some gardeners worry that it introduces fungal diseases, but the spores of these are already in the air and the bark does not appreciably increase the risk.

4 Special black plastic, with holes in it to allow water to pass through to the soil, is readily available from garden centres and nurseries. If you lay the plastic before you plant the climber or shrub, cut holes in it and plant through it. On the other hand, if the plant is already in position, cut the plastic to shape and lay it on the surface of the soil.

5 Plastic would be the perfect mulch were it not so unattractive. However, it can be covered with gravel or small stones. Make certain that the plastic is flat, with no ridges or wrinkles in it that will poke up through the stones, then pour the gravel on to cover the plastic completely.

Above: *Gravel makes an ideal background against which to see the plants. It is easy to maintain and can be raked to keep its fresh appearance. Make certain that the plastic does not show through, as this can spoil the effect.*

Watering

Once shrubs and climbers are established it is not often necessary to water them, unless there are periods of extreme drought. It is, however, important to water them when they are first planted and while they are developing their root system. Lack of attention at this stage can easily kill the plant. Some shrubs show stress much more readily than others. Hydrangeas, for example, are some of the first shrubs whose leaves hang limply when there is a shortage of moisture. They can be used as an indicator that conditions are worsening and that it will soon be time for general watering.

ADVICE ON WATERING

The best water to use on your garden is rain water. If at all possible, it is a very practical idea to use water butts (barrels) or tanks that are connected to the down-water pipe in order to collect any water falling on the roof. However, if you do have to use your tap water, it is important to be careful with hard water that comes from chalky (alkaline) areas. Although your local soil may be acidic, the water from your tap may have been collected miles away, where the soil is alkaline. The golden rule when using tap water is that hard water should not be used on acid-loving or ericaceous plants.

Another useful tip when you are watering your garden with tap water is that it should also be poured first into a barrel and then left to breathe before you use it on your plants. This procedure allows time for any chlorine that has been used in the treatment of the water to be given off.

Selected areas of the garden such as small beds and borders are best watered by hand with a watering can or perhaps a hand-held spray. Larger areas can be dealt with by using a sprinkler. Before you start watering, it is advisable to check to see if there are any local restrictions on the type of watering you may undertake: in drought years or areas of low rainfall, there may well be bans on sprinklers or the use of any method that involves hosepipes (garden hoses).

Whatever method you choose, watering is best carried out in the early morning or evening, when the sun is not too strong. This minimizes wastage of water through evaporation. In addition, drops of water on the plants can act as magnifying lenses, causing the sun to burn small brown spots on the foliage or petals, which though not harmful, are not very attractive. You will also find the chore of watering less arduous on a cool morning rather than in the heat of midday!

1 When watering by hand, have patience and give the ground around the plant a thorough soaking. If in doubt, dig a small hole and check the water has soaked right down to the roots. Sinking tubes around a shrub and pouring water down these is a good way of ensuring the water reaches the right place.

2 A sprinkler has the advantage that you can turn it on and then get on with something else. Place a jam jar or a similar container under the spray, to gauge roughly how much has fallen. There should be at least 2.5 cm (1 in) of water in the jar for the sprinkler to have done any good.

3 A spray attached to a hosepipe (garden hose) can be used as an effective alternative to a sprinkler. This delivers at a greater rate than a sprinkler but, even so, it must still be held in place until the ground is well and truly soaked. It is very easy to under-water using this method, as the gardener can become impatient. Freshen up the plant by spraying over the leaves, to wash away any dirt or dust.

4 A seep (soaker) hose with holes in it is snaked around those plants that need to be watered and left permanently in position. It can be covered with a bark mulch, to hide it. When connected, it provides a slow dribble of water. It is an efficient method of supplying water to exactly where it is needed, avoiding the evaporation that occurs with sprinklers and sprays.

AUTOMATIC WATERING

In areas where there is a constant need to water, a permanent irrigation system employing drip-feed pipes may be well worth considering. Alternatively, you can use a watering system with a timing device, which will save you time and is also beneficial to the plants. There are many systems to choose from, so visit your local garden centre and look at advertisements to find out what is best for your needs.

WATERING ERICACEOUS PLANTS

Ericaceous plants such as rhododendrons and heathers should not be watered with water containing chalk or lime. For this reason, it is advisable not to use tap water on these plants if it is collected from an area with chalky (alkaline) soil. When watering this type of plant, use rain water that has been collected in water butts (barrels) or tanks. Other ericaceous plants include *Andromeda, Camellia, Cassiope, Enkianthus, Gaultheria, Kalmia, Phyllodoce, Pieris* and *Vaccinium.*

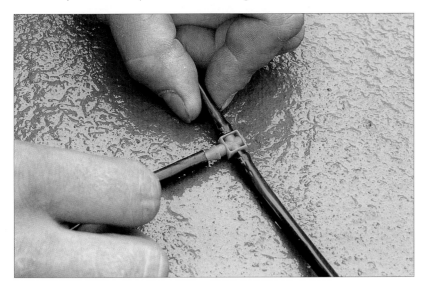

1 If you bury a pipeline just beneath the ground you can plug in various watering devices. A sprinkler can be pushed on to this fitting which lies flush with the turf.

2 Control systems can be fitted to the hose system so that you can alter the pressure of the water. These can also act as a filter.

3 Drip-feed systems can be used for beds, borders and containers. "T" joints allow tubes to be attached for individual drip heads.

4 The delivery tube of the hosepipe (garden hose) can be held in position with a pipe peg, if necessary.

Feeding

Most shrubs and climbers do not need regular feeding, particularly if you apply a mulch on a regular basis. Another effective method that cuts down on the amount of feeding you have to do is to allow the leaves to remain on the ground, under and around the plants, so that they will provide a mulch once they have rotted down. When you prepare the soil for planting a new shrub or climber, remember to incorporate plenty of organic material as well as a slow-release fertilizer. This should be sufficient for the plant for at least a year. If more is needed, particularly on light, free-draining soils, a general fertilizer may be applied in spring or a liquid feed in midsummer. The golden rule is never to overfeed.

ADVICE ON FEEDING

As well as water, a plant needs nutrients to keep healthy and produce the maximum number of blooms. These nutrients take the form of minerals and trace elements. In the garden, where plants are more crowded than in nature, the competition for nutrients is intense. If you use an organic mulch regularly, a sprinkling of a slow-release fertilizer, such as bonemeal, may be all that is required for the health of the plant. (When you are handling bonemeal, make sure that you wear vinyl or latex gloves and use a respirator.)

However, when there is regular watering, such as to a plant in a container, the soil can become drained of its nutrients and you will need to replace them. This can be done by adding a dry mixture by hand or by adding a liquid feed. Roses, in particular, benefit from an annual feed, which should be applied in spring or early summer after the dormant season of winter is over.

Whenever possible, choose a slow-release or controlled-release fertilizer that will provide the plant with the nutrients it needs throughout the summer. If you apply fertilizer in the form of concentrated mixes of blood, fish and bone, apply them during warm weather in the spring, when the activity of organisms in the soil will help in their slow release into the soil.

1 Water-soluble fertilizer should be sprinkled around the edges of the shrub, where most of the active root growth is.

2 Gently hoe the fertilizer into the soil in order to help it penetrate the roots more quickly.

3 Water in thoroughly, particularly if the ground is very dry.

OTHER FEEDING METHODS

1 An alternative method of feeding is to use a liquid feed. This is most useful for shrubs or climbers in containers. Add the fertilizer to one of the waterings; in the case of container shrubs, this could be once every three weeks, but it would not be required so frequently in the open soil – once every three months or as recommended by the manufacturer.

2 Granular fertilizer can be applied by hand, spreading it over the area covered by the roots below. Follow the instructions on the bag.

3 Apply a layer of well-rotted organic material, such as farmyard manure or garden compost, to the surface of the soil around the plant. If the plant is not shallow-rooted, lightly fork the material into the top layer of the soil.

Above: *Regular watering and feeding helps to keep plants at their best as the healthy foliage of this* Spiraea japonica *'Goldflame' shows.*

Above: *Walls offer perfect support and protection for climbers. Here,* Rosa *'Zéphirine Droubin',* Clematis *'Lady Betty Balfour' and* Vitis coignetiae *happily grow together.*

Moving a Shrub

The ideal, when planting shrubs, is to place them in the right position first time round, but, occasionally, it becomes necessary to move one. If the shrub has only been in the ground a few weeks, this is not too much of a problem: simply dig around the plant, lifting it with as big a ball of earth as possible on the spade and move it to a ready-prepared new hole. Moving a well-established shrub requires more thought and planning.

MOVING A WELL-ESTABLISHED SHRUB TO A NEW HOME

If the move is part of a long-term plan, there may well be time to root-prune the shrub first, a few months before you intend to move it. This involves digging a trench or simply slicing a sharp spade into the soil around the shrub, to sever the roots. This encourages the shrub to produce more fibrous feeding roots on the remaining roots and makes it easier for it to become established once it is moved.

Once you have moved the shrub, keep it well-watered and, as with all newly-planted shrubs, if it is in a windy situation, protect it with windbreak netting to prevent excessive transpiration. Shrubs that have been moved are likely to be vulnerable to wind-rock and so it is important to stake them firmly.

A shrub with a large ball of earth around its roots is a very heavy and unwieldy object to move. This can be a recipe for a back injury, so be very careful. Always get somebody to help, if possible. This will also ensure you don't drop the plant, causing the soil around the roots to drop off, which makes it far more difficult to re-establish the plant.

1 If possible, root-prune the shrub a few months before moving, to encourage the formation of new fibrous roots. Water the plant well the day before moving it.

2 Dig a trench around the plant, leaving a rootball that two people can comfortably lift. Sever any roots you encounter to release the rootball.

3 Dig under the shrub, cutting through any tap roots that hold it in place.

4 Rock the plant to one side and insert some hessian (burlap) sacking or strong plastic sheeting as far under the plant as you can. Push several folds of material under the rootball.

5 Rock it in the opposite direction and pull the hessian sacking or plastic sheeting through, so that it is completely under the plant.

6 Pull the sheeting round the rootball so that it completely encloses the soil and tie it firmly around the neck of the plant. The shrub is now ready to move. If it is a small plant, one person may be able to lift it out of the hole and transfer it to its new site.

7 If the plant plus the soil is heavy, it is best moved by two people. This can be made much easier by tying a bar of wood or metal to the trunk of the shrub or to the sacking. With one person on each end, lift the shrub out of the hole.

8 Prepare the ground and hole as for a new shrub and lower the transplanted shrub into it. Follow the reverse procedure, unwrapping and removing the sheeting from the rootball. Ensure the plant is in the right position and refill the hole.

Right: *Once the shrub has been replanted in its new position, water it thoroughly and mulch the soil around it. In more exposed positions place netting round it to prevent winds from drying the plant out and scorching it. It may also need protection from fierce sun. Moving a shrub in autumn or winter, as long as it is not too cold or wet, will allow it to become established in time for its first summer.*

Staking a Shrub

In a well protected garden or in a border where a new shrub is surrounded by other supportive shrubs or plants, it may well be unnecessary to stake, but where the wind is likely to catch a shrub it is important to stake it until it is established.

SHORT AND TALL STAKING

The aim of staking a shrub is to allow the new roots to move out into the soil while anchoring the plant firmly. If the wind rocks the plant, the ball of soil that came with the plant is likely to move as well, severing the new roots that are trying to spread out into the surrounding soil.

The modern technique for staking trees and shrubs is to ensure that the base of the shrub is firmly anchored, preventing the rootball from moving, while the top is free to move in the wind, which will strengthen it. Thus, only a short stake is required, with a single tie about 25 cm (10 in) or so above the ground. If the shrub is top-heavy – for example, a standard rose – it is important to use a taller stake and tie it in two places, or the top of the shrub may well snap off. Unlike other forms of staking, this support should be left in place rather than removed once the shrub is established.

Both short and tall staking is best done when first planting the shrub so that the roots can be seen. If the stake is knocked in afterwards it is likely to sever unseen roots. If it becomes necessary to stake a mature or already-planted shrub, use two stakes set some way out on either side of the shrub, with a crossbar to tie the stems to.

USEFUL SUPPORTS

A number of items can be used as stakes for shrubs. You can buy a variety of specially-designed plastic or wire supports from your local garden centre; alternatively, twiggy sticks pushed into the ground around a plant can be effective. Use short garden canes for fragile plants, tall canes for plants with tall, flowering stems and thicker pieces of wood for shrubs that need a stronger or more permanent means of support.

STAKING A STANDARD SHRUB

1 For a standard shrub, make sure you use a strong stake. It should be of a rot-resistant wood or one that has been treated with preservative. Firmly place the stake in the planting hole, knocking it into the soil so that it cannot move.

2 Plant the shrub, pushing the rootball up against the stake, so that the stem and stake are approximately 7.5–10 cm (3–4 in) apart.

3 Firm the soil down around the plant with the heel of your boot.

4 Although it is possible to use string, a proper rose or tree tie provides the best support. Fix the lower one 15 cm (6 in) above the soil.

5 Then fix the second tie near the top of the stake, just below the head of the standard shrub.

6 Water the ground around the plant thoroughly and mulch with a chipped bark or similar material.

Right: *Regularly check the ties, to make certain they are not too tight; otherwise they will begin to cut into the wood as the stems of the shrub increase in girth.*

Shrubs and Weather Problems

Weather, in particular winter weather, can cause problems for the shrub gardener. Throughout the year, winds can break branches of shrubs and, if there is any danger of this, shrubs should be firmly staked. If boughs or stems do break, cut them neatly back to a convenient point. If the wind is a constant problem, it becomes necessary to create a windbreak of some sort or shrubs will become permanently bent and, frequently, damaged.

PROTECTING AGAINST THE ELEMENTS

Frost can cause a lot of damage to shrubs, especially late or early frosts, which can catch new growth and flowers unexpectedly. General cold during the winter can be dealt with more easily, because it is relatively predictable: either cover the plants or plant them next to a wall, which will provide warmth and shelter.

Drought can be a problem, especially if it is not expected. Defend against drought when preparing the bed by incorporating plenty of moisture-retaining organic material. Once planted, shrubs benefit from a thick mulch, which will help hold the moisture in.

There are some plants that do not tolerate wet weather. Most plants with silver leaves, such as *Convolvulus cneorum* and lavenders prefer to grow in fairly dry conditions. Unfortunately there is little that can be done to protect such shrubs from the rain, although making their soil more free-draining by adding grit to the soil, or by growing them in well-drained containers usually helps.

Some shrubs prefer a shady position away from the sun. Many rhododendrons and azaleas, for example, prefer to be out of the hot sun. These can either be planted in the shade of a building or under trees or beneath taller shrubs.

WINDBREAKS

If there are perpetual problems with wind, it is essential to create some sort of windbreak. In the short term this can be plastic netting, but a more permanent solution is to create a living windbreak. A number of trees and shrubs can be used for this: *Leylandii* are often used, because they are one of the quickest-growing, but they are really best avoided for more suitable alternatives. They are thirsty and hungry plants that take a lot of the nutrients from the soil for some distance around their roots. They also continue growing rapidly past their required height.

It is best to get the windbreak established before the shrubs are planted but, if time is of the essence, plant them at the same time, shielding both from the winds with windbreak netting.

SHRUBS AND TREES FOR WINDBREAKS

Acer pseudoplatanus (sycamore)
Berberis darwinii
Buxus sempervirens (box)
Carpinus betulus (hornbeam)
Choisya ternata
Corylus avellana (hazel)
Cotoneaster simonsii
Crataegus monogyma (hawthorn)
Elaeagnus x ebbingei
Escallonia 'Langleyensis'
Euonymus japonicus 'Macrophyllus'
Fraxinus excelsior (ash)
Griselinia littoralis
Hippophaë rhamnoides (sea buckthorn)
Ilex (holly)
Ligustrum ovalifolium (privet)
Lonicera nitida (box-leaf honeysuckle)
Picea sitchensis (sitka spruce)
Pinus sylvestris (Scots pine)
Pittosporum tenuifolium
Prunus laurocerasus (cherry laurel)
Prunus lusitanica (Portuguese laurel)
Pyracantha (firethorn)
Rosmarinus officinalis (rosemary)
Sorbus aucuparia (rowan)
Tamarix (tamarisk)
Taxus baccata (yew)
Viburnum tinus (laurustinus)

Above: *Hedges are frequently used as windbreaks to protect the whole or specific parts of the garden. Whilst they are becoming established, they themselves may also need some protection, usually in the form of plastic netting. Here privet (Ligustrum) has been chosen.*

PROTECTING FROM WINTER COLD

1 Many shrubs, like this bay (*Laurus nobilis*) need some degree of winter protection. This shrub is in a container, but the same principles can be applied to free-standing shrubs. Insert a number of canes around the edge of the plant, taking care not to damage the roots.

2 Cut a piece of fleece, hessian (burlap) or bubble polythene (plastic) to the necessary size, making sure you allow for an overlap over the shrub and pot. Fleece can be bought as a sleeve, which is particularly handy for enveloping shrubs.

3 Wrap the protective cover around the plant, allowing a generous overlap. For particularly tender plants, use a double layer.

4 Tie the protective cover around the pot, or lightly around the shrub if it is in the ground. Fleece can be tied at the top as moisture can penetrate through, but if using plastic, leave it open for ventilation and watering.

5 Protecting with hessian (burlap) or plastic shade netting should be enough for most shrubs, but if a plant should require extra protection, wrap it in straw and then hold this in place with hessian or shade netting.

Above: *Late frost can ruin the flowering of a bush. This azalea has been caught on the top by the frost, but the sides were sufficiently sheltered to be unaffected. A covering of fleece would have given it complete protection.*

Right: *Lilac (Syringa) can be affected by late frosts which nip out the flowering buds preventing displays such as this.*

Caring for Climbers

Climbers are relatively maintenance-free and look after themselves, apart from one or two essential things. These essentials are, however, crucial not only to ensuring a good "performance" from your climbers, but also in making your garden safe for you and other users; so don't neglect these jobs, as they are important.

ESSENTIAL JOBS

The most important task is to be certain that the climber is well supported. Make regular checks that the main supports are still secure to the wall or that posts have not rotted or become loose in the wind.

Tie in any stray stems as they appear. If they are left, the wind may damage them. A worse situation can arise with thorned climbers, such as roses, whose thrashing stems may damage other plants or even passers-by. If they are not essential, cut off any stray stems to keep the climber neat and safe.

Throughout the flowering season, a climbing plant's appearance is improved by removing old flower heads. Dead-heading also prevents the plant from channelling vital resources into seed production, and thus frees energy for more flowering and growth.

WINTER PROTECTION

In winter, it may be important to protect the more tender climbers from the weather. Walls give a great deal of protection and may be sufficient for many plants but, even here, some plants may need extra protection if there is the possibility of a severe winter. One way is simply to drape hessian (burlap) or shade netting over the plant, to give temporary protection against frosts. For more prolonged periods, first protect the climber with straw and then cover this with hessian.

Keep an eye on climbers with variegated foliage, as some have the habit of reverting, that is, the leaves turn back to their normal green. If the stems bearing these leaves are not removed, the whole climber may eventually revert, losing its attractive foliage.

ROUTINE CARE

1 When vigorous climbers are grown against a house wall, they can become a nuisance once they have reached roof level.

4 Most climbers will produce stems that float around in space and that will need attention to prevent them being damaged or causing damage to other plants or passers-by. This *solanum* definitely needs some attention.

5 Regularly tie in any stray stems to the main supports. In some cases, it will be easier to attach them to other stems, rather than the supports. Always consider the overall shape of the climber and how you want to encourage it to grow in the future.

6 Sometimes it is better to cut off stray stems, either because there are already ample in that area or because they are becoming a nuisance. Trim them off neatly back to a bud or a branch. Sometimes, such stems will make useful cutting material from which to grow new plants.

2 At least once a year, cut back the new growth to below the level of the gutters and around the windows.

3 Dead-head regularly. If the dead flower is part of a truss, just nip out that flower; if the whole truss has finished, cut back the stem to a bud or leaf.

7 For light protection, especially against unseasonal frosts, hang shade netting or hessian (burlap) around the climber.

8 If the plant is against a wall, hang the shade netting or hessian from the gutter or from some similar support. This is a useful method of protecting new shoots and early flowers. For really tender plants, put a layer of straw around the stems of the climber and then hold it in place with a sheet of shade netting or hessian. Remove as soon as the plant begins to grow.

Above: *The overall effect of tying-in will be a neater and more satisfying shape. If possible, spread out the stems so that the climber looks fuller and less crowded.*

Providing Support for Climbers 1

When considering the choice and position of a climbing plant, it is important to take into account the method by which it climbs. While an ivy will support itself with modified roots on a brick wall, a rose, which is used to scrambling through bushes in the wild, will need to be tied to wires or trellis that has been attached to the wall.

CLIMBING HABITS

When buying a climbing plant, always consider the way it climbs and check that it is suitable for your purpose. If you want to cover a wall, and money is tight, an ivy is the best choice as it will cost no more than the plant, whereas the rose will also incur the price of the supporting structure. On the other hand, if you later want to paint the wall, it will be impossible to remove the ivy to do so, while a rose on a hinged or clipped trellis can be moved away from the wall to allow the operation to go ahead.

CLINGING CLIMBERS

True climbers are able to attach themselves to their supports. To do this, they have roots or modified roots that grip firmly on the surface of the support. They will attach themselves to any surface, including smooth ones such as glass and plastic. They need little attention, except for cutting them back from around windows and periodically cutting them off at the top of the wall so that they do not foul gutters or creep under tiles. If a wall is in good condition, there is little to fear from these climbers in terms of damage that they might inflict.

Above: Hydrangea anomala petiolaris *clings to wall surfaces by putting out modified roots.*

Right: *Clinging plants will cover any vertical surface without needing any support.*

CLINGING CLIMBERS

Hedera canariensis (Canary Island ivy)
Hedera colchica (Persian ivy)
Hedera helix (common ivy)
Hydrangea anomala petiolaris (climbing hydrangea)
Parthenocissus henryana (Chinese Virginia creeper)
Parthenocissus quinquefolia (Virginia creeper)
Parthenocissus tricuspida (Boston ivy)

CLIMBERS THAT USE TENDRILS

Many climbing plants have adapted themselves so that, although they do not cling to a smooth support, they can attach themselves to branches and other protrusions by means of tendrils. These are modified stems, or even leaves, which curl round the support.

Tendril plants will not climb up a wall unless there is already another plant on it or unless there is a mesh that they can attach themselves to. If a trellis or wires are used and the supporting strands are far apart, the stems will wave about until they are long enough to find something to which to cling; you may need to tie them in, to prevent them from breaking off. Closely woven mesh or another well-branched plant or tree provide the best supports for this type of climber.

CLIMBERS THAT USE TENDRILS

Campsis radicans
   (trumpet creeper)
Clematis
Cobaea scandens
   (cathedral bells)
Lathyrus (peas)
Mutisia
Vitis (vine)

Right: *The overall effect of a wall covered entirely by clematis is a mass of flower and foliage.*

Below: *Clematis puts out tendrils that entwine round a supporting structure, such as wire netting or another plant.*

Providing Support for Climbers 2

SCRAMBLING CLIMBERS

In the wild, apart from those that cling to cliffs, most climbers are supported by other plants. While some have adapted themselves to twine or use tendrils, the majority just push themselves up through the supporting plant, using its framework of branches and twigs as their support. Use this technique in the garden by allowing climbers to ramble up through shrubs and trees.

However, if the climbers are needed for a more formal situation, such as over a pergola or up a trellis or wall, artificial supports will be required. As the plants have no natural way of attaching themselves to wires or trellis, the gardener will have to tie them in with string or plant ties. This should be done at regular intervals, to ensure that the plant is well supported along its whole length.

TYPES OF TIES

There are various different materials for tying in stems. String is the most readily available and the cheapest. Use soft garden string for short-term (up to a year) tying in and tarred string for longer periods. Special twists made from thin wire covered with plastic "wings" are sold for garden use, although the version provided with plastic food bags is just as good.

Above: *Materials for tying in climbers* (left to right): *heavy-duty plastic tie; plastic twist tie; narrow plastic tie; tarred string; soft garden string.*

These are best used as temporary ties. Of more permanent use are plastic ties, which come in various sizes, from those suitable for holding stems, to those that will cope with small tree-trunks.

1 Use special lead-headed nails to attach the stems of scramblers to walls.

2 The malleable lead head can be wrapped around the stem to secure it.

Right: *Take advantage of scrambling climbers' natural habit of growing through other plants by growing a rose through an old apple tree.*

SCRAMBLING CLIMBERS

Akebia	*Rhodochiton atrosanguineus*
Actinidia (some)	*Rosa* (rose)
Bougainvillea	*Solanum* (nightshade)
Eccremocarpus scaber (Chilean glory flower)	*Thunbergia alata* (black-eyed Susan)
Fallopia baldschuanica (Russian vine)	*Trachelospermum*
Passiflora (passion-flower)	*Tropaeolum* (nasturtium)
Plumbago capensis	*Vinca* (periwinkle)

TWINING PLANTS

Some climbers twine their stems round the support as they grow. Plants that adopt this technique can be grown up poles or trellis, or through trees and shrubs. The stems automatically twist round their support, so little attention is required except to tie in any wayward shoots that might thrash around in the wind and get damaged.

Right: *The stems of twining climbers wind themselves round any support they can find as they grow, so, once you have provided the support, they will do the rest.*

Below: *Here, a hop has covered a metal arch with a shower of green leaves, supported by a mass of curling stems.*

TWINING CLIMBERS
Actinidia (some)
Humulus lupulus (hop)
Ipomoea (morning glory)
Lonicera (honeysuckle)
Phaseolus (climbing beans)

WALL SHRUBS

In gardening parlance, the term "climbing plants" is often liberally interpreted to include any plants that are grown up against walls. This can, in fact, include more or less any shrub. Generally, however, there are some shrubs that are best suited to this position, either because of their appearance or because they need the protection of the wall against the vagaries of the weather. Some are strong enough shrubs not to need support, except, perhaps, to be tied the wall to prevent them from being blown forward. Others need a more rigid support and should be tied into wires or a framework to keep them steady.

Above: Pyracantha *is a perfect wall shrub; it has flowers in the early summer and colourful berries in the autumn. Its branches are viciously thorned, making it a good burglar deterrent to plant on walls around windows.*

WALL SHRUBS
Abutilon
Azara
Carpenteria californica
Ceanothus (Californian lilac)
Cotoneaster
Euonymus fortunei
Magnolia
Pyracantha (firethorn)
Teucrium fruticans
   (shrubby germander)

PRUNING

Principles of Pruning

Pruning is the one thing that gardeners worry about more than anything else. The upshot is that many are frightened to do any pruning, feeling that it is probably best to leave things alone. While this may work with some plants, it is best to get into the habit of regularly checking all shrubs and climbers, and pruning those that need it. Certainly, the plants will benefit from this and will eventually deteriorate if left to their own devices.

BASIC PRUNING

There are several basic elements to pruning and taking them one step at a time makes the process easier. The first step is to remove all dead wood. This opens up the plant and makes it easier to see what is happening. The second is to remove any diseased wood. These are easy steps as it is not difficult to decide what to remove. The third stage is more difficult but becomes easier with practice. This is to remove any weak wood from the plant and to cut off stems that cross or rub others. Finally, to keep a plant vigorous it is important to encourage new growth. The way to do this is to remove a few of the oldest stems. Up to a third of the plant can be removed at any one time. Finally, check to see if any stems need removing to give the plant an attractive shape. Use sharp secateurs (pruners) or a saw for thicker branches, and keep your pruning cuts clean.

GOOD CUTS

1 A good pruning cut is made just above a strong bud, about 3 mm (⅛ in) above the bud. It should be a slanting cut, with the higher end above the bud. The bud should generally be outward bound from the plant rather than inward; the latter will throw its shoot into the plant, crossing and rubbing against others, which should be avoided. This is an easy technique and you can practise it on any stem.

2 If the stem has buds or leaves opposite each other, make the cut horizontal, again about 3 mm (⅛ in) above the buds.

PRUNING THICKER BRANCHES

Most stems can be removed with secateurs (pruners), but thicker branches of large shrubs and rambling roses will require the use of a sharp pruning saw.

The major problem of cutting thicker stems is that they usually have a considerable weight. If cut straight through, this weight bends the stem before the cut has been completed, tearing the branch below the cut back to the main stem or trunk. The following technique avoids this. It is no longer considered necessary to paint large cuts to protect them.

1 Make a cut from the underside of the stem. Cut about half-way through or until the saw begins to bend as the weight of the stem closes the gap, pinching the saw.

2 Next, make a second cut from the upper edge of the stem, this time about 2.5 cm (1 in) away from the previous cut and further away from the main stem. The weight of the stem will then cause it to split across to the first cut so that the main part of the branch falls to the ground.

3 Make the third cut straight through the stem at the place to which you want to cut back. This should not tear the stem, because the weight has gone.

BAD CUTS

 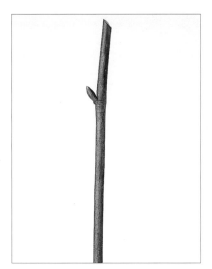 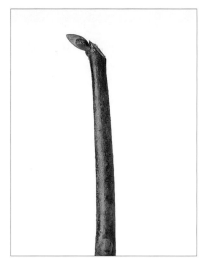 

3 Always use a sharp pair of secateurs (pruners). Blunt ones will produce a ragged or bruised cut, which is likely to introduce disease into the plant.

4 Do not cut too far above a bud. The piece of stem above the bud is likely to die back and the stem may well die back even further, causing the loss of the whole stem.

5 Do not cut too close to the bud otherwise the bud might be damaged by the secateurs (pruners) or disease might enter. Too close a cut is likely to cause the stem to die back to the next bud.

6 It is bad practice to slope the cut towards the bud as this makes the stem above the bud too long, which is likely to cause dieback. It also sheds rain on to the bud, which may cause problems.

DECIDING WHEN TO PRUNE

Perhaps the most difficult aspect of pruning is deciding when to do it. Gardeners worry that if they do it at the wrong time they might kill the plant. This is possible but unlikely. The worst that usually happens is that you cut off all the stems that will produce the year's flowers and so you miss a season. As a rule of thumb, most shrubs need to be pruned immediately after they have flowered, so that they have time to produce new mature stems by the time they need to flower again.

Above: Rosa *'Bantry Bay'* climbing up a metal obelisk. Roses need to be dead-headed and pruned to keep them at their best. If you don't care for them properly, the plants become very straggly and flowering diminishes.

Above: *Wisterias are grown for their magnificent flowers and are suitable for growing against walls, buildings and even trees. They also make good climbers for pergolas. They should be pruned after flowering and again in the winter. This is Japanese wisteria* (Wisteria floribunda*).*

Pruning Shrubs

Apart from pruning a shrub to improve its shape, you may also need to prune out potential problems, such as damage and disease. Once a year, thoroughly check whether your plant needs attention.

CUTTING OUT DEAD WOOD

Cut out all dead wood from the shrub. This can be done at pruning time or at any other time of year when you can see dead material. Cut the dead wood out where it reaches live wood, which may be where the shoot joins a main stem or at the base of the plant. If the shrub is a large, tangled one, it may be necessary to cut out the dead branches bit by bit, as the short sections may be easier to remove than one long piece, especially if the stems have thorns that catch on everything.

CUTTING OUT CROSSING STEMS

Most shrubs grow out from a central point, with their branches arching gracefully outwards. However, sometimes a shoot will grow in towards the centre of the bush, crossing other stems in its search for light on the other side of the shrub. While there is nothing intrinsically wrong with this growth pattern, it is best to remove such branches as they will soon crowd the other branches and will often chafe against them, rubbing off the bark from the stem.

CUTTING OUT DIEBACK

▮ Tips of stems often die back, especially those that have carried bunches of flowers. Another cause is the young growth at the tip of shoots being killed by frost. If this dieback is not cut out, it can eventually kill off the whole shoot. Even if die-back proceeds no further it is still unsightly and the bush looks much tidier without these dead shoots. Cut the shoot back into good wood, just above a strong bud.

CUTTING OUT CROSSING STEMS

▮ Cut out the stems while they are still young and free from damage and disease. Using secateurs (pruners), cut the stem at its base where it joins the main branch.

CUTTING OUT DISEASED OR DAMAGED WOOD

▮ Cut any diseased or damaged wood back to sound wood, just above a strong bud. The wood is usually quite easy to spot. It may not be dead yet but still in the process of turning brown or black.

HARD PRUNING

1 There are a few shrubs – buddlejas are the main example – which benefit from being cut hard back each spring, much improving the foliage. Elders (*Sambucus*) and the purple smoke bush (*Cotinus*) are best treated in this way. *Rosa glauca* also responds very well to this type of pruning.

2 Cut the shoots right back almost to the ground, making the cuts just above an outward-facing bud and leaving little more than a stump. It may seem a little drastic, but the shrubs will quickly grow again in the spring. If they are not cut back, they become very leggy and do not make such attractive bushes.

3 Several plants that have attractive coloured bark in the winter are best cut to the ground in the spring.

4 So by the following winter, new attractive shoots will be displayed. The various coloured-stemmed *Rubus*, such as *R. cockburnianus* as well as some of the dogwoods (*Cornus* 'sibirica') and willows (*Salix*) are good candidates for this treatment.

DEAD-HEADING

1 Regular dead-heading will keep the shrub looking tidy and will also help promote further flowering. Roses, in particular, appreciate regular attention. Cut the flowering stems back to a bud or stem division.

Right: *The flowering on roses will always be improved if they are regularly dead-headed. This vigorous, multi-coloured rose is 'Miss Pam Ayres'.*

Basic Pruning for Climbers

The basics of pruning are not at all difficult, although the task of tackling a huge climber that covers half the house may seem rather daunting. Break it into three logical stages to make it more manageable.

THREE-STAGE PRUNING

The first pruning stage is to remove all dead wood. These stems are now of no use and only make the climber congested. Moreover, clearing these first will enable you to see where to prune next.

The second stage is to remove diseased and dying wood. This type of wood is usually obvious and should be taken out before it affects the rest of the plant.

The third stage is to remove some of the older wood. This has the effect of causing the plant to throw up new growth, which ensures the plant's continuing survival and keeps it vigorous, producing plenty of healthy flowers.

DISPOSAL OF WASTE

How to get rid of the mass of waste material pruned from climbing plants has always been a problem. The traditional method was to burn it but this is a waste of organic material and creates environmental problems, especially in urban areas. The best way is to shred it (avoiding diseased material). The waste is then composted for a couple of months and then returned to the beds as a valuable mulch. If you do not own a shredder then perhaps it is possible to borrow or hire one. Some local authorities run recycling schemes in which they compost all organic garden waste for reuse. The last resort is to take it to the local refuse tip. Do not dump waste in the countryside.

PRUNING OUT DEAD WOOD

1 Most climbers produce a mass of dead wood that has to be removed so that the plant does not become congested. Dead wood is normally quite clearly differentiated from the live wood, by its colour and lack of flexibility.

2 Thin out the dead wood, removing it in sections, if necessary, so that the remaining stems are not damaged when it is pulled out.

PRUNING OUT DISEASED WOOD

1 Remove any diseased wood, cutting it back to a point on the stem where the wood is again healthy. If the cut end shows that the wood is still diseased on the inside of the stem, cut back further still.

REMOVING OLD WOOD

1 Up to a third of the old wood should be removed, to encourage the plant to produce new growth. If possible, cut some of this out to the base; also remove some of the upper stems, cutting them back to a strong growing point.

TYING IN

1 Tie in the remaining stems, spreading them out rather than tying them in a tight column of stems. If possible, spread at least some of the stems horizontally: this will not only produce a better wall or trellis cover but also encourage flowering.

Right: *At their peak, roses are amongst the loveliest of climbing plants. Here the rambling* Rosa *'Excelsa' is seen climbing up a pillar.*

Pruning Climbing Roses

Roses climbing through a tree are usually left to their own devices, because they are difficult to get at; any roses climbing up a wall, trellis or pergola, however, should be regularly pruned, not only to remove dead and old wood but also to keep them vigorous and flowering well. Unpruned roses become old before their time, their flowering decreases and they look scruffy.

ONCE-FLOWERING CLIMBING ROSES

As with most woody plants, the time to prune is immediately after flowering. For once-flowering climbing roses, this normally means in midsummer.

However, if you want to see the rose's colourful hips in the autumn, leave the pruning and wait until the birds come and remove the hips or until the fruits have lost their brilliance and are no longer attractive.

1 Pruning in summer means that the plant will be in full leaf and growth. Although this may seem a daunting task to tackle, it makes it easy to see what is dead and what is alive. If possible, it is often easier to prune climbing roses by removing them from their supports and laying the stems on the ground.

2 First, remove all dead main stems and side-shoots. Cut these right back to living wood; if they are difficult to remove, take them out in sections rather than all at once. Next, remove one or two of the oldest stems. This will promote new vigorous shoots. Cut back some of the older wood growing at the top of the plant to a vigorous new shoot lower down. Do not remove more than a third of the old wood, unless you want to reduce the size of the climber drastically.

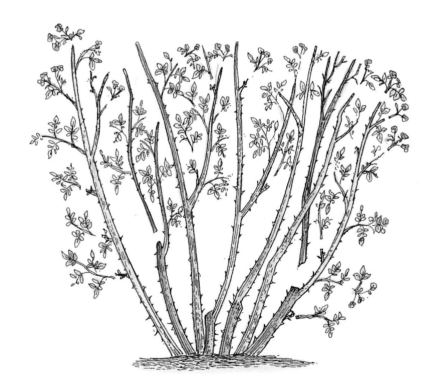

Above: *Cut out some of the older stems as soon as they have flowered, cutting back to a strong growing point, either at the base or higher up.*

3 Tie in the remaining shoots, if they are loose. Any young shoots that come from the base will need to be regularly tied in as they grow, to prevent them from thrashing around.

4 Once secure, prune back any of the shorter side shoots to three or four buds. At the same time, cut back the tips of any new main shoots that have flowered, to a sound bud.

REPEAT-FLOWERING ROSES

There are now many roses that continue to flower throughout the summer and well into the autumn. It is obviously not desirable to prune these during the summer or you will lose the later flowers. Light pruning, restricted to removing dead flowers and any dead wood, can be carried out throughout the summer, but the main pruning is best left until the winter, when the rose is dormant. It is easier to see where to prune, too.

Below: *The abundance of flowers on Rosa 'Alba maxima' makes it impossible to prune in summer.*

REPEAT-FLOWERING ROSES

'Agatha Christie' (pink)
'Aloha' (pink)
'Bantry Bay' (pink)
'Casino' (yellow)
'Coral Dawn' (pink)
'Danse du Feu' (red)
'Gloire de Dijon' (buff)
'Golden Showers' (yellow and cream)
'Handel' (white and pink)
'Parkdirektor Riggers' (red)
'Pink Perpétue' (pink)
'Royal Gold' (yellow)
'Schoolgirl' (orange)
'Summer Wine' (pink)

1 One advantage of pruning in the winter is that the leaves are missing, giving you a clearer picture of what you are doing. The structure of the rose, in particular, is more obvious.

2 First, remove any dead or diseased wood, cutting right back into living wood. Next, take out a few of the oldest shoots from the base, to encourage new growth for a compact shape.

3 If any flowering shoots remain on the tips of the stems, cut these out, taking the stem back to a sound bud. The side shoots can be shortened to about half their length. Tie in all loose stems.

4 In the summer, dead-head the roses as the flowers go over. This not only makes the climber tidier but promotes further flowering. With tall climbers, however, this may be impractical!

Pruning Rambling Roses

Ramblers only flower once during the summer. These flowers are formed on old wood produced during the previous season, so it is important to prune as soon as possible after flowering. This allows plenty of time for new shoots to grow, ready for next season's crop of flowers.

1 Because they are pruned in summer, the plants look congested and it is difficult to see what to prune. If possible, untie the shoots from their support and lay them out on the ground, so that you can see what you are doing. If this is not possible, remove the stems that need cutting out in sections and keep checking as you go.

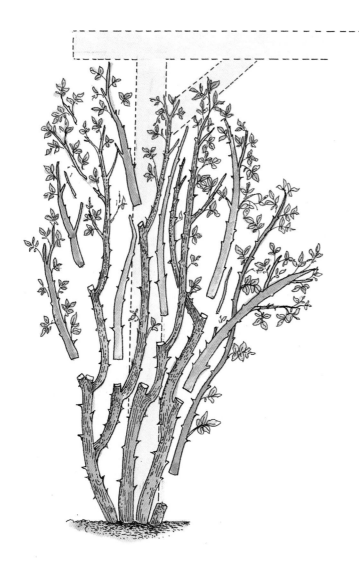

Above: *Remove older stems as soon as they have flowered, cutting back to a strong growing point, either at the base or higher up.*

2 Remove any diseased, dead or dying stems at the base. This may well reduce the rambler considerably and make subsequent pruning easier.

3 Cut out to the base any wood that has flowered during the summer. This should only leave new growth. However, if there is not much new growth, leave some of the older stems intact, to flower again the following season.

4 If you have retained any older shoots, cut back their side shoots to two or three buds. Tie in all remaining shoots. If possible, tie these to horizontal supports, to encourage flowering and new growth.

BARE AT THE BASE?

Sometimes rambler roses are reluctant to produce new shoots from the base of the plant. In that case, if there are new stems arising higher up the plant, cut back the old ones to this point.

Right: Rosa *'Bobby James' is a vigorous rambling rose that needs regular pruning to keep it flowering well. Gloves should be worn as it has vicious thorns.*

Pruning Clematis

Many gardeners worry about pruning clematis: the task seems complex, and is made more difficult because different clematis plants require different treatment. While this is true, the actual treatment is quite simple and soon becomes routine. If you grow a lot of clematis, keep a record of which plant needs what treatment. Alternatively, attach a label to each one, stating what type it is. This will make pruning very much easier.

Above: *There is always room to grow yet another clematis. Here the double* C. viticella *'Purpurea Plena Elegans' climbs over a wooden shed. For pruning it belongs to Group 3.*

CLEMATIS PRUNING GROUPS

There are three groups of clematis, as far as pruning is concerned. Most clematis catalogues or plant labels state what type each belongs to. However, it is possible to work it out. Small-flowered spring varieties such as *Clematis montana* belong to Group 1. Several of the early-flowering species also belong to this pruning group.

Group 2 consists of large-flowered clematis that bloom in early to midsummer, on old wood produced during the previous year.

Group 3 are the large-flowered climbing plants that bloom later in the summer on new wood produced during the spring.

PRUNING GROUPS FOR SOME OF THE MORE POPULAR CLEMATIS

C. 'Abundance'	3	C. macropetala	1
C. alpina	1	C. 'Madame Julia Correvon'	3
C. 'Barbara Jackman'	2	C. 'Marie Boisselot'	2
C. 'Bill Mackenzie'	3	C. 'Miss Bateman'	2
C. cirrhosa	1	C. montana	1
C. 'Comtesse de Bouchard'	3	C. 'Mrs Cholmondeley'	2
C. 'Daniel Deronda'	2	C. 'Nelly Moser'	2
C. 'Duchess of Albany'	3	C. 'Perle d'Azur'	3
C. 'Elsa Späth'	2	C. 'Royal Velours'	3
C. 'Ernest Markham'	2	C. 'Star of India'	2
C. 'Etoile Violette'	3	C. tangutica	3
C. 'Hagley Hybrid'	3	C. tibetana (orientalis)	3
C. 'Jackmanii'	3	C. 'The President'	2
C. 'Lasurstern'	2	C. viticella	3
C. 'Little Nell'	3	C. 'Vyvyan Pennell'	2

WHICH GROUP?

Does it flower in spring or early summer and have relatively small flowers?
Yes = It is probably Group 1.
No = Go to the next question.

Does it bloom in early or midsummer, possibly with a few flowers later, and are the flowers large?
Yes = It is probably Group 2.
No = Go to the next question.

Does it flower from mid- or late summer and into autumn?
Yes = It is probably Group 3.
No = There is an area of doubt, so consult a clematis expert or specialist nursery if you cannot find the variety listed on this page.

Pruning Group 1 Clematis

This group consists mainly of small-flowered clematis. Most flower early in the year, usually in spring, such as *C. montana*, although *C. cirrhosa* flowers in winter. This is the easiest group to deal with as you can, generally, leave them to their own devices, resorting to pruning only when they grow too big and need to be cut back.

1 Keep the climber looking healthy by removing any dead growth. This will help to reduce the bulk and weight of the climber, which can become considerable over the years.

2 If space is limited, remove some stems immediately after flowering. Cut them back to where they join a main shoot. Stray shoots that are thrashing around can also be removed.

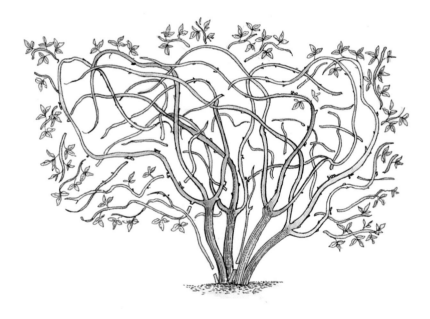

Above: *Group 1 clematis only need pruning when they outgrow their space. Just cut out sufficient branches to reduce congestion, and take those that encroach beyond their space back to their point of origin.*

Right: *Typical of Group 1 is this* C. montana.

Pruning Group 2 Clematis

Group 2 clematis need a little more care and attention to make them flower well. If they are left alone, they become very leggy, so that all the flowering is taking place at the top of the plant, out of view. The basic pruning goal is to reduce the number of shoots while leaving in a lot of the older wood. You can do this immediately after flowering but it is more usual to wait until late winter, before the clematis comes into growth.

1 First, cut out all dead or broken wood. If this is tangled up, cut it out a little at a time, so that it does not damage the wood that is to remain.

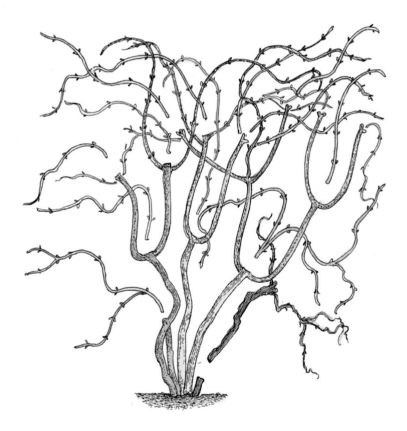

Above: *After cutting out all the dead, damaged or weak growth, remove any wood that is making the clematis congested, cutting back to a pair of buds.*

2 Cut out all weak growths, to a strong bud. If the climber is still congested, remove some of the older stems.

3 Do not remove too much material or the flowering for the following season will be reduced. If a plant has been cut back too drastically, it will often flower much later in the season than usual, and is likely to produce smaller flowers.

4 Spread out the remaining shoots, so that the support is well covered. If left to find their own way, the shoots will grow up in a column.

Right: *Correctly pruned, Group 2 clematis, such as this* Clematis *'Niobe', will provide an abundance of flowers throughout the summer.*

Pruning Group 3 Clematis

Once you have recognized that you have one of the plants that constitute this group, the actual process of pruning is very straightforward. The flowers appear on wood that grows during the current year, so all the previous year's growth can be cut away. These make good plants to grow through early-flowering shrubs, because the shrub will have finished blooming by the time that the new growth on the clematis has begun to cover its branches.

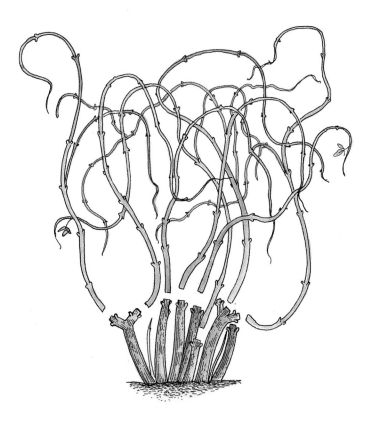

Above: *Group 3 clematis should have all the growth cut back in midwinter to the first pair of sound buds above the ground.*

1 Once Group 3 clematis become established, they produce a mass of stems at the base. If they are allowed to continue growing naturally, the flowering area gets higher and higher, leaving the base of the plant bare.

2 In mid- to late winter cut back all the shoots to within 1 m (3 ft), and preferably much less, of the ground. If the clematis is growing through a shrub, carefully untangle the stems from the shrub's branches and remove them.

3 Cut the stems back to a sound pair of plump buds. As the wood gets older, so the cuts for subsequent years are likely to get higher, but there is always plenty of new growth from the base, which should be cut low down.

4 Once cut back, the clematis looks quite mutilated but the buds will soon produce new shoots and new growth will also appear from the base; by midsummer, the support will, once again, be covered with new growth bearing a profusion of flowers.

Pruning Wisterias

Gardeners often complain that their wisteria never flowers. One of the reasons that this might happen is that they never prune the climber and consequently all the plant's energy seems to go in producing ever-expanding, new growth rather than flowers. Gardeners often seem reluctant to prune wisteria, possibly because it is usually done in two stages, one in summer and the other in winter. However, it is not at all difficult once you know the idea behind it. For the first few years allow the wisteria to grow out to form the basic framework, removing any unwanted stems.

1 During the spring and early summer, the wisteria produces long, wispy new growth that looks like tendrils. Around midsummer, this new growth should be trimmed back, leaving only four leaves on each shoot. Any shoots that are required to extend the range or shape of the wisteria should be left unpruned.

2 From early to midwinter, cut back the summer-pruned shoots even further, to about half their length, leaving two to three buds on each shoot. This generally means that the previous season's growth will now be about 7.5 cm (3 in) long, thus drastically reducing the overall growth rate of the climber.

Above: *Cut back the new growth each summer to about four leaves and reduce this even further with a winter pruning.*

Right: *All the effort is worthwhile when you achieve a display as stunning as this one.*

PROPAGATION

Advice on Seed

Growing a plant from seed is one of the easiest methods of propagation as well as a satisfying one. There is great pleasure to be had from seeing a tiny seed develop into a soaring plant that climbs up the side of a house, or seeing a fully mature shrub, perhaps covered in flowers, and knowing that you grew it from a small seed. Growing shrubs from seed requires more patience than propagating climbers: many shrubs take a number of years between sowing and growing to reach flowering size.

PROPAGATION

Seed can be obtained from seed merchants, friends or one of the many seed exchanges run by horticultural clubs. More exotic and rare seed can be bought from various seed-collecting expeditions that advertise their products in specialist gardening magazines.

Sow the seed as soon as you get it in one of the many soil mixes available (see the opposite page for details of their various properties). For climbers, stand the pot in a sheltered position outside or in a greenhouse or heated propagator for faster germination. For shrubs, put the pots out in an open, shady place where they experience whatever the weather throws at them. Keep them watered in dry weather, but do not cover them in cold weather, as the cold will often help over-ride any dormancy that there might be in the seed, which would prevent it from germinating. Bear in mind that germination might take a couple of years, so be patient. Seed that is encased in berries needs to have the fleshy part removed before it is sown.

Unless you want to grow a huge number of one particular variety of shrub or climber, a 9 cm (3½ in) pot is a large enough container, as this will produce up to twenty seedlings.

1 Fill the pot right up to the rim with compost (soil mix). Settle it by tapping it sharply on the bench or table. Very lightly press down and level the surface with the base of a similar sized pot. Do not press too hard. The level of the compost should now be below the rim of the pot.

PLANTING SEED IN POTS

2 Shrub and climber seeds are, on the whole, quite large and can be sown individually. Space them out evenly on the surface of the compost (soil mix). Do not be tempted to overfill the pot. If you have a lot of seed, use two pots. Smaller seed can be scattered over the surface but, again, do not overcrowd and ensure that they are well spaced.

4 Before you do anything else, label the pot. One pot of seed looks exactly like any other pot and they will soon get into a muddle if the pots are not labelled. Include the name of the plant and the date on which you sowed the seed on the labels. The source of the seed can also be useful additional information. Some gardeners like to keep a "sowing book", in which they record complete details of sowing and what happens afterwards, such as germination time and survival rates.

3 Cover the seed and compost (soil mix) with a layer of fine grit, which should be at least 1 cm (½ in) thick. This will make it easier to water the pot evenly as well as making it easier to remove any weeds, moss or liverwort that may start to grow on the surface. It also provides a well drained area around the rot-prone neck of the emerging seedling.

5 Water the pot with a watering can with a fine rose (nozzle). Place pots containing shrub seed in the open, but shielded from the sun; climber seeds should stand in a sheltered position or in a warmer atmosphere for faster growth. Do not let the compost dry out.

TAKING HARDWOOD CUTTINGS

In many ways, hardwood cuttings are even easier to take than semi-ripe ones, but they will take longer to root.

Once you have planted the cuttings, leave them in the ground until at least the next autumn, by which time they should have rooted. They will often produce leaves in the spring but this is not necessarily a sign that they have rooted.

Once you think they have rooted, test by digging one up. If they have, they can be transferred to pots or a nursery bed where they can be grown on to form larger plants before being moved to a permanent position.

1 Cut about 30 cm (12 in) of straight, fully ripened (hard) stem from a shrub.

2 Trim the stem off just below a leaf joint and remove any soft tip, so that the eventual length is about 23 cm (9 in) long. Remove any leaves.

3 Although a rooting hormone is not essential, it should increase the success rate, especially with plants that are difficult to root. Moisten the bases of the cuttings in water.

4 Choose a sheltered, shady spot in the garden and dig a slit in the ground with a spade. If the soil is heavy dig out a narrow trench and fill it with either cutting compost or sharp sand.

5 Insert the cuttings in the ground, leaving the top 7 cm (3 in) or so of the stem above ground.

6 Firm the soil around the cuttings to eliminate pockets of air that would cause the cuttings to dry out. Once the cuttings have rooted, dig them up and pot them on in the normal way. This will normally be the following autumn.

SHRUBS TO TRY

These are just some shrubs that will root from hardwood cuttings:
Aucuba japonica (spotted laurel)
Buddleja (butterfly bush)
Cornus (dogwood)
Forsythia
Ligustrum
Philadelphus (mock orange)
Ribes (currant)
Rosa
Salix (willow)
Sambucus (elder)
Spiraea
Viburnum (deciduous species)

Climbers from Cuttings

While using seed to increase plants is a simple procedure, it has the disadvantage that the resulting plant may not be like its parent, because not all plants will come "true" from seed. Seed-raised plants may vary in flower or leaf colour, in the size of the plant and in many other ways. When you propagate from cuttings, however, the resulting plant is identical in all ways to its parent (it is, effectively, a clone).

TAKING CUTTINGS

Taking cuttings is not a difficult procedure and nearly all climbers can easily be propagated in this way without much trouble. It is not necessary to have expensive equipment, although, if you intend to produce a lot of new plants, a heated propagator will make things much easier.

The most satisfactory method of taking cuttings is to take them from semi-ripe wood, that is, from this year's growth that is firm to the touch but still flexible and not yet hard and woody. If the shoot feels soft and floppy, it is too early to take cuttings. The best time for taking such cuttings is usually from mid- to late summer.

When taking cuttings it is vital that you always choose shoots that are healthy: they should be free from diseases and pests and not be too long between nodes (leaf joints). This usually means taking the cuttings from the top of the climber, where it receives plenty of light.

Do not take cuttings from any suckers that may rise from the base of the plant; if the climber was grafted on to a different rootstock, you might find that you have propagated another plant entirely.

CHOOSING COMPOST (SOIL MIX)

Specialist cutting compost (soil mix) can be purchased from most garden centres and nurseries. However, it is very simple to make your own. A half and half mix, by volume, of peat (or peat substitute) and sharp sand is all that is required. Alternatively, instead of sharp sand, use vermiculite.

1 Choose a healthy shoot that is not too spindly. Avoid stems that carry a flower or bud, as these are difficult to root. Cut the shoot longer than is required and trim it to size later. Put the shoot in a polythene (plastic) bag, so that it does not wilt while waiting for your attention.

2 Remove the shoot from the bag when you are ready to deal with it. Cut at an angle just below a leaf joint (node). Use a sharp knife, so that the cut is clean and not ragged.

3 Trim off the rest of the stem just above a leaf, so that the cutting is about 10 cm (4 in) long. For long-jointed climbers, this may be the next leaf joint up; for others there may be several leaves on the cutting.

4 Trim off all leaves except the upper one or pair. Cut the leaves off right against the stem, so that there are no snags. However, be careful not to damage the stem. Dip the base of the cutting into a rooting compound, either powder or liquid. This will not only promote rooting but also help protect the cutting against fungal attack.

5 Fill a 9 cm (3½ in) pot with cutting compost (soil mix) and insert the cuttings round the edge. Pushing them into the compost removes the rooting powder and damages the stems, so make a hole with a small dibber or pencil. Several cuttings can be put into one pot but do not overcrowd. Tap the pot on the bench, to settle the compost. Water gently. Label the pot.

6 If a propagator is available, place the pot in it and close the lid so that fairly high humidity and temperature are maintained. A less expensive alternative is to put the pot into a polythene (plastic) bag, with its sides held away from the leaves. Put it in a warm, light, but not sunny, position.

7 After a few weeks, the base of the cutting will callus over and roots will begin to appear. Carefully invert the pot, while supporting the compost with your other hand. Remove the pot and examine the roots. Once the roots are well developed, pot the cuttings up individually. Put the pot back in the propagator if roots are only just beginning to appear.

INTERNODAL CUTTINGS

A few plants, of which clematis is the main example, are propagated from internodal cuttings. The procedure is the same as for conventional cuttings, except that the bottom cut is through the stem, between two pairs of leaves, rather than under the bottom pair.

Right: *Your cuttings will eventually grow into hearty plants like this 'Rosa Cedric Morris'. These rambling roses can be grown through a large tree, as long as the tree is strong enough to take all the extra weight.*

Layering Shrubs

Layering is a good way of producing the odd few extra plants without a propagator. It is a useful method of producing one or two plants from a bush that somebody might want, without all the bother of what might be termed "formal" propagation. It is not a difficult technique and, after the initial work, nothing has to be done until the new plant is ready for transplanting – and it does not require any special equipment.

FOLLOWING NATURE

Basically, layering is simply persuading the plant to do what it often does in the wild (and in the garden, for that matter) and that is to put down roots where a branch or stem touches the ground. Encourage this by burying the stem and holding it in position with a peg or stone, so that the wind does not move it and sever any roots that are forming. It is as simple as that. Frequently, you will find that nature has already done it for you and a search around the base of many shrubs will reveal one or more layers that have already rooted on their own.

While layering might sound a casual way of propagating, it is a good one to try if you have difficulty in rooting cuttings. Being connected to the parent plant, the shoot still has a supply of nutrients and is, therefore, still very much alive, whereas a cutting may well have used up all its reserves and died before it has had a chance to put down roots. A layer is also far less prone to being killed off by a fungal disease.

DIVISION

Shrubs suitable for division produce multiple stems from below the ground or increase by suckering or running (self-layering). At any time between autumn and early spring, dig up one of the suckers or a portion of the shrub, severing it from the parent plant with secateurs (pruners) or a sharp knife and replant or pot up the divided portion. Suitable shrubs include *Arctostaphylos*, *Calluna*, *Clerodendrum bungei*, *Cornus alba*, *C. canadensis*, *Erica*, *Gaultheria*, *Holodiscolor*, *Kerria*, *Leucothoe*, *Mahonia*, *Nandina*, *Pachysandra*, *Rubus*, *Sarcococca* and *Sorbus reducta*.

1 Choose a stem that will reach the ground without breaking and prepare the ground beneath it. In most cases, the native soil will be satisfactory but if it is heavy clay add some potting compost (potting soil) to improve its texture.

2 Trim off any side-shoots or leaves. Dig a shallow hole and bend the shoot down into it.

3 To help hold the shoot in place, peg it down with a piece of bent wire.

4 Fill in the hole and cover it with a stone. In many cases, the stone will be sufficient to hold the layer in place and a peg will not be required. The stone will also help to keep the area beneath it moist.

5 It may take several months, or even years, for shrubs that are hard to propagate to layer but, eventually, new shoots will appear and the layer will have rooted. Sever it from its parent and pot it up into a container.

6 If the roots are well developed, transfer the layer directly to its new site.

IMPROVING ROOTING

Although it is not essential, rooting can be improved with difficult subjects by making a slit in the underside of the stem at a point where it will be below ground. This slit can be propped open with a thin sliver of wood or a piece of grit. This cut interrupts the passage of hormones along the stem and they accumulate there, helping to promote more rapid rooting.

If several plants are required, it is quite feasible to make several layers on the same shoot, allowing the stem to come above the surface between each layer. This is known as "serpentine layering".

Above: *Rhododendrons frequently self-layer in the wild and may also do so in the garden, but the prudent gardener always deliberately makes a few layers just in case a visiting friend takes a liking to one of the varieties that he grows.*

Layering Climbers

Layering is a simple technique, useful for propagating plants that are difficult to root from cuttings. It can be a slow process: occasionally, some plants can take several years to root. If one or two layers can be laid down at regular intervals, however, you should have a continuous supply of new plants at your disposal.

TIMING LAYERING

Layering can be carried out at any time of year. The time taken for roots to appear on the chosen stem depends on various factors and varies considerably from one type of plant to another. Usually, growth appearing from the area of the layer indicates that it has rooted and is ready for transplanting to another position.

ACHIEVING SUCCESS

One way of increasing the success rate with layering is to make a short slit in the underside of the stem at its lowest point. This checks the flow of the sap at this point and helps to promote rooting. Alternatively, a notch can be cut or some of the bark removed. Sometimes, just the act of forcing the stem down into a curve will wound the bark enough.

1 Make a shallow depression in the soil and place the selected stem in it. If the soil is in poor condition, remove some of it and replace it with potting compost (soil mix).

2 Use a metal pin or a piece of bent wire to hold the stem in place, if necessary, so that it cannot move in the wind.

3 Cover the stem with good soil or potting compost, and water it.

4 If you haven't pinned the stem down, place a stone on the soil above the stem, to hold it in position.

5 Once growth starts – or the stem feels as if it is firmly rooted when gently pulled – cut it away from the parent plant, ensuring that the cut is on the parent-plant side. Dig up the new plant and transfer it to a pot filled with potting compost. Alternatively, replant it elsewhere in the garden.

6 An alternative method is to insert the layer directly into a pot of compost, which is buried in the ground. Once the stem has rooted, sever it from the parent as above and dig up the whole pot. This is a good technique for making tip layers, as with this fruit-bearing tayberry. Tip layers are made by inserting the tip of a stem, rather than a central section, in the ground, until it roots; it is a suitable propagation technique for fruiting climbers, such as blackberries.

Right: *Roses are just one of the types of climber that can be propagated by layering.*

SHRUBS

Shrubs have a place in any garden and it is, in fact, impossible to imagine a garden without them. They provide so much: colour, shape, bulk, a habitat for wildlife, screens from the neighbours, dividers and even "camps" for children to play in. Flowering shrubs provide sudden bursts of colour. Some flower over a long period, but even those that do not are usually glorious while they last. In many cases, the visual power of the flowers is enhanced by a wonderful fragrance which wafts throughout the whole garden. There are flowering shrubs for every month of the year, including the depths of winter. Some can simply be enjoyed in the garden, while others may be cut to provide material for bunches of flowers for indoors or to give away.

Left: *This* Cotinus coggygria *'Royal Purple' is blessed with strikingly handsome, dark purplish-red leaves.*

DESIGNING A BORDER

Drawing a Border Plan

There are several ways of designing a border. The majority of gardeners undoubtedly go for the hit-and-miss approach, simply putting in plants as they acquire them. Then, if they feel inclined, they may move them around a bit to improve the scheme. Many good gardens have been created in this way but a more methodical approach tends to produce better results from the outset. However, do not be fooled: no method produces the best results first time. Gardening is always about adjustment, moving plants here and there to create a better picture or to change the emphasis or mood.

MAKING A SKETCH

The most methodical approach to designing a border is to draw up a plan and to work from this. Making a plan is one of the many enjoyable parts of gardening. It involves choosing the plants that you want to grow, sorting them into some form of pattern and committing this to paper, so that you can follow it through. A further refinement is to produce a drawing of what the border will roughly look like at different stages of the year. You do not have to be an artist to do this; it is for your own satisfaction and, since no one else need see it, the drawing can be quite crude!

The plan itself should, preferably, be drawn up on squared paper (graph). This will help considerably in plotting the size and relationship of plants. The sketches can be on any type of paper, including the back of an envelope, if you can't find anything else at the time.

Decide whether you are going to treat the garden as a whole or whether you are going to concentrate on a single border. This border will need to be accurately measured if it is already in existence or you must firmly decide on its intended shape and dimensions.

Draw up a list of the plants that you want to grow, jotting details alongside as to their colour, flowering period, eventual height and spread and their shape.

Plot the plants on the plan, making sure you show them in their final spread, not the size they are in their pots. Bear in mind details such as relative heights, foliage and flower colour. These can be further explored by making an elevation sketch of the border as seen from the front. It can be fun to colour this in with pencils or watercolours, to show roughly what it will look like in the different seasons.

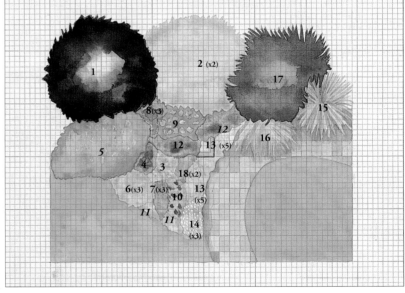

Key

1. *Cotinus coggyria* 'Royal Purple'
2. *Weigela florida* 'Florida Variegata'
3. *Perovskia atriplicifolia* 'Blue Spire'
4. *Allium chrisophii*
5. *Daphne x burkwoodii* 'Somerset'
6. *Sedum spectabile* 'September Glow'

7. *Eryngium giganteum*
8. *Digitalis purpurea*
9. *Rosa* 'Wenlock Castle'
10. *Papaver somniferum*
11. *Astrantia major*
12. *Salvia forsskaolii*

13. *Stachys byzantina*
14. *Lychnis coronaria* 'Alba'
15. *Yucca gloriosa* 'Variegata'
16. *Phormium cookianum*
17. *Berberis thunbergii* 'Rose Glow'
18. *Dictamnus albus purpureus*

Above: *It will take a few years before your plans and sketches develop into the established border you would like to see.*

Designing with Shrubs

Of all aspects of gardening, designing a garden or border is probably one of the most exciting and, at the same time, one of the most difficult. It requires the ability to see things that are not yet there and to assemble whole groups of different plants in the mind's eye.

THE BASIC ELEMENTS

Most people have an awareness of the basic elements of garden design from other disciplines; most of us, for example, are adept at choosing what clothes to wear. We know what colours go together and what suits our shape and height. We are aware that certain fabrics add a touch of luxury to an outfit and that certain colours create a bright effect, while others produce a more subtle image. Similarly, most people are at least involved in decorating their home, where again the choice of colours, textures and finishes have become almost second nature over the years.

PERSONAL TASTE

The same principles we apply to choosing clothes and items for the home are used when designing in the garden, with many of the choices coming from an innate feeling for what the gardener likes and dislikes. This means that, like clothing, gardens are personal, with the fortunate result that each garden is different from the next. By all means be inspired by ideas seen in other gardens, but do not slavishly imitate another garden: the chances are that it will not work in your situation – the climate might be slightly different or the soil might be wrong. There are no definite rules with regards to design; there is no ultimate garden. However, there are a few guidelines that the experience of many centuries of gardening have produced, and it is worth bearing these in mind.

THE SHAPE OF THE BORDER

A border can be any shape, to suit the garden. Curved edges tend to create a more informal, relaxed feeling, while straight edges are more formal. The one point to remember is that the border should not be too narrow. Shrubs look better in a border where they have room to spread without being too crowded. A border that is only wide enough to take one shrub at a time has a habit of looking more like a hedge than a border. A wider border also allows the gardener to build up a structure of planting, which is more visually satisfying.

Left: *An attractive border filled with a mixture of shrubs and herbaceous plants designed to provide interest over a long period of time. Shrubs in flower include the blue* Ceanothus, *white* Olearia, *purple* Lavandula stoechas *and the white* Prostanthera cuneata, *with a purple rhododendron in the background.*

PART OF THE SCHEME

Shrubs need not be confined to borders – they can become part of the overall scheme of the garden. This is particularly important where the garden is small and there is little room for formal borders. Shrubs can be mixed with other plants or simply used in isolation, as focal points that draw the eye. They can be taken out of the ground and used in pots or other containers, or grown against walls and fences. Besides being part of the design, they can have a sense of purpose, perhaps to screen a dustbin (trash can) or to create a perfumed area near where people sit in the evening.

HEIGHT AND SHAPE

Shrubs have a lot to offer the designer as there is such a wide choice of attributes that can be applied to them. Shrubs come in all sorts of shapes and sizes, from tiny dwarf ones to those that are difficult to distinguish from trees. The general principle of design is to put the tallest at the back and smallest at the front. This must not be rigidly adhered to or the the border will begin to look like choir stalls, all regularly tiered. Bring a few of the taller ones forward and place some of the shorter ones in gaps between bigger ones. This makes the border much more interesting and prevents the viewer from taking in the whole border at a glance.

The different shapes of the plants also add variety. Some are tall and thin, others short and spreading. The latter are particularly useful as ground cover and can be woven in and out of other shrubs as if they were "poured" there. Heathers are especially useful for this.

Above: *In this small garden, shrubs are not only used to make an interesting background of different textures, shapes and colours, but are also planted in containers to break up the foreground. To complete the picture, formal hedges hold the whole scheme together.*

Right: *This attractive border builds up beautifully from the front but, at the same time, is not regimented as the heights vary along its length. It demonstrates well the effectiveness of differently-shaped shrubs and other plants while, at the same time, illustrating the importance of colour and leaf shapes.*

Using Colour in the Border

Colour is an extremely important aspect of shrub gardening, perhaps more so than other areas because shrubs not only offer a large range of flower colours but also a vast range of foliage colour and texture.

MIXING COLOURS

Colour is the most tricky thing to get right in the garden. It is essential to spend time looking at other gardens and looking at pictures in books and magazines, to see how colours are best handled. It is not just a question of saying that reds mix well with purples: some do, others do not. Orange-reds and blue-reds are quite different from each other and cannot all be used in the same way.

A good garden will combine all the colours in a variety of ways in all areas. Sticking to just one style, especially in a large garden, can become boring. In a small garden, trying to mix too many different colour schemes has the reverse effect and may become uncomfortable.

Using shrubs gives colour in both leaves and flowers. When planning, it is important that the foliage of the various plants blends well together as they are generally around for a long time – all year, in fact, if they are evergreen. Try not to use too many different colours of foliage together and avoid too many variegated shrubs in one place as this can look too "busy". The colour of nearby flowering plants can also enhance the foliage.

Colours can also be affected by the texture of the leaves. A shiny green leaf can light up a dull area almost as brilliantly as a gold leaf while a soft, hairy foliage adds a sense of luxury.

Right: *The sharp contrast between the silver leaves of the* Elaeagnus *'Quicksilver' and the purple of the flowers of* Erysimum *'Bowles Mauve' makes a beautiful, if startling, combination.*

Below: *Here, the purple flowers of* Lavandula stoechas pedunculata *make a much softer contrast to the purple-leaved sage* Salvia officinalis *'Purpurascens'.*

Left: *The bright red stems of* Cornus alba *'Sibirica' add a great deal of interest to the winter scene, especially if sited so that the low sun strikes them.*

Right: *A dwarf willow,* Salix repens, *grows with the ground-hugging* Lithodora diffusa. *The contrast in the flowers makes this an exciting combination in the spring and, for the rest of the year, the different foliage shapes make them an interesting ground cover.*

COLOURFUL STEMS

It is not only the leaves and flowers of shrubs that have colour: stems, too, can provide it. This is particularly true in the winter, when the leaves are off most shrubs and there is little to lighten the grey scene. White, yellow, green, red and black stems then come into their own. Plants grown for their winter stems are often uninteresting for the rest of the year and so should be planted where they will not be noticed in summer but will stand out in winter.

Right: *It is possible to jazz up the appearance of the garden with bright colour combinations, such as this azalea and alyssum,* Aurinia saxatilis. *The dazzling picture they create is wonderful but, fortunately, neither plant lasts in flower too long, otherwise the effect would become tiresome.*

Mixing Shrubs

Shrub borders or shrubberies have died out as gardens have become smaller. In many ways, the border devoted to only shrubs would be a labour-saving form of gardening, but being able to mix in a few other plants helps to make it more interesting.

GROWING SHRUBS WITH PERENNIALS AND ANNUALS

As well as being more interesting from a visual point of view, mixing shrubs and other plants creates a greater variety of different habitats in the garden for a greater range of plants. For example, there are many herbaceous plants, many coming from wooded or hedgerow habitats in the wild, that need a shady position in which to grow. Where better than under shrubs? Many of these, such as the wood anemone, *Anemone nemorosa*, appear, flower and die back in early spring before the leaves appear on the shrubs, thus taking up a space that would be unavailable later in the season once the foliage has obscured the ground beneath the shrub.

Herbaceous plants can also be used to enliven a scene where all the shrubs have already finished flowering. For example, if you have a number of rhododendrons, most will have finished flowering by early summer and will be comparatively plain for the rest of the year. Plant a few herbaceous plants between them and retain interest for the rest of the year.

Herbaceous plants also extend the range of design possibilities. For example, it might not be possible to find a shrub of the right height that blooms at the right time with the right-coloured flowers. One of the thousands of hardy perennials may offer the perfect solution. Similarly, the combination of textures and shapes might not be available in shrubs, so look to see if there are herbaceous or annual plants that will help solve the problem.

In the early stages of the establishment of a shrub border or a mixed border, the shrubs are not likely to fill their allotted space. To make the border look attractive in the meantime, plant annuals or perennials in the gaps. These can be removed as the shrubs expand. As well as improving the appearance of the border, the plants will also act as a living mulch and help to keep weeds at bay.

WOODLAND PLANTS FOR GROWING UNDER SHRUBS

Anemone nemorosa (wood anemone)
Brunnera macrophylla
Campanula latifolia
Convallaria majalis (lily-of-the-valley)
Cyclamen hederifolium
Eranthis hyemalis
Euphorbia amygdaloides robbiae (wood spurge)
Galanthus (snowdrop)
Geranium
Helleborus (Christmas rose)
Polygonatum
Primula

Above: *This* Lychnis chalcedonica *adds the final touch to a good combination of foliage. Without it, the grouping might seem dull compared with other parts of the garden in the summer.*

Above: *The geranium in the foreground is the right height and colour to match the roses and the ceanothus behind. It would be hard to find a shrub to fit in with this combination.*

Left: *Sometimes, one startling combination acts as a focal point and draws the eye straight to it. This combination of the blue flowers of a ceanothus and the silver bark of the eucalyptus is extraordinarily beautiful. There are many such combinations that the gardener can seek and this is one of the things that makes gardening so satisfying and even, at times, exhilarating.*

Above: *A good combination of textures, shapes and colours is achieved here with the cardoon (*Cynara cardunculus*) providing interesting colour and structure, while the* Salvia sclarea *in the front provides the subtle flower colour.*

CHOOSING SHRUBS

Hedges

Few gardens are without a hedge of some sort. They are used as a defensive barrier around the garden as well as having a more decorative purpose within. The defensive role is to maintain privacy both from intruders and prying eyes (and, increasingly, against noise pollution). This type of hedge is thick and impenetrable, often armed with thorns to discourage animals and humans pushing through. Hedges also have less sinister functions, more directly related to gardening. One is the important role of acting as a windbreak to help protect plants. Another is to act as a foil for what is planted in front of it. Yew hedges, for example, act as a perfect backdrop to herbaceous and other types of border.

Above: *A formal beech hedge (*Fagus sylvatica*) makes a neat and tidy boundary to any garden. Beech, yew (*Taxus baccata*) and hornbeam (*Carpinus betulus*) also make good formal hedges as long as they are kept neat. They are all slow growing and need less attention than many others.*

USING HEDGES

Hedges are widely used within the garden, where they are perhaps better described as screens or frames. Screens are used to divide up the garden, hiding one area from view until you enter it. In some cases, the hedges are kept so low that they can hardly be called hedges; they are more like decorative edging to a border. Box reigns supreme for this kind of hedge. Others are informal hedges, in which the plants are allowed to grow in a less restricted way, unclipped, so they are able to flower, adding to their attraction. Roses and lavender are two popular plants for using like this.

We all want hedges that grow up as quickly as possible and usually end up buying one of the fastest growers. However, bear in mind that once grown to the intended height, these fast growers do not stop, they just keep growing at the same pace. This means that they need constant clipping to keep them under control. A slower growing hedge may take longer to mature, but once it does, its stately pace means that it needs far less attention. In spite of its slow-growing reputation, in properly prepared ground, yew will produce a good hedge, 1.5–2 m (5–6 ft) high in about 5 to 6 years from planting.

Right: *Although often much maligned, leyland cypress (*x Cupressocyparis leylandii*) makes a good hedge. The secret is to keep it under control and to clip it regularly. Here, although soon due a trim, it still looks attractive, as the new growth makes a swirling movement across the face of the hedge.*

Above: *This tapestry hedge is made up of alternate stripes of blue and gold conifers. Here, the bands have been kept distinct but, if deciduous shrubs are used, the edges often blend together, which gives a softer appearance.*

Above: A *country hedge makes an attractive screen around the garden. This one is a mixture of shrubs, all or most of them being native trees: there is box (*Buxus sempervirens*), hawthorn (*Crataegus monogyna*), hazel (*Corylus avellana*) and holly (*Ilex aquifolium*). The only problem with this type of hedge is that the growth rates are all different so it can become ragged looking, but then country hedges always are!*

Left: *An informal flowering hedge is formed by this firethorn (*Pyracantha*). The flowers make it an attractive feature while the powerful thorns give it a practical value as an impenetrable barrier. Flowering hedges should not be clipped as frequently as more formal varieties and trimming should be left until flowering is over.*

Above: *Informal hedges of lavender border a narrow path. The joy of such hedges is not only the sight of them but the fact that, as you brush along them, they give off the most delicious scent. Such hedges fit into a wide variety of different situations within a garden.*

Maintaining a Hedge

Planting a hedge in most respects is like planting any shrub. Prepare the ground thoroughly as the hedge is likely to stay in place for many years, possibly centuries.

INGREDIENTS FOR A HEALTHY HEDGE

Add plenty of organic material to the soil, both for feeding the hedge and for moisture retention. If the ground lies wet, either add drainage material or put in drains. Plant the hedge between autumn and early spring. For a thick hedge plant the shrubs in two parallel rows, staggering the plants in each. Water as soon as it is planted and keep the ground covered in mulch. Use a netting windbreak to protect the hedge if it is in an exposed position.

CLIPPING HEDGES

If a hedge is neglected, it soon loses a lot of its beauty. Regular trimming soon helps to restore this but it is also necessary for other reasons. If the hedge is left for too long, it may be difficult to bring it back to its original condition. Most can be restored eventually but this can take several years. A garden can be smartened up simply by cutting its hedges. Untrimmed hedges look ragged and untidy. Some types of hedging material need more frequent trimming than others, to keep them looking neat.

1 Cutting a hedge also includes clearing up the trimmings afterwards. One way of coping with this task is to lay down a cloth or plastic sheet under the area you are clipping and to move it along as you go.

2 When using shears, try to keep the blades flat against the plane of the hedge as this will give an even cut. If you jab the shears forward with a stabbing motion, the result is likely to be uneven.

WHEN TO CLIP HEDGES

Buxus (box)	late spring and late summer
Carpinus betulus (hornbeam)	mid/late summer
Chamaecyparis lawsoniana (Lawson's cypress)	late spring and late summer
Crataegus (hawthorn)	early summer and early autumn
x Cupressocyparis leylandii (leyland cypress)	late spring, midsummer or late spring, early autumn
Fagus sylvatica (beech)	mid/late summer
Ilex (holly)	late summer
Lavandula (lavender)	spring or early autumn
Ligustrum (privet)	late spring, midsummer and early autumn
Lonicera nitida (box-leaf honeysuckle)	late spring, midsummer and early autumn
Prunus laurocerasus (laurel)	mid-spring and late summer
Prunus lusitanica (Portuguese laurel)	mid-spring and late summer
Thuja plicata (thuja)	late spring and early autumn
Taxus (yew)	mid/late summer

3 A formal hedge looks best if it is given a regular cut. The top, in particular, should be completely flat. This can be best achieved by using poles at the ends or intervals along the hedges, with strings tautly stretched between them. These can be used as a guide. Take care not to cut the strings! If you have room to store it, make a template out of cardboard in the desired shape of the hedge so that the shape of the hedge is the same each time you cut it.

4 Keep the blades flat when you cut the top of a hedge. If it is a tall hedge, you will need to use steps rather than trying to reach up at an angle.

5 Power trimmers are much faster than hand shears and, in consequence, things can go wrong faster as well, so concentrate on what you are doing and have a rest if your arms feel tired. Wear adequate protective gear and take the appropriate precautions if you are using an electrically operated tool. Petrol- (gasolene-) driven clippers are more versatile, in that you are not limited by the length of the cord or by the charge of the battery, but they are much heavier than the electrically-powered equivalent.

6 Some conifers are relatively slow growing and only produce a few stray stems that can be cut off with secateurs (pruners) to neaten them. Secateurs should also be used for large-leaved shrubs, such as laurel (*Prunus laurocerasus*). This avoids leaves being cut in half by mechanical or hand shears, which always looks a bit of a mess.

Above: *A well-shaped hedge should be wider at the bottom than it is at the top. This allows the lower leaves to receive plenty of light and thus prevents the bottom branches from drying out.*

Ground Cover

One of the most valuable uses of shrubs is as ground cover. Ground cover is what its name implies, planting that covers the ground so that no bare earth shows. While there are obvious visual attractions in doing this, the main benefit is that ground cover prevents new weeds from germinating and therefore reduces the amount of maintenance required.

PLANTS FOR COVER

In the main, ground-covering plants are low-growing, but there is no reason why they should not be quite large as long as they do the job. Large rhododendron bushes form a perfect ground cover, for example, as nothing can grow under them.

Some ground-covering plants have flowers to enhance their appearance – heather (*Erica* and *Calluna*) and *Hypericum calycinum*, for example – while others depend on their attractive foliage – ivy (*Hedera*) and euonymus are examples.

Ground cover will not stop established weeds from coming through; it does inhibit the introduction of new weeds by creating a shade that is too dense for the seed to germinate and that starves any seedlings that do manage to appear.

SHRUBS SUITABLE FOR PLANTING AS GROUND COVER

Acaena
Arctostaphylos uva-ursi
Berberis
Calluna vulgaris (heather)
Cistus (rock rose)
Cotoneaster
Erica (heather)
Euonymus fortunei
Hebe pinguifolia 'Pagei'
Hedera (ivy)
Hypericum calycinum
Juniperus communis 'Prostrata'
Juniperus sabina tamariscifolia
Juniperus squamata 'Blue Carpet'
Lithodora diffusa
Pachysandra terminalis
Potentilla fruticosa
Salix repens
Stephandra incisa
Vinca minor (periwinkle)

Above: *A solid block of gold shimmers above the soil. The evergreen Euonymus fortunei 'Emerald 'n' Gold' makes a perfect ground cover plant because it is colourful and dense.*

Right: *Prostrate conifers perform well. One plant can cover a large area and the texture and colour of the foliage makes it a welcome feature. They have the advantage of being evergreen and thus provide good cover all year round.*

Above: *The periwinkles, especially* Vinca minor, *make good ground cover. They are evergreen and will thrive in quite dense shade. However, if you want them to flower well it is better that they are planted more in the open.*

Above: *In the rock garden, the ground-hugging* Salix repens *rapidly covers a lot of territory. It can be a bit of a thug and needs to be cut back from time to time, to prevent it from spreading too far.*

Above: Lithodora diffusa *is one of those plants that straddles the divide between hardy perennials and shrubs, because it is classed as a subshrub. It provides a very dense ground cover for the rock garden and, in the early spring, makes a wonderful carpet of blue.*

Right: *By late summer and into autumn, much ground cover is looking a bit tired and jaded. However,* Ceratostigma plumbaginoides *is still flowering and presents a good choice of plant for providing colour at this time of year.*

Planting Ground Cover

The benefits of ground cover only occur if the ground has been thoroughly prepared. Any perennial weeds left in the soil when the shrubs are planted will soon come up through the cover as it will not control existing weeds, it will only prevent new ones germinating.

TENDING GROUND COVER

Once planted, the space between the shrubs should be constantly tended until the plants have grown together, and from then on they truly create ground cover. Take care when planning ground cover as it is not something you want to replant too often.

Although one of the aims of using ground cover is to reduce maintenance by cutting out weeding, it still requires some attention and may need trimming once a year. Ivy, for example, looks much better if it is sheared in the late winter or early spring and hypericum should be cut back after flowering.

1 It is important to remove any weeds from the soil where you are going to grow ground cover, otherwise the weeds will grow through the shrubs which will make them very difficult to eradicate.

2 Thoroughly prepare the soil in the same way as you would for any other type of shrub. Dig in plenty of well rotted organic material.

3 Position the plants in their pots so that you get the best possible layout, estimating how far each plant will spread. The aim is to cover all the bare earth eventually.

4 Dig holes and plant the shrubs. Firm them in so that there are no air pockets around the plants and then water the shrubs well.

5 The gaps between the plants may take a year or more to close up. In the meantime, plant annuals, perennials or other shrubs to act as temporary ground cover while the main plants spread. Arrange the "fillers" in their pots first, so you can create the most effective planting.

Right: *When you are satisfied with the arrangement you have, plant the fillers and water them in. Remove them when the main ground cover takes over.*

MAINTAINING GROUND COVER

GROUND COVER PLANTS FOR SHADY AREAS
Acuba
Cassiope
Cornus canadensis (dogwood)
Euonymus
Gaultheria
Hedera (ivy)
Lonicera pileata
Pachysandra
Rhododendron
Sarcococca
Vaccinium
Vinca minor (periwinkle)

1 Ground cover is often neglected and, because it is a low, permanent planting, it tends to collect all kinds of litter and rubbish. Take time to regularly clean through all your ground cover, removing any litter that is lurking between the leaves.

2 Most ground cover benefits from being trimmed back at least once a year. Here, the periwinkle *Vinca minor* is given a much-needed trim.

3 Regular trimming means that the ground cover grows at a more even rate, with fewer straggly stems. It looks tidier and healthier.

Dwarf Shrubs

In the small garden and the rock garden, dwarf shrubs are much more in keeping with the scale of things than large plants. Being small, they also have the advantage that you can grow more varieties in the same space.

USING DWARF SHRUBS

Size apart, dwarf shrubs are no different from the larger ones and are treated in exactly the same way. They can be used by themselves in rock gardens or separate beds. Or they can be mixed in with taller shrubs, perhaps in front of them or even under them. Many dwarf shrubs make very good ground cover plants. They can also be used in pots and other containers, either in groups or as specimen plants.

ROCK GARDEN SHRUBS

The really small dwarf shrubs are usually grown in the rock garden and even in troughs. Many are not much more than a few centimetres high. Like their larger brethren, they are equally grown for their foliage and flowers. Some are perfect miniatures of larger plants. *Juniperus communis* 'Compressa', for example, could be a large conifer seen through the reverse end of a telescope.

Above: *For those who like bright colours, nothing could fit the bill better than* Genista lydia. *In spring, it is absolutely covered with a mound of bright, gold-coloured, pea-like flowers. It looks good tumbling over rocks or a wall but can be used anywhere. It requires very little attention.*

Above: *Most ceanothus are large shrubs, often needing wall protection to bring them through the winter. C. 'Pin Cushion' is a miniature version for the rock garden. It still retains both the good foliage and the blue flowers that attract so many gardeners to this group of plants and has the advantage that it needs little attention.*

Above: *As well as the more common dwarf shrubs, there are many varieties that will appeal to those who may want to start a collection of unusual shrubs:* x Halimiocistus revolii *is one example. This beautiful plant spreads to form a mat of dark green leaves, dotted with white flowers in midsummer. It likes a well-drained soil but needs little attention.*

Above: *The rock rose* (Helianthemum) *is one of the great joys of dwarf shrubs. There are many different varieties, with a wide range of colours, some bright while others are more subtle. The colour of their foliage also varies, from silver to bright green. Rock roses are suitable for the rock garden, raised beds or mixed borders. They spread to make large sheets, but rarely get tall. They need to be sheared over after flowering, to prevent them from becoming too sprawling.*

Above: *There are a number of dwarf willows of which this,* Salix helvetica, *is one of the best. It forms a compact shrub with very good silver foliage. It can be used in a rock garden or wherever dwarf shrubs are required. It looks especially good with geraniums –* G. sanguineum, *for example – growing through it. This willow needs very little attention.*

Left: *The group of dwarf conifers growing in this rock garden is* Juniperus communis *'Compressa'. This is one of the very best varieties of dwarf conifer, because it never grows very high, usually not more than 45 cm (18 in), and it takes many years to reach that height. Their slow growth rate means they are useful for alpine troughs and they have the advantage that they need very little attention.*

Above: *Using a few dwarf shrubs and conifers in a trough or sink adds to the height of the planting, giving it more structure and interest than if it were simply filled with low-growing alpine plants.*

Planting a Gravel Bed

Most dwarf rock garden plants need a well-drained soil with plenty of grit or sharp sand added to it. Plant between autumn and spring, as long as it is not too wet or cold. They look best grown with other alpine plants, set amongst rocks or in gravel beds. The miniature landscape of the trough can be designed in the same way.

DWARF SHRUBS FOR THE ROCK GARDEN

Aethionema	*Hypericum* (many dwarf
Berberis (dwarf forms)	forms)
Ceanothus prostratus	*Juniperus communis*
Chamaecyparis obtusa	'Compressa'
(and various 'Nana' forms)	*Leptospermum scoparium*
Convolvulus cneorum	'Nanum'
Convolvulus sabatius	*Lithodora diffusa*
Daphne	*Lonicera pyrenaica*
Dryas octopetala	*Micromeria corsica*
Erica (heather)	*Ononis*
Euonymus nana	*Salix helvetica*
Euryops acreus	*Salix repens* (and several
Fuchsia procumbens	other forms)
Genista lydia	*Sorbus reducta*
x *Halimiocistus revolii*	*Teucrium* (various dwarf forms)
Hebe (many dwarf forms)	*Thymus* (many forms)
Helianthemum (most forms)	*Verbascum* 'Letitia'

1 Prepare the ground for planting. Dig the ground to allow about 5 cm (2 in) of gravel. Level the ground and lay heavy-duty black plastic or a mulching sheet over the area, overlapping strips by about 5 cm (2 in).

2 Tip the gravel on top of the plastic and level it off with a rake.

3 Draw the gravel back from the planting area and make a slit in the plastic. Plant in the normal way.

4 Firm in the plants and pull back the plastic, then cover again with gravel.

Right: *A rock garden with dwarf and slow-growing shrubs.*

WOODLAND BEDS

As well as a rock garden built in the sun, with free-draining material, many rock gardeners also have what is traditionally known as a woodland or peat bed, although other materials besides peat are now used for planting. The beds are positioned in part shade, where they catch dappled sunlight or sun only at the end of the day. Here, in a woodland-type soil, a wide range of plants that like damp, shady conditions can be grown. Amongst these are many dwarf shrubs, perhaps the most popular being the dwarf rhododendrons.

The soil here is usually a mixture of leaf mould and good garden soil. In the past, quantities of peat were also used, although a peat substitute, such as coir, is now commonly used instead. The soil is usually acidic in nature, suiting many of the plants that grow in woodland conditions. The peat, or peat substitute, gives it the right pH balance, although it is possible to make soil more acid by adding rotted pine needles to it.

DWARF SHRUBS FOR A WOODLAND BED

Andromeda
Arctostaphylos
Cassiope
Daphne
Erica (heather)
Gaultheria
Kalmia
Kalmiopsis
Pernyetta
Phyllodoce
Rhododendron (many dwarf forms)
Vaccinium

Above: *Daphnes are excellent dwarf shrubs to use in the garden. They all have deliciously scented flowers and many, such as this D.* tangutica, *are evergreen. They have the advantage that they very rarely need any pruning, just the removal of dead wood should any occur. They can be used in rock gardens or elsewhere.*

Top right: *Heathers make good all-year-round plants and appreciate the acid nature of a woodland bed.*

Right: *A colourful woodland bed can be made up of heathers and conifers. This kind of bed is low maintenance, although the heathers stay tighter and more compact if they are sheared over once a year.*

Evergreens

The great feature of evergreens is the fact that they hold on to their leaves throughout the winter. They can be used as a permanent part of the structure of any border or garden. This has advantages and disadvantages. The advantage is that throughout the year there is always something in leaf to look at; on the other hand, unless carefully sited, evergreens can become a bit dull, so plan your planting with care.

WORK-FREE GARDENING

In many respects, evergreen shrubs form the backbone of a work-free garden, because they need very little attention unless they are used as hedging, where they need regular clipping. Although they do not drop their leaves in autumn, as deciduous bushes do, they still nonetheless shed leaves. This is usually done continuously through the year.

Many evergreens have dark green leaves, which can make the scene in which they are used a bit sombre but this effect can be brightened with the use of plants with variegated leaves. Because evergreen leaves have to last a long time, many are tough and leathery, with a shiny surface. This shine also helps to brighten up dull spots, reflecting the light back towards the viewer.

Evergreens are no more difficult to grow than other shrubs; indeed they are easier because they need less maintenance.

Above: *Conifers can become boring and so familiar that you do not even see them. However, there are some that provide a wonderful selection of shapes and textures. This juniper produces an attractive "sea of waves" effect that can never become boring.*

Left: *Privet is a good evergreen shrub although in its common form it is better known as a hedging plant. This is* Ligustrum lucidum *'Excelsum Superbum'. In the open the variegation is golden but in shade it becomes a yellowish green.*

Above: *One tends to think of evergreens as being dull green and without flowers, but there are many that put on a magnificent display of flowers each year. Rhododendrons are a good example of this.*

Left: *Choisya is a good evergreen. The leaves are shiny and catch the sun and it produces masses of white flowers in spring and often again later in the year. These perfume the air for a good distance around. This form with golden foliage is* C. ternata *'Sundance'.*

Below: *This* Pieris japonica *is an evergreen that will grace any garden, as long as the area is not prone to late frosts. The foliage alters its colour as it matures, providing a constantly changing picture. This is enhanced by long plumes of white flowers.*

Above: *Many of the hebes are evergreen. This one,* H. cupressoides, *belongs to the whipcord group; it has very small leaves pressed tightly against its stems and, when out of flower, it could easily be mistaken for a conifer.*

Shrubs with Coloured Foliage

Most foliage is green, but the discerning gardener will soon notice that the number of different greens is almost infinite. A lot can be done by careful arrangement of these various greens, but even more can be achieved by incorporating into the garden the large number of shrubs that have foliage in other colours besides green.

VARYING SHADES OF GREEN

Leaves need green chlorophyll to function, so leaves are never completely devoid of green, another colour may just dominate. For example, yellow foliage still has a green tinge to it and purple likewise. Scrape back the hairs that make a leaf look silver or grey and, again, there will be green. When grown out of the sun, particularly later in the season, this green becomes more apparent. Occasionally, stems bearing paper-white leaves appear on some shrubs. It would be wonderful if one could propagate these by taking cuttings but, unfortunately, their total lack of chlorophyll means they will not grow.

MAINTAINING THE COLOUR

Purple leaves need the sun to retain their colour. Silver-leaved plants must always be grown in the sun; they will not survive for long in shade. Golden and yellow foliage often need a dappled shade – too much sun and the leaves are scorched. However, too much shade and the leaves turn greener, so the balance is a delicate one. The thing to avoid is midday sun.

Growing coloured-leaved shrubs is no different from any other shrub. They need the same pruning, except that if a reversion occurs, this must be cut out.

As well as shrubs with single-coloured foliage, there are shrubs with foliage in two or more colours, known as "variegated" foliage, and shrubs which are planted for their autumn foliage – just two other interesting aspects of the coloration of shrubs.

SILVER FOLIAGE

Caryopteris x clandonensis
Convolvulus cneorum
Elaeagnus 'Quicksilver'
Hebe pinguifolia 'Pagei'
Hippophaë rhamnoides
Lavandula angustifolia
Pyrus salicifolia 'Pendula'
Rosa glauca
Salix lanata
Santolina chamaecyparis
Santolina pinnata neapolitana

BETTER FOLIAGE

Coppicing or pollarding some coloured-leaved shrubs improves the quality of the leaves. It produces bigger and often richer-coloured foliage. Cut the plants back in the early spring, before growth begins. They will quickly regain their original size but the foliage will be bigger and better. *Sambucus* (elder), *Cotinus* (smoke tree) and *Rosa glauca* all benefit from this.

Above: Rosa glauca *has the most wonderful glaucous (grey- or blue-green) foliage with a purple-blue tint which contrasts well with the pink and white flowers. The foliage is improved by coppicing.*

POLLARDING

1 Cut back the stems to very short stubs, leaving perhaps one or two buds on each stem to grow. The treatment looks a bit drastic, but a mass of new shoots will be produced during the summer, with colourful stems in winter.

2 A head of brightly-coloured branches will stem from the base in the winter as on this *Salix alba vitellina* 'Britzensis'.

Left: *Silver foliage is very desirable. All silver plants need a sunny position and a well drained soil, this cotton lavender,* Santolina chamaecyparis *being no exception. Shear the plant over in the spring, just as new growth begins, to keep it compact. Many gardeners also prefer to cut off the flowering stems, because they find the sharp yellow flowers too harsh.*

Below: *This shrub grows in areas that are too dry to grow many other plants. It has had many names over the years and is now called* Brachyglottis *(Dunedin Group) 'Sunshine'.*

Above: *The silver leaves of plants can often set off the colour of their flowers beautifully. Here, the silvery-grey leaves of* Helianthemum *'Wisley Pink' are a perfect foil for its pink flowers. Shear over the plant after flowering, to keep it from becoming straggly.*

Above: *A favourite silver-leaved shrub is* Elaeagnus *'Quicksilver' which in the sunshine looks like burnished pewter. During the spring, the leaves are supplemented by masses of small, pale primrose-yellow flowers which as well as being attractive have a delicious scent that wafts all over the garden.*

Shrubs with Purple Foliage

Purple foliage is a very useful component when designing a garden. It forms a pleasant alternative to the normal green, without being quite as stark in contrast as silver, yellow or one of the variegated foliages.

A PLEASANT CONTRAST

Purple is ideal as a main background colour or in combination with other plants as it goes with most other colours. It works well, in particular, as a background to various coloured flowers, so can be used with herbaceous or annual plants.

The one big drawback with purple foliage is that it can look very heavy and leaden if used in too great a quantity. A few shrubs will work better than too many. But purple can look superb if placed where the evening sunlight comes from behind the shrub so that the leaves are backlit. They then positively glow with colour and no other shrub can match them.

PURPLE-LEAVED SHRUBS

Acer palmatum
  'Atropurpureum'
Berberis thunbergii
  'Atropurpurea'
Berberis thunbergii
  'Bagatelle'
Cordyline australis
  'Atropurpurea'
Corylus maxima 'Purpurea'
Cotinus coggygria 'Royal
  Purple'
Fagus sylvatica 'Riversii'
Prunus cerasifera 'Nigra'
Salvia officinalis
  'Purpurascens'
Weigela florida 'Foliis
  Purpurea'

Above: *A really rich purple is to be seen on* Prunus x cistena. *This is beautifully enhanced in the spring by numerous pink flowers with purple centres. The total effect can be stunning.*

Left: *This* Cercis canadensis *'Forest Pansy' has purple foliage, exquisitely flushed with green and greenish blue. The heart-shaped leaves add to the attraction of this bush. In the autumn, the leaves take on a bright scarlet hue.*

Left: *The hazels (Corylus) have several purple forms to offer. They generally have large, imposing leaves. However, if they are in too shady a place they are liable to turn green.*

Right: *Another very good series of purples are the various smoke bushes,* Cotinus. *They look especially effective when they are planted so that the evening sun shines through the leaves. Cutting this shrub back hard in the spring produces much larger leaves the following year.*

Above: *In some shrubs, the colour is in the young leaves and once they begin to mature, they revert to their original colour. Although in some ways this is disappointing, in others, as here with this purple sage, the effect can be stunning.*

Above: *A good source of purple foliage is* Berberis thunbergii 'Atropurpurea' *in its various forms, including a dwarf one. In the autumn, the leaves colour-up beautifully and the shrub has the added attraction of red berries.*

Shrubs with Variegated Foliage

There has been a steady increase of interest in variegated shrubs and today they can be seen in one form or another in most gardens. This increase of interest is most welcome, because it has stimulated the search for more types of variegated plants and now there are many more from which to choose.

TYPES OF VARIEGATION

There are many different types of variegation. First there is the aspect of colour. Most variegations in shrubs are gold, followed very closely by cream and white. These have the effect of lightening any group of plants they are planted with. They are particularly useful in shade or in a dark corner, because they shine out, creating interest where it is often difficult to do so. Other colours include different shades of green. Again, these have a lightening effect. On the other hand, variegation that involves purples often introduces a more sombre mood. Sometimes, there are more than two colours in a variegation and this leads to a sense of gaiety, even if combined with sombre colours.

When looked at closely there are several different patterns of variegation. From a distance the differences blur and the leaves just register as variegated, but if you get closer you can see how the variegation can alter the appearance of the leaves. In some cases, it is the edges of the leaves that are variegated, sometimes as a ribbon and in others as an irregular margin, perhaps penetrating almost to the centre of the leaves. Another common type is where the centre of the leaves are variegated. Sometimes this is an irregular patch in the centre and in others the variegation follows the veins of the leaf. Yet a third form of variegation is where the leaves are splashed with an alternative colour, as though paint has been flicked onto their surface. A final type is where the variegation appears as long parallel strips down the leaves.

All these are attractive and it is worth looking out for and collecting at least one of each type. The more one looks at this group of plants, the more fascinating they become.

SILVER AND WHITE VARIEGATION

Cornus alternifolia 'Argentea'
Cornus alba 'Elegantissima'
Cornus controversa 'Variegata'
Euonymus fortunei 'Emerald Gaiety'
Euonymus fortunei 'Silver Queen'
Euonymus fortunei 'Variegatus'
Euonymus japonicus 'Macrophyllus Albus'
Fuchsia magellanica 'Variegata'
Prunus lusitanica 'Variegata'
Rhamnus alaternus 'Argenteovariegata'
Vinca minor 'Argenteovariegata'

Above: *The variegated* Weigela florida *'Albomarginata' is seen here against a spiraea. The white-striped leaves blend well with the white flowers of the spiraea in spring, and in summer the interest is continued because the weigela produces pink flowers.*

Below: Cornus mas *'Aureoelegantissima' creates a very different effect here, by being planted next to a different type of plant. Here the colours are more muted and do not provide such a contrast as they do against the leaves of the* Geranium x oxonianum.

Above: *One of the most popular of variegated plants,* Cornus mas *'Aureoelegantissima', is shown here with* Geranium x oxonianum *growing through it. This is an easy plant to grow and its subtle coloration means it can grow in a wide variety of situations.*

Left: Rhamnus alaternus *'Argenteovariegata', as its name implies, has a silver variegation. This is present as stripes down the margins of the leaves and sets the whole shrub shimmering. It can grow into quite a large shrub, up to 3.5–4.5 m (12–15 ft) high.*

CUTTING OUT REVERSION IN SHRUBS

Variegation is an abnormality that comes about in a number of different ways. Frequently, the process is reversed and the variegated leaves revert to their original green form. These green-leaved stems are more vigorous than the variegated ones, because they contain more chlorophyll for photosynthesis and thus produce more food. If these vigorous shoots are left, they will soon dominate the shrub and it may eventually all revert to green. The way to prevent this is to cut out the shoots as soon as they are seen.

Above: *Green-leaved shoots have appeared in this* Spiraea japonica *'Goldflame'. If left, they may take over the whole plant. The remedy is simple. Remove the affected shoots back to that part of the stem or shoot where the reversion begins.*

Shrubs with Variegated Foliage 2

USING VARIEGATED PLANTS

Variegated plants should be used with discretion. They can become too "busy": if several are planted together they tend to clash. Reserve them to use as accent plants, to draw the eye. Also use them to leaven a scene, brightening it up a bit.

On the whole, variegated shrubs are no different in terms of planting and subsequent maintenance to any other plants, although you may need to consider how much sunlight they can tolerate.

Although many variegated shrubs will tolerate full sun, many others prefer to be away from the hot midday sun, in a light, dappled shade. Always check the planting instructions when you buy a new shrub, to see what situation it requires.

Above: *Several of the herbs, such as thyme, rosemary and sage, can be variegated. Here, the sage* Salvia officinalis *is shown in the yellow and green form 'Icterina'. As well as providing a visual attraction throughout the year, these evergreen variegated forms of herbs are also always available for use in the kitchen.*

Above: *This elder,* Sambucus racemosa *'Plumosa Aurea', is not, strictly speaking, a variegated plant, but the variation from the young brown growth to the golden mature leaves gives the overall impression of a variegated shrub. In order to keep this effect, prune the elder almost to the ground each spring.*

YELLOW AND GOLD VARIATIONS

Abutilon metapotamicum
    'Variegatum'
Aucuba japonica 'Picturata'
Aucuba japonica 'Mr Goldstrike'
Aucuba japonica 'Crotonifolia'
Caryopteris x clandonensis
    'Worcester Gold'
Cornus alba 'Spaethii'
Daphne x burkwoodii
    'Somerset Gold Edge'
Euonymus fortunei 'Sunshine'
Euonymus fortunei 'Gold Spot'
Euonymus japonicus
    'Aureopictus'
Ilex aquifolium 'Golden
    Milkboy' (centre)
Ilex aquifolium 'Aurifodina'
    (edge/centre)
Ilex x altaclerensis 'Golden
    King' (edge)
Ilex aquifolium 'Crispa
Aureopicta' (centre)
Ilex x altaclerensis
'Lawsoniana' (centre)
Ligustrum ovalifolium 'Aureum'
Osmanthus heterophyllus
    'Goshiki'
Sambucus nigra
    'Aureomarginata'

Above: *There are many variegated evergreens that can add a great deal of interest to what could otherwise be a collection of plain, dark green shrubs. The hollies, in particular, provide a good selection. This one is* Ilex x altaclerensis *'Lawsoniana'. Its green berries have yet to change to their winter colour of red.*

Above right: Berberis thunbergii *'Rose Glow' is a beautifully variegated shrub, its purple leaves splashed with pink. It is eye-catching and fits in well with purple schemes. Avoid using it with yellows.*

Right: *An exotic variegation is seen on this* Abutilon megapontamicum *'Variegatum', with its green leaves splashed with gold. It has the added attraction of red and yellow flowers that appear in the latter half of the summer and continue into the autumn. It is on the tender side and in colder areas should be grown in pots and moved inside for the winter.*

Shrubs with Fragrant Foliage

There are a surprising number of shrubs with fragrant foliage. Some fragrances might not be immediately apparent, because they need some stimulant to produce it. Rosemary, for example, does not fill the air with its perfume until it is touched. Some of the rock roses (*Cistus*) produce a wonderfully aromatic scent after they have been washed with rain. Similarly, the sweet-briar rose (*Rosa rubiginosa*) and its hybrids, such as 'Lady Penzance', produce a delightfully fresh scent after rain.

WHERE TO PLANT

It is a good idea to plant shrubs with aromatic foliage near where you walk, so that when you brush against them they give out a delicious aroma. Few gardeners can resist running their fingers through rosemary foliage as they pass, and a lavender path is a pleasure to walk along, because the soothing smells of the herb are gently released along the path as you go.

For hot, dry gardens, *Camphorosma monspeliaca* is one of the best plants to grow, because it smells of camphor when the new shoots are touched. Thyme planted in the ground may be too low to touch with the hands, but it releases its fine fragrance if it is walked on in paving. Many conifers have a pleasant, resinous smell when they are rubbed. Juniper, in particular, is good.

But, of course, not all smells are pleasant. *Clerodendron bungei* has sweetly-scented flowers, but its leaves smell revolting if they are crushed. Many people dislike the sharp smell of the foliage of broom (*Cytisus*) and elder (*Sambucus*).

Above right: *While it is sensible to plant thyme used for the kitchen in a more hygienic position, it does make a wonderful herb for planting between paving stones because when crushed by the feet it produces a delicious fragrance – and trampling on it does not seem to harm the plant. Beware doing so in bare feet though, because there may well be bees on the thyme.*

Right: Prostanthera cuneata *is an evergreen shrub that has leaves with a curious aromatic scent that is very appealing. In spring, and again in the summer, white, scented flowers are produced, which look very attractive against the dark foliage.*

SHRUBS WITH FRAGRANT FOLIAGE

Aloysia triphylla
Laurus nobilis (bay)
Lavandula (lavender)
Myrica
Myrtus communis (myrtle)
Perovskia
Rosmarinus (rosemary)
Salvia officinalis (sage)
Santolina

Above: *One of the most beguiling of garden scents is that of rosemary, another culinary herb. If given a sunny well-drained site, this shrub will go on growing for many years, until its trunk is completely gnarled and ancient looking.*

Above: *Culinary herbs are a great source of scented foliage. Sage, for example, has a dry sort of herby smell, which will usually evoke in the passer-by thoughts of delicious stuffing mixtures. This is an evergreen and provides fragrance all year round.*

Right: Hebe cupressoides, *like so many plants, has a smell that is characteristically its own. It is a resinous type of fragrance that is reminiscent of the cypresses after which it is named.*

Shrubs with Fragrant Flowers

It is always worthwhile to include at least a few shrubs in the garden that have fragrant flowers. Unlike foliage scents, which generally need to be stimulated by touch, flower fragrances are usually produced unaided, and flowers will often fill the whole garden with their scent. This is particularly noticeable on a warm evening.

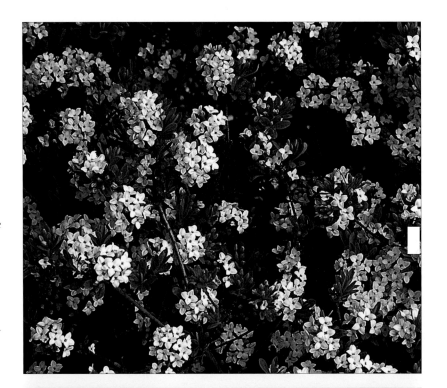

SOOTHING SCENTS

A good position for fragrant shrubs is next to a place where you sit and relax, especially after the day's work. The soft fragrance from the shrubs helps to soothe tiredness if put next to a seat or perhaps near an arbour or patio where you sit and eat. Psychologically, it can help to plant a shrub that has evening fragrance near the front gate or where you get out of the car, so that you are welcomed home by characteristically soothing scents. Choose an evening-scented shrub so that you do not get the scent on your way out in the morning, or you might not get to work at all! Another good position for a fragrant shrub is near a window or door that is often open, so the scents drift into the house.

As with foliage scents, some flowers smell unpleasant. Many dislike the smell of privet flowers, while the scent from *Cestrum parqui* is foetid in the day but sweet in the evening and at night.

One way to store summer fragrances is to turn some of the flowers into *potpourri*. Roses, in particular, are good for this.

In the winter, a surprising number of winter-flowering shrubs have very strong scents that attract insects from far away. Always try to include a few of these, such as the winter honeysuckles, in the garden.

FRAGRANT FLOWERS

Azara
Berberis x stenophylla
Clethra
Corylopsis
Daphne
Elaeagnus
Hamamelis (witch hazel)
Itea
Magnolia
Mahonia
Myrtus (myrtle)
Osmanthus
Philadelphus (mock orange)
Rhododendron luteum
Sarcococca (sweet box)
Skimmia

Above right: *Daphnes are a good genus of plants for fragrance, because they nearly all have a very strong, sweet scent.* Daphne x burkwoodii *is one of the largest of the genus, seen here in its variety 'Somerset'. When in full flower in the spring, it will perfume a large area.*

Right: *The Mexican orange-blossom,* Choisya ternata, *is another sweet-smelling shrub. It flowers in the spring and then sporadically again through the summer. The delightful flowers contrast with the glossy foliage.*

Above: *Not everybody likes the smell of elder flowers, and even fewer people like the smell of elder leaves, but the flowers do have a musky scent that is popular with many country people.*

Left: *Many flowers produce a sweet scent in the spring and early summer and this* Viburnum x juddii *and its close relatives are always amongst the best examples. It produces domes of pale pink flowers with a delicious perfume that spreads over quite a wide area.*

Above: Philadelphus *(mock orange) is one of the most popular of fragrant shrubs. The combination of the pure white flowers (sometimes tinged purple in the centre) and the sweet perfume seems to remind many people of purity and innocence. They flower after many of the other sweet-smelling flowers are over.*

Above: *The most popular perfumed shrub of all must surely be the rose. One of the advantages of many modern varieties of rose is that they continue to flower and produce their scent over a long period, often all the summer and well into the autumn. 'Zéphirine Drouhin' has a wonderful scent and is repeat-flowering. It can be grown either as a bush or as a climber and has the added advantage of being thornless.*

Shrubs with Berries and Fruit

It is not just the leaves and flowers that make a shrub worth growing. Flowering usually produces some form of seed, which is often carried in an attractive casing of fruit or berry. Two of the oldest fruiting shrubs to be appreciated, even back in ancient times, are the holly and the mistletoe.

THE APPEAL OF FRUIT

Fruit, either as berries, seed pods or even fluffy heads, often enhances the appearance of a shrub, especially if the fruit is brightly-coloured. Fruit bushes, such as gooseberries and red currants, can be fan-trained or grown as standards, and many berried shrubs have been specially bred to increase the range of colours. The firethorn (*Pyracantha*) can now be found with red, orange or yellow berries, for example.

Berries and fruit are not only attractive to gardeners, but to birds and other animals, so if you want to keep the berries buy a shrub like skimmia which will not be eaten by them.

One thing to bear in mind with berrying shrubs is that the male and female flowers may be on separate plants (skimmias and hollies, for example). Although they will both flower, only the female with bear fruit. So if you want fruit or berries, make sure you buy a male and a female.

Left: *Pyracantha makes a very decorative display of berries in the autumn. There are several varieties to choose from, with the berry colour varying from yellow, through orange to red. The berries are not only attractive but good food for the birds.*

Below: *It is important when buying pernettyas (Gaultheria mucronata) that you buy both a male and a female plant to ensure that pollination takes place. One male will suffice for several females that carry the berries.*

BERRIED SHRUBS

Chaenomeles (japonica)
Cotoneaster
Crataegus (hawthorn)
Daphne
Euonymus europaeus
Hippophaë rhamnoides
Ilex (holly)
Ligustrum
Rosa
Symphoricarpo
Viburnum opulus

Right: Piptanthus *is not totally hardy and is normally grown against a wall for protection. After its yellow flowers in spring, it produces these attractive pods, which decorate the plant in midsummer.*

Left: *When buying holly, ensure that you buy a berry-bearing form as not all carry them. Seen here in flower is* Ilex aquifolium *'Ferox Argentea'.*

Right: *Skimmias are good plants for the winter garden as they have very large, glossy berries, with the advantage that the birds do not like them, so they remain for a long period. Ensure you get a berrying form and buy a male to pollinate them.*

Below: *The cotoneasters produce a brilliant display of berries, as well as having attractive leaves and flowers. The berries are not too popular with birds and are often left until all the other berries have been eaten.*

Above: *Rose heps or hips provide an extension to the rose's season. The colour varies from variety to variety, with some being red and others orange, and some, such as* R. pimpinellifolia, *bearing black berries.*

Shrubs for Containers

Such is the versatility of shrubs that they can be grown successfully in containers as well as in the open ground. Container shrubs can be positioned on hard surfaces such as patios, walls or on steps. They can also be grown in roof gardens, on balconies or in basement plots.

WHY CHOOSE CONTAINERS?
If the garden is small or paved, there is no reason why all the plants should not be grown in containers, particularly because they can be attractive in their own right. Any kind of shrub can be grown in a container, so long as the shrub is not too big or the container too small.

One advantage of growing shrubs in pots is that you can tailor the soil to the shrub's requirements. Probably the best thing about this is the fact that it is possible to grow acid-loving plants, such as rhododendrons and azaleas, in areas where the soil is naturally alkaline and where such plants would not normally grow. Camellias, pieris, gaultherias, vacciniums and heathers are among other such plants which need special soil.

Above: *A glazed ceramic container is used to house a combination of lavender and* Euonymous fortunei *'Emerald Gaiety'; as long as they do not outgrow their container, such combinations can create a most attractive picture.*

Right: *Most elders make a large shrub after a few years, but they can still be used as pot plants, especially if cut to the base each spring. Here* Sambucus racemosa *'Plumosa Aurea' is growing in a large substitute-stone container. It is used as part of a larger planting.*

Above: *Fuchsias make exceptionally attractive container plants. The more tender varieties need to be over-wintered inside or started again each year, but hardier varieties can be left outside in milder climates.*

Above: *It is often possible to plant shrubs that form large bushes in containers for a few years while they are still small and then replace them with the same or another plant. Here* Cornus mas *'Aureoelegantissima' which could eventually grow to 6 m (20 ft) or more is being used.*

Right: *Acid-loving shrubs like this rhododendron benefit from being grown in containers, where they can have the soil they need.*

SHRUBS FOR CONTAINERS

Ballota pseudodictamnus	*Ilex* (holly)
Buxus sempervirens (box)	*Indigofera*
Callistemon citrinus (bottlebrush)	*Kalmia*
Camellia	*Laurus nobilis* (bay)
Convolvulus cneorum	*Lavandula* (lavender)
Cordyline australis	*Myrtus communis* (myrtle)
Cotoneaster	*Olearia* (daisy bush)
Erica (heather)	*Phormium* (New Zealand flax)
Fuchsia	*Rhododendron*
Hebe	*Rosa*
Helianthemum	*Rosmarinus* (rosemary)
Hydrangea	*Skimmia*
Hypericum	*Yucca*

Planting Shrubs in Containers

There is no great difficulty in growing plants in containers, so long as you remember that the pots are likely to need watering every day, except when it rains, and possibly more often than this in the summer.

CONTAINER CARE

When planting shrubs in containers, it is essential to use a good potting compost (potting soil) that contains plenty of grit or sharp sand, to help with drainage, and to add small stones to the pot so that excess water can drain away. In addition, a slow-release fertilizer and some water-retaining granules will encourage the plant to flourish.

Bear in mind that your plant will not grow indefinitely if it is kept in the same pot or compost (soil mix) for ever. Every year or so, remove the shrub and repot it using fresh compost. If the shrub is becoming pot-bound, that is,

the roots are going round the edge of the container, forming a tight knot, either put it in a larger pot or trim back some of the offending roots.

POSITIONING CONTAINERS

If you have a large enough garden, it is possible to keep the containers out of sight and only bring them into view when the shrubs are at their best, in full flower, for example. In a smaller garden, where this is more difficult, move the pots around so that the best ones are always in the most prominent position and even hiding the others if this is possible.

1 All containers should have a drainage hole in the bottom. Loosely cover this and the bottom of the pot with broken pottery, bits of tile or small stones, so that any excess water can freely drain away.

2 Partially fill the container with compost (soil mix) and then mix in some water-retaining granules. These essential granules will swell up and hold many times their own weight in water to give up to the plant's roots when they want it. While not considerably reducing the amount of water needed, water-retaining granules will make it easier for the shrub to come through really hot and dry times in midsummer. Follow the instructions on the packet as to quantities you need for the size of the pot you have.

3 Place the container in the position you finally want to have it and continue filling it with compost (the pot will be heavy to move once it is fully-planted). Plant the shrub to the same level as it was in its original container. Firm the compost down lightly and top up, if necessary, with some further compost.

4 Most composts contain fertilizers but the constant watering will soon leach (wash) it out. A slow-release fertilizer can be mixed with the compost or a tablet, as here, can be added to the pot, which will give six months' supply of nutrients. Read the packet for any special instructions.

5 Leave the top of the compost as it is, or cover it with stones of some sort, such as large pebbles, as here, or gravel. These not only give the container an attractive finish but help keep the compost cool and prevent water from evaporating.

6 Finally, water the container thoroughly and continue to do so at regular intervals. During hot weather, this is likely to be at least daily.

7 You may want to keep the newly-planted pot out of sight until the shrub has matured or comes into flower. However, if the container is large, it is often best to fill it *in situ*, because it will be very heavy once filled with compost.

Right: *This variegated pieris, which likes an acid soil, would soon languish and die in a chalky garden.*

Shrubs for Topiary

Most shrubs are grown naturally. They may be cut back if they get too big, or trimmed if they are part of a hedge, but their natural shape is not generally altered. However, there is one class of shrub-growing in which the shape is drastically altered, so much so that it takes a close look to identify the plants involved. These are topiaries.

PRODUCING A SHAPE

Topiaries can be cut to any shape the gardener desires. They can be formed into abstract or geometrical shapes, such as balls, cones or pyramids, or they can be made into something more intricate, perhaps depicting a bird, a person or even a teapot. There is little limit to what the imagination can produce in topiary.

Tight, slow-growing shrubs are the ones to choose for topiary, with yew and box being the best. Holly (*Ilex*), privet (*Ligustrum*) and box-leaf honeysuckle (*Lonicera nitida*) are also recommended. Several others can also be used, but they need a lot more attention to keep them neat.

The simplest topiaries are "carved" out of solid shrubs, particularly if they are yew or box, because these will easily regenerate and slowly fill out to their new shape. However, the most satisfactory way to produce topiary is to train the shrubs to their shape from the very beginning. A metal or wooden former or template helps with this. The shoots are tied in and trimmed as they grow, until the shrub has acquired the desired shape. Some formers are just a rough guide to the shape, intended to hold the main pieces in position, especially if they are

vulnerable, such as a peacock's tail, but others are shaped like the finished work and can be used as a trimming guide when the work is complete.

Topiaries can take several years to reach completion, so do not get too impatient. Several projects can be started in pots at the same time, so there is always something going on to keep the interest alive.

TOOLS FOR TOPIARY

Unless the topiary is on a large scale, avoid using powered tools. It is too easy to lose concentration or momentary control and disaster follows. In preference, use hand tools, which take longer but which give you more control. For cutting thicker stems, especially in the initial training, use secateurs (pruners), snipping out one stem at a time. Once the shape has been formed, trim it over with normal hedging shears or a pair of clippers of the type usually used for sheep-shearing. The latter give excellent control, but can only be used for light trimming, such as removing the tips of new growth. If the topiary is made from a shrub with large leaves, then use secateurs to trim it to avoid cutting the leaves in half, otherwise they will die back with a brown edge and the overall appearance will be spoiled.

Above: *In this topiary a four-masted ship in full sail glides across the garden. Here, the complicated design is slightly obscured by other topiaries in the background.*

Above: *This practical piece of topiary has a wooden seat worked into the bottom of the shrub, supported on a metal frame. A complete set round a table would be a novel feature for a barbecue or outdoor meal.*

Above: *These simple shapes worked in box can be used to advantage in a wide variety of positions in the garden. They will take several years of dedication to produce, but the effort is definitely worth it.*

Above: *Gardens do not have always to be serious: there is a sense of fun about this jolly witch, sitting around her cauldron with her cat and its mouse, which would cheer up anybody looking at it.*

Above: *Topiary shapes can be as precise or as free as you wish. In this free interpretation of a simple windmill, cut from yew, you can sense the pleasure of the person who created it.*

SHRUBS FOR ALL SEASONS

Shrubs in Spring

Shrubs come into their own in the spring. This is the time when everything is waking up and looking fresh and the gardener's own enthusiasm is at its greatest.

SPRING FLOWERS

Many shrubs flower in spring, which gives them ample time to produce seed and for it to ripen and be distributed to ensure the next generation.

The one big enemy of spring-flowering shrubs is the severe late frosts that occur in some areas. A false start to the spring brings warm weather and then a sudden frost kills all the new shoots and knocks off the flower buds. Rhododendrons, azaleas, pieris, magnolias and many others frequently suffer this fate. One solution is to give some protection if hard frost is forecast. Placing a sheet of fleece over them is often sufficient.

It is tempting to put all the spring shrubs together, for one glorious display, but resist this or, at least, mix in a few later-flowering ones as well or the area could become dull for the rest of the year. One solution is to plant *viticella* clematis through them. These are cut back to the ground in late winter so that they do not interfere with the shrubs' flowering, but grow up and cover them in blooms from midsummer onwards.

Try and finish planting any new shrubs by early spring and, as the various shrubs finish flowering, prune them as necessary. Remember to feed those that are in containers.

Above: *The flowering currant,* Ribes sanguineum, *is a beautiful spring-flowering shrub, but its foliage has a distinctive 'foxy' smell that not everyone likes.*

Above: *Camellias flower from the late winter through to the middle of spring. They are best planted where they do not get the early-morning sun, as this will destroy the buds if they have been frosted overnight.*

Right: *One of the earliest shrubs to flower is* Spiraea *'Arguta' which produces a frothy mountain of pure white flowers over quite a long period. Sometimes it will even produce a few blooms in midwinter, to brighten the gloom.*

Above: Exochorda x macrantha *'The Bride'* is a showy, spring-flowering plant. *When in full flower, it is so covered in pure white flowers that the leaves are barely visible. Here, many of the flowers are still in bud, forming attractive ribbons of white balls.*

Above: *Rhododendrons are many gardeners' favourite spring shrub. They need an acid soil and a position out of hot sunlight. They can be bought in a wide variety of colours, some soft and subtle and others bright and brash.*

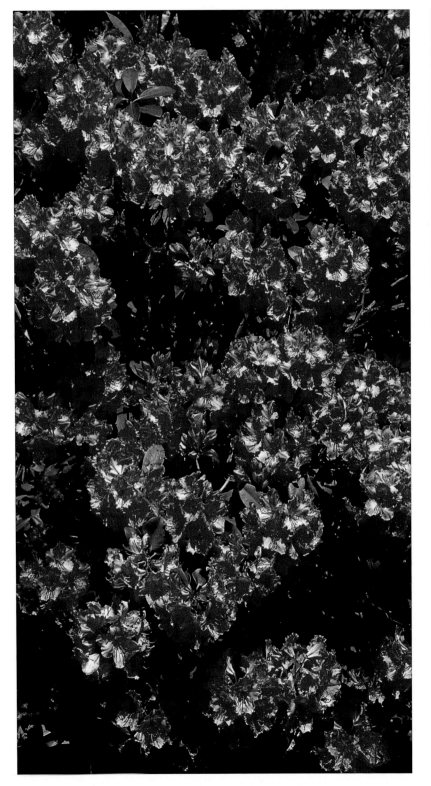

Above: *Forsythia creates one of the biggest splashes of colour in the spring. Here it is used as an informal hedge. It should be cut immediately after flowering to ensure that new flowering shoots grow in time for next season.*

Right: *One of the best-loved spring shrubs is* Magnolia stellata. *Each year it is a mass of delicate star-like flowers in glistening white or tinged with pink. The effect is enhanced because the flowers appear on naked stems, before the leaves develop.*

Left: *Azaleas are a form of rhododendron. There are ever-green and deciduous forms, both producing masses of flowers in a good year. Many of the deciduous forms have a wonderful scent. Like other rhododendrons, they need an acid soil and shelter from hot sun.*

Left: *Berberis are versatile plants, because they are attractive for much of the year: they have spectacular flower displays in spring and good foliage until summer, which then becomes beautifully tinted in the autumn. As an extra, many varieties produce red berries, which often last throughout the winter. Shown here is* Berberis linearifolia *'Orange King'*.

Left: *Lilac (*Syringa*) flowers in the late spring. It has one of the most distinctive smells of all spring-flowering shrubs and is popular for cutting to take indoors. When the flowers die they can look ugly, especially the white forms, and should be removed.*

Above: *A close up of a berberis in flower. This one is* Berberis *'Goldilocks'. Many varieties have sweetly-scented flowers, and all are much loved by bees.*

SPRING-FLOWERING SHRUBS

Berberis	*Magnolia*
Camellia	*Mahonia*
Chaenomeles	*Pieris*
(japonica)	*Prunus* (cherry)
Corylopsis	*Rhododendron*
Corylus (hazel)	*Ribes* (currant)
Cytisus (broom)	*Rosmarinus* (rosemary)
Daphne	*Salix* (willow)
Exochorda	*Spiraea*
Forsythia	*Viburnum*

Shrubs in Summer

While spring is noted for its fresh, young flowers, summer, especially early summer, is the time of mainstream flowering. This is the time for heady scents, particularly on long, warm, summer evenings. It is also a time when insects are at their busiest, with flowering shrubs full of bees and butterflies. Buddleja, in particular, is good for both.

ENJOYING THE SUMMER

Mix in a few summer-flowering shrubs with those from earlier in the year, so that the garden or borders have some form of continuity. Plant fragrant shrubs near where you sit or relax, and use those with thick foliage to create areas of privacy.

There are many types of shrub or dwarf tree that can be used for producing fruit. Currants, gooseberries, cherries, plums and apples can all be grown as small shrubs. These have decorative blossoms in the spring and then provide the delights of picking your own fruit in the summer and autumn. They need not be in a special fruit garden; grow them in ordinary borders, but beware that the soft fruits may need netting, as they ripen, to prevent birds from eating them.

In a small garden, use large shrubs, rather than trees, to create a shady sitting area. There are many that can be used and they are better suited to being cut to shape than trees.

Generally, there is not much to be done to shrubs during the summer. If the garden is in a town or near a road where there is a lot of dust and grime, wash off the leaves with a sprinkler, or spray if there is a prolonged period of drought, because the film over the surface of the foliage will impair the shrub's ability to make food. Also water, if necessary. Continue to feed those shrubs in containers until the end of the summer.

Above: *In summer the bush* Olearia x haastii *resembles a snowy mountain. Shown in full flower, this one is delicately fronted by a variegated grass,* Phalaris arundinacea *'Picta', more commonly known as "gardener's garters". Always consider the relationship between plants, rather than simply putting them in at random.*

Left: *Roses are at their best in summer. Some are once-flowering and do so in the early summer, but many go on flowering throughout the whole summer. Some gardeners prefer to have a separate garden or special beds for roses, while others like to mix them in with other plants. This lovely old rose is* R. *'Stanwell Perpetual'.*

Above: *From midsummer onwards, the hydrangeas begin to flower. There is a wide range available. The delicate lace-caps are popular because of the shape of the flowers. Here, the beautiful* H. quercifolia, *or oak-leafed hydrangea, combines good flowers and good foliage. Another very attractive hydrangea to consider is* H. aspera *'Villosa', which has soft, furry leaves and subtle, mauvish-blue and pink flowers.*

Above: *Many hydrangeas have white flowers. On the whole, they prefer a shady position and here the whites come into their own, illuminating their surroundings.*

Left: *The vexed question with these mop-headed (*H. macrophylla*) varieties of hydrangea is the colour. The same plant can have blue flowers on acid soil, red ones on a neutral soil and pink ones on an alkaline soil. It is possible to vary the colour by changing the acidity of your soil but, in the long run, it is more satisfactory to go with what you have. If you want to have different colours, plant hydrangeas in containers with the appropriate soil.*

Left: *The rock roses, or* Cistus, *make very fine summer-flowering plants. They are especially good in hot summers as they need a dry soil and can happily cope with droughts. The flowers only last a day, but are replaced by fresh ones the following morning. Some species drop their petals in the early afternoon so they are not much use to the evening gardener. This one is* C. x skanbergii, *with white-centred pink flowers set off against soft, greyish-green foliage.*

Below: *The kalmias are not seen so frequently as they should be. This may be because they need an acid soil and light shade, but even gardeners with alkaline soils should be able to grow them in containers. They flower in early summer, covering the branches with pink or red flowers. These are held in bunches, each flower being cup-shaped in a way that is unique to the plant.*

Above: *Allied to the rock rose, and liking the same kind of hot, dry conditions, are the halimiums. These are evergreen, with white or yellow flowers, some varieties having brown blotches at the base of the petals. This one is* Halimium x pauanum, *a form with pure golden flowers. Again, the flowers are produced afresh each day over a long period through the summer and sometimes well into autumn.*

Above: *The lavateras have become popular with gardeners, and justifiably so. They produce flowers over a long period, from early summer right through to the first frost. Sometimes, after a severe winter, the stems are cut to the ground and, because the new shoots take a time to grow, the flowering does not start until much later in the summer. They are not long-lived plants and it is wise to take cuttings regularly, which is not a difficult task as they root easily.*

Above: *Californian lilacs, Ceanothus, are good-value plants. Although a few of them are deciduous, the majority in cultivation have evergreen foliage that stays attractive throughout the year. In the early summer, they are covered with masses of blue flowers, the shade of blue varying from light to dark, depending on the variety. This is the dwarf form, 'Pin Cushion'.*

Above: *Being closely related, the halimiums and the cistus produce crossbreeds of which this* x Halimiocistus revolii *is an example. The first part of the name is a combination of those of its parents. This shrub makes a low-spreading carpet of green foliage, which contrasts well with its myriad snow-white flowers.*

Above: *The New Zealand tea tree,* Leptospermum *is becoming increasingly popular, especially in milder areas. They flower over a long period, with masses of small, saucer-shaped flowers in red, pink or white, often with a dark centre. There are also double-flowered varieties and several dwarf forms that are good for rock gardens. This one is* L. scoparium *'Lyndon'.*

Above: *The New Zealand hebes are amongst some of the best summer-flowering plants. They make beautifully-shaped shrubs, with good foliage and masses of flowers that are produced over a long period. The long spikes of flowers seem to whizz around in all directions, like fireworks.*

SUMMER-FLOWERING SHRUBS

Abutilon	*Hydrangea*
Brachyglottis	*Hypericum*
Buddleja	*Indigofera*
Callistemon (bottlebrush)	*Jasminum*
Carpenteria	*Kalmia*
Ceanothus (Californian lilac)	*Lavandula* (lavender)
Cistus (rock rose)	*Lavatera*
Cornus (dog wood)	*Leptospermum*
Deutzia	*Leycesteria*
Erica (heather)	*Olearia* (daisy bush)
Fremontodendron	*Philadelphus* (mock orange)
Fuchsia	*Potentilla*
Halimium	*Rosa*
Hebe	*Sambucus* (elder)
Hibiscus	*Viburnum*
Hoheria	*Weigela*

Above: *Another plant from the same region as the New Zealand hebes is the Australian bottlebrush,* Callistemon. *This shrub has curious bottle-shaped flowers, that explain its common name. Being of Australian origin, they are on the tender side, but some can be brought through to survive most winters by planting against a warm wall. If in doubt, plant in a container and keep inside during the cold months. This species is* C. sieberi.

Right: *Various forms of* Abutilon vitifolium *are appearing in more and more gardens, because it is realized that they are frost hardy. They will not survive a severe winter, but they are quick-growing and can easily be replaced. They come in a range of colours, including red, white and mauve, as here.*

Shrubs in Autumn

Autumn sees the closing of the annual growing cycle.
With it come the autumn tints and hues both of the
foliage and of the many berries and other fruits. Autumn
is the season of reds and browns.

LONG-FLOWERING SHRUBS

There are not many shrubs that
flower just in the autumn, but
some summer ones continue
right through to the frosts.
Fuchsias are particularly useful.
Buddlejas, hibiscus, hydrangeas,
hypericums and indigoferas also
continue to flower. One of the
true autumn-flowering plants is
Osmanthus heterophyllus, with
its fragrant flowers more
reminiscent of spring than of
summer. Other plants that are
associated with autumn
flowering are the ceratostigmas
and Eucryphia glutinosa.

AUTUMN LEAVES

The true glory of the autumn
belongs to foliage. In a small
garden, in particular, it is a wise
choice to make every plant earn
its keep, and those that provide
a fiery end to the year's gardening certainly deserve their place.
Berries and other fruit are an
added bonus; they are not only
attractive but also supply birds
and other animals with food for
the harsh months ahead.

Autumn is the time to start
preparing beds for new planting
and indeed to actually start
planting. It is also a time to
check that those plants that need
staking are still securely held in
place, before the winter winds
begin. Once the leaves have
fallen, it is a good idea to go
round and examine each shrub,
removing any dead or dying
wood. Autumn is also the time

for clearing up fallen leaves and
stopping them from smothering
other plants and lawns. Do not
waste them by burning or
throwing them away. Compost
them and return them to the soil
once they have rotted.

Right: *While the best-known
Osmanthus flower in the spring,
O.* heterophyllus *flowers in late
autumn, perfuming the air.*

Below: *Hydrangeas are really
summer-flowering shrubs, but
their flowers last such a long time
that they are still flourishing well
into autumn, when their leaves
lose their green colour and take
on autumn tints.*

SHRUBS WITH GOOD AUTUMN FOLIAGE

Amelanchier
Berberis thunbergii
Ceratostigma willmottianum
   (leaves and flowers)
Cotinus (smoke bush)
Enkianthus
Euonymus alatus
Fothergilla
Rhus hirta
Stephandra incisa

SHRUBS WITH GOOD AUTUMN FLOWERS

Buddleja
Ceratostigma
Eucryphia glutinosa
Fuchsia
Hibiscus
Hydrangea
Hypericum
Indigofera
Osmanthus heterophyllus

Above: *The Judas tree is a curious shrub. In spring, purple flowers fill the naked branches; in autumn the leaves take on beautiful colours.*

Left: *Some of the most brilliant of autumn colours are presented by the spindle trees and bushes,* Euonymus. *The colourful* E. alatus *'Compactus' is suitable for the smaller garden. Interest in winter is maintained by its corky wings on the stems.*

Above: *Berberises provide the gardener with a valuable group of plants. They are attractive at all seasons of the year, providing flower, berry and foliage interest. Most produce fiery-coloured foliage and waxy red berries in the autumn, including this* B. thunbergii *'Red Pillar.'*

Above: *Blue is not a colour that one normally associates with the autumn; indeed there are not many shrubs that produce flowers of this colour at any time of year.* Ceratostigma willmottianum *has piercingly blue flowers that carry over from summer well into autumn.*

Right: *Most of the* eucryphias *soon become large trees, but* E. glutinosa, *although it can become large, usually remains small enough to be considered a shrub. The beauty of this plant is the late-season flowers. They are glisteningly white bowls, with a central boss of stamens.*

Left: *As well as its beautiful flowers,* Eucryphia glutinosa *is deciduous, and its leaves take on autumnal tints.*

Above: *Fothergill (*Fothergilla major*) is another good-value shrub with good flowers in late spring or early summer and wonderfully-coloured foliage in autumn. It is very slow growing and although it can eventually become quite large, it will take many years to do so.*

Below: *Many of the cotinus, or smoke bushes, have foliage that is attractive throughout the growing seasons. Many are dark purple, which beautifully set off their smoky plumes of flowers.*

Above: Amelanchier lamarckii *frequently grows into a small tree but, if required, it can be pruned to produce several stems instead of a trunk, so that it becomes a large shrub. It is covered with delicate white flowers in spring and then in autumn its leaves colour beautifully.*

Shrubs in Winter

Winter is often considered the dead month in the garden and many may be tempted to stay indoors. But, in fact, there is a lot going on. A number of shrubs flower at this time of year, some of them with beautiful scents that are particularly noticeable on warm winter days. There are also evergreen shrubs that can look particularly good in the low winter light, especially those with shiny leaves.

WINTER TASKS

There is a lot going on during the winter months and the garden should reflect this. Because many of the shrubs that provide winter interest are dull at other times, they should be planted in less prominent positions. In this way, they will show up in winter when other plants have died back, but will be masked by more interesting plants for the rest of the year.

If the weather is fine and the soil not waterlogged, work can proceed. The more achieved during these winter months, the less there will be to do later in the year. If all the beds are forked over, the weeds removed and the soil mulched, the need for weeding throughout the spring and summer will be considerably reduced. Indeed, one hour spent weeding in winter will save several later on. Provided that the ground is neither waterlogged nor frozen, this is also the best time of year for planting and moving shrubs.

During snowy weather, make certain that shrubs, especially evergreen ones, are not weighed down and broken by excessive falls. Knock the snow off at the earliest opportunity. Light falls should be left if there is a cold wind, because these will help protect the plants.

Above left: *The winter jasmine,* Jasminum nudiflorum, *is truly a winter plant, flowering from the end of autumn through into the early spring, totally ignoring the frost and snow. Stems taken indoors make attractive winter flower decorations.*

Above right: *The winter hazels,* Corylopsis, *make excellent winter plants, with yellow catkins that defy the frosts.*

Right: *Witch hazels,* Hamamelis, *produce curious flowers like clusters of ribbons. As well as being attractive, they have a strident smell that fills the air on sunny days.*

SHRUBS WITH WINTER INTEREST

Corylus (hazel)
Cornus mas (dog wood)
Corylopsis
Hamamelis (witch hazel)
Jasminum nudiflorum
Lonicera purpusii
Lonicera standishii
Lonicera fragrantissima
Mahonia
Viburnum bodnantense
Viburnum farreri
Viburnum tinus

Above and below: *Like many winter-flowering shrubs, the mahonias are beautifully scented. This is possibly to make certain that they attract what few insect pollinators there are at this time of year. Mahonia is a prickly subject and plants can look a bit tatty at some times of year, but in winter it is supreme, with its long spikes of yellow flowers and wafting scent.*

Left: *Viburnums are a versatile group of plants, with at least one variety in flower at each time of year, including two or three in winter. Viburnum tinus is evergreen and is covered with flat heads of flowers throughout most of the winter and often through to the spring as well. On warm days the flowers have a delicate perfume.*

Shrubs with Coloured Stems

Those shrubs that have coloured bark and are grown for their winter stems such as *Rubus cockburnianus, R. thibetanus* and *Salix alba* 'Britzensis' are very worthwhile and are of great value to the winter gardener.

WINTER STEMS

When the leaves have fallen from the shrubs it is time to appreciate what is left: the bare outline of the stems and branches and, more importantly, the colour of the bark. Not all shrubs are coloured in this way but a number provide a wonderful display, especially if they are planted so they catch the low winter sunshine. The shrubs are best cut to the ground each spring, so that there is new growth for the following winter.

SHRUBS WITH COLOURED WINTER STEMS

Cornus alba
Corylus avellana contorta
Rubus cockburnianus
Rubus thibetanus
Salix alba 'Britzensis'

Above: *The red glow of the stems of* Cornus alba *is seen here on a typical winter's day.*

Above: *The ghostly stems of* Rubus cockburnianum *shine out in the winter landscape. The white is a "powdery" bloom, which is lost on older stems, and the whole plant should be cut to the ground each spring to produce new stems for the following winter.*

Above: Cornus stolonifera *'Flaviramea' is quite vibrant with its yellowish green bark. If left to mature, the stems lose their rich colour and hard pruning every spring will ensure plenty of new growth for the following winter.*

Above: Rubus *'Golden Veil'* is an extremely attractive plant, with bright yellow foliage in the summer and white stems in the winter. Here the leaves have nearly all fallen, revealing the attractive winter stems beneath.

Right: *Several of the willows have beautiful winter stems as well as providing their distinctive catkins or pussies at the end of the season.* Salix alba *produces some of the best coloured stems. Here it is represented by* S.a. vitellina *and its variety* S.a.v. *'Britzensis'. The stems should be cut back each spring to encourage new growth for the following winter.*

Left: *Here* Salix gracilistyla *'Melanostachys' displays the catkins typical of so many willows in the winter. As well as being attractive in the garden, the stems are very popular for adding to indoor winter flower arrangements.*

CLIMBERS

Climbers do not seem to have any shape: they just go straight up – or do they? When you stop to think about it you realize they are actually much more versatile. For a start, they can be trained to spread sideways, thus covering a considerable area, or even grown through trees and shrubs. Climbers are slightly more difficult to grow than shrubs, simply because they need something to climb up and usually an element of training. However, the choice of training method gives the gardener plenty of scope. Climbers can be grown on walls with a variety of supports, including wires and trellis panels. Trellising can also be used to form fences or screens, either around the outside of the garden or within it. Archways, arbours and pergolas are other ideal supports for climbers.

Left: *Golden hop* (Humulus lupulus *'Aureus') is an attractive, self-supporting perennial climber with bristly twining stems.*

TYPES OF CLIMBERS

Annual Climbers

When considering climbers, most gardeners automatically think of woody climbing plants, such as clematis or roses, and forget about the annuals. However, annual climbers are extremely useful plants and should never be overlooked.

INSTANT COLOUR

One of the great virtues of annual climbers is that they are temporary; they allow the gardener the opportunity of changing the plants or changing their position every year. This means that it is possible to fill gaps at short notice or simply to change your mind as to the way the garden should look.

Another virtue of annuals is that they come in a wide range of colours, some of which are not so readily available in other climbers. The "hot" colours – red, orange, yellow – in partic-ular, are of great use. Annuals, on the whole, have a very long flowering season, much longer than most perennials. This also makes them very useful.

The one drawback of annuals is that they must be raised afresh each year. Many can be bought as young plants from garden centres but all can be raised from seed. This doesn't require a lot of time or space: the majority will germinate quite happily on a kitchen windowsill. With the exception of sweet peas, which are hardy and should be sown in winter, most annuals should be sown in spring, pricked out into pots, hardened off and then planted out in the open ground as soon as the threat of frosts has passed.

Annuals can be grown up any type of support, both permanent and temporary. Although they are only in place for a few months, some, such as *Cobaea scandens* (cathedral bells), can cover a very large area. Nasturtiums (*Tropaeolum*) are also annuals that can put on a lot of growth in a season.

Above: *Many climbers can be used as trailing plants as well as climbing ones. Annual nasturtiums are a good example of this. Here the nasturtium 'Jewel of Africa' is seen around a purple-leaved* Canna *'Wyoming'.*

ANNUAL CLIMBERS

Asarina	*Lagenaria* (gourds)
Caiophera	*Lathyrus odoratus* (sweet peas)
Cobaea scandens (cathedral bells)	*Lathyrus sativus*
Convolvulus tricolor	*Maurandia*
Eccremocarpus scaber	*Mikania scandens*
Ipomoea (morning glory)	*Rhodochiton atrosanguineus*
Lablab purpureus (syn. *Dolichos lablab*)	*Thunbergia alata* (black-eyed Susan)
	Tropaeolum (nasturtium)

Above: *Not all "annuals" are strictly annual.* Eccremocarpus scaber, *shown here, is really a perennial but it is often treated as an annual and planted afresh every year. It is shown with an everlasting pea,* Lathyrus latifolius.

Above: *Annuals are not restricted to just flowers. Many vegetables also make attractive climbers as well as being productive. Here, scarlet runner beans are grown up a wigwam (tepee) of canes. This is not only attractive but allows the gardener to produce quite a large crop in a small space.*

Above: *Sweet peas are amongst everyone's favourite climbers. Not only do they look good in the garden; they are also wonderful flowers for cutting for the house. Most have a delicious scent.*

Right: Cobaea scandens *is a vigorous annual climber. For success it must be planted in a warm position, preferably against a wall, and given as long a growing season as possible.*

Left: *The morning glories,* Ipomoea, *are just that, glorious. Soak seeds overnight before sowing and germinate in a warm place or propagator. Harden off thoroughly before planting or they are unlikely to do well. Plant them in a sheltered sunny position.*

Evergreen Climbers

Climbing plants are mainly valued for their flowers, but there are a few that hold their place in the garden because of their evergreen foliage. Probably the best known is ivy. Its glossy, three-pointed leaves make a permanent cover for whatever they climb up.

FOLIAGE SCREENS

One of the best uses of evergreens is as a cover for eyesores. They can be grown directly over an ugly wall or allowed to clamber over trellising judiciously positioned to hide a fuel tank or messy utility area. There are some places in the garden, moreover, where it is preferable that the appearance does not change with the seasons. A gateway, perhaps, may be surrounded by an evergreen climber over an arch, so that it presents the same familiar image to the visitor all year round.

From a design point of view, evergreen climbers provide a permanent point of reference within the garden. They form part of the structure, around which the rest of the garden changes season by season.

Plain green can be a little uninspiring; green works extremely well, however, as a backdrop against which to see other, more colourful, plants. Climbers such as ivy have glossy leaves, which reflect the light, giving a shimmering effect as they move. Evergreen leaves can vary in shape, and they can also be variegated, providing contrasting tones of green and sometimes colour variation.

Right: Laurus nobilis *provides attractive green foliage.*

EVERGREEN CLIMBERS
Clematis armandii
Clematis cirrhosa
Fremontodendron
   californicum
Hedera (ivy)
Lonicera japonica
Solanum crispum
Solanum jasminoides
Vinca major (periwinkle)

EVERGREEN WALL SHRUBS
Azara
Callistemon citrinus
Carpenteria californica
Ceanothus
Coronilla glauca
Cotoneaster
Desfontainea spinosa
Elaeagnus x ebbingei
Elaeagnus pungens
Escallonia
Euonymus fortunei
Euonymus japonicus
Garrya elliptica
Itea ilicifolia
Laurus nobilis
Magnolia grandiflora
Piptanthus laburnifolius
Pyracantha (firethorn)
Teucrium fruticans

Above: *Variegated ivies can make a big impact. Those with golden variegation are excellent for lighting up dark corners and they are especially good in helping to brighten the grey days of winter.*

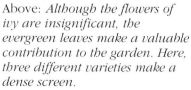

Above: *Although the flowers of ivy are insignificant, the evergreen leaves make a valuable contribution to the garden. Here, three different varieties make a dense screen.*

Right: *This* Solanum crispum *'Glasnevin' is one of the very best climbers. Unless the weather gets very cold, it retains its shiny leaves throughout the winter and then is covered with its blue flowers from late spring right through to the autumn. The leaves may drop during severe winters, but they soon recover.*

Above: Vinca major *(periwinkle) can be considered a shrub if it is kept rigorously under control by cutting back, but it is often used as a climber, scrambling through shrubs and hedges, as here. It retains its glossy green leaves throughout the winter and produces bright blue flowers from midwinter onwards.*

Below: *There is a brightly variegated periwinkle, 'Variegata', which looks good against dark hedges.*

Climbers with Spring Interest

Spring is one of the most joyous times of the year in the garden; the winter is over and ahead lie the glories of summer. Many of the plants that flower at this time of year have a freshness about them that almost defies definition.

PROTECTING FROM FROST

Spring is a time of varying weather and plants can suffer badly from late frosts. This is made worse when frosts are preceded by a warm spell, in which a lot of new growth appears. These young shoots are susceptible to sudden cold weather and can be burnt off. Buds are also likely to be harmed and it is not uncommon to see a *Clematis montana*, for example, covered in buds and full of promise one day, only to be denuded of buds the next after a night of hard frost. This, however, should never deter you from growing spring-flowering climbers; such frosts do not occur every year and, in most springs, these climbers perform at their best. If frosts are forecast, it is possible to guard against them.

Many of the more tender early-flowering shrubs need walls for protection and are usually grown as wall shrubs. Shrubs such as camellias are particularly prone to frost damage and so are grown in this way.

Once they have finished flowering, many spring-flowering climbers are a bit dreary for the rest of the year. One way to enliven them is to grow another, later-flowering, climber through their stems. This is very useful where space is limited.

SPRING-FLOWERING CLIMBERS AND WALL SHRUBS
Abeliophyllum distichum
Akebia quinata
Akebia trifoliata
Azara serrata
Ceanothus arboreus 'Trewithen Blue'
Chaenomeles (japonica or ornamental quince)
Clematis alpina
Clematis armandii
Clematis macropetala
Clematis montana
Forsythia suspensa
Garrya elliptica
Lonicera (honeysuckles)
Piptanthus laburnifolius
Ribes laurifolia
Rosa (early roses)
Schisandra
Solanum cripsum 'Glasnevin'
Wisteria

Above: *Spring is the time when all plants are beginning to burst forth. Clematis are some of the earliest climbers, one of the earliest and most impressive being* C. montana, *which frequently has so much bloom that the leaves cannot be seen.*

Right: Clematis armandii *is one of the few evergreen clematis. It is also one of the earliest to flower, doing so in late winter or early spring.*

Above: *Another early clematis, more delicate in appearance, is* C. macropetala. *It is here seen with* C. montana, *which will flower a week or so later.*

Above: *Honeysuckles* (Lonicera) *are a great feature of the spring. This one* (L. periclymenum) *is in a natural habitat – scrambling through a bush. In this case, the supporting plant is a berberis, whose purply-bronze leaves make a good contrast to the yellow flowers.*

Left: Rosa *'Maigold' is one of the many roses that although strictly a shrub, have a tendency to climb. They can be used as low climbers up pillars, as here, or on tripods, trellis or low walls. It starts flowering early in the season and often repeats later in the year.*

Right: *When in full flower, wisteria must be one of the most beautiful of climbers. It can be grown as a free-standing tree but it is best supported on a wall or pergola. Walls help to protect it against late frosts which can damage the flower buds.*

Climbers with Summer Interest

Summer is when many climbers are at their best. Clematis and roses, in particular, produce plenty of blooms, covering pergolas and arches as well as climbing up walls and through trees and shrubs. They make a valuable contribution to the summer scene, giving vertical emphasis to a garden that would otherwise be flat and less interesting.

SHADE AND FRAGRANCE

During hot, sunny summers, climbers are most welcome for providing dappled shade as they cover arbours and pergolas. There is nothing better than to sit on a summer's day in the shade of an arbour or relax there with a meal or a drink in the evening after work. Relaxation is further enhanced if the climbers are fragrant – and many are. Roses, honeysuckle and jasmine are three of the most popular scented climbers.

Many shrubs and trees are spring-flowering and climbers can be used to enliven them during the summer months, when they are, perhaps, at their dullest. *Clematis viticella* is probably the best to use for this purpose; because it is cut back almost to the ground during the winter, it doesn't smother the tree or shrub when it is in flower. Later in the season, when the tree or shrub has finished flowering, the clematis grows up through its branches and produces its own colour, usually over a long period.

Similarly, climbers can be used in herbaceous borders, where there are gaps left by perennials that flower early in the season and are then cut back. Clematis can be left to scramble through the border, either without any support or over a simple framework of twigs.

Above: Campsis radicans *is a beautiful climber for the second half of the summer. Its large tubular flowers, here just opening, contrast well with the green of the foliage. It is not a common climber but it is not difficult to find or to grow.*

SUMMER CLIMBERS

Campsis
Clematis
Cobaea scandens (cathedral bells)
Eccremocarpus scaber (Chilean glory flower)
Fallopia baldschuanica (Russian vine)
Ipomoea (morning glories)
Jasminum (jasmines)
Lapageria rosea
Lathyrus (peas)
Lonicera (honeysuckles)
Mutisia
Passiflora (passion-flowers)

Phaseolus coccineus (runner beans)
Plumbago auriculata (Cape leadwort)
Rosa (roses)
Schisandra
Schizophragma
Solanum crispum 'Glasnevin'
Solanum jasminoides
Thunbergia alata (black-eyed Susan)
Trachelospermum
Tropaeolum (nasturtium)
Wisteria

Above: Clematis florida *'Sieboldii' is a very distinct clematis, with creamy white outer petals and an inner button of purple ones. It is a beautiful flower even when still in bud and while opening.*

Right: Clematis *'Perle d'Azur' must be one of the best of the blue clematis. It produces flowers of a delicate lilac blue in tremendous profusion around midsummer.*

Above: *Bougainvillea is a climber from hot climates. In more temperate areas, it has to be grown under glass, such as in a conservatory, but, in warmer districts, it can be grown outside. Its brilliant colours continue for months as it is the papery bracts rather than the flowers that provide the colour.*

Right: *Scrambling plants are a neglected area. There are very many of them and they can provide a lot of vertical interest through the summer months. Here a* Euonymus fortunei *'Emerald Gaiety' scrambles up through a large bush, with* Geranium x oxonianum *pushing its way up through both.*

Left: *Unlike the sweet pea, the perennial* Lathyrus grandiflorus *does not smell, but it is a most beautiful small climber. The round pea flowers are large and full of rich colour. They are best planted under shrubs, through which they will happily scramble.*

Above: *Another scrambler is* Tropaeolum speciosum. *This, like* Lathyrus grandiflorus, above, *has a more common annual relative, the nasturtium. However,* Tropaeolum speciosum *is a perennial and has small flowers of an intense flame red. It will scramble up through any shrub.*

Right: Tropaeolum peregrinum *(canary creeper) is tender to frosts, but if protected will flower throughout the summer.*

Left: *Not all climbers need to climb to great heights to be attractive. This herbaceous climber scrambles up through other plants with gay abandon. It is* Convolvulus althaeoides *and has delicate pink flowers, which are set off well against its silver foliage. It likes a sunny, well-drained spot.*

Above: *Passion-flowers are tender climbers, best grown against walls. Most should be grown under glass but* Passiflora caerulea *is hardy enough to be grown outside. The flowers are amongst the most extraordinary of all climbers.*

Right: *For many people, roses are the best summer climbing plants. They can be grown in a wide variety of ways, including up tripods, as seen here. This is* Rosa *'Dortmund'.*

Climbers with Autumn Interest

Most climbers have finished flowering by the time the autumn arrives but many have qualities that make them still desirable in the garden at this time of year.

FOLIAGE AND BERRIES

Perhaps the biggest attraction of autumn climbers is the change in colour of the leaves, prior to their fall. Many take on autumnal tints, some of the most fiery red. This will completely transform the appearance of the climber itself and, often, that of the surrounding area. Another benefit that some climbers have to offer is that they produce berries or fruit. Most produce seed of some kind or other but these are often visually insignificant; others produce an abundance of bright berries – honeysuckle (*Lonicera*), for example – or large luxurious fruit, such as the passion-flowers (*Passiflora*). Others carry their seeds in a different but, none the less, very attractive way. The fluffy or silky seed heads of clematis, for example, always make an interesting feature.

As well as providing an important visual element in the garden, the berries and other forms of seed are also a good source of food for birds. Birds will be attracted to the fruit for as long as they last, which may be well beyond the autumn and into the winter. Not only birds like fruit: man also likes the garden's edible bounty and many fruiting plants, ranging from currants and gooseberries to apples, plums, pears and apricots, can be grown against a wall, which provides not only support but also warmth and protection. Fruiting trees, such as apples and pears, also make good plants to train up and over arches and pergolas.

Right: Pyracantha *offers the choice of yellow, red or orange berries, depending on the variety. This is* P. *'Orange Charmer'.*

AUTUMNAL-FOLIAGED CLIMBERS

Actinidia (kiwi fruit)
Akebia quinata
Campsis
Chaenomeles (japonica or flowering quince)
Clematis alpina
Clematis flammula
Clematis tibetana vernayi
Cotoneaster
Fallopia baldschuanica (Russian vine)
Hydrangea anomala petiolaris
Hydrangea aspera
Hydrangea quercifolia
Jasminum officinale (jasmine)
Lonicera tragophylla (honeysuckle)
Parthenocissus (Boston ivy or Virginia creeper)
Passiflora (passion-flower)
Ribes speciosum
Rosa (roses)
Tropaeolum (nasturtium)
Vitis (grapevine)

BERRIED AND FRUITING CLIMBERS AND WALL SHRUBS

Actinidia (kiwi fruit)
Akebia
Clematis
Cotoneaster
Hedera (ivy)
Humulus lupulus (hop)
Ilex (holly)
Lonicera (honeysuckle)
Malus (crab apple)
Passiflora (passion-flower)
Prunus (plums, apricots, peaches)
Pyracantha (firethorn)
Pyrus (pears)
Rosa (roses)
Vitis (grapevine)

Above: Clematis cirrhosa *flowers in late autumn and carries its fluffy seed heads well into winter.*

Left: *The berries of* Cotoneaster horizontalis *are set off well against the foliage of* Helleborus foetidus.

Above and right: Parthenocissus henryana *is seen here in both its summer and autumn colours.*

Left: *Clematis display a mass of silky heads as beautiful as any flowers throughout the autumn.*

Below: *Fruit trees are attractive as wall shrubs as they carry blossom in spring and fruit in the autumn. This pear, 'Doyenne du Comice', has attractive foliage, too.*

Climbers with Winter Interest

While there are not many climbers that are interesting in winter, they are still a group of plants that are worth thinking about. Valuable wall space should not be taken up with plants that do not earn their keep for the greater part of the year, but it is often possible to find space for at least one that brightens up the winter scene.

Above: Hedera colchica *'Dentata Variegata'* is in perfect condition even in these frosty conditions. The gold variegation is good for lightening up dark winter days.

Above: *The winter jasmine,* Jasminum nudiflorum, *flowers throughout winter, supplying cut flowers for indoors and decorating walls and fences outside.*

WINTER-FLOWERING CLIMBERS

Surprisingly, there is one clematis that is in full flower during the bleaker winter months. *Clematis cirrhosa* is available in several forms, some with red blotches on their bell-shaped flowers. *Clematis armandii* appears towards the end of winter and heralds the beginning of a new season. There are three honeysuckles that flower in the winter and, although they are, strictly speaking, shrubs, they can be grown against a wall. As an added bonus, these are very strongly scented and they will flower throughout the whole of the winter. Another wall shrub that flowers early is *Garrya elliptica*, with its long, silver catkins. This is the more valuable because it will grow on a north-facing wall.

One of the most commonly grown wall shrubs is the winter jasmine, *Jasminum nudiflorum*, which produces a wonderful display of bright yellow flowers. Unfortunately, unlike its summer relatives, it is not scented.

EVERGREEN CLIMBERS

While not so attractive as the flowering plants, evergreen climbers, such as ivy (*Hedera*), can be used as winter cover both for walls and for other supports. These evergreen climbers afford valuable winter protection for birds and insects, especially if grown by a warm wall. Different green tones and, especially, variegated leaves, can add a surprising amount of winter cheer, even on dark days.

Climbers and wall shrubs that still carry berries from the previous autumn can add interest in the winter. Cotoneaster and pyracantha are good examples.

Right: Clematis armandii *flowers in late winter, with a wonderful display of pure-white flowers.*

WINTER CLIMBERS AND WALL SHRUBS

Chaenomeles (japonica or flowering quince)
Clematis armandii
Clematis cirrhosa
Elaeagnus x ebbingei
Elaeagnus pungens
Garrya elliptica
Hedera (ivy)
Jasminum nudiflorum (winter jasmine)
Lonicera fragrantissima (winter honeysuckle)
Lonicera x purpusii
Lonicera standishii

Above: Garrya elliptica *is an excellent plant for winter. It has beautiful silver catkins and is one of the few plants suitable for growing on north-facing walls.*

Above: Clematis cirrhosa *is the earliest clematis to flower, starting in early winter and continuing until spring. The many varieties include this one, 'Balearica'.*

Right: Chaenomeles, *known as* japonica, *or Japanese or ornamental quince, flowers from midwinter to spring, then has hard fruit that often lasts through until the next spring.*

Fragrant Climbers

When choosing plants, the main consideration is, often, what the flowers are like, followed by the foliage. Something that is often forgotten, or just considered as a bonus, is fragrance; and yet it is something that most people enjoy and it enhances the pleasure of all uses of the garden.

USING FRAGRANCE

Climbers include some of the loveliest and most scented plants in the garden. Some of them, such as honeysuckle or jasmine, will perfume the air over a long distance. They are always worth growing on house walls near windows that are often open, so that the beautiful smells waft in and fill the rooms. Another good place to locate fragrant climbers is over an arbour or where there is a seat. Fragrance can be a tremendous aid to relaxation: just think about the idea of sitting in the evening, after a hard day, with the air filled with the smell of honeysuckle, for example.

Most scented climbers are at their best in the evening. This is a bonus if you are at work all day and, again, makes them very suitable for planting where you relax or have your evening meal. Some scented climbers, such as sweet peas, make ideal flowers for cutting to bring indoors.

Check carefully that a climber is fragrant. Honeysuckles (*Lonicera*) are amongst the most fragrant of climbers, but not all of them are scented, by any means. *Lonicera tragophylla* and *L. × tellmanniana* are both very attractive honeysuckles, but neither has any smell at all. Roses, too, vary in the intensity of their scent, and it is worth finding out which ones you like

best. Another thing to be beware of is that not all smells are nice. The privets (*Ligustrum*), which are sometimes used as wall shrubs, have a smell that many people find revolting.

FRAGRANT CLIMBERS AND WALL SHRUBS
Azara
Clematis montana
Itea ilicifolia
Jasminum (jasmine)
Lathyrus odoratus
  (sweet peas)
Lonicera (honeysuckle)
Magnolia grandiflora
Osmanthus
Passiflora (passion-flower)
Rosa (roses)

Above: *The fragrance of this* Rosa 'Wedding Day' *climbing through a tree will be carried far in the warm summer evenings.*

Above: *Honeysuckle has a very heady perfume, from flowers that first appear in spring and then continue through the summer; odd flowers are still being produced in autumn.*

Left: *Not all honeysuckles are fragrant but* Lonicera periclymenum *and its varieties are amongst the best. They can be vigorous growers and need strong supports.*

Above: *Growing Rosa 'Zéphirine Drouhin' around a summer house is ideal. This rose has a delightful perfume and flowers on and off throughout the summer and well into the autumn. It has the advantage that it is thornless and so is safe to use near places where people are sitting or walking.*

Above: *Jasmine has a very distinctive fragrance and is most appreciated on a warm summer evening. This variety,* Jasminum officinale *'Aureum', has gold-splashed leaves. This gives the climber an attraction even when it is out of flower.*

Right: *Roses grown on walls next to windows will fill the adjoining rooms with relaxing perfumes. Here Rosa 'Iceberg' and Rosa 'Albertine' mingle colour and fragrance near a bedroom window.*

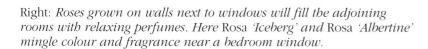

Wall Shrubs

Not all plants that one sees climbing up walls or supported on trellis are true climbers. Many are just ordinary shrubs that are growing against a wall for a variety of reasons. In the wild, some of these might scramble through others if they are next to them, but, generally, they are free-standing shrubs. These shrubs are used as surrogate climbers in the garden, partly because they look good in positions where climbers are grown and partly because some need the protection that walls and fences provide.

ADVANTAGES OF WALL SHRUBS
From the design point of view, wall shrubs are often more compact and controllable than climbers. They can be used in smaller spaces, which climbers would soon outgrow. If so desired, they can be clipped into topiary shapes and they will retain their shape for some time, unlike climbers, which have a constant tendency to throw out new shoots. Wall shrubs increase the range of flowering colours and periods available to the gardener, as well as offering a greater range of foliage effects.

Walls offer winter protection to many shrubs that could otherwise not be grown. The warmth that comes from a house wall might horrify the conservationally minded but, to the gardener, it offers the opportunity to grow plants, such as *Ceanothus*, which might otherwise succumb to the cold weather and die.

It is sometimes difficult to tell what is a climber and what is a wall shrub. *Pyracantha* cut tight against a wall, for example, has every appearance of being a climber, as has a large *Magnolia grandiflora. Euonymus fortunei,*
which grows like any other shrub in the open ground, will, given the chance, shin up a wall as if that were its normal habitat. But, in fact, the difference between climbers and wall shrubs does not matter. Most gardeners are concerned about the appearance of the garden and are not worried about categories. Sad would be the case if a plant were banished from a wall or some other support simply because it was not, strictly speaking, a climber.

WALL SHRUBS

Abutilon
Azara
Carpenteria californica
Ceanothus (Californian lilac)
Chaenomeles (japonica, ornamental quince)
Clianthus puniceus (parrot's bill)
Cotoneaster
Euonymus fortunei

Ficus carica (fig)
Fremontodendron californicum (fremontia)
Garrya elliptica
Itea ilicifolia
Jasminum (jasmine)
Magnolia
Pyracantha (firethorn)
Teucrium fruticans (shrubby germander)

Above: Piptanthus nepalensis *blooms in the spring, producing bright yellow, pea-like flowers. As summer moves on, so these attractive pods are formed, adding yet another dimension to the plant. Both the flowers and pods show up well against a brick wall.*

Left: Fremontodendron californicum *is usually grown against a wall. Wear a mask when pruning or handling as the stems are covered with fine hairs that can get into the lungs.*

Right: *Although most frequently used as a free-standing shrub,* Euonymus fortunei *'Emerald 'n' Gold' will happily climb up a wall or fence.*

Above: Carpenteria californica *is one of the glories of the summer, with its large white flowers, surmounted by a boss of yellow stamens. These are set off well by the dark green foliage. This plant is usually grown as a wall shrub, because it is slightly tender and appreciates the protection of the wall.*

Left: Calistemon citrinus, *with its curious, bottle-brush-like flowers, is a tender shrub that needs the warm protection of a wall if it is to survive. It flowers during the summer months.*

Above: Ceanothus *produces some of the best blue flowers of any wall shrubs. Many can be grown free-standing, but most do best if grown against a wall or a fence as here.*

TRAINING CLIMBERS

Training Methods 1

Training is an important aspect of growing climbers. The general shape and well-being of the plant is taken care of by pruning, but how it is trained and where it is positioned are the most important things to consider when thinking about how your climber will look.

POSITIONING THE PLANT

The overall shape of the plant depends on its position. Those against a wall, for example, need to be tied in so that they do not protrude too far. Similarly, climbers over arches must be constrained on at least the inner side, so that they do not catch people walking through the arch. In some places, the plants can be left to show off the way they froth out over their supports. Vigorous climbers covering large trees, for example, are best left natural and untrained. Plants on trellis can be allowed a certain amount of ebullient freedom but they may also need some restraint.

SPREADING OUT THE STEMS

The climber's natural tendency is to go straight up through its support or host until it reaches the light. This frequently means that the climber forms a tight column without much deviation on either side. To make a good display the gardener should spread out the stems at as early a stage as possible so that the main stems fan out, covering the wall, fence or trellis. This not only means that the climber covers a wider area but also that its stems all receive a good amount of light, and thus flowering is encouraged at a lower level.

EARLY DAYS

At the time of planting it can be a good policy to train individual stems along canes until they reach the wires, trellis or whatever the support may be. This will prevent them from all clustering together, making it difficult to train them at a later stage. Once the plant starts to put on growth, tie this in rather than tucking it behind the trellis or wires. This will enable you to release it at a later stage to re-organize it.

Right: *Horizontal training produces some of the best flowering. Here,* Rosa *'Seagull' has been trained along swags of rope suspended between wooden pillars. Do not pull the ropes too tight: a graceful curve gives a much better effect. If it is not self-clinging, tie the climber in well to the rope or it will become loose and thrash about.*

Above: *Tying in climbers under overhanging tiles can be a problem, because it may be difficult to find anchor points. A criss-cross arrangement of vertical wires can normally be fixed between the end of the eaves and the wall below the tiles; it makes an attractive feature in its own right. Here,* Rosa *'Zéphirine Drouhin' is supported on wires.*

Above: *A similar effect to climbing on ropes can be had by training the climber along poles attached to pillars. These form a rustic trellis and can look very effective, even during the winter when the climber is not in leaf Here, Rosa 'Felicia' clambers over the structure.*

Right: *Vigorous climbers, such as rambling roses, some clematis and Russian vines, can be grown through trees. This is an easy way of training because, once the plant has been pointed in the right direction (by tying it to a cane angled into the tree), it can be left to its own devices. Make certain that the tree can support the weight of the climber, especially in high winds. Here Rosa 'Paul's Himalayan Musk' begins its ascent.*

Training Methods 2

ENCOURAGING FLOWERS

Once the climber has thrown up some nice long shoots, bend these over in a curving arc and attach them to the wires or trellis. From these will come new shoots which should be treated in the same manner so that the wall, fence or trellis is covered in a increasing series of arching stems. This method has the advantage, besides creating a good coverage of the wall, of making the plant produce plenty of flowers. The chemistry of the stems is such that flower buds are laid down on the top edge of the curving branches. Roses, in particular, benefit greatly from this method of training.

Curving branches over to encourage growth can also be used for climbers growing around tripods or round a series of hooped sticks, where the stems are tied around the structure rather than in a vertical position. This will encourage a much thicker coverage and many more blooms as well as allowing you to use vigorous plants in a limited amount of space.

CHOOSING YOUR METHOD OF TRAINING

There are endless possibilities for training your climber, and really the choice will affected by the constraints of the garden and personal choice. You may have something particular in mind – for example, you may want to construct a shady arbour or romantic walkway – or you may have simply bought a climber you took a fancy to and now want to find a good place for it where it will flourish and add to the beauty of the garden.

TRAINING CLIMBERS OVER EYESORES

Climbers that grow quickly and produce lots of flowers are well-suited to covering unsightly features in the garden such as refuse areas, grey concrete walls belonging to a neighbouring property or ugly fences you are not allowed to pull down.

CLIMBERS TO TRAIN OVER EYESORES

Clematis montana
Clematis rehderiana
Fallopia baldschuanica (Russian vine)
Hedera (ivy)
Humulus (hops)
Hydrangea anomala petiolaris
Lonicera (honeysuckles)
Rosa (roses)

CLIMBERS AND WALL SHRUBS FOR NORTH- AND EAST-FACING WALLS

Akebia quinata
Camellia
Chaenomeles (Japonica or ornamental quince)
Clematis 'Marie Boisselot'
Clematis 'Nelly Moser'
Euonymous fortunei
Jasminum nudiflorum
Hedera (Ivy)
Hydrangea anomala petiolaris
Lonicera x tellemanniana
Parthenocissus (Boston ivy or virginia creeper)
Pyracantha (Firethorn)
Rosa 'New Dawn'
Schizophragma

Above: Rosa *'New Dawn' has a very long flowering period and has the added benefit that it can be grown on a north-facing wall. Here it has been tied into trellising on a wall.*

Left: *Climbers planted near doorways should be kept under control to avoid injury. Clematis, such as this C. 'Rouge Cardinal', are safer than roses as they have no thorns to catch the unwary.*

Above: *When roses are well-trained they can produce an abundance of flowers. The curiously coloured R. 'Veilchenblau', shown here growing up a wooden trellis, puts on a fine show during midsummer.*

Above: *If possible, train climbers that have scented flowers near open windows, so that their fragrance can be appreciated indoors. Here Rosa 'Albertine' is in full flower, while beyond is a wisteria that has finished flowering.*

Right: *To obtain extra height for the more vigorous roses a trellis can be erected on top of a wall. When well-trained they present a backdrop of colour against which to view the border in front and below.*

Growing Climbers on Wires

If a large area of wall is to be covered with non-clinging climbers, wires are the only realistic way of supporting them. Alternative methods, such as covering the whole wall with wooden trellis, are expensive and, if the wall is at all attractive, may detract from its appearance.

HOW TO USE WIRES

Wires can be used for most types of climbers, except for clinging ones, which should be able to cling directly to the surface of the wall. If the wires are too far apart, however, plants with tendrils may have difficulty finding the next wire up and may need to be tied in. Wires are also suitable for wall shrubs, which while not needing support, benefit from being tied in to prevent them from being blown forward by wind rebounding from the wall. Wires are unobtrusive and can be painted the same colour as the wall, to make them even less visible. Galvanized wire is best, as it will not rust. Rusty wires are not only liable to break but may also cause unsightly rust marks that may show up on the wall. Plastic-covered wire can be used but the coating is not as permanent as a galvanized one.

Do not use too thin a wire or it will stretch under the weight of the plants. If there is a chance that the wires will stretch, use bottle screws or tension bolts at one end. These can be tightened as the wire slackens.

1 Before it is fixed to wires, the young plant is loose and growing in all directions.

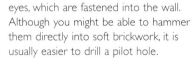

2 The wires are supported by vine eyes, which are fastened into the wall. Although you might be able to hammer them directly into soft brickwork, it is usually easier to drill a pilot hole.

3 If you are using vine eyes with a screw fixing, you need to insert a plastic or wooden plug in the wall first. The eye is then screwed into the plug. This type of vine eye varies in length, the long ones being necessary for those climbers, such as wisteria, that grow large and need wires further from the wall.

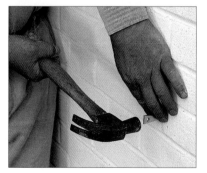

4 The simplest vine eyes are wedge shaped. Hammer them directly into the masonry and then feed the wire through a hole. While wedge-shaped eyes are suitable for brick and stone walls, the screw type are better for wooden fences and posts.

5 Thread the galvanized wire through the hole in the vine eye and wrap it round itself, forming a firm fixing. Thread the other end through the intermediate eyes (set at no more than 180 cm/6 ft intervals and preferably closer) and then fasten the wire round the end eye, keeping it as taut as possible.

6 Curve over the long stems and attach them to the wires, using either plastic ties or string. Tie at several points, if necessary, so that the stems lie flat against the wall and do not flap about.

7 When all the stems are tied in, you should have a series of arches. Tying them in like this, rather than straight up the wall, covers the wall better and encourages the plant to produce flowering buds all along the top edge of the stems.

Above: *Climbers such as roses and clematis can be trained up the whole side of a house with wires. Here* Rosa *'Madame Isaac Pereire' completely covers its wires.*

Fixing Trellis to Walls

Permanent wooden trellis, fixed to a wall, is not only a strong method of supporting climbers but also an attractive one. However, large areas of trellis can look overpowering, especially on house walls; wires are a better choice for these situations. Apart from self-clinging plants, which support themselves, any type of climber can be held up by such trellis.

HOW TO USE TRELLIS

The trellis should be well fixed to the wall, preferably with screws. It should be held a short distance from the brickwork or masonry, so that the stems of the climber can easily pass up behind it. This can be simply achieved by using spacers – wooden blocks will do – between the trellis and the wall.

If the wall is a painted one, or might need future attention for other reasons, it is possible to make the trellis detachable. The best method is to fix hinges along the bottom edge of the trellis. This allows the framework to be gently eased away from the wall, bringing the climber with it, so that maintenance can

take place. The top is held by a catch. Alternatively, the trellis can be held in position by a series of clips or catches. This is not so easy to manoeuvre as one held on hinges, however.

Any shape of trellis can be used, such as square, rectangular or fan shaped, depending on the climber and the effect of the shape on the building or wall. It is possible to be more imaginative and devise other shapes, perhaps creating a two-dimensional topiary. The mesh can be either square or diagonal, the former being better with brickwork, because the lines of the trellis then follow those of the brick courses rather than contradicting them.

CLIMBERS FOR TRELLIS

Akebia
Clematis
Cobaea scandens (cathedral bells)
Humulus (hop)
Ipomoea (morning glory)
Lathyrus odoratus (sweet peas)
Lonicera (honeysuckle)
Rosa (roses)
Solanum crispum
Solanum jasminoides
Thunbergia alata (black-eyed Susan)

1 Take the trellis to the wall and mark its position. Drill holes for fixing the spacers and insert plastic or wooden plugs.

2 Drill the equivalent holes in the wooden batten and secure it to the wall, checking with a spirit level that it is horizontal. Use a piece of wood that holds the trellis at least 2.5 cm (1 in) from the wall. Fix a similar batten at the base and one half-way up for trellis above 1.2 m (4 ft) high.

3 Drill and screw the trellis to the battens, first fixing the top and then working downwards. Check that the trellis is not crooked.

4 The finished trellis should be tightly fixed to the wall, so that the weight of the climber, and any wind that blows on it, will not pull it away from its fixings.

Above: *The rose 'Dublin Bay' here climbs up a wooden trellis secured to the wall. This rose is fragrant and flowers over a very long period.*

Growing Climbers on Netting

A cheap but effective method of providing support for climbers on a wall is to use a rigid plastic netting. This can be used for large areas but it is more effective for smaller climbers, where a limited area is covered.

HOW TO USE NETTING

Rigid plastic netting is suitable for covering brick or stone walls as well as wooden walls and panel fences. It can also be wrapped around poles or pillars, to give plants something to grip. You can string netting between upright posts, as a temporary support for annual climbing plants such as sweet peas, but it is not really suitable for a permanent structure of this sort.

Netting is readily available from garden centres and nurseries. It can generally be bought in green, brown or white, which allows you to choose a colour that matches the wall, so that the netting does not show up too obviously. It is also possible to buy special clips, which make fixing the netting to a surface very simple.

The clips are designed to be used either with masonry nails or with screws. They have the advantage that they hold the netting away from the wall, so that there is room for the plant to climb through it or wrap its tendrils round the mesh, whereas if the netting is nailed directly to the wall there is no space between them.

A further advantage of this method of fixing is that the net can be unclipped and eased away from the wall, allowing the latter to be painted or treated with preservative before the net is clipped back into position.

Plastic netting can be used either with plants that support themselves with tendrils or by twining, or with plants that need to be tied in. It does not look as attractive as the more expensive wooden trellising but, once it has been covered with the climber, it is not noticeable, especially if the right colour has been chosen. After a few years you will not be able to see the netting at all; it will be covered in a mass of foliage and flowers.

1 Position the first clip just below the top of where the net will be and drive in a masonry nail. Alternatively, drill a hole, plug it and screw the clip into it.

2 With a spirit level, mark the position of the other upper clip, so that it is level with the first. Fix the second clip.

3 Place the top of the net in position, with one horizontal strand in the jaw of the clip. Press it home so it is securely fastened. Repeat with the other clip.

4 Smooth the net down against the wall and mark where the next set of clips will come. They should be at about 60 cm (2 ft) intervals down the wall. Move the net out of the way, fix the clips and press the net into the clips. Follow the same procedure with the bottom clips.

5 When the netting is securely in place, train the climber up into it. Even those that are self-supporting may need tying in to get them going. If the plant is a little way out from the wall, train it towards the netting along canes.

Above: *Netting is rather ugly and it is best used with vigorous climbers that will soon cover it. Here, the netting has only been used well above the ground, where the main support is needed. Unsightly supports won't show around the base of the climbers, where the main stems make an attractive feature in their own right.*

Trellis and Fences

One of the simplest and yet most decorative ways of displaying climbers is to grow them over free-standing trellises or fences. Used in the garden, to define its major routes, this is an impressive way of bringing planting right in to the garden's fundamental structure.

BOUNDARIES AND SCREENS

Fences tend to be functional, in that they create a boundary; this is usually between the garden and the outside world but a fence is sometimes used as an internal divider. Many existing fences are ugly and covering them with climbers is a good way of hiding this fact. Those erected by the gardener need not be ugly but they still provide an opportunity for climbers.

Trellises are usually much more decorative than fences. They are not so solid and allow glimpses of what lies on the other side. They are either used as internal dividers within the garden, as screens, or simply as a means of supporting climbers. Used in this way, trellis can make a tremendous contribution to a garden design, as they can provide horizontal as well as vertical emphasis. As screens, they are useful for disguising eyesores such as fuel tanks, garages or utility areas.

ERECTING TRELLIS

The key to erecting a good trellis is to make certain that it is firmly planted in the ground. Once covered with climbers, it will come under enormous pressure from the wind and will work loose unless firmly embedded in concrete. Do not try to take a short cut by simply back-filling the post-hole with earth; unless the trellis is in a very protected position, it will eventually fall over. Panel fences are erected in a similar way.

Virtually any climber can be grown over trellis. But unless it is in a sheltered position, trellis will not offer the same protection as a wall to tender climbers.

1 Dig a hole at least 60 cm (2 ft) deep, deeper in light soils.

2 Put the post in the prepared hole and partly fill the hole with a dry-mix concrete. Check that the post is upright and not sloping, using a spirit level. Adjust the position of the post, if necessary, and then continue filling the hole, tamping down firmly as you go to hold the pole still.

3 Continue filling the hole with concrete, ramming it down firmly; frequently check that the post is still upright. The post should now be firm enough in the ground to work on and, once the concrete has "cured", it will be permanently secure.

4 Lay the panel on the ground, to work out where the next hole should be. Dig the hole, again to at least 60 cm (2 ft) deep.

5 Nail the panel on to the first post, while a helper supports the free end.

6 Place the second post in its hole and nail it to the panel, checking that the tops of the posts are level and the panel is horizontal. Fill the second hole with dry-mix concrete, tamping it down as you proceed. Check that the post is upright and adjust, if necessary.

7 Repeat the steps by digging the third post hole, nailing on the second panel, positioning and nailing the third post and so on, until the length of trellising is complete. This is more accurate than putting in all the posts and then fixing the panels, when, inevitably, some gaps will be too large and some too small.

Above: *Honeysuckles will quickly cover trellis.*

Hoops

Training over hoops allows you to direct the growth of the plant, so that it covers all the available space. If the plant is allowed to shoot heavenwards, the result can be disappointing, whereas, if you spread out the initial stems at the base when you first plant, you can encourage the plant to make a much better display.

THE AIMS OF TRAINING

Bending the new young growth into curving arches encourages flowering buds to be formed along the whole length of the stem, rather than just at the tip, as happens if the branch is tied in a vertical position. Frequently, new shoots will also develop from the curving stems and these should, in turn, also be tied into an arch, gradually encouraging the climber to cover the whole hoop. This will encourage a much thicker coverage and many more blooms.

Training plants over hoops helps keep their final height in proportion to the border in which they are growing. It is a very useful method for growing reasonably vigorous plants in a limited space. Very vigorous plants are best avoided; they will soon outgrow their space, however much training you do!

1 In early spring, make a series of hoops around the rose, pushing each end of the pole into the ground. The wood used should be pliable, hazel (*Corylus avellana*) being one of the best to use. Bend each stem carefully, so that it does not crack.

2 Allow each hoop to overlap the previous one.

3 Sort out the long shoots of the rose, carefully bend them over and then tie them to a convenient point on the hoop. In some cases, it may be easier to tie the shoot to a stem that has already been tied down.

4 To start with, the "bush" will look rather untidy but, gradually, the leaves will turn to face the light and it will produce new buds all along the upper edges of the curved stems.

5 Gradually the plant will fill out, and by midsummer it should be a mass of blooms. Every year, remove a few of the older stems and tie in all new ones. After a few years, remove the old hoops and replace them with new ones.

Above: *Roses grown over hoops form a dense bush that is covered with flowers. Here R. 'Isphahan' puts on a good display of flowers as well as putting on plenty of new growth for the following year.*

Growing Climbers up Tripods

Tripods provide a useful opportunity for growing climbers in borders and other areas of limited space. A tripod helps to create vertical emphasis in gardens and may become a striking focal point if eye-catching climbers are allowed to cover it with foliage and flowers.

USING TRIPODS

Tripods can be formal, made to a classic design, or they can be made from rustic poles. The former are better where they are still partly on show after the climber is in full growth. The latter, on the other hand, in spite of their rustic and informal charm, are more suitable for carrying heavy, rampant climbers that will cover them completely. Tripods provide a more substantial support than a single pole.

More formal designs can be bought complete, ready to be installed in the garden. Tripods can, of course, also be made by the competent woodworker. A rustic-pole tripod is much more basic and can easily be constructed by most gardeners. They can be made to any height, to suit the eventual height of the plants and the visual aspects of the site.

Although any type of climber can be grown up a tripod, self-clingers would not be so good because there isn't enough flat surface for them to attach their modified roots. Tripods are ideal for carrying two or more climbers at once. If possible, choose climbers that flower at different times. Alternatively, choose two that flower at the same time but look particularly well together.

An ideal combination is a rose and a *Clematis viticella*. The latter is pruned almost to the ground each winter and so is still growing while the rose is in flower and, therefore, does not smother it. Later in the summer, the clematis comes into its own when the rose is past its best.

1 Position three posts in the ground. The distance apart will depend on the height; balance the two to get a good shape. The posts can be driven into the ground but a better job is done if you dig holes at least 60 cm (2 ft) deep. For a really solid job, backfill the holes with dry-mix concrete, but it will normally be sufficient just to ram the earth back around the poles.

2 Nail cross-pieces between the posts. These will not only help support the plants but also give the structure rigidity. Rails at 40–45 cm (15–18 in) apart should be sufficient for tying in stems. If you want more support for self-clingers, wrap a layer of wire netting around the structure. The plants will soon hide it.

3 When you nail the cross-pieces to the poles, the ends may well split if they have already been cut to the exact length. Nail the pieces on first and then cut them to the right length. Alternatively, cut to length and then drill holes in the appropriate places before nailing to the poles.

4 Plant the climbers in and around the tripod. Avoid planting them too close to the upright poles as the earth here will either be rammed down hard or have been replaced with concrete. Before planting, dig in some well-rotted organic material.

5 Water all the plants in well. If the weather continues dry, keep watering until the plants have become established. Always soak the ground well: a dribble on the surface will not help the plants send roots out into the surrounding soil.

6 The finished tripod will look a bit raw at first but it will soon weather and become covered in plants.

CLIMBERS SUITABLE FOR TRIPODS
Clematis
Humulus (hop)
Lonicera (honeysuckle)
Rosa (roses)
Solanum jasminoides
Tropaeolum (nasturtiums)
Vitis (vines)

Right: *As an alternative, a tripod can be constructed so that the tops meet, forming a three-sided pyramid. Here, Clematis 'Jackmanii' is seen clambering up such a design; once fully grown, the clematis will cover the support completely, so that the tripod cannot be seen.*

Simple Pillars for Climbers

A very effective way of displaying climbers is to grow them up a single pole, which is usually called a pillar. This can look very elegant and also means it is possible to grow a large number of climbers in a relatively small space. Pillars create vertical emphasis in borders or small gardens, without creating a barrier.

CLIMBERS FOR PILLARS

Clematis
Humulus (hop)
Lonicera (honeysuckle)
Rosa (roses)
Solanum jasminoides
Tropaeolum (nasturtiums)
Vitis (vines)

USING PILLARS

A surprising number of climbers are suited to growing up pillars. Most climbing roses, for example, look particularly good growing up them, although it is probably best to avoid vigorous climbers or rambling roses.

An advantage of using pillars for your climbers is that they are inexpensive and simple to erect and take down.

The pillar shown here is permanently positioned in a border but is possible to place the posts in a collar of concrete or a metal tube, so that they can be taken down during the winter when they are bare.

Movable columns are best suited to annuals or *Clematis viticella*, which can be cut down almost to the ground before the posts are removed. Permanent climbers, such as roses, will need a permanent structure.

If space is available, a very attractive walkway can be created by using a series of pillars along a path. This can be further improved by connecting the tops with rope, along which swags of climbers can grow. This is a very good way of growing roses and creates a very romantic, fragrant route through the garden. The effect is suited to formal designs, but is so soft and flowing that it gives a very relaxing feel.

1 Dig a hole at least 60 cm (2 ft) deep. Put in the post and check that it is upright. Backfill with earth, ramming it firmly down as it is filled. In exposed gardens, a more solid pillar can be created by filling the hole with concrete.

2 Plants can be tied directly to the post but a more natural support is created if wire netting is secured to the post. Plants such as clematis will then be able to climb by themselves with little attention from you other than tying in wayward stems.

3 Plant the climber a little way out from the pole, to avoid the compacted area. Lead the stems to the wire netting and tie them in, to get them started. Self-clingers will now take over but plants such as roses will need to be tied in as they climb. Twining plants, such as hops, can be grown up the pole without the wire.

Left: Clematis *'W.E. Gladstone'* *climbing up a pillar. If the pole was covered with wire netting the plant would have more to grip on, which would prevent it suddenly collapsing down the pole under its own weight as it may do later here.*

Right: *Although single-post pillars are rather slim, they can accommodate more than one climber. Here there are two roses, 'American Pillar' and 'Kew Rambler'. Another option is to choose one rose and a later-flowering clematis.*

Above: *Single-post pillars help to break up what would, otherwise, be a dull, rather two-dimensional border. Although it is only a thin structure, when clothed with a climber it becomes a well-filled-out, irregular shape, as this 'American Pillar' rose shows.*

Growing Climbers Through Trees and Shrubs

In the wild, many climbing plants that are also used in the garden find support by scrambling up through trees and shrubs. In thick woodland or forests, they may grow to 50 m (150 ft) plus, in search of light. In the garden, supports of this height are rarely available, and, if they were, the flowers of the climbers using them would be out of sight.

CHOOSING GOOD PARTNERS

A smaller support is required for cultivated climbers in the garden, with a large apple tree, therefore, usually being the highest used. Clematis and roses will scramble through the branches, creating huge fountains of flowers. On a more modest scale, even dwarf shrubs can be used to support some low-growing climbers.

One of the advantages of growing climbers through shrubs is that it is possible to obtain two focuses of interest in one area. This is particularly true of early-flowering shrubs, which are relatively boring for the rest of the year. Through these, it is possible to train a later-flowering climber to enliven the area further on in the season. Clematis are particularly good for this, especially the later-flowering forms, such as the viticellas. These can be cut nearly to the ground during the winter, so that the shrub is relatively uncluttered with the climber when it is in flower itself earlier on in the next season.

Fruit trees that have finished their fruiting life can be given new appeal if you grow a rose through them. However, it is important to remember that old trees may be weak and that the extra burden of a large rose, especially in a high wind, may be too much for it to carry.

1 Any healthy shrub or tree can be chosen. It should preferably be one that flowers at a different time to the climber. Choose companions that will not swamp each other. Here, a relatively low *Salix helvetica* is to be planted with a small form of *Clematis alpina*. The two will make a delicate mix, especially the blue clematis flowers against the silver foliage of the *Salix helvetica*.

CLIMBERS SUITABLE FOR GROWING THROUGH TREES

Akebia
Clematis
Fallopia baldschuanica
   (Russian vine)
Humulus (hop)
Lonicera (honeysuckle)
Rosa (roses – vigorous varieties)
Solanum crispum
Solanum jasminoides

CLIMBERS SUITABLE FOR GROWING THROUGH SHRUBS

Clematis
Cobaea scandens (cathedral
   bells)
Eccremocarpus scaber (Chilean
   glory flower)
Ipomoea (morning glory)
Lathyrus odoratus
   (sweet peas)
Thunbergia alata (black-eyed
   Susan)
Tropaeolum (nasturtiums)
Vinca major

2 Dig the planting area at a point on the perimeter of the shrub and prepare the soil by adding well-rotted organic material. For clematis, choose a position on the shady side of the plant, so that its roots are in shade but the flowers will be up in the sun. Dig a hole bigger than the climber's rootball and plant it. Most climbers should be planted at the same depth as they were in their pots but clematis should be 5 cm (2 in) or so deeper.

3 Using a cane, train the clematis into the bush. Once the clematis has become established, you can remove the cane. Spread the shoots of the climber out so that it spreads evenly through the shrub, not just in one area.

4 If possible, put the climber outside the canopy of the shrub or tree, so that it receives rain. However, it is still important to water in the new plant and, should the weather be dry, to continue watering until the plant is established.

Above: *The beautiful white clematis 'Marie Boisselot' grows up through a small apple tree.*

Archways

Arches are very versatile features in a garden and are well suited for growing a variety of climbers. Archways can be incorporated into a dividing feature, such as a wall, hedge or fence, or can be free-standing along a path as nothing more than a means of supporting climbers.

Above: *A simple arch, constructed from rustic poles and covered with a variegated ivy. The simplicity of the foliage allows the eye to pass through to the garden beyond, without distraction.*

USING ARCHES

Archways exert a magnetic effect on visitors to your garden. No matter how interesting the area you are in, an archway draws the eye to what lies beyond. It creates mystery with tantalizing glimpses of other things.

Those forming entrances are important features. They are often the first thing that a visitor is aware of on entering a garden. Arches frame the scene beyond and create atmosphere. A cottage garden, for example, looks particularly fine when seen through a rose arch, while a formal town garden may be better suited to a simple arch of foliage, such as ivy.

The possibilities of creating an arch are almost endless. They can be purchased in kit form, made to order or made by the gardener. They can be made from metal, wood, brick or stone work. Plastic ones are also available, but are neither very attractive nor long lasting. Wooden ones present the biggest range. They can be formal ones created from panels of trellis, or informal ones made from rustic poles. The choice is normally limited by cost and the appearance that is required – climbers themselves will generally climb over anything.

Always choose or make one that is big enough for people to walk through when it is fully clad with climbers – which may stick out as far as 60 cm (2 ft) or more from the supports. Make certain that the supports are well sunk into the ground, preferably concreted in. When covered with a voluminous climber, an arch may be under great pressure from the wind and a storm may push over a badly constructed one, destroying your display.

Virtually any climbers can be used with archways, although over-vigorous ones can become a nuisance – they seem to be constantly growing across the entrance itself. Other types of climbers to avoid, unless there is plenty of room, are thorned roses which may cause injury, or coarse-stemmed plants such as hops. These can be dangerous to the unwary. If you want a rose, use something like 'Zéphirine Drouhin', which is thornless.

CLIMBERS FOR ARCHWAYS

Akebia
Campsis radicans
Clematis
Phaseolus (climbing beans)
Humulus (hop)
Lonicera (honeysuckle)
Rosa (roses)
Vitis (vines)

Above: *Wisteria makes a good covering for an arch because, once it has finished flowering, its foliage still retains a great deal of interest. It is accompanied here by* Vitis coignetiae, *whose foliage turns a magnificent purple colour in autumn. Together, these climbers provide interest from spring to autumn.*

Above: *A golden hop,* Humulus lupulus aureus, *and a honeysuckle,* Lonicera periclymenum, *combine to decorate this archway. Again, interest should be provided from spring to autumn.*

Above left: *This wonderfully romantic arch seems to come from the middle of nowhere. The roses and long grass create a soft image that provides nothing but delight.*

Left: *Roses make excellent subjects for archways. Repeat-flowering ones provide the longest interest; once-flowering roses can be combined with late-flowering clematis, to extend the season.*

Arbours

An arbour is a framework over which climbers are trained to create a shady outdoor room. It can be just big enough to take a chair or bench, but best of all is an arbour large enough to accommodate a table and several chairs, where you can sit and linger over alfresco meals.

DESIGNING AN ARBOUR

The structure can be of metal or wood or the arbour can have brick or stone piers with a wooden roof. The design can be any shape that takes the fancy or fits the site. It may be triangular, semi-circular, rectangular or octagonal, to suggest but a few. The climbers can be any that you like. If you do not like bees, stick to climbers grown for their foliage. In areas designed for relaxation, fragrant climbers are most welcome. Honeysuckle provides a delicious scent, particularly in the evening. Jasmine is another good evening plant. For daytime enjoyment, fragrant roses are ideal.

An arbour may have to remain in place for many years, so make sure you build it well. Take trouble to use timbers treated with preservative (not creosote, which may kill many climbers) and make certain that it is a strong design, well supported in the ground. As with similar structures covered in heavy climbers, the wind can wreak havoc on weak construction.

Right: *Here, the overhanging fig,* Ficus carica, *and the surrounding rose, clematis and other climbers create an intimate area for sitting and relaxing, which fulfils all the functions of an arbour, even though there is no supporting structure.*

Above: *This arbour is dappled with shade from a number of roses. It is big enough for small supper parties as well as simply sitting in the evening with a drink.*

Above: *A large arbour, built for entertaining, this example is covered in a variety of climbers, including a purple grapevine. This provides a wonderfully dappled shade, as well as colourful foliage and grapes at the end of the autumn.* Clematis montana *supplies the colour in the spring and early summer.*

Above: *A dual-purpose arbour: the newly planted beans will provide shade during the hotter part of the year, as well as a constant supply of runner beans for the kitchen. As a bonus, the flowers provide an added attraction.*

Walkways and Pergolas

Extending the use of arches and trellis brings the possibility of pergolas and walkways. This is an ideal way of providing a shady path. On the whole, these are not suitable for the smaller garden, although it is surprising what can be achieved with a bit of imagination.

PLANT IDEAS

Akebia
Campsis radicans
Clematis
Phaseolus (climbing beans)
Humulus (hop)
Lonicera (honeysuckle)
Rosa (roses)

USING WALKWAYS AND PERGOLAS

Walkways are open pergolas, with no roof. They can be double-sided, that is, down both sides of a path, or you can use a single piece of trellis down one side. The simplest way is to build them out of either trellis or rustic poles. For a romantic version, use a series of pillars linked with swags of ropes.

Both can become massive structures that have to support a great deal of weight, especially when there is a strong wind blowing, so it is important to make certain that, whatever the material, the walkway or pergola is well constructed.

A wide range of climbing plants can be used to clothe the pergola or walkway; fragrant plants are especially pleasing. Roses are ideal, as long as they are either thornless or well tied in so that they do not catch passers-by with their thorns. Evergreen climbers, such as ivy, make a dark and intriguing tunnel and will keep passers-by dry in wet weather throughout the year.

Right: *An arch leads through into another part of the garden. The poles are covered with* Rosa 'American Pillar' and R. 'Albertine'. *On the side of the arch is* Clematis 'Alba Luxurians'.

Above: *Clematis tumbling over the corner of a pergola. Here, C. 'Etoile Violette' combines with some late flowers of* C. montana *to create an attractive picture.*

Above: *Colourful foliage makes a long-lasting covering for a pergola. Here* Vitis vinifera *'Purpurea' creates an attractive screen up a wooden pillar. As the year proceeds, the colour of the foliage will deepen, so there is a change of appearance, even without flowers.*

Above: *A romantic walkway created from a series of arches, passing along a clipped path through long grass. The arches provide a delightful tunnel effect, while the statue at the end draws the eye and adds to the romantic image.*

Temporary Supports

It is not always desirable to have fixed screens or supports for climbers. It can be fun to move them around the garden, using a different position each year. This allows a much more flexible design. While this is not really practical with perennial climbers, especially those that might take several years to establish themselves, it is entirely possible with annuals.

USING TEMPORARY SUPPORTS

In some cases, temporary supports can undertake two functions at once: to provide an attractive screen and to provide vegetables for the kitchen. Thus, peas and beans make good traditional subjects, while more novel ideas might include climbing marrows, courgettes (zucchini), gourds (squashes) and cucumbers.

Temporary screens are easy to make and a variety of materials can be used. Many are rustic in nature, such as pea-sticks simply pushed into the ground or traditional bean poles tied together in a row or wigwam (tepee). More modern materials would include plastic netting held on poles or a metal frame. However, it is best not to use materials that are unattractive, as the plants trained up temporary supports do not often get under way until the early summer, not covering them until midsummer.

Temporary structures can also be used for a few perennials that are cut to the ground each year, such as the everlasting pea *Lathyrus latifolius* or some of the clematis that are either herbaceous or a pruned to near the ground each year. Since the latter can grow quite tall, they can be supported by large branches stuck in the ground, to imitate small trees.

Left: *Climbing plants can often be used in this somewhat more horizontal way than is usual. It is an ideal way to utilize space left after spring flowers have finished blooming.*

Above: *A typical bean row, with the scarlet-flowered runner beans climbing up poles that have been tied together for support. The poles can be kept for several seasons before they need to be replaced.*

Above: *Peas growing up a wigwam (tepee) of canes. The canes are pushed into the ground in a circle, with their tops pointing towards the centre, where they are all tied together to keep them rigid. Poles of any wood or metal can be used, as well as the traditional bamboo canes shown here.*

Above right: *Sweet peas growing up a temporary screen of pea-sticks. Hazel* (Corylus avellana) *is one of the best types of wood, but any finely branched sticks will do. They usually only last one season and then need to be replaced.*

Right: *A framework of hazel sticks have been woven into a dome, over which a clematis is growing.*

Growing Climbers in Containers

Although most climbers are grown in the open ground, there is no reason why they should not be grown in containers. This is a particularly good idea for a balcony, roof garden or patio. While it is not really feasible to grow vigorous plants in this way, a surprising number of climbers are suitable.

SUPPORTING CLIMBERS IN POTS

The main problem when growing climbers in pots is finding a method of supporting the plant. If they are only short plants or annuals, such as black-eyed Susan (*Thunbergia*) or nasturtiums, it is perfectly feasible to include the support in the container. You can use canes or a V-shaped piece of trellising, burying the lower end in the pot.

For more vigorous plants, set the containers against a wall on which trellis has been fixed. An alternative is to have strings or tall canes rising from the pot to some suitable fixing on the wall.

One of the main secrets of success with container climbers is to keep them watered well. Feeding also becomes very important, as constant watering leaches out many of the nutrients in the soil.

1 To ensure that the compost in the container is adequately drained it is important to place a layer of small stones or broken pots in the bottom. This will allow any excess water to drain away quickly.

2 Partly fill the pot with a good-quality potting compost (soil mix). Add to this some water-retaining granules and stir these into the compost. Use the quantity recommended on the packet. The granules will expand when they become wet and hold the moisture until the plant wants it, without making the soil too wet, something that most plants hate.

3 Put the narrow end of the trellis into the container. The trellis will be held in position by the weight of the compost, so the base should be as low down in the pot as possible. This type of frame is not suitable for tall, narrow pots, which may be blown over easily.

4 Put the plant in position so that the top of the rootball comes level with the intended surface of the compost. Put in the remaining compost and lightly firm it down. Train the stems of the climber against the trellis and tie them in, if necessary.

5 Water the pot and top it up with compost (soil mix) if the level falls. Cover the top with pebbles or gravel, partly to give it a pleasant appearance but also to help suppress weeds and make watering easier. When creating such a display, put it in its final position before you fill the container as the complete container may be very heavy.

6 As an alternative, fix a piece of trellis to a wall and stand the pot next to it. This will take heavier climbers and be less inclined to blow or fall over. Being next to a wall may put the pot in a rain shadow, however, so be prepared to water it even if you have had rain.

Above: *Grouping containers together presents an attractive display. Here, Clematis 'Prince Charles' is planted in a chimney pot next to some potted chives.*

Above: *A variety of different frameworks can be used in large containers, to support annual and temporary climbers. The metal frameworks will last the longest but will be most expensive. The willow wicker support, at the back of the group, is attractive in its own right.*

Shrubs List

Lists of shrubs for specific purposes (e.g. ground cover) are given in the relevant sections

d = deciduous
e = evergreen

YELLOW-FLOWERED SHRUBS
Azara (e)
Berberis (d & e)
Buddleja globosa (d)
Chimonanthus (d)
Colutea arborescens (d)
Cornus mas (d)
Coronilla (e)
Corylopsis (d)
Corylus (d)
Cytisus (d)
Forsythia (d)
Fremontodendron californicum (e)
Genista (d)
Halimium (e)
Hamamelis (d)
Helianthemum (e)
Hypericum (d)
Jasminum (d & e)
Kerria japonica (d)
Mahonia (e)
Phlomis (e)
Piptanthus (e)
Potentilla (d)
Rhododendron (d & e)
Senecio (d)

Azara lanceolata

ORANGE-FLOWERED SHRUBS
Berberis (d & e)
Buddleja x weyeriana (d)
Colutea orientalis (d)
Embothrium coccineum (e)
Helianthemum (e)
Potentilla (d)
Rhododendron (d & e)

Fuchsia 'Genii'

RED-FLOWERED SHRUBS
Callistemon citrinus (e)
Calluna (e)
Camellia (e)
Chaenomeles (d)
Crinodendron hookerianum (e)

Fremontodendron californicum

Desfontainia spinosa (e)
Erythrina crista-galli (d)
Escallonia (e)
Fuchsia (d)
Helianthemum (e)
Hydrangea (d)
Leptospermum (e)
Rhododendron (d & e)
Ribes speciosum (d)
Weigela (d)

PINK-FLOWERED SHRUBS
Abelia (e)
Andromeda (e)
Buddleja (d)
Calluna (e)
Camellia (e)
Chaenomeles (d)
Cistus (e)

Chaenomeles speciosa 'Moerloosii'

Calluna vulgaris 'Darkness'

Clerodendrum bungei (d)
Cotinus coggygria (d)
Cytisus (d)
Daphne (d & e)
Deutzia (d)
Erica (e)
Escallonia (e)
Fuchsia (d)
Hebe (e)
Helianthemum (e)
Hibiscus (d)
Hydrangea (d)
Indigofera (d)
Kalmia (e)
Kolkwitzia (d)
Lavatera (d)
Leptospermum (e)
Lonicera (d)
Magnolia (d & e)
Nerium (e)
Prunus (d)
Rhododendron (d & e)
Ribes sanguineum (d)
Spiraea (d)
Syringa (d)
Viburnum (d & e)
Weigela (d)

Ceanothus impressus

BLUE-FLOWERED SHRUBS
Buddleja (d)
Caryopteris (d)
Ceanothus (d & e)
Ceratostigma (d)
Hebe (e)
Hibiscus (d)
Hydrangea (d)
Lavandula (e)
Perovskia (d)
Rhododendron (d & e)
Rosmarinus (e)
Vinca (e)

Syringa vulgaris

PURPLE-FLOWERED SHRUBS
Buddleja (d)
Elsholtzia stauntonii (d)
Erica (e)
Hebe (e)
Hydrangea (d)

Rhamnus alaternus 'Variegata'
with Campanula pyramidalis

Lavandula stoechas (e)
Rhododendron (d & e)
Salvia officinalis (e)
Syringa (d)
Vinca (e)

WHITE-FLOWERED SHRUBS
Aralia (d)
Berberis thunbergia (d)
Buddleja (d)
Calluna (e)
Camellia (e)
Carpenteria californica (e)
Chaenomeles (d)

Choisya (d)
Cistus (e)
Clerodendrum trichotomum (d)
Clethra alnifolia (d)
Cornus (d)
Cotoneaster (e)
Crataegus (d)
Cytisus (d)
Daphne blagayana (d)
Erica (e)
Escallonia (e)
Eucryphia (d & e)
Exochorda x *macrantha* (d)
Fuchsia (d)
Gaultheria (e)
Halesia (d)
Hebe (e)
Helianthemum (e)
Hibiscus (d)
Hoheria (d)
Hydrangea (d)
Itea (d & e)
Jasminum (d & e)
Leptospermum (e)

Ligustrum (e)
Magnolia (d & e)
Myrtus (e)
Olearia (e)
Osmanthus (e)
Philadelphus (d)
Pieris (e)
Potentilla (d)
Prunus (d)
Pyracantha (e)
Rhododendron (d & e)
Romneya (d)
Rubus 'Tridel' (d)
Sambucus (d)
Skimmia (e)
Spiraea (d)
Stephanandra (d)
Syringa (d)
Viburnum (d & e)
Vinca (e)

GREEN-FLOWERED SHRUBS
Daphne laureola (e)
Garrya elliptica (d)

Carpenteria californica

SHRUBS FOR DRY SHADE
Aucuba japonica (e)
Ilex (d & e)
Pachysandra terminalis (e)
Buxus sempervirens (e)
Daphne laureola (d & e)
Elaeagnus × ebbingei (e)
Gaultheria shallon (e)
Hypericum × inordum 'Elstead' (d)
Lonicera pileata (e)

SHRUBS FOR MOIST SHADE
Camellia (e)
Clethra (d & e)
Corylopsis (d)
Crataegus laevigata (d)
Enkianthus (d)
Fatsia japonica (e)
Fothergilla (d)
Mahonia aquifolium (e)
Osmanthus decorus (e)
Pieris formosa var. *forrestii*
    'Wakehurst' (e)

Rhododendron (d & e)
Salix magnifica (d)
Sarcococca ruscifolia (e)
Skimmia japonica (e)
Viburnum davidii (e)
Vinca major (e)
Vinca minor (e)

SHRUBS FOR SUNNY AND DRY AREAS
Caryopteris × clandonensis (d)
Cistus (e)
Convolvulus cneorum (e)
Cytisus (d & e)
Hamamelis mollis (d)
Helianthemum
    nummularium (e)
Santolina chamaecyparissus (e)
Senecio (e)
Yucca (e)

SHRUBS FOR ACID SOIL
Azalea (d & e)
Calluna vulgaris (e)
Camellia (e)
Corylopsis pauciflora (d)
Daboecia (e)
Enkianthus (d)
Erica cinerea (e)
Fothergilla (d)
Gaultheria mucronata (e)
Halesia carolina (d)
Hamamelis (d)
Kalmia latifolia (e)
Pieris (e)
Rhododendron (d & e)
Ulex europaeus (e)

SHRUBS FOR CHALKY SOIL
Berberis darwinii (e)
Buddleja davidii (d)
Ceanothus impressus (e)
Choisya ternata (e)
Cistus (e)

Clematis (d & e)
Cotoneaster (d & e)
Deutzia (d)
Helianthemum (e)
Lavandula (e)
Nerium oleander (e)
Paeonia suffruticosa (d)
Potentilla (shrubby species) (d)
Pyracantha (e)
Rosa rugosa (shrub species)
Syringa (d)
Viburnum tinus (e)

SHRUBS FOR SANDY SOIL
Calluna vulgaris (e)
Ceanothus thyrsiflorus (e)
Cistus (e)
Cytisus scoparius (d)
Erica arborea alpina (e)
Gaultheria mucronata (e)
Genista tinctoria (d)
Lavandula (e)
Rosa pimpinellifolia (d)

Below: *Rosemary (*Rosmarinus*) has a distinctive scent.*

Below: *The foliage of* Pieris japonica *changes through the year.*

Below: Helianthemum *'Wisley Pink' has unusual silver leaves.*

Rosmarinus officinalis (e)
Spartium junceum (d)
Yucca gloriosa (e)

SHRUBS FOR CLAY SOIL
Clethra alnifolia (d)
Cornus alba 'Sibirica' (d)
Kalmia latifolia (e)
Magnolia (some) (d & e)
Salix caprea (d)
Sambucus racemosa (d)
Viburnum opulus (d)

SHRUBS FOR GROUND COVER
Cotoneaster cochleatus (e)
Erica carnea (e)
Euonymus fortunei (e)
Hypericum calycinum (e)
Juniperus horizontalis (e)
Lonicera pileata (e)
Pachysandra terminalis (e)
Persicaria affinis (e)
Rosa (ground cover species)

Thymus (e)
Vinca minor (e)

SHRUBS THAT ATTRACT WILDLIFE
Buddleja davidii (d)
Cotoneaster species (d & e)
Hebe (e)
Lavandula (e)
Ilex (e)
Pyracantha (e)

SHRUBS WITH FRAGRANT FLOWERS
Buddleja davidii (d)
Chimonanthus praecox (d)
Choisya ternata (e)
Cytisus battandieri (e)
Daphne mezereum (d)
Lavandula (e)
Lonicera fragrantissima (d & e)
Philadelphus (d)
Rosa (d)

Sarcococca (e)
Syringa (d)
Viburnum × *bodnantense* (d)
Viburnum carlesii (d)

SHRUBS WITH SCENTED FOLIAGE
Aloysia triphylla (d)
Artemisia abrotanum (d)
Helichrysum italicum (e)
Hyssopus officinalis (d)
Lavandula (e)
Pelargonium (scented-leaved forms) (e)
Rosmarinus officinalis (e)
Salvia officinalis (e)

SHRUBS FOR HEDGES AND WINDBREAKS
Berberis darwinii (e)
Buxus sempervirens (e)
Cotoneaster simonsii (d)
Elaeagnus × *ebbingei* (e)

Escallonia (e)
Euonymus japonicus (e)
Griselinia littoralis (e)
Lavandula (e)
Ligustrum ovalifolium (e)
Lonicera nitida (e)
Photinia × *fraseri* 'Red Robin' (e)
Pittosporum tenuifolium (e)
Prunus laurocerasus (e)
Prunus lusitanica (e)
Tamarix ramosissima (d)

SHRUBS FOR EXPOSED SITES
Elaeagnus pungens 'Maculata' (e)
Erica cinerea (e)
Euonymus japonicus (e)
Genista hispanica (e)
Hibiscus rosa-sinensis (e)
Hippophäe rhamnoides (d)
Lavandula 'Hidcote' (e)
Pyracantha coccinea (e)
Senecio 'Sunshine' (e)
Viburnum tinus (e)

Below: Choisya ternata *'Sundance' has fragrant white flowers.*

Below: Pyracantha *has very decorative autumn berries.*

Below: Salvia officinalis *'Icterina' or sage is often used in cooking.*

Climbers List

Plant lists for specific types of climbers (e.g. fragrant climbers) are given in the relevant sections.

Where only the genus is given several species and cultivars are suitable.

ac = annual climber
c = climber
wf = wall fruit
ws = wall shrub

YELLOW-FLOWERED CLIMBERS AND WALL SHRUBS

Abutilon megapotamicum (ws)
Azara dentata (ws)
Billardiera longiflora (c)
Clematis (c)
   C. 'Moonlight'
   C. 'Paten's Yellow'
   C. rehderiana
   C. tangutica
   C. tibetana

Clematis tangutica

Eccremocarpus scaber (c)
Fremontodendron californicum (ws)
Humulus lupulus 'Aureus' (c)
Jasminum (c & ws)
Lathyrus (ac & c)
Lonicera (c)
Magnolia grandiflora (ws)
Piptanthus laburnifolius (ws)
Rosa (c)
   R. 'Dreaming Spires'
   R. 'Emily Grey'
   R. 'Gloire de Dijon'
   R. 'Golden Showers'
Thunbergia alata (ac)
Tropaeolum (ac)

Lonicera japonica *'Halliana'*

ORANGE-FLOWERED CLIMBERS AND WALL SHRUBS

Bignonia capreolata (c)
Bougainvillea spectabilis (c)
Campsis (c)
Eccremocarpus scaber (c)
Lonicera (c)
Rosa (c)
   R. 'Autumn Sunlight'
   R. 'Danse du Feu'
Tropaeolum (ac)

RED-FLOWERED CLIMBERS AND WALL SHRUBS

Akebia quinata (c)
Bougainvillea spectabilis (c)
Callistemon citrinus (ws)
Camellia (ws)
Chaenomeles (ws)

Clematis *'Madame Julia Correvon'*

Clematis (c)
   C. 'Niobe'
   C. 'Ruby Glow'
Clianthus puniceus (ws)
Crinodendron hookerianum (ws)
Desfontainea spinosa (ws)
Eccremocarpus scaber (c)
Erythrina crista-galli (ws)
Lathyrus (ac & c)
Lonicera (c)
Phaseolus coccineus (ac)
Rhodochiton atrosanguineum (c)
Ribes speciosum (ws)
Rosa (c)
   R. 'American Pillar'
   R. 'Danny Boy'
   R. 'Excelsa'
   R. 'Galway Bay'
   R. 'Symphathie'
Tropaeolum (ac & c)

Clematis *'Duchess of Albany'*

Clematis *'Comtesse de Bouchard'*

PINK-FLOWERED CLIMBERS AND WALL SHRUBS

Bougainvillea spectabilis (c)
Camellia (ws)
Chaenomeles (ws)
Cistus (ws)
Clematis (c)
   C. 'Comtesse de Bouchard'
   C. 'Hagley Hybrid'
   C. 'Margot Koster'

Lathyrus grandiflorus

Hoya carnosa (c)
Jasminum beesianum (c)
Jasminum x *stephanense* (c)
Lapageria rosea (c)
Lathyrus (ac & c)
Lonicera (c)
Malus (wf)
Mandevilla splendens (c)

Nerium oleander (ws)
Prunus (wf)
Rosa (c)
   R. 'Albertine'
   R. 'Bantry Bay'
   R. 'New Dawn'
   R. 'Pink Perpétue'
   R. 'Zéphirine Drouhin'

Vinca major

BLUE-FLOWERED CLIMBERS AND WALL SHRUBS
Aloysia triphylla (ws)
Ceanothus (ws)
Clematis (c)
   C. 'Beauty of Richmond'
   C. 'Lady Betty Balfour'
   C. macropetala
   C. 'Mrs Cholmondeley'
   C. 'Perle d'Azur'
Hydrangea aspera villosa (ws)
Ipomoea (ac)
Lathyrus (ac & c)
Passiflora caerulea (c)
Plumbago capensis (c)
Rosmarinus officinalis (ws)
Solanum crispum (ws)
Solanum jasminoides (c)
Sollya fusiformis (c)
Teucrium fruticans (ws)
Vinca major (c)
Wisteria (c)

PURPLE-FLOWERED CLIMBERS AND WALL SHRUBS
Clematis (c)
   C. 'Etoile Violette'

Clematis *'Lasurstern' and*
Clematis *'Nelly Moser'*

   C. 'Gipsy Queen'
   C. 'The President'
Cobaea scandens (ac)
Lathyrus (ac & c)
Rosa (c)
   R. 'Bleu Magenta'
   R. 'Veilchenblau'
   R. 'Violette'
Solanum dulcamara 'Variegata' (c)

Vitis vinifera *'Purpurea'*

GREEN-FLOWERED CLIMBERS AND WALL SHRUBS
Garrya elliptica (ws)
Hedera (c)
Itea ilicifolia (ws)
Ribes laurifolium (ws)
Vitis (c)

Clematis *'Mrs George Jackman'*

WHITE-FLOWERED CLIMBERS AND WALL SHRUBS
Camellia (ws)
Carpenteria californica (ws)
Chaenomeles (ws)
Cistus (ws)
Clematis (c)
   C. 'Edith'
   C. 'Miss Bateman'
   C. 'Snow Queen'
Clianthus puniceus (ws)
Cotoneaster (ws)
Dregea sinensis (c)
Fallopia baldschuanica (c)
Hoheria (ws)
Hoya carnosa (c)
Hydrangea anomala petiolare (c)
Jasminum (c & ws)

Clematis florida *'Sieboldii'*

Lathyrus (ac & c)
Mandevilla suaveolens (c)
Myrtus (ws)
Nerium oleander (ws)
Pileostegia viburnoides (c)
Prunus (wf)
Pyracantha (ws)
Pyrus (wf)
Rosa (c)
   R. 'Albéric Barbier'
   R. 'Kiftsgate'
   R. 'Mme Alfred Carrière'
Solanum jasminoides 'Album' (c)
Trachelospermum (c)
Wisteria (c)

Rosa *'Iceberg' and* Clematis
tangutica

Clematis *'Marie Boisselot'*

CLIMBERS FOR DRY SHADE
Hedera canariensis (c)
Lapageria rosea (c)
Parthenocissus tricuspidata (c)

CLIMBERS FOR MOIST SHADE
Humulus lupulus 'Aureus'
   (h & c)
Hydrangea petiolaris (c)
Lonicera tragophylla (c)
Pileostegia viburnoides (c)
Schizophragma
   integrifolium (c)

Trachelospermum
   jasminoides (c)

CLIMBERS FOR ACID SOIL
Berberidopsis corallina (c)

CLIMBERS FOR CHALKY SOIL
Campsis radicans (c)
Celastrus orbiculatus (c)
Clematis (all)
Eccremocarpus scaber (c & a)
Hedera (c)
Lonicera (some) (c)

Passiflora caerulea racemosa (c)
Rosa banksiae 'Lutea' (c)
Rosa 'Albertine' (c)
Trachelospermum jasminoides (c)
Wisteria sinensis (c)

CLIMBERS FOR SANDY SOIL
Vitis vinifera 'Purpurea' (c)

CLIMBERS FOR CLAY SOIL
Humulus lupulus 'Aureus' (c)
Rosa filipes 'Kiftsgate' (c)
Vitis coignetiae (c)

CLIMBERS FOR QUICK COVER
Hedera helix (small cvs) (c)
Hydrangea petiolaris (c)
Polygonum
   baldschuanicum (c)
Trachelospermum
   jasminoides (c)

Below: Rosa *'Iceberg' is a beautiful, highly fragrant rose.*

Below: *Hops* (Humulus lupulus) *are good at disguising eyesores.*

Below: Passiflora *is a stunning climber that loves walls.*

CLIMBERS FOR GROUND COVER

Hedera colchica 'Dentata Variegata' (c)
Schizophragma hydrangeoides (c)
Vitis coignetiae (c)

CLIMBERS WITH FRAGRANT FLOWERS

Azara (c)
Clematis montana 'Elizabeth' (c)

Itea ilicifolia (c)
Jasminum (most) (c)
Lathyrus odoratus (c & a)
Lonicera (many) (c)
Osmanthus (c)
Passiflora (c)
Trachelospermum (c)
Wisteria (c)

CLIMBERS WITH ARCHITECTURAL FOLIAGE

Hedera colchica 'Dentata Variegata' (c)

Schizophragma hydrangeoides (c)
Schizophragma integrifolium (c)
Vitis coignetiae (c)

CLIMBERS FOR CONTAINERS

Eccremocarpus scaber (c)
Hedera helix and cvs (c)
Ipomoea (some) (c & a)
Lathyrus (climbing species) (c & a)
Passiflora (c)

CLIMBERS FOR EXPOSED SITES

Euonymus fortunei (c)
Hedera helix (c)
Wisteria sinensis (c)

Below: Campsis radicans *is a beautiful late summer climber.*

Below: Rosa *'Zéphirine Drouhin' is adaptable and has no thorns.*

Below: *The flowers of* Clematis *'Perle d'Azur' open in summer.*

INDEX

Abeliophyllum distichum, 134
Abutilon, 39, 118, 146
    A. metapotamicum 'Variegatum', 97
    A. vitifolium, 119
Acaena, 80
Acer palmatum 'Atropurpureum', 92
    A. pseudoplatanus, 32
acid soil: climbers for, 184
    shrubs for, 180
Actinidia, 38, 39, 140
Aethionema, 86
Akebia, 38, 140, 154, 166, 168, 172
    A. quinata, 134, 140, 150
    A. trifoliata, 134
alkaline soil, 25, 104
Allium christophii, 69
Aloysia triphylla, 98
Amelanchier, 121
    A. lamarckii, 123
Ampelopsis glandulosa var. *brevipedunculata* 'Elegans', 14
Andromeda, 25, 87
Anemone nemorosa, 74
annual climbers, 130–1
aphids, 58
apples, 114, 140, 167
apricots, 140
arbours, 136, 170–1
architectural foliage, climbers, 185
archways, 148, 168–9
Arctostaphylos, 62, 87
    A. uva-ursi, 80
Asarina, 130
ash trees, 32
Astrantia major, 69
Aucuba, 83
    A. japonica, 59
        A. j. 'Crotonifolia', 97
        A. j. 'Mr Goldstrike', 97
        A. j. 'Picturata', 97
Aurinia saxatilis, 73
automatic watering, 25
autumn climbers, 140–1
autumn shrubs, 120–3
azaleas, 32, 73, 104, 110, 112
Azara, 39, 100, 132, 144, 146
    A. lanceolata, 178
    A. serrata, 134

Ballota pseudodictamnus, 105
bark, coloured stems, 126–7
bark mulches, 23
bay, 33, 98, 105
beans, climbing, 39, 168, 171, 172, 174
beech, 76, 78
Berberis, 11, 80, 86, 113, 135
    B. darwinii, 32
    B. 'Goldilocks', 113

    B. linearifolia 'Orange King', 113
    B. × *stenophylla*, 100
    B. thunbergii, 121
        B. t. 'Atropurpurea', 92, 93
        B. t. 'Bagatelle', 92
        B. t. 'Red Pillar', 122
        B. t. 'Rose Glow', 69, 97
berries, 102–3, 120, 140, 142
bindweed, 22
birds, 140
black-eyed Susan, 38, 130, 136, 154, 166, 176
blood, fish and bone, 26
blue-flowered climbers, 183
blue-flowered shrubs, 179
bonemeal, 26
borders: colour, 72–3
    designing, 68–71
    making new beds in lawns, 17
    mixed borders, 74–5
    shapes, 70
    shrubs in, 9–10
Boston ivy, 36, 140, 150
bottlebrush, 105, 119
Bougainvillea, 38, 137
box, 32, 76, 77, 78, 105, 108, 109
box-leaf honeysuckle, 32, 78, 108
Brachyglottis, 118
    B. 'Sunshine', 91
branches, pruning, 40
broom, 98, 113
Brunnera macrophylla, 74
Buddleja, 43, 59, 118, 120, 121
buds, pruning and, 40–1
butterfly bush, 59
Buxus, 78
    B. sempervirens, 32, 77, 105

Caiophora, 130
calico bush, 9
Californian lilac, 39, 117, 118
Callistemon, 118
    C. citrinus, 105, 132, 147
    C. sieberi, 119
Calluna, 62, 80
    C. vulgaris, 80
        C. v. 'Darkness', 178
Camellia, 25, 104, 105, 110, 113, 134, 150
Campanula latifolia, 74
    C. pyramidalis, 179
Camphorosma monspeliaca, 98
Campsis, 136, 140
    C. radicans, 37, 136, 168, 172, 185
canary creeper, 138
Canary Island ivy, 36
canes, staking, 30
Canna 'Wyoming', 130
Cape leadwort, 136
cardoons, 75
Carpentaria, 118
    C. californica, 39, 132, 146, 147, 179
Carpinus betulus, 32, 76, 78
Caryopteris × *clandonensis*, 90
    C. × *clandonensis* 'Worcester Gold', 97
Cassiope, 25, 83, 87
cathedral bells, 37, 130, 136, 154, 166
Ceanothus, 39, 70, 75, 118, 132, 146, 147
    C. arboreus 'Trewithen Blue', 134
    C. impressus, 179
    C. 'Pin Cushion', 84, 117
    C. prostratus, 86

Ceratostigma, 120, 121
    C. plumbaginoides, 81
    C. willmottianum, 121, 122
Cercis canadensis 'Forest Pansy', 92
Cestrum parqui, 100
Chaenomeles, 102, 113, 134, 140, 142, 143, 146, 150
    C. speciosa 'Moerloosii', 178
chalky soil, 180, 184
Chamaecyparis lawsoniana, 78
    C. obtusa, 86
cherries, 113, 114
cherry laurel, 32
Chilean glory flower, 38, 136, 166
Chinese jasmine, 7
Chinese Virginia creeper, 36
chlorophyll, 90, 95
Choisya ternata, 32, 100
    C. t. 'Sundance', 89, 181
Christmas rose, 74
Cistus, 80, 98, 118
    C. × *skanbergii*, 116
clay soil, 181, 184
Clematis: arbours, 170
    on archways, 168
    in autumn, 140, 141
    climbing habit, 37
    cuttings, 61
    as ground cover, 11
    growing through trees and shrubs, 166–7
    on pillars, 164
    planting, 20
    pruning, 50–4
    in summer, 136
    temporary supports, 174, 175
    on trellis, 154
    on tripods, 163
    on walkways and pergolas, 172
    C. 'Abundance', 50
    C. 'Alba Luxurians', 172
    C. alpina, 50, 134, 140, 166–7
    C. armandii, 132, 134, 142
    C. 'Barbara Jackman', 50
    C. 'Bill Mackenzie', 50
    C. cirrhosa, 50, 51, 132, 140, 142
        C. c. 'Balearica', 143
    C. 'Comtesse de Bouchard', 50, 182
    C. 'Daniel Deronda', 50
    C. 'Duchess of Albany', 50, 182
    C. 'Elsa Späth', 50
    C. 'Ernest Markham', 50
    C. 'Etoile Violette', 50, 173
    C. flammula, 140
    C. florida 'Sieboldii', 136, 183
    C. 'Hagley Hybrid', 50
    C. 'Jackmanii', 50, 163
    C. 'Lady Betty Balfour', 27
    C. 'Lasurstern', 50, 183
    C. 'Little Nell', 50
    C. macropetala, 50, 134

C. 'Madame Julia Correvon', 50, 182
C. 'Marie Boisselot', 50, 150, 167, 183
C. 'Miss Bateman', 50
C. 'Mrs Cholmondeley', 50
C. 'Mrs George Jackman', 183
C. montana, 50, 51, 134, 144, 150, 171, 173
C. 'Nelly Moser', 50, 150, 183
C. 'Niobe', 53
C. 'Perle d'Azur', 50, 136
C. 'Prince Charles', 177
C. rehderiana, 150
C. 'Rouge Cardinal', 150
C. 'Royal Velours', 50
C. 'Star of India', 50
C. tangutica, 50, 182, 183
C. 'The President', 50
C. tibetana, 50
   C. t. vernayi, 140
C. viticella, 21, 50, 110, 136, 162, 164
   C. v. 'Purpurea Plena Elegans', 50
C. 'Vyvyan Pennell', 50
C. 'W.E. Gladstone', 165
Clerodendrum bungei, 62, 98
Clethra, 100
Clianthus puniceus, 146
climbers, 129–85
  annual climbers, 130–1
  in autumn, 140–1
  colour, 182–3
  in containers, 185
  cuttings, 60–1
  evergreens, 132–3, 142
  fragrant climbers, 144–5
  as ground cover, 11
  layering, 64–5
  maintenance, 34–5
  north- and east-facing walls, 150
  planting, 20–1
  propagation, 12
  pruning, 12, 44–7
  in spring, 134–5
  in summer, 136–9
  supports, 11, 21, 34, 36–9
  training, 148–77
  tying in, 34
  in winter, 142–3
clinging climbers, 36
clipping hedges, 78–9
Cobaea scandens, 37, 130, 131, 136, 154, 166
coir, potting compost, 57
colour, 7
  annual climbers, 130
  climbers, 182–3
  designing borders, 72–3
  foliage, 90–1

shrubs, 178–9
  stems, 126–7
compost, garden, 16, 27
compost (soil mix): containers, 106, 176
  for cuttings, 60
  seedlings, 57
conifers, 88
  fragrant foliage, 98
  hedges, 77, 79
containers: climbers in, 176–7, 185
  dwarf shrubs, 85
  shrubs in, 10–11, 104–7
Convallaria majalis, 74
Convolvulus althaeoides, 138
  C. cneorum, 32, 86, 90, 105
  C. sabatius, 86
  C. tricolor, 130
coppicing, 90
Cordyline australis, 105
  C. a. 'Atropurpurea', 92
Cornus, 59, 118
  C. alba, 62, 126
    C. a. 'Elegantissima', 94
    C. a. 'Sibirica', 43, 73
    C. a. 'Spaethii', 97
  C. alternifolia 'Argentea', 94
  C. canadensis, 62, 83
  C. controversa 'Variegata', 94
  C. mas, 124
    C. m. 'Aureoelegantissima', 95, 105
  C. stolonifera 'Flaviramea', 126
Coronilla glauca, 132
Corylopsis, 100, 113, 124
Corylus, 93, 113, 124
  C. avellana, 32, 77, 160, 175
    C. a. contorta, 126
  C. maxima 'Purpurea', 92
Cotinus, 43, 90, 93, 121, 123
  C. coggygria 'Royal Purple', 67, 69, 92
Cotoneaster, 39, 80, 102, 103, 105, 140, 142, 146
  C. horizontalis, 140
  C. simonsii, 32
cotton lavender, 91
country hedges, 77
courgettes (zucchini), 174
crab apple, 140
Crataegus, 78, 102
  C. monogyna, 32, 77
cucumbers, 174
× *Cupressocyparis leylandii*, 32, 76, 78
currants, 59, 114, 140
  flowering, 110, 113
cutting compost, 60
cuttings, 58–61
Cyclamen hederifolium, 74
Cynara cardunculus, 75
Cytisus, 98, 113

daisy bush, 105, 118
Daphne, 86, 87, 100, 102, 113
  D. × *burkwoodii* 'Somerset', 11, 69, 100
  D. × *burkwoodii* 'Somerset Gold Edge', 97
  D. tangutica, 87
dead-heading, 34, 35, 43
dead wood, pruning, 44
deciduous shrubs, 9
Desfontainea spinosa, 132
designing borders, 68–71
Deutzia, 118
Dictamnus albus purpureus, 69
dieback, 42
digging, 16
Digitalis purpurea, 69
diseased wood, pruning, 42, 44
diseases, 58, 62
division, 62
dogwood, 43, 59, 83, 118, 124
drainage, 16, 106
drought, 32
dry areas, 180, 184
Dryas octopetala, 86
dwarf shrubs, 84–7

east-facing walls, 150
Eccremocarpus scaber, 38, 130, 136, 166
Elaeagnus, 100
  E. × *ebbingei*, 32, 132, 142
  E. pungens, 132, 142
  E. 'Quicksilver', 72, 90, 91
elder, 43, 59, 90, 96, 98, 101, 104, 118
Enkianthus, 25, 121
Eranthis hyemalis, 74
Erica, 62, 80, 86, 87, 105, 118

ericaceous plants, watering, 25
Eryngium giganteum, 69
Erysimum 'Bowles Mauve', 72
Escallonia, 132
  E. 'Gwendolyn Anley', 16
  E. 'Langleyensis', 32
Etruscan honeysuckle, 11
Eucalyptus, 75
Eucryphia glutinosa, 120, 121, 122
Euonymus, 80, 83
  E. alatus, 121
    E. a. 'Compactus', 121
  E. europaeus, 102
  E. fortunei, 39, 80, 132, 146, 150
    E. f. 'Emerald Gaiety', 94, 104, 137
    E. f. 'Emerald 'n' Gold', 8, 80, 146
    E. f. 'Gold Spot', 97
    E. f. 'Silver Queen', 94
    E. f. 'Sunshine', 97
    E. f. 'Variegatus', 94
  E. japonicus, 132
    E. j. 'Aureopictus', 97
    E. j. 'Macrophyllus', 32
    E. j. 'Macrophyllus Albus', 94
  E. nana, 86
Euphorbia amygdaloides robbiae, 74
Euryops acreus, 86
evergreens: climbers, 132–3, 142
  shrubs, 8, 88–9
Exochorda, 113
  E. × *macrantha* 'The Bride', 8, 111
exposed sites, 181, 185
eyesores, screening, 9, 150

Fagus sylvatica, 76, 78
  F. s. 'Riversii', 92

Fallopia baldschuanica, 38, 136, 140, 150, 166, 170
fences, 158
fertilizers, 18, 20, 26–7, 106
Ficus carica, 146, 170
figs, 146, 170
firethorn, 32, 39, 77, 102, 132, 140, 146, 150
fleece, winter protection, 33
flowers: annual climbers, 130–1
autumn shrubs, 120–3
colours, 7
fragrant, 100–1, 181, 185
hedges, 77
spring climbers, 134–5
spring shrubs, 110–13
summer climbers, 136–9
summer shrubs, 114–19
training climbers, 150
winter climbers, 142–3
focal points, 8, 10
foliage: autumn, 120, 121, 140
colour, 7, 72, 90–1
evergreen climbers, 132
evergreen shrubs, 88
fragrant foliage, 98–9, 181
purple foliage, 90, 92–3
reversion, 95
silver-leaved plants, 32, 90, 91
texture, 72
variegated, 34, 90, 94–7
formers, topiary, 108
Forsythia, 59, 112, 113
F. suspensa, 134
Fothergilla, 121
F. major, 123
fragrance: climbers, 136, 144–5, 185
shrubs, 98–101, 181
Fraxinus excelsior, 32
Fremontodendron, 118
F. californicum, 132, 146, 178
frost damage: climbers, 34, 35, 134
shrubs, 32, 33, 110
fruit, 102–3, 114, 120, 140, 141
fruit trees, growing climbers through, 166
Fuchsia, 105, 118, 120, 121
F. 'Genii', 178
F. magellanica 'Variegata', 94
F. procumbens, 86
fungal diseases, 62

Galanthus, 74
gardener's garters, 114
Garrya elliptica, 132, 134, 142, 143, 146
Gaultheria, 25, 62, 83, 87, 104
G. mucronata, 102
Genista lydia, 84, 86
Geranium, 74, 75
G. × *oxonianum*, 95, 137
G. sanguineum, 85

germander, shrubby, 39, 146
glyphosate, 22
golden foliage, 90, 97
gooseberries, 102, 114, 140
gourds (squashes), 130, 174
grapevines, 140, 171
grass clippings, mulches, 23
gravel beds, 86–7
gravel mulches, 23
green-flowered climbers, 183
green-flowered shrubs, 179
Griselinia littoralis, 32
ground cover: climbers as, 11, 185
shrubs, 80–3, 181
ground elder, 22

× *Halimiocistus revolii*, 84, 86, 117
Halimium, 118
H. × *pauanum*, 116
Hamamelis, 100, 124
hardwood cuttings, 58, 59
hawthorn, 32, 77, 78, 102
hazel, 32, 77, 93, 113, 124, 160, 175
heather, 25, 71, 80, 86, 87, 104, 105, 118
Hebe, 86, 105, 118
H. cupressoides, 89, 99
H. pinguifolia 'Pagei', 80, 90
Hedera, 80, 83, 132, 140, 142, 150, 170
H. canariensis, 36
H. colchica, 36
H. c. 'Dentata Variegata', 142
H. helix, 36
hedges, 76–9
clipping, 78–9
shrubs for, 9, 181
as windbreaks, 32
Helianthemum, 85, 86, 105
H. 'Wisley Pink', 91, 180
Helleborus, 74
H. foetidus, 140
herbaceous plants, mixed borders, 74–5
herbicides, 16, 22
herbs, 99
hessian, winter protection, 34, 35
Hibiscus, 118, 120, 121
Hippophaë rhamnoides, 32, 90, 102
hips, 46, 103
hoeing, 22
Hoheria, 118
holly, 32, 77, 78, 97, 102, 103, 105, 108, 140
honeysuckle: arbours, 170
on archways, 168, 169
in autumn, 140
climbing habit, 39
growing through trees and shrubs, 166
hiding eyesores, 150
on pillars, 164

scent, 100, 144
in spring, 134, 135
on trellis, 154, 159
on tripods, 163
on walkways and pergolas, 172
in winter, 142
hoops, training climbers on, 160–1
hops, 39, 128, 140, 150, 154, 163, 164, 166, 168, 169, 170, 172, 184
hornbeam, 32, 76, 78
hosepipes, 24–5
Humulus, 150, 154, 163, 164, 166, 168, 170, 172
H. lupulus, 39, 140, 184
H. l. 'Aureus', 128, 169
Hydrangea, 24, 105, 118, 120, 121
H. anomala petiolaris, 8, 36, 140, 150
H. aspera, 140
H. a. 'Villosa', 115
H. macrophylla, 115
H. quercifolia, 115, 140
Hypericum, 86, 105, 118, 120, 121
H. calycinum, 80

Ilex, 32, 78, 102, 105, 108, 140
I. × *altaclerensis* 'Golden King', 97
I. × *altaclerensis* 'Lawsoniana', 97
I. aquifolium, 77
I. a. 'Aurifodina', 97
I. a. 'Crispa Aureopicta', 97
I. a. 'Ferox Argentea', 103
I. a. 'Golden Milkboy', 97
Indigofera, 105, 118, 120, 121
internodal cuttings, 61
Ipomoea, 39, 130, 131, 136, 154, 166

Itea, 100
I. ilicifolia, 132, 144, 146
ivy, 11, 36, 80, 82, 83, 132, 140, 142, 150, 168, 170, 172

Japanese hydrangea vine, 10
Japanese wisteria, 41
japonica, 113, 134, 140, 142, 143, 146, 150
Jasminum, 6, 118, 136, 144, 146, 170
J. nudiflorum, 124, 142, 150
J. officinale, 140
J. o. 'Aureum', 145
Judas tree, 121
Juniperus, 88, 98
J. communis 'Compressa', 84, 85, 86
J. c. 'Prostrata', 80
J. sabina tamariscifolia, 80
J. squamata 'Blue Carpet', 80

Kalmia, 25, 87, 105, 116, 118
K. latifolia, 9
Kalmiopsis, 87
Kerria, 62

Lablab purpureus, 130
Lagenaria, 130
Lapageria rosea, 136
Lathyrus, 37, 136
L. grandiflorus, 138, 182
L. latifolius, 130, 174
L. odoratus, 130, 144, 154, 166
L. sativus, 130
laurel, 78, 79
Laurus nobilis, 33, 98, 105, 132
laurustinus, 32
Lavandula (lavender), 32, 76, 77, 78,

98, 104, 105, 118
L. angustifolia, 90
L. stoechas, 70
L. s. pedunculata, 72
Lavatera, 117, 118
lawns, making new beds in, 17
Lawson's cypress, 78
layering, 62–5
leaves *see* foliage
Leptospermum, 118
L. scoparium 'Lyndon', 118
L. s. 'Nanum', 86
Leucothoe, 62
Leycesteria, 118
Leyland cypress, 76, 78
Ligustrum, 59, 78, 102, 108, 144
L. lucidum 'Excelsum Superbum', 88
L. ovalifolium, 32
L. o. 'Aureum', 97
lilac, 6, 33, 113
lily-of-the-valley, 74
liquid fertilizers, 27
Lithodora diffusa, 73, 80, 81, 86
Lonicera, 39, 134, 136, 140, 144, 150, 154, 163, 164, 166, 168, 170, 172
L. etrusca, 11
L. fragrantissima, 124, 142
L. japonica, 132
L. j. 'Halliana', 182
L. nitida, 32, 78, 108
L. periclymenum, 135, 144, 169
L. pileata, 83
L. × *purpusii*, 124, 142
L. pyrenaica, 86
L. standishii, 124, 142
L. × *tellmanniana*, 144, 150
L. tragophylla, 140, 144
Lychnis chalcedonica, 74
L. coronaria 'Alba', 69

Magnolia, 39, 100, 110, 113, 146
M. grandiflora, 132, 144, 146
M. stellata, 112
Mahonia, 62, 100, 113, 124, 125
M. aquifolium, 9
M. media 'Charity', 8
Malus, 140
manure, 27
marrows, 174
Mexican orange-blossom, 100
Micromeria corsica, 86
Mikania scandens, 130
minerals, 26
mixed borders, 74–5
mock orange, 7, 59, 100, 101, 118
moist shade, 180, 184
morning glory, 39, 130, 131, 136, 154, 166
moving shrubs, 28–9
mulches, 20, 21, 23

Mutisia, 37, 136
Myrica, 98
Myrtus, 98, 100, 105
M. communis, 98, 105

Nandina, 62
nasturtiums, 38, 130, 136, 140, 163, 164, 166, 176
netting: growing climbers on, 156–7
windbreaks, 32
winter protection, 34, 35
New Zealand flax, 105
New Zealand tea tree, 118
nightshade, 38
north-facing walls, 150

oak-leafed hydrangea, 115
Olearia, 70, 105, 118
O. × *haastii*, 114
Ononis, 86
orange-flowered climbers, 182
orange-flowered shrubs, 178
Oregon grape, 9
organic material, 16, 27
Osmanthus, 100, 144
O. heterophyllus, 120, 121
O. h. 'Goshiki', 97

Pachysandra, 62, 83
P. terminalis, 80
Papaver somniferum, 69
parrot's bill, 146
Parthenocissus, 140, 150
P. henryana, 36, 141

P. quinquefolia, 36
P. tricuspida, 36
Passiflora, 38, 136, 140, 144, 184
P. caerulea, 139
passion-flower, 38, 136, 139, 140, 144
pea-sticks, 174, 175
pears, 140, 141
peas, 37, 136, 174, 175
peat: peat beds, 87
potting compost, 57
perennial weeds, 16, 22, 23
pergolas, 136, 172–3
periwinkle, 38, 80, 81, 83, 132, 133
pernettya, 87, 102
Perovskia, 98
P. atriplicifolia 'Blue Spire', 69
Persian ivy, 36
Phalaris arundinacea 'Picta', 114
Phaseolus, 39, 168, 172
P. coccineus, 136
Philadelphus, 59, 100, 101, 118
P. coronarius, 7
Phormium, 105
P. cookianum, 69
Phyllodoce, 25, 87
Picea sitchensis, 32
Pieris, 25, 104, 107, 110, 113
P. japonica, 89, 180
pillars, training climbers on, 164–5
pink-flowered climbers, 182–3
pink-flowered shrubs, 178
Pinus sylvestris, 32
Piptanthus, 102
P. laburnifolius, 132, 134

P. nepalensis, 146
Pittosporum tenuifolium, 32
plans, designing borders, 68
planting: climbers, 20–1, 166–7
ground-cover shrubs, 82–3
hedges, 78
planting times, 18, 20
shrubs, 18–19
shrubs in containers, 106–7
plastic mulches, 23
Plumbago auriculata, 136
P. capensis, 38
plums, 114, 140
pollarding, 90
Polygonatum, 74
Portuguese laurel, 32, 78
Potentilla, 23, 118
P. fruticosa, 80
pricking out seedlings, 57
Primula, 74
privet, 32, 78, 88, 100, 108, 144
propagation, 12, 56–65
cuttings, 58–61
division, 62
layering, 62–5
seed, 56–7
propagators, 58, 61
Prostanthera cuneata, 70, 98
pruning, 40–55
clematis, 50–4
climbers, 12, 44–7
climbing roses, 46–7
hedges, 78–9
rambling roses, 48–9
root-pruning, 28
shrubs, 12, 40–3
topiary, 108
wisteria, 55
pruning saws, 40
Prunus, 113, 140
P. cerasifera 'Nigra', 92
P. × *cistena*, 92
P. laurocerasus, 32, 78, 79
P. lusitanica, 32, 78
P. l. 'Variegata', 94
purple-flowered climbers, 183
purple-flowered shrubs, 179
purple foliage, 90, 92–3
Pyracantha, 32, 39, 77, 102, 132, 140, 142, 146, 150, 181
P. 'Orange Charmer', 140
Pyrus, 140
P. 'Doyenne du Comice', 141
P. salicifolia 'Pendula', 90

quince, flowering, 134, 140, 142, 143, 146, 150

rambling roses, pruning, 48–9
red currants, 102
red-flowered climbers, 182
red-flowered shrubs, 178

repeat-flowering roses, pruning, 47
reversion, 95
Rhamnus alaternus
    R. a. 'Argenteovariegata', 94, 95
    R. a. 'Variegata', 179
Rhodochiton atrosanguineus, 38, 130
Rhododendron, 25, 32, 63, 70, 74, 80,
    83, 87, 89, 104, 105, 110, 111,
    113
    R. luteum, 100
Rhus hirta, 121
Ribes, 59, 113
    R. laurifolia, 134
    R. sanguineum, 110
    R. speciosum, 140
rock gardens, dwarf shrubs, 84, 86
rock roses, 80, 85, 98, 116, 118
"rooms", 9
roots: layering, 63
    pruning, 28
ropes, training climbers on, 148, 164
Rosa (roses), 59, 102, 105, 118
    arbours, 170, 171
    on archways, 168, 169
    in autumn, 140
    climbing habit, 38
    dead-heading, 43
    feeding, 26
    growing through trees and
        shrubs, 166
    hedges, 76
    hiding eyesores, 150
    hips, 103
    layering, 65
    on pillars, 164
    pruning, 46–9
    scent, 100, 144
    in spring, 134
    staking, 30
    in summer, 136
    supports, 36, 38
    training, 150
    training on hoops, 160–1
    on trellis, 154
    on tripods, 162, 163
    tying in, 34
    walkways and pergolas, 172
    R. 'Agatha Christie', 47
    R. 'Alba maxima', 47
    R. 'Albertine', 145, 151, 172
    R. 'Aloha', 47
    R. 'American Pillar', 165, 172
    R. 'Bantry Bay', 41, 47
    R. 'Bobbie James', 49
    R. 'Casino', 47
    R. 'Cedric Morris', 61
    R. 'Coral Dawn', 47
    R. 'Danse du Feu', 47
    R. 'Dortmund', 139
    R. 'Dublin Bay', 155
    R. 'Excelsa', 45
    R. 'Felicia', 149

R. glauca, 43, 90
R. 'Gloire de Dijon', 47
R. 'Golden Showers', 47
R. 'Handel', 47
R. 'Iceberg', 145, 183, 184
R. 'Isphahan', 161
R. 'Kew Rambler', 165
R. 'Lady Penzance', 98
R. 'Madame Isaac Pereire', 153
R. 'Maigold', 135
R. 'Miss Pam Ayres', 43
R. 'New Dawn', 150
R. 'Parkdirektor Riggers', 47
R. 'Paul's Himalayan Musk', 149
R. pimpinellifolia, 103
R. 'Pink Perpétue', 47
R. 'Royal Gold', 47
R. rubiginosa, 98
R. 'Schoolgirl', 47
R. 'Seagull', 148
R. 'Stanwell Perpetual', 114
R. 'Summer Wine', 47
R. 'Veilchenblau', 151
R. 'Wedding Day', 144
R. 'Wenlock Castle', 69
R. 'Zéphirine Drouhin', 27, 101,

    145, 148, 168, 185
Rosmarinus, 32, 98, 99, 105, 113, 180
    R. officinalis, 32
rowan, 32
Rubus, 62
    R. cockburnianus, 43, 126
    R. 'Golden Veil', 127
    R. thibetanus, 126
runner beans, 130, 136, 171, 174
Russian vine, 38, 136, 140, 150, 166,
    170

sage, 72, 93, 96, 98, 99, 181
Salix, 43, 59, 113
    S. alba vitellina, 127
        S. a. v. 'Britzensis', 90, 126, 127
    S. gracilistyla 'Melanostachys', 127
    S. helvetica, 85, 86, 166
    S. lanata, 90
    S. repens, 73, 80, 81, 86
Salvia forsskaolii, 69
    S. officinalis, 96, 98
        S. o. 'Icterina', 181
        S. o. 'Purpurascens', 72, 92
    S. sclarea, 75
Sambucus, 43, 59, 90, 98, 118

    S. nigra 'Aureomarginata', 97
    S. racemosa 'Plumosa Aurea', 96,
        104
sandy soil, 180–1, 184
Santolina, 98
    S. chamaecyparis, 90, 91
    S. pinnata neapolitana, 90
Sarcococca, 62, 83, 100
scent *see* fragrance
Schisandra, 134, 136
Schizophragma, 136, 150
    S. hydrangeoides, 10
Scots pine, 32
scrambling climbers, 38
screens, 9, 76, 132, 150, 158
sea buckthorn, 32
secateurs (pruners), 41
Sedum spectabile 'September Glow',
    69
seed, sowing, 56–7
seedlings, pricking out, 57
seep (soaker) hose, 24
semi-ripe cuttings, 58, 60
"serpentine layering", 63
shade: climbers for, 136, 184
    shrubs for, 32, 180
shapes, shrubs, 8–9
shredders, 44
shrubs, 67–127
    in autumn, 120–3
    berries and fruit, 102–3
    in borders, 9–10
    colour, 178–9
    coloured foliage, 72, 90–1
    coloured stems, 73, 126–7
    in containers, 10–11, 104–7
    cuttings, 58–9
    designing borders, 68–71
    division, 62
    dwarf shrubs, 84–7
    evergreen shrubs, 88–9
    form and shape, 8–9
    fragrance, 98–101, 181
    ground cover, 80–3, 181
    growing climbers through, 166–7
    hedges, 76–9, 181
    height and shape, 71
    layering, 62–3
    mixed borders, 74–5
    moving, 28–9
    planting, 18–19
    propagation, 12
    pruning, 12, 40–3
    purple foliage, 90, 92–3
    in spring, 110–13
    staking, 30–1
    in summer, 114–19
    topiary, 108–9
    variegated foliage, 94–7
    wall shrubs, 39, 132, 144, 146–7
    as windbreaks, 32
    in winter, 124–7

silver foliage, 32, 90, 91
Skimmia, 100, 102, 103, 105
smoke bush, 43, 90, 93, 121, 123
snow, 124
snowdrops, 74
soil: preparation, 16–17
    woodland beds, 87
soilless potting compost, 57
Solanum, 34–5, 38
    S. crispum, 132, 154, 166
        S. c. 'Glasnevin', 133, 134, 136
    S. jasminoides, 132, 136, 154,
        163, 164, 166
Sorbus aucuparia, 32
    S. reducta, 62, 86
sowing seed, 56–7
spindle tree, 121
Spiraea, 59, 94, 113
    S. 'Arguta', 19, 110
    S. japonica 'Goldflame', 27, 95
    S. nipponica 'Snowmound', 8
spotted laurel, 59
spring climbers, 134–5
spring shrubs, 110–13
sprinklers, 24
spruce, sitka, 32
Stachys byzantina, 69
staking, shrubs, 30–1
stems: coloured, 73, 126–7
    dieback, 42
    hard pruning, 43
    pollarding, 90
    pruning crossing stems, 42
Stephandra incisa, 80, 121
suckers, climbers, 60
summer climbers, 136–9
summer shrubs, 114–19
sunny areas, shrubs for, 180
supports: arbours, 170–1
    on archways, 168–9
    climbers, 11, 21, 34, 36–9
    in containers, 176–7
    hoops, 160–1
    pillars, 164–5
    staking shrubs, 30–1
    temporary, 174–5
    trellis, 158–9
    tripods, 162–3
    walkways and pergolas, 172–3
sweet box, 100
sweet-briar rose, 98
sweet peas, 130, 131, 144, 154, 156,
    166, 175
sycamore, 32
Symphoricarpos, 102
Syringa, 33, 113
    S. × henryi, 6
    S. vulgaris, 179

Tamarix, 32
tap water, 24
tapestry hedges, 77

Taxus, 78
    T. baccata, 12, 32, 76, 185
temporary supports, 174–5
tendrils, climbers, 37
Teucrium, 86
    T. fruticans, 39, 132, 146
texture, 8, 72
Thuja plicata, 78
Thunbergia, 176
    T. alata, 38, 130, 136, 154, 166
Thymus, 86, 98
ties: climbers, 38
    staking shrubs, 30–1
    training climbers on wires, 153
topiary, 16, 108–9
trace elements, 26
Trachelospermum, 38, 136
    T. jasminoides, 7
training climbers, 148–77
    on arbours, 170–1
    on archways, 168–9
    in containers, 176–7
    erecting trellis, 158–9
    fixing trellis to walls, 154–5
    on hoops, 160–1
    on netting, 156–7
    over eyesores, 150
    on pillars, 164–5
    temporary supports, 174–5
    through trees and shrubs, 166–7
    on tripods, 162–3
    on walkways and pergolas, 172–3
    on wires, 152–3
trees: growing climbers through,
    149, 166–7
    as windbreaks, 32
trellis: in containers, 176–7
    erecting, 158–9
    fixing to walls, 154–5
    walkways, 172
tripods, training climbers on, 162–3
Tropaeolum, 38, 130, 136, 140, 163,
    164, 166
    T. 'Jewel of Africa', 130
    T. peregrinum, 138
    T. speciosum, 138
troughs, dwarf shrubs, 85, 86
trumpet creeper, 37
twining climbers, 39

Vaccinium, 25, 83, 87, 104
variegated foliage, 34, 90, 94–7

Verbascum 'Letitia', 86
Viburnum, 59, 113, 118
    V. bodnantense, 124
    V. farreri, 124
    V. × juddii, 101
    V. opulus, 102
    V. tinus, 32, 124, 125
Vinca, 38
    V. major, 132, 133, 166, 183
        V. m. 'Variegata', 133
    V. minor, 80, 81, 83
        V. m. 'Argenteovariegata', 94
vine eyes, 152
vines, 37, 140, 163, 164, 168, 170,
    171
viral diseases, 58
Virginia creeper, 36, 140, 150
Vitis, 37, 140, 163, 164, 168, 170
    V. coignetiae, 27, 168
    V. vinifera 'Purpurea', 173, 183

walkways, training climbers on,
    172–3
wall shrubs, 39, 132, 144, 146–7
walls: fixing trellis to, 154–5
    growing climbers on netting,
        156–7
    planting climbers, 20
    training climbers on wires, 152–3
water butts, 24
watering, 18, 20, 24–5, 106
weather problems, 32–3
weedkillers, 16, 22
weeds, 16, 22, 23, 80
Weigela, 118
    W. florida 'Albomarginata', 94
        W. f. 'Florida Variegata', 69
        W. f. 'Foliis Purpurea', 92
white-flowered climbers, 183
white-flowered shrubs, 179
wigwams (tepees), 174, 175
wildlife, 181
willow, 43, 59, 73, 85, 113, 127
wind-rock, 28, 30
windbreaks, 9, 18, 32, 181
winter climbers, 142–3
winter jasmine, 124, 142
winter protection, 33, 34, 35
winter shrubs, 124–7
wires, growing climbers on, 152–3
Wisteria, 55, 134, 135, 136, 168
    W. floribunda, 41
witch hazel, 100, 124
wood spurge, 74
woodland plants, 74, 87

yellow-flowered climbers, 182
yellow-flowered shrubs, 178
yellow foliage, 90, 97
yew, 12, 32, 76, 78, 108, 109, 185
Yucca, 105
    Y. gloriosa 'Variegata', 69

Acknowledgements

The publishers would like to thank the following for their permission to photograph their plants and gardens: Hilary and Richard Bird, Ken Bronwin, Mr and Mrs R Cunningham, Chris and Stuart Fagg, Della and Colin Fox, Christopher Lloyd, Merriments Gardens, Eric Pierson, the RHS Garden Wisley, Mavis and David Seeney, Lyn and Brian Smith.

They would also like to thank the following people for allowing their pictures (to which they own the copyright) to be reproduced in this book:

Key: t = top; b = bottom; r = right; l = left; c = centre

Richard Bird for the picture on p. 61 (br); **Jonathan Buckley** for the pictures on p. 41 (br), p. 81 (br), p. 137 (tr), p. 137 (br), p. 153 (tr), p. 153 (bl), p. 153 (br), p. 162 (tr), p. 170 (b), p. 171 (r), p. 173 (l), p. 174 (br), p. 175 (br), p. 175 (l), p. 176 (all), p. 177 (all); **The Garden Picture Library** for the picture on p. 70; **Andrew Lawson** for the front cover picture; **Peter McHoy** for the pictures on p. 32, p. 33 (br), p. 39 (r), p. 43, p. 52, p. 53, p. 54 (tr), p. 54 (bl), p. 55 (tl), p. 79 (br), p. 97 (tr), p. 102 (tr), p. 103 (tr), p. 110 (tl), p. 110 (tr), p. 112 (br), p. 113 (bl), p. 120 (tr), p. 121 (l), p. 122 (all), p. 123 (tr), p. 123 (br), p. 124 (tl), p. 124 (tr), p. 125 (br), p. 131 (b), p. 135 (bl), p. 138 (br), p. 140 (b), p. 141 (r), p. 142 (br), p. 143 (bl), p. 144 (tr), p. 144 (bl), p. 178 (bl), p. 178 (tc), p. 178 (bc), p. 179 (t), p. 179 (br), p. 182 (c), p. 185 (tl); and **Derck St Romaine** for the picture on p. 69.

EYEWITNESS TRAVEL GUIDES

THE
WORLD'S
MUST-SEE
PLACES

DK

LONDON, NEW YORK,
MELBOURNE, MUNICH AND DELHI
www.dk.com

PUBLISHER Douglas Amrine
PUBLISHING MANAGER Kate Poole
MANAGING EDITOR Anna Streiffert
PROJECT EDITOR Lucinda Cooke
SENIOR ART EDITOR Marisa Renzullo
SENIOR DESIGNER Tessa Bindloss
DESIGNER Maite Lantaron
SENIOR DTP DESIGNER Jason Little
DTP DESIGNER Conrad Van Dyk
SENIOR MAP-COORDINATOR Casper Morris
EDITORS Sherry Collins, Vandana Mohindra,
Mani Ramaswarmy
PRODUCTION Joanna Bull, Sarah Dodd
PICTURE RESEARCH Taiyaba Khatoon,
Ellen Root

Reproduced by Colourscan (Singapore)
Printed and bound in Italy by Graphicom

First published in Great Britain in 2005 by
Dorling Kindersley Limited
80 Strand, London WC2R 0RL

Copyright 2005 © Dorling Kindersley Limited, London
A Penguin Company

A CIP CATALOGUE RECORD IS AVAILABLE FROM THE BRITISH LIBRARY.

ISBN 1 4053 1109 6

FLOORS ARE REFERRED TO THROUGHOUT IN ACCORDANCE WITH
EUROPEAN USAGE; IE THE "FIRST FLOOR" IS THE FLOOR ABOVE
GROUND LEVEL.

Château de Chenonceau, France

CONTENTS

INTRODUCTION 6-9

EUROPE

NORWAY
Borgund Stave Church 12

SWEDEN
Vasa Museum, Stockholm 14

IRELAND
Newgrange 16
Trinity College, Dublin 18
Rock of Cashel 20

GREAT BRITAIN
Stirling Castle 22
Edinburgh Castle 24
York Minster 28
Westminster Abbey,
London 30
St Paul's Cathedral,
London 32
The Tower of London 34
Hampton Court Palace 36
Stonehenge 38
Canterbury Cathedral 42

BELGIUM
Rubens' House, Antwerp 44

THE NETHERLANDS
Het Loo Palace, Apeldoorn 46

FRANCE
Amiens Cathedral 48
Mont-St-Michel 50
Notre-Dame, Paris 54
Arc de Triomphe, Paris 56
Château de Versailles,
Paris 58
Chartres Cathedral 60
Château de Chenonceau 62
Rocamadour 66

GERMANY
Bremen Town Hall 68
Cologne Cathedral 70
Würzburg Residence 72
Heidelberg Castle 74
Neuschwanstein Castle 76

SWITZERLAND
St Gallen Monastery 80

AUSTRIA
Stephansdom, Vienna 82
Schönbrunn Palace 84

POLAND
Royal Castle, Warsaw 86

CZECH REPUBLIC
Old-New Synagogue,
Prague 88
Charles Bridge, Prague 92

HUNGARY
Parliament, Budapest 94

RUSSIA
The Winter Palace,
St Petersburg 96
St Basil's Cathedral,
Moscow 98

PORTUGAL
Palace of Pena, Sintra *102*

SPAIN
Santiago de Compostela Cathedral *104*
Guggenheim, Bilbao *106*
Sagrada Família, Barcelona *110*
El Escorial, Madrid *112*
The Alhambra, Granada *114*

ITALY
St Mark's Basilica, *116*
Doge's Palace, Venice *120*
Campo dei Miracoli, Pisa *122*
Cathedral and Baptistry, Florence *124*
Basilica of St Francis, Assisi *126*
Colosseum, Rome *128*
St Peter's, Rome *130*
Pompeii *132*

CROATIA
Basilica of Euphrasius, Poreč *134*

GREECE
Acropolis, Athens *136*
Monastery of St John, Pátmos *140*
Palace of the Grand Masters, Rhodes *142*

TURKEY
Topkapı Palace, Istanbul *144*
Haghia Sophia, Istanbul *148*
Ephesus *150*

Fresco by Giotto, Basilica of St Francis, Assisi

Ruins of Machu Picchu, high in the Peruvian Andes

AFRICA

MOROCCO
Mosque of Hassan II, Casablanca *154*

TUNISIA
Great Mosque, Kairouan *156*

LIBYA
Leptis Magna *158*

EGYPT
The Great Pyramid, Giza *160*
Abu Simbel *162*

MALI
Djenné Mosque *166*

SOUTH AFRICA
Castle of Good Hope, Cape Town *168*

ASIA

SYRIA
Krak des Chevaliers *172*

ISRAEL
Church of the Holy Sepulchre, Jerusalem *174*
Dome of the Rock, Jerusalem *178*
Masada *180*

JORDAN
Petra *182*

UZBEKISTAN
The Registan, Samarkand *184*

CHINA
Potala Palace, Lhasa *186*
The Great Wall of China *188*
Forbidden City, Beijing *192*
Temple of Heaven, Beijing *194*

JAPAN
Tosho-gu Shrine, Nikko *196*
Todai-ji Temple, Nara *198*

INDIA
Golden Temple, Amritsar *202*
Taj Mahal, Agra *204*
Fatehpur Sikri *206*
The Great Stupa, Sanchi *208*

THAILAND
Grand Palace and Wat Phra Kaeo, Bangkok *210*
Wat Arun, Bangkok *212*

CAMBODIA
Angkor Wat *216*

INDONESIA
Borobodur Temple, Java *218*
Pura Ulun Danu Batur, Bali *220*

Sydney Opera House, Australia

AUSTRALASIA

AUSTRALIA
Sydney Opera House *224*

NEW ZEALAND
Dunedin Railway Station *226*

NORTH, CENTRAL & SOUTH AMERICA

CANADA
Sainte-Anne-de-Beaupré *230*
CN Tower, Toronto *232*

UNITED STATES OF AMERICA
Old State House, Boston *234*
Solomon R Guggenheim Museum, New York *236*
Empire State Building, New York *238*
Statue of Liberty, New York *242*
The White House, Washington DC *244*
United States Capitol, Washington DC *246*
Golden Gate Bridge, San Francisco *248*
Chaco Culture National Historical Park *250*

MEXICO
Chichén Itzá *252*
Metropolitan Cathedral, Mexico City *256*

PERU
Machu Picchu *258*

BRAZIL
Brasília *260*

INDEX/ ACKNOWLEDGMENTS
262-264

INTRODUCTION

Travellers in the Classical age, whose ideas of enjoyment were probably little different from our own, had few sites to visit. It was therefore not difficult for Greek writers to list the seven best and call them the "wonders of the world". Civilizations have come a long way since then, the world has shrunk with high-speed travel and there has been no let up in the desire to build. These days, it would be hard to pinpoint the seven most wondrous efforts in the world. But here are 103 sites that should not be missed.

Created for people of vision and flair to glorify themselves, their gods and their power as well as their genius, these buildings are landmarks that tell us about the past, where we have come from and what we are capable of achieving. Each one needs close inspection to appreciate its setting, structure, style and ornament. Palaces, castles, religious houses and places of entertainment have been handed to artists and artisans to embellish. Around and within these walls masons, carpenters, wood carvers, ceramicists, sculptors, painters, glassmakers, metalworkers, cabinet makers, embroiderers, tapestry makers and landscape gardeners have all sought some kind of perfection. Some are well known, but most were journeymen whose names were never meant to last. In the creation of these buildings they caught the glory of their age for all the world to see, for ever.

It is astonishing that some have lasted so long. With few exceptions, such as Norway's stave churches and the Todai-ji Temple in Japan, most wooden structures have not survived. Even stone buildings have frequently come to grief in earthquakes, war, fire and flood. As a result many are like palimpsests, written over again and again. In Europe a single building can have within it half a

St Basil's Cathedral in Moscow, crowned with colourful domes

dozen cultures dating back more than 2,000 years. Their uses change: castle to palace, church to fort, and many now flourish today as museums.

UNESCO
WORLD HERITAGE SITES

The Great Pyramid at Giza in Egypt is the only surviving wonder of the ancient world. In 1979 it was designated a World Heritage Site by the United Nations Educational, Scientific and Cultural Organisation (UNESCO), an agency of the United Nations set up in 1945. The idea of a fund to preserve the world's heritage was sparked in 1959 when the temples at Abu Simbel were in danger of drowning in Lake Nasser by the building of the Aswan High Dam. Following an appeal from the governments of Egypt and Sudan, UNESCO raised US$80 million to move the temples of Ramses II and Nefertari over 60 m (197 ft) out of harm's way.

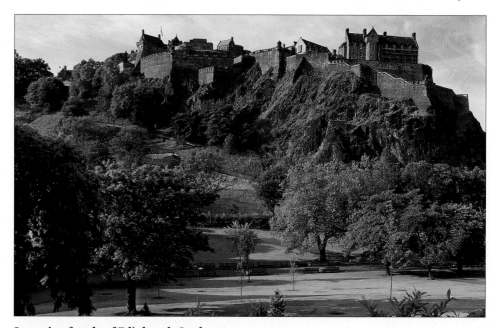

Imposing façade of Edinburgh Castle

◁ **The Taj Mahal built by Shah Jahan, in memory of his wife Mumtaz**

The work was completed in 1968 and as a result of this success, UNESCO with the International Council on Monuments and Sites (ICOMOS) went on to draft a new convention to protect the world's cultural heritage. Joined by ideas from the International Union for the Conservation of Nature (IUCN), proposals for safeguarding both cultural and natural sites were formally adopted by UNESCO's General Conference in 1972.

There are some 800 UNESCO World Heritage Sites around the world today, more than 600 of them cultural, as opposed to natural, sites. Italy and Spain have the most, followed by France and Germany. Each year a dozen or more sites are added to the list. Proposals can come from any one of the signed-up member countries who give one per cent of their UNESCO dues to the fund. With voluntary contributions, the Fund

Striking Gothic exterior of Cologne Cathedral, Germany

receives around US$3.5 million a year. The money goes towards preserving the sites, while some is set aside for those currently deemed at risk through man-made or natural calamities.

TOURISM

The feet of thousands of visitors also put sites at risk, and many have had to restrict access because of this. Conservation, however, is also helped by tourism which can provide funds from charging an entrance fee.

We now have a chance to see inside these buildings, to wander their corridors and squares,

and our curiosity is unbounded. Today, many of these spectacular sites are only a weekend break away. Some provide exhibitions, talks, conferences or concerts, while others are the keepers of colourful rituals and traditions.

Not all sites are so easily accessible. Religious devotees often sought remote places for their contemplations.

Some were strategically remote, for example Macchu Pichu in Peru, so hard to find that it was lost to the world for centuries. For a traveller, perhaps the longer the journey, the greater the reward.

Many ancient and prehistoric sites were based on the movement of the sun and stars, and being there at dawn or at a solstice is to feel their potent magic. Other sites have their special times: when choirs and music fill the churches; when festivals recall the buildings' heydays; when a full moon hovers over the Taj Mahal, the sun sets on San Francisco's Golden Gate or when snow is snug around St Petersburg's Winter Palace. Some museums are gratis on a particular day, while visiting any site early always tends to be best to avoid crowds of visitors. Rainy or baking-hot seasons are to be avoided, and sometimes buildings, or parts of them, are closed for renovation. However, you might want to visit Mali in the spring to watch the renovation of Djenné Mosque, when around 4,000 townspeople gather to replaster the mud-brick building in a splendid festival.

The White House, Washington DC, the official residence of the President of the USA

The Alhambra's Patio de los Leones, typifying the sensual architecture of the Moors

MEN AND MATERIALS

Conservation requires skilled crafts-people. A stonemason these days may be as much in demand as any in the Middle Ages. The right materials are important, too. They are not only required to be authentic, but they must work within their limitations. Stone can only reach a certain height and it wasn't until the 19th century that the 147m (482 ft) high Great Pyramid at Giza was surpassed.

In the 20th century new shapes became possible through the use of reinforced concrete, notable in the structures of Oscar Niemeyer's Brasília and in Frank Lloyd Wright's Solomon R Guggenheim Museum, completed in 1959, the year that Jørn Utzon's Sydney Opera House was begun. These were among the first buildings to make use of computer technology, too. Less than half a century later this technology helped produce marvels such as the titanium waves of Frank O Ghery's Guggenheim Museum in Bilbao.

Buildings are monuments to patrons and architects – through them their names have been handed down to us. In ancient sites the archaeologists are also remembered, men driven by the desire to be the first to find treasures lost for millennia: imagine the delight of Burckhardt when his eyes first fell on Abu Simbel.

Discoveries pepper the 19th century, a time when steam power made travel easier and artifacts from sites seemed waiting to be revealed. Many ideas were revived too, and the century saw the rebirth of many styles. The Arc de Triomphe revisited the Classical style, while the parliament building in Budapest revived Gothic. Castle building was spectacularly revived in King Ludwig's Bavarian fantasy, Neuschwanstein Castle, and at the Palace of Pena in Sintra, where various styles were incorporated into the stately pile.

Cartouche at Abu Simbel, Egypt

Buildings have become emblems of whole nations: the Statue of Liberty, the Registan, St Peter's, Angkor Wat, the Taj Mahal. Romantic, exotic, seductive, the names speak volumes. By the same token religious houses, churches, monasteries, mosques, temples and shrines, have become defining symbols of different faiths, and their spaces may produce an inner peace. More modestly, they help to conjure up the lives of their former occupants, be they homes of artists such as Rubens in Antwerp, or palaces for rulers, like the Forbidden City in Beijing, home to emperors of dynastic China.

Whatever a building's form and function, and whatever its age and condition, it always has many stories to tell.

Through these pages, their walls are peeled back and the layers of history are revealed to provide the opportunity to step inside and let the imagination roam.

The Great Wall of China snakes through the landscape, a major tourist attraction and powerful symbol of China

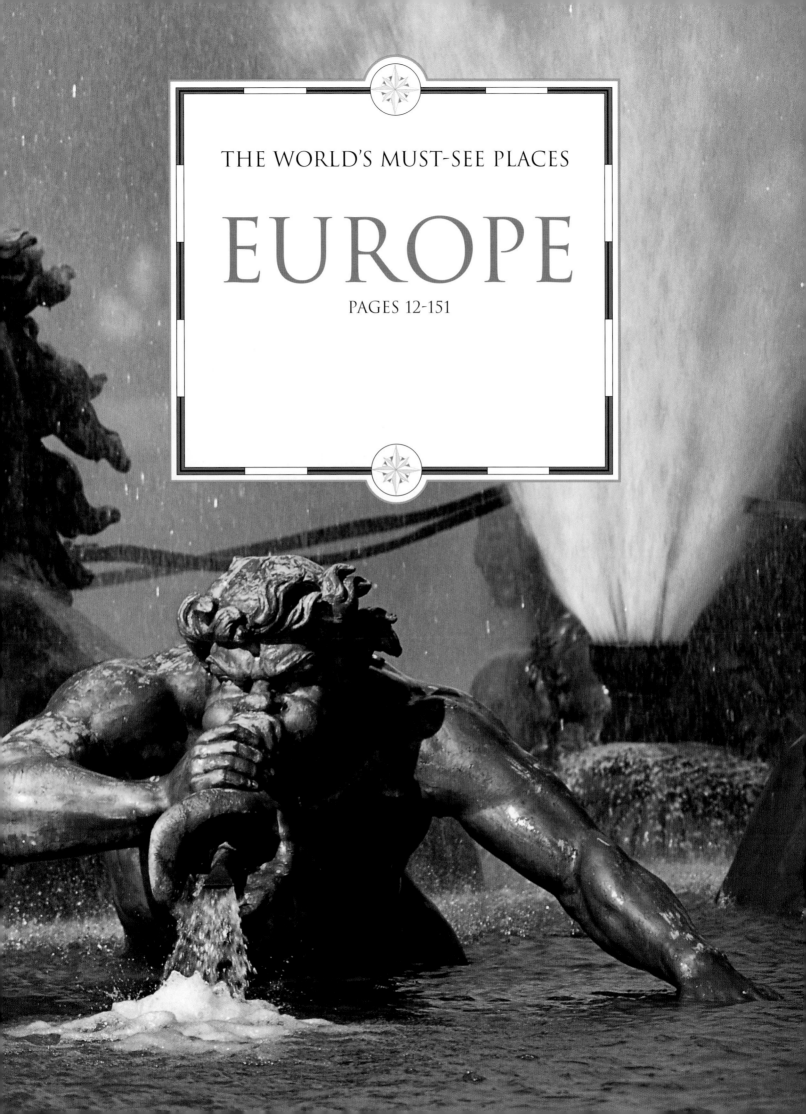

THE WORLD'S MUST-SEE PLACES

EUROPE

PAGES 12-151

Borgund Stave Church

**Urnes Stave Church,
constructed c. 1130–50**

CONSTRUCTION METHODS

The earliest stave churches, built in the 11th century, had wooden wall columns which were set directly into the ground. These churches lasted no more than 100 years, as moisture in the earth caused the column bases to rot away. As construction techniques developed, it became customary to set the wooden framework on sills which rested on a stone foundation. This raised the entire wooden skeleton above ground level, protecting it from humidity. This method proved so effective that churches built in the 12th century are still standing today. Among these is Borgund Stave Church, which was built from almost 2,000 carefully crafted pieces of wood.

STAVE CHURCH DESIGN

Borgund Stave Church is one of the largest and most ornately designed of the almost 30 remaining stave churches in Norway. Commonly they were simple, relatively small structures with a ▷ *nave* and narrow chancel. Borgund's chancel also has a distinctive semicircular apse. Stave posts mark a division between the two. The interior is dark, as light can only filter through from small round openings (▷ *the windows*) under the three-tiered roof, which is crowned by a turret. An ▷ *external gallery* frequently encircles stave churches.

T HE ONLY STAVE CHURCH to have remained unchanged since the Middle Ages is Borgund Stavkirke at Lærdal in western Norway. Dedicated to the apostle St Andrew, it dates from around 1150 and is built entirely of wood. The interior is very simple: there are no pews or decorations, and the lighting is limited to a few small openings high up on the walls. The exterior is richly decorated with carvings: dragon-like animals in life-and-death struggles, dragon-heads and runic inscriptions. There is a free-standing belfry with a medieval bell. The pulpit dates from the 16th century.

Stave Church Location
Many of the surviving stave churches are in remote locations. High, exposed sites which were noticeable and remarkable were generally chosen to create a dramatic visual effect.

Nave
Twelve posts (staves) around the central part of the nave support the roof. Disappearing into the semi-darkness of the roof, they give an increased sense of height.

Crosses decorate the gables above the door-ways and apse tower.

West Door
The exterior of the church is richly adorned. The decorations on the Romanesque west door show vine-like ornamentation and dragon battles.

A spire sits at the top of the three-tiered roof.

The roofs are clad in pine shingles.

KING OLAV THE HOLY

Olav Haraldsson was declared King of a united Norway in 1016. He went on to convert the entire country to Christianity. Pagan statues were torn down all over the country and stave churches were built. He died in battle at Stiklestad in 1030. A year after his death, his undecayed body was exhumed and he was declared a saint.

King Olav the Holy

VIKING HERITAGE

Rich ornamentation in stave churches is evidence of Norway's Viking era, when skilled carving techniques were developed to combine art and wood-working in construction. The depiction of animals such as dragons and serpents in these carvings is thought to derive from Viking art.

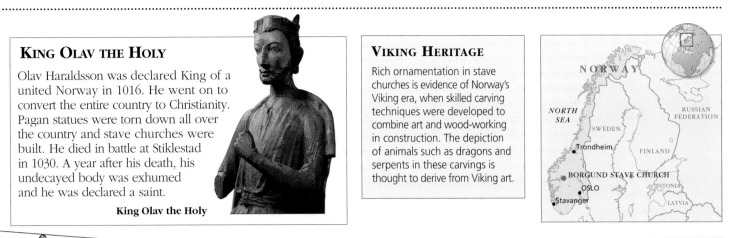

The windows are simply circular openings in the outer walls.

The central tower has a three-tiered roof. The first tier is decorated with dragonheads on the gables, similar to those on the main roof. These were meant to cleanse the air, purging it of the evil spirits of unlawful pagan worship.

Roof Construction

Carved and constructed out of timber, this spectacular Gothic church (▷ Gothic Style p55) contains richly decorated gables, colonnades and capitals. Seen from below, the roof is composed of an intricate framework using numerous rafters and joists.

External gallery

Altarpiece

The interior of Borgund Church contains no ornate embellishment apart from a simple pulpit and altar. This altarpiece dates from 1654.

Crosses of St Andrew, in the shape of the letter "X", border the central nave.

KEY DATES

1150 Borgund Stave Church is erected.

Late 1500s The pulpit is constructed.

Mid-1600s The altarpiece is added.

1870 The church goes out of regular service when a larger church is constructed nearby.

ORNAMENTATION

The introduction of Christianity to Norway around the year 1000 saw the merging of pagan and Christian cultures and beliefs. Most stave churches were erected on the sites of old temples which were destroyed in the wake of Christianity. The impact of this can be seen in the richly decorated carvings in stave churches, which unite pre-Christian and Christian symbolism. Pagan gods were represented in disguise alongside medieval Christian saints. The door frame designs (▷ *West Door*) are particularly elaborate, and demonstrate the skill of the carpenters who embellished them from top to bottom with intricate carvings. Wood from pine trees was commonly used as this was most readily available. Branches and bark were removed from the trees, which were then left to dry out before being chopped down. This method meant that the wood was more weather-resistant and durable.

Borgund Stave Church

Vasamuseet, designed by Marianne Dahlbäck and Göran Månsson

THE SHIP

The *Vasa* was built as a symbol of Swedish might by King Gustav II Adolf. He was steadily increasing Swedish influence over the Baltic region during the 1620s, through war with Poland. It was constructed by Dutch shipbuilder Henrik Hybertsson. *Vasa* was the largest ship in the history of the Swedish fleet and was capable of carrying 64 cannons and over 445 crew. From its high ▷ *stern* it would have been possible to fire down on smaller ships. It was equipped for both traditional close combat and artillery battles. The musketeers had shooting galleries for training, and on the upper deck were so-called "storm pieces", erected as protection against musketry fire.

LIFE ON BOARD

Vasa's destination on its maiden voyage was intended to be the Älvsnabben naval base in the southern Stockholm archipelago, where more soldiers were to embark. Each man's life on the ship would have been determined by his rank. The officers would have slept in bunks and the Admiral in his cabin. They also had better food than the crew whose meals were very basic, and consisted of beans, porridge, salted fish and beer. The decks would have been very crowded – the small space between every two guns was the living and sleeping quarters for seven men (▷ *Gun Deck*). There was no fresh food, so a lot of the crew would have had scurvy and died from deficiency diseases before they reached battle.

Vasa Museum, Stockholm

S WEDEN'S MOST VISITED museum enshrines the royal warship *Vasa*, which capsized on its maiden voyage of just 1,300 m (4,265 ft) in calm weather, on 10 August 1628 in Stockholm's harbour. About 50 people went down with what was supposed to be the pride of the Navy. Guns were all that were salvaged from the vessel in the 17th century and it was not until 1956 that a marine archaeologist's persistent search led to the rediscovery of *Vasa*. After a complex salvage operation followed by a 17-year conservation programme, the city's most popular museum was opened in June 1990, less than a nautical mile from the scene of the disaster.

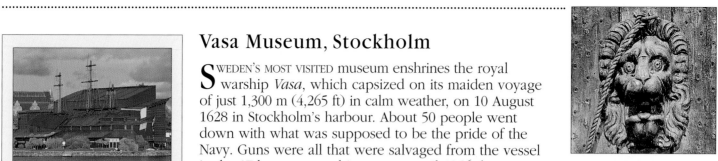

★ **Lion Figurehead**
King Gustav II Adolf, who commissioned Vasa, *was known as the Lion of the North. So a springing lion was the obvious choice for the figurehead. It is 4 m (13 ft) long and weighs 450 kg (990 lb).*

Gun-port Lion
More than 200 carved ornaments and 500 sculpted figures decorate Vasa.

The rigging has been meticulously reconstructed to reflect that of a 17th–century warship.

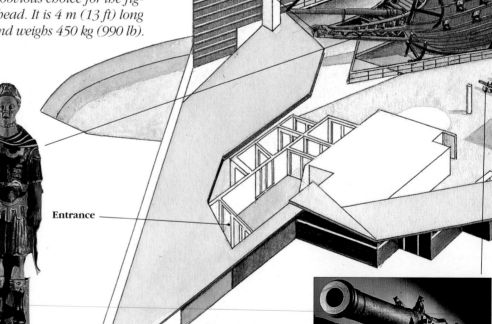

Entrance

Emperor Titus
Carvings of 20 Roman emperors stand on parade on Vasa.

Bronze Cannon
More than 50 of Vasa's *64 original cannons were salvaged already in the 17th century. Three 11 kg (24 lb) bronze cannons are on display in the museum.*

★ **Stern**
Vasa's *stern was badly damaged but has been painstakingly restored to reveal the ship's magnificent ornamentation.*

The main mast
was originally 52 m (170 ft) high.

The Gun Ports
Vasa *carried more heavy cannons on its two gundecks than earlier ships of the same size. This contributed to its capsizing.*

Reconstruction of the upper gun deck

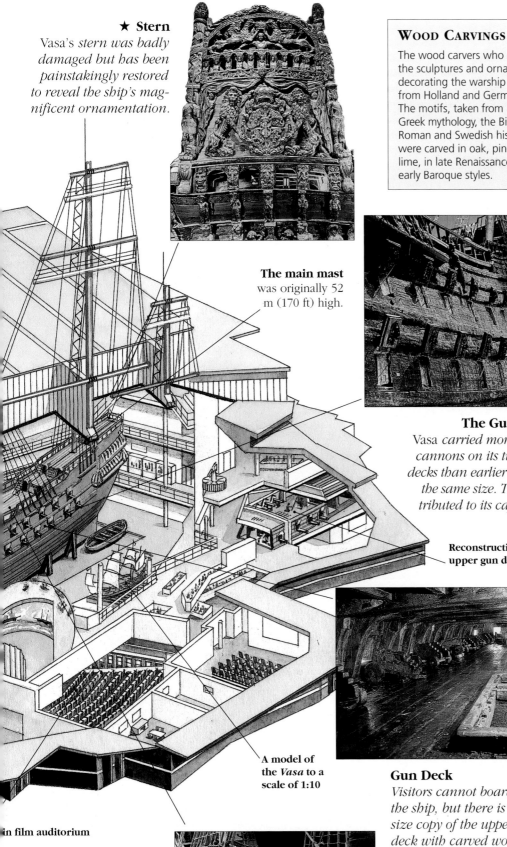

A model of the Vasa to a scale of 1:10

in film auditorium

Upper Deck
The entrance to the cabins was towards the stern. This area was the grandest part of the ship, reserved for senior officers. Part of the original mainmast can be seen on the right.

Gun Deck
Visitors cannot board the ship, but there is a full-size copy of the upper gun deck with carved wooden dummies of sailors, which gives a good idea of conditions on board.

STAR FEATURES

★ **Lion Figurehead**

★ **Stern**

WOOD CARVINGS

The wood carvers who made the sculptures and ornaments decorating the warship came from Holland and Germany. The motifs, taken from Greek mythology, the Bible, Roman and Swedish history, were carved in oak, pine and lime, in late Renaissance and early Baroque styles.

NORTH SEA
SWEDEN FINLAND
NORWAY
RUSSIAN FEDERATION
VASA MUSEUM, STOCKHOLM
ESTONIA
• Göteborg
LATVIA
DENMARK BALTIC SEA LITHUANIA

Vasa Museum

KEY DATES

1625 King Gustav II Adolf orders new warships including *Vasa*.

1628 *Vasa* is ready for its maiden voyage, but capsizes in Stockholm's harbour.

1956 Archaeologist Andérs Franzen locates *Vasa*.

1961 *Vasa* is raised to the surface after 333 years on the sea bed.

1962 The temporary *Vasa* museum, Wasavarvet opens.

1990 The Vasa Museum opens as a permanent museum, showing the restored *Vasa* and its treasures.

THE SALVAGE OPERATION

The marine archaeologist Andérs Franzen had been looking for *Vasa* for many years. On 25 August 1956 his patience was rewarded when he brought up a piece of blackened oak on his plumb line from *Vasa*, located 30 m (100 ft) beneath the surface. From the autumn of 1957, it took divers two years to clear tunnels under the hull for the lifting cables. The first lift with six cables was a success, after which *Vasa* was lifted in 16 stages into shallower water. Thousands of plugs were then inserted into holes left by rusted iron bolts. The final lift started on the morning of 24 April 1961, and on 4 May *Vasa* was finally towed into dry dock after 333 years under water.

TARA AND ITS KINGS

A site of mythical importance, Tara was the political and spiritual centre of Celtic Ireland and the seat of the High Kings until the 11th century. Whoever ruled Tara could claim supremacy over Ireland. It is thought that many of Tara's kings were buried in pagan ceremonies at Newgrange. Tara's importance as a spiritual centre diminished as Christianity flourished. Legend says that Tara's most famous king, Cormac Mac Art who ruled in the 3rd century, did not wish to be buried at Newgrange among pagan kings. His kinsmen, disregarding his wish, tried to cross the River Boyne to Newgrange but failed due to the huge waves and so he was buried elsewhere according to his wishes.

WINTER SOLSTICE AT NEWGRANGE

The shortest day and the longest night occurs each year on 21 December and is known as the Winter Solstice. At Newgrange, on the morning of 21 December, rays of sunlight shine into the roof box of the passage grave and light up the ▷ *passage* illuminating the north recess of the cruciform burial ▷ *chamber*. At all other times of the year the tomb is shrouded in darkness. Newgrange is the only passage grave currently excavated which has this characteristic – temples tend to be the usual locations for this type of event. Many believe that because of this, Newgrange was originally used as a place of worship, and only later as a burial ground for pagan kings.

Megalithic motifs adorning the walls of Newgrange

Newgrange

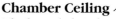

Tri-spiral carving on stone in chamber

THE ORIGINS OF Newgrange, one of the most important passage graves in Europe, are steeped in mystery. According to Celtic lore, the legendary kings of Tara were buried here, but Newgrange predates them. The grave was left untouched by all invaders except the Danish, who raided its burial chambers in the 9th century. In 1699, it was rediscovered by local landowner, Charles Campbell Scott. When it was excavated in the 1960s, archaeologist Professor M J O'Kelly discovered that on the winter solstice, 21 December, rays of sun enter the tomb and light up the burial chamber – making it the world's oldest solar observatory.

The chamber has three recesses or side chambers: the north recess is the one struck by sunlight on the winter solstice.

Basin Stone
The chiselled stones, found in each recess, would have once contained funerary offerings and the bones of the dead.

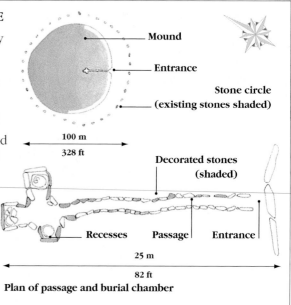

Chamber Ceiling
The burial chamber's intricate corbelled ceiling, which reaches a height of 6 m (20 ft) above the floor, has survived intact. The overlapping slabs form a conical hollow, topped by a single capstone.

CONSTRUCTION OF NEWGRANGE

The tomb at Newgrange was designed by people with clearly exceptional artistic and engineering skills, who had use of neither the wheel nor metal tools. About 200,000 tons of loose stones were transported to build the mound, or cairn, which protects the passage grave. Larger slabs were used to make the circle around the cairn (12 out of a probable 35 stones have survived), the kerb and the tomb itself. Many of the kerbstones and the slabs lining the passage, the chamber and its recesses are decorated with zigzags, spirals and other geometric motifs. The grave's corbelled ceiling consists of smaller, unadorned slabs and has proved completely waterproof for the last 5,000 years.

Mound
Entrance
Stone circle (existing stones shaded)
100 m
328 ft
Decorated stones (shaded)
Recesses Passage Entrance
25 m
82 ft
Plan of passage and burial chamber

MYTHOLOGICAL TALE

In Irish mythology, Aenghus Mac Og was the God of Love, who tricked his way to owning Newgrange. It is said that he was away when the magical places of Ireland were being divided up. On his return, he asked to borrow Newgrange for the day and night, but refused to give it back, claiming it was his, as all of time can be divided by day and night.

KEY DATES

c.3200 BC Construction of Newgrange.

c.860 Danish invaders raid the burial chambers of Newgrange and remove most of its treasures.

c.1140 Newgrange is used as farmland for grazing cattle until the 14th century.

1962–75 Newgrange is restored and the roof box is discovered.

1967 Archaeologists discover that rays of sun light up the burial chamber on winter solstice, 21 December.

1993 Newgrange is listed as a World Heritage Site.

DOWTH AND KNOWTH

Described as the "cradle of Irish civilization", the Boyne Valley contains two other prehistoric burial sites not far from Newgrange. The nearest is Knowth, which is only 1.5 km (1 mile) away. Excavation of this site began in 1962 and it was found to contain two tomb passages and the greatest concentration of megalithic art in Europe. Archaeologists also found evidence that the site was occupied from the Neolithic period and was used for habitation as well as for burials up until about 1400. Dowth, another passage grave 3 km (2 miles) from Newgrange, is less spectacular. Its tombs are smaller and most of its artifacts were stolen by Victorian souvenir hunters. The site has not yet been fully excavated by archaeologists.

Restoration of Newgrange

Located on a low ridge north of the river Boyne, Newgrange took more than 70 years to build. Between 1962 and 1975 the passage grave and mound were restored as closely as possible to their original state.

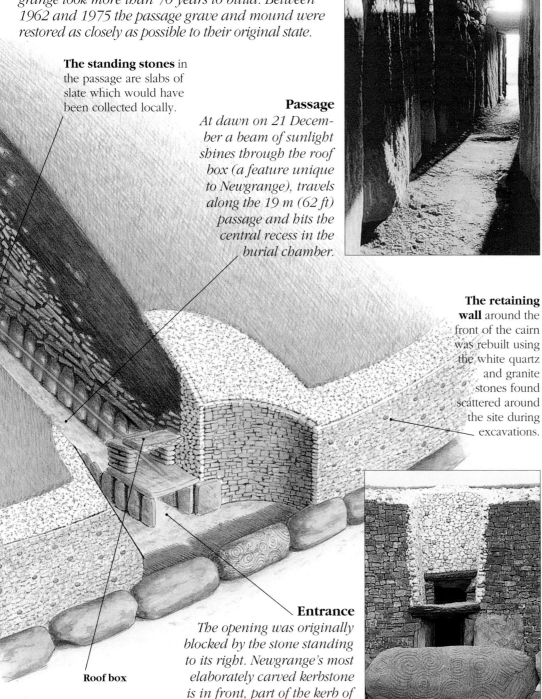

The standing stones in the passage are slabs of slate which would have been collected locally.

Passage
At dawn on 21 December a beam of sunlight shines through the roof box (a feature unique to Newgrange), travels along the 19 m (62 ft) passage and hits the central recess in the burial chamber.

The retaining wall around the front of the cairn was rebuilt using the white quartz and granite stones found scattered around the site during excavations.

Roof box

Entrance
The opening was originally blocked by the stone standing to its right. Newgrange's most elaborately carved kerbstone is in front, part of the kerb of huge slabs around the cairn.

THE BOOK OF KELLS

The most richly decorated of Ireland's medieval illuminated manuscripts, the *Book of Kells* may have been the work of monks from the island of Iona in Scotland, who fled to Kells in County Meath in AD 806 after a Viking raid. The book, moved to Trinity College (▷ *Treasury*) in the 17th century, contains the four gospels in Latin. The scribes who copied the texts also embellished their calligraphy with intricate interlacing spirals as well as human figures and animals. Some of the dyes used were imported from as far as the Middle East. The monogram page is the most elaborate page of the book and contains the first three words of St Matthew's account of the birth of Christ. The first word "XRI" is an abbreviation of "Christi".

Marble bust of Jonathan Swift in the Old Library

FAMOUS ALUMNI

Trinity College is Dublin's most famous seat of learning and since its foundation it has cultivated many distinguished writers and historical figures. Their time spent here had a discernible impact on their lives. Outstanding graduates include writers and dramatists such as Jonathan Swift, Oliver Goldsmith, Oscar Wilde, Bram Stoker, William Congreve and Samuel Beckett; philosopher George Berkeley; statesman and political philosopher Edmund Burke; Nobel prizewinning physicist Ernest Walton; Ireland's first President Douglas Hyde; and Ireland's first female President Mary Robinson. Statues in tribute to its famous scholars stand throughout the college.

Trinity College, Dublin

Q UEEN ELIZABETH I founded Trinity College, Dublin's oldest and most famous educational institution, in 1592. Originally a Protestant college, it only began to take Catholics in numbers after 1970, when the Catholic Church relaxed its opposition to them attending. Among Trinity's many famous students were playwrights Oliver Goldsmith and Samuel Beckett, and political writer Edmund Burke. The college's lawns and cobbled quads provide a pleasant haven in the heart of the city. The major attractions are the Old Library and the *Book of Kells*, housed in the Treasury.

Trinity College coat of arms

★ Campanile
The 30-m (98-ft) bell tower was built in 1853 by Sir Charles Lanyon, architect of Queen's University in Belfast.

Reclining Connected Forms (1969) by Henry Moore

Dining Hall (1761)

Parliament Square

Chapel *(1798)*
This was the first university chapel in the Republic to accept all denominations. The painted window above the altar is from 1867.

Statue of Edmund Burke (1868) by John Foley

Main entrance

Statue of Oliver Goldsmith (1864) by John Foley

Provost's House (c.1760)

SAMUEL BECKETT (1906–89)

Nobel prizewinner Samuel Beckett was born at Foxrock, south of Dublin. In 1923 he entered Trinity, and later graduated with a first in modern languages and a gold medal. He was also an avid member of the college cricket team. Forsaking Ireland, Beckett moved to France in the early 1930s. Many of his major works such as *Waiting for Godot* (1951) were written first in French, and later translated, by Beckett, into English.

Examination Hall
Completed in 1791 to a design by Sir William Chambers, the hall features a gilded oak chandelier and ornate ceilings by Michael Stapleton.

THE DOUGLAS HYDE GALLERY

Situated in the Trinity College grounds, this is one of Ireland's leading contemporary art venues. Exhibits feature film, painting, installation and sculpture work by emerging as well as recognised artists.

Library Square
The redbrick building (known as the Rubrics) on the east side of Library Square was built around 1700 and is the oldest surviving part of the college.

Entrance to Old Library

Entrance to Old Library

New Square

Fellows' Square

The Museum Building, completed in 1857, is noted for its Venetian exterior, and its magnificent multicoloured hall and double-domed roof.

Sphere within Sphere
(1982) was given to the college by its sculptor Arnaldo Pomodoro.

Berkeley Library Building by Paul Koralek (1967)

Entrance from Nassau Street

The Douglas Hyde Gallery
was built in the 1970s to house temporary art exhibitions.

★ Old Library *(1732)*
The spectacular Long Room measures 64 m (210 ft) from end to end. It houses 200,000 antiquarian texts, marble busts of scholars and the oldest surviving harp in Ireland.

★ Treasury
This detail is from the Book of Durrow, *one of the other magnificent illuminated manuscripts housed in the Treasury along with the celebrated* Book of Kells.

STAR FEATURES

★ **Campanile**

★ **Treasury**

★ **Old Library**

KEY DATES

1592 Trinity College is founded.

c.1661 The *Book of Kells* is given to Trinity by the Bishop of Meath.

1689 The college is turned temporarily into barracks.

1712 Work begins on the Old Library.

1793 Religious restrictions on entry are abolished.

1853 The Campanile is erected.

1987 Restoration of the Dining Hall is completed following the fire of 1984.

PARLIAMENT SQUARE

Trinity College stands on what was once part of the All Hallows Monastery grounds. The wood-tiled archway at the main entrance leads to Trinity's main quadrangle (▷ *Parliament Square*). Fine green lawns and an array of fine 18th- and 19th-century buildings characterize the cobbled square. An imposing centrepiece (▷ *Campanile*) marks the original site of All Hallows monastery. The ▷ *chapel* was designed by Sir William Chambers in 1798. Beside it is the ▷ *dining hall*, built by Richard Castle in 1742, where Trinity's students eat. This building has been considerably altered over the past 250 years, particularly after a fire caused severe damage in 1984. The walls are hung with huge portraits of college dignitaries.

Trinity College, Dublin

CASHEL MUSEUM

The 15th-century two-storey ▷ *Hall of the Vicars' Choral*, was once the residential quarters of the cathedral choristers and today displays copies of medieval artifacts and furnishings. Its lower level houses the Cashel museum, which exhibits rare silverware, stone carvings and the ▷ *St Patrick's Cross*, a 12th-century crutched cross with a crucifixion scene on one side and animals on the other. The cross stands on a supporting coronation stone dating from the 4th century. Tradition held that the kings of Cashel, including King Brian Boru of Munster (977–1014), were crowned at the base of the cross.

Romanesque carvings decorating the buildings of Cashel

CORMAC'S CHAPEL

The King of Munster, Cormac MacCarthy, donated this chapel to the Church in 1134, because they had helped to protect the Rock of Cashel from being invaded by the Eoghanachta clan. Romanesque in style, it was constructed in sandstone with a stone roof and two towers on either side of the nave and chancel. The interior is decorated with various motifs, some showing dragons and human heads. At the west end of the chapel there is a stone sarcophagus embellished with serpent carvings. This is thought to have once contained the body of Cormac MacCarthy. The chancel is decorated with the only surviving Romanesque frescoes in Ireland, which include a representation of the Baptism of Christ.

Rock of Cashel

A SYMBOL OF ROYAL and priestly power for more than a millennium, this is one of the most spectacular archeological sites in Ireland. From the 5th century, it was the seat of the Kings of Munster, whose kingdom extended over much of southern Ireland. In 1101, they handed Cashel over to the Church, and it flourished as a religious centre until a siege by a Cromwellian army in 1647 culminated in the massacre of its 3,000 occupants. The cathedral was finally abandoned in the late 18th century. A good proportion of the medieval complex is still standing, and Cormac's Chapel is one of the most outstanding examples of Romanesque architecture in the country (▷ *Romanesque Style p122*).

Hall of the Vicars' Choral
This hall was built in the 15th century for Cashel's most privileged choristers. The ceiling, a modern reconstruction based on medieval designs, features several decorative corbels including this painted angel.

Entrance

The museum
in the undercroft contains a display of stone carvings and religious artifacts.

Dormitory block

★ St Patrick's Cross
The carving on the east face of this cross is said to be of St Patrick, who visited Cashel in 450. The cross is a copy of the original that stood here until 1982 and is now in the museum.

Outer wall

Limestone rock

★ Cormac's Chapel
Superb Romanesque carving adorns this chapel – the jewel of Cashel. The tympanum over the north door shows a centaur in a helmet aiming his bow and arrow at a lion.

STAR FEATURES

★ **St Patrick's Cross**

★ **Cormac's Chapel**

★ **St Patrick's Cathedral**

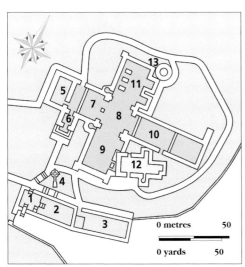

Rock of Cashel

KEY

☐ **12th Century**
 4 St Patrick's Cross (replica)
12 Cormac's Chapel
13 Round tower

☐ **13th Century**
 6 Cathedral porch
 7 Nave
 8 Crossing
 9 South transept
10 Choir
11 North transept

☐ **15th Century**
 1 Ticket office
 2 Hall of the Vicars' Choral (museum)
 3 Dormitory
 5 Castle

0 metres 50
0 yards 50

ST PATRICK AND KING AENGHUS

During the baptism ceremony of King Aenghus, St Patrick accidentally stabbed him in his foot with his crozier and the king, thinking it was part of the initiation, bore the pain without complaint.

The Rock
The 28 m (92 ft) round tower, oldest and tallest building on the rock, enabled Cashel's inhabitants to scour the surrounding plain for potential attackers.

KEY DATES

AD 450 St Patrick visits Cashel and converts King Aenghus to Christianity.

1101 Cashel is handed over to the Church by King Muircheartach O'Brien.

1127–1134 King Cormac MacCarthy builds Cormac's Chapel as a gift for the Church.

1647 Cashel is invaded and besieged by a Cromwellian army under Lord Inchiquin.

1975 Hall of Vicars' Choral is restored.

LIFE OF ST PATRICK

Born in Wales in AD 385, St Patrick lived his early life as a pagan. When he was 16 years old, he was captured and sold as a slave to work in Ireland. During his captivity, he converted to Christianity and dedicated his life to religion. He escaped and travelled to France, where he entered St Martin's monastery to study the Scriptures, under the guidance of St Germain of Auxerre. He was appointed Bishop to Ireland in AD 432. He went on to found over 300 churches and baptized over 120,000 people, including King Aenghus, when he visited Cashel in AD 450. Today the death of St Patrick, the Patron Saint of Ireland, is celebrated on 17 March all over the world with special religious services and the wearing of shamrocks – the three-tipped clover leaf which is the national emblem of Ireland.

Round tower

Crossing

The Choir contains the 17th-century tomb of Miler Magrath, who caused a scandal by being both a Protestant and a Catholic archbishop at the same time.

Graveyard

The O'Scully Monument, an ornate memorial erected in 1870 by a local landowning family, was damaged during a storm in 1976.

★ St Patrick's Cathedral
The roofless Gothic cathedral has thick walls riddled with hidden passages; in the north transept these are seen emerging at the base of the windows.

North Transept
Panels from three 16th-century tombs in the north transept are decorated with remarkably fresh and intricate carvings. This one, against the north wall, features a vine-leaf design and strange stylized beasts.

THE BATTLE OF BANNOCKBURN

Stirling Castle was strategically vital to Scotland's military resistance to the English throughout history and was frequently under siege as a result. In 1296, Edward I of England led a devastating invasion that defeated the Scots, but William Wallace led a revolt, recapturing the castle in 1297, only to lose it again the following year. On 23 June 1314 Scotland, led by Robert the Bruce, won back her independence at the Battle of Bannockburn. However, the wars with England continued for another 300 years. The castle's last military use was against an attack by the Jacobite Army in 1746, after which the English army set up barracks here until 1964.

Engraving depicting the Battle of Bannockburn

THE GREAT HALL

This splendid royal hall, the largest ever built in Scotland, was erected by James IV between 1501 and 1504 to host lavish state events and banquets. When the focus of the monarchy shifted to London after the Union of the Crowns in 1603 – when King James VI of Scotland became King James I of England – the ▷ *Great Hall* was no longer required for state occasions. Changes were made to the hall in the 18th century to reinforce the castle's defences and to create space for military barracks. After more than 30 years' work the Great Hall, restored as closely as possible to its original condition, was reopened by Queen Elizabeth II on 30 November 1999.

Stirling Castle

R ISING HIGH on a rocky crag, this magnificent castle, which dominated Scottish history for centuries, now remains one of the finest examples of Renaissance architecture in Scotland (▷ *Renaissance Style p131*). Legend says that King Arthur wrested the original castle from the Saxons, but there is no evidence of a castle at this location before 1124. The present building dates from the 15th and 16th centuries and was last defended in 1746 against the Jacobites, who were mainly Catholic Highlanders wishing to restore the Stuart monarchy to the throne. From 1881 to 1964 the castle was used as a depot for recruits into the Argyll and Sutherland Highlanders, though today it serves no military function.

Gargoyle on castle wall

The Prince's Tower erected in the 16th century is still standing today.

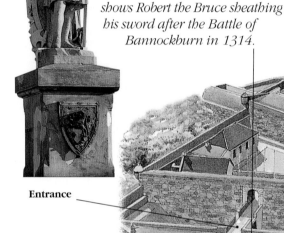

Robert the Bruce
In the esplanade, this modern statue shows Robert the Bruce sheathing his sword after the Battle of Bannockburn in 1314.

Forework

Entrance

The French Spur was an artillery spur that formed part of a line of defences built in the mid-16th century, to improve the defence of the castle in an age of modern artillery.

The Elphinstone Tower was reduced to half its original height to allow it to be made into a gun platform in 1714.

Stirling Castle in the Time of the Stuarts, **painted by Johannes Vorsterman (1643–99)**

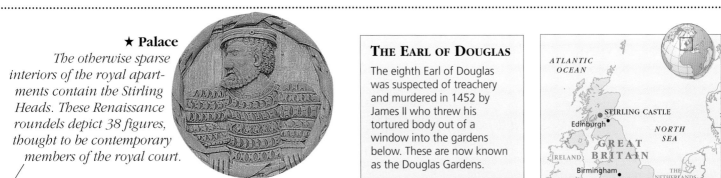

★ Palace
The otherwise sparse interiors of the royal apartments contain the Stirling Heads. These Renaissance roundels depict 38 figures, thought to be contemporary members of the royal court.

The King's Old Building houses the Regimental Museum of the Argyll and Sutherland Highlanders.

★ Chapel Royal
Seventeenth-century frescoes by Valentine Jenkins adorn the chapel, reconstructed in 1594.

THE EARL OF DOUGLAS
The eighth Earl of Douglas was suspected of treachery and murdered in 1452 by James II who threw his tortured body out of a window into the gardens below. These are now known as the Douglas Gardens.

Nether Bailey

The Great Hall, built in 1500, has been restored to its former splendour.

STAR FEATURES
★ Palace

★ Chapel Royal

STIRLING BATTLES
At the highest navigable point of the Forth and holding the pass to the Highlands, Stirling occupied a key position in Scotland's struggles for independence. Seven battlefields can be seen from the castle; the 67 m (220 ft) Wallace Monument at Abbey Craig recalls William Wallace's defeat of the English at Stirling Bridge in 1297, foreshadowing Robert the Bruce's victory in 1314.

The Victorian Wallace Monument

Grand Battery
Seven guns stand on this parapet overlooking the town of Stirling. They were built in 1708 during a strengthening of defences.

Stirling Castle

KEY DATES

1296 Edward I captures Stirling Castle.

1297 The castle yields to the Scots after the Battle of Stirling Bridge led by William Wallace.

1314 Robert the Bruce defeats the English at the Battle of Bannockburn.

1496 James IV begins extensive construction. Work begins on the Chapel Royal.

1501 Work begins on the Great Hall.

1503 Building work starts on the Forework.

1855 The King's Old Building is badly damaged by fire.

1964 The army leaves the castle barracks.

THE KING'S OLD BUILDING

Built for James IV in 1496, the King's Old Building stands on the highest point of the castle rock. Following the completion of the palace in the 1540s, the King's Old Building was no longer the ruling monarch's residence and so was put to varied use. Additional floors and walls were added in the 1790s to provide accommodation for a military garrison. It was also rebuilt after fire damage in the mid-19th century. The building now houses the Regimental Museum of the Argyll and Sutherland Highlanders and contains a collection of memorabilia including medals, uniforms and weapons.

Edinburgh Castle

STONE OF DESTINY

The origins of this famous stone are steeped in myth and legend. It is said to have been Jacob's pillow when he dreamt that the angels of God were descending to earth from heaven. Scottish kings, from Kenneth I in 847, sat on the stone during coronation ceremonies. It was kept in Scone, Perthshire, after which it is sometimes called The Stone of Scone. The stone was seized on Edward I's invasion of Scotland in 1296 and taken to Westminster Abbey, where it was kept for 700 years. The 1326 Treaty of Northampton promised return of the stone, but this was not honoured until 1996, when a handover ceremony took place at the English-Scottish border and the stone was transported to Edinburgh Castle, where it remains today.

Edinburgh Castle viewed from Princes Street

VOLCANIC GEOLOGY

Edinburgh Castle is located in the Midland Valley of Scotland. The rocky volcanic outcrops of Arthur's Seat, measuring 251 m (823 ft) high, and Salisbury Crags, 122 m (400 ft) high, dominate the Edinburgh skyline. Salisbury Crags are igneous rocks exposed by the tilting of local rock and erosion by glaciers. Arthur's Seat is the remnant of a Carboniferous volcano, partly eroded by glacial activity. Edinburgh Castle is situated on a rock that plugs a vent of this volcano. The "crag" of basalt on which the castle stands was resistant to glacial erosion in the last ice-age. This left a "tail" of soft sedimentary rock lying behind it, which forms the main street (▷ *Royal Mile*) of Edinburgh.

Beam support in the Great Hall

STANDING UPON the basalt core of an extinct volcano, Edinburgh Castle is a remarkable assemblage of buildings dating from the 12th to the 20th centuries, reflecting its changing role as fortress, royal palace, military garrison and state prison. There is evidence of Bronze Age occupation of the site, which takes its name from Dun Eidin, a Celtic fortress captured by King Oswald of Northumbria in the 7th century. The castle was a favourite royal residence until the Union of Crowns in 1603, after which the king resided in England. After the Union of Parliaments in 1707, the Scottish regalia were walled up in the palace for over a hundred years. The castle is now the zealous possessor of the so-called Stone of Destiny, a relic of ancient Scottish kings which was seized by the English and not returned until 1996.

Governor's House
Complete with Flemish-style crow-stepped gables, this building was constructed for the governor in 1742 and now serves as the Officers' Mess for the castle garrison.

Old Back Parade

MONS MEG

Positioned outside St Margaret's Chapel, the siege gun (or *bombard*) Mons Meg was made in Belgium in 1449 for the Duke of Burgundy, who subsequently gave it as a present to his nephew, James II of Scotland (r.1437–60), in 1457. It was used by James IV (r.1488–1513) against Norham Castle in England in 1497. After exploding during a salute to the Duke of York in 1682, it was kept in the Tower of London until it was returned to Edinburgh in 1829, at Sir Walter Scott's request.

Scottish Crown
Now on display in the palace, the Crown was restyled by James V of Scotland in 1540.

Military Prison

Vaults
This French graffiti, dating from 1780, recalls the many prisoners who were held in the vaults during the wars with France in the 18th and 19th centuries.

STAR FEATURES

★ **Palace**

★ **Great Hall**

STOLEN STONE

Long before the Stone of Destiny was returned to Scotland, a group of Scottish students stole the Stone in 1950 from Westminster Abbey. A search was mounted by the British, but it was not found until a year later in Scotland's Arbroath Abbey.

Argyle Battery

This fortified wall commands a spectacular view to the north of the city's New Town.

Mons Meg

★ Palace

Mary, Queen of Scots (1542–87) gave birth to James VI in this 15th-century palace, where the Scottish regalia are on display.

KEY DATES

638 King Oswald of Northumbria's army capture the site and build a fortress.

1296 Edward I takes the castle after an eight-day siege and installs a garrison of 347 men.

1496–1511 James I adds more buildings to the castle, including the Palace.

1573 After a failed siege by Mary, Queen of Scots, the castle is remodelled and the Half Moon Battery is built.

1650 The castle is fortified with barracks, officers' quarters and storehouses.

1995 Edinburgh and its castle are inscribed a World Heritage Site.

Entrance

Royal Mile →

The Esplanade is the location of the Military Tattoo.

The Half Moon Battery was built in the 1570s as a platform for the artillery defending the northeastern wing of the castle.

St Margaret's Chapel

This stained-glass window depicts Malcolm III's saintly queen, to whom the chapel is dedicated. Probably built by her son, David I, in the early 12th century, the chapel is the castle's oldest existing building.

★ Great Hall

With its restored open-timber roof, the hall dates from the 15th century and was the meeting place of the Scottish parliament until 1639.

THE MILITARY TATTOO

Since 1947, for three weeks over the summer, Edinburgh has played host to one of the world's most important arts festivals, with every available space overflowing with international artists and performers (from theatres to street corners). It is an exciting fusion of film, music, theatre, dance, comedy and literature. The most popular event is the Edinburgh Military Tattoo, held every night on the ▷ *Esplanade*. The world's finest military bands perform with bagpipers and drummers from Scottish regiments, in full regalia. The music and marching, against the backdrop of the illuminated Edinburgh Castle, make for a marvellous spectacle.

Edinburgh Castle

The spectacular Military Tattoo held at Edinburgh Castle ▷

STAINED GLASS

York Minster has an exceptional collection of medieval stained glass. The glass was generally coloured during production, using metal oxides to produce the desired colour, then worked on by craftsmen on site. When a design had been produced, the glass was first cut, then trimmed to shape. Details were painted on, using iron oxide-based paints which were fused to the glass by firing in a kiln. Individual pieces were then leaded together to form the finished window. Part of the fascination of the minster glass is its variety of subject matter. Some windows, including the ▷ *Great East Window*, were paid for by lay donors who specified a particular subject; others reflect ecclesiastical patronage.

DECORATED GOTHIC STYLE

An example of this second period of Gothic architecture from the late 13th to mid-14th century is the ▷ *Chapter House,* which radiates elegantly against the backdrop of York Minster. Delicate carvings, fine stained-glass windows, elaborate tracery and experimental vaulting typify the Decorated Gothic style. Carvings of foliage, animals and human figures can be viewed above the stalls inside the cathedral. Inside the ▷ *nave,* complex tracery can be seen throughout.

The Octagonal Chapter House in York Minster

York Minster

Central sunflower in rose window

T HE LARGEST Gothic cathedral in northern Europe (▷ *Gothic Style p55),* York Minster is 158 m (519 ft) long and 76 m (249 ft) wide across the transepts, and houses the largest collection of medieval stained glass in Britain. The word "minster" usually refers to a cathedral served by monks, but priests always served at York. The first minster began as a wooden chapel used to baptize King Edwin of Northumbria in 627. There have been several cathedrals on or near the site, including an 11th-century Norman structure. The present minster was begun in 1220 and completed 250 years later. In July 1984, the south transept roof was destroyed by fire. Restoration cost £2.25 million.

Central Tower
Reconstructed in 1420–65 (after partial collapse in 1407) from a design by the master stonemason William Colchester, its geometrical roof design has a central lantern.

East transept

★ **Great East Window**
Measuring the size of a tennis court, this is the largest expanse of surviving medieval stained glass in the world. The Bishop of Durham, Walter Shirlaw, paid glazier John Thornton four shillings a week to complete the celebration of the Creation, between 1405–8.

Five Sisters' Window

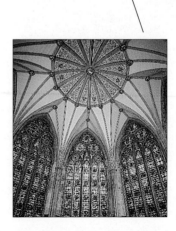

The Choir has a vaulted entrance with a 15th-century boss of the Assumption of the Virgin.

★ **Chapter House**
A Latin inscription near the entrance of the wooden-vaulted Chapter House (1260–85) reads: "As the rose is the flower of flowers, so this is the house of houses."

The Nave
Building works on the nave began in 1291 and were completed in the 1350s. It was severely damaged by fire in the 19th century. Rebuilding costs were heavy, but it was reopened with a new peal of bells in 1844.

THE FIVE SISTERS
The north transept is adorned with the ▷ *Five Sisters' Window*. It is the largest example of grisaille glass in Britain. This 13th-century design involved creating fine patterns on clear glass and decorating it with black enamel.

West Towers
The 15th-century decorative panelling and elaborate pinnacles on the west towers contrast with the simpler design of the north transept.

Exit in south transept

16th-century rose window

The Great West Window was added between 1338–9 by master stonemason Ivo de Raghton. The glazier was Robert Ketelbarn and it was commissioned by Archbishop Melton. The heart shape in the tracery symbolizes the Sacred Heart of Christ.

The Great West Door leads into the main body of the cathedral.

Nave pulpit

KEY DATES

1220 Construction of the present York Minster begins.

1472 The cathedral is completed.

1730–36 The entire floor is relaid in patterned marble.

1840 Fire damages the nave.

1985 The roof in the south transept is rebuilt following a fire in 1984.

YORK MYSTERY PLAYS

These 48 medieval dramas, which relate the history of the world from the mystery of God's creation to the Last Judgment, were originally performed between the 14th and the 16th centuries for the feast of Corpus Christi. The York Mystery Plays, or cycles, are one of only four which have survived. They are divided into short episodes and performed by actors standing on a wagon. The entertainers then ride through the city streets, pausing at a number of venues to perform. It was customary for different guilds to adopt the productions which often bore a connection to their trade. For example, shipbuilders were responsible for the portrayal of Noah's Ark, bakers played the Last Supper and butchers staged the Death of Christ. This cycle tradition was revived for the Festival of Britain in 1951 and has been performed every three to four years since. In 2000, York Minster staged a lavish millennium performance of the biblical plays in the ▷ *nave*.

STAR FEATURES

★ **Great East Window**

★ **Chapter House**

★ **Choir Screen**

★ **Choir Screen**
Sited between the choir and the nave, this beautiful 15th-century stone screen depicts kings of England from William I to Henry VI, and has a canopy of angels.

Lady Nightingale's Memorial by Roubiliac (1761), North Transept

FAMOUS TOMBS AND MONUMENTS

Many sovereigns and their consorts are buried in Westminster Abbey. Some tombs are deliberately plain, while others are lavishly decorated. The shrine of the Saxon king Edward the Confessor and various tombs of medieval monarchs are located at the heart of the abbey (▷ *St Edward's Chapel*). The *Grave of the Unknown Warrior* in the ▷ *Nave* commemorates those killed in World War I who had no formal resting place. One un-named soldier is buried here. Monuments to a number of Britain's greatest public figures – from politicians to poets – crowd the aisles. Memorials to countless literary giants such as Chaucer, Shakespeare and Dickens can be found in the South Transept (▷ *Poets' Corner*).

HENRY VII CHAPEL

Work on the chapel began in 1503, on the orders of King Henry VII. It was intended to enshrine Henry VI, but it was Henry VII himself who was finally laid to rest here in an elaborate tomb. The highlight of this chapel, completed in 1519, is the vaulted roof, a glorious example of Perpendicular architecture. The undersides of the choir stalls (1512) are beautifully carved with exotic and fantastic creatures. Inside the chapel is the fine tomb of Elizabeth I, who reigned 1558–1603, also containing the body of her half-sister, Mary I, who ruled 1553–8.

Westminster Abbey, London

SINCE THE 13TH CENTURY, Westminster Abbey has been the burial place of Britain's monarchs and the setting for many coronations and royal weddings. It is one of the most beautiful buildings in London, with an exceptionally diverse array of architectural styles, ranging from the austere French Gothic of the nave to the astonishing complexity of Henry VII's Chapel. Half national church, half national museum, the abbey aisles and transepts are crammed with an extraordinary collection of tombs and monuments honouring some of Britain's greatest public figures, ranging from politicians to poets.

★ Nave
At a height of 31 m (102 ft), the nave is the highest in England. The ratio of height to width is 3:1.

CORONATION

The coronation ceremony is over 1,000 years old. The last occupant of the Coronation Chair was the present monarch, Queen Elizabeth II. She was crowned on 2 June 1953 by the Archbishop of Canterbury in the first televised coronation.

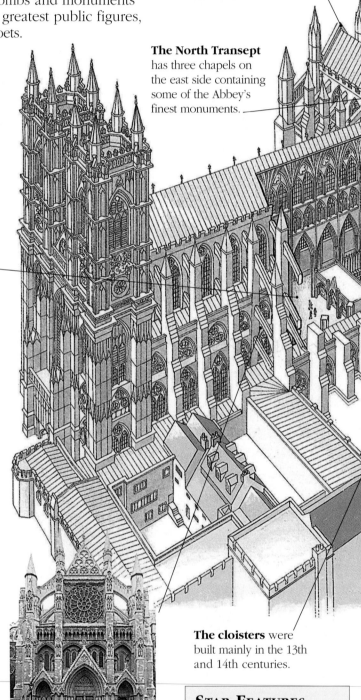

North Entrance
The mock-medieval stonework is Victorian.

The North Transept
has three chapels on the east side containing some of the Abbey's finest monuments.

The cloisters were built mainly in the 13th and 14th centuries.

Flying Buttresses
The abbey's enormous flying buttresses help to redistribute the great weight of the soaring nave roof.

STAR FEATURES

★ **Nave**

★ **Henry VII Chapel**

★ **Chapter House**

★ Henry VII Chapel

The chapel, built in 1503–12, has superb late Perpendicular vaultings and choir stalls dating from 1512.

The Sanctuary, built by Henry III, has been the scene of 38 coronations.

WILLIAM SHAKESPEARE 1564–1616 BURIED AT STRATFORD-ON-AVON

THE CORONATION CHAIR

This magnificent chair, used for all coronations since 1308, used to hold the supposedly biblical Stone of Destiny that Edward I seized from Scotland in 1296. It can now be seen at Edinburgh Castle. The chair remains in the abbey (▷ *St Edward's Chapel).*

Poets' Corner

A host of great poets are honoured here, including Shakespeare, Chaucer and T S Eliot.

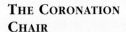

The Museum has many of the abbey's treasures including wood, plaster and wax effigies of monarchs.

★ Chapter House

A beautiful octagonal room, remarkable for its 13th-century tile floor. It is lit by six huge stained-glass windows showing scenes from the abbey's history.

The Pyx Chamber is where the coinage was tested in medieval times.

St Edward's Chapel

The shrine of Edward the Confessor is housed here, along with the Coronation Chair and many tombs.

HISTORICAL PLAN OF THE ABBEY

The first abbey church was established as early as the 10th century, but the present French-influenced Gothic structure (▷ *Gothic Style p55)* was begun in 1245 at the behest of Henry III. Because of its unique role as the coronation church, the abbey escaped Henry VIII's onslaught on Britain's monastic buildings in 1540.

KEY

- ▪ Built before 1500
- ▪ Built in 1500–20
- ▪ Completed by 1745
- □ Remodelled after 1850

KEY DATES

1065 Edward the Confessor founds the original abbey.

1245 Henry III demolishes the old abbey and begins work on Westminster Abbey as we know it today.

1503 Work commences on the stunning Henry VII Chapel.

1734 Construction of the west towers begins.

1953 Queen Elizabeth II's coronation is the most recent in the abbey's history.

THE CORONATION CEREMONY

Every monarch since William the Conqueror, except Edward V and Edward VIII, has been crowned in Westminster Abbey. Many elements in this solemn and mystical ceremony date from the reign of Edward the Confessor (1042–66). The king or queen proceeds to the abbey and is accompanied by some of the crowns, sceptres, orbs and swords that form the royal regalia. The jewelled State Sword, one of the most valuable in the world, represents the monarch's own sword. He or she is anointed with holy oil, to signify divine approval, and invested with ornaments and royal robes. The climax of the ceremony is when St Edward's Crown is placed on the sovereign's head; there is a cry of "God Save the King" (or Queen), the trumpets sound, and guns at the Tower of London are fired.

Westminster Abbey

Admiral Lord Nelson's tomb in the crypt

FAMOUS TOMBS

St Paul's Cathedral is the final resting place of Sir Christopher Wren whose tomb is marked by a slab. The inscription states: "Reader, if you seek a monument look around you." Around 200 tombs of famous figures and popular heroes can be found in the crypt, such as Nelson, naval hero of the Battle of Trafalgar (1805) and the Duke of Wellington, hero of the Battle of Waterloo (1815). Other tombs and memorials include those of Sir Arthur Sullivan the composer, Sir Henry Moore the sculptor and the artists Sir John Everett Millais and Joshua Reynolds. Florence Nightingale, famous for her pioneering work in nursing standards and the first woman to receive the Order of Merit, is also buried here, as well as Alexander Fleming who discovered penicillin.

THE INTERIOR

St Paul's cool, beautifully ordered, ornate and spacious interior is instantly striking. The nave, transepts and choir are arranged in the shape of a cross, as in a medieval cathedral, but Wren's Classical vision shines through this conservative floor plan, forced on him by the cathedral authorities. The interior is dominated by the vast cupola (▷ *Dome*) which is decorated with monochrome frescoes by Sir James Thornhill. Master woodcarver Grinling Gibbons produced intricate carvings of cherubs, fruits and garlands (▷ *Choir Stalls*), while wrought ironwork genius Jean Tijou created the sanctuary gates.

St Paul's Cathedral, London

THE GREAT FIRE OF LONDON in 1666 left the medieval cathedral of St Paul's in ruins. Wren was commissioned to rebuild it, but his design for a church on a Greek Cross plan (where all four arms are equal) met with considerable resistance. The authorities insisted on a conventional Latin cross, with a long nave and short transepts, to focus the congregation's attention on the altar. Despite the compromises, Wren created a magnificent, world-renowned Baroque cathedral which was built between 1675 and 1710 and has since formed the lavish setting for many state ceremonies.

The Nave
An imposing succession of massive arches and saucer domes open out into the vast space below the cathedral's main dome.

CHRISTOPHER WREN

Trained as a scientist, Sir Christopher Wren (1632–1723) began his impressive architectural career at the age of 31. He became a leading figure in the rebuilding of London after the Great Fire of 1666, building a total of 52 new churches. Although Wren never visited Italy, his work was influenced by Roman, Baroque and Renaissance architecture, as is apparent in his masterpiece, St Paul's Cathedral.

★ **Dome**
At 113 m (370 ft), the elaborate dome is one of the highest in the world.

The balustrade along the top was added in 1718 against Wren's wishes.

★ **West Front and Towers**
The towers were added by Wren in 1707. Their design was inspired by the Italian Baroque architect, Boromini.

The West Portico consists of two storeys of coupled Corinthian columns, topped by a pediment carved with reliefs showing the Conversion of St Paul.

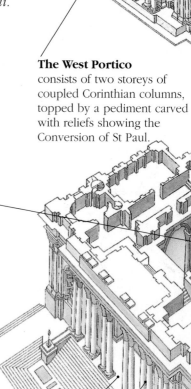

West Porch

Main entrance approached from Ludgate Hill

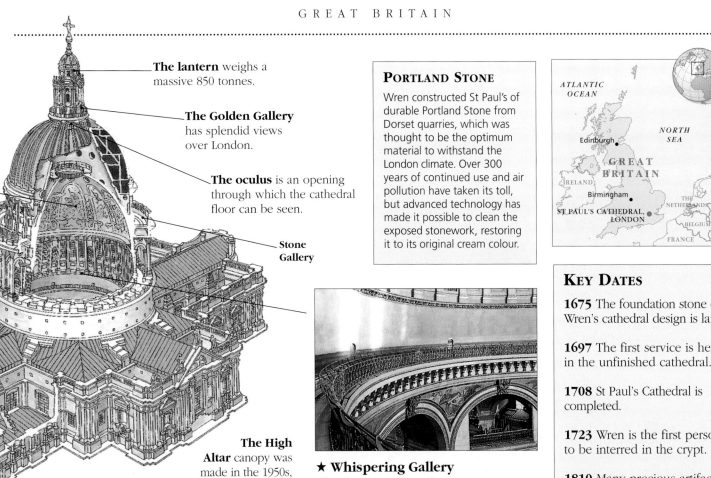

The lantern weighs a massive 850 tonnes.

The Golden Gallery has splendid views over London.

The oculus is an opening through which the cathedral floor can be seen.

Stone Gallery

The High Altar canopy was made in the 1950s, based on designs by Wren.

Entrance to crypt, which has many memorials to the famous.

Entrance to Golden, Whispering and Stone galleries

The South Portico was inspired by the porch of Santa Maria della Pace in Rome. Wren absorbed the detail by studying a friend's collection of architectural engravings.

PORTLAND STONE

Wren constructed St Paul's of durable Portland Stone from Dorset quarries, which was thought to be the optimum material to withstand the London climate. Over 300 years of continued use and air pollution have taken its toll, but advanced technology has made it possible to clean the exposed stonework, restoring it to its original cream colour.

★ Whispering Gallery
The dome's unusual acoustics mean that words whispered against the wall can be heard clearly on the opposite side.

Choir
Jean Tijou, a Huguenot refugee, created much of the fine wrought ironwork in Wren's time, including these choir screens.

STAR FEATURES

★ **Dome**

★ **West Front and Towers**

★ **Whispering Gallery**

Choir Stalls
The 17th-century choir stalls and organ case were made by Grinling Gibbons (1648–1721), a wood-carver from Rotterdam. He and his team of craftsmen worked on these intricate carvings for two years.

KEY DATES

1675 The foundation stone of Wren's cathedral design is laid.

1697 The first service is held in the unfinished cathedral.

1708 St Paul's Cathedral is completed.

1723 Wren is the first person to be interred in the crypt.

1810 Many precious artifacts are lost in a major robbery.

1937 The St Paul's Heights Code is introduced to limit development which would block the cathedral's profile on the London skyline.

1940–1 Slight bomb damage occurs during World War II when the cathedral is targeted in the Blitz.

SPECIAL EVENTS

Aided by some of the finest craftsmen of his day, Christopher Wren created an interior of grand majesty and Baroque splendour (▷ *Baroque Style p81*), a worthy setting for the many great ceremonial events that have taken place here. These include the funerals of Admiral Lord Nelson (1806), the Duke of Wellington (1852) and Sir Winston Churchill (1965). Celebrated royal occasions have included the wedding of Prince Charles and Lady Diana Spencer (1981) and the Queen's Golden Jubilee (2002). The cathedral also provided the venue for a special service to mark the 11 September 2001 attacks in America.

THE LEGEND OF THE RAVENS

The Tower's most celebrated residents are a colony of eight ravens. It is not known when they first settled here, but these scavenger birds would have arrived soon after the castle was constructed to feed off the abundant refuse. Their presence has been protected by the legend that should the birds desert the Tower, the kingdom will fall. In fact they have their wings clipped on one side, making flight impossible. Unfortunately, as the ravens court in flight, this also makes breeding difficult. The Ravenmaster, one of the Yeoman Warders (▷ *"Beefeaters"*), looks after the birds. A memorial in the moat commemorates some of the ravens who have died at the Tower since the 1950s.

FAMOUS PRISONERS

The Tower has been prison to kings and notorious characters throughout its history. One of the first monarchs to be held here was Henry VI, who was murdered while at prayer in 1471. The Duke of Clarence, brother of Edward IV, was convicted of treason and assassinated in 1478 by drowning in a cask of wine. Two of Henry VIII's wives and his former chancellor Sir Thomas More were beheaded here. Even Elizabeth I was held in the tower for two months, and on her death in 1603 her favourite explorer Sir Walter Raleigh was imprisoned and later executed. The last prisoner, held in the ▷ *Queen's House* in 1941, was deputy leader of the Nazi party, Rudolf Hess.

The 19th-century Tower Bridge overlooking the Tower

The Tower of London

SOON AFTER HE BECAME KING in 1066, William the Conqueror built a castle here to guard the entrance to London from the Thames Estuary. In 1097 the White Tower, standing today at the centre of the complex, was completed in sturdy stone; other fine buildings were added over the centuries to create one of the most powerful and formidable fortresses in Europe. The Tower has served as a royal residence, armoury, treasury and most famously as a prison for enemies of the crown. Many were tortured and among those who met their death here were the "Princes in the Tower", the sons and heirs of Edward IV. Today the Tower is a popular attraction, housing the Crown Jewels and other priceless exhibits which remain powerful reminders of royal might and wealth.

"Beefeaters"
Thirty-seven Yeoman Warders guard the Tower and live here. Their uniforms hark back to Tudor times.

Queen's House
This Tudor building is the sovereign's official residence at the Tower.

Beauchamp Tower
Many high-ranking prisoners were held here, often with their own retinues of servants. The tower was built by Edward I around 1281.

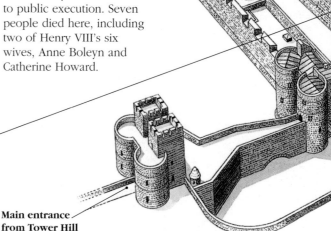

Two 13th-century curtain walls protect the tower.

Tower Green was the execution site for favoured prisoners, away from crowds on Tower Hill, where many had to submit to public execution. Seven people died here, including two of Henry VIII's six wives, Anne Boleyn and Catherine Howard.

Main entrance from Tower Hill

THE CROWN JEWELS

The world's best-known collection of precious objects, now displayed in a splendid exhibition room, includes the gorgeous regalia of crowns, sceptres, orbs and swords used at coronations and other state occasions. Most date from 1661, when Charles II commissioned replacements for regalia destroyed by Parliament after the execution of Charles I (r.1625–49). Only a few older pieces survived, hidden by royalist clergymen until the restoration of the monarchy in 1660 – notably, Edward the Confessor's (r.1327–77) sapphire ring, now incorporated into the Imperial State Crown. The crown was made for Queen Victoria in 1837 and has been used at every coronation since.

The Sovereign's Ring (1831)

The Sovereign's Orb (1661), a hollow gold sphere encrusted with jewels

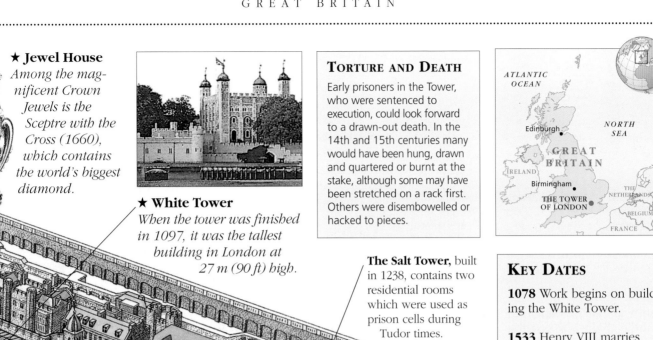

★ Jewel House
Among the magnificent Crown Jewels is the Sceptre with the Cross (1660), which contains the world's biggest diamond.

★ White Tower
When the tower was finished in 1097, it was the tallest building in London at 27 m (90 ft) high.

The Salt Tower, built in 1238, contains two residential rooms which were used as prison cells during Tudor times.

TORTURE AND DEATH
Early prisoners in the Tower, who were sentenced to execution, could look forward to a drawn-out death. In the 14th and 15th centuries many would have been hung, drawn and quartered or burnt at the stake, although some may have been stretched on a rack first. Others were disembowelled or hacked to pieces.

★ Chapel of St John
This austerely beautiful Romanesque chapel is a particularly fine example of Norman architecture.

Traitors' Gate
The infamous entrance was used for prisoners brought from trial in Westminster Hall.

Bloody Tower
Edward IV's two sons were put here by their uncle, Richard of Gloucester (subsequently Richard III), after their father died in 1483. The princes, depicted here by John Millais (1829–96), disappeared mysteriously and Richard was crowned later that year. In 1674 the skeletons of two children were found nearby.

THAMES

STAR FEATURES

★ Jewel House

★ White Tower

★ Chapel of St John

KEY DATES

1078 Work begins on building the White Tower.

1533 Henry VIII marries Anne Boleyn at the Tower.

1601 Last victim of the axe is beheaded on Tower Green.

1841 Fire destroys part of the White Tower.

THE WHITE TOWER

Begun by William I in 1078, the ▷ *White Tower* is the oldest surviving building in the Tower of London. It was designed as a palace-fortress to accommodate the king and the Constable of the Tower, the garrison commander. Each had self-contained rooms including a hall, for public occasions, a partitioned chamber and a chapel. When the fortress was enlarged a century later, both king and constable moved to new residences. On the upper two storeys, the monarch's elegant Royal Suite was used to hold distinguished prisoners. The ceremonial chambers would have been twice their present height; a pitched roof was removed in 1490 so that extra floors could be built on top. Rising through two floors is the ▷ *Chapel of St John*, an exquisite example of an early Norman church. Originally this would have been decorated with rich furnishings, painted stonework and stained-glass windows. These were removed in 1550 during the English Reformation. By the 1600s, the tower was used as a storehouse and armoury.

The Tower of London

ROYAL TENNIS COURT AND THE MAZE

Henry VIII had the ▷ *royal tennis court* built in the 16th century, as he was very fond of the game. Legend says that he was playing tennis at Hampton Court while his second wife Anne Boleyn was being executed. When William III moved into the palace in 1689, he had the gardens and the buildings remodelled. Wren's design for the gardens included the ▷ *Fountain Garden* and the ▷ *Maze*. The Maze was planted with hornbeams until the 18th century, when they were replaced with yews and hollies.

The Chapel Royal decorated with carved pendants and royal arms

THE CHAPEL ROYAL AND THE GREAT HALL

Cardinal Wolsey had the ▷ *Chapel Royal* built during his time at Hampton Court. As soon as King Henry VIII moved in, he refurbished the chapel and installed its impressive vaulted ceiling in 1535–6. The chapel subsequently became the location for many decisive moments in Henry's life – he learnt of his fifth wife Katherine Howard's infidelity and married his last wife Catherine Parr here. The ▷ *Great Hall*, with its delightful hammerbeam roof and Gothic fireplaces, was also part of Henry's rebuilding of Hampton Court. Stained-glass windows were added to the beautiful hall, showing him flanked by the coats of arms of his six wives.

Hampton Court Palace

Ceiling decoration from the Queen's Drawing Room

Cardinal Wolsey, influential Archbishop of York to Henry VIII, began building Hampton Court in the early 16th century. Originally it was not a royal palace, but was intended as Wolsey's riverside country house. Later, in 1528, Hampton Court was seized by the king when Wolsey fell from royal favour. The buildings and gardens were then twice rebuilt and extended into a grand palace, first by Henry himself and then, in the 1690s, by William III and Mary II, who employed Christopher Wren as architect. There is a striking contrast between Wren's Classical royal apartments and the Tudor turrets, gables and chimneys elsewhere. The inspiration for the gardens as they are today comes largely from the time of William and Mary, for whom Wren created a vast formal Baroque landscape, radiating avenues of majestic limes and many collections of exotic plants.

★ Clock Court

The so-called Anne Boleyn's Gateway is at the entrance to Clock Court. Henry VIII's Astronomical Clock, created in 1540 by Nicholas Oursian, is also located here.

The Pond Garden

This sunken water garden was part of Henry VIII's elaborate designs.

★ The Maze

Its yew and holly hedges are approximately 2 m (7 ft) high and 0.9 m (3 ft) wide.

Royal tennis court

Chapel Royal

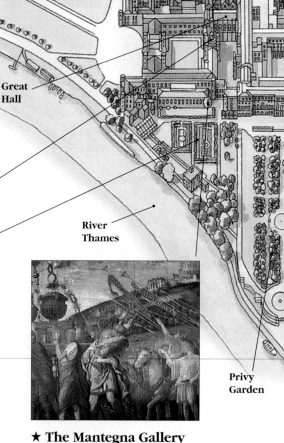

Great Hall

River Thames

Privy Garden

★ The Mantegna Gallery

Andrea Mantegna's nine canvases depicting The Triumphs of Caesar *(1490s) are housed here.*

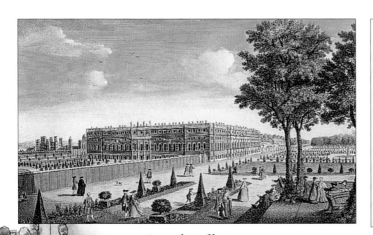

HAMPTON COURT FLOWER SHOW

The large ornamental gardens at Hampton Court host one of Britain's most popular horticultural events each summer. Some of the best gardeners from all over the country showcase their garden designs, surrounded by flowers and exotic plants. Creators of the most captivating gardens are awarded medals.

Broad Walk

A contemporary print shows the East Front and the Broad Walk during the reign of George II (1727–60).

Long Water

A man-made lake runs almost parallel to the Thames, from the Fountain Garden across the Home Park.

Fountain Garden

A few of the clipped yews here were planted in the reign of William and Mary.

The East Front

The windows of the Queen's Drawing Room, designed by Wren, overlook the central avenue of the Fountain Garden.

STAR FEATURES

★ **The Maze**

★ **Clock Court**

★ **The Mantegna Gallery**

KEY DATES

c.1236 The Knights Hospitallers of St John of Jerusalem acquire the manor of Hampton and begin to use the site as a grange.

1514 Cardinal Thomas Wolsey obtains the lease of Hampton Court from the Knights Hospitallers.

1532 As part of Henry VIII's rebuilding of Hampton Court, work on the Great Hall begins.

1838 Hampton Court Palace opens to the public for the first time.

CARDINAL WOLSEY AND HENRY VIII

The English statesman and Cardinal, Thomas Wolsey (c.1475–1530), was considered the most powerful person in England after the king. During Henry VIII's reign from 1509, Wolsey was given the role of managing England's foreign affairs, as well as being the king's advisor. This important position earned Wolsey a lot of wealth, but he also had enemies. His downfall came when Henry wanted a church annulment from his first wife Catherine of Aragon so he could marry Anne Boleyn. Wolsey, aware that his life would be in danger if he did not achieve Henry's demand, proceeded slowly with a request to the Pope. This angered the king and also Anne who used her influence to remove Wolsey from court. A few years later, Wolsey died suddenly on his way to face trial for treason.

THE BELL BEAKER CULTURE

It is believed that the Beaker people emerged in Britain around 2200 BC. Their name derives from the distinctive bell-shaped pottery cups found in their burial mounds. They are credited with building ▷ *the Bluestone Circle* at Stonehenge because concentric circles were typical of their culture and much of their pottery was unearthed in the vicinity. Their advanced construction technique suggests that the Beaker Folk were sun worshippers as well as highly organized and skilled craftsmen. They created ▷ *the Avenue* which runs directly towards the midsummer sun, and widened the entrance to the henge, aligning it more precisely with the sunrise of the summer solstice.

THE SITE

Despite centuries of archaeo-logical, religious and mystical interest in Stonehenge, the site's original purpose remains unknown. The building of this inscrutable prehistoric megalith has been attributed to Druids, Greeks, Phoenicians and Atlanteans. Theories on the reason it was built range from sacrificial ceremonies to astronomical calendars. Unearthed evidence of burials suggests that human sacrifices took place here and most experts agree that Stonehenge has religious foundations. The arrangement of the stones fuels beliefs in an astronomical purpose. The significance of this site must have been great as the stones used were not quarried locally but brought from as far away as Wales (▷ *the Bluestone Circle*).

An impression of the completed prehistoric monument

Stonehenge

BUILT IN SEVERAL STAGES from about 3000 BC, Stonehenge is Europe's most famous prehistoric monument. We can only guess at the rituals that took place here, but the alignment of the stones leaves little doubt that the circle is connected with the sun and the passing of the seasons, and that its builders possessed a sophisticated understanding of both arithmetic and astronomy. Despite popular belief, the circle was not built by the Druids; this Iron Age priestly cult flourished in Britain from around 250 BC, more than 1,000 years after Stonehenge was completed.

The Winter Solstice
There are many lunar and solar alignments. The inner horseshoe faces the winter solstice sunrise.

The Heel Stone, a large sarsen stone quarried in the Marlborough Downs, stands at the entrance to the site. It casts a long shadow straight to the heart of the inner circle on Midsummer's Day.

The Avenue is a dirt path built by the Beaker Folk which forms a ceremonial approach to the site.

The Slaughter Stone, named by 17th-century antiquarians who be-lieved Stonehenge to be a place of human sacrifice, was in fact one of a pair forming a doorway.

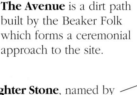

The Prehistoric Site
This was possibly a ceremonial area for fertility, birth and death rituals. Evidence of burials and cremations exists nearby and inside the circle.

The Outer Bank, dug around 3000 BC, is the oldest part of the historic Stonehenge site.

RECONSTRUCTION OF STONEHENGE

This illustration shows what Stonehenge probably looked like about 4,000 years ago. The stones remaining today create a strong impression of how incredible the original site would have been to see.

BUILDING OF STONEHENGE

Stonehenge's monumental scale is more impressive given that the only tools available were made of stone, wood and bone. The labour involved in quarrying, transporting and erecting the huge stones was such that its builders must have been able to command immense resources and vast numbers of people. One method is explained here.

A sarsen stone *was moved on rollers and levered down into an awaiting pit.*

With levers *supported by timber packing, it was gradually raised by 200 men.*

Stonehenge as it is Today
The ruins of Stonehenge reflect the grand structure that existed 4,000 years ago. Only half of the original stones remain due to natural weathering and human destruction.

PREHISTORIC WILTSHIRE

Ringing the horizon around Stonehenge are scores of circular barrows, or burial mounds, where ruling class members were honoured with burial close to the temple site. Ceremonial bronze weapons, jewellery and other finds excavated around Stonehenge can be seen in the museums at Salisbury and Devizes.

The Bluestone Circle was built around 2000 BC out of some 80 slabs quarried in south Wales. It was never completed.

The Horseshoe of Sarsen Trilithons was built around 2300 BC out of sandstone from the Marlborough Downs.

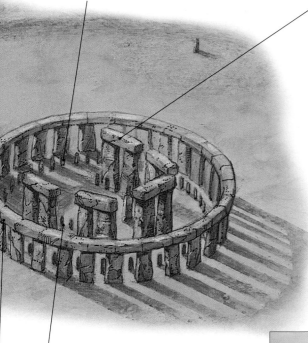

Finds
From a burial mound near Stonehenge, these prehistoric finds are now part of Devizes museum's exceptional collection.

The Horseshoe of Bluestones is likely to have been transported from Wales on a combination of sledges and rafts.

The Sarsen Circle was erected around 2300 BC and is capped by lintel stones held in place by mortice and tenon joints.

Restoration
Formal excavation and restoration work on the site only began during the 20th century.

KEY DATES

3000–1000 BC Stonehenge is constructed in three phases.

1648 The site is recognized as a prehistoric religious base.

1900 Two stones on the site fall down.

1978 The government prohibits visitors from walking within the stone circle.

1984 Stonehenge is added to UNESCO's World Heritage Site list.

THE DRUIDS

Archaeologists initially claimed that Stonehenge was built by Druids, priests of a pre-Christian, Celtic society, who performed ritualistic ceremonies and sacrifices here. Although the site is still associated with Druids, radiocarbon dating has proved that it was raised over a thousand years before Druids were established in the region, and they may have used the existing site as a temple of worship. Today Stonehenge is famous for the Druid ceremonies and festivals. English Heritage, who control the site, permit Druid gatherings in the inner circle each year for the solstices and equinoxes, however the site itself is cordoned off to protect against damage caused by an increasing number of tourists. Many Druids associate Stonehenge with the magician Merlin. Said to have been a Druid master, legend claims he taught and advised the fabled King Arthur of Britain.

The pit *round the base was packed tightly with stones and chalk.*

Alternate ends *of the lintel were levered up.*

The weight *of the lintel was supported by a timber platform.*

The lintel *was then levered sideways onto the uprights.*

Midsummer sunrise over Stonehenge ▷

Stonehenge

Canterbury Cathedral

Sculpture of a seated Jesus on Christ Church Gate

ST THOMAS BECKET

When Archbishop Theobold died in 1161, King Henry II saw the opportunity to increase his power over the church by consecrating his faithful advisor, Thomas Becket, as the Archbishop of Canterbury – the most prominent ecclesiastical role in the kingdom. The king mistakenly believed that this would allow him to exert pressure on the Church. Becket's loyalty shifted and the struggle between Church and monarch for ultimate control of the realm culminated in the murder of Becket in 1170 by four knights attempting to gain the king's favour. People flocked to mourn him and three days later, a series of miracles took place which were attributed to Becket. After Becket's canonization in 1173, Canterbury became a major centre of pilgrimage.

THE REFORMATION

In 1534, Henry VIII broke with the Church of Rome when the Pope refused to divorce him from Catherine of Aragon. The Archbishop of Canterbury, Thomas Cranmer, was made to do so instead. The Church of England was created, with Henry as its supreme head and the Archbishop of Canterbury its ecclesiastical guide. The *Book of Common Prayer*, compiled by Cranmer, became the cornerstone of the Church of England.

THIS GLORIOUS HIGH-VAULTED cathedral was designed in the French Gothic style (▷ *Gothic Style p55*) by William of Sens in 1070 and became the first Gothic church in England. It was built to reflect the city's growing ecclesiastical rank as a major centre of Christianity by the first Norman archbishop, Lanfranc, on the ruins of an Anglo-Saxon cathedral. Enlarged and rebuilt many times it remains, however, an exceptional example of the different styles of medieval architecture. The most significant moment in its history came in 1170 when Archbishop Thomas Becket was murdered here. In 1220 Becket's body was moved to a new shrine in Trinity Chapel which, until Henry VIII destroyed it, soon became one of Christendom's chief pilgrimage sites.

★ Medieval Stained Glass
This depiction of the 1,000-year-old Methuselah is a detail from the southwest transept window. The cathedral's unique collection of stained glass gives a precious glimpse into medieval thoughts and practices.

The nave seen today was rebuilt by Henry Yevele in the Perpendicular style from 1377–1405.

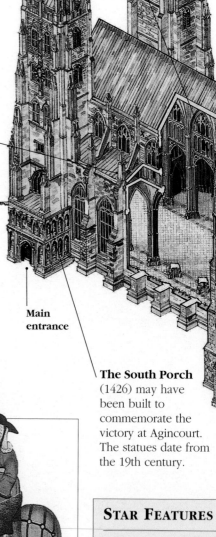

The Nave
At 100 m (328 ft), the nave makes Canterbury Cathedral Europe's longest medieval church. In 1984, parts of an Anglo-Saxon cathedral were found below the nave.

Main entrance

The South Porch (1426) may have been built to commemorate the victory at Agincourt. The statues date from the 19th century.

THE CANTERBURY TALES

Considered to be the first great English poet, Geoffrey Chaucer (c.1345–1400) is chiefly remembered for his rumbustious and witty saga of a group of pilgrims who travel from London to Becket's shrine in 1387, called *The Canterbury Tales*. Chaucer's pilgrims represent a cross-section of 14th-century English society and the tales remain one of the greatest and most entertaining works of early English literature.

Wife of Bath, *The Canterbury Tales*

STAR FEATURES

★ **Medieval Stained Glass**

★ **Site of the Shrine of St Thomas Becket**

★ **Black Prince's Tomb**

Bell Harry Tower

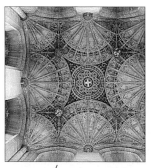

The central tower was built in 1496 to house a bell donated by Prior Henry (Harry) of Eastry. The present Bell Harry was cast in 1635. The fan vaulting is a superb example of this late Gothic style.

St Augustine

In 597, Pope Gregory the Great sent Augustine on a mission to convert the English to Christianity. Augustine founded a church on the present-day site of Canterbury Cathedral and became its first Archbishop.

★ Site of the Shrine of St Thomas Becket

This Victorian illustration (anon) portrays Becket's canonization. The Trinity Chapel was built to house his tomb which stood here until 1538. The spot is now marked by a lighted candle.

Great Cloister

Chapter House

★ Black Prince's Tomb

This copper effigy is on the tomb of Edward, Prince of Wales, who died in 1376.

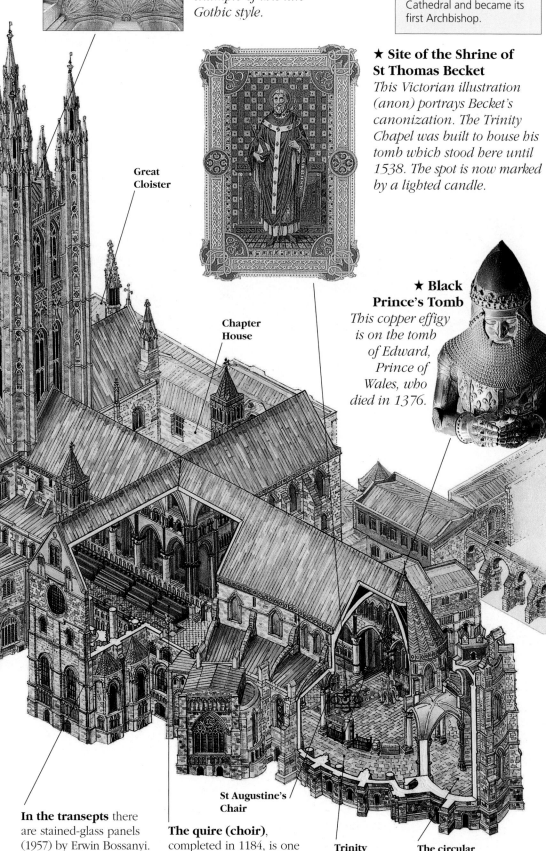

In the transepts there are stained-glass panels (1957) by Erwin Bossanyi.

St Augustine's Chair

The quire (choir), completed in 1184, is one of the longest in England.

Trinity Chapel

The circular Corona Chapel

Key Dates

597 St Augustine founds the first cathedral at Canterbury.

1070 The cathedral is rebuilt by Archbishop Lanfranc.

1170 Archbishop Thomas Becket is murdered at the altar and canonized in 1173.

1534 Henry VIII splits from the Church of Rome and forms the Church of England.

1538 St Thomas Becket's shrine is destroyed by Henry VIII.

1982 Pope John Paul II and Archbishop Robert Runcie pray at Thomas Becket's tomb.

The Black Prince

Edward, Prince of Wales (1330–76), known as "The Black Prince", gained popularity as leader of the English at the Battle of Crécy in 1346. He again emerged victorious in 1356 at the Battle of Poitiers when the French King, John the Good, was captured and brought to Canterbury Cathedral to worship at St Thomas' tomb. As heir to the throne, the prince wished to be buried in the crypt but it was throught appropriate that this hero be laid to rest alongside the tomb of St Thomas in the ▷ *Trinity Chapel*. The copper effigy in the ▷ *Black Prince's Tomb* is one of the most impressive in the cathedral. Edward was outlived by his father Edward III but the Prince's son was crowned Richard II in 1377.

PIETER PAUL RUBENS (1577–1640)

Rubens had apprenticeships with prominent Antwerp artists from an early age and was inspired to visit Italy in 1600 to study the work of the Italian Renaissance masters. It was here that his majestic style was largely founded. On returning to Antwerp in 1608, his reputation earned him his appointment as court painter to Archduke Albert and his wife, the Infanta Isabella. He became the most renowned Baroque painter in Europe, combining Flemish realism with the classical imagery of Italian Renaissance art. After 1626, he was assigned diplomatic missions, nominated to the courts of Charles I in England, Marie de' Medici in France and Felipe IV in Spain. Having helped to conclude a treaty between England and Spain in 1629, he was knighted by Charles I for his peacemaking efforts. Rubens spent the later years of his life distancing himself from diplomatic duties and focusing once again on his painting.

Baroque portico of the inner courtyard, Rubens' House

RUBENS IN ANTWERP

On his return to Antwerp in 1608, Rubens was swamped by commissions from the nobility, Church and state. He was asked to paint pictures for church altar pieces, to etch, engrave, design tapestries and plan entire pageants. His well-run ▷ *studio*, modelled on those in Italy, was able to meet the demand. Under his guidance, a school of superior artists flourished. His most significant undertaking was for the decoration of the Jesuit church in Antwerp. Sadly, most of his work there was destroyed by a fire in 1718.

Rubens' House, Antwerp

Statue of Neptune

PIETER PAUL RUBENS' home and studio for the last thirty years of his life, from 1610 to 1640, is found on Wapper Square in Antwerp. The city bought the premises just before World War II, but the house had fallen into ruin, and what can be seen today is the result of careful restoration and is a fascinating insight to how the artist lived and worked. Rubenshuis is divided into two sections. To the left of the entrance are the narrow rooms of the artist's living quarters, equipped with period furniture. Behind this part of the house is the *kunstkamer*, or art gallery, where Rubens exhibited both his own and other artists' work, and entertained his friends and wealthy patrons, such as the Archduke Albert and the Infanta Isabella. To the right of the entrance lies the main studio, a spacious salon where Rubens worked on – and showed – his works.

Façade of Rubens' House
The older Flemish part of the house sits next to the later house, whose elegant early Baroque façade was designed by Rubens.

Formal Gardens
The small garden is laid out formally and its charming pavilion dates from Rubens' time. He was influenced by such architects of the Italian Renaissance as Vitruvius when he built the Italian Baroque addition to his house in the 1620s.

★ Rubens' Studio
It is estimated that Rubens produced some 2,500 paintings in this large, high-ceilinged room. In the Renaissance manner, Rubens designed the work which was usually completed by a team of other artists employed in his studio.

STAR FEATURES

★ Rubens' Studio

★ Kunstkamer

Bedroom

The Rubens family lived in the Flemish section of the house, with its small rooms and narrow passages. The portrait by the bed is said to be of Rubens' second wife, Helena Fourment.

The Familia Kamer,

or family sitting room, is cosy and has a pretty tiled floor. It overlooks Wapper Square.

RELIGIOUS WORKS

Rubens was a fervent Roman Catholic prompting magnificent religious and allegorical masterpieces, some of which can be seen in Antwerp's cathedral.

Dining Room

Intricately fashioned leather panels line the walls of this room, which also displays a noted work by Frans Snyders.

KEY DATES

1610 Rubens buys a house on Wapper Square, Antwerp.

1614 The studio is enlarged to satisfy growing demand for Rubens' work.

1628 Rubens is knighted by English king Charles I.

1628 Rubens dies in his house.

1937 Rubens' House is bought and renovated by the city of Antwerp and opened to the public in 1946.

RUBENS' HOUSE DESIGN

Rubens' sojourn in Italy (1600–08) influenced his views on architecture as well as painting. Rubens' House was embellished to reflect his love of Italian Renaissance forms, incorporating classical arches and sculpture (▷ *Renaissance Style p131*). His style boldly contrasted with the architectural traditions of the day and bears witness to the artist's voracious creativity. It was here that Rubens received prominent guests throughout his career. The house is entered as Rubens intended: through the main gate leading to the inner courtyard which created an imposing impression of the surrounding features. The opulent Baroque portico (▷ *Baroque Style p81*) between the courtyard and the ▷ *Formal Gardens* was designed by Rubens. The renovations completed in 1946 were based on the artist's original sketches.

★ Kunstkamer

This art gallery contains a series of painted sketches by Rubens. At the far end is a semi-circular dome, modelled on Rome's Pantheon, displaying a number of marble busts.

Chequered mosaic tiled floor

Baroque Portico

One of the few remaining original features, this portico was designed by Rubens, and links the older house with the Baroque section. It is adorned with a frieze showing scenes from Greek mythology.

Engraving of William III of Orange (1650–1702)

THE HOUSE OF ORANGE-NASSAU

The marriage of Hendrik III of Nassau-Breda to Claudia of Chalon-Orange established the House of Orange-Nassau in 1515. Since that time the family has played a central role in governing the Netherlands. The House of Orange is also important in British history. In 1677, William III of Orange married the English princess Mary Stuart. William and Mary became king and queen of England in 1689 when Mary's father James II went into exile in France, and the couple ruled as joint monarchs.

THE HET LOO PALACE INTERIOR

The Orange-Nassau family continued to use Het Loo Palace as a royal summer house until 1975. The palace is now a museum, and painstaking restoration has recreated its 17th-century look. The interior, sumptuously decorated with rich materials, is laid out symmetrically, with the royal apartments to the east and west of the Great Hall. The wings of the palace contain exhibitions of court costumes, as well as documents, paintings, silver and china relating to the House of Orange-Nassau over three centuries.

Het Loo Palace, Apeldoorn

STADTHOLDER WILLIAM III, the future king of England, built the magnificent Het Loo Palace, regarded as the "Versailles of the Netherlands", as a royal hunting lodge in the 17th century. Generations of the House of Orange used the lodge as a summer palace. The main architect was Jacob Roman (1640–1716); the interior decoration and layout of the gardens were the responsibility of Daniel Marot. The building's Classical façade belies the opulence of its lavish interior; extensive restoration work was completed on both in 1984.

★ **Royal Bedroom** *(1713)*
The wall coverings and draperies in this luxuriously furnished bedroom are of rich orange damask and purple silk.

Stadtholder William III's Closet *(1690)*
The walls of William's private study are covered in embossed scarlet damask. His favourite paintings and Delftware pieces are exhibited here.

Coat of arms (1690) of William and Mary, future king and queen of England.

King William III's bedroom

King's Garden

Classic Cars
This 1925 Bentley, nick-named Minerva, was owned by Prince Hendrik, husband of Queen Wilhelmina. It is one of the Dutch royal family's vintage cars on display in the stable block (1910).

STAR FEATURES

★ **Royal Bedroom**

★ **Old Dining Room**

★ **Formal Gardens**

QUEEN WILHELMINA

After the death of the Dutch King William III (r.1848–90), his daughter Wilhelmina was the first female to rule the country as Queen (r.1890–1948). During her reign she used the Het Loo Palace as her summer retreat.

★ **Old Dining Room** *(1686)*
In 1984, six layers of paint were removed from the marbled walls, now hung with tapestries depicting scenes from Ovid's poems.

NORTH SEA

AMSTERDAM

HET LOO PALACE, APELDOORN

THE HAGUE

THE NETHERLANDS

GERMANY

BELGIUM

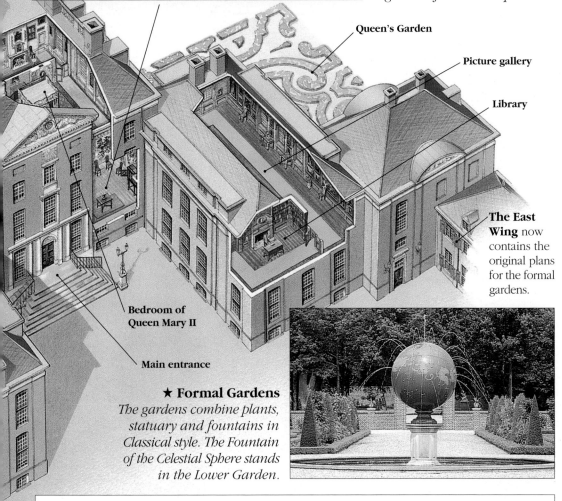

Queen's Garden

Picture gallery

Library

The East Wing now contains the original plans for the formal gardens.

Bedroom of Queen Mary II

Main entrance

★ **Formal Gardens**
The gardens combine plants, statuary and fountains in Classical style. The Fountain of the Celestial Sphere stands in the Lower Garden.

THE FORMAL GARDENS

Old prints, records and plans were used as the guidelines for recreating Het Loo's formal gardens, which lie in the vast acres behind the palace. Grass was planted over the original walled and knot gardens in the 18th century, and this was cleared in 1975. By 1983, the intricate floral patterns had been re-established, replanting had begun, the Classical fountains were renovated and the water supply fully restored. The garden reflects the late 17th-century belief that art and nature should operate in harmony.

Upper Garden

Het Loo Palace

Queen's Garden

Lower Garden

King's Garden

Layout of the formal section of the gardens

KEY DATES

1684–6 Building of the Het Loo Palace, for Prince William III and Princess Mary.

1691–4 King William III commissions new building works on the palace.

1814 Het Loo becomes the property of the Dutch state.

1984 Restoration of the house and garden comes to an end; Het Loo reopens.

THE GARDENS AND FOUNTAINS

In 1686 the ▷ *formal gardens* surrounding Het Loo Palace were laid and quickly became celebrated. The designer was Daniel Marot (1661–1752), who added a host of small details such as wrought-iron railings and garden urns. The gardens, which include the ▷ *Queen's Garden* and ▷ *King's Garden*, were designed to be strictly geometrical. They were decorated with formal flower beds and embellished with fountains, borders, topiary and cascades. Statues were also placed throughout. Today, the King's Garden features clipped box trees and pyramid-shaped juniper trees. At the centre stands an octagonal white marble basin with a spouting triton and gilt sea dragons. The slightly raised ▷ *Upper Garden* is home to the impressive King's Fountain, which is fed by a natural spring and operates 24 hours a day. It is a classic, eye-catching feature in a royal garden.

Het Loo Palace

Illustration of the façade of
Amiens cathedral

GOTHIC ORNAMENTATION

Like all Gothic churches,
Amiens' cathedral is richly
decorated. Sculpture served
to detract attention from
structural features, making a
virtue out of a necessity, as
with grotesque gargoyles that
disguise waterspouts, or
natural forms decorating
columns. Even where the
carvings would not be seen
at close hand, they were still
produced with tremendous
skill and care. The ▷ *choir
stalls* alone are decorated
with over 4,000 wooden
carvings of figures, many representing local trades of the
day, residents of Amiens and
biblical figures.

VIOLLET-LE-DUC

The renowned theorist and
designer Eugène Emmanuel
Viollet-le-Duc (1814–79)
worked on the restoration of
the cathedral in the 1850s.
Trained in both architecture
and medieval archaeology,
he was a leading figure in
France's Commission for
Historical Monuments, which
undertook early restoration
work on many architectural
landmarks, including Notre-
Dame in Paris. Today, he is
best known for his encyclo-
pedic writings on French
architecture and design,
especially the *Analytical
Dictionary of French Architecture from the 11th–16th
Centuries* (1854–68).

Amiens Cathedral

A MASTERPIECE OF ENGINEERING and Gothic architecture
(▷ *Gothic Style p55*) carried to a bold extreme,
Amiens' Notre-Dame Cathedral is also the largest cathedral
in France. It was begun around 1220 and took only fifty
years to build, financed by profits from the cultivation
of woad, a plant valued for its blue dye. Built to house
the head of St John the Baptist brought back from the
Crusades, which is still displayed, the cathedral became
a magnet for pilgrims. After restoration by Viollet-le-Duc,
and miraculously surviving two World Wars, the cathedral is famous for its wealth of statues and reliefs, which
inspired John Ruskin's *The Bible of Amiens* in 1884.

★ West Front
*The King's Gallery, a row of 22 colossal statues
representing the kings of France, spans the west front.
They are also thought to symbolize the Kings of Judah.*

Weeping Angel
*Sculpted by Nicolas Blasset
in 1628, this sentimental
statue in the ambulatory
became a popular image
during World War I.*

St Firmin Portal is decorated
with figures and scenes from
the life of St Firmin, the martyr
who brought Christianity to
Picardy and became the
first bishop of Amiens.

The Calendar shows
signs from the Zodiac,
with the corresponding
monthly labours below.
It depicts everyday life
in the 13th century.

North Tower

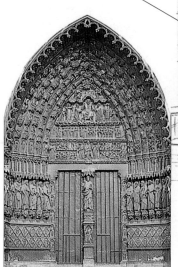

Central Portal
*Above the doors are scenes
from the Last Judgment and
there is a statue of Christ
between the doors.*

STAR FEATURES
★ **West Front**
★ **Nave**
★ **Choir Stalls**
★ **Choir Screens**

Amiens Cathedral

Towers

Two towers of unequal height frame the west front. The south tower was completed in 1366; the north in 1402. The spire was replaced twice, in 1627 and 1887.

The flamboyant tracery of the rose window was created in the 16th century.

Amiens Cathedral

St Firmin

The patron saint of Amiens, St Firmin was born in Pamplona, Spain c.272. After ordination, he was sent to northern France, where he pursued his mission boldly, unafraid of persecution, and soon settled in Amiens. Because of his persuasive preaching, he was beheaded by the Romans in c.303.

KEY DATES

1220 Work begins on the foundations of the cathedral.

1279 The relics of St Firmin and St Ulphe are presented, attended by the kings of France and England.

1849 Restoration of the cathedral under the direction of Viollet-le-Duc.

1981 Amiens Cathedral joins the list of UNESCO World Heritage Sites.

BUILDING AMIENS CATHEDRAL

The cathedral was designed by the French architect Robert de Luzarches, and inspired by the Gothic cathedral at Reims. Work began in 1220 and by 1236 the façade, rose window and portals were complete. By this stage the architect Thomas de Cormont had taken over from de Luzarches, who had died prematurely in about 1222. De Cormont directed the building of the choir and apse. The cathedral was finished by 1270 and this speed of execution perhaps explains the building's coherence and purity of style. Research has shown that the figures on the beautiful west portal would originally have been brightly painted. Modern laser technology has now enabled experts to assess the original colouring of the sculptures, and a light show is put on periodically to illuminate the portal, recreating the look of over 700 years ago.

A double row comprising 22 elegant flying buttresses supports the construction.

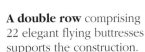

★ Nave
Soaring 42 m (138 ft) high, with support from 126 slender pillars, the brightly illuminated interior of Notre-Dame is a hymn to the vertical.

★ Choir Stalls
The 110 oak choir stalls (1508–19) are delicately carved with over 4,000 biblical, mythical and real life figures.

★ Choir Screens
Vivid scenes from the lives of St Firmin and St John, carved in the 15th–16th centuries, adorn the walkway.

The flooring was laid down in 1288 and reassembled in the late 19th century. The faithful followed its labyrinthine path on their knees.

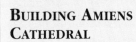

BISHOP AUBERT

For centuries, the Mont was recognised as a sacred site of devotion, where both Druids and Romans worshipped. In 708 Aubert, Bishop of the nearby town of Avranches, had a vision in which the Archangel Michael commanded that a chapel be built in his honour on Mont-St-Michel. In response, Bishop Aubert had an oratory erected on the summit, his belief inspiring one of Christianity's most spectacular holy sites. The faithful came to appeal for the archangel's protection and Mont-St-Michel soon became an important place of pilgrimage. Although nothing remains of Bishop Aubert's original oratory, it is thought to have been situated on the west side of the rock, on the ground where ▷ *St Aubert's Chapel* now stands.

Early 13th-century Anglo-Norman style cloisters

THE ABBEY

The three levels of the abbey reflect the monastic hierarchy. The monks lived at the highest level, in an enclosed world of the church, refectory and the elegant columns of the cloister. In 1776, three bays in the church's nave were pulled down to create the West Terrace which has fine views of the coastline. Monks ate in the long, narrow refectory which is flooded with light through tall windows. On the middle level, the abbot entertained his noble guests. Soldiers and pilgrims further down on the social scale were received at the lowest level of the abbey, in the almonry. The three-storey complex of La Merveille (The Miracle), added to the north side in the early 13th century, is a Gothic masterpiece (▷ *Gothic Style p55*).

Mont-St-Michel

St Michael

Shrouded by mist and encircled by sea, the enchanting silhouette of Mont-St-Michel soars proudly above glistening sands. Now linked to the mainland by a causeway, the island of Mont-Tombe (Tomb on the Hill) stands at the mouth of the river Couesnon, crowned by an abbey that almost doubles its height. This superb example of a fortified abbey ranks as one of the most significant sites of pilgrimage in Christendom. Lying strategically on the frontier between Brittany and Normandy, Mont-St-Michel grew from a humble 8th-century oratory to become a Benedictine monastery of great influence. Pilgrims known as *miquelots* journeyed from afar to honour the cult of St Michael, and the monastery was a renowned centre of medieval learning. After the Revolution the abbey became a prison. It is now a national monument that draws one million visitors a year.

OVER THE CENTURIES

The 10th-century abbey
Richard I, Duke of Normandy, founded this great Benedictine abbey in 966.

The 11th-century abbey
The Romanesque church was built between 1017 and 1144 (▷ Romanesque Style p122).

The 18th-century abbey
Few monks remained in the abbey by the end of the 18th century when it became a political prison.

★ Ramparts
Fortified walls with imposing towers were build to withstand English attacks during the Hundred Years' War (1337–1453).

Gabriel Tower
was built in 1524 by military engineer, Gabriel du Puy.

Entrance

St Aubert's Chapel
A small 15th-century chapel built on an outcrop of rock is dedicated to St Aubert, the founder of Mont-St-Michel.

Tides of Mont-St-Michel

Extremely strong tides in the Baie du Mont-St-Michel act as a natural defence. They rise and fall with the lunar calendar and can reach speeds of 10 km/h (6 mph) in spring.

★ Abbey

Protected by high walls, the abbey and its church occupy an impregnable position on the island.

THE FORTIFICATIONS

Mont-St-Michel became a symbol of national identity when its defensive 15th-century walls protected it against fierce cannon attacks in the Hundred Years' War. All of Normandy was conquered by the English except this well-fortified island.

Gautier's Leap

At the top of the Inner Staircase, this terrace is named after a prisoner who leaped to his death.

Église St Pierre

King's Tower

The Arcade Tower provided lodgings for the abbot's soldiers.

Liberty Tower

★ Grande Rue

Now crowded with restaurants, the pilgrims' route, followed since the 12th century, climbs up past Église St-Pierre to the abbey gates.

STAR FEATURES

★ Ramparts

★ Abbey

★ Grande Rue

KEY DATES

708 St Aubert builds an oratory on Mont-Tombe, dedicated to St Michael.

966 Duke Richard I founds the Benedictine abbey.

1446–1521 The late Gothic choir is built.

1874 The abbey is declared a national monument.

1877–9 A causeway is built, linking Mont-St-Michel to mainland France.

1895–7 The Belfry, spire and statue of St Michael are added.

1922 Services are again held in the abbey church.

1979 Mont-St-Michel is added to UNESCO's World Heritage Site list.

THE MONT PRISON

The monastery first served as a prison in the 15th century under the reign of Louis XI whose political opponents were kept here in famously severe conditions. During the French Revolution, the monks were dismissed and the abbey once again functioned as a penitentiary with aristocrats, priests and political adversaries imprisoned within its walls. Recognised figures, including writers such as Chateaubriand and Victor Hugo, protested against this practice but Mont-St-Michel remained a state prison for 73 years until 20 October, 1863 when a decree was passed, returning the abbey to divine worship.

The buttressed apse of Notre-Dame

THE HUNCHBACK OF NOTRE-DAME

The novel *Notre-Dame de Paris*, published in English as *The Hunchback of Notre-Dame*, was the work of the Romantic French novelist Victor Hugo (1802–85) and was published in 1831. The hunchback of the title is the bell-ringer Quasimodo, ward of the cathedral, and the novel tells the story of his doomed love for the dancer Esmeralda. The cathedral features strongly in the work and Hugo used his book to rail against its neglect, declaring that medieval cathedrals were "books in stone" and should be deeply treasured. The novel aroused widespread interest in the restoration of Notre-Dame.

THE INTERIOR

Notre-Dame's interior grandeur is strikingly apparent in its high-vaulted central nave. This is bisected by a huge ▷ *transept*, at either end of which is a medieval ▷ *rose window*, 13 m (43 ft) in diameter. Works by famous sculptors adorn the cathedral. Among them are Jean Ravy's choir-screen carvings, Nicolas Coustou's *Pietà*, which stands on a gilded base sculpted by François Girardon, and Antoine Coysevox's statue of Louis XIV. The 13th-century stained-glass North Rose Window depicts the Virgin encircled by figures from the Old Testament. Against the southeast pillar of the transept stands a 14th-century statue of the Virgin and Child.

Notre-Dame, Paris

NO OTHER BUILDING is so associated with the history of Paris as Notre-Dame. It stands majestically on the Ile de la Cité, in the heart of the city. When the first stone was laid in 1163, it marked the start of 170 years of toil by armies of Gothic architects and medieval craftsmen. Since then, a series of coronations and royal marriages have passed through its doors. Built on the site of a Roman temple, the cathedral is a masterpiece of Gothic architecture. When it was finished, in about 1330, it was 130 m (430 ft) long and featured flying buttresses, a large transept, a deep choir and 69-m (228-ft) high towers.

★ **West Façade and Portals**
Two huge towers, three main doors, superb statuary, a central rose window and an openwork gallery are impressive features of the west façade.

The south tower houses the cathedral's famous Emmanuel bell.

★ **Galerie des Chimères**
The cathedral's legendary gargoyles (chimères) hide behind a large upper gallery between the towers.

★ **West Rose Window**
This window depicts the Virgin in a medallion of rich reds and blues.

STAR FEATURES

★ **West Façade and Portals**

★ **Galerie des Chimères**

★ **West Rose Window**

★ **Flying Buttresses**

The Kings' Gallery features 28 Kings of Judah.

Portal of the Virgin
The Virgin surrounded by saints and kings is a fine composition of 13th-century statues.

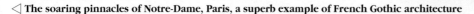

◁ **The soaring pinnacles of Notre-Dame, Paris, a superb example of French Gothic architecture**

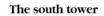

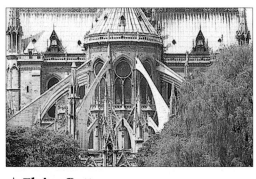

★ Flying Buttresses
Jean Ravy's spectacular flying buttresses at the east end of the cathedral have a span of 15 m (50 ft).

The spire, designed by Viollet-le-Duc, soars to a height of 90 m (295 ft).

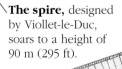

The transept was built at the start of Philippe-Auguste's reign, in the 13th century.

The treasury houses the cathedral's religious treasures, including ancient manuscripts and reliquaries.

South Rose Window
This south façade window, with its central depiction of Christ, is an impressive 13 m (43 ft) high.

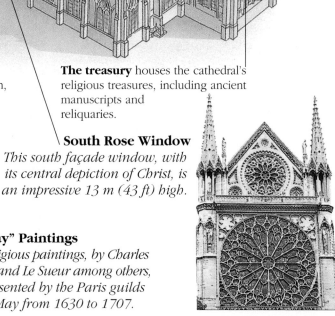

The "May" Paintings
These religious paintings, by Charles Le Brun and Le Sueur among others, were presented by the Paris guilds every 1 May from 1630 to 1707.

View of Interior
From the main entrance the high-vaulted central nave, choir and high altar give an impression of great height and grandeur.

KEY DATES

1163 Work begins when Pope Alexander III lays the foundation stone.

1793 Revolutionaries loot the cathedral and rename it the Temple of Reason.

1845 Architect Viollet-le-Duc undertakes restoration work of the cathedral.

1991 Notre-Dame becomes a UNESCO World Heritage Site.

GOTHIC STYLE

The Gothic style emerged in France around the end of the 12th century, with the Basilica of St-Denis (1137–1281), north of Paris, where most of the French monarchs are buried. The pointed arch, the ribbed vault, tracery and the rose window were all used to great effect there and were important features of the Gothic style. The desire to build ever taller, more magnificent light-filled ecclesiastical buildings grew. Another key feature emerged with the use of flying buttresses, which provided support for high walls and helped redistribute their weight. With its soaring interior and stained-glass filtered light from the large ▷ *rose windows*, the Notre-Dame Cathedral is one of the best known and most impressive examples of the Gothic style. Across Europe in many countries, including Italy, Germany, Belgium, Switzerland and Great Britain, architects took to the style with enthusiasm.

Notre-Dame

Arc de Triomphe, Paris

CARVED RELIEFS

The west façade of the arch is adorned with colossal reliefs. *The Resistance of the French in 1814* is depicted on the right. Here, a soldier defends his family and is encouraged by the embodiment of the future. *The Peace of 1815* on the left shows a man, protected by Minerva, Goddess of Wisdom, returning his sword to its scabbard. These reliefs are by the sculptor Antoine Étex. Above this are two bas-reliefs. The left frame depicts the *Capture of Alexandria* (1798) as General Kléber urges his troops forward. The right-hand panel shows the *Passage of the Bridge of Arcola* (1796) with Napoleon advancing against the Austrians. The south façade details the Battle of Jemmapes in 1792.

THE BATTLE OF AUSTERLITZ

Napoleon commissioned the arch in 1806 to honour his soldiers who achieved a masterful victory at the Battle of Austerlitz in 1805. Heavily outnumbered, Napoleon led the Allies to believe that his army was weak and successfully lured them into a vulnerable position. Fierce battle ensued, forcing the Allies to retreat across frozen Lake Satschan. It is believed that Napoleon's army fired on the ice in an attempt to drown the fleeing enemy. The armies of Russia and Austria, members of the Third Coalition alliance against France in the Napoleonic Wars, were destroyed. The French had 9,000 casualties whereas the Allies suffered three times as many.

The east façade of the Arc de Triomphe

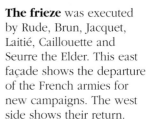

AFTER HIS greatest victory, the Battle of Austerlitz in 1805, Napoleon promised his men, "You shall go home beneath triumphal arches." The first stone of what was to become the world's most famous and largest triumphal arch was laid the following year. But disruptions to architect Jean Chalgrin's plans and the demise of Napoleonic power delayed the completion of this monumental building until 1836. Standing 50 m (164 ft) high, the arch is now the customary starting point for victory celebrations and parades.

The Battle of Aboukir, a bas-relief by Seurre the Elder, depicts a scene of Napoleon's victory over the Turkish army in 1799.

Triumph of Napoleon
J P Cortot's high-relief celebrates the Treaty of Vienna peace agreement of 1810. Victory, History and Fame surround Napoleon in this relief.

Thirty shields just below the arch's roof each bear the name of a victorious Napoleonic battle fought in either Europe or Africa.

The frieze was executed by Rude, Brun, Jacquet, Laitié, Caillouette and Seurre the Elder. This east façade shows the departure of the French armies for new campaigns. The west side shows their return.

East façade

★ **Tomb of the Unknown Soldier**
An unknown French soldier from World War I is buried here.

Arc de Triomphe viewed from the west

Place Charles de Gaulle
Twelve avenues radiate from the triumphal arch at the centre. Some bear the names of important French military leaders. Baron Haussman, in charge of urban planning under Napoleon III, created the star-shaped configuration.

NAPOLEON'S NUPTIAL PARADE

Napoleon divorced Josephine in 1809 because she was unable to bear him children. A diplomatic marriage was arranged in 1810 with Marie-Louise, daughter of the Austrian emperor. Napoleon was determined to impress his bride by going through the Arc on their way to the wedding at the Louvre, but work had barely been started. So Chalgrin built a full-scale model of the arch on the site for the couple to pass beneath.

THE BATTLE OF VERDUN

On the day this battle started in 1916, the sword carried by the figure representing France broke off from ▷ *Departure of the Volunteers in 1792.* The relief was covered up so that the public would not interpret it as a sign of misfortune.

The viewing platform affords one of the best views in Paris, overlooking the grand Champs-Élysées on one side. Beyond the other side is La Défense.

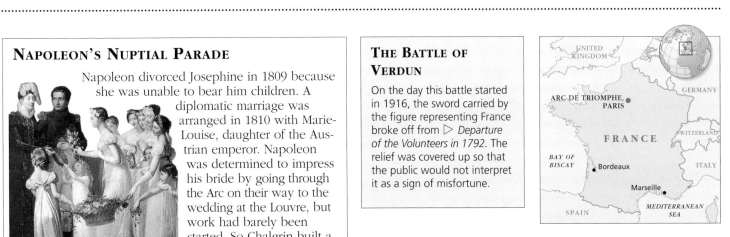

General Marceau's Funeral
Marceau defeated the Austrians in 1795, only to be killed in fighting them the next year.

The Battle of Austerlitz by Gechter shows Napoleon's army breaking up the ice on the Satschan lake in Austria to drown thousands of enemy troops who were marching across.

Officers of the Imperial Army are listed on the walls of the smaller arches.

Entrance to museum

STAR FEATURES

★ **Tomb of the Unknown Soldier**

★ **Departure of the Volunteers in 1792**

★ **Departure of the Volunteers in 1792**
François Rude's work shows citizens leaving to defend the nation. This patriotic relief is commonly known as "La Marseillaise".

KEY DATES

1806 Napoleon commissions Jean Chalgrin to build the triumphal arch.

1815 With Napoleon's downfall, work ceases.

1836 The arch is completed.

1885 The body of French poet and novelist Victor Hugo is laid in state beneath the Arc.

1920 An unknown World War I soldier is buried here.

NEO-CLASSICAL STYLE

The power, might and learning of Western Europe was represented in the 18th and the first half of the 19th centuries by architecture inspired by that of ancient Greece and Rome. The traditional principles of the Classical style were extended and adapted as the culture of the ancient world was increasingly revealed, documented and disseminated. This new Classicism was seen as an ideal match for the ambition of the powerful European states, whether autocratic or witnessing the birth pangs of democracy, and of the young United States of America for which it symbolized a connection with the Republican ideals of pre-Augustan Rome and the democracy of Athens and the Greek states. The Neo-Classical style is defined by elaborate details and a refined sense of proportion, hallmarks of ancient Classical architecture, which could be adapted to every conceivable purpose.

Arc de Triomphe

RESIDENTS OF VERSAILLES

In 1682, Louis XIV declared Versailles the official seat of the government and court. During his reign, life in this sumptuous Baroque palace (▷ *Baroque Style p81*) was ordered by rigid etiquette. Under Louis XV (1715–74), it became increasingly opulent with the help of Madame de Pompadour, the king's mistress, who set a taste for elegance which soon spread across Europe. In 1789, Louis XVI was forced to leave Versailles when it was invaded by the Revolutionary Parisian mob. It was subsequently looted and left until the reign of Louis-Philippe (1830–48), who converted part of it into a museum of French history.

Madame de Pompadour, a renowned patron of the arts

THE GARDENS

André Le Nôtre (1613–1700), the greatest French landscape gardener, created a number of magnificent château gardens. His superb architectural orchestration, Classical vision and sense of symmetry are seen in the sweeping vistas of Versailles, his greatest triumph. The gardens are styled into regular patterns of flowerbeds and box hedges, paths and groves, ornate pools of water and fountains. The Water Parterre's vast pools of water are decorated with fine bronze statues. Geometric paths and shrubberies are features of the formal gardens. The Petit Trianon, a small château built in 1762 as a retreat for Louis XV, is found in the gardens. This became a favourite of Marie-Antoinette.

Château de Versailles

Gold crest from the Petit Trianon

AMAGNIFICENT palace with sumptuous interiors and splendid gardens, Versailles represents the glory of Louis XIV's reign. Starting in 1668 with his father's modest hunting lodge, he commissioned the largest palace in Europe, with 700 rooms, 67 staircases and 730 ha (1,800 acres) of landscaped parkland. Architect Louis Le Vau built a series of wings that expanded into an enlarged courtyard. They were decorated with marble busts, antique trophies and gilded roofs. Jules Hardouin-Mansart took over in 1678 and added the two immense north and south wings. He also designed the chapel, which was finished in 1710. Charles le Brun planned the interiors and André Le Nôtre redesigned the gardens.

Louis XIV's statue, erected by Louis-Philippe in 1837, stands where a gilded gateway once marked the beginning of the Royal Courtyard.

STAR FEATURES

★ **Marble Courtyard**

★ **L'Opéra**

★ **Chapelle Royale**

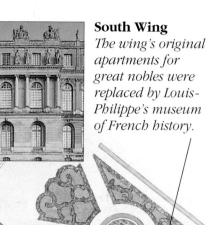

South Wing
The wing's original apartments for great nobles were replaced by Louis-Philippe's museum of French history.

Ministers' Courtyard

Main Gate
Mansart's original gateway grille, surmounted by the royal arms, is the entrance to the Ministers' Courtyard.

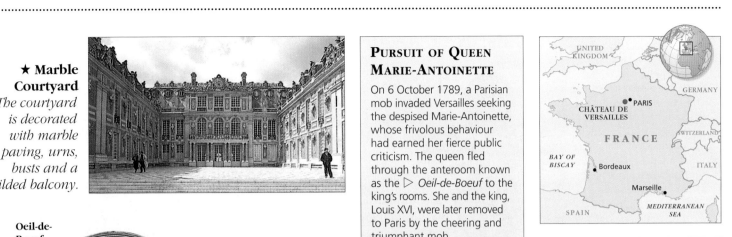

★ Marble Courtyard
The courtyard is decorated with marble paving, urns, busts and a gilded balcony.

Oeil-de-Boeuf

The Clock
Hercules and Mars flank the clock overlooking the Marble Courtyard.

Hall of Mirrors

Salon d'Apollon

Salon d'Hercule

North Wing
The chapel, opera and picture galleries occupy this wing, which originally housed royal apartments. Masses, concerts and operas are still held in this extravagant setting.

★ L'Opéra
The Opéra was completed in 1770, in time for the marriage of the future Louis XVI and Marie Antoinette. It was intended for lavish spectacles.

★ Chapelle Royale
Mansart's last great work, this two-storey Baroque chapel, was Louis XIV's last addition to Versailles.

The Royal Courtyard
was separated from the Ministers' Courtyard by elaborate grillwork during Louis XIV's reign. It was accessible only to royal carriages.

PURSUIT OF QUEEN MARIE-ANTOINETTE

On 6 October 1789, a Parisian mob invaded Versailles seeking the despised Marie-Antoinette, whose frivolous behaviour had earned her fierce public criticism. The queen fled through the anteroom known as the ▷ *Oeil-de-Boeuf* to the king's rooms. She and the king, Louis XVI, were later removed to Paris by the cheering and triumphant mob.

KEY DATES

1668 Le Vau starts construction of the château.

1671 The interior decoration is begun by Le Brun.

1833 Louis-Philippe turns the château into a museum.

1919 The Treaty of Versailles is signed in the Hall of Mirrors, ending World War I.

INSIDE THE CHÂTEAU

The lavish main apartments are on the first floor of the vast château complex. Around the ▷ *marble courtyard* are the private apartments of the king and the queen. On the garden side are the state apartments where official court life took place. These were richly decorated by Charles Le Brun with coloured marbles, stone and wood carvings, murals, velvet, silver and gilded furniture. Starting with the ▷ *Salon d'Hercule*, each state room is dedicated to an Olympian deity. The ▷ *Salon d'Apollon*, dedicated to the god Apollo, was Louis XIV's throne room. A copy of Hyacinthe Rigaud's famous portrait of the king (1701) hangs here. The climax is the ▷ *Hall of Mirrors* stretching 70 m (230 ft) along the west façade. Great state occasions were held in this room where 17 mirrors face tall arched windows. Another highlight is the ▷ *Chapelle Royale*, with the first floor reserved for the royal family and the ground floor for the court. The chapel's interior is richly decorated in white marble, gilding and Baroque murals.

Château de Versailles

Chartres Cathedral

THE ROYAL PORTAL

Following the devastating fire of 1194, a decision was taken to retain the magnificent, still-standing west entrance (▷ *Royal Portal*), which was a survivor of the earlier Romanesque church (▷ *Romanesque Style p122*). Although this created a variation in architectural styles, it was an astute decision which resulted in the survival of some of the finest sculpture of the early Middle Ages. The Royal Portal, carved between 1145 and 1155, is the most ornamental of the cathedral's three entrances. The features of the statues in the portal are lengthened in Romanesque style (▷ *Elongated Statues*) and depict figures from the Old Testament. The portal represents the glory of Christ.

Stained-glass panels of the Blue Virgin Window

THE STAINED GLASS OF CHARTRES

Donated by aristocracy, the merchant brotherhoods and royalty between 1210 and 1240, this glorious array of ▷ *stained-glass windows* is world-renowned. Over 150 windows illustrate biblical stories and daily life in the 13th century. Each window is divided into panels, usually read from left to right, bottom to top (earth to heaven). The bottom panel of the Blue Virgin window depicts Christ's conversion of water into wine. During both World Wars the windows were dismantled piece by piece and removed for safety. There is an on-going programme, begun in the 1970s, to restore the windows.

Part of the Vendôme Window

THE EPITOME OF EARLY GOTHIC architecture (▷ *Gothic Style p55*), Chartres Cathedral established a style which soon spread throughout Christendom. It was built around the remains of an earlier Romanesque church which had been partly destroyed by fire. The result is a blend of styles, with the original north and south towers, south steeple, west portal and crypt enhanced by lofty Gothic additions. Peasant and lord alike helped to rebuild the church in just 25 years. Few alterations were made after 1250, and fortunately Chartres was unscathed by the Wars of Religion and the French Revolution.

STAR FEATURES

★ **Royal Portal**

★ **Stained-Glass Windows**

★ **South Porch**

Gothic Nave
As wide as the Romanesque crypt below it, the nave reaches a soaring height of 37 m (121 ft).

★ Royal Portal
The central tympanum of the Royal Portal (1145–55) shows Christ in Majesty.

Elongated Statues

These statues on the Royal Portal represent Old Testament figures.

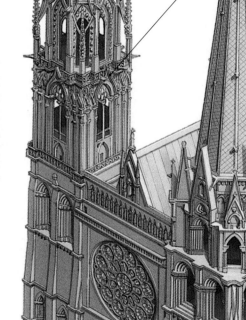

The steeple of the north tower dates from the start of the 16th century. Flamboyant Gothic in style, it contrasts sharply with the solemnity of its Romanesque counterpart.

The lower half of the west front is a survivor of the original Romanesque church.

Labyrinth

THE LABYRINTH

The 13th-century labyrinth, inlaid in the nave floor, was a feature of most medieval cathedrals. As a penance, pilgrims used to follow the tortuous route on their knees, echoing the Way of the Cross. The journey of 262 m (859 ft), around 11 bands of broken concentric circles, took at least one hour to complete.

VEIL OF THE VIRGIN

The miraculous survival of this relic after the fire of 1194 made Chartres a holy pilgrimage site and attracted generous donations. The veil is said to have been worn by the Virgin Mary when she gave birth to Jesus.

Apsidal Chapel
This chapel houses the oldest cathedral treasure, the Veil of the Virgin *relic, which miraculously survived the fire of 1194. More artifacts can be found in the St Piat Chapel.*

Vaulted Ceiling
A network of ribs supports the vaulted ceiling.

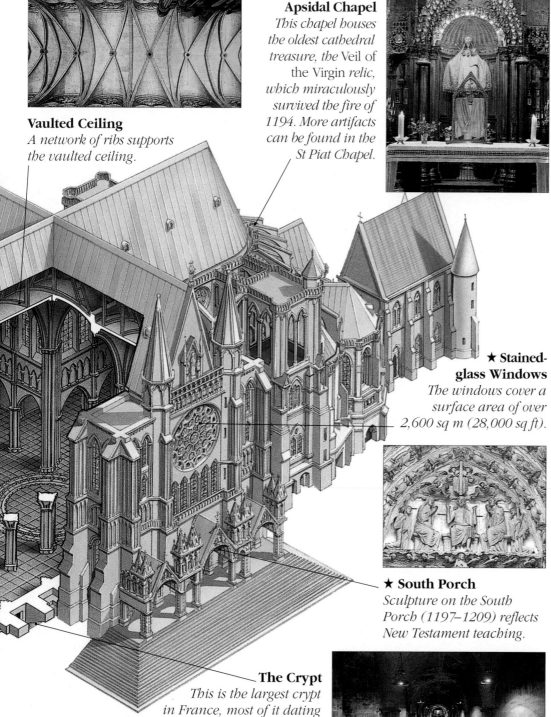

★ **Stained-glass Windows**
The windows cover a surface area of over 2,600 sq m (28,000 sq ft).

★ **South Porch**
Sculpture on the South Porch (1197–1209) reflects New Testament teaching.

The Crypt
This is the largest crypt in France, most of it dating from the early 11th century. It comprises two parallel galleries, a series of chapels and the 9th-century St Lubin's vault.

KEY DATES

1020 Romanesque cathedral is begun.

1194 A fire partly destroys the Romanesque cathedral.

1220s The cathedral is rebuilt, with new parts in the early Gothic style.

1260 The cathedral is formally consecrated.

1507 A Flamboyant Gothic steeple is added to the north tower.

1836 The cathedral's wooden roof is damaged by fire.

1974 The cathedral is added to UNESCO's World Heritage Site list.

GOTHIC STATUARY

There are approximately 4,000 statues at Chartres Cathedral. Fortunately, having remained virtually untouched since being sculpted in the 13th century, they are in a remarkable state of preservation. Incredible examples, tracing the evolution of Gothic sculpture, are clustered around the north and south portals. The north porch is devoted to representations of such Old Testament figures as Joseph, Solomon, the Queen of Sheba, Isaiah and Jeremiah. Scenes from Christ's childhood and the Creation of the World are also illustrated. The ▷ *South Porch* portrays the Last Judgment, and episodes in the lives of the Saints. The hundreds of figures decorating both portals were originally painted in bright colours.

The gardens' current design, dating from the 19th century

THE FORMAL GARDENS

As the mistress of Henri II, Diane de Poitiers wanted a surrounding fit for a king and set about creating her grand garden along the banks of the River Cher. Divided into four triangles and kept from flooding by elevated stone terraces, it was planted with an extensive selection of flowers, vegetables and fruit trees. When Catherine de' Medici arrived at Chenonceau, she created her own garden from a design by Bernard Palissy in his *Drawings of a Delectable Garden*. Today, over 4,000 flowers are planted in the gardens each year.

THE CREATION OF CHENONCEAU

Catherine Briçonnet, wife of the royal chamberlain, was the first of many females who added their feminine touches to Chenonceau. During King Henri II's reign (1547–59) he gave the castle to his mistress Diane de Poitiers, who went on to dramatically transform it. She redecorated its interiors, built a bridge over the River Cher and constructed a ▷ *formal garden*. When the king died, his wife Catherine de' Medici reclaimed the château from Diane and set about erasing her presence. She redesigned the castle and built a ▷ *Grande Galerie* on the bridge above the Cher. Over the centuries other ladies have shaped Chenonceau's destiny and design, including Louise de Lorraine who was bequeathed the castle in 1589, the enlightened Louise Dupin, friend of Voltaire and Rousseau, in the 18th century and Madame Pelouze in the 19th century.

Château de Chenonceau

STRETCHING ROMANTICALLY across the River Cher, this French Renaissance château (▷ *Renaissance Style p131)* was the residence for queens and royal mistresses, including Catherine de' Medici and Diane de Poitiers. Transformed over the centuries from a modest manor and water mill into a castle designed solely for pleasure, it is surrounded by elegant formal gardens and wooded grounds. The interior rooms have been restored to their original style and a small waxworks museum illustrates the building's history. The site also includes a stable with a miniature train ride down the lovely tree-lined drive and a restaurant.

Chapelle
The chapel has a vaulted ceiling and pilasters sculpted with acanthus leaves and cockle shells. The stained glass, ruined by a bomb in 1944, was replaced in 1953.

★ Cabinet Vert
The walls of Catherine de' Medici's study were originally covered with green velvet.

To Formal Gardens

Louise de Lorraine's room was painted black and decorated with monograms, tears and knots in white after the death of her husband, King Henri III in 1589.

The Tour des Marques survives from the 15th-century castle of the Marques family.

STAR FEATURES

★ **Cabinet Vert**

★ **Tapestries**

★ **Grande Galerie**

The Three Graces
Painted by Charles-André Van Loo (1705–65), The Three Graces depicts the pretty Mailly-Nesle sisters, all royal mistresses.

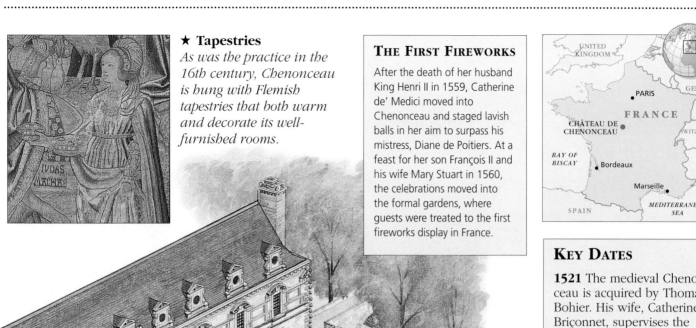

★ Tapestries
As was the practice in the 16th century, Chenonceau is hung with Flemish tapestries that both warm and decorate its well-furnished rooms.

THE FIRST FIREWORKS
After the death of her husband King Henri II in 1559, Catherine de' Medici moved into Chenonceau and staged lavish balls in her aim to surpass his mistress, Diane de Poitiers. At a feast for her son François II and his wife Mary Stuart in 1560, the celebrations moved into the formal gardens, where guests were treated to the first fireworks display in France.

KEY DATES

1521 The medieval Chenonceau is acquired by Thomas Bohier. His wife, Catherine Briçonnet, supervises the rebuilding of the château.

1526 The château is seized from the Bohier family by King François I for unpaid debts to the crown.

1547 Diane de Poitiers, King Henri II's lifelong mistress moves into the château.

1559 On the death of King Henri II, Catherine de' Medici takes the building from Diane de Poitiers.

1789 The castle is spared in the French Revolution thanks to its liberal owner, Madame Dupin.

1913 The Menier family buys Chenonceau and still owns it today.

CHÂTEAU GUIDE

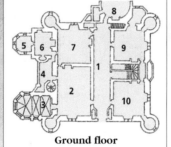

Ground floor

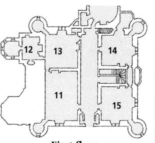

First floor

1 Vestibule
2 Salle des Gardes
3 Chapelle
4 Terrasse
5 Librairie de Catherine de' Medici
6 Cabinet Vert
7 Chambre de Diane de Poitiers
8 Grande Galerie
9 Chambre de François I
10 Salon Louis XIV
11 Chambre des Cinq Reines
12 Cabinet des Estampes
13 Chambre de Catherine de' Medici
14 Chambre de Vendôme
15 Chambre de Gabrielle d'Estrées

★ Grande Galerie
Catherine de' Medici added this elegant gallery to the bridge designed by Philibert de l'Orme in 1556–9 for Diane de Poitiers.

THE INTERIOR

The elegant ▷ *Grande Galerie* designed by Catherine de' Medici to hold her festivities dominates Chenonceau. Lit by 18 windows stretching from an exposed-joists ceiling, its enamelled tiled floor leads into royal bedrooms, including Diane de Poitiers', covered in Flemish ▷ *tapestries*. The small tiles in the first floor hall are stamped with fleur de lys crossed by a dagger. Marble medallions brought from Italy by Catherine de' Medici hang above the doors, including those in her bedroom, which is full of 16th-century furnishings and tapestries depicting biblical scenes.

Chenonceau's Florentine-style Grande Galerie, which stretches across the River Cher for 60 m (197 ft)

Catherine de' Medici's graceful Grande Galerie, Château de Chenonceau ▷

ST AMADOUR

There are various stories about the life of St Amadour. One legend claims that he was Zaccheus of Jericho, who knew and conversed with Jesus during his time on earth. His wife, St Veronica, gave Jesus a cloth to wipe his face during his journey to Calvary. After Jesus's crucifixion, Zaccheus and his wife fled from Palestine to escape religious persecution. On their travels, they met the Bishop St Martial, another disciple of Jesus in Aquitaine, France, who was preaching the Gospel, but continued to Rome. While in Rome they witnessed the martyrdoms of St Peter and St Paul. The death of his wife led Zaccheus back to France and the place later named after him, where he stayed until he died in 70 AD.

CHAPEL OF NOTRE-DAME

This Romanesque chapel (▷ *Romanesque Style p122*) was built in the 15th century near the site where St Amadour's body was found. It houses the statue of the Black Virgin and Child. Pilgrims who heard about the statue flocked to the shrine, climbing the ▷ *Grand Stairway* on their knees as they prayed for the forgiveness of their sins. A 9th-century bell hangs in the chapel's vault and is thought to ring when a miracle occurs. Saints and kings also visited the chapel, including England's King Henry II. Legend says that he was cured of his ailment when he prayed before the Black Virgin and Child.

Rocamadour, both a place of pilgrimage and a tourist sight

Rocamadour

Black Virgin and Child

PILGRIMS HAVE FLOCKED to Rocamadour since the discovery in 1166 of an ancient grave and sepulchre containing an undecayed body, said to be that of the early Christian hermit St Amadour. King Louis IX, St Bernard and St Dominic were among many who visited the site as a spate of miracles were heralded, it is claimed, by the bell above the Black Virgin and Child in the Chapel of Notre-Dame. Although the town suffered with the decline of pilgrimages in the 17th and 18th centuries, it was heavily restored in the 19th century. Still a holy shrine, as well as a popular tourist destination, the site above the Alzou valley is phenomenal. The best views of the town can be had from the hamlet of L'Hospitalet.

The Château stands on the site of a fort which protected the sanctuary from the west.

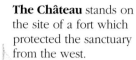

General View
Rocamadour is at its most breathtaking in the sunlight of early morning: the cluster of medieval houses, towers and battlements seems to sprout from the base of the cliff.

St Michael's Chapel contains well-preserved 12th-century frescoes.

The Tomb of St Amadour once held the body of the hermit from whom the town took its name (Rock of Amadour).

Museum of Sacred Art

Grand Stairway
Pilgrims would climb this broad flight of steps on their knees as they said their rosaries. The stairway leads to a square on the next level, around which the main pilgrim chapels are grouped.

The Chapel of St John the Baptist faces the fine Gothic portal of the Basilica of St-Sauveur.

Ramparts

The Basilica of St-Sauveur, a late 12th-century sanctuary, backs on to the bare rock face.

St Anne's Chapel dates from the 13th century, and contains a 17th-century gilded altar screen.

Cross of Jerusalem

Chapel of St Blaise

THE SPORTELL

Crafted in either lead, bronze, tin, silver or gold, the Sportell or medal displays the Virgin Mary and Child. It is worn by pilgrims who have visited Rocamadour and was once used as a pass to cross war-torn countries.

Stations of the Cross
Pilgrims encounter the Cross of Jerusalem and 14 stations marking Jesus's journey to the Cross on their way up the hillside to the château.

Rocamadour Town
Now a pedestrian precinct, its main street is lined with souvenir shops to tempt the throngs of pilgrims.

Chapel of Notre-Dame
A statue of the 12th-century Black Virgin and Child, made of walnut wood and covered in blackened silver, stands on the altar.

KEY DATES

1166 The preserved body of Zaccheus, later named St Amadour, is discovered.

1172 The *Book of Miracles* is drafted with the testimonies of miracles granted to pilgrims.

1193–1317 Over 30,000 pilgrims flock to the religious site.

1479 The Chapel of Notre-Dame is constructed.

1562 The chapels are plundered by Protestants.

1858–72 Rocamadour's restoration is supervised by abbot Jean-Baptiste Chevalt.

ROCAMADOUR'S MUSEUM

The ▷ *Museum of Sacred Art* is housed in the Bishop's Palace, which was constructed by the abbots of Tulle in the 13th century. The museum was restored in 1996 and is dedicated to the French music composer Francis Poulenc (1899–1963), who was inspired to compose *Litanies to the Black Virgin* after he visited Rocamadour. The museum's collection of statues, paintings and religious artifacts has been assembled from different sites around Rocamadour. Particularly interesting is the 17th-century statue of the prophet Jonah, carved in wood, and the fine lanterns, vases and chalices, which are still used in various religious ceremonies at Rocamadour.

Rocamadour

Roland (right) on the Market Square in Bremen

THE STATUE OF ROLAND

This 10-m (33-ft) high statue of Roland has been a fixture of Bremen's Market Square for 600 years. A Christian knight and nephew of Charlemagne, the Holy Roman Emperor (r.800–814), Roland symbolizes a town's independence. His gaze is directed towards the cathedral, the residence of the bishop, who often sought to restrict Bremen's autonomy. Roland's sword of justice symbolizes the judiciary's independence, and the engraved motto confirms the emperor's edict, conferring town rights on Bremen. The statue was carved in 1404 by a member of the Parléř family, a well-known clan of architects and sculptors. It was the prototype for 35 similar statues in other German towns.

WESER RENAISSANCE

Bremen's Gothic Town Hall owes much of its splendour to its magnificent ▷ façade. Having been completely reworked by the architect Lüder von Bentheim in 1595–1612, this façade is considered an outstanding example of Weser Renaissance architecture, the style that predominated throughout the Weser region of northern Germany between 1520 and 1630. Nobles who had toured Italy returned home inspired by the Renaissance architecture they had seen and attempted to replicate it in their own designs. The ▷ ornamental gables and frieze along the arcade are both typical of this style, as are the richly sculptured projecting oriels.

Bremen Town Hall

THE BRICK FAÇADE IN THE STYLE of the Weser Renaissance makes Bremen Town Hall one of the northernmost Renaissance masterpieces to be found in mainland Europe (▷ *Renaissance Style p131*). Behind the façade lies a magnificent late-Gothic manifestation of civic pride (▷ *Gothic Style p55*). The rectangular building is decorated with medieval statuary, including life-size sandstone sculptures of Emperor Charlemagne and the seven Electors, four prophets and four wise men. The frieze above the arcade represents an allegory of human history.

Façade
The original Gothic building was clad with a magnificent Weser Renaissance façade designed by Lüder von Bentheim in 1595–1612.

Fireplace Room
Adjoining the Gobelin Room, the Fireplace Room owes its name to a high, French marble fireplace.

★ Upper Hall
New laws were passed in the splendid Upper Hall, which occupies the entire first floor. Model sailing ships suspended from the ceiling are reminiscent of Bremen's role as a major port.

Main entrance

★ Ratskeller
The Gothic Ratskeller stores hundreds of different wines. Murals by Max Slevogt (1927) decorate the walls.

Gobelin Room

This room derives its charm from a large, exquisitely wrought tapestry produced by the 17th-century Gobelin workshop in Paris.

MUSICIANS OF BREMEN

On the north side of the Town Hall is a bronze statue of the four animals – a donkey, dog, cat and cockerel – immortalised in the Grimm Brothers' fairytale of *The Musicians of Bremen*. It was cast by Gerhard Marcks in 1951.

★ Ornamental Gable

The architect Lüder von Bentheim gave the Town Hall façade a local touch by adding a decorative Flemish-style stepped gable that is five storeys high.

Bremen Town Hall

KEY DATES

1251 Inauguration of Bremen's first civic building, the *domus consulum*.

1405–10 The dilapidated town hall is replaced by a new Gothic structure.

1491 The plaque bearing the "12 Cautions" for the benefit of councillors is mounted in the Upper Hall.

1620 The Bacchus and what is now the Hauff Room for the storage of wine are built.

1905 Completion of the Jugendstil Room.

1909–13 Addition of the New Town Hall on the east side of the building.

1927 Completion of the murals in the Hauff Room.

THE RATSKELLER

To the west side of the Town Hall is the entrance to the ▷ *Ratskeller*, which has been serving wine since 1405. Today, more than 650 different wines can be sampled here, all of which are from German wine-growing regions and some of which are stored in decoratively carved wine casks. The atmosphere in the Ratskeller is known to have inspired many an artist. Wilhelm Hauff, for example, wrote his *Fantasies in the Bremer Ratskeller* in 1827 and these later inspired the German Impressionist painter, Max Slevogt, to paint the humorous frescoes that now decorate the Hauff Room.

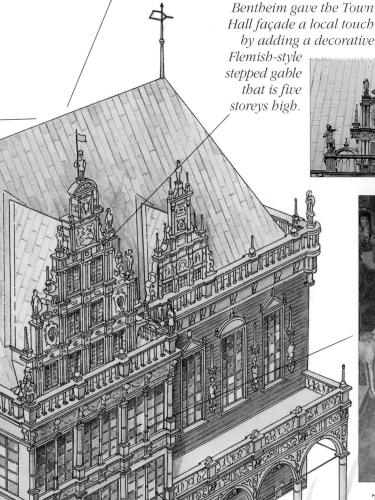

The Judgment of Solomon

The mural (1532) of Solomon's court in the Upper Hall is a reference to the room's dual function as a council chamber and courtroom.

STAR FEATURES

★ **Upper Hall**

★ **Ratskeller**

★ **Ornamental Gable**

Jugendstil Room

The lower room of the two-storey Gülden-kammer owes its 1905 Jugendstil makeover to the artist Heinrich Vogeler. The gilded leather wallpaper dates from the 17th century.

Cologne Cathedral at night

THE CATHEDRAL BELLS

The 3.4-tonne bell cast in 1418 in honour of the Three Kings was tuned to the note B. It hung in a belfry adjacent to the cathedral, but in 1437 was moved to the south tower. Eleven years later, it was joined by Europe's largest bell, the 10-tonne "Pretiosa" ("Precious One"), tuned to G. When rung together, the bells produced a G-major chord. In 1449, the 4.3-tonne "Speciosa" ("Beautiful One") was added. It is tuned to A so that Cologne Cathedral became the first church to have its bells tuned to a melody rather than a chord. The first bell has since been replaced.

THE CHOIR

About 30 years after the cathedral's foundation stone was laid, the pillars of the choir were decorated with early-Gothic statues of Christ, the Virgin Mary and the 12 Apostles. These larger-than-life figures are clad in splendid robes. Above them there is a choir of angels playing musical instruments, symbolizing the heavenly music played to celebrate the celestial coronation of Mary the Virgin. The coronation itself is depicted in the figures of Christ and Mary. A similar interpretation, dating from 1248, can be seen in the church of Sainte-Chapelle in Paris. There, too, 12 of the pillars supporting the building symbolize the 12 Apostles as the most important pillars of the Christian church.

Cologne Cathedral

10th-century Gero Cross

THE MOST FAMOUS Gothic structure in Germany, Cologne Cathedral is also unusually complex, whether in terms of its splendour, its size or even simply the date of its construction. The foundation stone of the current cathedral was laid on 15 August 1248 and the presbytery consecrated in 1322. The cathedral was built gradually until c.1520, but remained unfinished until the 19th century. The building was finally completed in 1842–80, according to the rediscovered, original Gothic designs (▷ *Gothic Style p55*).

Cathedral Interior
The presbytery, the ambulatory and the chapels retain a large number of Gothic, mainly early-14th-century, stained-glass windows.

Engelbert Reliquary (c.1630)
The cathedral treasury is famous for its large collection of golden objects, vestments and the fine ornamentation of its liturgical books.

Pinnacles
Elaborately decorated pinnacles top the supporting pillars.

Main entrance

Petrusportal, or the portal of St Peter, the only one built in the second half of the 14th century, has five Gothic figures.

STAR FEATURES

★ **Gothic Stalls**

★ **Shrine of the Three Kings**

★ **Altar of the Magi**

★ **Gothic Stalls**
The massive oak stalls, built in 1308–11, were the largest that have ever been made in Germany.

Semicircular arches
transfer the thrust of the vaults onto the buttresses.

Buttresses support the entire bulk of the cathedral.

High Altar
The Gothic altar slab, which dates back to the consecration of the presbytery, depicts the Coronation of the Virgin Mary, flanked by the 12 Apostles.

★ **Shrine of the Three Kings**
This huge Romanesque reliquary was made by Nikolaus von Verdun in 1181–1220 to hold the relics of the Three Kings. These relics were brought to Cologne in 1164 for Emperor Friedrich I Barbarossa.

Mailänder Madonna
This fine early-Gothic carving of the Milan Madonna and Child dates from around 1290. It is currently displayed in the Marienkapelle.

★ **Altar of the Magi**
This splendid altar (c.1445), the work of Stephan Lochner, is dedicated to the Three Kings, the patrons of Cologne.

KEY DATES

1248 The cathedral's foundation stone is laid.

1265 The outer walls of the choir and adjacent chapels are completed.

c.1530 Work on the cathedral halts with the south tower at 58 m (190 ft) high.

1794 French troops use the cathedral as a warehouse.

1801 The cathedral is reconsecrated.

1842–80 Completion of the cathedral according to historical plans.

1996 Cologne Cathedral becomes a UNESCO World Heritage Site.

SHRINE OF THE THREE KINGS

The ▷ *Shrine of the Three Kings*, the largest reliquary in the western world, is located near the ▷ *High Altar*. Studded with precious and semi-precious stones, this shrine is a masterpiece of medieval goldsmithery. Its sides are decorated with images of the prophets and apostles, the adoration of the Kings and the baptism of Christ. The rear depicts a portrait of Rainald von Dassel, Archbishop of Cologne (1159–67). As chancellor to Emperor Barbarossa (r.1152–90), he is said to have brought the mortal remains of the Three Kings from Milan to Cologne in 1164. On 6 January every year, the front of the shrine is opened to reveal the skulls.

Cologne Cathedral

TIEPOLO

Born in Venice, the Italian painter, Giovanni Battista Tiepolo (1696–1770) is considered the last great master of Venetian art. He created numerous altarpieces and frescoes for churches, castles, palaces and villas in Italy and Germany. His ceiling in the ▷ *Treppenhaus* is an allegorical depiction of the four continents and an outstanding example of fresco painting.

ROCOCO STYLE

The Würzburg Residence is such a fine example of German Rococo that it had a style named after it, Würzburg Rococo. Typical of this style are the vast *trompe-l'oeil* painted ceilings and large, domed rooms. Rococo derives from the French word *rocaille*, meaning "rock-work", a decorative trend for both interiors and façades featuring abstract, shell-like forms and curves. Trees, flowers and Chinese scenes were among the most popular motifs. Stucco craftsmen and wood-carvers became just as revered as architects and painters for the quality and splendour of their work.

An example of the decorative stucco work typical of Rococo

Würzburg Residence

Sculpture in the Residence garden

A MASTERPIECE OF GERMAN ROCOCO, the Residence was commissioned by two prince-bishops, the brothers Johann Philipp Franz and Friedrich Karl von Schönborn, as an episcopal palace. Its construction between 1720 and 1744 was supervised by several architects, including Johann Lukas von Hildebrandt and Maximilian von Welsch. However, the Residence is mainly associated with the name of Balthasar Neumann, the creator of its remarkable Baroque staircase (▷ *Baroque Style p81*).

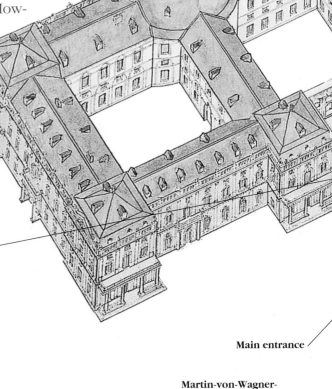

Napoleon's bedroom

Main entrance

Martin-von-Wagner-Museum entrance

★ Treppenhaus

The work of the Venetian artist Giovanni Battista Tiepolo, the largest fresco in the world adorns the vault of the stairwell.

Frankonian Fountain

A fountain, designed by Gabriel von Seidel, was constructed in the parade square in front of the Residence in 1896. It was funded by donations from the inhabitants of Würzburg.

The Arms of the Patron

The richly decorated façade by Johann Wolfgang von der Auwery bears the personal arms of Friedrich Karl von Schönborn, Prince-Bishop of Bamberg and Würzburg.

★ Emperor's Chamber

The centrepiece of the palace, the sumptuous Kaisersaal testifies to the close relationship between Würzburg and the Holy Roman Empire.

Garden Chamber

This vast, low hall has Rococo stucco work by Antonio Bossi, dating from 1749. There is also a painting on the vaulting by Johan Zick, dating from 1750, depicting The Feast of the Gods and Diana Resting.

Venetian Room

This room is named after a tapestry depicting the Venetian Carnival. Further ornaments include decorative panels with paintings by Johann Thalhofer, a pupil of Rudolph Byss.

★ Hofkirche

The church interior is richly decorated with paintings, sculptures and stucco ornaments. The side altars were designed by the architect Johann Lukas von Hildebrandt and feature paintings by Giovanni Battista Tiepolo.

Würzburg Residence

KEY DATES

1720–44 Building of the Würzburg Residence.

1732–92 The Residence garden is landscaped.

1751–53 Decoration of the Residence with ceiling frescoes by Tiepolo.

1765 Ludovico Bossi oversees the decorative stucco work in the stairwell.

1945 The palace is damaged in a bombing raid.

1981 The Residence becomes a UNESCO World Heritage Site.

1987 The completion of the Mirror Cabinet marks the end of the reconstruction work.

2003 The restoration of the stairwell frescoes begins.

THE PATRONS

Many of the people who were involved in the building of the Residence were members of the Schönborn family, a powerful 18th-century dynasty of princes and electors on the Main, Rhine and Moselle. Among them was Johann Philipp von Schönborn, who became Prince Bishop of Würzburg in 1719. He was succeeded by his brother, Friedrich Karl, one of the chief instigators of the Residence project. They engaged architects and painters of international renown, such as Tiepolo, for what was to become a truly unique *Gesamtkunstwerk*, combining all the arts.

STAR FEATURES

★ Treppenhaus

★ Emperor's Chamber

★ Hofkirche

HEIDELBERG ROMANTICISM

Heidelberg is widely held to be Germany's most romantic city and Heidelberg Castle was a favourite target of early 19th-century revisionism, with poets such as Achim von Arnim, Clemens Brentano, Joseph von Eichendorff and Ludwig Görres recasting it as the cradle of German Romanticism. The ruins came to symbolize the artistic, intellectual and political return to Germany's national roots that the poets so much wanted to see. It was at this period that Count Charles de Graimberg acted to prevent further looting of stone from the site in an attempt to preserve the ruins. Even today, the sprawling castle complex provides an extraordinarily majestic scene. Since being destroyed by the French in the 17th century, this once important residence is regarded as Germany's most palatial ruin.

Heidelberg's Church of the Holy Ghost housing the electors' tombs

RUPRECHT III

One of the most important figures in the history of Heidelberg Castle was Elector Ruprecht III, a member of the Wittelsbach dynasty. Born in Amberg in 1352, he became Elector of the Palatinate in 1398 and spearheaded a successful campaign to depose Wenceslas, the Holy Roman Emperor, in 1400. Ruprecht was elected emperor in his place, although his election was not universally recognized. He died in Oppenheim in 1410, having failed to restore the crown to its former glory.

Heidelberg Castle

TOWERING OVER THE town, the majestic Heidelberg Castle is a vast residential complex that was built between the 12th and 17th centuries. Originally a supremely well-fortified Gothic castle (▷ *Gothic Style p55*), but now mostly in ruins, this was the seat of the House of Wittelsbach palatines. After remodelling in the 16th century, the castle became one of Germany's most beautiful Renaissance residences (▷ *Renaissance Style p131*). However, its splendour was extinguished during the Thirty Years' War (1618–48) and the 1689 war with France, when most of the structure was destroyed.

Ruprecht's coat of arms

★ **Ottheinrich's Palace**
The German Pharmacy Museum is housed within the shell of this Renaissance building. It features Baroque and Rococo workshops and a travelling pharmacy.

★ **Friedrich's Palace**
One of the latest parts of the castle is Friedrich's Palace, which dates from 1601–07. Inside are statues of members of the Wittelsbach dynasty, including Charles the Great.

The bell tower, which was erected in the early 15th century, was remodelled frequently in subsequent years.

Castle moat

English Palace
These imposing ruins in the castle complex are the remains of a 17th-century building that Friedrich V built for his wife Elizabeth Stuart.

Gunpowder Tower
Built during the reign of the Elector Ruprecht, this 14th-century tower once formed part of the castle defences. It was damaged by lightning in 1764, after which the townspeople took its stone for building.

THE GIANT WINE CASK
To the left of ▷ *Friedrich's Palace*, a staircase leads to the cellars where a giant wine cask is stored. This symbol of the electors' love of good wine was built in 1750 and holds 221,000 litres (48,620 gallons). The wine was piped directly from the cask to the King's Hall.

Fountain Hall
This Gothic loggia features early-Romanesque columns taken from the palace of Charles the Great in Ingelheim.

Gate Tower

Panoramic View
Heidelberg Castle has survived as a picturesque ruin, and its imposing structure occupies a commanding position above the town. From its terrace there is a beautiful view of the medieval old town of Heidelberg.

Main entrance

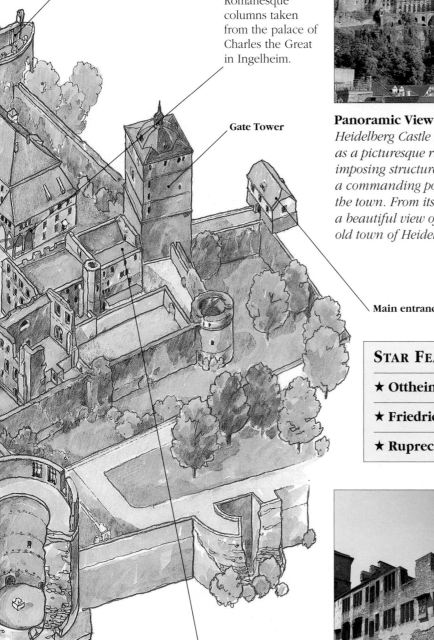

STAR FEATURES

★ **Ottheinrich's Palace**

★ **Friedrich's Palace**

★ **Ruprecht's Palace**

★ Ruprecht's Palace
Built around 1400 by a master builder from Frankfurt, this is the oldest surviving part of the castle.

KEY DATES

Mid-12th century
Construction begins under Count Palatine Conrad.

1400 Ruprecht's Palace is built.

1556–9 Ottheinrich builds his Renaissance-style palace.

1614–19 The castle garden is landscaped.

1689–93 The castle is destroyed in the War of the Palatine Succession.

1742–64 Reconstruction takes place under Elector Karl Theodor.

1810 Attempts are made to preserve the ruins.

STYLISTIC ACCRETIONS

Inside the Gothic-style ▷ *Ruprecht's Palace*, there are two models of the castle showing the various additions over the ages. In 1524, Ludwig V added a residential building known as Ludwig's Palace. The Glazed Palace (1549), named after its mirrored hall, symbolizes the architectural transition from Gothic to Renaissance style. ▷ *Ottheinrich's Palace* is a splendid example of German early-Renaissance architecture, while ▷ *Friedrich's Palace* has a typical late-Renaissance façade. This was followed by the ▷ *English Palace*. The jewel in the crown was undoubtedly the castle garden of Friedrich V (r.1613–19), once described as the eighth wonder of the world.

Heidelberg Castle

The Tapestry Room in Linderhof

LUDWIG'S BUILDINGS

Today, Ludwig II of Bavaria (1845–86) is known above all for his extravagant building projects, including Linderhof, near Neuschwanstein, and the palace at Herrenchiemsee in eastern Bavaria. While Neuschwanstein was an attempt to recreate the Middle Ages (▷ *Castle Building*), Herrenchiemsee was inspired by the Château de Versailles. Linderhof was originally a hunting lodge that from 1869 onwards was repeatedly rebuilt, its interior shaped largely by Ludwig's fantasy world. The main inspiration here, as at Herrenchiemsee, was the French Rococo style of Louis XIV, as is evident from the Gobelin tapestries that adorn the Tapestry Room (▷ *Rococo Style p72*).

A MODERN CASTLE

The medieval character of Neuschwanstein is purely illusory, for hidden behind the façade is what, for the 19th century, was state-of-the-art technology. The royal chambers, for example, all have central heating and there is running water on every floor with both hot and cold water in the kitchens. There is a dumb-waiter linking the kitchens and the ▷ *dining room*. The third and fourth floors of the castle even have telephone jacks and an electric bell system, which Ludwig II could use to summon his servants and adjutants.

Neuschwanstein Castle

SET AMIDST MAGNIFICENT mountain scenery on the shores of the Schwansee (Swan Lake), the fairy-tale Neuschwanstein Castle was built in 1869–91 for the eccentric Bavarian king, Ludwig II, to a design by the theatre designer Christian Jank. When deciding to build this imposing residence, the king was undoubtedly inspired by Wartburg Castle in Thuringia, which he visited in 1867. But Neuschwanstein is no ordinary castle: behind the pale grey granite exterior, which draws on a variety of styles, the interior is fitted with the latest 19th-century comforts. The castle offers spectacular views of the surrounding landscape.

Vestibule
The walls of the vestibule and of other rooms in the castle are lavishly covered with paintings depicting scenes from old German myths and legends.

★ Throne Room
The gilded interior of the throne room reminds one of Byzantine temples and the palace church of All Saints in the Residence in Munich.

★ Singing Room
The Sängersaal was modelled on the singing room at Wartburg Castle in Eisenach.

Study

Dining Room
Like other rooms in the palace, the dining room includes fabulous pictures, intricately carved panels and beautifully decorated furniture, all bearing witness to the skill and artistry of the 19th-century craftsmen.

Neuschwanstein Castle

★ **Castle Building**

Neuschwanstein Castle is the archetypal fairy-tale castle and has provided the inspiration for countless toy models, book illustrations and film sets.

THE SWAN MOTIF

Ludwig was fascinated by swans (hence his early identification with Lohengrin, the Knight of the Swan) and not just as a symbol of purity, but also because he regarded himself as successor to the Lords of Schwangau, whose heraldic beast was the swan. Not surprisingly, the swan motif dominates the interior décor.

LUDWIG'S CHILDHOOD HOME

The skyline of Schwangau is dominated by another castle, the majestic Hohenschwangau Castle. Ludwig's father, Maximilian II, acquired the castle when he was crown prince and had it rebuilt in 1832 in a Neo-Gothic style (▷ *Gothic Style p55*). As a child, Ludwig was captivated by its frescoes depicting various legends.

Hohenschwangau Castle

The Kemanate was completed after Ludwig's death and was planned to feature statues of female saints.

Two-storey arcades surround the castle courtyard.

The Knight's House connects the gatehouse with the main building.

KEY DATES

1868 Ludwig makes known his plans to build a new castle.

1869 The foundation stone is laid.

1873 Completion of the gatehouse.

1880 A ceremony marks the completion of all five floors.

1884 The castle is occupied.

1886 Seven weeks after Ludwig II drowns, the castle is opened to visitors.

1891 Completion of the castle.

PICTURE CYCLE

Ludwig II's choice of interior decoration was inspired by the operas of Richard Wagner (1813–83). Yet although Ludwig commissioned set painter Christian Jank with the interior design, most of the murals depict scenes taken not from operas, but from the same medieval sagas that Wagner himself used as a source. They feature Tannhäuser the poet, Lohengrin, the Knight of the Swan, and his father, Parsifal, King of the Holy Grail. Murals in the ▷ *Singing Room* show one of the legendary singing contests held at Wartburg Castle in the 13th century. Scenes from Wagner's *Lohengrin* (1846–48) decorate the King's Chambers. Among the artists employed were Josef Aigner, Wilhelm Hauschild and Ferdinand Piloty.

Courtyard

The heart of the castle was supposed to have been a mighty 90-m (295-ft) high tower with a Gothic castle church. It was never built, but in 1988 its planned position was marked in white stone.

The Gatehouse, completed in 1872, served as temporary accommodation for the king. He had an apartment on the second floor.

Main entrance

STAR FEATURES

★ **Singing Room**

★ **Throne Room**

★ **Castle Building**

The magnificent setting of the fairy tale Neuschwanstein Castle ▷

THE CRYPT

Several calamitous fires destroyed much of the Romanesque Episcopal church erected in 830–37 on the site where the Cathedral of St Gall now stands. The only part of the building to survive the ravages of time is the 9th–10th century ▷ *crypt*, which became an integral part of the Baroque cathedral. The bishops of St Gall have long found their final resting place here – a tradition that has continued to the present day. Among those buried in the cathedral are Abbot Otmar, who founded the abbey and who, ten years after his death in 769, was interred in St Otmar's Crypt beneath what is now the west gallery, and Bishop Otmar Mäder, who died in 2003.

THE ABBEY LIBRARY

Built in the second half of the 18th century according to plans drawn up by Peter Thumb, the Abbey Library is richly decorated with ceiling frescoes, intricate stuccowork, wood carving and intarsia. The two-storey reading room, containing walnut and cherry bookcases reaching to the ceiling, is especially impressive. Around 130,000 leather-bound volumes and 2,000 manuscripts are housed here. These include such biblio-philic treasures as a copy of the *Song of the Nibelungen* and *Codex Abrogans* (790), a dictionary of synonyms presumed to be one of the oldest existing written documents in German. The liturgical collection is renowned for its *Psalterium Aureum*, a psalter composed c.900. The best-known item in the collection is the *St Gallener Klosterplan*, showing the layout of an ideal Benedictine monastery. Copied from an earlier manuscript by the monks of Reichenau on Lake Constance in the early 9th century, this document is thought to have been the blueprint for the St Gallen Monastery.

St Gallen Monastery

THE BENEDICTINE ABBEY in St Gallen, established in 720, was one of the most important monasteries in Europe as well as being a foremost centre for the arts, letters and sciences. A priceless library was gathered and monks came from far and wide to copy manuscripts, many of which still exist. Only the crypt remains of the early Romanesque church and monastery built in the 9th century. The present Baroque cathedral and abbey, by architects Peter Thumb and Johann Michael Beer, were completed in 1766 and feature exquisite Rococo decorations (▷ *Rococo Style p 72*).

★ Ceiling Frescoes
The ceiling is decorated with frescoes by Joseph Wannenmacher.

Main Altarpiece
The painting on the high altar of the Assumption of the Virgin *is by Francesco Romanelli. Dating from 1645, it was later heavily retouched.*

High altar

Thrones
Two thrones by Franz Joseph Anton Feucht-mayer and decorated with paintings by Franz Joseph Stälzer, stand in the choir stalls.

STAR FEATURES

★ **Ceiling Frescoes**

★ **Choir Stalls**

St Gallen Monastery

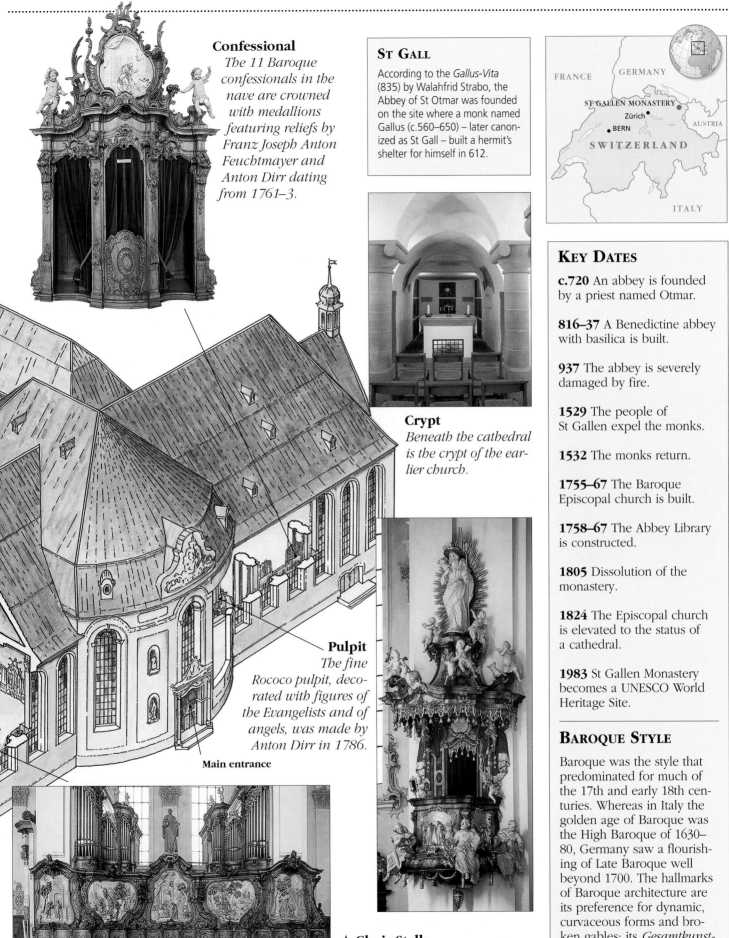

Confessional
The 11 Baroque confessionals in the nave are crowned with medallions featuring reliefs by Franz Joseph Anton Feuchtmayer and Anton Dirr dating from 1761–3.

Pulpit
The fine Rococo pulpit, decorated with figures of the Evangelists and of angels, was made by Anton Dirr in 1786.

Main entrance

St Gall

According to the *Gallus-Vita* (835) by Walahfrid Strabo, the Abbey of St Otmar was founded on the site where a monk named Gallus (c.560–650) – later canonized as St Gall – built a hermit's shelter for himself in 612.

Crypt
Beneath the cathedral is the crypt of the earlier church.

★ **Choir Stalls**
The Baroque choir stalls (1763–70), made of walnut and decorated with painting and gilding, are by Franz Joseph Anton Feuchtmayer and Franz Joseph Stälzer.

Key Dates

c.720 An abbey is founded by a priest named Otmar.

816–37 A Benedictine abbey with basilica is built.

937 The abbey is severely damaged by fire.

1529 The people of St Gallen expel the monks.

1532 The monks return.

1755–67 The Baroque Episcopal church is built.

1758–67 The Abbey Library is constructed.

1805 Dissolution of the monastery.

1824 The Episcopal church is elevated to the status of a cathedral.

1983 St Gallen Monastery becomes a UNESCO World Heritage Site.

Baroque Style

Baroque was the style that predominated for much of the 17th and early 18th centuries. Whereas in Italy the golden age of Baroque was the High Baroque of 1630–80, Germany saw a flourishing of Late Baroque well beyond 1700. The hallmarks of Baroque architecture are its preference for dynamic, curvaceous forms and broken gables; its *Gesamtkunstwerk*, or fusion of the arts to create an exuberant whole; and its liberal use of ornamentation and sculpture.

St Gallen Monastery

RUDOLF THE FOUNDER

In 1359, Duke Rudolf IV of Austria, later known as Rudolf the Founder, laid the foundation stone for the Gothic enlargement of what was then a Romanesque church (▷ *Romanesque Style p122*). Born in 1339, Rudolf became a duke in 1358 and campaigned tirelessly to have St Stephen's Church granted its independence from the Bishop of Passau and elevated to the status of a cathedral. But it was not until 1469 that Vienna, under Frederick III, became a diocese in its own right. On Rudolf's death in 1365 a monument to him was placed in front of the ▷ *High Altar*. In 1945, it was moved to the Ladies' Choir. Rudolf is buried in the ducal vault next to his wife, Katharina.

The catacombs

CATACOMBS

The extensive ▷ *catacombs* beneath St Stephen's Cathedral were excavated around 1470 to relieve pressure on Vienna's main cemetery. For the next 300 years, the people of Vienna were interred here and by the time Emperor Joseph II put a stop to the practice in 1783, some 10,000 people had been laid to rest in the catacombs. At the heart of the complex is the Habsburg Vault built by Rudolf IV in 1363. This houses 15 sarcophagi belonging to the early Habsburgs and 56 urns, which contain the entrails of the later Habsburgs who, from 1633 onwards, were buried in the imperial vault of the Capuchin Monastery Church. Vienna's archbishops are interred beneath the Apostles' Choir in the Episcopal vault, completed in 1953.

St Stephen's Cathedral, Vienna

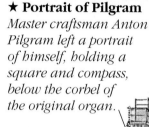

Carving of Rudolf IV

Sɪᴛᴜᴀᴛᴇᴅ ɪɴ ᴛʜᴇ medieval centre of Vienna, St Stephen's Cathedral is the soul of the city itself; it is no coincidence that the urns containing the entrails of some of the Habsburgs lie in a vault beneath its main altar. A church has stood on the site for more than 800 years, but all that remains of the original 13th-century Romanesque structure are the Giants' Doorway and Heathen Towers. The Gothic nave, choir and side chapels are the result of a major rebuilding programme in the 14th and 15th centuries (▷ *Gothic Style p55*). The lofty vaulted interior contains an impressive collection of works of art spanning several centuries.

STAR FEATURES

- ★ **Portrait of Pilgram**
- ★ **Singer Gate**
- ★ **Steffl or Spire**
- ★ **Tiled Roof**

The symbolic number "O5" of the Austrian Resistance Movement was carved here in 1945.

★ **Portrait of Pilgram**
Master craftsman Anton Pilgram left a portrait of himself, holding a square and compass, below the corbel of the original organ.

The Heathen Towers and Giant's Doorway stand on the site of an earlier heathen shrine.

The North Tower, according to legend, was never completed because its master builder, Hans Puchsbaum, broke a pact he had made with the devil, by pronouncing a holy name. The devil then caused him to fall to his death.

Entrance to the catacombs

Main entrance

Pilgram's Pulpit

Lower Vestry

★ **Singer Gate**
This was once the entrance for male visitors. A sculpted relief above the door depicts scenes from the life of St Paul.

★ Steffl or Spire

The 137-m high (450-ft) Gothic spire is a famous landmark. From the Sexton's Lodge, it is possible to climb the stairs as far as a viewing platform.

TOOTHACHE FIGURE

According to legend, the "Zahnwehherrgott", a sculpture of a man in agony, punished those who ridiculed him by inflicting them with toothache. Only when they atoned for their sins did the pain subside. The figure is located beneath the ▷ North Tower.

★ Tiled Roof

Almost a quarter of a million glazed tiles cover the roof; they were meticulously restored after the damage caused in the last days of World War II.

Wiener Neustädter Altar

Friedrich III commissioned the elaborate altarpiece in 1447. Painted panels open out to reveal an earlier carved interior of the life of Christ. This panel shows the Adoration of the Magi *(1420).*

The High Altar is adorned with an altarpiece by Tobias Pock showing the martyrdom of St Stephen.

KEY DATES

1137–47 The first Romanesque church is built.

1304 Work begins on a Gothic choir.

1433 The south tower is completed.

1556–78 The dome is added to the north tower.

1722 The church is elevated to cathedral status.

1945–60 Reconstruction of the cathedral after it was severely damaged during World War II.

2001 The historic centre of Vienna, including St Stephen's Cathedral, becomes a UNESCO World Heritage Site.

ANTON PILGRAM

One of the cathedral's foremost craftsmen was Anton Pilgram, a master-builder from Brünn (c.1460–1515). His sandstone ▷ *pulpit* (1514–15) inside the nave contains portraits of the Four Fathers of the Church (theologians representing four physiognomic temperaments) and is considered a masterpiece of late-Gothic stone sculpture. Pilgram even included a portrait of himself as a "watcher at the window" beneath the pulpit steps. There is another ▷ *portrait of Pilgram* in the cathedral. Here, the builder and sculptor is shown peeping through a window into the church. Pilgram signed this work with the monogram "MAP 1513".

JOHANNES CAPISTRANO

On the exterior northeastern wall of the choir is a pulpit built after the victory over the Turks at Belgrade in 1456. It was from here that the Italian Franciscan, Johannes Capistrano (1386–1456), is said to have preached against the Turkish invasion while on a visit to Austria in 1451. Capistrano had trained as a lawyer. He was appointed governor of Perugia, but while on a peace mission to the neighbouring state of Malatesta he was imprisoned. After some soul-searching and the appearance of St Francis in a dream, he joined the Franciscans and became a priest in 1425. In 1454 he assembled troops for the successful crusade against the Turks. This event is depicted in the 18th-century statue above the pulpit showing Capistrano trampling on a Turkish invader. He was canonized in 1690.

Baroque statue of St Johannes Capistrano

Schönbrunn Palace, Vienna

THE FORMER SUMMER RESIDENCE of the imperial Habsburg family takes its name from a beautiful spring found on the site. Leopold I asked Johann Bernhard Fischer von Erlach to design a grand residence here in 1695, but it was not until Empress Maria Theresa employed the Rococo architect Nikolaus Pacassi in the mid-18th century that it was completed (▷*Rococo Style p72*). Glorious gardens complement the architecture.

**Empress
Maria Theresa**

MARIA THERESA

The daughter of Emperor Charles VI, Maria Theresa (1717–80) became Archduchess of Austria and Queen of Hungary and Bohemia on her father's death in 1740. Five years later her husband, Duke Francis Stephen of Lorraine, was recognized as Holy Roman Emperor. Maria Theresa instigated numerous reforms in the spirit of the Enlightenment. She initiated state-supported elementary schools, introduced a new penal code and reduced taxation. She also worked towards unifying Habsburg lands by centralizing control over the empire. Among her 16 children was Marie Antoinette, who married Louis XVI of France.

PREVIOUS PALACES

Schönbrunn stands on the site of the Katterburg, a 14th-century castle that belonged to the Neuburg Convent. By the time Emperor Maximilian II bought the property in 1569, it included a mansion, mill and stables. Maximilian intended to turn it into a pleasure palace and zoo, and indeed a palace was finally built in the mid-17th century by the widow of Emperor Ferdinand II. She named it "Schönbrunn" after the "Schönen Brunnen" ("beautiful spring"), discovered by Emperor Matthew II, while hunting on the estate in 1612. This first palace was destroyed by the Turks during the siege of Vienna in 1683. Emperor Leopold I acquired the estate in 1686 and commissioned today's palace.

Round Chinese Cabinet
Maria Theresa used this white and gold room for private discussions with her State Chancellor, Prince Kaunitz. The walls are adorned with lacquered panels.

★ Great Gallery
Used for imperial banquets, the gallery has a lovely ceiling fresco by Gregorio Guglielmi.

A hidden staircase leads to the apartment of the State Chancellor, above which he had secret conferences with the Empress.

Blue Chinese Salon
The last Austrian emperor, Karl I, signed his abdication in 1918 in this Rococo room with its Chinese scenes.

Chapel

Napoleon Room

The Millions' Room, featuring superb Rococo decor, was Maria Theresa's conference room.

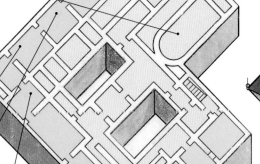

★ Vieux-Lacque Room
During her widowhood Maria Theresa lived in this room, which is decorated with exquisite oriental lacquered panels.

Main entrance

Breakfast Room
The imperial family's breakfast room has white wood panelling inlaid with appliqué floral designs worked by Maria Theresa and her daughters.

A MILITARY MAN

When visiting Schönbrunn, Emperor Franz Joseph I would sleep in a simple, iron-framed bed, as befit a man who felt more at home in the field. He died at the palace in 1916, after nearly 68 years on the throne.

CZECH REPUBLIC

SCHÖNBRUNN PALACE, VIENNA

GERMANY
• Salzburg

Innsbruck •

AUSTRIA

ITALY
SLOVENIA

CROATIA

KEY DATES

1696 Work begins on Emperor Leopold I's residence.

1728 Emperor Charles VI purchases Schönbrunn and later makes a gift of it to his daughter, Maria Theresa.

1743–63 Nikolaus Pacassi enlarges the palace in the Rococo style.

1775–80 Johann Ferdinand Hetzendorf von Hohenberg redesigns the park.

1880–82 The Palm House is created.

1904 The Sundial House is built.

1996 Schönbrunn becomes a UNESCO World Heritage Site.

Large Rosa Room
This is one of three rooms decorated with monumental Swiss and Italian landscape paintings by Josef Rosa, after whom the room is named.

PALACE GUIDE
On the first floor, the suite of rooms to the right of the Blue Staircase was occupied by Franz Joseph I and Elisabeth. The rooms in the east wing include Maria Theresa's bedroom and rooms used by Grand Duke Karl.

STAR FEATURES

★ **Great Gallery**

★ **Vieux-Lacque Room**

The Billiard Room is the first of a suite of rooms that provide a glimpse of Emperor Franz Joseph's life at the palace.

The Blue Staircase is so-called because of its original decorative scheme.

KEY

- Franz Joseph I's apartments
- Empress Elisabeth's apartments
- Ceremonial and reception rooms
- Maria Theresa's rooms
- Grand Duke Karl's rooms
- Closed to visitors

THE COACH MUSEUM

One wing of Schönbrunn Palace, formerly housing the Winter Riding School, now contains a marvellous collection of coaches – one of the most interesting in the world. It includes more than 60 carriages dating back to the 17th century, as well as riding uniforms, horse tack, saddles, coachmen's liveries, and paintings and drawings of horses and carriages. The pride of the collection is the coronation coach of Emperor Charles VI. Exhibits include sleighs and sedan chairs belonging to Maria Theresa, among others.

Coronation coach of Charles VI

CEREMONIAL STATE ROOMS

As architect to the court of Empress Maria Theresa, Nikolaus Pacassi oversaw the enlargement and redesigning of Schönbrunn. Together with Rococo artists and craftsmen such as Albert Bolla, Gregorio Guglielmi, Isidor Canevale and Thaddaeus Adam Karner, Pacassi was responsible for creating the interiors of both the state rooms and the private quarters. The ▷ *Large Rosa Room* and the ▷ *Millions' Room*, for example, feature frescoes and stuccowork in the Rococo style commissioned by Maria Theresa herself. The palace is renowned for its intricate gilded stuccowork, elegant mirrored galleries and exotic chinoiserie.

Royal Castle

INSIDE THE CASTLE

The Royal Castle's fascinating interiors are the result of its dual role: both as a royal residence and as the seat of the *Sejm* (Parliament). A tour of the castle features lavish royal apartments as well as the ▷ *Deputies' Chamber* and the Senate. Throughout it has been meticulously reconstructed in the style of the 18th century, and many of the furnishings and *objets d'art* are original to the castle. These include statues, paintings and even fragments of woodwork and stucco, notably used in the New Audience Room, which were rescued from the building and hidden during World War II. The ▷ *Canaletto Room* displays 18th-century paintings of Warsaw by the Italian artist that were used as source material for the rebuilding of the Old Town of Warsaw and the castle.

THE GALLERIES

Among the many permanent exhibitions in the castle, two galleries are of particular interest. The Gallery of Decorative Arts, opened in 1998, is a showcase for 17th- and 18th-century ceramics, glass, furniture, textiles, bronzes, silverware and jewellery. Around 200 pieces are on display including an Etruscan vase saved from the original castle. In the ▷ *Lanckoroński Gallery* there are paintings from the former royal gallery of King Stanisław August Poniatowski, donated by the Lanckoroński family in 1994. The collection includes works by Rembrandt, Teniers the Younger and Anton von Maron.

The New Audience Room featuring original stucco-work

Royal Castle, Warsaw

Tabletop from 1777

A GRAND EXAMPLE of Baroque architecture, the original Royal Castle (Zamek Królewski) was planned on the site of a Mazovian fortress when Zygmunt III Vasa decided to move the capital from Cracow to Warsaw in 1596. It was designed in the early Baroque manner (▷ *Baroque Style p81*) by the Italian architects Giovanni Trevano, Giacomo Rodondo and Matteo Castelli between 1598 and 1619. Successive rulers remodelled the castle many times. Following its destruction during World War II, the castle was rebuilt between 1971 and 1984, and many of the original furnishings were returned. This massive undertaking was funded largely by donations from the Polish people.

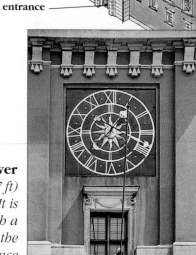

★ **Ballroom**
Decorated with 17 pairs of golden columns, the ballroom is one of the castle's most elaborate interiors.

Royal Princes' Rooms
Historical paintings by Jan Matejko are displayed here.

Deputies' Chamber
In this room, the Constitution of 3 May was formally adopted in 1791. The coats of arms of all the administrative regions and territories of the Republic are depicted on the walls. A reconstructed royal throne is also on show.

Main entrance

STAR FEATURES

★ **Ballroom**

★ **Marble Room**

★ **Canaletto Room**

Zygmunt Tower
This tower, 60 m (197 ft) high, was built in 1619. It is crowned by a cupola with a spire. It is also known as the Clock Tower (Zegarowa), since a clock was installed in 1622.

★ **Marble Room**
The interior dates from the time of Władysław IV Vasa (r.1632–48). The magnificent portraits of Polish rulers by Marcello Bacciarelli are the only later additions.

The Lanckoroński Gallery on the second floor contains two paintings by Rembrandt: *Portrait of a Young Woman* and *Scholar at his Desk.*

Knights' Hall
The finest piece in this beautiful interior is the Neo-Classical sculpture of Chronos by le Brun and Monaldi.

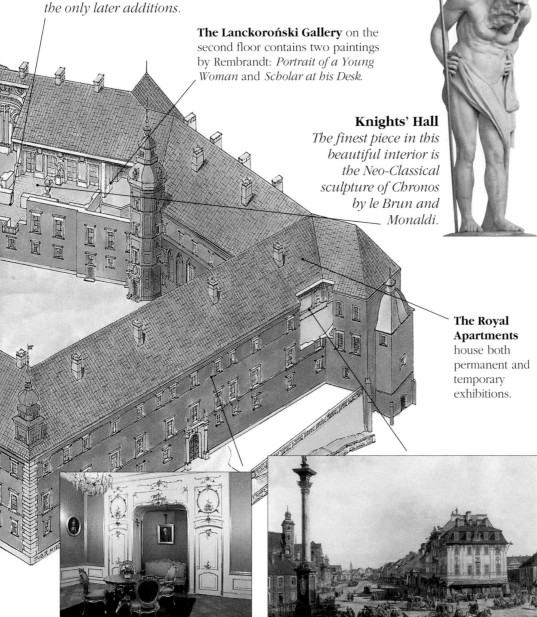

The Royal Apartments house both permanent and temporary exhibitions.

KEY DATES

Early 1300s The dukes of Mazovia build a fortress on the site of the Royal Castle.

1598 Construction begins on the Baroque addition.

1939–44 The Royal Castle is destroyed in World War II.

1980 The rebuilt Old Town of Warsaw, including the Royal Castle, is designated a UNESCO World Heritage Site.

1984 The restored Royal Castle opens to the public.

POLAND'S LAST KING

Born in 1732, King Stanisław August Poniatowski (r.1764–95) was the son of the palatine of Mazovia. He spent his early life in St Petersburg where he was introduced to the future empress, Catherine the Great, who took him as her lover. Russia was keen to add Poland to its empire and perhaps to this end, Catherine promised the Polish crown to Poniatowski. When he fell out of favour and was sent back to Warsaw she was true to her word and in 1764 engineered his election as king of Poland. As king he notably introduced economic reforms, promoted the arts and sciences and presided over the adoption of the Constitution of 3 May 1791. But he was unable to repel his mighty neighbours: the country was partitioned between Russia, Prussia and Austria and by 1795 Poland had lost its statehood. The king abdicated and died in St Petersburg in 1798.

Apartment of Prince Stanisław Poniatowski
The Rococo panelling, thought to be by Juste-Aurèle Meissonier, was taken from the former Tarnowski Palace.

★ **Canaletto Room**
The walls of this room are decorated with scenes of Warsaw by Canaletto, the Venetian painter who was one of the most commercially successful artists of his day.

Royal Castle

THE INTERIOR

This Gothic hall, with its distinctive crenellated gable, has been a house of prayer for over 700 years. Its twin-nave has a ribbed, vaulted ceiling. To avoid the sign of the cross, a fifth rib was added (▷ *five-rib vaulting*) and decorated with vine leaves, symbolizing the fertility of the land, and ivy. In a two-storey building the women's gallery would be upstairs, but here it is located in the vestibule. The number 12 recurs in features throughout the synagogue, probably a reference to the 12 tribes of Israel.

The Old-New Synagogue and the Jewish Town Hall

THE JEWISH GHETTO

The Old-New Synagogue stands in Josefov, once Prague's Jewish Ghetto. The area is named after Emperor Josef II, who partially relaxed the discrimination against Jews during his reign in the 18th century. For centuries Prague's Jews had suffered from oppressive laws – in the 16th century they had to wear a yellow circle as a mark of shame. In the 1890s the ghetto slums were razed, but a handful of buildings survived, including the Jewish Town Hall and a number of synagogues. During World War II the Nazis occupied Prague and almost two-thirds of the city's Jewish population perished in the Holocaust, mainly in Terezín concentration camp, situated northwest of Prague.

Old-New Synagogue, Prague

Star of David in Červená Street

BUILT AROUND 1270, this is the oldest surviving synagogue in Europe and one of the earliest Gothic buildings in Prague (▷ *Gothic Style p55*). The synagogue has survived fires, slum clearances in the 19th century and several Jewish pogroms. Residents of the city's Jewish Quarter (Josefov) have often had to seek refuge within its walls and today it is the religious centre for Prague's Jewish community. It was originally called the New Synagogue until another synagogue was built nearby – this was later destroyed.

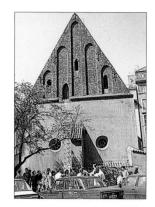

The synagogue's eastern side

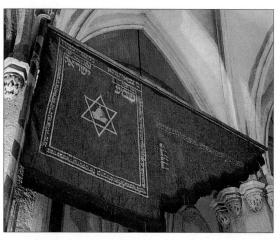

★ **Jewish Standard**
The historic banner of Prague's Jews is decorated with a Star of David and within it the hat that had to be worn by Jews in the 14th century.

These windows formed part of the 18th-century extensions built to allow women a view of the service.

RABBI LÖW AND THE GOLEM

The scholar and philosophical writer Rabbi Löw, director of the Talmudic school (which studied the Torah) in the late 16th century,

was also thought to possess magical powers. He was supposed to have created a figure, the Golem, from clay and then brought it to life by placing a magic stone tablet in its mouth. The Golem went berserk and the Rabbi had to remove the tablet. He hid the creature among the Old-New Synagogue's rafters.

14th-century stepped brick gable

Candlestick holder

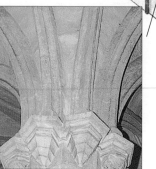

★ **Five-rib Vaulting**
Two massive octagonal pillars inside the hall support the five-rib vaults.

Old-New Synagogue

Right-hand Nave
The glow from the bronze chandeliers provides light for worshippers using the seats lining the walls.

OLD JEWISH CEMETERY

Near the Old-New Synagogue is the Old Jewish Cemetery. For over 300 years, this was the only burial ground permitted for Jews. Over 100,000 people are estimated to be buried here. The oldest gravestone dates from 1439, and the last burial was in 1787.

The tympanum above the Ark is decorated with 13th-century leaf carvings.

★ **Rabbi Löw's Chair**
A Star of David marks the chair of the Chief Rabbi, placed where the distinguished 16th-century scholar used to sit.

The cantor's platform and its lectern are surrounded by a wrought-iron Gothic grille.

Entrance to the Synagogue

Entrance Portal
The tympanum above the door in the south vestibule is decorated with clusters of grapes and vine leaves growing on twisted branches.

The Ark
This shrine is the holiest place in the synagogue and holds the sacred scrolls of the Torah.

STAR FEATURES

★ **Jewish Standard**

★ **Five-rib Vaulting**

★ **Rabbi Löw's Chair**

KEY DATES

Mid- to late 13th century Work starts on building the New Synagogue.

18th century Construction of the women's gallery on the western and northern sides of the synagogue.

1883 The architect Joseph Mocker begins renovation work on the building.

1992 The Historic Centre of Prague becomes a UNESCO World Heritage Site.

WORSHIPPING IN THE SYNAGOGUE

The Old-New Synagogue is one of three synagogues in Prague where services are held today. Admonishing worshippers on their way into the synagogue are the following words inscribed on the ▷ *entrance portal*: "Revere God and observe his commandments! For this applies to all mankind". Inside, men and women are segregated for religious rituals. Services are held in the main prayer hall and are reserved for men only; those attending must keep their heads covered. Women may follow the rituals from the adjacent women's gallery, where they can stand and watch through small slot ▷ *windows*. In the centre of the hall is the *bima*, similar to a wrought-iron cage, with a lectern from which the Torah is read daily (▷ *the cantor's platform*). Above this is a red ▷ *Jewish Standard*, which is a copy of the 1716 original.

THE SCULPTORS

Matthias Braun (1684–1738), who was born near Innsbruck and learned his craft in Austria and Italy, came to Prague in 1710. His first work, the statue of ▷ *St Luitgard*, was produced when he was only 26. Other sculptors were Johann Brokoff (1652–1718), of German origin, and his sons Michael and Ferdinand. The latter produced some of the bridge's most dynamic figures, such as ▷ *St Adalbert*, and his statue of ▷ *St Francis Xavier* which shows the Jesuit missionary supported by three Moorish and two Oriental converts.

EMULATING ROME

Charles Bridge was named after Charles IV, crowned Holy Roman Emperor in 1355, who wanted the bridge to echo the ancient Rome of the Caesars. However, it was not until the late 17th century that statues inspired by Roman sculptures were placed on the bridge. The statues mainly depict saints including ▷ *St Vitus*, the bridge's patron saint. Cherubs, dice and a centurion's gauntlet form part of the statue of the ▷ *Madonna and St Bernard*. Nearby, the Dominicans are shown with the Madonna and their emblem, a dog (▷ *The Madonna, St Dominic and St Thomas*).

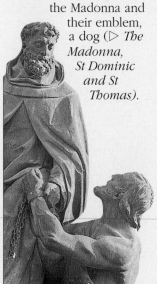

Detail from the statue of St John de Matha, St Felix de Valois and the Blessed Ivan

Charles Bridge, Prague

Prague's most familiar monument, connecting the city's Old Town with the Little Quarter, was the city's only crossing over the Vltava river until 1741. It is 520 m (1,706 ft) long and built of sandstone blocks. Now pedestrianized, at one time it could take four carriages abreast. Today, due to wear and tear, many of the statues are copies. The Gothic Old Town Bridge Tower (▷ *Gothic Style p55*) is one of the finest buildings of its kind.

LITTLE QUARTER SIDE

Little Quarter Bridge Tower

Tower entrance

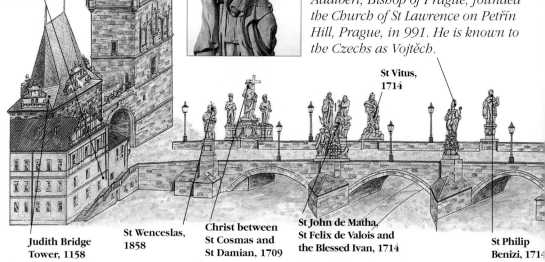

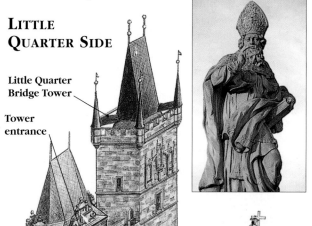

Judith Bridge Tower, 1158

St Wenceslas, 1858

Christ between St Cosmas and St Damian, 1709

St John de Matha, St Felix de Valois and the Blessed Ivan, 1714

St Vitus, 1714

St Philip Benizi, 1714

OLD TOWN SIDE

Thirty Years' War
In the last hours of this war, the Old Town was saved from the invading Swedish army. The truce was signed in the middle of the bridge in 1648.

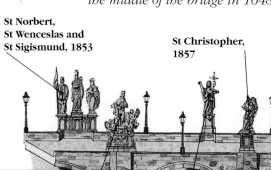

St Norbert, St Wenceslas and St Sigismund, 1853

St Christopher, 1857

St Francis Borgia, 1710

St John the Baptist, 1857

St Cyril and St Methodius, 1938

St Ann, 1707

St Francis Xavier, 1711

St Joseph, 1854

View from Little Quarter Bridge Tower
The tall pinnacled wedge tower gives a superb view of the city of 100 spires.

St Adalbert, 1709
Adalbert, Bishop of Prague, founded the Church of St Lawrence on Petřín Hill, Prague, in 991. He is known to the Czechs as Vojtěch.

★ **St Luitgard, 1710**
This statue, sculpted by Matthias Braun, is based on a blind Cistercian nun's celebrated vision in which Christ appeared and permitted her to kiss his wounds.

A VITAL INGREDIENT

Large quantities of egg white were needed to strengthen the mortar used in building the bridge and Emperor Charles IV asked everyone with chickens to supply eggs for this purpose. Legend has it that one village misunderstood and sent wagonloads of useless hard-boiled eggs.

St John Nepomuk, 1683
Reliefs on the bridge depict the martyrdom of St John Nepomuk. Here the saint is polished bright from people touching it for good luck.

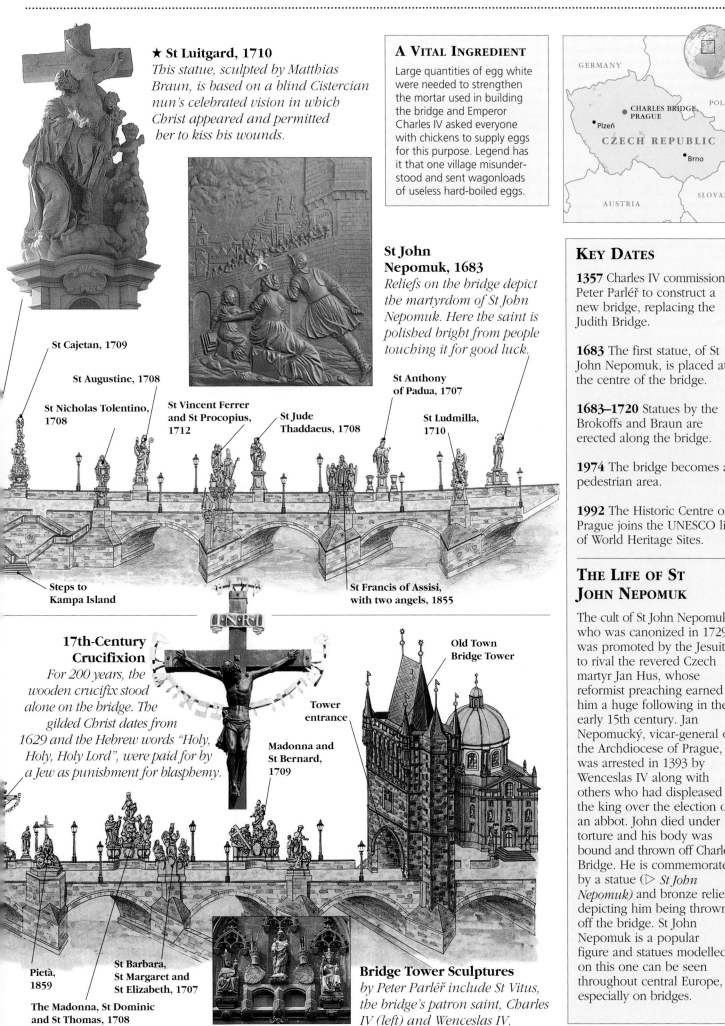

St Cajetan, 1709

St Augustine, 1708

St Nicholas Tolentino, 1708

St Vincent Ferrer and St Procopius, 1712

St Jude Thaddaeus, 1708

St Anthony of Padua, 1707

St Ludmilla, 1710

Steps to Kampa Island

St Francis of Assisi, with two angels, 1855

17th-Century Crucifixion
For 200 years, the wooden crucifix stood alone on the bridge. The gilded Christ dates from 1629 and the Hebrew words "Holy, Holy, Holy Lord", were paid for by a Jew as punishment for blasphemy.

Madonna and St Bernard, 1709

Tower entrance

Old Town Bridge Tower

Pietà, 1859

St Barbara, St Margaret and St Elizabeth, 1707

The Madonna, St Dominic and St Thomas, 1708

Bridge Tower Sculptures
by Peter Parléř include St Vitus, the bridge's patron saint, Charles IV (left) and Wenceslas IV.

KEY DATES

1357 Charles IV commissions Peter Parléř to construct a new bridge, replacing the Judith Bridge.

1683 The first statue, of St John Nepomuk, is placed at the centre of the bridge.

1683–1720 Statues by the Brokoffs and Braun are erected along the bridge.

1974 The bridge becomes a pedestrian area.

1992 The Historic Centre of Prague joins the UNESCO list of World Heritage Sites.

THE LIFE OF ST JOHN NEPOMUK

The cult of St John Nepomuk, who was canonized in 1729, was promoted by the Jesuits to rival the revered Czech martyr Jan Hus, whose reformist preaching earned him a huge following in the early 15th century. Jan Nepomucký, vicar-general of the Archdiocese of Prague, was arrested in 1393 by Wenceslas IV along with others who had displeased the king over the election of an abbot. John died under torture and his body was bound and thrown off Charles Bridge. He is commemorated by a statue (▷ *St John Nepomuk*) and bronze relief depicting him being thrown off the bridge. St John Nepomuk is a popular figure and statues modelled on this one can be seen throughout central Europe, especially on bridges.

Charles Bridge

IMRE STEINDL

Professor of architecture at Hungary's Technical University, Imre Steindl (1839–1902) won the competition to design Hungary's Parliament. The building was to symbolize the country's thriving democracy. Steindl drew inspiration from Charles Barry and A W Pugin's Neo-Gothic Houses of Parliament in London. However, for the internal spaces, including the superb ▷ *Dome Hall*, he used references from the Baroque (▷ *Baroque Style p81*) and Renaissance (▷ *Renaissance Style p131*) styles as well.

Parliament building's exterior adorned with lace-like pinnacles

SACRED CROWN OF ST STEPHEN I

The first Hungarian king, St Stephen I (c.975–1038), received the royal crown from Pope Sylvester II in the year 1000. The crown became a symbol of Christianity and all Hungarian kings who followed after Stephen I were crowned with the sacred diadem. Many today believe that the crown bears little resemblance to the original crown, because over the centuries it has been lost and stolen. Battles and wars have also been fought for possession of the crown. At the end of World War II it was taken to America for safekeeping and returned to Hungary with much fanfare in 1978. The crown now resides in Hungary's Parliament.

Parliament, Budapest

IMRE STEINDL's rich Neo-Gothic Parliament (▷ *Gothic Style p55*) is Hungary's largest building and a symbol of Budapest. Hungarian materials, techniques and master craftsmen were used in its construction. The building is 268 m (880 ft) long and 96 m (315 ft) high. The north wing houses the offices of Hungary's Prime Minister, while the south wing contains those of the President of the Republic.

One of the pair of lions at the main entrance

Aerial View
The magnificent dome marks the central point of the Parliament building. Although the façade is elaborately Neo-Gothic, the ground plan follows Baroque conventions.

★ Dome Hall
Adorning the massive pillars that support Parliament's central dome are figures of some of the rulers of Hungary.

Façade facing River Danube

★ National Assembly Hall
Formerly the upper house, this hall is now where the National Assembly convenes. Two paintings by Zsigmond Vajada hang on either side of the Speaker's lectern. These were especially commissioned for the building.

South wing

Gables
Almost every corner of the Parliament building features gables with pinnacles based on Gothic sculptures.

Lobby
Lobbies, the venues for political discussions, line the corridors lit by stained-glass windows.

Dome
The ceiling of the 96-m (315-ft) high dome is covered in an intricate design of Neo-Gothic gilding combined with heraldic decoration.

PARLIAMENT VASE
In 1954, the Herend Porcelain Manufacturers made the first Parliament Vase. It stood in the ▷ *Dome Hall* for ten years and was then moved to the Herend Museum. A new vase was created in 2000 to mark Hungary's 1000 years of Statehood.

Gobelin Hall
This hall is decorated with a Gobelin tapestry illustrating Prince Árpád, with seven Magyar leaders under his command, signing a peace treaty and blood oath.

North wing

Main Entrance

The Royal Insignia, excluding the Coronation Mantle, are kept in the Dome Hall.

STAR FEATURES
★ **Dome Hall**

★ **National Assembly Hall**

Congress Hall
This vast hall is virtually a mirror image of the National Assembly Hall. Both halls have public galleries running around a horseshoe-shaped interior.

Main Staircase
The best contemporary artists were invited to decorate the interior. The sumptuous main staircase features ceiling frescoes by Károly Lotz and sculptures by György Kiss.

KEY DATES
1882 Imre Steindl wins the competition for the design of the Parliament building.

1885 The first foundation stone is laid as construction of the Parliament building begins.

1902 Work on the Parliament building is completed.

1987 The historical area of Budapest, which includes the Parliament building, is inscribed a UNESCO World Heritage Site.

PARLIAMENT'S STATUES
Surrounding the external façade of Parliament are 90 statues, which include some of Hungary's past monarchs, writers, revolutionaries and Prime Ministers. A statue of the Transylvanian prince, Ferenc Rákóczi II (1676–1735), who fought the Habsburgs for Hungary's freedom, is at the southern end. Nearby is a seated statue of the Hungarian writer József Attila (1905–37). His first collection of poems was published at the age of 17. Adorning the ▷ *north wing* is the statue of Lajos Kossuth (1802–94), who fought for Hungary's independence for six months in 1849 before being driven into exile. Next to Kossuth's statue is that of the democratic Prime Minister and revolutionary, Mihály Károlyi (1875–1955). He ruled Hungary for five months in 1919 until he was forced into exile, after the government was overthrown by the Communists.

Parliament

THE SMALL AND LARGE HERMITAGE

Catherine hired architect Yuriy Velten to erect the Small Hermitage so she could privately entertain her chosen friends at court. The building was designed in the Late Baroque style with Early Classical features to blend alongside Rastrelli's Baroque Winter Palace. After the Small Hermitage was constructed, Catherine decided to house her newly acquired collection of over 255 paintings in the building as well. The Large Hermitage was built a few years later to accommodate the tsarina's vast library and works of art. Over the centuries, Catherine's original collection has been added to. There are now over 3 million pieces of art displayed in the Small and Large Hermitage, as well as in an ensemble of buildings, which includes the Winter Palace. There are exhibits from the Stone Age up to the 20th century, including works by Matisse, Rembrandt and Cézanne.

BARTOLOMEO RASTRELLI

The Italian architect Rastrelli (1700–71) studied under his father and assisted him during his appointment as architect for Tsar Peter I. In 1722 Rastrelli took on his own commissions in Moscow and St Petersburg, which established him as a brilliant Baroque architect. During Elizabeth's reign, he was appointed Chief Court Architect and went on to design several buildings, including the grandiose Winter Palace. When Catherine the Great ascended the throne, Rastrelli retired from court as she preferred a stricter Classical design.

Rastrelli, court architect until 1763

The Winter Palace, St Petersburg

THIS SUPERB EXAMPLE of Baroque architecture (▷ *Baroque Style p81*)was the home of the Russian tsars and tsarinas from the late 18th century, including Catherine the Great. Built for Tsarina Elizabeth (r.1741–62), this opulent winter residence was the finest achievement of Italian architect Bartolomeo Rastrelli. Though the exterior has changed little, the interiors were altered by a number of architects and then largely restored after a fire gutted the palace in 1837. After the assassination of Alexander II in 1881, the imperial family rarely lived here. In July 1917, the Provisional Government took the palace as its headquarters, which led to its storming by the Bolsheviks.

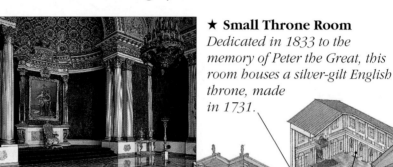

★ Small Throne Room
Dedicated in 1833 to the memory of Peter the Great, this room houses a silver-gilt English throne, made in 1731.

The 1812 Gallery (1826) has portraits of Russian military heroes of the Napoleonic War, most by English artist George Dawe.

The Armorial Hall (1839), with its vast gilded columns, covers over 800 sq m (8,600 sq ft). It now houses the European silver collection and a restored imperial carriage.

The Field Marshals' Hall (1833) was the reception room where the devastating fire of 1837 broke out.

To Large Hermitage ↓

The Hall of St George (1795) has monolithic columns and wall facings of Italian Carrara marble.

The Nicholas Hall, the largest room in the palace, was always used for the first ball of the season.

North façade overlooking the River Neva

★ Jordan Staircase
This vast, sweeping staircase (1762) was Rastrelli's masterpiece. It was from here that the imperial family watched the Epiphany ceremony of baptism in the Neva, which celebrated Christ's baptism in the Jordan.

★ Malachite Room
Over two tonnes of ornamental stone were used in this sumptuous room (1839) which is decorated with malachite columns and vases, gilded doors and rich parquet flooring.

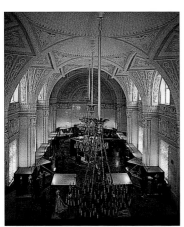

Alexander Hall
Architect Aleksandr Bryullov employed a mixture of Gothic vaulting and Neo-Classical stucco bas-reliefs of military themes in this reception room of 1837.

STORMING THE PALACE
On the evening of 25 October 1917, the Bolsheviks fired some blank shots at the Winter Palace, storming it soon after to arrest the Provisional Government who resided there. The communists took over power and the Revolution was a fact.

The White Hall
was decorated for the wedding of the future Alexander II in 1841.

The French Rooms, designed by Bryullov in 1839, house a collection of 18th-century French art.

South façade on Palace Square

Dark Corridor
The French and Flemish tapestries here include The Marriage of Emperor Constantine, *made in Paris in the 17th century to designs by Rubens.*

KEY DATES

1754–62 The Winter Palace is constructed.

1764–75 The Small Hermitage by Yuriy Velten is built for Catherine II's art collection.

1771–87 The Large Hermitage, also by Yuriy Velten, is added.

1917 Anatoly Lunacharsky of the Soviet Government declares the Winter Palace and the Hermitage state museums.

1990 The historical city of St Petersburg, which includes the Winter Palace and the Hermitage, is inscribed a UNESCO World Heritage Site.

CATHERINE II

Tsarina Elizabeth chose the German-born princess Catherine (1729–96), the future Catherine the Great, as a wife for her successor Peter III. When he ascended the throne in 1762, Catherine had resided in Russia for 18 years and had fully immersed herself in the Russian culture. She was also widely read and corresponded with French intellectuals such as Voltaire and Diderot. Six months into Peter's reign, Catherine and her allies at the Imperial Guard had the tsar killed. She was then crowned ruler of Russia in 1763. During her reign she implemented many reforms and expanded the Russian territory. Art and trade flourished and new academies were built, including the Russian Academy of Sciences and the Academy of Fine Art.

The Rotunda (1830) connected the private apartments in the west with the state apartments on the palace's north side.

West wing

The Gothic Library and other rooms in the northwest part of the palace were adapted to suit Nicholas II's bourgeois lifestyle. This wood-panelled library was created by Meltzer in 1894.

The Gold Drawing Room
Created in the 1850s, this room was extravagantly decorated in the 1870s with all-over gilding of walls and ceiling. It houses a display of Western European carved gems.

STAR FEATURES

★ **Small Throne Room**

★ **Jordan Staircase**

★ **Malachite Room**

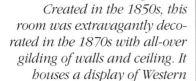

The Winter Palace

St Basil's Cathedral, Moscow

Detail, Chapel of the Entry of Christ into Jerusalem

R EGARDED AS ONE OF THE MOST beautiful monuments to the Russian Orthodox Church, St Basil's has come to represent Moscow and Russia to the outside world. Commissioned by Ivan the Terrible to celebrate the capture of the Mongol stronghold of Kazan in 1552, the cathedral was completed in 1561. It is reputed to have been designed by the architect Postnik Yakovlev. According to legend, Ivan was so amazed at the beauty of Postnik's work that he had him blinded so that he could never design anything as exquisite again. The church was officially called the Cathedral of the Intercession because the final siege of Kazan began on the Feast of the Intercession of the Virgin. However, it is more usually known as St Basil's after the "holy fool" Basil the Blessed whose remains are interred here in the cathedral's ninth chapel.

BASIL, THE "HOLY FOOL"

Born in 1464 into a peasant family in the village of Yelokhovoe, Basil worked as an apprentice in a shoemakers. His skill at divining the future soon became apparent and at the age of 16 he left for Moscow. There he undertook the ascetic challenge of walking the city's streets barefooted, educating Muscovites in piety. Although he was often derided and beaten for his sermonizing, his fortune changed in 1547 when he foresaw the fire of Moscow and was credited with preventing it from destroying the entire city. On Basil's death, at the age of 88, Tsar Ivan the Terrible carried his body to the cathedral for burial. He was canonized in 1579.

Colourful, onion-shaped dome, part of the façade of St Basil's

CATHEDRAL DESIGN

St Basil's Cathedral consists of nine churches dedicated to different saints. Each of these, except the ▷ *Central Chapel of the Intercession*, symbolizes the eight assaults on Kazan and is topped by a multi-coloured ▷ *dome*. All of the churches are uniquely decorated and different in size from each other, giving the structure an all-round balance. The building is designed to be viewed from every angle, hence there is no single main façade. In plan the eight churches form an eight-pointed star. The four larger domes form the endpoints of an imaginery cross with the Central Chapel in the middle, and the smaller churches between the larger ones.

★ **Domes**

Following a fire in 1583 the original helmet-shaped cupolas were replaced by ribbed or faceted onion domes. It is only since 1670 that the domes have been painted many colours; at one time St Basil's was white with golden domes.

Chapel of St Cyprian

This is one of eight main chapels commemorating the campaigns of Ivan the Terrible against the town of Kazan, to the east of Moscow. It is dedicated to St Cyprian, whose feast is on 2 October, the day after the last attack.

MININ AND POZHARSKIY

A bronze statue by Ivan Martos depicts two heroes from the Time of Troubles (1598–1613), the butcher Kuzma Minin and Prince Dmitriy Pozharskiy. They raised a volunteer force to fight the invading Poles and, in 1612, led their army to victory when they drove the Poles out of the Kremlin. The statue was erected in 1818, in the triumphal afterglow of the Napoleonic Wars. Originally placed in the centre of Red Square facing the Kremlin, it was moved to its present site in front of St Basil's during the Soviet era.

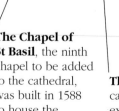

Monument to Minin and Prince Pozharskiy

Bell tower

Chapel of the Trinity

The Chapel of St Basil, the ninth chapel to be added to the cathedral, was built in 1588 to house the remains of the "holy fool", Basil the Blessed.

Chapel of the Three Patriarchs

The entrance to the cathedral contains an exhibition on its history, armour and weapons dating from the time of Ivan the Terrible.

Tent roof on the Central Chapel

Chapel of St Nicholas

Central Chapel of the Intercession
Light floods in through the windows of the tent-roofed central church, which soars to a height of 61 m (200 ft).

★ Main Iconostasis
The Baroque-style iconostasis in the Central Chapel of the Intercession dates from the 19th century. However, some of the icons contained in it were painted much earlier.

Chapel of St Varlaam of Khutynskiy

Tiered gables

Chapel of Bishop Gregory

RED SQUARE

St Basil's Cathedral is located in Red Square in the heart of Moscow. The name of the square derives from the Russian word *krasnyy*, which originally meant "beautiful" but later came to denote "red".

STAR FEATURES

★ **Domes**

★ **Main Iconostasis**

★ **Gallery**

The Chapel of the Entry of Christ into Jerusalem
was used as a ceremonial entrance during the annual Palm Sunday procession. On this day the patriarch rode from the Kremlin to St Basil's Cathedral on a horse disguised to look like a donkey.

★ Gallery
Running around the outside of the Central Chapel, the gallery connects it to the other eight chapels. It was roofed over at the end of the 17th century and the walls and ceilings were decorated with floral tiles in the late 18th century.

RUSSIA

St Petersburg

ST BASIL'S CATHEDRAL, MOSCOW

FINLAND

BELARUS

POLAND

UKRAINE

KAZAKHSTAN

KEY DATES

1555 Building work commences, and St Basil's is completed six years later.

1583 Onion-shaped domes are built to replace the original cupolas destroyed by fire.

1812 Napoleon's cavalry stable their horses in St Basil's during his invasion of Russia.

1918 Communist authorities close the cathedral down.

1923 St Basil's reopens as a museum.

1990s St Basil's Cathedral is declared a World Heritage Site in 1990, and returned to the Orthodox Church in 1991.

THE ART OF ICON PAINTING IN RUSSIA

The Russian Orthodox Church uses icons for both worship and teaching and there are strict rules for creating each image. Iconography is a symbolic art, expressing in line and colour the theological teaching of the Church. Icons are thought to be imbued with power from the saint they depict and are often invoked for protection during wars. The first icons were brought to Russia from Byzantium. Kiev, today the capital of Ukraine, was Russia's main icon painting centre until the Mongols conquered it in 1240. The Moscow school was born in the late 15th century when Ivan the Terrible decreed that artists must live in the Kremlin. Dionysius and Andrey Rublev were members of this renowned school.

St Basil's Cathedral

Onion-shaped domes of St Basil's Cathedral, Moscow ▷

BARON VON ESCHWEGE

In 1839, Ferdinand of Saxe-Coburg-Gotha acquired the well-positioned land of a former monastery and appointed German architect Baron von Eschwege (1777–1855) to construct his fabulous summer palace. Von Eschwege turned the king's extravagant dreams into reality and, over the following decade, he erected a fantasy palace around the restored ruins of the monastery. On a nearby crag stands the statue of a warrior-knight which supposedly guards the palace. It is an enormous stone sculpture whose base bears an engraving of the Baron's coat of arms.

DESIGN

Ferdinand's passion for the arts and for scientific progress resulted in an eclectic mix of architectural styles that included Gothic (▷ *Gothic Style p55*), Renaissance (▷ *Renaissance Style p131*) and Portuguese elements. Painted in shades of pink, blue and yellow, the exterior of the building is lavishly carved or covered with *azulejo* tile arrangements, with golden domes, crenellated turrets and gargoyles. Inside the palace, highlights include the Renaissance retable by sculptor Nicolau Chanterène (▷ *Chapel Altarpiece*) and the exotic furniture which contribute to the prevailing air of decadence.

Parque da Pena overlooked by the Palace of Pena

Palace of Pena, Sintra

Triton Arch

ON THE HIGHEST PEAKS of the Serra de Sintra stands the spectacular Palace of Pena. This eclectic medley of architectural styles was built in the 19th century for the husband of the young Queen Maria II (r.1834–53), Ferdinand of Saxe-Coburg-Gotha – King Dom Fernando II of Portugal. It stands over the ruins of a Hieronymite monastery founded here in the 15th century on the site of the chapel of Nossa Senhora da Pena. The outlandish rooms of the enchanting summer palace are filled with oddities from all over the world. The monarchy was overthrown in 1910 and with the declaration of the Republic, the palace became a museum, preserved as it was when the royal family lived here.

Entrance Arch
A studded archway with crenellated turrets greets the visitor at the entrance to the palace. The palace buildings are painted the original daffodil yellow and strawberry pink.

Manuel II's Bedroom
The oval-shaped room is decorated with bright red walls and a stuccoed ceiling. A portrait of Manuel II, the last king of Portugal, hangs above the fireplace.

In the kitchen the copper pots and utensils still hang around the iron stove. The dinner service bears the coat of arms of Ferdinand II.

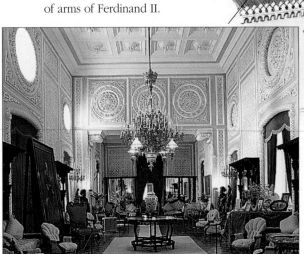

★ Ballroom
The spacious ballroom is sumptuously furnished with German stained-glass windows, precious Oriental porcelain and four life-size turbaned torchbearers holding giant candelabra.

★ Arab Room
Marvellous trompe-l'oeil frescoes cover the walls and ceiling of the Arab Room, one of the loveliest in the palace. The Orient was a great inspiration to Romanticism.

ENTERTAINMENT

The palace hosts a number of live events throughout the year. These include concerts of classical music, exhibitions, ballets and historical plays performed by internationally acclaimed artistes.

★ Chapel Altarpiece
The impressive 16th-century alabaster and marble retable was sculpted by Nicolau Chanterène. Each niche portrays a scene of the life of Christ, from the manger to the Ascension.

The Triton Arch is encrusted with Neo-Manueline decoration and is guarded by a fierce sea monster.

The cloister, decorated with colourful patterned tiles, is part of the original monastery buildings.

Entrance

KEY DATES

15th century A Hieronymite monastery is founded here.

1839 Ferdinand of Saxe-Coburg-Gotha buys the ruins of the monastery.

1840s Baron von Eschwege puts the king's ideas into effect and transforms the site into a palace residence, preserving the original monastery cloister and chapel.

1910 The palace opens to the public as a museum.

1995 The city of Sintra is added to UNESCO's World Heritage list.

ROMANTICISM

Sintra has long been recognized as an enchanting place of outstanding beauty, internationally revered by kings, noblemen and artists. In 1809 the English poet Lord Byron described its verdant beauty as "glorious Eden" and further praise was given in *Os Lusíadas*, Portugal's celebrated 16th-century epic poem by Luís Vaz de Camões. The Palace of Pena's garish union of styles including exotic Gothic traces made it a forerunner of European Romanticism. Largely inspired by Bavarian palaces, Arab, Portuguese, German, Classical and Romantic influences are combined to create a unique and at times bizarre effect. The surrounding grounds of Pena park are also of striking romantic beauty, comprising thousands of delicately arranged trees imported from all over the world.

STAR FEATURES

★ **Ballroom**

★ **Arab Room**

★ **Chapel Altarpiece**

FERDINAND: KING CONSORT

Ferdinand was known in Portugal as Dom Fernando II, the "artist" king. Like his cousin Prince Albert, who married the English Queen Victoria, he loved art, nature and the new inventions of the time. He was himself a watercolour painter. Ferdinand enthusiastically adopted his new country and devoted his life to patronizing the arts. In 1869, 16 years after the death of Maria II, Ferdinand married his mistress, the opera singer Countess Edla. His lifelong dream of building the extravagant palace at Pena was completed in 1885, the year he died.

Palace of Pena

JAMES THE GREAT

According to legend, having spent time preaching in Spain, James returned to Jerusalem and was the first apostle to be martyred. His body is thought to have been translated, some claim miraculously, to a burial site in Galicia. A bishop is said to have discovered the relics some 800 years later in 813, guided by a divine vision. A cathedral was erected in St James' honour on the sacred spot. Invading Moors devastated Santiago in 997 yet fortunately the saint's tomb was spared (▷ *Crypt*). This and subsequent Christian victories led to St James becoming Spain's patron saint and forged the cathedral's reputation as one of Christendom's major pilgrimage sites.

THE ROAD TO SANTIAGO

In the Middle Ages, half a million pilgrims a year flocked to Santiago Cathedral from all over Europe. Several pilgrimage roads converge on Santiago. The main road from the Pyrenees is known as the French Route. The various routes, marked by the cathedrals, churches and inns built along them, are still used by travellers today. To qualify for a certificate, pilgrims must produce a stamped and dated pilgrim passport and have covered the final 100 km (62 miles) on foot or horseback, or have cycled the final 200 km (125 miles). They must also declare a spiritual or religious motivation. A crucial medieval manuscript on St James' life and miracles, the 12th-century *Codex Calixtinus*, is kept in the cathedral library. Named in Pope Calixtus II's honour, it includes a practical guide for pilgrims en route to Santiago.

A certificate awarded to pilgrims

Santiago Cathedral

The gigantic *botafumeiro*

AS BEFITS ONE OF THE GREAT SHRINES of Christendom, this monument to St James is a majestic sight, dominated by its soaring twin Baroque towers (▷ *Baroque Style p81*). The rest of the cathedral dates from the 11th–13th centuries although it stands on the site of Alfonso II's 9th-century basilica. Through the famous Pórtico da Gloria is the same interior that met pilgrims in medieval times. The choir, designed by Maestro Mateo, has been completely restored.

"Passport" – proof of a pilgrim's journey

★ **West Façade**
The richly sculpted Baroque Obradoiro façade was added in the 18th century.

★ **Pórtico da Gloria**
Statues of apostles and prophets decorate the 12th-century Doorway of Glory.

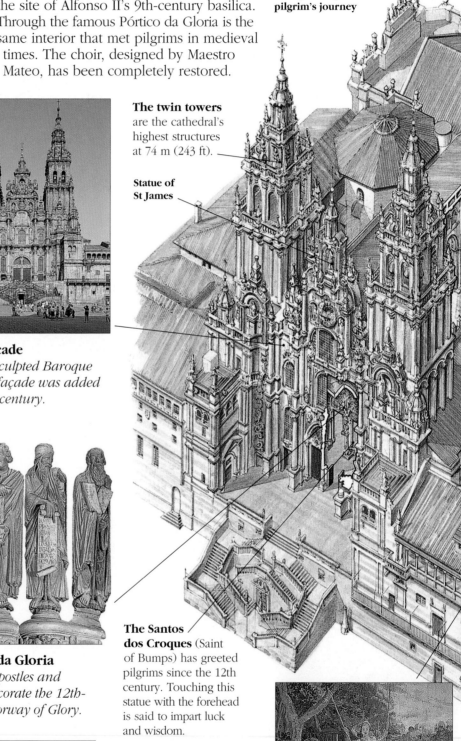

The twin towers are the cathedral's highest structures at 74 m (243 ft).

Statue of St James

The Santos dos Croques (Saint of Bumps) has greeted pilgrims since the 12th century. Touching this statue with the forehead is said to impart luck and wisdom.

STAR FEATURES

★ **West Façade**

★ **Pórtico da Gloria**

★ **Porta das Praterias**

Tapestry Museum
Tapestries dating from the early 16th century are displayed in the museum above the chapterhouse and library. Some later tapestries are based on Goya's works.

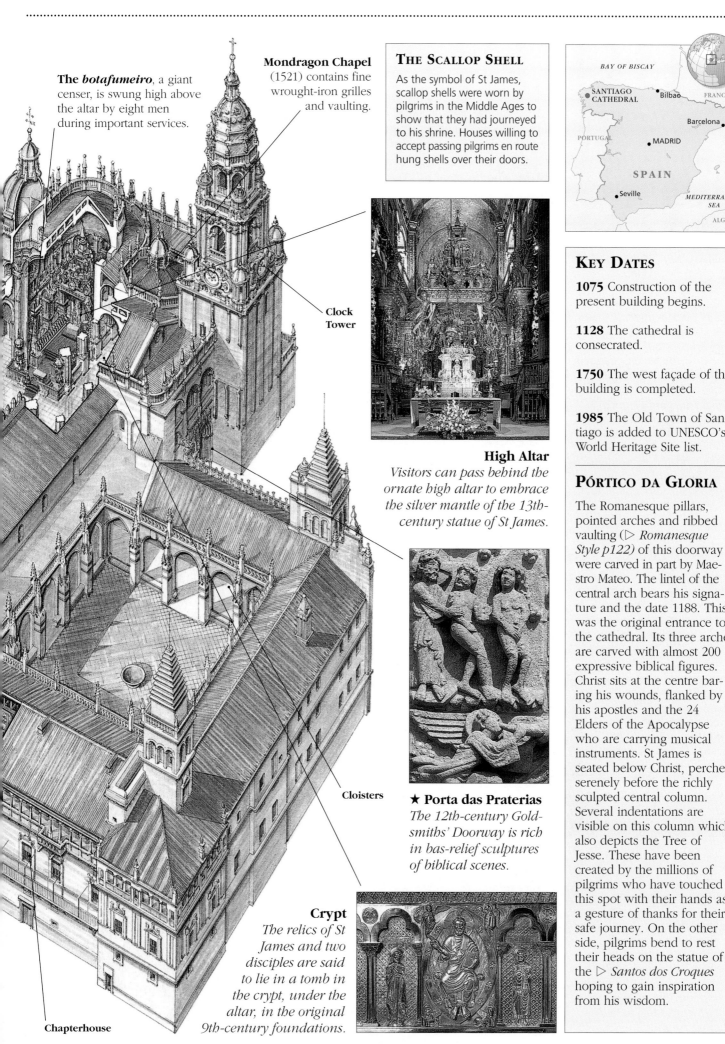

The *botafumeiro*, a giant censer, is swung high above the altar by eight men during important services.

Mondragon Chapel (1521) contains fine wrought-iron grilles and vaulting.

Clock Tower

Cloisters

Chapterhouse

THE SCALLOP SHELL

As the symbol of St James, scallop shells were worn by pilgrims in the Middle Ages to show that they had journeyed to his shrine. Houses willing to accept passing pilgrims en route hung shells over their doors.

High Altar
Visitors can pass behind the ornate high altar to embrace the silver mantle of the 13th-century statue of St James.

★ Porta das Praterias
The 12th-century Gold-smiths' Doorway is rich in bas-relief sculptures of biblical scenes.

Crypt
The relics of St James and two disciples are said to lie in a tomb in the crypt, under the altar, in the original 9th-century foundations.

KEY DATES

1075 Construction of the present building begins.

1128 The cathedral is consecrated.

1750 The west façade of the building is completed.

1985 The Old Town of Santiago is added to UNESCO's World Heritage Site list.

PÓRTICO DA GLORIA

The Romanesque pillars, pointed arches and ribbed vaulting (▷ *Romanesque Style p122*) of this doorway were carved in part by Maestro Mateo. The lintel of the central arch bears his signature and the date 1188. This was the original entrance to the cathedral. Its three arches are carved with almost 200 expressive biblical figures. Christ sits at the centre baring his wounds, flanked by his apostles and the 24 Elders of the Apocalypse who are carrying musical instruments. St James is seated below Christ, perched serenely before the richly sculpted central column. Several indentations are visible on this column which also depicts the Tree of Jesse. These have been created by the millions of pilgrims who have touched this spot with their hands as a gesture of thanks for their safe journey. On the other side, pilgrims bend to rest their heads on the statue of the ▷ *Santos dos Croques* hoping to gain inspiration from his wisdom.

Guggenheim Museum

FRANK O GEHRY

Canadian-born architect Frank O Gehry designed the extraordinary Guggenheim museum in Bilbao. He studied architecture at the University of Southern California and then Urban Planning at Harvard

Architect Frank O Gehry

before setting up his own firm in 1962. His early work was notable for its unusual materials including chain-link and corrugated metal. More recent works have possessed an almost sculptural quality, made possible by computer design, creating distinctly unique modern landmarks. In the course of his career, Gehry has been awarded large-scale public and private commissions in America, Japan and Europe. His impressive work has received worldwide praise and numerous awards.

THE BUILDING

The edifice is a breathtaking combination of curling fragmented shapes, limestone blocks, glass walls and panels which beam light into the building. The central space (▷ *Atrium)*, one of the most pioneering design features, is crowned by a metal dome and skylight. Framing this vast area is a futuristic vision of suspended curved walkways, glass lifts and soaring staircases that lead to the 19 galleries. Ten of these have a classic rectangular form and are recognized from the outside by their stone finish. The other rooms are erratically shaped and identified by their exterior titanium panelling (▷ *Titanium façade)*. Volumes and perspectives have been manipulated throughout to blend the overall sculpted design with the surrounding landscape, embracing Bilbao's industrial identity.

Guggenheim Museum, Bilbao

THE JEWEL IN BILBAO's development programme, the Museo Guggenheim unites art and architecture. The building itself is a star attraction: a mind-boggling array of silvery curves by the architect Frank O Gehry, which are alleged to resemble a ship or flower. The Guggenheim's collection represents an intriguingly broad spectrum of modern and contemporary art, and includes works by Abstract Impressionists such as Willem de Kooning and Mark Rothko. Most of the art shown here is displayed as part of an ongoing series of temporary exhibitions and major retrospectives. Some of these are also staged at the Guggenheim museums in New York, Venice and Berlin.

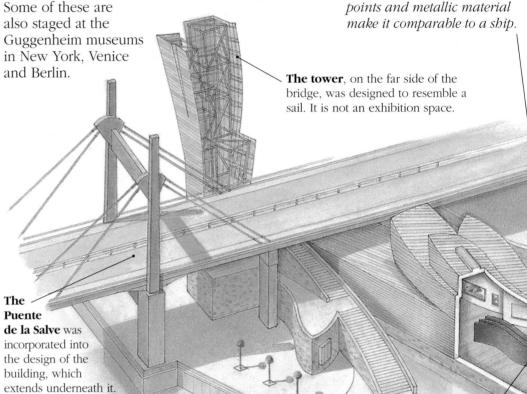

The Puente de la Salve was incorporated into the design of the building, which extends underneath it.

The tower, on the far side of the bridge, was designed to resemble a sail. It is not an exhibition space.

Roofscape
The Guggenheim's prow-like points and metallic material make it comparable to a ship.

★ **Titanium Façade**
Rare in buildings, titanium is more commonly used for aircraft parts. In total 60 tonnes were used, but the layer is only 3 mm (0.1 inch) thick.

The Snake, by Richard Serra, was created in hot-rolled steel. It is over 30 m (100 ft) long.

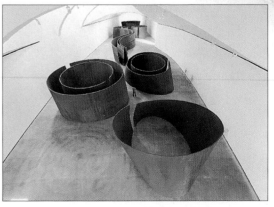

Fish Gallery
Dominated by Richard Serra's Snake, *this gallery is the museum's largest. The fish motif, seen in the flowing shape, is one of architect Frank O Gehry's favourites.*

★ **Atrium**
The space in which visitors to the museum first find themselves is the extraordinary 60-m (197-ft) high atrium. It serves as an orientation point and its height makes it a dramatic setting for exhibiting large pieces.

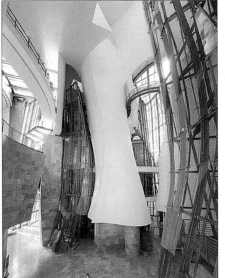

Second-floor balcony

SYMBOLISM

Built to rescue the city from economic decline, the museum uses materials and shapes to convey Bilbao's industrial past of steel and shipbuilding while simultaneously symbolizing the city's commitment to its future.

Puppy, by American artist Jeff Koons, has a coat of flowers irrigated by an internal system. Originally a temporary feature, the sculpture's popularity with Bilbao's residents earned it a permanent spot.

BAY OF BISCAY

GUGGENHEIM MUSEUM, BILBAO — FRANCE

Barcelona

PORTUGAL — MADRID

SPAIN

Seville — MEDITERRANEAN SEA

ALGERIA

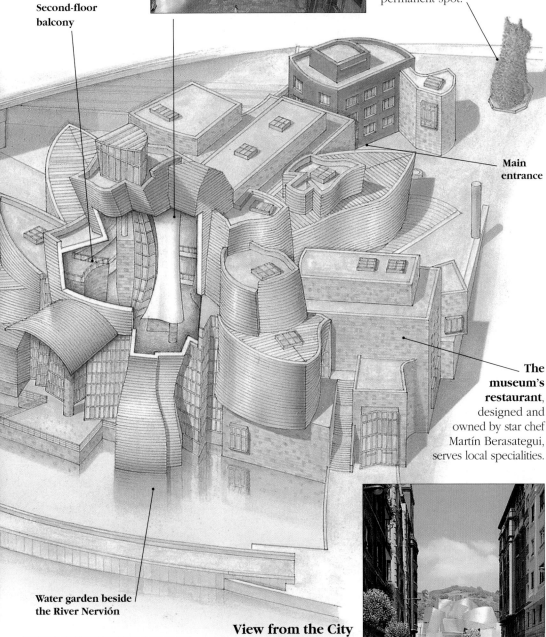

Main entrance

The museum's restaurant, designed and owned by star chef Martín Berasategui, serves local specialities.

Water garden beside the River Nervión

View from the City
Approaching along the Calle de Iparraguirre, the "Guggen", as the museum has been nicknamed by locals, stands out amid traditional buildings.

KEY DATES

1991 Plans to build the museum are approved.

1993 Frank O Gehry presents his museum design model.

1994 Work begins on the museum building.

1997 The museum is opened to the public.

THE COLLECTION

The collection is arranged over three levels around the ▷ *atrium* with Mark Rothko's *Untitled* (1952) marking the chronological start. The collection comprises works by significant artists of the late 20th century, ranging from the earliest avant-garde movements to present-day genres. Prominent artists featured include Eduardo Chillida, Yves Klein, Willem de Kooning, Robert Motherwell, Clyfford Still, Antoni Tàpies and Andy Warhol. There are also a number of works by emerging Basque and Spanish artists. The museum's own permanent collection is supplemented by important artworks from the extensive collection of the Solomon R Guggenheim Museum in New York and the Peggy Guggenheim Collection in Venice. These include significant examples of Pop Art, Minimalism, Arte Povera, Conceptual Art, Abstract Expressionism and Surrealism. This sharing of works allows the collection to assume a constantly evolving, versatile role as it presents different aspects of contemporary art.

STAR FEATURES

★ **Titanium Façade**

★ **Atrium**

Guggenheim Museum

Titanium curves at the Guggenheim Museum, Bilbao ▷

MODERNISME

Towards the end of the 19th century a new style of art and architecture, a variant of Art Nouveau, was born in Barcelona. It became a means of expression for Catalan nationalism and attempted to re-establish a local identity that had waned under the rule of Castilian Madrid. It is characterized by curved lines, a profusive use of coloured tiles and tiled mosaics. Modernisme counted Josep Puig i Cadafalch, Lluís Domènech i Montaner and, above all, Antoni Gaudí among its major exponents, and its radical style is one of the principal attractions of Barcelona today.

ANTONI GAUDÍ

Born into a family of artisans, Antoni Gaudí (1852–1926) was the leading exponent of Modernisme. Following a stint as a blacksmith's apprentice, he studied at Barcelona's School of Architecture. Inspired by a nationalistic search for a romantic medieval past, his work was supremely original. His most celebrated building is the extravagant church of the Sagrada Família, to which he devoted his life from 1883. He gave all his money to the project and often went from house to house begging for more, until his death a few days after being run over by a tram. Gaudí designed, or collaborated on designs, for almost every known medium. He combined bare, undecorated materials – wood, rough-hewn stone, rubble and brickwork – with meticulous craftwork in wrought iron and stained glass.

Stained-glass window in the Sagrada Família

Sagrada Família, Barcelona

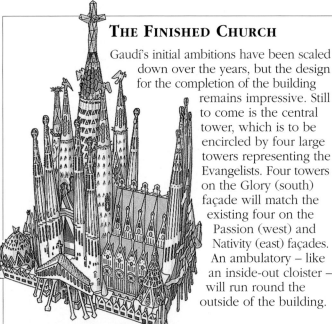

A carved whelk

EUROPE'S MOST unconventional church, the Temple Expiatori de la Sagrada Família is an emblem of a city that likes to think of itself as individualistic. Crammed with symbolism inspired by nature, and striving for originality, it is Antoni Gaudí's greatest work. In 1883, a year after work had begun on a Neo-Gothic church on the site (▷ *Gothic Style p55*), the task of completing it was given to Gaudí who changed everything, extemporizing as he went along. It became his life's work; he lived like a recluse on the site for 16 years and is buried in the crypt. At his death only one tower on the Nativity façade had been completed, but work continued after the Spanish Civil War and several more have since been finished to his original plans. Work continues today, financed by public subscription.

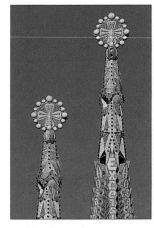

Bell Towers
Eight of the 12 spires, one for each apostle, have been built. Each is topped by Venetian mosaics.

THE FINISHED CHURCH

Gaudí's initial ambitions have been scaled down over the years, but the design for the completion of the building remains impressive. Still to come is the central tower, which is to be encircled by four large towers representing the Evangelists. Four towers on the Glory (south) façade will match the existing four on the Passion (west) and Nativity (east) façades. An ambulatory – like an inside-out cloister – will run round the outside of the building.

Tower with lift

The apse was the first part of the church Gaudí completed. Stairs lead down from here to the crypt below.

The altar canopy, designed by Gaudí, is still waiting for the altar.

★ **Passion Façade**
This bleak façade was completed in the late 1980s by artist Josep Maria Subirachs. A controversial work, its sculpted figures are angular and often sinister.

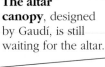

Entrance to Crypt Museum

Spiral Staircases
Viewed from the top, the spiral of stone steps is reminiscent of a snail or a sea shell. The steps allow access to the towers and upper galleries.

Tower with lift

★ **Nativity Façade**
The most complete part of Gaudí's church, finished in 1904, has doorways representing Faith, Hope and Charity. Scenes of the Nativity and Christ's childhood are embellished with symbolism, such as doves representing the congregation.

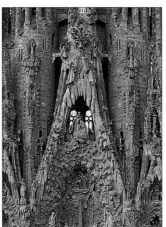

★ **Crypt**
The crypt, where Gaudí is buried, was built by the original architect, Francesc de Paula Villar i Lozano, in 1882. On the lower floor a museum traces the careers of both architects and the church's history.

Nave
In the nave, which is still under construction, fluted pillars will support four galleries above the aisles, while skylights let in natural light.

Main entrance

THE CIVIL WAR

The church was attacked in 1936, at the height of the Civil War. The ▷ *Crypt* and Gaudí's workshop were damaged by fire. Charred remains of site models and drawings are on display in the Crypt Museum.

BAY OF BISCAY
Bilbao
FRANCE
SAGRADA FAMÍLIA, BARCELONA
PORTUGAL
● MADRID
SPAIN
● Seville
MEDITERRANEAN SEA
ALGERIA

KEY DATES

1882 The foundation stone of the Sagrada Família is laid.

1885 The church is inaugurated.

1893 Work on the Nativity façade begins.

1954 Work resumes on the church after it was halted during the Spanish Civil War (1936–39). The church is still incomplete.

SYMBOLISM

Gaudí united nature and religion in his symbolic vision of the Sagrada Família. The church has three monumental façades. The east front (▷ *Nativity Façade*) is directed towards the rising sun and dedicated to the birth of Christ. Flora and fauna, spring and summer symbols, fruits, birds and flowers adorn this façade. The west front (▷ *Passion Façade*) represents Christ's Passion and death, with columns eerily reminiscent of bones combined with a sombre lack of decoration to reflect the loss which death brings. The Glory façade to the south has not yet been constructed, but is projected to be the largest of all. It will depict the Christian virtues and show that ascension to heaven can only be attained through prayer and sacraments. Gaudí intended the interior of the church to evoke the idea of a forest (▷ *nave*). Columns are "planted" symbolically like tree trunks, and dappled light filters in through the skylights.

STAR FEATURES

★ **Passion Façade**

★ **Nativity Façade**

★ **Crypt**

Sagrada Família

THE LIBRARY

Established by Felipe II (r.1556–98), this was Spain's first public library. In 1619, a decree was issued demanding that a copy of each new publication in the empire be sent here. At its zenith, it contained some 40,000 books and manuscripts, mainly from the 15th and 16th centuries. The long Print Room has a marble floor and a glorious vaulted ceiling. The ceiling frescoes by Pellegrino Tibaldi (1527–96) depict Philosophy, Grammar, Rhetoric, Dialectics, Music, Geometry, Astrology and Theology. The wooden shelving was designed by Juan de Herrera (1530–97). On the four main pillars hang portraits of the royal House of Habsburg – Carlos I (Emperor Charles V), Felipe II, Felipe III and Carlos II.

Marble sarcophagi in El Escorial's octagonal Royal Pantheon

THE PANTHEONS

Directly beneath the high altar of the basilica is the ▷ *Royal Pantheon*, where almost all Spanish monarchs since Carlos I are laid to rest. This pantheon, with Spanish black marble, red jasper and Italian gilt bronze decorations, was finished in 1654. Kings lie on the left of the altar and queens on the right. The most recent addition to the pantheon was the mother of Juan Carlos I in 2000. Of the eight other pantheons, one of the most notable is that of Juan de Austria, Felipe II's half-brother, who became a hero after defeating the Turks at the Battle of Lepanto in 1571. Also worth seeing is La Tarta, a white marble polygonal tomb that resembles a cake, where royal children are buried.

El Escorial, Madrid

Fresco by Luca Giordano

Felipe II's imposing grey palace of San Lorenzo de El Escorial stands out against the foothills of the Sierra de Guadarrama to the northwest of Madrid. It was built between 1563 and 1584 in honour of St Lawrence, and its unornamented severity set a new architectural style which became one of the most influential in Spain. The interior was conceived as a mausoleum and contemplative retreat rather than a splendid residence. Its artistic wealth, which includes some of the most important works of art of the royal Habsburg collections, is concentrated in the museums, chapterhouses, church, royal pantheon and library. In contrast, the royal apartments are remarkably humble.

★ **Royal Pantheon**
The funerary urns of Spanish monarchs line the marble mausoleum.

Basilica
The highlight of this huge decorated church is the lavish altarpiece. The chapel houses a superb marble sculpture of the Crucifixion by Cellini.

The Alfonso XII College was founded by monks in 1875 as a boarding school.

Main entrance

Bourbon Palace

Architectural Museum

Sala de Batallas

Patio de los Reyes

Entrance to Basilica only

★ **Library**
This impressive array of 40,000 books incorporates King Felipe II's personal collection. On display are precious manuscripts, including a poem by Alfonso X the Learned. The 16th-century ceiling frescoes are by Tibaldi.

STAR FEATURES

★ Royal Pantheon

★ Library

★ Museum of Art

The royal apartments, on the second floor of the palace, consist of Felipe II's modestly decorated living quarters. His bedroom opens directly on to the high altar of the basilica.

★ Museum of Art
Flemish, Italian and Spanish paintings hang in the museum, located on the first floor. One of the highlights is The Calvary, *by 15th-century Flemish artist Rogier van der Weyden.*

ST LAWRENCE

On 10 August 1557 – St Lawrence's Day – King Felipe II defeated the French in battle, immediately vowing to build a monastery in the saint's honour. El Escorial's gridiron plan is said to recall the instrument of St Lawrence's martyrdom.

The Patio de los Evangelistas has a magnificent pavilion by Juan de Herrera at its centre.

Chapterhouses
On display here is Charles V's portable altar. The ceiling frescoes depict monarchs and angels.

The monastery was founded in 1567, and has been run by Augustinian monks since 1885.

The Glory of the Spanish Monarchy by Luca Giordano
This beautiful fresco, above the main staircase, depicts Charles V and Felipe II, and scenes of the building of the monastery.

The Building of El Escorial
When chief architect Juan Bautista de Toledo died in 1567 he was replaced by Juan de Herrera, royal inspector of monuments. The plain architectural style of El Escorial is called desornamentado, *literally "unadorned".*

KEY DATES

1563 The foundation stone of the monastery is laid.

1581 Work on the Basilica is finished.

1654 The Royal Pantheon is completed.

1984 El Escorial is added to UNESCO's World Heritage Site list.

THE BASILICA

Historically, only the aristocracy were permitted to enter the ▷ *Basilica*, and the townspeople were confined to the vestibule at the entrance. The basilica contains 45 altars. Among its highlights are the exquisite statue of Christ Crucified (1562) in Carrara marble by Benvenuto Cellini. It is found in the chapel to the left of the entrance, with steps leading up to it. Either side of the high altar, above the doors leading to the ▷ *royal apartments,* are fine gilded bronze cenotaphs of Charles V and Felipe II worshipping with their families. The enormous altarpiece was designed by Juan de Herrera with coloured marble, jasper, gilt-bronze sculptures and paintings. The central tabernacle, backlit by a window, took Italian silversmith Jacoppo da Trezzo (1515–89) seven years to craft. The paintings are by Federico Zuccaro (1542–1609) and Pellegrino Tibaldi, who also executed the fresco above. The wood for the cross (also used for Felipe II's coffin) came from a Spanish ship, the *Cinco Llagas* (Five Wounds).

El Escorial

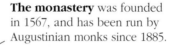

Patio de la Acequia, Generalife

THE GENERALIFE

Located west of the Alhambra, the Generalife was the country estate of the Nasrid kings. Here, they could escape the intrigues of the palace and enjoy tranquillity high above the city, a little closer to heaven. The name Generalife, or Yannat al Arif, has various interpretations, perhaps the most pleasing being "the garden of lofty paradise". The gardens, begun in the 13th century, have been modified over the years. They originally contained orchards and pastures for animals.

THE NASRID DYNASTY

The wars of the Reconquest of land lost to the Moors since 711 started in northern Spain, arriving in Andalusia with a landmark Christian victory at Las Navas de Tolosa in 1212. As the Christians infiltrated the Muslim empire, Granada became the principal Arab stronghold in Spain. The Nasrids came to power in the Kingdom of Granada in 1236, bringing a prolonged period of peace and prosperity. Muhammad I, founder of the Nasrid Dynasty, undertook the construction of the Alhambra and Generalife in 1238, building a fortified complex of singular beauty that became the official residence of the Nasrid sultans. Granada finally fell in 1492 to Fernando and Isabel of Aragón and Castilla, the Catholic Monarchs. According to legend, Boabdil, the last Moorish ruler, wept as he was expelled from the kingdom.

The Alhambra, Granada

A MAGICAL USE of space, light, water and decoration characterizes this most sensual piece of Moorish architecture. The Moors first arrived in Spain in 710. By the late 13th century only the Nasrid kingdom of Granada remained under Muslim control, and the Alhambra is one of the most remarkable structures that remains from this period. Seeking to belie an image of waning power, they created their idea of paradise on Earth. Modest materials were used, but they were superbly worked. Restored after suffering from pillage and decay, the Alhambra's delicate craftsmanship still dazzles the eye.

★ Salón de Embajadores
The ceiling of this sumptuous throne room, built from 1334 to 1354, represents the seven heavens of the Muslim cosmos.

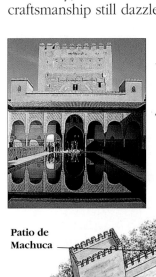

★ Patio de Arrayanes
This pool, set amid myrtle hedges and graceful arcades, reflects light into the surrounding halls.

Sala de la Barca

Patio de Machuca

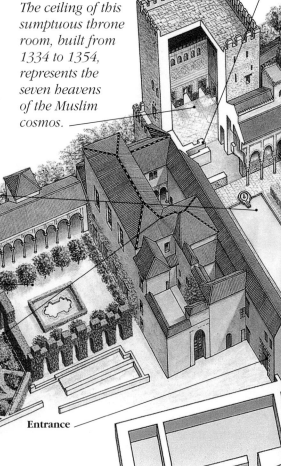

Entrance

Patio del Mexuar
This council chamber, completed in 1365, was where the reigning sultan listened to the petitions of his subjects and held meetings with his ministers.

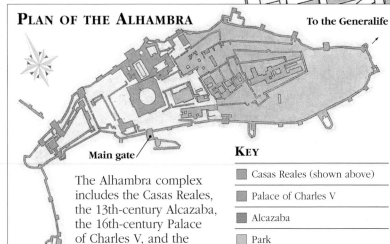

PLAN OF THE ALHAMBRA

To the Generalife

Main gate

The Alhambra complex includes the Casas Reales, the 13th-century Alcazaba, the 16th-century Palace of Charles V, and the Generalife which is located just off the map.

KEY

- Casas Reales (shown above)
- Palace of Charles V
- Alcazaba
- Park
- Other buildings

The Alhambra

Palacio del Partal
A pavilion with an arched portico and a tower is all that remains of this palace, the oldest building in the Alhambra.

The Alhambra

THE ALHAMBRA AT NIGHT

Night visits provide a magical view of the Alhambra complex, allowing subtle, indirect lighting to contrast with the bright city lights. Nocturnal visits only give access to the outdoor areas of the Nasrid palaces.

Washington Irving's apartments, where the celebrated author wrote *Tales of the Alhambra.*

Baños Reales

Jardín de Lindaraja

Sala de las Dos Hermanas, with its honeycomb dome, is regarded as the ultimate example of Spanish Islamic architecture.

Puerta de la Rawda

Sala de los Reyes
This great banqueting hall was used to hold extravagant parties and feasts. Beautiful ceiling paintings on leather, from the 14th century, depict tales of hunting and chivalry.

★ Sala de los Abencerrajes
This hall takes its name from a noble family, who were rivals of Boabdil. According to legend, he had them massacred while they attended a banquet here. The geometrical ceiling pattern was inspired by Pythagoras' theorem.

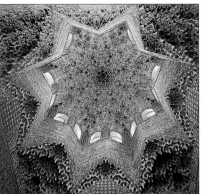

The Palace of Charles V (1526) houses a collection of Spanish-Islamic art, whose highlight is the Alhambra vase.

★ Patio de los Leones
Built by Muhammad V (1354–91), this patio is lined with arcades supported by 124 slender marble columns. At its centre, a fountain rests on 12 marble lions.

STAR FEATURES

★ **Salón de Embajadores**

★ **Patio de Arrayanes**

★ **Sala de los Abencerrajes**

★ **Patio de los Leones**

KEY DATES

1236 The Nasrid Dynasty comes to power in the sole remaining Islamic state in Spain, the Kingdom of Granada.

1238 Construction of the Alhambra complex begins

1492 The Nasrid Dynasty falls to the Catholic Monarchs.

1984 Alhambra is added to UNESCO's World Heritage list.

MOORISH ARCHITECTURE

The palaces of the Moors were designed with gracious living, culture and learning in mind. Space, light, water and ornamentation were combined to harmonious effect. The superbly crafted Alhambra possesses all the enduring features of Moorish architecture: arches, stucco work and ornamental use of calligraphy. The elaborate stucco work (▷ *Sala de los Abencerrajes*) typifies the Nasrid style. Reflections in water combined with an overall play of light are another central feature. Water cooled the Moors' elegant courtyards and served a contemplative purpose. Often water had to be pumped from a source far below (▷ *Patio de los Leones*). The Moors introduced techniques for making fantastic mosaics of tiles in sophisticated geometric patterns to decorate their palace walls. The word *azulejo* derives from the Arabic *az-zulayj* or "little stone". Exquisite Moorish *azulejos* made of unicoloured stones can be seen throughout the Alhambra complex.

One of the ornate, jewelled panels from the Pala d'Oro

PALA D'ORO

The most valuable treasure held in the St Mark's Basilica is the Pala d'Oro (Golden Altar Screen). This jewel-spangled altarpiece is situated behind the high altar, beyond the chapel of St Clement. The Pala consists of 250 enamel paintings on gold foil, enclosed within a gilded silver Gothic frame. The subjects include scenes from the life of Christ and the life of St Mark. Originally begun in Byzantium in 976, the altarpiece was enlarged and embellished over the centuries. Following the fall of the Republic in 1797, Napoleon removed some of the precious stones, but the screen still gleams with jewels such as pearls, rubies, sapphires and amethysts.

ST MARK'S TREASURY

Although the treasury was plundered after the French invasion in the late 18th century, and much depleted by a fund-raising sale of jewels in the early 19th century, it nevertheless possesses a precious collection of Byzantine silver, gold and glasswork. Today, the treasures, 283 pieces in all, are mostly housed in a room whose remarkably thick walls are believed to have been a 9th-century tower of the Doges' Palace. A dazzling array of exhibits by Byzantine and Venetian craftsmen includes chalices, goblets, reliquaries, two intricate icons of the archangel Michael and an 11th-century silver-gilt reliquary made in the form of a five-domed basilica.

St Mark's Basilica, Venice

THIS STUNNING BASILICA, built on a Greek cross plan and crowned with five huge domes, clearly shows the influence of Byzantine architecture (▷ *Byzantine Style p149*) which had been brought to Venice through the city's extensive links with the East. Today's basilica is the third church to stand on this site. The first, built to enshrine the body of St Mark, was destroyed by fire. The second was pulled down in the 11th century in order to make way for a more spectacular edifice, reflecting the escalating power of the Republic. In 1807, it succeeded San Pietro in the administrative district of Castello as the cathedral of Venice; it had until then served as the Doge's chapel for State ceremonies.

The Pentecost Dome, showing the Descent of the Holy Ghost as a dove, was probably the first dome to be decorated with mosaics.

St Mark and Angels
The statues crowning the central arch are additions from the early 15th century.

Museo Marciano

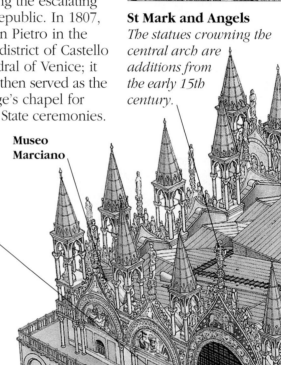

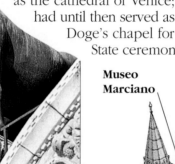

★ **Horses of St Mark**
The four horses are replicas of the gilded bronze originals, now protected inside the Basilica.

★ **Central Doorway Carvings**
The central arch features 13th-century carvings of the Labours of the Month. The grape harvester represents September.

★ **Façade Mosaics**
A 17th-century mosaic shows the smuggling out of Alexandria of St Mark's body, reputedly under slices of pork to deter prying Muslims.

Ciborium
The fine alabaster columns of the altar canopy, or ciborium, are adorned with scenes from the New Testament.

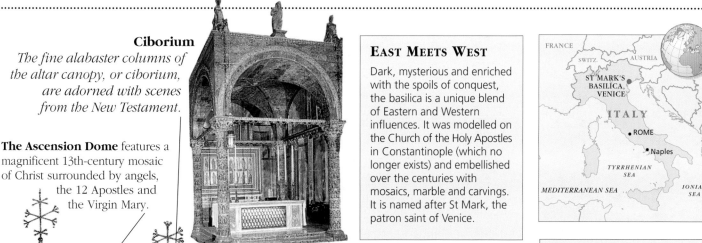

The Ascension Dome features a magnificent 13th-century mosaic of Christ surrounded by angels, the 12 Apostles and the Virgin Mary.

St Mark's body, believed lost in the fire of AD 976, supposedly reappeared when the new church was consecrated in 1094. The remains are housed in the altar.

Allegorical mosaics

St Mark's Treasury

Baptistry

Baptistry Mosaics
Herod's Banquet *(1343–54)* is one of the mosaics in a cycle of scenes from the life of St John the Baptist.

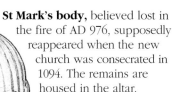

EAST MEETS WEST
Dark, mysterious and enriched with the spoils of conquest, the basilica is a unique blend of Eastern and Western influences. It was modelled on the Church of the Holy Apostles in Constantinople (which no longer exists) and embellished over the centuries with mosaics, marble and carvings. It is named after St Mark, the patron saint of Venice.

★ The Tetrarchs
This charming sculptured group in porphyry (4th-century Egyptian) is thought to represent Diocletian, Maximian, Valerian and Constance. Collectively they were the tetrarchs, appointed by Diocletian to help rule the Roman Empire.

The so-called Pilasters of Acre in fact came from a 6th-century church in Constantinople.

STAR FEATURES

- ★ **Horses of St Mark**
- ★ **Central Doorway Carvings**
- ★ **Façade Mosaics**
- ★ **The Tetrarchs**

KEY DATES

832 A shrine is built to house the body of St Mark the Evangelist, brought from its tomb in Alexandria.

1063–94 The third church is built on the site, much as it is seen today.

1345 Pala d'Oro is finally completed. It was first commissioned in 976.

1987 The city of Venice and its Lagoon are added to UNESCO's World Heritage list.

ST MARK'S MUSEUM

A stairway from the atrium of the basilica leads up to the ▷ *Museo Marciano,* or church museum. There are splendid views into the basilica interior from the gallery, and from the exterior loggia the Piazza San Marco can be seen. Doges and dignitaries once looked down on ceremonies in the square from this vantage point. Four replica chariot horses stand here. The original ▷ *Horses of St Mark* are housed at the far end of the museum. They were stolen from the Hippodrome (ancient race-course) in Constantinople (now Istanbul) in 1204 but their origin, either Roman or Hellenistic, remains a mystery. The same room contains Paolo Veneziano's 14th-century *Pala Feriale,* painted with stories from the life of St Mark, which once covered the Pala d'Oro. Also on display are medieval illuminated manuscripts, fragments of ancient mosaics and antique tapestries.

St Mark's Basilica

Ornate exterior of St Mark's Basilica, Venice ▷

Doge's Palace, Venice

SALA DEL CONSIGLIO DEI DIECI

This was the meeting room of the awesomely powerful Council of Ten, founded in 1310 to investigate and prosecute people for crimes concerning the security of the State. Napoleon pilfered some of the Veronese paintings from the ceiling but two of the finest found their way back in 1920: *Age and Youth* and *Juno Offering the Ducal Crown to Venice* (both 1553–54). Offenders awaited sentence in the next room, the ▷ *Sala della Bussola*. In the same room is a *bocca di leone* (lion's mouth), used to post secret denunciations, one of several in the palace. Convicts were sent across ▷ *the Bridge of Sighs* for incarceration.

THE BRIDGE OF SIGHS

According to legend, the Bridge of Sighs, built in 1600 to link the Doge's Palace with the new prisons, takes its name from the lamentations of the prisoners as they made their way over to the offices of the feared State Inquisitors. Just below the leaded roof of the Doge's Palace are the *piombi* cells. Prisoners here were more comfortable than those in the *pozzi* in the dungeons at ground level. One of the more famous inmates was the Venetian libertine Casanova, incarcerated here in 1755. He made a daring escape from his cell in the *piombi* through a hole in the roof.

The Bridge of Sighs, with the Ponte della Paglia beyond

A T THE HEART of the powerful Venetian Republic, the magnificent Doge's Palace was the official residence of the Doge (ruler). Originally built in the 9th century, the present palace dates from the 14th and early 15th centuries and is adorned with glorious paintings and sculptures. To create their airy Gothic masterpiece (▷ *Gothic Style p55*), the Venetians perched the bulk of the palace (built in pink Veronese marble) on top of an apparent fretwork of loggias and arcades (built from white Istrian stone).

Mars by Sansovino

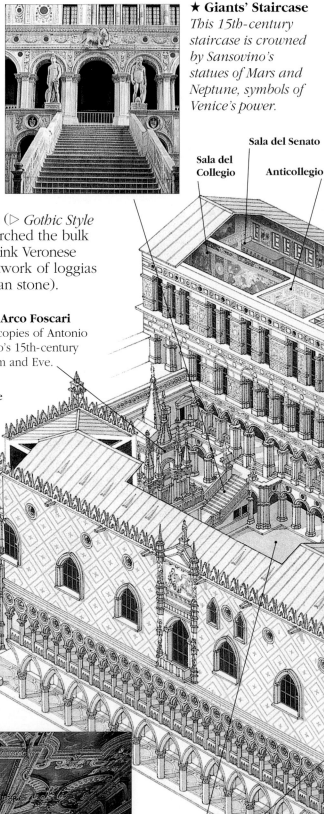

★ **Giants' Staircase**
This 15th-century staircase is crowned by Sansovino's statues of Mars and Neptune, symbols of Venice's power.

Sala del Senato

Sala del Collegio

Anticollegio

The Arco Foscari has copies of Antonio Rizzo's 15th-century Adam and Eve.

Main entrance

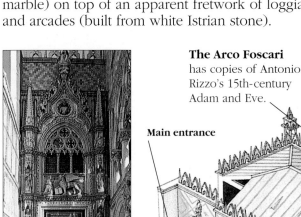

★ **Porta della Carta**
This 15th-century Gothic gate is the principal entrance to the palace. From it, a vaulted passageway leads to the Arco Foscari and the internal courtyard.

Courtyard

★ **Sala del Maggior Consiglio**
This vast hall was used as a meeting place for members of Venice's Great Council. Tintoretto's huge Paradise *(1590) fills the end wall.*

Sala dello Scudo
The walls of this room, once part of the doge's private apartments, are covered with maps of the world. In the centre of the room are two giant 18th-century globes.

PALACE DECORATION
Large and allegorical historical paintings by artists such as Veronese and Tintoretto embellish the palace walls and ceilings. The ornamentation was designed to impress and overawe visitors.

Sala delle
Quattro Porte

Sala del Consiglio
dei Dieci

Sala della
Bussola

Torture Chamber
Interrogations took place in the Torture Chamber. Suspects were hung by their wrists from a cord in the centre of the room.

The Bridge
of Sighs

Drunkenness of Noah
This early 15th-century sculpture, symbolic of the frailty of man, is set on the corner of the palace.

KEY DATES

Early 9th century Square fortress is built on the site, but destroyed by fire in 976.

1106 Another fire destroys replacement building.

1340–1424 Building of Gothic palace to house the Great Council.

1419 Inauguration of Sala del Maggior Consiglio.

1600 Bridge of Sighs is built.

CHOOSING A DOGE

The Doge's Palace was the Republic's seat of power and home to its rulers. New doges were nominated in the Sala dello Scrutinio and were chosen from the members of the Maggior Consiglio, Venice's Great Council. A lengthy and convoluted system was used to count votes during dogal elections; a method designed to prevent candidates bribing their way to power. Once elected, the doge occupied the post for the rest of his lifetime, but numerous restrictions were placed on him in an attempt to prevent him from exploiting his position. Despite the precautions, numerous doges met their deaths in office or were sent into exile for activities such as conspiring against the state. One of the most famous was Doge Marin Falier, beheaded in 1355 for conspiring to overthrow the councils of Venice. Others survived in office for many years: the diplomat Doge Leonardo Loredan ruled for 20 years.

The Ponte della Paglia, built of Istrian stone, has a pretty balustrade of columns and sculpted pinecones.

STAR FEATURES

★ **Giants' Staircase**

★ **Porta della Carta**

★ **Sala del Maggior Consiglio**

The Loggia
Each arch of the ground level portico supports two arches of the loggia, which commands fine views of the lagoon.

Doge's Palace

ROMANESQUE STYLE

When Charlemagne was crowned head of the Holy Roman Empire in AD 800, he encouraged a wave of ambitious church building throughout Western Europe. Massive Roman vaults and arches, characteristic of the ancient Roman Empire, fused with elements from Byzantium and the Middle East, and from the Germans, Celts and other northern tribes in Western Europe. These combinations created a number of local styles known as Romanesque, meaning "in the manner of the Romans". Romanesque structures are characterized by their vast size, huge piers and round arches. Decorations are carved into the structural fabric rather than painted on. An outstanding achievement of the architects was the development of stone vaulted buildings.

Detail from the Duomo pulpit by Giovanni Pisano

CARRARA MARBLE

The pure white marble of Massa Carrara is world-famous and was the stone of choice for many sculptors and architects. During the Renaissance it was a great favourite with Michelangelo and many of his most famous works are sculpted from Carrara marble. The 300 or so quarries near Carrara date back to Roman times, making this the oldest industrial site in continuous use in the world. In Carrara itself today there are showrooms and workshops where the marble is worked into sheets or made into ornaments. The town also contains the house where Michelangelo used to stay when buying marble. It is marked by a plaque.

Campo dei Miracoli, Pisa

PISA'S WORLD-FAMOUS Leaning Tower is just one of the splendid buildings rising from the lawns of the "Field of Miracles". It is joined by the Duomo, a triumph of marble decorations; Italy's largest Baptistry, with an acoustically perfect interior; and the Campo Santo cemetery, containing Roman sarcophagi. The buildings combine Moorish elements, such as inlaid marble in geometric patterns (arabesques), with delicate Romanesque colonnading and spiky Gothic niches and pinnacles.

Cemetery memorial

Campo Santo
The cemetery contains earth from the Holy Land and carved Roman sarcophagi.

The Triumph of Death
These late 14th-century frescoes depict various allegorical scenes such as this of a knight and lady overwhelmed by the stench of an open grave.

The domed Cappella del Pozzo was added in 1594.

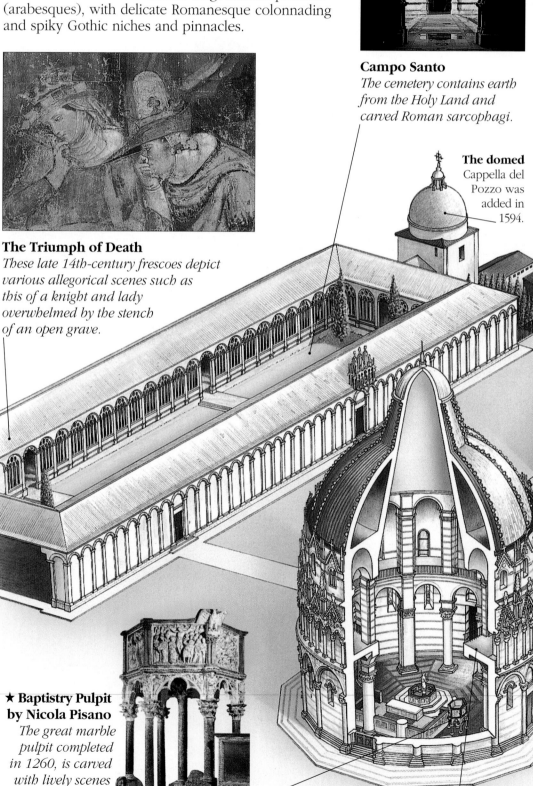

★ Baptistry Pulpit by Nicola Pisano
The great marble pulpit completed in 1260, is carved with lively scenes from the life of Christ.

Upper gallery

★ Portale di San Ranieri

Bonanno Pisano's bronze panels for the south transept doors depict the life of Christ. Palm trees and Moorish buildings show Arabic influence.

PISAN ARCHITECTURE

The Romanesque architectural style of Pisa, with its tiers of open colonnades on a background of marble and arcaded themes, was to spread widely and examples can be found throughout Italy and as far afield as Zadar in Croatia.

Frescoes were added to the dome's interior after a fire in 1595.

Fragments of the 11th-century marble floor survive beneath the dome.

The Leaning Tower was completed in 1350, when its seven bells were hung.

A frieze shows that work began in 1173.

KEY DATES

1063 Work starts on the Duomo.

1152 Building work on the Baptistry begins.

1173 Construction starts on the Leaning Tower.

1260 Nicola Pisano completes the marble Baptistry pulpit.

1311 Giovanni Pisano finishes sculpting the Duomo pulpit.

1987 Campo dei Miracoli buildings are declared a UNESCO World Heritage Site.

THE LEANING TOWER OF PISA

The tower is not the only leaning building on this site; the shallow foundations and sandy silt subsoil also create problems for all of the surrounding structures. However none tilts so famously as the *Torre Pendente* or ▷ *Leaning Tower*. The tower began to tip sideways even before the third storey was completed. Despite this, construction continued until its completion in 1350, when the addition of the bell chamber at the top of the tower brought its total height to 54.5 m (179 ft). Recent engineering interventions have corrected the tilt by 38 cm (15 in). Measures adopted include excavations at below soil level, the removal of soil on the north side, the use of counterweights (1993–4) and the introduction of ten anchors (1994–5). The tower was reopened to visitors in December 2001.

Gleaming white Carrara marble decorates the walls.

Duomo Pulpit *The carved supports for Giovanni Pisano's pulpit (1302–11) symbolize the Arts and Virtues.*

This 12th-century wall tomb is for Buscheto, the Duomo's original architect.

★ Duomo Façade

Coloured sandstone, glass and majolica plates decorate the Lombard-style 12th-century façade. Its patterned surface includes knots, flowers and animals in inlaid marble.

STAR FEATURES

★ Baptistry Pulpit by Nicola Pisano

★ Portale di San Ranieri

★ Duomo Façade

Campo dei Miracoli

THE CATHEDRAL WORKS MUSEUM

This highly informative museum consists of a series of rooms dedicated to the history of the cathedral. The main ground floor room holds statues from Arnolfo di Cambio's workshop, which once occupied the cathedral's niches. Nearby is Donatello's *St John* and Michelangelo's *Pietà* can be seen on the staircase. The upper floor contains two choir lofts from the 1430s by Luca della Robbia and Donatello. The haunting statue of *La Maddalena* is also by Donatello.

THE EAST DOORS

Lorenzo Ghiberti's famous bronze Baptistry doors were commissioned in 1401 to mark the city's deliverance from the plague. Ghiberti was chosen for the project after a competition involving seven leading artists of the day including Donatello, Jacopo della Quercia and Brunelleschi. The trial panels by Ghiberti and Brunelleschi are so different from the Florentine Gothic art of the time, notably in the use of perspective and individuality of figures, that they are often regarded as the first works of the Renaissance. The great Michelangelo enthusiastically dubbed the East Doors the "Gate of Paradise". Ghiberti worked on them from 1424 to 1452, after spending 21 years on the ▷ *North Doors*. The original ten relief panels are now on display in the Museo dell'Opera del Duomo.

Door panel depicting Abraham and the Sacrifice of Isaac

Cathedral and Baptistry, Florence

Sir John Hawkwood by Paolo Uccello, in the Duomo

RISING ABOVE THE heart of the city, the richly-decorated cathedral (Santa Maria del Fiore) and its massive dome have become Florence's most famous symbols. Typical of the Florentine determination to lead in all things, the cathedral is Europe's fourth-largest church, and is still the Tuscan city's tallest building. The Baptistry, with its celebrated bronze doors and host of mosaic panels inside, is one of Florence's oldest buildings. The Campanile, designed by Giotto in 1334, was finally completed in 1359, 22 years after his death.

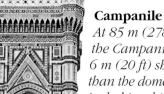

Campanile
At 85 m (278 ft), the Campanile is 6 m (20 ft) shorter than the dome. It is clad in white, green and pink Tuscan marble.

★ Baptistry
Colourful 13th-century mosaics illustrating the Last Judgment *decorate the ceiling above the octagonal font, where many famous Florentines, including Dante, were baptized. The doors are by Andrea Pisano (south) and Lorenzo Ghiberti (north, east).*

Gothic windows

The Neo-Gothic marble façade echoes the style of Giotto's Campanile, but was only added in 1871–87.

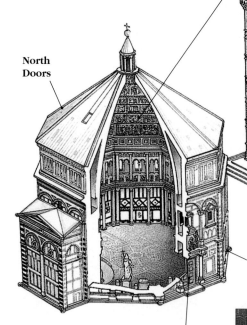

North Doors

South Doors

East Doors

Main entrance

Campanile Reliefs
Copies of reliefs by Andrea Pisano on the Campanile's first level depict the Creation of Man, and the Arts and the Industries. The originals are kept in the Museo dell'Opera del Duomo.

The top of the dome offers spectacular views over the city.

★ Dome by Brunelleschi
Brunelleschi's dome, finished in 1436, was the largest of its time to be built without scaffolding. The outer shell is supported by a thicker inner shell that acts as a platform for it.

CLASSICAL INSPIRATION

Brunelleschi was inspired by the purity and simplicity of Classical Roman buildings. His first Renaissance work, the elegantly arched loggia of the Ospedale degli Innocenti in Florence, reflects this style.

The *Last Judgment* frescoes (1572–4) were started by Vasari and completed by Zuccari.

Bricks were set between marble ribs in a self-supporting herringbone pattern – a technique Brunelleschi copied from the Pantheon in Rome.

Chapels at the East End
The three apses, crowned by smaller copies of the dome, have five chapels each. The 15th-century stained glass is by Ghiberti.

Entrance leading to the dome

The marble sanctuary around the High Altar was created by Baccio Bandinelli in 1555.

Marble Floor
The colourful, intricately inlaid floor (16th century) was designed in part by Baccio d'Agnolo and Francesco da Sangallo.

Dante Explaining the Divine Comedy *(1465)*
This painting by Michelino shows the poet outside Florence against a backdrop of Purgatory, Hell and Paradise.

STAR FEATURES

★ **Baptistry**

★ **Dome by Brunelleschi**

KEY DATES

c.1059–1150 Probable construction of the current Baptistry.

1294–1302 Building work begins on the duomo, to a design by Arnolfo di Cambio.

1334–59 Campanile is built, supervised by Giotto, Andrea Pisano and Francesco Talenti.

1875–87 Neo-Gothic façade is added, designed by Emilio de Fabris and Augustino Conti.

1982 As part of the historic city of Florence, the cathedral and baptistry are declared a UNESCO World Heritage Site.

BRUNELLESCHI'S DOME

A stunning feat of technical as well as artistic skill, Brunelleschi's ▷ *Dome* was unprecedented for its time and epitomizes Florentine Renaissance architecture (▷ *Renaissance Style p131*). Construction took over 14 years and only began after a lengthy period of planning and model building, during which Brunelleschi worked hard to convince the sceptics that the project was feasible. At one point he even built a large-scale model by the river to demonstrate that the dome was technically achievable. The dome spans 43 m (140 ft) and is not buttressed; instead, a double wall of spirally laid bricks has been strengthened by the use of stone chains. Despite his brilliance as an engineer and architect, Brunelleschi was not made Chief Architect until 1445, a year before his death.

Cathedral and Baptistry, Florence

Engraving of the Basilica of St Francis in Assisi

ST FRANCIS

A highly revered and loved Christian saint, St Francis was born in 1182 in Assisi to a rich family. During his mid-20s he decided to reject the family's wealth and embrace a life of poverty, chastity, meditation and prayer. He looked after the sick and extended his care to birds and animals. His humble spirituality soon attracted numerous followers and he established a religious order, the Friars Minor, in 1209. This new order was orally recognized by Pope Innocent III the same year, and in 1223 it was officially confirmed by Pope Honorius III. A Franciscan order of nuns, the Poor Clares, was founded in 1215. St Francis died in Assisi in 1226 and was canonized two years later. He became the patron saint of Italy in 1939.

THE EARTHQUAKES OF 1997

The earthquakes that hit Umbria in September and October 1997 killed 11 people and left tens of thousands homeless. A large number of centuries-old buildings were also badly damaged. The eastern part of Umbria was the most affected, with the basilica in Assisi suffering the worst structural upheaval. In the ▷ *Upper Church* the vaults in the two bays collapsed, shattering ancient frescoes by Cimabue and others attributed to Giotto. However, the great St Francis cycle (▷ *frescoes by Giotto*) survived, as did the stained-glass windows. Painstaking restoration followed, and the church reopened to the public in November 1999.

Basilica of St Francis, Assisi

ONE OF THE GREATEST Christian shrines in the world, the Basilica of St Francis is visited by a vast number of pilgrims throughout the year. It is the burial place of St Francis, and building work began two years after the saint's death in 1226. Over the next century its Upper and Lower Churches were decorated by the foremost artists of their day, among them Cimabue, Simone Martini, Pietro Lorenzetti and Giotto, whose frescoes on the *Life of St Francis* are among the most renowned in Italy.

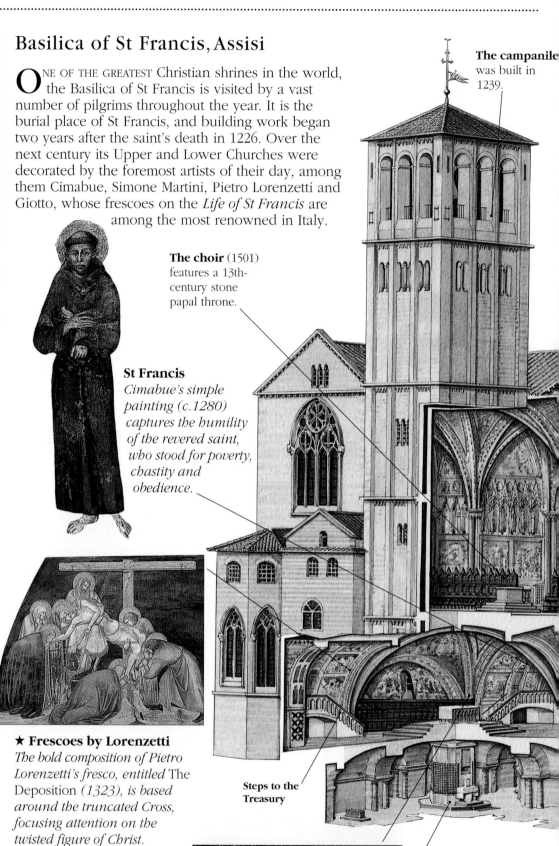

The campanile was built in 1239.

The choir (1501) features a 13th-century stone papal throne.

St Francis
Cimabue's simple painting (c.1280) captures the humility of the revered saint, who stood for poverty, chastity and obedience.

★ **Frescoes by Lorenzetti**
The bold composition of Pietro Lorenzetti's fresco, entitled The Deposition *(1323), is based around the truncated Cross, focusing attention on the twisted figure of Christ.*

Steps to the Treasury

The crypt contains the tomb of St Francis.

Lower Church
Side chapels were created here in the 13th century to accommodate the growing number of pilgrims.

STAR FEATURES

★ **Frescoes by Lorenzetti**

★ **Capella di San Martino**

★ **Frescoes by Giotto**

Upper Church
The soaring Gothic lines (▷ Gothic Style p55) of the 13th-century Upper Church symbolize the heavenly glory of St Francis. This style also influenced later Franciscan churches.

▷ Gothic Style p55

THE POETRY OF ST FRANCIS

In order to reach a wide audience, St Francis preached and wrote in his native tongue, instead of using the Latin texts of the Church of Rome. He wrote simple, lyrical hymns that everyone could understand. In the *Laudes Creaturarum* (1224), a milestone in Italian vernacular poetry, he praised all of God's creation.

KEY DATES

1228 Building begins on the Basilica of St Francis.

September 1997 An earthquake damages the basilica; the vault collapses and many frescoes are shattered.

October 1997 Restoration work on the basilica begins.

2000 The Basilica of St Francis is added to UNESCO's list of World Heritage Sites.

GIOTTO'S FRESCOES

The work of the great Tuscan architect and artist Giotto di Bondone (1267–1337) is often seen as the inspirational starting point for Western painting. He broke away from the ornate but highly formulated Byzantine style to visualize naturalness and human emotions, placing three-dimensional figures in convincing settings. The Assisi cycle (▷ *Frescoes by Giotto*) was painted "al fresco" by spreading paint onto a thin layer of damp, freshly laid plaster. Pigments were drawn into the plaster by surface tension and the colour became fixed as the plaster dried. The pigments reacted with the lime in the plaster to produce strong, rich colours. The technique is not suited to damp climates but was widely used in hot, dry Italy and had been for centuries. Many of the frescoes found buried in Pompeii after the eruption of Mount Vesuvius in 79 AD were produced by adopting the same methods.

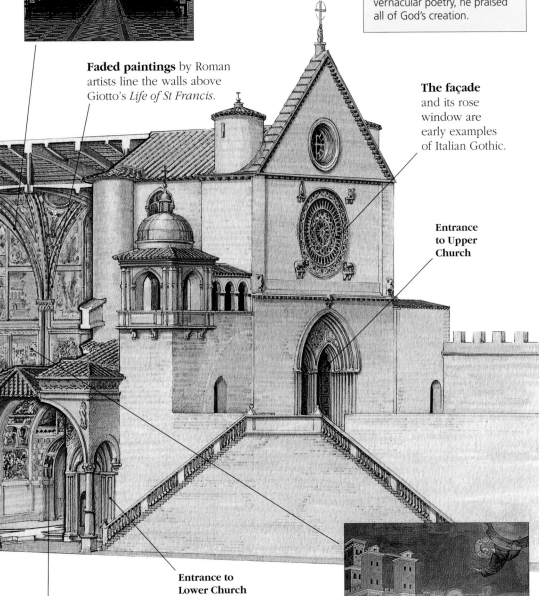

Faded paintings by Roman artists line the walls above Giotto's *Life of St Francis*.

The façade and its rose window are early examples of Italian Gothic.

Entrance to Upper Church

Entrance to Lower Church

Basilica of St Francis

★ Cappella di San Martino
The frescoes in this chapel on the Life of St Martin *(1315) are by the Sienese painter Simone Martini. This panel shows the* Death of the Saint. *Martini was also responsible for the fine stained glass in the chapel.*

★ Frescoes by Giotto
The Ecstasy of St Francis *is one of 28 panels that make up Giotto's cycle on the* Life of St Francis *(c.1290–95).*

GLADIATORIAL FIGHTS IN THE ARENA

The emperors of Rome held impressive shows which often began with animals performing circus tricks. Then on came the gladiators, who fought each other to the death. Gladiators were usually slaves, prisoners of war or condemned criminals. When one was killed, attendants dressed as Charon, the mythical ferryman of the dead, carried his body off on a stretcher, and sand was raked over the blood in preparation for the next bout. A badly wounded gladiator would surrender his fate to the crowd. The "thumbs-up" sign from the emperor meant he could live, while "thumbs-down" meant that he would die. The victor became an instant hero and was some-times rewarded with freedom.

EMPEROR VESPASIAN

Titus Flavius Vespasianus (▷ *Founder of the Colosseum*) was Roman emperor for a decade from AD 69. At that time Rome was in total disarray, the legacy of Emperor Nero. Vespasian's rule is noted for the stability and relative peace he brought to the empire. He instigated a number of building projects, including a temple dedicated to Claudius on the Celian Hill, a Temple of Peace near the Forum and most famously, the Colosseum. At the time of his death in AD 79 the amphi-theatre was still incomplete, and it was left to his sons and successors, Titus and Domitian, to finish the work.

Looking across the ancient Forum to the Colosseum in Rome

Colosseum, Rome

ROME'S GREATEST amphitheatre was commissioned by the Emperor Vespasian in AD 72 on the marshy site of a lake in the grounds of Nero's palace, the Domus Aurea. Deadly gladiatorial combats and wild animal fights were staged free of charge by the emperor and wealthy citizens for public viewing. The Colosseum was built to a practical design, with its 80 arched entrances allowing easy access to 55,000 spectators, but it is also a building of great Classical beauty (▷ *Classical Style p137*). The drawing here shows how it looked at the time of its inauguration in AD 80. It was one of several similar amphitheatres built in the Roman Empire, and some survive – at El Djem in North Africa, Nîmes and Arles in France and Verona in northern Italy. Despite being damaged over the years by neglect and theft, it remains a majestic sight.

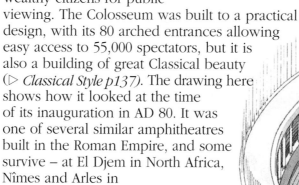

Outer Wall of the Colosseum
Stone plundered from the façade in the Renaissance was used to build several palaces, bridges and parts of St Peter's.

Founder of the Colosseum
Vespasian was a professional soldier who became emperor in AD 69, founding the Flavian dynasty.

The outer walls are made of travertine.

FLORA OF THE COLOSSEUM

By the 19th century the Colosseum was heavily overgrown. Different microclimates in various parts of the ruin had created an impressive variety of herbs, grasses and wild flowers. Several botanists were inspired to study and catalogue them and two books were published, one listing 420 different species.

Borage, a herb

The bollards anchored the velarium.

The velarium was a huge awning which shaded spectators from the sun. Supported on poles fixed to the upper storey of the building, it was then hoisted into position with ropes anchored to bollards outside the stadium.

Internal Corridors

These were designed to allow the large and often unruly crowd to move freely and to be seated within ten minutes of arriving at the Colosseum.

The vomitorium was the exit used from each numbered section.

A GLADIATOR'S LIFE

Gladiator fights were not mere brawls but were professional affairs between trained men. Gladiators lived and trained in barracks and a range of different fighting styles was practised, each with its own expert coach. Larger barracks had a training arena where men could get used to fighting in front of noisy spectators.

KEY DATES

AD 72 The Colosseum is commissioned by Vespasian.

81–96 Amphitheatre is completed during the reign of Emperor Domitian.

248 Games are held to mark the thousandth anniversary of Rome's founding.

1980 Historic Centre of Rome is added to UNESCO's World Heritage list.

INSIDE THE COLOSSEUM

The stadium was built in the form of an ellipse, with tiers of seats around a vast central arena. The different social classes were segregated and the consul and emperor had their own separate entrances and boxes. A complex of rooms, passages and lifts lay in the subterranean area (▷ *Beneath the Arena)*, and this was where animals, men and scenery were moved around. Cages for the animals were found at the lowest level beneath the wooden arena floor. When the animals were needed, the cages were moved upwards to the arena by means of winches and the animals were released. A system of ramps and trap doors enabled them to reach the arena. Animals were brought here from as far away as North Africa and the Middle East. The games held in AD 248 to mark the thousandth anniversary of Rome's founding saw the death of hundreds of lions, elephants, hippos and zebras.

Entry routes to take the spectators to their seats were reached by means of staircases to the various levels of the amphitheatre.

Colossus of Nero
The Colosseum may have acquired its name from this huge gilt bronze statue that stood near the amphitheatre.

Corinthian columns

Ionic columns

Doric columns

The podium was a large terrace where the emperor and the wealthy upper classes had their seats.

Brick formed the inner walls.

Arched entrances, 80 in total, were all numbered to let in the vast crowds that attended the fights. Each spectator had a *tessera* (small square tile) with an entrance number stamped on it.

Beneath the Arena
Late 19th-century excavations exposed the network of underground rooms where the animals were kept.

Colosseum

The interior of St Peter's, looking towards the great Baldacchino

MICHELANGELO

The great Florentine artist, sculptor, architect and poet Michelangelo Buonarroti (1475–1564) was one of the towering figures of the Renaissance. One of his very early works, the ▷ *Pietà*, a technically accomplished masterpiece, produced when the artist was only 25, is in St Peter's. Michelangelo felt that he was primarily a sculptor, but in 1508 he accepted Pope Julius II's commission to paint the ceiling of the Sistine Chapel in the Vatican. When it was completed in 1512 it was immediately hailed as a masterpiece of the age. In 1546 he was appointed chief architect of St Peter's and devoted the last decades of his life to completing the building.

GIANLORENZO BERNINI

The Italian sculptor, architect, set designer and painter was the outstanding figure of the Baroque age in Italy. Born in Naples in 1598, the son of a sculptor, the young Bernini was quickly acknowledged to have a precocious talent for marble. He became the favourite architect, sculptor and town planner to three successive popes, and transformed the look of Rome with his churches, palaces, piazzas (he designed the colonnaded ▷ *Piazza San Pietro* in front of St Peter's), statues and fountains. He worked on various parts of St Peter's for over 57 years.

St Peter's, Rome

CATHOLICISM'S most sacred shrine, the sumptuous, marble-clad Basilica of St Peter, draws pilgrims and tourists from all over the world. It holds hundreds of precious works of art, some salvaged from the original 4th-century basilica built by Constantine, others commissioned from Renaissance and Baroque artists. The dominant tone is set by Bernini, who created the baldacchino twisting up below Michelangelo's huge dome. He also created the Cathedra in the apse, with four saints supporting a throne that contains fragments once thought to be relics of the chair from which St Peter delivered his first sermon.

Baldacchino
Commissioned by Pope Urban VIII in 1624, Bernini's extravagant Baroque canopy stands above St Peter's tomb.

The church is 186 m (610 ft) long.

HISTORICAL PLAN OF THE BASILICA OF ST PETER

St Peter was buried in AD 64 in a necropolis near his crucifixion site at the Circus of Nero. Constantine built a basilica on the burial site in AD 324. In the 15th century, the old church was found to be unsafe and had to be demolished. It was rebuilt in the 16th and 17th centuries. By 1614 the façade was ready and in 1626 the new church was consecrated.

KEY

- Circus of Nero
- Constantinian
- Renaissance
- Baroque

Dome of St Peter's
The 136.5 m (448 ft) high Renaissance dome was designed by Michelangelo, although it was not completed in his lifetime.

A staircase of 537 steps leads to the summit of the dome.

Entrance to Historical Artistic Museum and Sacristy

The Papal Altar stands over the crypt where St Peter is reputedly buried.

Monument to Pope Alexander VII
Bernini's last work in St Peter's was finished in 1678 and shows the Chigi pope among the allegorical figures of Truth, Justice, Charity and Prudence.

The Grottoes
A fragment of this 13th-century mosaic by Giotto, salvaged from the old basilica, can be found in the Grottoes, where many popes are buried.

ST PETER
One of the most important and popular saints, Peter was one of the first two disciples of Christ. Peter's apostolate brought him to Rome in the year AD 44 where he established the Church of Rome. The saint is traditionally associated with two keys, one for earth and one for heaven.

Two minor cupolas by Vignola (1507–73)

The foot of St Peter by Arnolfo di Cambio, 13th century, has worn thin from the touch of pilgrims over the centuries.

Michelangelo's Pietà
Protected by glass since an attack in 1972, this famous marble sculpture was created in 1499.

Filarete Doors
These bronze doors from the old basilica were decorated with biblical reliefs by Filarete between 1439 and 1445.

Façade by Carlo Maderno (1614)

The Holy Door is used only in Holy Years.

Entrance

Markings on the floor of the nave show how other churches compare in length.

Atrium by Carlo Maderno

Piazza San Pietro
On Sundays, religious festivals and special occasions such as canonizations, the pope blesses the crowds from a balcony.

KEY DATES

AD 64 St Peter is buried in Rome.

324 Emperor Constantine builds a basilica over St Peter's tomb.

1506 Pope Julius II lays first stone of new basilica.

1546 Michelangelo is appointed chief architect.

1980 Properties of the Holy See join the list of UNESCO World Heritage Sites.

RENAISSANCE STYLE

Brunelleschi's design for the Ospedale degli Innocenti (1419–24) in Florence ushered in a new era of architecture in Italy with its Classically-inspired slender columns and semi-circular arches. In the following decades the Renaissance style spread to the other urban centres in Italy. The vanguard of the movement relocated to Rome in the late 15th and early 16th centuries. By this point, Renaissance styles had reached most of Europe even as far as Moscow, via Venice. The Renaissance (or "rebirth") in building design was intended to be rational and humane. Taking inspirations from the principal elements of architecture – square, cube, circle and sphere – architects began to plan buildings according to mathematical proportions. City landscapes changed as rational principles were applied to urban designs. Streets were widened and planning led to a focus on monuments and fountains.

Pompeii

VILLA OF THE MYSTERIES

This large villa outside the city walls on Via dei Sepolcri was built in the early 2nd century BC. First designed as an urban dwelling, it was extended into an elegant country house. The villa is famous for its interior decoration and contains a series of well-preserved fresco cycles. The most famous is in the salon and features 29 brightly coloured, life-size figures against a red background. They represent a bride's initiation into the Dionysian mysteries or a postulant's initiation to the Orphic mysteries. Some scholars say this subject was depicted because the owner was a priestess of the Dionysian cult, which was widespread in southern Italy.

Scene from the famous fresco cycle in the Villa of the Mysteries

VIA DELL'ABBONDANZA AND VIA STABIANA

Once the liveliest, busiest street in Pompeii, ▷ *Via dell'Abbondanza* was lined with private homes and shops selling a wide range of goods. Felt and tanned hide were sold at the shop of Verecundus and further along there is also a well-preserved laundry. Among the inns, the most famous belonged to Asellina, whose obliging foreign waitresses are depicted in graffiti on the wall. The inn *(thermopolium)* still has the record of the proceeds of that fateful day in AD 79: 683 sesterces. The Via Stabiana was a major thoroughfare, used by carriages travelling between Pompeii and the port and coastal districts. On the west side stood the Stabian Baths.

Pompeii

WHEN MOUNT VESUVIUS erupted in AD 79, the entire town of Pompeii was buried in 6 m (20 ft) of pumice and ash. It was discovered in the 16th century, but serious excavation only began in 1748. This amazing find revealed an entire city petrified in time. Houses, temples, works of art and everyday objects have been unearthed, all remarkably preserved, providing a unique insight to how people lived at this moment in history.

★ House of the Faun
This famous villa of the wealthy patrician Casii is named after its bronze statuette. The mosaic Battle of Alexander, *in the Museo Archeologico Nazionale in Naples, originated here.*

```
0 metres          100
0 yards           100
```

Sacrarium of the Lares
Close to the Temple of Vespasian, this building housed the statues of Pompeii's guardian deities, the Lares Publici.

Villa of the Mysteries

★ House of the Vettii
This partly reconstructed patrician villa of the wealthy merchants Aulus Vettius Conviva and Aulus Vettius Restitutus contains wonderful frescoes.

Forum Baths

Forum

In the bakery
of Modesto, carbonized loaves of bread were found.

Macellum
Pompeii's market place was fronted by a portico with two money-changers' kiosks.

STAR SIGHTS
★ House of the Vettii
★ House of the Faun

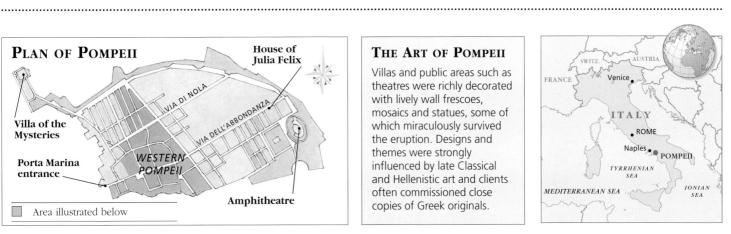

PLAN OF POMPEII

House of Julia Felix

VIA DI NOLA

VIA DELL'ABBONDANZA

Villa of the Mysteries

WESTERN POMPEII

Porta Marina entrance

Amphitheatre

Area illustrated below

THE ART OF POMPEII

Villas and public areas such as theatres were richly decorated with lively wall frescoes, mosaics and statues, some of which miraculously survived the eruption. Designs and themes were strongly influenced by late Classical and Hellenistic art and clients often commissioned close copies of Greek originals.

SWITZ. AUSTRIA
FRANCE
Venice
ITALY
ROME
Naples
POMPEII
TYRRHENIAN SEA
MEDITERRANEAN SEA
IONIAN SEA

Pompeii

WESTERN POMPEII

This illustration shows part of the western area of Pompeii, where the most impressive and intact Roman ruins are located (▷ *Classical Style p137*). There are several large patrician villas in the eastern area where some wealthy residents built their homes; however much of eastern Pompeii still awaits excavation.

Amphitheatre and sports ground

Teatro Grande

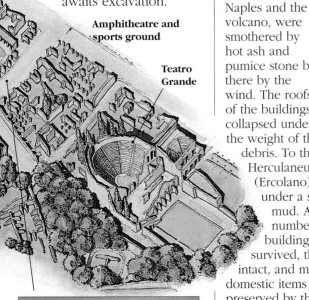

Via dell'Abbondanza
This was one of the original and most important roads through ancient Pompeii. Many inns lined the route.

VESUVIUS AND THE CAMPANIAN TOWNS

Nearly 2,000 years after the eruption of Mount Vesuvius, the Roman towns in its shadow are still being released from the petrification that engulfed them. Both Pompeii and Stabiae (Castellammare di Stabia), to the southeast of Naples and the volcano, were smothered by hot ash and pumice stone blown there by the wind. The roofs of the buildings collapsed under the weight of the volcanic debris. To the west, Herculaneum (Ercolano) vanished under a sea of mud. A large number of its buildings have survived, their roofs intact, and many domestic items were preserved by the mud. About 2,000 Pompeiians perished but few, if any, of the residents of Herculaneum died.

In AD 79 Pliny the Elder, the Roman soldier, writer and naturalist, was the commander of a fleet stationed off Misenum (present-day Miseno, west of Naples) and with his nephew Pliny the Younger observed the ongoing eruption from afar. Eager to see this natural catastrophe closer to hand, Pliny the Elder

Pompeiian vase in Museo Nazionale Archeologico

proceeded to Stabiae, but was overcome by fumes and died. Based on reports by survivors, Pliny the Younger related the first hours of the eruption and his uncle's death in detail in two letters to the Roman historian Tacitus.

Much of our knowledge of the daily lives of the ancient Romans derives from the excavations of Pompeii and Herculaneum. Most of the objects from them as well as Stabiae are now in Naples' Museo Archeologico Nazionale, creating an outstanding and fascinating archaeological collection.

Although Mount Vesuvius has not erupted since 1944, it rumbles occasionally, causing minor earthquakes.

Casts of a dying mother and child in the museum in Naples

KEY DATES

c.8th century BC Building of early Pompeii.

August, AD 79 Vesuvius erupts and Pompeii and Stabiae are showered with debris and completely buried for centuries.

1594 Workers digging a trench discover traces of the ancient town.

1860 Giuseppe Fiorelli becomes director of excavations; the town is gradually uncovered by archaeologists.

1997 The Archaeological Area of Pompeii is added to UNESCO's World Heritage list.

LIFE IN POMPEII

In the 1st century AD, Pompeii was a prosperous commercial town. Once Etruscan, and later Greek, by AD 79 it was a thriving Roman town with baths, amphitheatres, temples and luxurious villas for the wealthy. The ▷ *House of Julia Felix* occupies an entire block, divided into the owner's quarters and rented dwellings and shops. The house also had baths that were open to the public. On the highest spot in Pompeii was the rectangular, paved ▷ *Forum*, formerly the market place. This was the centre of public life and the focus for the most important civic functions, both political and religious. The ▷ *Amphitheatre* (80 BC) was used for gladiatorial combat and is the oldest one of its kind.

ST MAURUS AND BISHOP EUPHRASIUS

Little is known about the early life of St Maurus, the first Bishop of Poreč and Bishop Euphrasius. In the 4th century St Maurus built an oratory which was used by early Christians for secret worship. Legend says that he endured a martyr's death during the Roman Emperor Diocletian's persecution of Christians. In the 6th century his body was transferred from a cemetery near the basilica and placed in the ▷ *Votive Chapel*. The influential 6th-century Bishop Euphrasius sought the best craftsmen for the construction of the basilica, and created one of the greatest architectural complexes of the period.

BYZANTINE MOSAIC TECHNIQUE

The art of mosaics, especially in churches, reached its peak during the Byzantine period. Small coloured glass pieces were inlaid onto the walls while more hard-wearing natural stones and marbles were encrusted into the floors. In the 6th century, mosaicists began to use gold and silver glass tesserae in their designs to help reflect the maximum amount of light. Most mosaics exclusively depicted Christian biblical scenes or saints and a few also included images of the builders. Bishop Euphrasius commissioned marvellous Byzantine designs for his basilica. The most impressive is that of the Virgin and Child in the apse, flanked by images of St Maurus and Euphrasius (▷ *apse mosaics*).

Virgin and Child mosaic in the apse

Basilica of Euphrasius, Poreč

A mosaic in the apse

THIS 6TH-CENTURY CHURCH, a Byzantine masterpiece (▷ *Byzantine Style p149*), is decorated with splendid mosaics on a gold background. The Basilica of Euphrasius was constructed for Bishop Euphrasius between 539 and 553 by enlarging the existing 4th-century Oratory of St Maurus, one of the earliest Christian religious sites in the world. Over the centuries the building has undergone several alterations. Some of the original floor mosaics still survive, many of which were rediscovered during the 19th-century restoration.

★ Ciborium
Dominating the presbytery is a beautiful 13th-century ciborium, supported by four marble columns. The canopy is decorated with mosaics.

★ Apse Mosaics
Mosaics from the 6th century cover the apse. On the triumphal arch are Christ and the Apostles (above), on the vault, the Virgin enthroned with Child and two Angels, to the left St Maurus, Bishop Euphrasius with a model of the basilica and Deacon Claud with his son.

Remains of a 4th-century mosaic floor from the Oratory of St Maurus are in the garden.

Sacristy and the Votive Chapel
Past the sacristy's left wall is a triple-apsed chapel with a mosaic floor from the 6th century. Here lie the remains of the saints Maurus and Eleuterius.

STAR FEATURES

★ Ciborium

★ Apse Mosaics

Interior

The entrance leads to a large basilica with a central nave and two side aisles. The 18 Greek marble columns have carved capitals featuring animals, some of Byzantine origin and others Romanesque. All bear the monogram of Euphrasius.

THE POREČ MUSEUM

Near the Basilica of Euphrasius is the regional museum which was opened in 1884. There are over 2000 exhibits, including mosaics from as early as the 3rd century, as well as crosses, altarpieces and choir stalls.

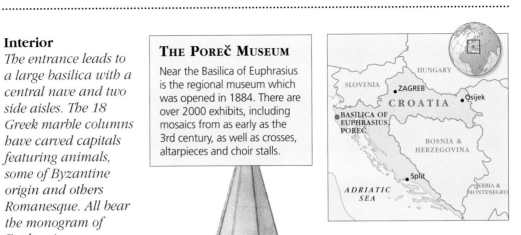

KEY DATES

Mid-6th century The Basilica of Euphrasius is built.

1277 The ciborium is constructed.

19th century The building undergoes extensive restoration work.

1997 The Basilica of Euphrasius is inscribed a UNESCO World Heritage Site.

THE INTERIOR

The basilica is entered through the ▷ *atrium*, which contains small traces of Byzantine mosaics that were restored in the 19th century. Nearby is the ▷ *Baptistry*, built with a wooden roof in the 5th century and remodelled during the construction of Euphrasius's basilica. Early Christian converts were baptized in the central font until the 15th century. Inside the basilica beautiful mosaics, partly made of semi-precious stones and mother-of-pearl, are still visible especially in the apse (▷ *apse mosaics*) and the ▷ *ciborium*. Several fires and earthquakes over the centuries have altered the shape of the building; the southern wall of the central nave was destroyed in the 15th century and later rebuilt with Gothic windows (▷ *Gothic Style p55*). On the western side of the basilica is the Holy Cross Chapel, adorned with a polyptych created in the 15th century by Antonio Vivarini, as well as an oil painting of *The Last Supper* by Jacobo Palma Junior.

Baptistry

This octagonal building dates from the 6th century. In the centre is a baptismal font and there are also fragments of mosaics; to the rear rises a 16th-century bell tower.

Atrium

This has a roughly square portico with two columns on each side. Tombstones and a variety of archaeological finds dating from the medieval period are displayed in this area.

The Bishop's Palace, a triple-aisled building dating from the 6th century, now houses several paintings by Antonio da Bassano, a polyptych by Antonio Vivarini and a painting by Palma il Giovane.

ACROPOLIS MUSEUM

Opened in 1878, the Acropolis Museum is located on the southeast corner of the site, and contains exhibits devoted to finds from the Acropolis. Divided chronologically, the collection begins with 6th-century BC works which include fragments of painted pedimental statues such as *Moschophoros*, or Calf-Bearer, a young man carrying a calf on his shoulders (c.570 BC). Two rooms in the museum house a unique collection of *korai* from c.500 BC. These were votive statues of maidens offered to Athena. Together they represent the development of ancient Greek art – moving from the formal bearing of *Peplos Kore* to the more natural body movement of the *Almond-Eyed Kore*. Elsewhere, a well-preserved *metope* from the ▷ *Parthenon* shows the battle between the Lapiths and centaurs. The collection ends with the original four caryatids from the south porch of Erechtheion (▷ *Porch of the Caryatids*).

THE PARTHENON

Built as an expression of the glory of ancient Athens, this temple (▷ *Parthenon)* was designed by Kallikrates and Iktinos to house the 12-m (40-ft) high statue of Athena Parthenos (Maiden) sculpted by Pheidias. Taking nine years to complete, the building was finally dedicated to the goddess in 438 BC. This peripteral temple was 70 m (230 ft) long and 30 m (100 ft) wide with a striking red, blue and gold entablature. Every aspect of the Parthenon was built on a 9:4 ratio. The sculptors used every visual trickery to counteract the laws of perspective to make the building completely symmetrical. Over the centuries the temple has served as a church, a mosque and an arsenal.

Moschophoros, Acropolis Museum

Acropolis, Athens

IN THE MID-5TH CENTURY BC, Perikles persuaded the Athenians to begin a grand programme of building work that has come to represent the political and cultural achievements of Ancient Greece. The work transformed the existing Acropolis with three new contrasting temples and a monumental gateway. The Theatre of Dionysos on the south slope was developed further in the 4th century BC, and the Theatre of Herodes Atticus was added in the 2nd century AD.

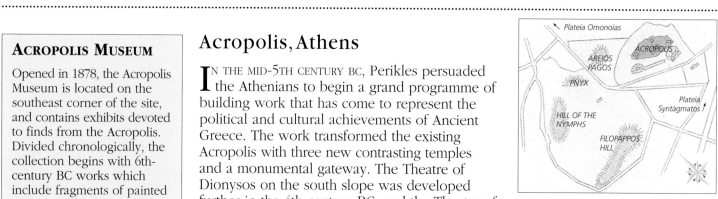

LOCATOR MAP

▨ Area illustrated below

★ Porch of the Caryatids
These statues of women were used in place of columns on the south porch of the Erechtheion. The originals, four of which are now in the Acropolis Museum, have been replaced by casts.

An olive tree now grows where Athena first planted her tree in a competition against Poseidon.

The Propylaia was built in 437–432 BC to form a new entrance to the Acropolis.

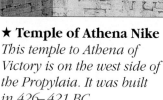

★ Temple of Athena Nike
This temple to Athena of Victory is on the west side of the Propylaia. It was built in 426–421 BC.

The Beulé Gate was the first entrance to the Acropolis.

STAR FEATURES

★ Porch of the Caryatids

★ Temple of Athena Nike

★ Parthenon

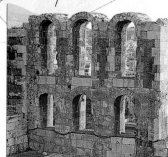

Theatre of Herodes Atticus
Also known as the Odeion of Herodes Atticus, this superb theatre was originally built in AD 161. It was restored in 1955 and is used today for outdoor concerts.

★ Parthenon
*Although few sculp-
tures are left on this
famous temple to
Athena, some can
still be admired,
such as this one on
the east pediment.*

THE ELGIN MARBLES

Lord Elgin acquired the famous
▷ *Parthenon* marbles in 1801–
3 and sold them to the British
in 1816. Controversy surrounds
the sculptures, now in London's
British Museum, as many
believe they belong in Athens.

The Acropolis Museum
exhibits stone sculptures
from the Acropolis monu-
ments and artifacts from
on-site excavations.

**Two Corinthian
columns** are the
remains of monu-
ments erected by
sponsors of suc-
cessful dramatic
performances.

**Panagía
Spiliótissa**
is a chapel set
in a cave in the
Acropolis rock.

**Shrine of
Asklepios**

Stoa of Eumenes

The Acropolis rock was
an easily defended site.
It has been populated for
nearly 5,000 years.

**Theatre of
Dionysos**
*This figure of the
comic satyr, Silenus,
can be seen here.
The theatre visible
today was built
by Lykourgos in
342–326 BC.*

KEY DATES

3000 BC First of the settlements on the Acropolis.

510 BC The Delphic Oracle
declares the Acropolis a holy
place of the gods.

451–429 BC Lavish building
programme is begun by
Perikles.

AD 267 Much of the Acropolis
is destroyed by the Germanic
Heruli tribe.

1987 UNESCO declares
the Acropolis a World
Heritage Site.

CLASSICAL STYLE

At the heart of Greek architecture were the Classical
"orders" – the types and
styles of columns, and the
forms of structures and
decoration that followed on
from them. Of these, Doric
is the earliest; the column has
no base, a fluted shaft and a
plain capital. The Ionic column is a lighter development
from the Doric; the fluted
shaft has a base and a volute
capital. The Corinthian, with
its plinth and fluted shaft,
is a variant of the Ionic,
and distinctive in its ornate
capital. The capitals of these
columns were representations
of natural forms, as in the
rams' horns of the Ionic or the
stylized acanthus leaves of
the Corinthian. Other architectural features included
pediments (triangular structures crowning the front of the
temples), caryatids (sculptures
used as columns) and friezes
of relief sculptures, used
to adorn exteriors.

The Acropolis today
*The Acropolis provides a
stunning backdrop to the
modern city of Athens and
is Greece's single most visited
site. Having survived earthquakes, fires and wars for
over 2,500 years, today its
monuments are under
threat from the atmospheric
pollution which is slowly
softening their marble.*

Statues adorning the south porch of the Erectheion on the Acropolis, Athens ▷

Acropolis

Holy Cave of the Apocalypse where St John lived and worked

St John and the Holy Cave

Inside the church of Agía Anna, near the Monastery of St John, is the Holy Cave of the Apocalypse. It is here that St John saw his vision of fire and brimstone inspiring the *Book of Revelation,* which he dictated to his disciple, Próchoros. Inside the cave is the rock where the *Book of Revelation* was written and the indentation where St John is said to have rested his head. There are 12th-century wall paintings and icons from 1596 of St John and the Blessed Christodoulos by the Cretan painter Thomás Vathás. St John is said to have heard the voice of God coming from a cleft in the rock, still visible today.

Christodoulos

Christian monk Christodolous (slave of Christ) was born in the early 11th century in Asia Minor. He spent much of his life building monasteries on several Greek islands. He was given permission by the Byzantine Emperor Alexios I Comnenos (r.1081–1118) to build a temple on Pátmos, in honour of the Apostles. Christodolous laid the first foundation stone for the Monastery of St John, but died in 1093 before it was completed. His remembrance celebrations are held each year in Pátmos on 16 March and 21 October.

Monastery of St John, Pátmos

THE MONASTERY OF ST JOHN is one of the most important places of worship among Orthodox and Western Christian faithful alike. It was founded in 1088 by a monk, the Blessed Christodoulos, in honour of St John the Divine, author of the *Book of Revelation*. One of the richest and most influential monasteries in Greece, its towers and buttresses make it look like a fairy-tale castle, but were built to protect its religious treasures, which are now the star attraction for the thousands of pilgrims and tourists.

Monastery of St John above Chóra

Chapel of John the Baptist

Kitchens

Inner courtyard

The Hospitality of Abraham
This is one of the most important of the 12th-century frescoes that were found in the chapel of the Panagía. They had been painted over but were revealed after an earthquake in 1956.

The monks' refectory has two tables made of marble taken from the Temple of Artemis, which originally occupied the site.

★ **Icon of St John**
This 12th-century icon is the most revered in the monastery and is housed in the katholikón, *the monastery's main church.*

The Chapel of Christodoulos contains the tomb and silver reliquary of the Blessed Christodoulos.

Star Features

★ **Icon of St John**

★ **Main Courtyard**

Chapel of the Holy Cross

This is one of the monastery's ten chapels built because church law forbade Mass being heard more than once a day in the same chapel.

SHIP OF STONE

Close to Pátmos is a rock which resembles an upturned ship. Legend says that Christodoulos, discovering that a pirate ship was on its way to Pátmos, seized an icon of John the Evangelist and pointed it at the ship, turning it to stone.

Chrysobull

This scroll of 1088 in the treasury is the monastery's foundation deed, sealed in gold by the Byzantine Emperor Alexios I Comnenos.

KEY DATES

11th century The Monastery of St John is constructed.

1999 The Monastery of St John and the Cave of the Apocalypse are inscribed a UNESCO World Heritage Site.

The treasury houses over 200 icons, 300 pieces of silverware and a dazzling collection of jewels.

★ **Main Courtyard**
Frescoes of St John from the 18th century adorn the outer narthex of the katholikón, *whose arcades form an integral part of the courtyard.*

The Chapel of the Holy Apostles lies just outside the gate of the monastery.

THE LIBRARY

The ▷ *treasury*, also known as the library, contains a vast and important collection of theological and Byzantine works. There is a central room, decorated with stone columns supporting plastered arches, off which are other rooms displaying religious artifacts. Priceless icons and sacred art, such as vestments, chalices and Benediction crosses, are on view. Floor-to-ceiling bookcases, built into the walls, store religious manuscripts and biographical materials, many written on parchment. Manuscripts of important note include the *Book of Job*, sermons by St George the Theologue, the Purple Code and a volume containing images of the Evangelists, dating from the 14th century, entitled *Gospel of Four*. The library also posesses 15th- to 18th-century embroidered stools and mosaics, as well as beautiful 17th-century furnishings. There are also garments worn by past bishops, some woven in gold thread. Patriarchal seals from Byzantine emperors and princes can be found in the library, along with the foundation deed (▷ *Chrysobull*) donated by Emperor Alexios I Comnenos.

NIPTIR CEREMONY

The Orthodox Easter celebrations on Pátmos are some of the most important in Greece. Hundreds of people visit Chóra to watch the *Niptír* (washing) ceremony on Maundy Thursday. The abbot of the Monastery of St John publicly washes the feet of 12 monks, re-enacting Christ's washing of His disciples' feet before the Last Supper. The rite was once performed by the Byzantine emperors as an act of humility.

Embroidery of Christ washing the disciples' feet

The main entrance has slits for pouring boiling oil over marauders. This 17th-century gateway leads up to the cobbled main courtyard.

MOSAIC FLOORS AND STATUES FROM KOS

During the restoration of the Palace of the Grand Masters, beautiful early Christian, Hellenistic and Roman mosaics were brought in from the nearby island of Kos. These were used to rebuild the floors throughout the palace, including those of the ▷ *Chamber with Colonnades* and the ▷ *Medusa Chamber*. The magnificent statues displayed in the ▷ *Central Courtyard* were also taken from Kos; they date from the Hellenistic and Roman periods.

THE KNIGHTS OF RHODES

Founded in the 11th century by merchants from Amalfi, the Order of Knights Hospitallers of St John guarded the Holy Sepulchre and defended Christian pilgrims in Jerusalem. They became a military order after the First Crusade (1096–9), but took refuge in Cyprus when Jerusalem fell in 1291 to the Mamelukes. They then bought Rhodes from the Genoese and conquered the Rhodians in 1309. A Grand Master was elected for life to govern the Order, which was divided into seven Tongues, or nationalities: France, Italy, England, Germany, Spain, Provence and Auvergne. Each Tongue protected an area of the city wall known as a Curtain. The Knights fortified the Dodecanese with around 30 castles and their defences are some of the finest examples of medieval military architecture.

Odos Ippotón – ancient street used by the Knights of Rhodes

Palace of the Grand Masters, Rhodes

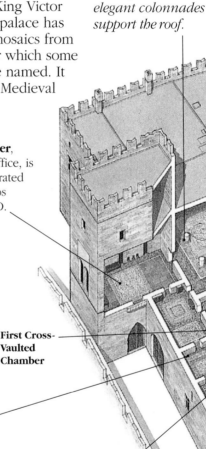

Gilded angel candleholder

A FORTRESS WITHIN a fortress, this was the seat of 19 Grand Masters, the nerve centre of the Collachium, or Knights' Quarter, and last refuge for the Rhodians in times of danger. Built in the 14th century, it survived earthquake and siege, but was blown up by an accidental explosion in the mid-19th century. It was restored by the Italians in the early 20th century for Mussolini and King Victor Emmanuel III. The palace has some priceless mosaics from sites in Kos, after which some of the rooms are named. It also houses two exhibitions: Medieval Rhodes and Ancient Rhodes.

Chamber with Colonnades
An early Christian mosaic from the 5th century AD decorates the floor. Two elegant colonnades support the roof.

Second Cross-Vaulted Chamber, once used as the governor's office, is paved with an intricately decorated early Christian mosaic from Kos dating from the 5th century AD.

★ **Medusa Chamber**
The mythical Gorgon Medusa, with hair of writhing serpents, forms the centrepiece of this important late Hellenistic mosaic. The chamber also features Chinese and Islamic vases.

Thyrsus Chamber

First Cross-Vaulted Chamber

Laocoön Chamber
A copy of the sculpture of the death of the Trojan Laocoön and his sons dominates the hall. The 1st-century BC original by Rhodian masters Athenodoros, Agesandros and Polydoros is in the Vatican.

The battlements and heavy fortifications of the palace were to be the last line of defence in the event of the city walls being breached.

Palace of the Grand Masters

★ Central Courtyard
Hellenistic statues taken from the Odeion in Kos line the central courtyard. Its north side is paved with geometric marble tiles.

Entrance to Ancient Rhodes exhibition

Chamber of the Nine Muses has a late Hellenistic mosaic featuring busts of the Nine Muses of Greek myth.

★ Main Gate
This imposing entrance, built by the Knights, has twin horseshoe-shaped towers with swallowtail turrets. The coat of arms is that of Grand Master del Villeneuve, who ruled from 1319–46.

Entrance

First Chamber, with its 16th-century choir stalls, features a late Hellenistic mosaic.

Grand staircase

Entrance to Medieval Rhodes exhibition

Second Chamber has a late Hellenistic mosaic and carved choir stalls.

KEY DATES

14th century The Palace of the Grand Masters is constructed.

1856 The palace is accidentally demolished by a gunpowder explosion.

1937–40 The building is restored by Italian architect Vittorio Mesturino.

1988 The Medieval City of Rhodes, which includes the Palace of the Grand Masters, is inscribed a UNESCO World Heritage Site.

EXHIBITIONS

In the south and west wings of the Palace of the Grand Masters is the splendid Medieval Rhodes exhibition. Covering the 4th century AD to the Turkish Conquest (1522), it gives an insight into trade and everyday life in Byzantine and medieval times, with Byzantine icons, Italian and Spanish ceramics, armour and military memorabilia. The Ancient Rhodes exhibition is situated off the ▷ *central courtyard* in the north wing. It details 45 years of archaeological investigations on the island with a marvellous collection of finds. Some of the exhibits include vases and figurines from the prehistoric period up to 408–7 BC, excavated from the Minoan site at Trianda. There are also grave stelae, jewellery and pottery from the tombs of Kamiros, Lindos and Ialysos, which date from the 8th and 9th centuries BC.

THE FIRST GRAND MASTER

The first Grand Master, or Magnus Magister of the Knights, was Foulkes de Villaret (1305–19), a French knight. He negotiated to buy Rhodes from the Lord of the Dodecanese, Admiral Vignolo de Vignoli, in 1306. This left the Knights with the task of conquering the island's inhabitants. The Knights of Rhodes, as they became known, remained here until their expulsion in 1522. The Villaret name lives on in Villaré, one of the island's white wines.

Foulkes de Villaret

STAR FEATURES

★ Medusa Chamber

★ Central Courtyard

★ Main Gate

LIFE IN THE HAREM

The word *harem* derives from the Arabic for "forbidden". It was the residence of the sultan's wives, concubines, children and mother (the most powerful woman), who were guarded by black slave eunuchs. The sultan and his sons were the only other men allowed into the harem. The concubines were slaves, gathered from the furthest corners of the Ottoman Empire and beyond. Their aim was to become a favourite of the sultan and bear him a son. Competition was stiff, for at its height the harem had more than 1,000 women. Topkapı's harem was laid out by Murat III in the 16th century. The last women eventually left in 1909.

The harem's Imperial Hall, used for staging entertainments

MEHMET II

Blowing apart the mighty city walls and capturing the strategically-important Constantinople from the Byzantines in 1453 was one of Mehmet II's greatest achievements. It marked a turning point in the development of the Ottoman Empire. Mehmet (1432–81) was the son of Murat II and a slave girl. He became known as "the Conqueror", not only for taking Constantinople, but for successful campaigns abroad in the Balkans, Hungary, Crimea and elsewhere, which enlarged his empire. In his 30 years as sultan, he rebuilt his new capital, reorganized government, codified the law and set up colleges which excelled in mathematics and astronomy.

Topkapı Palace, Istanbul

Süleyman I's *tuğra* (monogram)

THE OFFICIAL RESIDENCE of the Ottoman Sultans for more than 400 years, the splendid Topkapı Palace was built by Mehmet II between 1459 and 1465, shortly after his conquest of Constantinople. Rather than a single building, it was conceived as a series of pavilions contained by four enormous courtyards, a stone version of the tented encampments from which the nomadic Ottomans had emerged. Initially, the palace served as the seat of government and contained a school in which civil servants and soldiers were trained. However, the government was moved to the Sublime Porte in Istanbul in the 16th century. Sultan Abdül Mecid I left Topkapı in 1853 in favour of Dolmabahçe Palace. In 1924, two years after the sultanate was abolished, it was opened to the public as a museum.

★ **Harem**
This was a labyrinth of exquisite rooms where the sultan's wives and concubines lived.

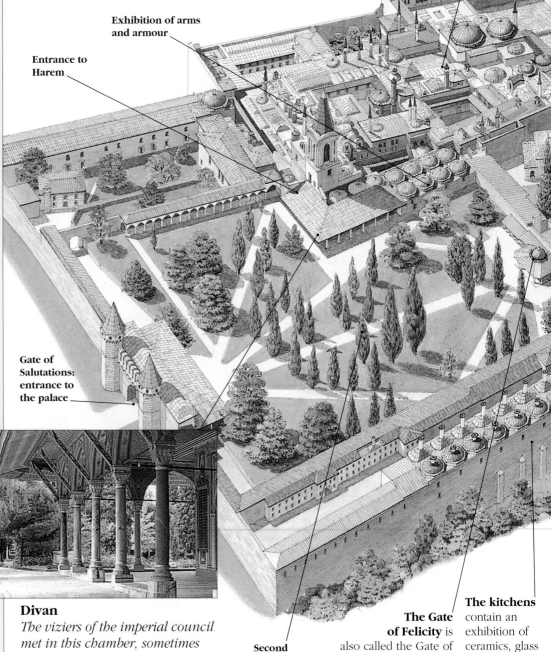

Exhibition of arms and armour

Entrance to Harem

Gate of Salutations: entrance to the palace

Divan
The viziers of the imperial council met in this chamber, sometimes watched covertly by the sultan.

Second courtyard

The Gate of Felicity is also called the Gate of the White Eunuchs.

The kitchens contain an exhibition of ceramics, glass and silverware.

İftariye Pavilion

Under the pavil-ion's golden roof, Sultan Ahmed III awarded gold coins to those who entertained him during a festival honouring the circumcision of his sons in 1720.

THE CAGE

A new sultan would order the execution of his brothers to avoid succession contests. From the 17th century, brothers were spared, but incarcerated in the notorious "Cage", a set of rooms in the harem.

Circumcision Pavilion

Exhibition of clocks

Pavilion of the Holy Mantle

Baghdad Pavilion

In 1639 Murat IV built this pavilion to celebrate his capture of Baghdad. It has exquisite blue-and-white tilework.

Exhibition of miniatures and manuscripts

The fourth courtyard is a series of gardens dotted with pavilions.

Third courtyard

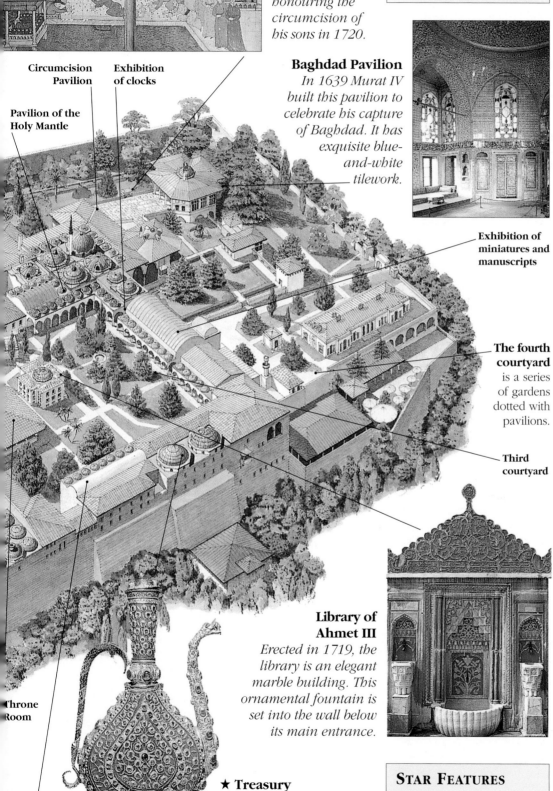

KEY DATES

1465 The palace is finished.

1574 Grand rebuilding to house Murat III's vast harem.

1640s The Circumcision Pavilion is built.

1665 A fire destroys parts of the Harem and Divan.

PALACE COLLECTIONS

During their 470-year reign, the Ottoman sultans amassed a glittering collection of trea-sures, which are on display in Topkapı Palace. As well as diplomatic gifts and articles commissioned from palace craftsmen, many items were booty brought back from military campaigns. ▷ *The kitchens* contain cauldrons and utensils used to prepare food for the 12,000 residents, and Chinese porcelain carried along the Silk Route. The ▷ *Treasury* holds thousands of precious and semi-precious stones: highlights include the bejewelled Topkapı dagger (1741), commissioned by the sultan as a gift for the Shah of Persia, and the 86-carat Spoonmaker's diamond said to have been found on an Istanbul rubbish heap in the 17th century. Mehmet II's sumptuous silk kaftan is among the imperial costumes in the ▷ *Hall of the Campaign Pages*. In the ▷ *Pavilion of the Holy Mantle* are some of the holiest relics of Islam, such as the mantle once worn by the Prophet Mohammed. Manuscripts and exquisite copies of the Koran are on display throughout the palace.

Topkapı Palace

Throne Room

Library of Ahmet III

Erected in 1719, the library is an elegant marble building. This ornamental fountain is set into the wall below its main entrance.

Hall of the Campaign Pages

★ Treasury

This 17th-century jewel-encrusted jug is one of the precious objects exhibited in the former treasury.

STAR FEATURES

★ Harem

★ Treasury

Haghia Sophia, Istanbul

THE "CHURCH OF HOLY WISDOM", Haghia Sophia is among the world's greatest architectural achievements. More than 1,400 years old, it stands as a testament to the sophistication of the 6th-century Byzantine capital and had a great influence on architecture in the following centuries. The vast edifice was built over two earlier churches and inaugurated by Emperor Justinian in 537. In the 15th century the Ottomans converted it into a mosque: the minarets, tombs and fountains date from this period. To help support the structure's great weight, the exterior has been buttressed on numerous occasions, which has partly obscured its original shape.

Imposing calligraphic roundels from the 19th century

THE GROUND FLOOR

The interior of Haghia Sophia succeeds in imparting a truly celestial feel. Highlights include the fine Byzantine ▷ *Mosaics,* mostly dating from the 9th century or later. The most conspicuous features at ground level are those added by the Ottoman Sultans after the conquest of Istanbul in 1453, when the church was converted into a mosque. These comprise the *mihrab,* a niche indicating the direction of Mecca; the *minbar,* a platform used by the *imam* to deliver sermons; the ▷ *Sultan's loge,* a safe place in which the sultan could pray; and the ▷ *Kürsü,* a throne used by the *imam* while reading from the Koran.

UPPER WALLS AND DOME MOSAICS

The apse is dominated by a large and striking mosaic showing the Virgin with the infant Jesus on her lap. Two other mosaics, unveiled in 867, depict the archangels Gabriel and Michael, yet only fragments of the latter now remain. Portraits of the saints Ignatius the Younger, John Chrysostom and Ignatius Theophorus adorn niches in the north tympanum. In the concave areas at the base of the dome are mosaics of the six-winged seraphim. The dome itself is decorated with Koranic inscriptions (▷ *Calligraphic roundels*). It was once covered in golden mosaic.

Print of Haghia Sophia from the mid-19th century

Seraphim adorn the pendentives at the base of the dome.

Calligraphic roundel

Kürsü

Byzantine Frieze
Among the ruins of the monumental entrance to the earlier Haghia Sophia (dedicated in AD 415) is this frieze of sheep.

Buttress

Imperial Gate

Entrance

Inner narthex

Outer narthex

The galleries were originally used by women during services.

HISTORICAL PLAN OF HAGHIA SOPHIA

Nothing remains of the first 4th-century church on this spot, but there are traces of the second one from the 5th century, which burned down in AD 532. Earthquakes have taken their toll on the third structure, strengthened and added to many times.

KEY

- ☐ 5th-century church
- ■ 6th-century church
- ☐ Ottoman additions

STAR FEATURES

★ **Nave**

★ **Mosaics**

★ **Ablutions Fountain**

◁ **The magnificent interior of Haghia Sophia, Istanbul**

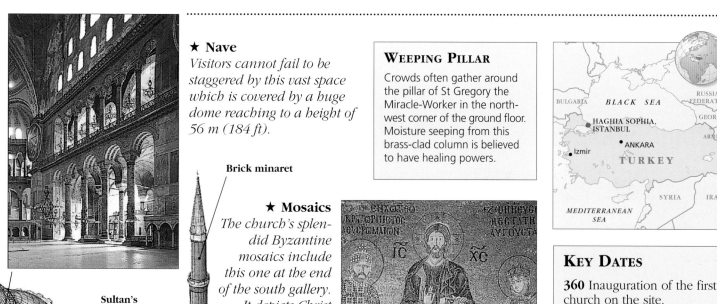

★ Nave

Visitors cannot fail to be staggered by this vast space which is covered by a huge dome reaching to a height of 56 m (184 ft).

WEEPING PILLAR

Crowds often gather around the pillar of St Gregory the Miracle-Worker in the north-west corner of the ground floor. Moisture seeping from this brass-clad column is believed to have healing powers.

Brick minaret

★ Mosaics

The church's splendid Byzantine mosaics include this one at the end of the south gallery. It depicts Christ flanked by Emperor Constantine IX and his wife, the Empress Zoe.

Sultan's loge

Muezzin mahfili

The Coronation Square served for the crowning of emperors.

Mausoleum of Mehmet III

KEY DATES

360 Inauguration of the first church on the site.

532 Architects Anthemius of Tralles and Isidore of Miletus are commissioned to build Haghia Sophia.

1453 Ottomans convert the church into a mosque.

1934 Haghia Sophia opens as a museum.

BYZANTINE STYLE

When Emperor Constantine I (r.306–337) chose Byzantium for his capital and renamed it Constantinople, he amassed artists, architects and craftsmen to build his new imperial city. They came mainly from Rome, bringing with them an early Christian style. To this were added eastern influences and a distinctive Byzantine style evolved. Churches once based on a longitudinal design became centralized, such as Haghia Sophia, with an eastern apse and three aisles. Mosaics covered the interiors, depicting angels, archangels and saints in strict hierarchy. The Virgin Mary would be pictured in one of the domes. Figures were front-on, with large, penetrating eyes, and set against a gold background. Individual features were flattened to give a spiritual look. Sculpture took the form of small relief carving and frescoes rather than figures. The Byzantines were also sophisticated metalworkers, producing great bronze doors inlaid with silver for their churches.

Library of Sultan Mahmut I

Mausoleum of Selim II

The oldest of the three mausoleums was completed in 1577 to the plans of Sinan, Süleyman I's imperial architect. Its interior is entirely decorated with İznik tiles.

The mausoleum of Murat III was used for his burial in 1599. Murat had by that time sired 103 children.

Exit

The Baptistry, part of the 6th-century church, now serves as the tomb of two sultans.

★ Ablutions Fountain

Built around 1740, this fountain is an exquisite example of Turkish Rococo style. Its projecting roof is painted with floral reliefs.

CHURCH OF ST MARY

Occupying a place of particular significance in the development of Christianity, the Church of St Mary is said to be the first church dedicated to the Blessed Virgin. It was here in AD 431 that the Council of the Church accepted that Jesus, son of the Virgin Mary, was indeed the son of God. Once a Roman warehouse, the long and narrow building has been altered over time and was at one point used for training priests. In the 4th century it was converted into a basilica with a central nave and two aisles. Later, an apse was created on the eastern wall and, to the western side of the church, a circular baptistry with a central pool was built. Additions dating from the 6th century include a domed chapel between the apse and the entrance of the original church. Geometric patterns feature in the balustrading panels between the columns of the nave and in the floor mosaics.

EPHESUS MUSEUM

The Archaeological Museum at Selçuk, 3 km (2 miles) from the excavations, is one of the most important in Turkey. It contains many of the remarkable artifacts uncovered at Ephesus. The museum displays items which have been excavated since World War II. An entire hall is devoted to Artemis, the Greek goddess of chastity, hunting and the Moon. Other exhibits feature marble and bronze statues, ancient frescoes and wall paintings, jewels, Mycenean vases, gold and silver coins, Corinthian column heads, tombs, bronze and ivory friezes, and the altar from the ▷ *Temple of Domitian.*

A statue of the goddess Artemis, Ephesus Museum

Ephesus

ONE OF THE GREATEST ruined cities in the western world, Ephesus defines Classical architecture (▷ *Classical Style p137<None>*). A Greek city was first settled here in about 1000 BC and it soon rose to fame as a centre for the worship of Cybele, the Anatolian Mother Goddess. The city we see today was built by Alexander the Great's successor, Lysimachus, in the 4th century BC. But it was under the Romans that Ephesus became the chief port on the Aegean. Most of the surviving structures date from this period. As the harbour silted up the city declined, but it played an important role in the spread of Christianity. Two great Councils of the early Church were held here in AD 431 and 449. It is said that the Virgin Mary spent her last days nearby and that St John the Evangelist came to care for her.

Statue of Artemis

★ Library of Celsus
Built in AD 114–117 by Consul Gaius Julius Aquila for his father, the library was damaged first by the Goths and then by an earthquake in AD 1000. The statues occupying the niches in front are Sophia (wisdom), Arete (virtue), Ennoia (intellect) and Episteme (knowledge).

THE HOUSE OF MARY

According to the Bible, Jesus asked St John the Evangelist to look after his mother Mary after his death. John brought Mary with him to Ephesus in AD 37, and she spent the last years of her life here in a modest stone house. The house

The house of the Blessed Virgin

of the Blessed Virgin is located at Meryemana, 8 km (5 miles) from the centre of Ephesus. The shrine, known as the Meryemana Kultur Parkı, is revered by both Christians and Muslims. Pilgrims visit the shrine, especially on 15 August (Assumption) every year.

Restored Mural
Murals in the houses opposite the Temple of Hadrian indicate that these were the homes of wealthy people.

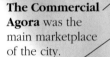

The Commercial Agora was the main marketplace of the city.

The brothel was adorned with a statue of Priapus, the Greek god of fertility.

Private houses featured murals and mosaics.

Temple of Domitian

0 metres   200

0 yards   200

STAR FEATURES

★ **Library of Celsus**

★ **Theatre**

★ **Temple of Hadrian**

★ **Theatre**
Carved into the flank of Mt Pion during the Hellenistic period, the theatre was later renovated by the Romans.

A FISH AND A BOAR

Androklos asked the oracle at Delphi where he should build his city. He was told, "A fish and a boar will show you the place." When he crossed the Aegean and went ashore to cook a fish, a bush caught fire and a boar ran out. Ephesus was founded on that spot.

Ephesus

The skene
(stage building) featured elaborate ornamentation.

Marble Street was paved with blocks of marble.

★ **Temple of Hadrian**
Built to honour a visit by Hadrian in AD 123, the relief marble work on the façade portrays mythical gods and goddesses.

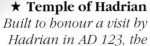

Gate of Hercules
The gate at the entrance to Curetes Street takes its name from two reliefs showing Hercules draped in a lion skin. Originally a two-storey structure, and believed to date from the 4th century AD, it had a large central arch with winged victories on the upper corners of the archway. Curetes Street was lined by statues of civic notables.

The Odeon (meeting hall) was built in AD 150.

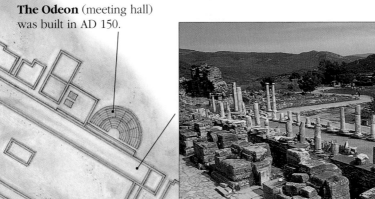

Baths of Varius

Colonnaded Street
Lined with Ionic and Corinthian columns, the street runs from the Baths of Varius to the Temple of Domitian.

KEY DATES

1000 BC The city of Ephesus is founded by Androklos, son of Kodros, King of Athens.

133 BC Ephesus comes under the rule of Rome. It is made capital of Asia Province.

4th century The harbour silts up, trade decreases and the city starts to decline.

1869 The first excavations of the city begin.

GENERAL LYSIMACHUS

On the death of Alexander the Great in 323 BC, the Macedonian empire – including Ephesus – was divided among his generals. Lysimachus (360–281 BC) was entrusted with Thrace. He soon added Asia Minor and in 286 BC took Ephesus, heralding a new era for the city. It was a strategic trading port, but the receding coastline and silt-filled harbour threatened its livelihood. Lysimachus dredged the harbour. Then he moved the city to its present site, fortified it with huge walls and renamed it (for a brief time) Arsinoe, after his third wife. The city was soon densely populated and began to prosper. Meanwhile, Arsinoe, eager to ensure that her son and not the son of Lysimachus's first wife would succeed him, persuaded her husband to execute the elder boy on the grounds that he was plotting to kill his father. During the ensuing furore, Asia Minor was attacked by King Seleucus of Syria. Lysimachus was killed in battle.

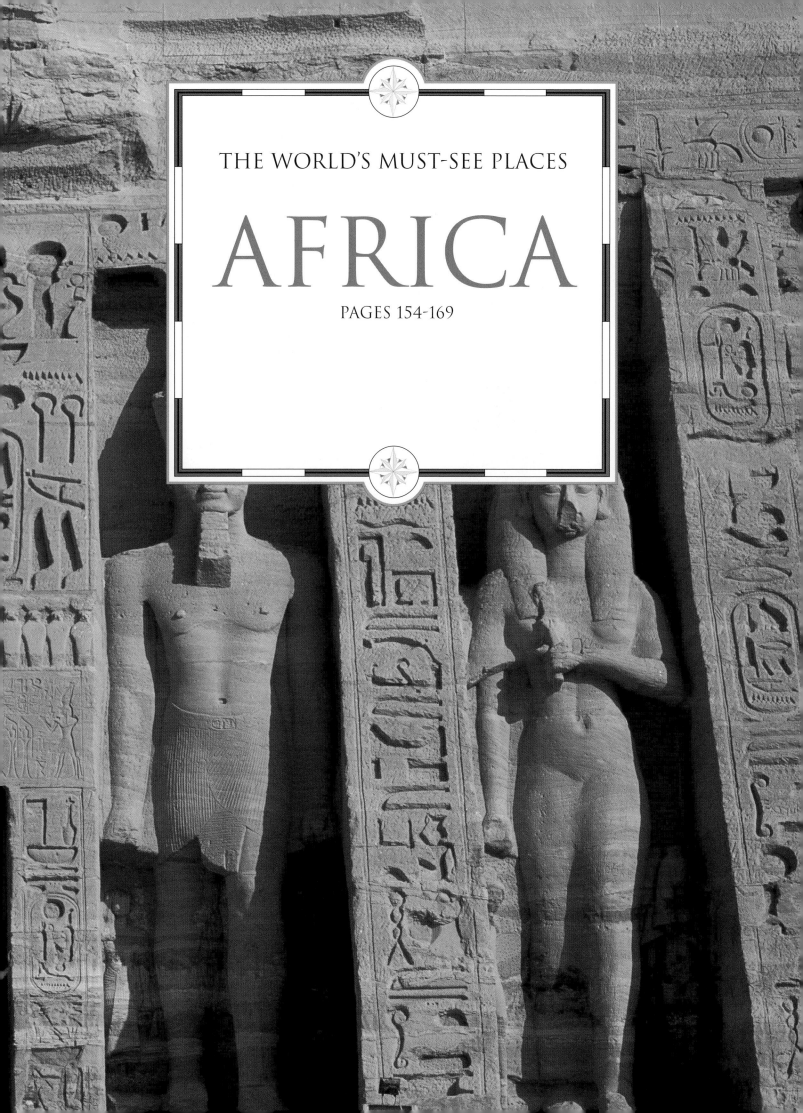

THE WORLD'S MUST-SEE PLACES

AFRICA

PAGES 154-169

HASSAN II

Moulay Hassan succeeded to the throne of Morocco on the death of his father, Mohammed V, in 1961. A skilful politician, he alternated liberalizing policies with repression. He introduced the country's first constitution (1962) and parliamentary elections (1963), but the road to reform was rocky. Hassan also sucessfully defended attempts to overthrow him as leader. Abroad, war raged with Algeria over border disputes (1963). When Spain withdrew from the mineral-rich Western Sahara in 1975, Hassan initiated the Green March of 350,000 civilians who crossed the border to assert Morocco's claim to the region. Spain agreed to the transfer of power, but Algerian-backed Polisario Front guerrillas began a violent campaign for independence. A ceasefire was agreed in 1991. Hassan II died in 1999. He was succeeded by Mohammed VI.

INSIDE THE MOSQUE

The waterfront Mosque of Hassan II in Casablanca is the crowning glory of the king's reign. Built for his 60th birthday, the mosque was mainly financed by donations from the Moroccan people. Inside, the massive marble-floored ▷ *prayer hall* sparkles in the glow of Venetian chandeliers. It is said that the hall is large enough to accommodate St Peter's in Rome. Cedar from Morocco's Middle Atlas has been shaped and carved to form ▷ *doors* and screens and the panelling of 70 cupolas. Even the sliding roof is painted and gilded. The ▷ *hammam* (traditional bathhouse) is below the prayer hall.

Mosque viewed from the sea

Mosque of Hassan II, Casablanca

Mosque door, interior view

WITH A PRAYER HALL that can accommodate 25,000, the Mosque of Hassan II is the second-largest religious building in the world after the mosque in Mecca. The complex covers 9,000 sq m (96,840 sq ft), with two-thirds of it built over the sea. The minaret, the lighthouse of Islam, is 200 m (656 ft) high, and two laser beams reaching over a distance of 30 km (18.5 miles) shine in the direction of Mecca. The building was designed by Michel Pinseau and it took 35,000 craftsmen to build it. With carved stucco, *zellij* tilework, a painted cedar ceiling and marble, onyx and travertine cladding, it is a monument to Moroccan architectural virtuosity.

★ Minaret
Its vast size and exquisite decoration make this minaret an exceptional building.

Fountains
These are decorated with zellij *tilework and framed with marble arches and columns.*

Marble
Used throughout the building on the columns of the prayer hall, doorways, fountains and stairs, marble is everywhere. It is also sometimes combined with granite and onyx.

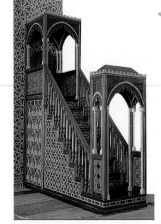

Minbar
The minbar, *or pulpit, located at the western end of the prayer hall, is particularly ornate. It is decorated with verses from the Koran.*

STAR FEATURES

★ **Minaret**

★ **Prayer Hall**

◁ **Huge statues of Queen Nefertari and Ramses II on Nefertari's temple at Abu Simbel, Egypt**

Women's Gallery
Above two mezzanines and hidden from view, this gallery extends over 5,300 sq m (57,000 sq ft) and can hold up to 5,000 women.

KEY DATES

1986 Construction begins on the Mosque of Hassan II.

1993 The mosque is completed.

MUSLIM BELIEFS AND PRACTICES

Muslims believe in one God (Allah), and their holy book, the Koran, shares many stories and prophets with the Christian Bible. However, whereas Christians believe that Jesus is the son of God, Muslims hold that he was just one in a line of prophets, the last being Mohammed, who brought the final revelation of God's truth to mankind. Muslims believe that Allah communicated the sacred texts of the Koran to Mohammed through the archangel Gabriel. In their belief in Allah, Muslims pray five times a day wherever they might happen to be. The calls to prayer are broadcast from the mosque. Worshippers who visit a mosque to pray remove their shoes and wash their feet, head and hands outside before entering the prayer hall. Once inside, depending on the size of the mosque, women and men pray in separate areas. When praying, Muslims face Mecca in Saudi Arabia, the birthplace of Mohammed and also the site of the Kaaba, a sacred shrine built by Abraham. In a prayer hall the direction is indicated by the *mihrab* (a niche in the wall). Kneeling and lowering the head to the ground are gestures of humility and respect for Allah.

Dome
The cedar-panelled interior of the dome, over the prayer hall, glistens with carved and painted decoration.

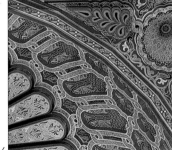

Royal Door
This is decorated with traditional motifs engraved on brass and titanium.

Columns

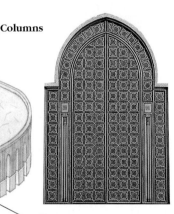

Doors
Seen from the exterior, these are double doors in the shape of pointed arches framed by columns. Many are clad in incised bronze.

Mashrabiyya screen-work at the windows protects those within from prying eyes.

Hammam

Stairway to the Women's Gallery
The stairway features decorative woodcarving, multiple arches and marble, granite and onyx columns, arranged in a harmonious ensemble.

★ Prayer Hall
Able to hold 25,000 believers, the prayer hall measures 200 m (656 ft) by 100 m (328 ft). The central part of the roof can be opened to the sky.

Mosque of Hassan II

Great Mosque, Kairouan

UQBA IBN NAFI AND KAIROUAN

At the time of the Prophet Mohammed's death in AD 632, Muslims only ruled Arabia. However, by 750 the Arab Muslims had achieved one of the most spectacular conquests in history, ruling over the Middle East, Central Asia and North Africa. In AD 670 the Muslim leader Uqba ibn Nafi crossed the desert from Egypt as part of the conquest of North Africa. Establishing military posts along the way, he stopped to camp at the location of present-day Kairouan (the word *Qayrawan* means "military camp" in Arabic). Legend tells of a golden cup being discovered in the sand, which was recognized as one that had previously disappeared from Mecca several years before. When the cup was picked up, a spring emerged from the earth which, it was declared, was supplied by the same source as that of the holy Zem-Zem well in Mecca. Uqba founded his capital and swept on to conquer Morocco. Returning home in 683, he was defeated and killed in battle by the Berbers.

ISLAM'S FOURTH HOLIEST CITY

Kairouan grew in importance to become the capital of the Aghlabid dynasty in the 9th century. When the Fatimids took power in AD 909 they moved their capital elsewhere. By the 11th century the city's political and economic power had been surpassed by other cities but it never lost its holy status. As a religious centre it continued to grow in prominence with the mosque proving a powerful magnet for Muslim pilgrims. Today, Kairouan is Islam's holiest city in North Africa and its fourth holiest city in the world after Mecca, Medina and Jerusalem. The pilgrims come to drink the waters of the holy spring and to visit the mosque built by the city's founder.

Ornately decorated capital

T HE MOSQUE OF SIDI UQBA is considered the first mosque to have been built in North Africa, and the city of Kairouan owes its fame as Islam's fourth holiest city to the Great Mosque. The founder of the city, Uqba ibn Nafi, built a small mosque on the site as long ago as AD 670. As the city thrived, the mosque was rebuilt and enlarged several times, in 703, again in 774, in 836 and 863, reaching its current dimensions by the end of the 9th century. Its design and ornamentation continued to evolve through to the 19th century.

Columns
Most of the arched colonnades and columns were salvaged from Roman and Byzantine buildings elsewhere. Some however, were carved by local craftsmen.

★ Minaret
Built between AD 724 and 728, the imposing square minaret is one of the oldest surviving towers of its kind, and is the oldest part of the Mosque. It rises in three sections, each diminishing in size, and is topped by a dome. The lower storeys are built of blocks taken from Roman buildings. There are 129 steps leading to its highest point.

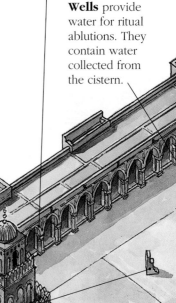

Wells provide water for ritual ablutions. They contain water collected from the cistern.

The sundial in the courtyard shows the times of prayer.

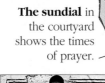

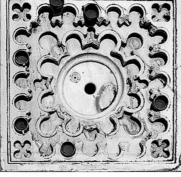

Cistern
The courtyard slopes down towards its centre where there is a latticed plate shielding a cistern. The plate has a decorative function but also prevents the water, which drains into the cistern, from being polluted.

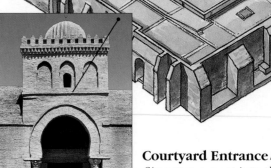

Courtyard Entrance
Six gates are set into the wall surrounding the courtyard. The main entrance is through a gate surmounted by a dome.

Cloisters
Surrounding the courtyard on three sides are cloisters giving shade and protection from the elements.

KAIROUAN CARPETS
Kairouan is a carpet-making centre, a tradition going back hundreds of years, and it is renowned for the quality of its rugs. However, the large rug in the ▷ *prayer hall* was a gift from Saudi Arabia.

Dome
The exterior of the mosque's dome shows the position of the mihrab, *which indicates the direction to Mecca. It is more richly decorated than the other domes.*

KEY DATES

670 Kairouan is founded by Uqba ibn Nafi who constructs a small mosque.

836 The Great Mosque is renovated and enlarged under the Aghlabids and takes the appearance of what can be seen today.

Mid-9th century The Great Mosque becomes a site for Islamic pilgrimage.

1988 Kairouan is declared a UNESCO World Heritage Site.

INSIDE THE PRAYER HALL

Entrance to the ▷ *prayer hall* at the southern end of the courtyard is through a set of beautiful, finely carved, wooden doors dating from the 19th century. Inside is a rectangular, domed chamber with arched aisles. Most of the stunning 400-odd marble and granite pillars that support the roof were taken from Roman and Byzantine sites, many from Carthage and Sousse. The imam leads the prayers from the ▷ *minbar*, a marvellous pulpit sculpted out of wood from Baghdad and thought to be one of the oldest in the Arab world. Behind the *mihrab* (▷ *dome)* at the end of the central aisle are 9th-century tiles also from Baghdad, surrounding carved marble panels. A carved wooden screen, the *maqsura*, dating from the 11th century stands nearby and many Kairouan carpets cover the floor.

★ **Prayer Hall**
This hall is divided into seventeen long naves divided by arcades. The two wider naves form a "T" shape.

The *minbar* (pulpit), made out of teak, was built around AD 863 and commissioned by the Aghlabid emir, Abu Ibrahim.

Entrance to the Mosque
There are two entrances to the prayer hall from the road. Non-Muslims are not permitted to enter but they may look in the open doors.

Decoration
The richly decorated mosque contains some rare examples of ceramic decorative features. Plant motifs and geometric forms are popular.

STAR FEATURES

★ **Minaret**

★ **Prayer Hall**

Great Mosque

Leptis Magna

THE CITY'S PORT

A promontory protects the harbour at the mouth of the Wadi Lebdah at Leptis Magna, and it is here that the Phoenicians settled in the 7th century BC. They exploited the fertile hinterland and traded olive oil, ivory and animal skins throughout the Carthaginian Empire and around the Mediterranean. During the early 3rd century AD, under the Roman Emperor Septimius Severus, the harbour was rebuilt and enlarged. New quays, 1-km (half-a-mile) long, were constructed with warehouses, a temple and a watchtower; a ▷ *lighthouse* was built on the promontory. Awnings were installed around the port to provide protection from the sweltering sun. The mooring blocks on the quay, which were covered in sand soon after completion, have been well preserved.

EMPEROR SEPTIMIUS SEVERUS

The Roman ruler Lucius Septimius Severus was born in Leptis Magna in Roman North Africa in AD 146. Regarded as an outstanding soldier, Severus rose to the rank of consul and by 190 was in command of the legions in Pannonia. Soon after the murder of Emperor Pertinax in 193, Severus was proclaimed emperor, but he had to fight off two rivals to secure his position. He was a strong but popular ruler, who was known for his lavish entertaining. He marked his victory over the Parthians in 199 with a triumphal arch in Rome (203), which still stands today. His final campaign was to England in 208 to secure the empire's northern border at Hadrian's Wall. Severus died in York in 211 while preparing to invade Scotland.

Bust of Emperor Septimius Severus

Column detail, Severan Basilica

O NE OF THE WORLD'S greatest ruined cities, Leptis Magna attests to the prosperity and status of the Roman empire in North Africa. Leptis was particularly fortunate in AD 193 when Septimius Severus, a native of the city, became emperor of Rome. During his reign the population grew to some 70,000, and buildings were raised to glorify his name. Attacks by nomadic tribes led eventually to the city's abandonment, at which point sand dunes engulfed it, preserving the site that is still being excavated by archaeologists.

Market

Once surrounded by arcades and centred on two beautiful kiosks, this grand trading place was endowed by one wealthy citizen, Annobal Rufus, in 9–8 BC.

← To Hunters' quarters   Arch of Septimius Severus   Arch of Trajan

Arch of Tiberius

★ Theatre

Like the market, this vast structure was given to the city by Annobal Rufus. The lowest, wider stone steps would have held chairs for distinguished visitors. From the top, the panoramic view of the ancient city is magnificent.

★ **Severan Basilica**
Begun during the reign of Septimius to house the law courts, this massive double-apsed building was converted into a church by Justinian in the 6th century AD, though part of it seems to have served as a synagogue from the 5th century AD.

HUNTERS' QUARTERS

To the west of the city lies a group of well-preserved, small domed buildings. Wall paintings indicate they belonged to hunters who supplied the amphitheatres of the Roman Empire with wild animals.

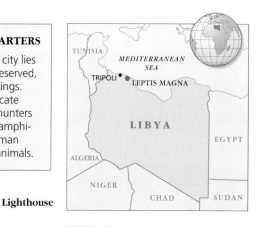

TUNISIA
MEDITERRANEAN SEA
TRIPOLI • LEPTIS MAGNA
ALGERIA
LIBYA
EGYPT
NIGER
CHAD
SUDAN

Leptis Magna

KEY DATES

600 BC A Phoenician trading post is founded on the site.

23 BC Leptis Magna forms part of the new Roman province of Africa.

523 The city is sacked by Berbers and abandoned.

1982 Leptis Magna becomes a UNESCO World Heritage Site.

1994 A new archaeological programme begins at Leptis Magna.

THE EMPEROR'S NEW BUILDING

Leptis Magna prospered under Roman rule as a major commercial centre, but at the beginning of the 3rd century, after the appointment of Septimius Severus as Roman emperor, the city underwent a transformation. Marble was imported from Asia Minor, Greece and Italy, granite columns from Egypt, and the limestone buildings took on a grand appearance (▷ *Classical Style p137*). In AD 200, Severus built a fine new ▷ *Severan Forum*, surrounded by colonnades topped with arches. At the northeastern end he constructed the three-aisled ▷ *Severan Basilica*. Its marble pilasters were carved with scenes from the lives of Hercules and Dionysus, his family's patron gods. The mighty four-sided ▷ *Arch of Septimius Severus*, constructed in white marble, was raised for his visit to the city in 203.

Lighthouse

0 metres   100

0 yards   100

Severan Forum
A series of vast reliefs of Medusa's head once adorned the arcade of the Severan Forum.

RECONSTRUCTION OF LEPTIS MAGNA
This shows the many magnificent buildings erected during the reigns of successive emperors up to and including Septimius Severus.

STAR FEATURES

★ **Theatre**

★ **Severan Basilica**

Hadrian's Baths
This baths complex includes an outdoor sports ground (palaestra), *hot and warm baths* (caldarium *and* tepidarium), *once heated by underfloor fires, and a huge cold bath* (frigidarium) *with two plunge pools, one still containing water.*

The Sphinx and Pyramid of Khafre viewed from the plateau

THE SPHINX

Dating back to 2500 BC, and positioned at the entrance to the Pyramid of Khafre, the Sphinx is the earliest known ancient Egyptian sculpture. It stands 20-m (66-ft) high with an elongated body, a royal headdress and outstretched paws. It is carved from an outcrop of natural rock, augmented by shaped blocks around the base, added during several renovations. It was once thought that the nose of the Sphinx was shot off by Napoleon's French army, but in reality it was lost before the 15th century.

THE GIZA PLATEAU

During the 4th Dynasty (2613–2498 BC), Giza became the royal burial ground for Memphis, capital of Egypt. In less than 100 years, the ancient Egyptians built three pyramid complexes to serve as tombs for their dead kings. These consisted of the Great Pyramid, the Pyramid of Khafre (r.2558–2532) and the Pyramid of Menkaure (r.2532–2530). The Sphinx was also added to guard the pyramids, while each king's close family and royal court were buried in satellite pyramids and ▷ *mastaba* tombs nearby. Of important note is the 6th-Dynasty (2345–2181 BC) tomb of Qar, a high-ranking official in charge of maintaining the Giza pyramids. His tomb is decorated with fine reliefs.

The Great Pyramid, Giza

THE FACTS OF KHUFU'S PYRAMID, commonly referred to as the Great Pyramid, are staggering. Until the 19th century it was the tallest building in the world. Yet for such a vast structure the precision is amazing – the greatest difference in length between the four 230-m (756-ft) sides is only 4 cm (2 inches). The construction methods and exact purpose of some of the chambers and shafts are unknown, but the fantastic architectural achievement is clear. It is estimated to contain over two million blocks of stone weighing on average around 2.5 tonnes, with some weighing as much as 15 tonnes.

Statue of Khufu (Cheops)
Khufu's only surviving statue is this 7.5-cm (3-inch) high ivory figure from Abydos, now kept in the Egyptian Museum in Cairo.

The Queen's Chamber probably held a statue representing the *ka* or life-force of the king.

Queens' Pyramids
These three small pyramids were built for members of the king's family, although the actual identity of the occupants is unknown.

Underlying bedrock

The "air shafts" may have been symbolic paths for the king's soul to ascend to the stars.

★ **King's Chamber**
Probably emptied 600 years after being built, the chamber, despite holding only a lidless sarcophagus, was often broken into by treasure seekers.

Unfinished underground chamber

★ **Great Gallery**
Soaring nearly 9 m (30 ft) high, this is thought to have been used as a slipway for the huge blocks that sealed the passageway.

STAR FEATURES

★ **King's Chamber**

★ **Great Gallery**

RECONSTRUCTION OF THE KING'S CHAMBER

Built to protect the chamber, the stress-relieving rooms also hold the only reference to Khufu in the Great Pyramid – gangs who built the pyramid left graffiti stating "How powerful is the great White Crown of Khufu".

King's Chamber

The "air shaft" would have been closed off by the outer casing.

SOLAR BOAT MUSEUM

Near the Great Pyramid sits the Solar Boat Museum. This holds a full-size solar boat found in 1954, which took experts 14 years to put its 1,200 pieces back together. Archaeologists believe that it might have been a funerary barque for Khufu.

Workers' graffiti

Stress-relieving chambers were built out of huge blocks of granite weighing up to 80 tonnes.

Counterbalanced slabs of granite were lowered to seal the tomb.

KEY DATES

2589–2566 BC King Khufu builds the Great Pyramid during his reign.

2555–2532 BC Construction of the Pyramid of Khafre.

1550–1295 BC The Sphinx is restored for the first time.

1979 The Giza Plateau is inscribed a UNESCO World Heritage Site.

KHUFU

Reigning for approximately 24 years, this 4th-Dynasty pharaoh (r.2589–2566 BC) is also known as Cheops or Suphis due to the late Greek influence on Egypt. His real name, Khnum-Khufwy, meaning "the god of Khnum protect me", was often shortened to Khufu. He built the most famous tomb in the ancient world, the Great Pyramid, one of the world's seven ancient wonders. His tomb was robbed long before archaeologists discovered it and all that remains is his modest statue (▷ *statue of Khufu*). He is believed to have been a wealthy ruler of a highly structured society. He led and coordinated his people in the building of the Great Pyramid which, contrary to popular belief, was not achieved through slave labour, but by a conscripted workforce. Despite his benevolent parentage, Khufu was reputedly both ruthless and cruel. He also enjoyed stories about the reigns of his predecessors and tales about magic and mystery.

This vertical shaft probably served as an escape route for the workers.

THE DEVELOPMENT OF PYRAMIDS

It took the ancient Egyptians around 400 years to progress from mudbrick *mastaba* to smooth-sided pyramid. The last stage, from stepped to "true" or smooth-sided pyramid took only 65 years. In this time each pyramid was a brave venture into the unknown. Rarely in the history of mankind has technology developed at such a rate.

The Red or North Pyramid, at Dahshur (c.2600 BC)

Mastaba
Around 3000 BC the sandy mounds of the graves of the upper echelons of society were formalized into low, box-like mastabas.

Stepped Pyramid (c.2665 BC)
A more impressive memorial was made by putting six stone mastabas on top of each other.

Prototype Pyramid (c.2605 BC)
The first smooth-sided pyramid was achieved by filling in the steps of a pyramid. This was followed by purpose-built, smooth-sided pyramids.

Entrance
The original entrance is blocked and a lower opening made by the Caliph Maamun in AD 820 is now used.

The Great Pyramid

A New Location

When the Aswan Dam proved too small to control the floodwaters of the Nile, the Egyptian government embarked on a project to build the High Dam and create Lake Nasser as a reservoir. But the rising waters of the lake threatened to submerge Abu Simbel. Concern over losing the temples led UNESCO to back an international relief scheme and in 1964 an ambitious four-year operation began to move the two monuments to safety. The temples, complete with their artifacts, were cut into 950 blocks and transferred to a higher site against the backdrop of a purpose-built mountain (▷ *Relocated Temples*). Care was taken to ensure that the ▷ *Inner Sanctuary* remained aligned with the sun.

The Aswan Dam, built in 1902 to regulate the flow of the Nile

The Great Statues

Three of the four 20-m (65-ft) high statues, the ▷ *Ramses II Colossi*, gaze southwards to deter even the most determined of the pharoah's enemies. Their enormous size is thought to illustrate Ramses' divinity as a supreme god. The gods and Ramses' family feature prominently among the other statues. At the feet of the colossi stand figures of the pharaoh's mother, his wife Queen Nefertari and the royal children. Above the entrance to the Great Temple is the falcon-headed statue of the sun god ▷ *Ra-Harakhty*. Hapi, the god of the Nile flood, associated with fertility, is featured holding lotus and papyrus, symbols of Upper and Lower Egypt respectively.

Abu Simbel

Carved baboon at Abu Simbel

HEWN OUT OF a solid cliff in the 13th century BC, the Great Temple of Abu Simbel and the smaller Temple of Hathor are a breathtaking sight. Although dedicated to the patron deities of Egypt's great cities – Amun of Thebes, Ptah of Memphis and Ra-Harakhty of Heliopolis – the Great Temple was built to honour Ramses II. Its 33-m (108-ft) high façade, with four colossal enthroned statues of Ramses II wearing the double crown of Upper and Lower Egypt, was intended to impress and frighten, while the interior revealed the union of god and king.

Relocated Temples at Abu Simbel
In the 1960s, as Lake Nasser threatened to engulf the temples, UNESCO cut them from the mountain and moved them to an artificial cliff 210 m (688 ft) back from and 65 m (213 ft) above their original position.

Ramses II Colossi
Accompanied by carved images of captives from the north and south, the four colossi on the temple façade boast of a unified Egypt. Ramses' names adorn the thrones in cartouche form.

STAR FEATURES

★ **Temple Façade**

★ **Inner Sanctuary**

★ **Hypostyle Hall**

★ **Temple Façade**
Buried in sand for centuries, this façade was discovered in 1813 by Swiss explorer Jean-Louis Burckhardt.

Store rooms held offerings to the gods and ritual items.

Baboons greeting the rising sun

Statue of Ra-Harakhty

The broken colossus lost its head in an earthquake in 27 BC.

Entrance to temple

The vestibule is adorned with scenes of Ramses and Nefertari making offerings to Amun and Ra-Harakhty.

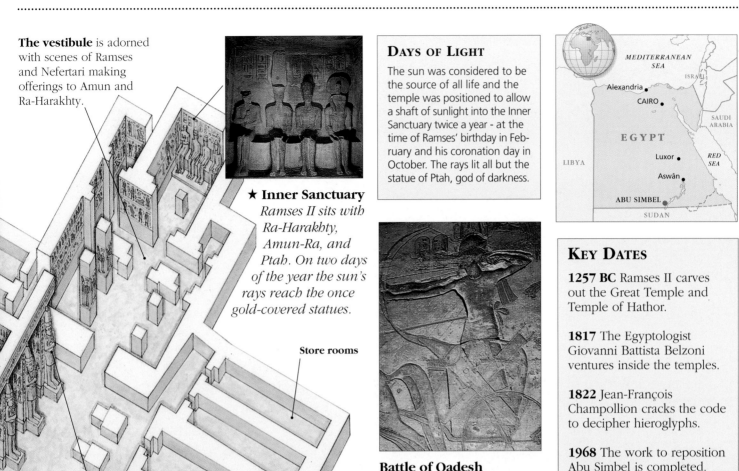

★ **Inner Sanctuary**
Ramses II sits with Ra-Harakhty, Amun-Ra, and Ptah. On two days of the year the sun's rays reach the once gold-covered statues.

Store rooms

10-m (33-ft) high statue of Ramses as Osiris

★ **Hypostyle Hall**
In this hall the roof is supported by pillars with colossi in Osiride form – carrying crook and flail. Those on the southern pillars wear the Upper Egypt crown, while the northern ones wear the double crown of Upper and Lower Egypt.

DAYS OF LIGHT

The sun was considered to be the source of all life and the temple was positioned to allow a shaft of sunlight into the Inner Sanctuary twice a year - at the time of Ramses' birthday in February and his coronation day in October. The rays lit all but the statue of Ptah, god of darkness.

Battle of Qadesh
Reliefs inside the hypostyle hall show Ramses II defeating Egypt's enemies including, on the right hand wall, the defeat of the Hittites in the Battle of Qadesh c.1275 BC.

TEMPLE OF HATHOR

Dedicated to the goddess Hathor, deity of love, pleasure and beauty, the smaller temple at Abu Simbel was built by Ramses II to honour his favourite wife, Nefertari. The hypostyle hall has Hathor-headed pillars and is decorated with scenes of Ramses slaying Egypt's enemies, watched by Nefertari. The vestibule shows the royal couple making offerings to the gods.

Statues of Nefertari as goddess Hathor alternating with Ramses II on the façade of Queen Nefertari's Temple

KEY DATES

1257 BC Ramses II carves out the Great Temple and Temple of Hathor.

1817 The Egyptologist Giovanni Battista Belzoni ventures inside the temples.

1822 Jean-François Champollion cracks the code to decipher hieroglyphs.

1968 The work to reposition Abu Simbel is completed.

1979 Abu Simbel is declared a UNESCO World Heritage Site.

WRITING ON THE WALL

Graphic wall paintings and reliefs found in the Great Temple of Abu Simbel and the ▷ *Temple of Hathor* glorify Ramses II as a divine pharaoh. They tell of his victories and show him fighting his enemies. In the Temple of Hathor Nefertari's consecration as divine queen is illustrated. Surrounding the paintings and reliefs are detailed rows of hieroglyphs. This pictorial script, thought to have developed around 3200 BC, is the world's oldest known form of writing. The word "hieroglyph" means "sacred carved letter" and a complex system of 6,000 symbols was used by the ancient Egyptians to write their names and express their religious beliefs. Stories of the life of Ramses and Nefertari have been engraved in this way on the walls. This painstaking work, undertaken by highly-trained scribes, fell from use in the 4th century AD.

Abu Simbel

The mosque's imposing mud-brick façade

THE HISTORY OF DJENNÉ MOSQUE

Djenné's present-day mosque was constructed in 1907 on the foundations of the town's first mosque. This was built in 1280 by Koi Konboro, the 26th king of Djenné, following his conversion to Islam. As a demonstration of his allegiance to the new faith, he had his royal palace knocked down and the mosque constructed on its site. His mosque survived until the early 19th century when the fundamentalist Islamic king, Cheikou Amadou, keen to reinforce local Islamic religious practices, allowed it to fall into ruin. Instead, a more austere mosque was built close by (now the site of a *medresa*).

MOSQUE DESIGN

With its thick, battlemented walls and towers, and the peculiar "spiky" appearance of the projecting ▷ *wooden beams*, the mosque seems more like a fortress than a religious building. Its imposing exterior is made up of ▷ *three sloping minarets*, which stand over 10 m (33 ft) high, some ▷ *towers*, and a large ▷ *base*, accessible via a number of ▷ *stepped entrances*. The interior is not accessible to non-Muslims, but views of it can be had from the roofs of nearby houses. The art and skill of the masons have been handed down from generation to generation since the 15th century. The master masons still mix the mud mortar by foot, and shape the mud bricks by hand. A simple iron trowel is their only tool, and is used for cutting the bricks and levelling the walls.

◁ **Fortress-like exterior of Djenné Mosque, Mali**

Djenné Mosque, Mali

WITH ITS STRIKING façade and unique architectural style, the Djenné Mosque ranks among the most unusual and beautiful buildings in the world. This large mud-brick structure is typical of the special African-Islamic "marriage" found on the continent – in which African societies have moulded Islam to fit their own traditional beliefs, values and concerns. Usually a mosque is made of the finest materials available, but the Djenné Mosque is made with the modest, humble material of sun-baked mud (also known as *adobe* or *pisé*), which in the skilled hands of the Mali master masons has resulted in one of the most remarkable expressions of faith in Africa.

The Market
A colourful market is set up in front of the Djenné Mosque every Monday, attracting traders from the surrounding area. Djenné and its region are famous for the mud cloth sold here, known as bogolan.

Mosque Interior
Inside the mosque the impressive prayer hall with its sandy floor is covered by a wooden roof supported by nearly 100 pillars.

Three sloping minarets
are used by the *muezzin* (mosque official) to call the faithful to prayer. Staircases inside each minaret lead directly to the roof.

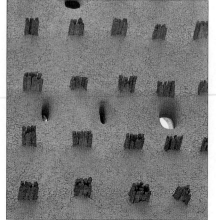

★ Wooden Beams
Giving the mosque its distinctive "spiky" appearance, the palm beams not only support the mud walls, but also serve as a kind of permanent scaffolding for the annual repairs, as well as aesthetically relieving the solidity of the structure.

The Spring Renovation

The annual restoration of the mosque is a communal concern, with up to 4,000 townspeople taking part in the work. Specialist masons, bareys (a kind of builder-magician caste dating back to the 15th century), carefully oversee the work.

WIND, SUN AND RAIN

The elements cause damage to the Djenné Mosque. Rainwater erodes the walls and damp can weaken the structure. Extreme temperature and humidity also cause stress to the building. However, the yearly replastering helps keep the building in good shape.

★ Base

The large base on which the mosque sits raises it some 3 m (10 ft) above the market area, and separates it both physically and symbolically from the pedestrian and profane activities of the market place.

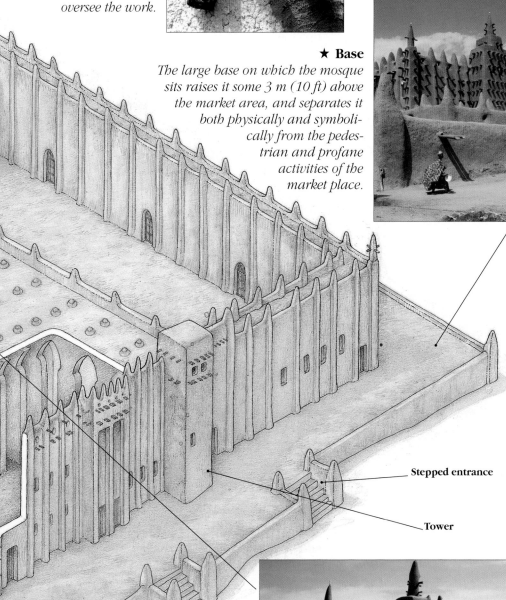

Stepped entrance

Tower

KEY DATES

c.1250–1300 Djenné town is founded and the first mosque is built.

1300–1468 Djenné forms part of the Mali Empire.

1468 The Songhay Empire captures and annexes the city.

1591 Moroccans take over the city.

1819 Cheikou Amadou abandons the old mosque and builds a new one on a different site.

1907 A third mosque is constructed on the foundations of the 13th-century original.

1988 Djenné is declared a UNESCO World Heritage Site.

DJENNÉ TOWN

Djenné is one of the oldest trading towns in the region. Founded in 1250 on the ancient trans-Saharan trade routes, Djenné quickly grew into a thriving centre of commerce, attracting merchants from north, east, west and central Africa. Textiles, brass, ceramics and copperware were exchanged for Sahel gold, ivory and precious Saharan salt. By the end of the 13th century, Islam had also arrived, brought to Djenné by Muslim merchants from North Africa, and the first mosque was built. By the 14th century, Djenné had not only become an important centre of Islamic learning, but also one of the wealthiest and most cosmopolitan towns of sub-Saharan Africa.

STAR FEATURES

★ **Wooden Beams**

★ **Base**

★ **Pillars and Roof**

★ Pillars and Roof

A forest of 90 wooden pillars supports the roof, which is perforated with small vents to allow light and air to penetrate. In the rainy season, the holes are covered with ceramic caps.

Djenné Mosque

Castle of Good Hope

THE WILLIAM FEHR COLLECTION

The Castle of Good Hope houses the famous ▷ *William Fehr Collection* of historical paintings and furnishings. Dr Fehr (1892–1968) was a local businessman who started collecting colonial pictures and objects at a time when the practice was unusual. His collection now forms an invaluable record of many aspects of social and political life in the Cape, from the early days of the Dutch East India Company (VOC in Dutch) to the end of the 19th century. As well as landscape paintings by English artists Thomas Baines and William Huggins, there are also exhibits of 17th-century Japanese porcelain and 18th-century Indonesian furniture.

COMMANDER JAN VAN RIEBEECK

In April 1652, the Dutchman Jan van Riebeeck arrived at the Cape with about 80 men and women to establish a staging post for the Dutch East India Company. This was needed to provision Dutch ships plying the lucrative trade route between Europe and Asia. Despite setbacks (20 men died during that first winter), the station flourished and began to provide ships with meat, milk and vegetables. Rivalry with the indigenous Khoina over water and grazing, however, soon turned into open hostility, escalating into bitter wars.

Commander Jan van Riebeeck, founder of Cape Town

Castle of Good Hope, Cape Town

Dutch East India (VOC) monogram, 17th century

SOUTH AFRICA'S OLDEST SURVIVING structure, the castle of Good Hope, was built between 1666–79, replacing an earlier clay-and-timber fort erected by Commander Jan van Riebeeck in 1652. The castle overlooks the Grand Parade and is now home to a military museum, an art collection, a banqueting hall and is the headquarters for Cape Army regiments.

The Castle Moat
Sections of the moat were rebuilt as part of an extensive restoration programme launched in the 1980s.

Old Slates
Slate, taken from a quarry on Robben Island in the 17th century, was used as the paving material inside the castle.

STAR FEATURES

★ **The Castle Military Museum**

★ **William Fehr Collection**

★ **De Kat Staircase**

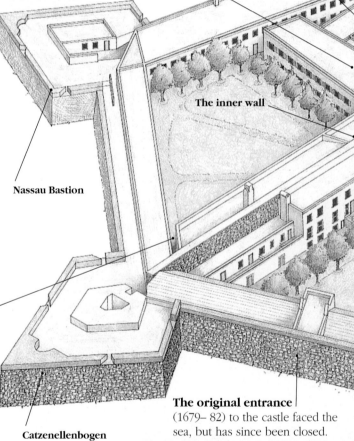

Dolphin Pool
Descriptions and sketches made by Lady Anne Barnard in the 1790s enabled the reconstruction of the dolphin pool over two hundred years later.

Bakery

The inner wall

Nassau Bastion

Catzenellenbogen Bastion

The original entrance
(1679– 82) to the castle faced the sea, but has since been closed.

★ **The Castle Military Museum**
On display is an array of military artifacts, including weapons and uniforms from the VOC and British periods in the Cape.

★ William Fehr Collection

Exhibits include paintings by artists such as Thomas Baines, as well as period furniture, glass, ceramics and metalware.

DUTCH TRADERS

In 1602 the Dutch East India Company (Verenigde Oost-indische Compagnie, or VOC) was founded to trade with Asia mainly for its prized spices. Successful and powerful, by 1669 the VOC fleet numbered 150 merchant ships and 40 warships.

Oranje Bastion

Entrance Gable

A teak copy of the original VOC gable reflects martial symbols: a banner, flags, drums and cannon balls.

Leerdam Bastion

Each bastion was named after titles held by Prince William of Orange – Leerdam, Oranje, Nassau, Catzenellenbogen and Buuren.

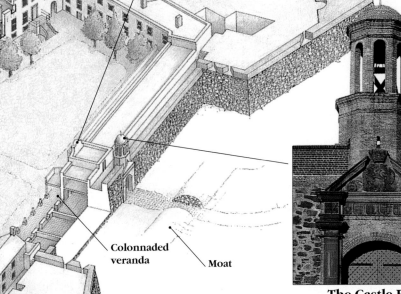

Colonnaded veranda

Moat

Buuren Bastion

★ De Kat Staircase

The original staircase, built in 1695 as part of a defensive crosswall, divided the square into an inner and outer court, and was remodelled between 1786 and 1790.

The Castle Entrance

The original bell, cast in Amsterdam in 1697, still hangs in the belfry. The coat of arms of the United Netherlands can be seen on the pediment above the gate.

KEY DATES

1652 First Dutch settlers, under the command of Jan van Riebeeck, land on the Cape.

1666–79 Settlers build a stone castle to replace van Riebeeck's earlier timber fort.

1795 Rule by the Dutch East India Company (VOC) ends and British forces occupy the Cape.

1952 The William Fehr art collection moves to the Castle.

THE CASTLE

The design of the castle was influenced by the work of the French military engineer Vauban, employed at the court of Louis XIV. The castle was built in the shape of a pentagon with five defensive bastions, from which the outside walls could be defended by cross-fire. The ▷ *original entrance* faced the sea but it was moved to its present position in 1684. From the beginning the castle was intended as a base for the Dutch East India Company in the Cape. In 1691 a line of rooms known as De Kat was added across the centre of the castle courtyard and this became the Governor's residence. Today this area houses the ▷ *William Fehr Collection*. In the past the Castle of Good Hope housed facilities to support a community, with living quarters, a church, a bakery, offices and a jail with a torture chamber. In the 1930s a new banqueting hall was created from a series of rooms on an upper floor.

Castle of Good Hope

THE WORLD'S MUST-SEE PLACES

ASIA

PAGES 172-221

Krak des Chevaliers, the Crusaders' magnificent fortress

INSIDE THE CASTLE

Krak des Chevaliers (Castle of the Knights) crowns a 650-m (2,133-ft) high hill at Homs Gap, commanding the route from Antioch to Beirut. The crusading Knights Hospitallers undertook a massive expansion programme in the mid-12th century, adding a 30-m (98-ft) thick outer wall, seven guard towers and ▷ *stables* for 500 horses. An inner reservoir filled by water from an ▷ *aqueduct* supplied the needs of the 4,000-strong garrison. Storerooms were stocked with food produced by local villagers. The castle had its own olive presses and a bakery. The later Muslim occupants converted the Crusaders' ▷ *Chapel* of St George into a mosque and also added refinements, such as ▷ *baths* and pools.

THE FINAL CONQUEST

While the Crusaders continued their campaigns in the Middle East throughout the 12th and into the 13th centuries, Krak des Chevaliers remained secure. In 1163, the knights successfully fought off the army of Nuradin, sultan of Damascus, in the valley below. Then in 1188, the Muslim leader, Saladin, attempted to lay siege to the castle, but finding it impenetrable, withdrew his forces. Finally, in 1271, the Mameluk sultan, Baibars I, devised a scheme. He forged a letter, said to be from the Crusader commander in Tripoli, instructing the army at Krak to surrender. Baibars' forces succeeded in taking the Crusaders' bastion without so much as a fight.

Krak des Chevaliers

O NE OF THE GREATEST castles in the world, Krak des Chevaliers was built in the middle of the 12th century by the Crusaders. Having captured Jerusalem and the Holy Land from the Muslims, they required strong bases from which to defend their newly won territories. The largest of a string of such fortresses, Krak des Chevaliers withstood countless attacks and sieges, but the Crusaders abandoned it after their defeat at the hands of the Arabs in 1271. Villagers settled within the walls and remained there until the 1930s, when the castle was cleared and restored.

General view of Krak des Chevaliers

RECONSTRUCTION OF KRAK DES CHEVALIERS

This shows how the castle would have looked over 800 years ago. In its heyday the castle would have housed a garrison of 4,000.

The glacis is an enormous sloping wall designed to stop attackers undermining the inner wall.

The Warden's Tower, containing the guard master's quarters, was the castle's innermost keep.

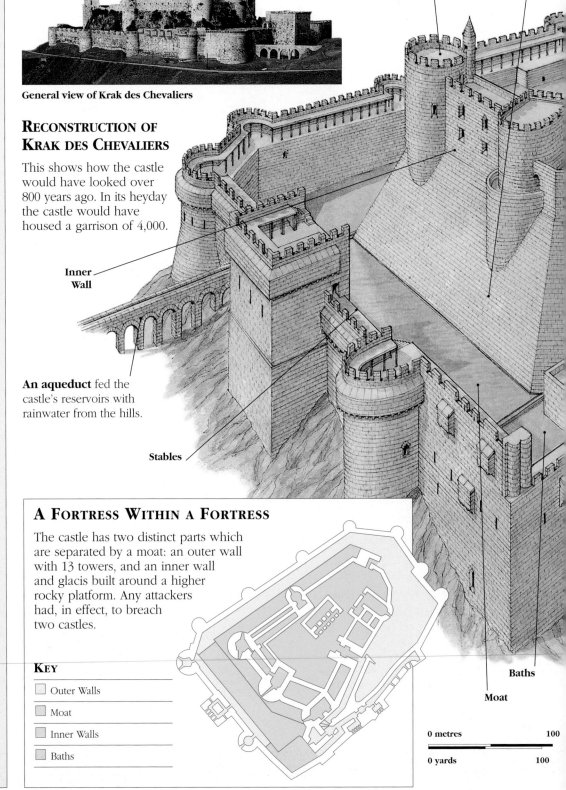

Inner Wall

An aqueduct fed the castle's reservoirs with rainwater from the hills.

Stables

Baths

Moat

A FORTRESS WITHIN A FORTRESS

The castle has two distinct parts which are separated by a moat: an outer wall with 13 towers, and an inner wall and glacis built around a higher rocky platform. Any attackers had, in effect, to breach two castles.

KEY

☐ Outer Walls

☐ Moat

☐ Inner Walls

☐ Baths

0 metres   100

0 yards   100

◁ **The Taj Mahal, a prime example of Mughal architecture**

★ Tower of the King's Daughter

The northern face of this tower has a large projecting gallery from which rocks could be hurled if the outer wall was breached. At ground level the tower is decorated with three blind arches.

Outer wall

Krak des Chevaliers

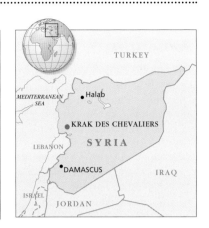

THE PERFECT CASTLE

The author T E Lawrence ("Lawrence of Arabia") described Krak des Chevaliers as "the most wholly admirable castle in the world". Indeed, it served as an inspiration to the English king, Edward I, who passed by on the ninth Crusade in 1272 and returned home to build his own castles across England and Wales.

KEY DATES

1031 The Emir of Aleppo builds the original fortress.

1110 Crusaders under Tancred take the bastion.

1142 The Knights Hospitallers occupy the castle and construct the outer wall.

1271 Baibars I, the Mameluk sultan, captures the castle and adds further fortifications.

1934 Restoration begins.

★ Main Entranceway

A long, stepped passage leads from the site of the former drawbridge to the upper castle. Small ceiling apertures throw light into the corridor, though they were also designed for pouring boiling oil over invaders. The passageways are high and wide enough to allow for mounted riders.

The chapel was built by the Crusaders and later converted into a mosque after the Muslim conquest. Its Islamic *minbar* (pulpit) can still be seen.

The entrance passage doubled back on itself to confuse any invaders who managed to get this far.

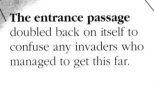

Inner Fortress

★ Loggia

Running along one side of the castle's innermost courtyard, the loggia is a graceful Gothic arcade with a vaulted ceiling (▷ Gothic Style p55). It is decorated with carved floral motifs and animals. Beyond the loggia is the Great Hall, which functioned as a refectory.

TANCRED, PRINCE OF ANTIOCH

In 1096 a young Norman lord from southern Italy, Tancred of Hauteville (1078–1112), set out with his uncle, Bohemund, and fellow Norman lords on the first Crusade to the Holy Land. Their object was to halt the advance of the Seljuk Turks, who were threatening the Byzantine Empire, and to claim Jerusalem for the Christians. Tancred soon made a name for himself when he captured Tarsus from the Turks. He played a major role in the siege of Antioch and led the march on Jerusalem (1099) and its occupation. A year later, when Bohemund was taken prisoner by the Turks, Tancred took control of the Principality of Antioch. As Prince of Antioch, he ruled supreme in northern Syria, mounting attacks on both the Turks and Byzantines. In 1110 he occupied the hilltop fortress, which the Crusaders were to transform into the mighty Krak des Chevaliers.

STAR FEATURES

★ Tower of the King's Daughter

★ Main Entranceway

★ Loggia

GOLGOTHA

Inside the church, two stair-cases lead up to Golgotha, meaning "Place of the Skull" in Hebrew. On the left is a Greek Orthodox chapel with its altar placed directly over the rocky outcrop on which the cross of Christ's Crucifixion is believed to have stood (▷ *Rock of Golgotha*). The crack in Golgotha, visible from the apse of the ▷ *Chapel of Adam* below, is believed to have been caused by the earthquake that followed Christ's death (*Matthew* 27:51). To the right is a Roman Catholic chapel containing a silver and bronze altar made in 1558 and donated by Cardinal Ferdinand de Medici. In between the two altars is the Stabat Mater, an altar commemorating Mary's sorrow at the foot of the cross.

The Holy Sepulchre seen from the roof of St Helena's chapel

THE STATUS QUO

No fewer than 17 churches are represented in Jerusalem, a result of many historical schisms. Fierce disputes, lasting centuries, between Christian creeds over ownership of the Church of the Holy Sepulchre were largely resolved by an Ottoman decree issued in 1852. Still in force and known as the Status Quo, it divides custody of the church among Armenians, Greeks, Copts, Roman Catholics, Ethiopians and Syrians. Some areas are administered communally. Every day, the church is unlocked by a Muslim keyholder acting as a "neutral" intermediary. This ceremonial task has been performed by a member of the same family for generations.

Church of the Holy Sepulchre, Jerusalem

BUILT AROUND WHAT IS BELIEVED to be the site of Christ's crucifixion, burial and resurrection, this complex church is the most important in Christendom. The first basilica here was built by Roman emperor Constantine between AD 326 and 335 at the suggestion of his mother, St Helena. It was rebuilt on a smaller scale by Byzantine emperor Constantine Monomachus in the 1040s following its destruction by Fatimid sultan Hakim in 1009, but was much enlarged again by the Crusaders between 1114 and 1170. A disastrous fire in 1808 and an earthquake in 1927 necessitated extensive repairs.

The mosaic of roofs and domes of the Church of the Holy Sepulchre

The Rotunda, heavily rebuilt after the 1808 fire, is the most majestic part of the church.

★ **Christ's Tomb**
For Christians, this is the most sacred site of all. Inside the 1810 monument, a marble slab covers the rock on which Christ's body is believed to have been laid.

The Crusader bell tower was reduced by two storeys in 1719.

Stone of Unction
This is where the anointing and wrapping of Christ's body after his death has been commemorated since medieval times. The present stone dates from 1810.

Chapel of the Franks

The main entrance is early 12th-century. The right-hand door was blocked up late in the same century.

Courtyard
The main entrance courtyard is flanked by chapels. The disused steps opposite the bell tower once led to the Chapel of the Franks, the Crusaders' ceremonial entrance to Golgotha.

THE HOLY FIRE

On the Saturday of Orthodox Easter, all the church's lamps are put out and the faithful stand in the dark, a symbol of the darkness at the Crucifixion. A candle is lit at Christ's Tomb, then another and another, until the entire basilica and courtyard are ablaze with light, symbolizing the Resurrection. Legend says the fire comes from heaven.

The Easter ceremony of the Holy Fire

THE FIRST CHURCHES

Christian churches did not appear in the Holy Land until AD 200. Roman suspicion of unauthorized sects kept these churches underground until the 4th century AD when Christianity became the dominant religion.

LEBANON

SYRIA

MEDITERRANEAN
SEA

Haifa

Tel Aviv

CHURCH OF THE
HOLY SEPULCHRE,
JERUSALEM

ISRAEL

EGYPT

JORDAN

IRAQ

KEY DATES

326–35 Emperor Constantine and St Helena have the first basilica built.

1114–70 Crusaders enlarge the building.

1981 Old City of Jerusalem joins the list of UNESCO World Heritage Sites.

The Seven Arches of the Virgin are the remains of an 11th-century colonnaded courtyard.

Catholikon Dome
Rebuilt after the 1927 earthquake and decorated with an image of Christ, this dome covers the central nave of the Crusader church. This part of the building is now used for Greek Orthodox services.

The Centre of the World, according to ancient map-makers, is marked here by a stone basin.

★ **Rock of Golgotha**
Through the glass around the Greek Orthodox altar can be seen the outcrop of rock venerated as the site of the Crucifixion.

Chapel of Adam

Rock of Golgotha

The Chapel of St Helena is now dedicated to St Gregory the Illuminator, patron saint of the Armenians.

Ethiopian Monastery
Living in the cluster of small buildings on the roof of the Chapel of St Helena is a community of Ethiopian monks.

Stairs to the Inventio Crucis Chapel

STAR FEATURES

★ **Christ's Tomb**

★ **Rock of Golgotha**

CHRIST'S TOMB

For the construction of the first church, in the 4th century, Emperor Constantine's builders dug away the hillside to leave the presumed rock-hewn tomb of Christ (▷ *Christ's Tomb*) isolated, with enough room to build a church around it. To achieve this end, an old temple had to be cleared from the site and in the process the ▷ *Rock of Golgotha*, believed to be the site where Christ was nailed to the cross, was found. A succession of shrines replaced the original 4th-century one. In 1555, a shrine was commissioned by the Franciscan friar Bonifacio da Ragusa. The present shrine was rebuilt in 1809–10, after a severe fire in 1808. The shrine contains two chapels. The outer Chapel of the Angel has a low pilaster with a piece of the stone said to have been rolled from the mouth of Christ's tomb by angels. It serves as a Greek Orthodox altar. A low door leads to the inner Chapel of the Holy Sepulchre which houses the place where Christ's body was said to have been laid.

Church of the Holy Sepulchre

MOHAMMED'S NIGHT JOURNEY

The Koran, the holy book of Islam, is regarded as the exact word of Allah. Muslims believe that it can never be truly understood unless read in Arabic; translations into other languages can only ever paraphrase. The Koran is divided into 114 chapters, covering many topics. One of the core episodes recounts the Night Journey of the Prophet Mohammed. In this he is carried from Mecca to Jerusalem and from there makes the *Miraj*, the ascent through the heavens to God's presence, returning to Mecca in the morning. The story is illustrated with geometric tiling and verses on the exterior of the ▷ *drum* of the Dome of the Rock.

Octagonal arcade of the Dome, above which are Koranic verses

HARAM ASH-SHARIF

The Temple Mount or *Haram ash-Sharif*, in the southeastern part of the Old City of Jerusalem, is an important Islamic religious sanctuary and home to a number of important buildings. The Dome of the Rock is its chief attraction. Traditionally the site of Solomon's Temple, it later housed the Second Temple, enlarged by Herod the Great and destroyed by the Romans. Left in ruins for more than half a century, the site became an Islamic shrine in 691 with the construction of the Dome of the Rock. Neighbouring Al-Aqsa Mosque, begun 20 years after the Dome, was twice razed by earthquakes. Its present form dates from the 11th century. Most of the surrounding buildings are Islamic colleges.

Dome of the Rock (side tab)

Dome of the Rock, Jerusalem

Tile above the south entrance

CONSIDERED ONE of the first and greatest achievements of Islamic architecture, the Dome of the Rock was built in AD 688–91 by the Omayyad caliph Abd el-Malik. Built to proclaim the superiority of Islam and provide an Islamic focal point in the Holy City, the majestic structure now dominates Jerusalem and has become a symbol of the city. More a shrine than a mosque, the mathematically harmonious structure echoes elements of Classical and Byzantine styles of architecture (▷ *Classical style p137* and ▷ *Byzantine style p149*).

View of the Dome of the Rock with the Muslim Quarter in the background

The drum is decorated with tiles and verses from the Koran which tell of Mohammed's Night Journey.

★ Tile Work
The multicoloured tiles that adorn the exterior are faithful copies of Persian tiles that Suleyman the Magnificent added in 1545 to replace the damaged original mosaics.

Koranic verses

The octagonal arcade is adorned with original mosaics (AD 692) and an inscription inviting Christians to recognize the truth of Islam.

Marble panel

Inner Corridor
The space between the inner and outer arcades forms a corridor around the Rock. The shrine's two corridors recall the ritual circular movement of pilgrims around the Qaaba in Mecca.

STAR FEATURES

★ **Tile Work**

★ **Interior of Dome**

Crescent Finial and Dome

The dome was originally made of copper but is now covered with gold leaf, thanks to the financial support of the late King Hussein of Jordan.

HOLY SITE

One of the oldest and most beautiful of all mosques, the Dome of the Rock is the third most holy site of Islam after Mecca and Medina. The mosque is also important for Judaism as it stands on the site of the two temples of the Jews - the first built by King Soloman and the second by Herod.

★ Interior of Dome

The dazzling interior of the cupola has elaborate floral decoration as well as various inscriptions. The large text commemorates Saladin, who sponsored restoration work on the building.

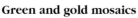

Green and gold mosaics create a scintillating effect on the walls below the dome.

Outer corridor

KEY DATES

691 Building work on the Dome of the Rock is completed.

16th century Suleyman the Magnificent commissions the dazzling tile work on the exterior.

1981 The Dome of the Rock joins the UNESCO list of World Heritage Sites.

THE DOME OF THE CHAIN AND THE GOLDEN GATE

Just east of the Dome of the Rock stands the small Dome of the Chain, set at the approximate centre of the *Haram ash-Sharif*. The reasons given for its construction are varied. According to one theory it sits at the site of the Holy of Holies (the most sacred and inaccessible place in Herod's Temple), which is thought of in Jewish tradition as the *omphalos*, the navel of the universe. The Dome of the Chain is a simple structure with a domed roof supported by 17 columns. It is famous for its marvellous 13th-century interior tiling which surpasses even that of the Dome of the Rock. Its name derives from the legend that a chain once hung from the roof and whoever told a lie while holding it would be struck dead by lightning. Further east is the Golden Gate, one of the original Herodian city gates. Jews believe the Messiah will enter Jerusalem through this gate, which is said to be the reason why the Muslims walled it up in the 7th century.

Well of Souls

This staircase leads down to a chamber under the Rock known as the Well of Souls. The dead are said to meet here twice a month to pray.

Stained-glass window

The Rock

The Rock is variously believed to be where Abraham was asked to sacrifice Isaac, where Mohammed left the Earth on his Night Journey, and the site of the Holy of Holies of Herod's Temple.

Each outer wall is 20.4 m (67 ft) long. This exactly matches the dome's diameter and its height from the base of the drum.

South entrance

INSIDE THE FORTRESS

The cliff-top plateau of Masada is surrounded by two walls 1,400 m (4,593 ft) long and 4 m (13 ft) wide. Within, King Herod built palaces, barracks and storehouses. His private retreat, the splendid northern ▷ Hanging Palace, extended over three terraces cut into the cliff-face and connected by steep staircases. The rooms were lavishly decorated with mosaic floors. Walls and ceilings were painted to resemble stone and marble, and elegant columns surrounded balconies and courtyards. His other palace, the larger ▷ Western Palace, served as the administrative centre and contained Herod's throne room and royal apartments. In the ruins of a stone-built storehouse complex, the remains of storage jars used for keeping wine, oil and grain were found.

THE ZEALOTS

Around the time of Herod's death in 4 BC, the inhabitants of Masada became embroiled in a rebellion against Rome. The uprising was led by Judas of Galilee, founder of the Zealots, a militant Jewish sect which vehemently opposed the Romans because of their pagan beliefs. The Romans crushed the rebellion and took Masada. In AD 66, at the start of the First Jewish Revolt, the Zealots regained the mountain-top. They lived among the palaces using the fortress as a base to conduct raids against the Romans. At the time of the ▷ Roman siege of Masada, there were 1,000 inhabitants.

The desert fort of Masada, site of the Zealots' last stand

Masada

THIS ISOLATED MOUNTAIN-TOP FORTRESS about 440 m (1,300 ft) above the banks of the Dead Sea, known as Masada, is believed to be the location of the oldest synagogue in the world. It was fortified as early as the 1st or 2nd century BC and then enlarged and reinforced by Herod the Great, who added two luxurious palace complexes. On Herod's death the fortress passed into Roman hands but it was captured in AD 66 during the First Revolt by Jews of the Zealot sect. After the Romans crushed the rebels in Jerusalem, Masada remained the last Jewish stronghold. It remained defended for over two years before the walls were breached by the Romans in AD 73.

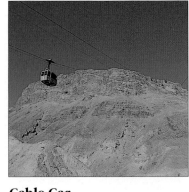

Cable Car
A large number of pilgrims visit this rocky mountain citadel every year. The cable car was installed to help with their tiring journey.

Upper terrace
Snake Path
Storerooms
Middle terrace
Lower terrace

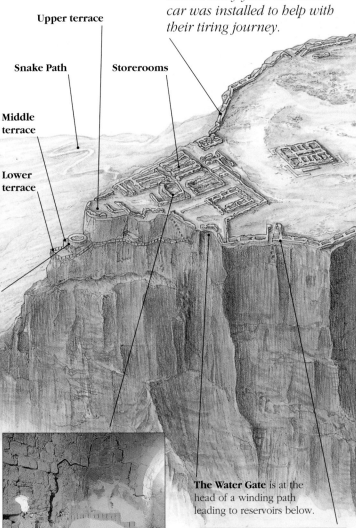

★ Hanging Palace
Part of the large Northern Palace complex, the Hanging Palace was Herod's private residence. It was built on three levels; the middle terrace had a circular hall used for entertaining, the lower had a bathhouse.

The Water Gate is at the head of a winding path leading to reservoirs below.

Calidarium
Masada's hot baths are one of the best preserved parts of the fortress. The columns remain, on which the original floor was raised to allow hot air to circulate underneath and heat the room.

Synagogue
Possibly built by Herod, this synagogue is thought to be the oldest in the world. The stone seats were added by the Zealots.

STAR FEATURES

★ Hanging Palace

★ Western Palace

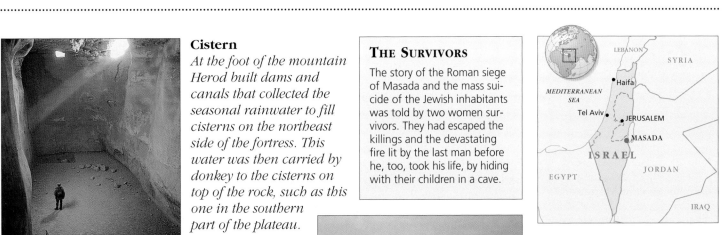

Cistern

At the foot of the mountain Herod built dams and canals that collected the seasonal rainwater to fill cisterns on the northeast side of the fortress. This water was then carried by donkey to the cisterns on top of the rock, such as this one in the southern part of the plateau.

THE SURVIVORS

The story of the Roman siege of Masada and the mass suicide of the Jewish inhabitants was told by two women survivors. They had escaped the killings and the devastating fire lit by the last man before he, too, took his life, by hiding with their children in a cave.

Southern
Citadel

Columbarium

This is a small building with niches for funerary urns; it is thought the urns held the ashes of non-Jewish members of Herod's court.

Western
Wall

West
Gate

The Roman ramp
is now the western
entrance to the site.

★ Western Palace

Used for receptions and the accommodation of Herod's guests, the Western Palace was richly decorated with mosaic floors and frescoes adorning the walls.

KEY DATES

37–31 BC Herod starts his grandiose building projects.

1963 Excavations of the Masada stronghold begin.

2001 UNESCO declares Masada a World Heritage Site.

HEROD THE GREAT

Herod was born in 73 BC, the son of a Jewish father, Antipater, and an Arab mother, Cyprus. Herod, like his father, was a practising Jew. Antipater was the right-hand man of Hyrcanus, king of Judaea (r.76–30 BC) – a vassal state of Rome – and instrumental in Herod's first appointment at the age of 16 as governor of Galilee. With cunning and ruthlessness, Herod moved up the political ladder, married the king's daughter, found favour with his Roman overlords and was ultimately crowned king of Judaea himself in 37 BC. He embarked on a massive building programme, which included a modern port, Caesarea, fortresses such as Masada, and the grand reconstruction of the Temple in Jerusalem. Orthodox Jews however, considered him racially impure and were incensed by his tyrannical rule and his excessive taxes. They despised the presence of the golden eagle – a symbol of Roman power – on the Temple gate. When he died in 4 BC his kingdom was divided among four of his sons - he had had two sons executed just before dying to prevent them from succeeding him.

THE ROMAN SIEGE OF MASADA (AD 70–73)

According to a 1st-century account by historian Flavius Josephus, the Roman legions laying siege to Masada numbered about 10,000 men. To prevent the Jewish rebels from escaping, the Romans surrounded the mountain with a ring of eight camps, linked by walls; an arrangement that can still be seen today. To make their attack, the Romans built a huge earthen ramp up the mountainside. Once this was finished, a tower was constructed against the walls. From the shelter of this tower the Romans set to work with a battering ram. The defenders hastily erected an inner defensive wall, but this proved little obstacle and Masada fell when it was breached. Rather than submit to the Romans the Jews inside chose to commit mass suicide. Josephus relates how each man was responsible for killing his own family. "Masada shall not fall again" is a swearing-in oath of the modern Israeli army.

Roman catapult missiles

Remains of one of the Roman base camps viewed from the fortress top

Access to Petra is through a deep ravine called the Siq, preceded by a wide valley called the Bab el-Siq. The entrance to the Siq is marked by the remains of a monumental arch and is the start of a gallery of intriguing insights into the Nabataeans' past. These include rock-cut water channels, Nabataean graffiti, carved niches with worn outlines of ancient deities, Nabataean paving stones and flights of steps leading nowhere. As the Siq descends it becomes almost imperceptibly deeper and narrower (at its narrowest the walls are only 1 m (3 ft) apart). At its deepest, darkest point the Siq opens out before Petra's most thrilling monument, the ▷ *Treasury*. From here the path leads into the ▷ *Outer Siq*.

The Palace Tomb, a three-storey imitation of a Roman palace

THE ROYAL TOMBS

Carved into the base of El-Khubtha mountain, where the ▷ *Outer Siq* opens out onto Petra's central plain, are the Urn, Palace and Corinthian Tombs. Together they are known as the Royal Tombs. Their monumental size suggests they were built for wealthy or important people, possibly Petran kings or queens. These tombs and their neighbours are also remarkable for the vivid striations of colour rippling through their sandstone walls, an effect heightened in the warm glow of late afternoon sun. Particularly striking are the Silk Tomb and the ceiling in the Urn Tomb.

Petra

SET DEEP IN THE ROCK and protected by the valley walls is one of the world's most marvellously preserved and impressive archaeological sites, Petra. There has been human settlement here since prehistoric times, but before the Nabataeans came, Petra was just another watering hole. Between the 3rd century BC and the 1st century AD they built a superb city, the centre of a vast trading empire. In AD 106 Petra was annexed by Rome. Christianity arrived in the 4th century, the Muslims in the 7th and the Crusaders in the 12th. Petra then lay forgotten until the early 19th century.

Treasury Tholos
The central figure may be the Petran fertility goddess El-Uzza. Bullet marks in the tholos and urn have been made over the years by Bedouins attempting to release hidden treasure.

The Outer Siq Designs
A range of intermediate design styles are displayed throughout, including on the Treasury and Theatre tombs. One, freestanding, uniquely combines Classical features with a crowstep used as a battlement.

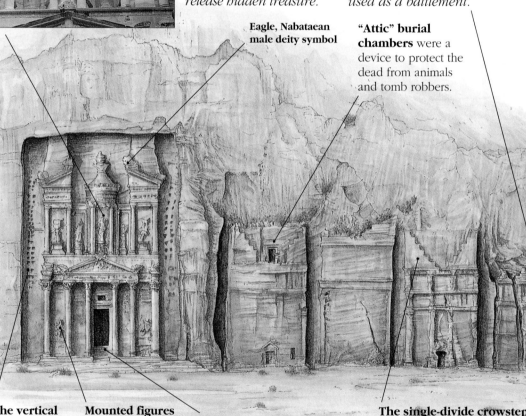

Eagle, Nabataean male deity symbol

"Attic" burial chambers were a device to protect the dead from animals and tomb robbers.

The vertical footholds may have been to aid the sculptors.

Mounted figures of Castor and Pollux, sons of Zeus, flank the portico.

THE OUTER SIQ

The artwork above shows some of the major constructions on the left-hand side of the Outer Siq leading from the Treasury to the Theatre. In reality, of course, the route bends and twists and on both the left and right sides are a great number of other tombs and features of architectural interest.

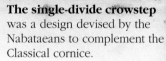

The single-divide crowstep was a design devised by the Nabataeans to complement the Classical cornice.

Treasury Interior
A colossal doorway dominates the outer court (left) and leads to an inner chamber of 12 sq m (129 sq ft). At the back of the chamber is a sanctuary with an ablution basin, suggesting that the Treasury was in fact a temple.

THE ARCHITECTURE OF PETRA

The Nabataeans were adventurous architects, inspired by other cultures but always creating a distinctive look. The multiple crowstep can be seen as a design of the first settlers, whereas complex Nabataean Classical buildings reflect a later period. The dating of façades is very difficult, as many examples of the "early" style appear to have been built during the Classical period (▷ *Classical style p137*) or even later.

This early design was probably Assyrian-inspired.

In Search of Petra

IN SEARCH OF PETRA

After the departure of the Crusaders in the 12th century, Petra lay almost forgotten for over 500 years. In 1812, lured by tales of a lost city, the explorer Johann Ludwig Burckhardt managed to persuade a guide to lead him to Petra.

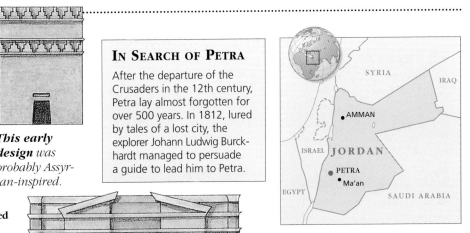

Stacked look, favoured by Nabataeans

Single-divide crowstep, lending height

This intermediate style, seen frequently in Petra, placed multiple crowsteps with a single-divide crowstep, adding Classical cornices and pillars and Hellenistic doorways. This style continued well into the 1st century AD.

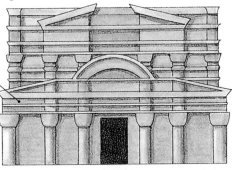

Nabataean Classical designs, such as the Bab el-Siq Triclinium (above), are complex, possibly experimental fusions of Classical and native styles.

KEY DATES

3rd century BC Nabataeans settle in Petra.

12th century AD Petra falls into decline after the Crusaders depart.

1812 The explorer Johann Burckhardt rediscovers Petra.

1985 Petra joins UNESCO's World Heritage list.

THE NABATAEANS

The Nabataeans' original homeland lay in northeastern Arabia but they migrated west in the 6th century BC, settling eventually in Petra. As merchants and entrepreneurs, they grasped the lucrative potential of Petra's position on the spice and incense trade routes from East Asia and Arabia to the Mediterranean. By the 1st century BC they had made Petra the centre of a rich, powerful kingdom extending from Damascus in the north to the Red Sea in the south and had built a city large enough to support 20–30,000 people. Key to their success was their ability to control and conserve water. Conduits and old terracotta piping can be seen along the walls of the ▷ *Siq* – part of an elaborate city water system. The Romans felt threatened by their achievements and took over the city in AD 106. Petra continued to thrive culturally for a time. In the end, changes in trade routes and two devastating earthquakes eventually brought about the city's demise.

Petra

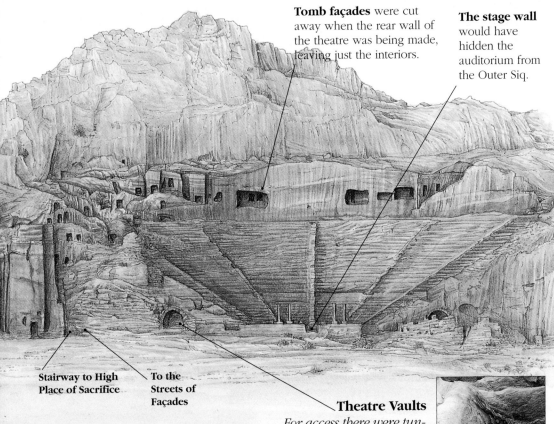

Tomb façades were cut away when the rear wall of the theatre was being made, leaving just the interiors.

The stage wall would have hidden the auditorium from the Outer Siq.

Stairway to High Place of Sacrifice

To the Streets of Façades

Theatre Vaults
For access there were tunnels either side of the stage. Inside (right) these were dressed with painted plaster or marble.

Streets of Façades
Carved on four levels, these tightly packed tombs may include some of Petra's oldest façades. Most are crowned with multiple crowsteps.

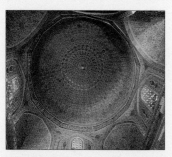

Stunning interior of the Tilla Kari Medresa

BUILDING THE REGISTAN

The three *medresas* were built over a period of 230 years. The first was the ▷ *Ulug Beg*, begun in 1417. Directly opposite, the ▷ *Sher Dor* ("Lion Bearer"), modelled on the Ulug Beg, was added two centuries later. Its unconventional façade depicts live animals and human faces (an interpretation of the Koran forbids this). The combined mosque and *medresa* of ▷ *Tilla Kari* ("Gold Decorated") was added in the mid-17th century. Its ceiling appears domed but is in fact flat – an effect created by the decreasing pattern size towards the centre. The two later buildings were the work of the architect Abd al-Jabbar, who drew his inspiration from the earlier Timurid style, hence the harmonious relationship between the three.

A CENTRE OF SCIENCE AND LEARNING

With room for over 100 students and teachers lodged in 52 cells around the courtyard, the ▷ *Ulug Beg* was effectively a university. Unlike the traditional *medresa*, which was wholly devoted to Islamic studies, students here also received an education in mathematics and the sciences. This was a reflection of Ulug Beg's own personal passions. Known as the "astronomer king" he also endowed Samarkand with one of the world's earliest observatories, a two-storey structure built on a hill and meant to serve as a giant astronomical instrument pointing at the heavens. Only its circular foundations survive today.

The Registan, Samarkand

T HE THREE BUILDINGS SURROUNDING Samarkand's Registan square comprise one of the world's most spectacular architectural ensembles. In the 15th century Ulug Beg, grandson of the Mongol warlord Tamerlane, built a group of mosques, *caravanserais* (merchants' inns) and the Ulug Beg, a *medresa* (Koranic school), around the city's sandy market square. With the exception of the Ulug Beg, the other buildings were later destroyed and replaced in the 17th century by two more *medresas*, the Sher Dor and Tilla Kari.

★ Tilla Kari Medresa
Lavish gold-leaf gilding covers the Mecca-facing mihrab *beneath the dome chamber.*

★ Ulug Beg Medresa
The façade consists of a central arched pishtaq *(porch) flanked by two minarets. The elaborate tiling of stars is in keeping with Ulug Beg's passion for astronomy.*

STAR FEATURES

★ Tilla Kari Medresa

★ Ulug Beg Medresa

★ Sher Dor Medresa

Ornamental gardens today replace the former single-storey buildings that stood in this area.

Prayer hall

The Courtyard has two arcaded tiers of cells for students and professors.

Arched Portals
The Sher Dor Medresa's marvellous courtyard contains large iwans (arched portals) that are covered with spectacular tiling.

MATHEMATICS

Ulug Beg employed a mathematical consultant in the building of his *medresa*, Ghiyath ad-Din Jamshid al-Kashi, whose treatise on mathematics and astronomy has survived to the present day.

Minarets have flared tops from which the *muezzin* called the people to prayer.

Bazaar

Ablutions pool

★ Sher Dor Medresa
The impressive tiling on the pishtaq (porch) depicts two lions stalking gazelles. Behind each lion is a sun portrayed with a human face.

Ulug Beg Medresa Tiling
The brilliant glazed tiles of vine scrolls and flowers in a polychromy of gold leaf and lapis lazuli is typical of Timurid decoration.

Registan Square
A vast space at the heart of the city, the Registan, meaning a "sandy place", is the most famous site in Samarkand.

The Registan

KEY DATES

c.1417–20 Construction of the Ulug Beg Medresa.

1619 Completion of the Sher Dor Medresa.

1647 The Tilla Kari is finished.

1932–52 Restoration of the Ulug Beg Medresa.

2001 The Registan is designated a UNESCO World Heritage Site.

GOLDEN SAMARKAND

Until recently isolated and largely forgotten, what is now known as Central Asia (formerly Turkestan and before that Transoxiana) was once the glittering centre of the Islamic world. Its cities, which included Bukhara and Khiva, boasted magnificent palaces, mosques and mausoleums. Most magnificent of all was Samarkand. The city was already renowned at the time of Alexander the Great but it owes its legendary reputation to Tamerlane (1336–1405), a distant relative of Genghis Khan. Brutal and despotic, Tamerlane was responsible for an estimated 17 million deaths as a result of his military campaigns. He is reported to have had walls and towers built with the skulls of his enemies. However, with the riches he accrued and the artisans he captured and sent back to Samarkand, he built a city that became a political, religious, commercial and cultural capital whose influence extended widely into all corners of the known world.

THE WHITE PALACE

The ▷ *White Palace* is seven storeys high and was used for primarily secular purposes. The top three levels were built around a large, central skywell. These levels contained accommodation and offices for senior monks and officials, as well as kitchens and storage areas. The Dalai Lama occupied two rooms on the top floor, called the ▷ *East and West Sunshine Apartments*. Beneath these three levels lies the Great East Hall, a vast 700-sq m (7,500-sq ft) assembly place for important political ceremonies. The lower levels of the palace provide a frame that supports the main buildings and are used for storage. The first hallway, after the entrance, has several large murals depicting the building of the Potala Palace and the arrival of Princess Wencheng in Tibet with all her retinue.

THE RED PALACE

The Red Palace, at the heart of the Potala complex, was intended for spiritual concerns. It is a complicated structure with numerous halls of worship as well as the remains of eight Dalai Lamas inside magnificent stupas. Like the ▷ *Chapel of the 13th Dalai Lama*, the ▷ *Chapel of the 5th Dalai Lama* holds an enormous funerary stupa that rises up over 12 m (40 ft). It is made of sandalwood and reputed to be covered with nearly four tons of gold and nearly 20,000 pearls and other gems. The rest of the stupas are much more modest and displayed in smaller chapels on all floors of the Red Palace. Other treasures on display include rare hand-written Buddhist sutras, and a great deal of statuary – one of the best statues is the statue of Maitreya in his own chapel on the east side of the top floor. Pilgrims circle the chapels clockwise, prostrating themselves before shrines and lighting votive yak butter lamps, whose distinctive smell is all-pervasive.

Potala Palace, Lhasa

PERCHED ON LHASA'S HIGHEST POINT, the Potala Palace is the greatest monumental structure in Tibet. Thirteen storeys high, with over a thousand rooms, it was once the residence of Tibet's chief monk and leader, the 14th Dalai Lama, and therefore the centre for both spiritual and temporal power. These days, after his escape to India in 1959, it is a vast museum, serving as a reminder of Tibet's rich and devoutly religious culture. The first palace on the site was built by Songtsen Gampo in 641, and this was incorporated into the larger building which stands today. There are two main sections – the White Palace, built by the fifth Dalai Lama in 1645, and the Red Palace which was completed in 1694.

★ **Golden Roofs**
Seemingly floating above the huge structure, the gilded roofs (actually copper) cover the funerary chapels dedicated to previous Dalai Lamas.

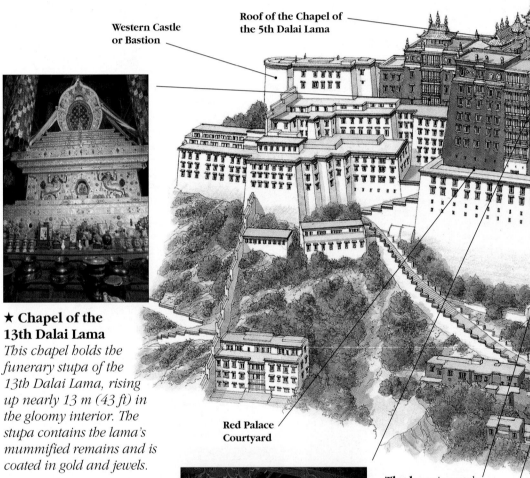

Western Castle or Bastion

Roof of the Chapel of the 5th Dalai Lama

★ **Chapel of the 13th Dalai Lama**
This chapel holds the funerary stupa of the 13th Dalai Lama, rising up nearly 13 m (43 ft) in the gloomy interior. The stupa contains the lama's mummified remains and is coated in gold and jewels.

Red Palace Courtyard

The base is purely structural, holding the palaces onto the steep hill.

Thangka Storehouse

★ **3D Mandala**
This intricate mandala of a palace, covered in precious metals and jewels, embodies aspects of the path to enlightenment.

STAR FEATURES

★ **Golden Roofs**

★ **Chapel of the 13th Dalai Lama**

★ **3D Mandala**

The Western Hall

The largest hall inside the Potala, the Western Hall is located on the first floor of the Red Palace and contains the holy throne of the 6th Dalai Lama.

Maitreya Chapel   **East Sunshine Apartment**

PRINCESS WENCHENG

Offered as a wife to Songtsen Gampo to broker peace, the Tang Dynasty (618–907) bride apparently converted the king and thus Tibet to Buddhism. She also instigated building many of Tibet's finest temples.

White Palace

The entrance to the main part of the building has a triple-stairway – the middle one is reserved for the sole use of the Dalai Lama.

The Eastern Court-yard is a huge open space used for important religious celebrations.

School of Religious Officials

The Eastern Bastion shows that the palace also had a defensive function.

KEY DATES

AD 641 The first Potala Palace is built.

9th century The Tubo kingdom collapses and the Potala Palace is almost completely destroyed in the struggle for power.

1642 After the 5th Dalai Lama unites Tibet and becomes its spiritual and political leader, he decides to reconstruct the Potala Palace.

1922 The 13th Dalai Lama renovates much of the White Palace and adds two storeys to the Red Palace.

1994 UNESCO adds the Potala Palace to its World Heritage List.

SONGTSEN GAMPO

The warrior king and founder of the Tubo kingdom, Songtsen Gampo was born in AD 617 and built the original Potala Palace for his wife, Princess Wencheng. Most of it has long since burned down – only the Dharma Cave, set almost into the mountain, and the Saints' Chapel remain from the 7th century. They are both in the northern part of the Red Palace. The Dharma Cave is said to be the place where King Songtsen Gampo meditated. Inside, statues of the king, Princess Wencheng and his chief ministers are venerated. In the Saints' Chapel on the floor above, several important Buddhist figures and the 7th, 8th and 9th Dalai Lamas are enshrined and worshipped.

View from the Roof

On a clear day the view of the valley and mountains is unequalled, although the newer parts of Lhasa are less impressive.

Heavenly King Murals

The East Entrance has sumptuous images of the Four Heavenly Kings, Buddhist guardian figures.

THE EXPANDING WALL

Sections of the bastion called the Great Wall were first built during the Warring States period (475–221 BC) by individual states to thwart incursions by northern tribes and to defend against aggressive neighbours. Simple and unconnected earthen ramparts, they were not joined together until the Qin dynasty (221–207 BC) first unified China under Shi Huangdi, the First Emperor. The maintenance and expansion of the wall reflected each succeeding dynasty's feelings of insecurity. Enlarged under the expansionist Han (206 BC–AD 220), the wall was neglected by the cosmopolitan Tang (AD 618–907), only to be heavily fortified by the more inward-looking Ming.

Qin Emperor Shi Huangdi, the so-called First Emperor

BUILDING ON SAND

The Qin wall was a simple tamped earth affair but the later Han dynasty adopted a more advanced technology that enabled them to build walls even in the bleak expanses of the Gobi desert. They would line wooden frames with a layer of willow reeds and twigs and then fill the frame with a mixture of mud, fine gravel and water. This would then be pressed firmly into place. When the mix dried, the frame could be removed, leaving behind a large slab of hard brick-like mud that could be built upon again in the same manner. This is much like modern construction when steel rods are use to reinforce concrete.

The Great Wall of China

SYMBOL OF CHINA'S HISTORIC DETACHMENT and sense of vulnerability, the Great Wall snakes through the Chinese landscape over deserts, hills and plains for over 4,000 km (2,500 miles). Yet despite its seemingly impregnable battlements the wall was ultimately an ineffective barricade. In the 13th century it was breached by the ferocious onslaught of the Mongols and then in the 17th century by the Manchu, helped by the decline of the Ming dynasty. Today, its dilapidated remains crumble across the rugged terrain of north China and only select sections have been restored.

★ Panoramic Views
Because the wall took advantage of the natural terrain for defensive purposes, following the highest points and clinging to ridges, it now offers some superb panoramic views.

Surface of stone slabs and bricks

Tamped layer of earth and rubble

Bigger rocks and stones

Kiln-fired bricks, cemented with a mortar of lime and glutinous rice

Large, locally quarried rocks

Crumbling Ruin
Away from Beijing, most of the wall is unrestored and has crumbled away with only the core remaining.

Ramparts enabled the soldiers to fire down on their attackers with relative impunity.

STAR FEATURES

★ Panoramic Views

★ Watchtowers

RECONSTRUCTION OF THE GREAT WALL

This shows a section of the wall as built by the most prolific wall builders of them all, the Ming dynasty (1368–1644). The section at Badaling, built around 1505, is similar to this and was restored in 1950s and 1980s.

★ Watchtowers
A Ming addition, these served as signal towers, forts, living quarters and storerooms for provisions, gunpowder and weapons.

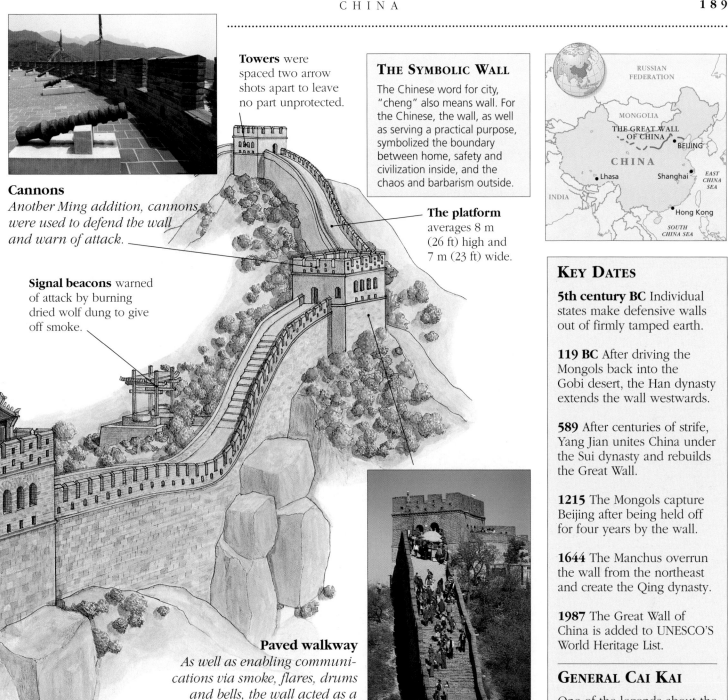

Cannons
Another Ming addition, cannons were used to defend the wall and warn of attack.

Towers were spaced two arrow shots apart to leave no part unprotected.

Signal beacons warned of attack by burning dried wolf dung to give off smoke.

THE SYMBOLIC WALL
The Chinese word for city, "cheng" also means wall. For the Chinese, the wall, as well as serving a practical purpose, symbolized the boundary between home, safety and civilization inside, and the chaos and barbarism outside.

The platform averages 8 m (26 ft) high and 7 m (23 ft) wide.

Paved walkway
As well as enabling communications via smoke, flares, drums and bells, the wall acted as a road for the rapid transport of troops over very difficult terrain.

The Great Wall of China

KEY DATES

5th century BC Individual states make defensive walls out of firmly tamped earth.

119 BC After driving the Mongols back into the Gobi desert, the Han dynasty extends the wall westwards.

589 After centuries of strife, Yang Jian unites China under the Sui dynasty and rebuilds the Great Wall.

1215 The Mongols capture Beijing after being held off for four years by the wall.

1644 The Manchus overrun the wall from the northeast and create the Qing dynasty.

1987 The Great Wall of China is added to UNESCO'S World Heritage List.

GENERAL CAI KAI

One of the legends about the wall tells that, during the Ming dynasty, General Cai Kai was put in charge of building the section of wall at Huanghua. Rumour got back to the emperor that the general was taking too long over the task and wasting too much money. The unfortunate general was therefore summarily executed. Later when the Mongols mounted a concerted attack, General Cai Kai's efforts paid off; Huanghua was the only fortress that successfully warded off the enemy. Realising his mistake the emperor exhumed General Cai Kai's body and it was reburied with full honours near the part of the wall that he built.

THE GREAT WALL OF CHINA (MING DYNASTY)

0 kilometres   500

0 miles   400

Inner Mongolia

Yellow River

Datong

② ③ ④

Beijing

Taiyuan

Tianjin

Bo Hai

⑤

Qinghai Lake

Lanzhou

Yellow Sea

①

THE GREAT MYTH

The story that the Great Wall is the only man-made object visible to the naked eye from the moon is obviously false – it is far too thin.

PLACES TO VISIT THE WALL

① Jiayuguan
② Juyongguan and Badaling
③ Huanghua
④ Simatai
⑤ Shanhaiguan

The immense Great Wall of China snaking over hills near Beijing ▷

DESIGN PRINCIPLES

The harmonious principle of Yin and Yang is core to Chinese design. The palace is arranged symmetrically on a north-south axis, with hall entrances facing south to avoid the malign Yin effects – cold wind, evil spirits and barbarian warriors – that come from the north. Odd numbers represent Yang, the masculine element associated with the emperor. Hence the frequent occurrence of three, five, seven, and the highest (and therefore best) single-digit odd number – nine – in architectural details. It is said that the Forbidden City has 9,999 rooms and as nine times nine is especially fortunate, imperial doors usually have 81 golden studs.

Door in the Forbidden City with an auspicious number of studs

SERVING THE EMPEROR

Because of the dual role of the Forbidden City — as living quarters of the Imperial family and the centre of administration – eunuchs, the only male servants allowed in the palace, were in a unique position. Allowed access to the emperor's family, a few influential eunuchs wielded great power, siphoning off vast fortunes from the imperial coffers. However, the fate of the majority was far more akin to that of a slave. Higher up the social scale, the emperor's concubines were kept in a series of palaces beside the Inner Court. Emperors could have several wives and many concubines. At night the emperor would decide which concubine would sleep with him. The number of times a concubine was chosen determined her social standing and bearing the emperor a son meant instant promotion.

Forbidden City, Beijing

Glazed decorative wall relief

FORMING THE HEART OF BEIJING, the Forbidden City is China's most magnificent architectural complex. Completed in 1420, the palace is a comprehensive compendium of Chinese imperial architecture and a lasting monument of dynastic China where 24 emperors ruled over 500 years, ending with the pitiful Last Emperor, Puyi. As the symbolic centre of the Chinese universe, the palace was the exclusive domain of the imperial court and dignitaries on royal business, but was opened to the public in 1949.

Golden Water
Five marble bridges, symbolizing the five cardinal virtues of Confucianism, cross the Golden Water, which flows from west to east in a course designed to resemble the jade belt worn by officials.

OUTER COURT
Despite its name, this forms the very core of the complex. The surrounding buildings, originally built to service this series of halls, now house a variety of interesting displays.

★ Meridian Gate
From the balcony over-looking the courtyard the emperor would review his armies and perform ceremonies marking the start of a new calendar.

Chinese Lions
Lions symbolized sovereign power and the splendour of the imperial palace. Males are portrayed with a ball under their paw, while females have a lion cub.

Gate of Supreme Harmony
Originally used for receiving visitors, the 24-m (78-ft) high, double-eaved hall was later used for banquets during the Qing dynasty (1644–1912).

★ **Marble Carriageway**
The central ramp carved with dragons chasing pearls among clouds was reserved for the emperor.

The Hall of Preserving Harmony held the Civil Service Exams.

FALL OF THE MING

In 1644, as peasant rebels were storming the capital, the last Ming emperor, Chong Zhen, killed his daughter and concubines before fleeing the Forbidden Palace to hang himself on nearby Coal Hill.

The Gate of Heavenly Purity leads to the Inner Court – reserved for the Imperial family only.

Bronze cauldrons filled with water were a practical precaution against fire.

The Hall of Middle Harmony was a place of preparation for the emperor when on official business.

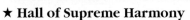

Roof Guardians
These figures, associated with water, were supposed to protect the building from fire.

★ **Hall of Supreme Harmony**
The largest hall in the palace, this was used for major occasions such as the enthronement of an emperor. Inside the hall, the ornate throne sits beneath a fabulously coloured ceiling.

STAR FEATURES

★ **Meridian Gate**

★ **Marble Carriageway**

★ **Hall of Supreme Harmony**

THE LAST EMPEROR

Henry (Aixinjueluo) Puyi ascended the Qing throne in 1908 aged three. His brief reign ended on 12 February 1912, when he abdicated in favour of the Republic of China. Puyi remained a virtual prisoner in the palace until 1924, before fleeing to the Japanese concession in Tianjin. Puyi never returned to the Forbidden City and died childless and anonymous in 1967 after working for seven years as a gardener at the Beijing Botanical Gardens.

Henry Puyi, the boy emperor

KEY DATES

1407 Construction of the Forbidden City starts.

1557 Fire destroys the main halls in the palace.

1925 The palace is renamed the Palace Museum.

1987 The Forbidden City is Listed by UNESCO as a World Heritage Site.

THE INNER COURT

The structure of the Inner Court mirrors that of the Outer Court but on a smaller scale. There are three main inner court palaces – the double-eaved Palace of Heavenly Purity was originally used as the imperial sleeping quarters and later for the reception of imperial officials. Banquets were held here for New Year and other important occasions. Beyond this palace lies the Hall of Union, which was used as a throne room by the empress as well as a depository for the imperial seals used to sign official documents. Still further on, the Palace of Earthly Tranquillity served as living quarters for the Ming empresses. During the Qing dynasty, the hall was used for Manchurian shaman rites, including the sacrifice of animals. Behind the inner court is the Imperial Garden, a typical Chinese recreation of nature in all its guises. On either side of the state apartments were the private residences of the whole imperial family and their attendants – reputed to number as many as 9,000 by the 18th century.

Forbidden City

Temple of Heaven

LAYOUT OF THE TEMPLE OF HEAVEN

The design of the Temple of Heaven is replete with cosmological significance. All the major structures lie on the favoured north-south axis. The ancient Chinese saying "sky round, earth square" is represented here by the interplay of squares and circles. Heaven is suggested in the round, conical roofing and the blue tiles of both the ▷ *Hall of Prayer for Good Harvests* and the ▷ *Imperial Vault of Heaven*. The ▷ *Round Altar* symbolizes Heaven, while Earth is there in its square enclosure. Numerology is also important, with odd numbers being the most fortunate, hence the triple eaves of the Hall of Prayer for Good Harvests and the Round Altar's three tiers. Nine is the most important of the single-digit odd numbers and the uppermost tier of the altar is designed with nine rings of stones, each ring itself a multiple of nine stones. The significance of numbers finds further refrain throughout the structure (▷ *Dragon Well Pillars)*.

CEREMONIES & RITES

The emperor would perform the ceremonies at the Temple of Heaven to pray for rain and good harvests or in the event of natural disasters that required the appeasement of Heaven. After fasting for three days, he would be conveyed in a spectacular procession from the Forbidden City to spend the night before the sacrifice in the Palace of Abstinence just inside the Temple of Heaven compound. The emperor would rise before dawn the next day and be ceremonially robed. Then proceeding north to south, with sacred music and dance, he would ascend the ▷ *Round Altar* to burn a freshly killed ox and bundles of silk before an array of wooden spirit tablets *(shenpai)*, including those of his ancestors who were thus also "participating".

Temple of Heaven, Beijing

Gate to the Round Altar

BUILT DURING THE MING Dynasty, Tiantan, commonly called the Temple of Heaven, is one of the largest temple complexes in China and a paradigm of Chinese architectural balance and symbolism. It was here that the emperor, after a ceremonial procession from the Forbidden City, would make sacrifices and pray to heaven at the winter solstice. As the Son of Heaven, the emperor could intercede with the gods on behalf of his people and ensure a good harvest. Off-limits to the common people during the Ming and Qing dynasties, the Temple of Heaven is situated in a large park that now attracts early-morning practitioners of Tai Chi.

The Hall of Prayer where the emperor prayed for a good harvest for his people

TEMPLE OF HEAVEN COMPLEX

The main parts of the complex are all connected by the Red Step Bridge (an elevated ceremonial path) to form the focal point of the park. The doorways at each triple gate are for the emperor (east), the gods (centre) and the officials (west). The circular Echo Wall is famed for its supposed ability to carry a whisper from one end of the wall to the other.

① Hall of Prayer for Good Harvests
② Red Step Bridge
③ Echo Wall
④ Imperial Vault of Heaven
⑤ Round Altar

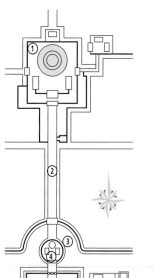

KEY
☐ Area illustrated

Three door gates to the Imperial Vault of Heaven

Imperial Vault of Heaven with the spirit tablets of the gods

The Centre of Heaven Stone at the heart of the Round Altar

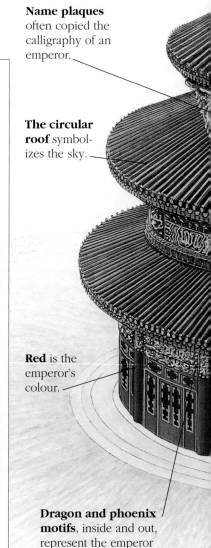

Name plaques often copied the calligraphy of an emperor.

The circular roof symbolizes the sky.

Red is the emperor's colour.

Dragon and phoenix motifs, inside and out, represent the emperor and empress.

STAR FEATURES

★ **Caisson Ceiling**

★ **Dragon Well Pillars**

The golden finial is 38 m (125 ft) high and prone to lightning strikes.

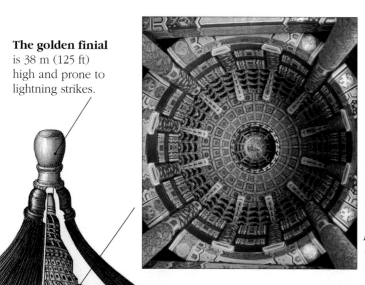

EMPEROR YONGLE

This Ming Emperor ruled from 1403–24 and was responsible not only for moving the capital from Nanjing to Beijing but also for starting work on the Forbidden City, Temple of Heaven and the Ming Tombs.

★ **Caisson Ceiling**

The splendidly decorated circular caisson ceiling has a beautiful gilded dragon and phoenix at its centre. The hall is entirely built of wood without using a single nail.

KEY DATES

1420 Qinian Dian is built – originally called the "Temple of Earth and Heaven".

1530 Round Altar is constructed by Emperor Shizong.

1889 Qinian Dian burns down after a lightning strike.

1918 The Temple of Heaven is opened to the public.

1998 UNESCO inscribes the Temple of Heaven onto the World Heritage List.

THE LAST CEREMONY

Observed by China's emperors since the Zhou dynasty (1100–771 BC), the winter solstice rites at the Temple of Heaven were last performed by the first president of the Republic of China, the former Qing general Yuan Shikai (1859–1916). The general had helped modernize the Chinese army and, as the head of such a force, could easily ask for positions of influence in return for his and the army's support. Once he was made president, he aimed to install himself as emperor and re-establish an imperial dynasty. Therefore Yuan performed the ceremony at the Temple of Heaven on the occasion of the winter solstice in 1914, clearly asserting his imperial ambitions. However, despite dressing in the appropriate robes, he failed to recreate the traditional majesty of the occasion, arriving in an armoured car. Yuan Shikai died in 1916, before he could ascend the throne.

Blue represents the colour of heaven.

★ **Dragon Well Pillars**

The roofs of the hall are supported on 28 highly-decorated pillars. At the centre, the four colossal columns, known as Dragon Well Pillars, represent the seasons, while the outer 12 pillars represent the months of the year and the inner circle of 12 pillars represent the 12 two-hour periods into which the Chinese divided the day.

Emperor's throne

Central "Dragon and Phoenix Stone"

Symbolic offerings

HALL OF PRAYER FOR GOOD HARVESTS

The Qinian Dian or Hall of Prayer for Good Harvests is the most famous structure at the complex and is often thought to be the "Temple of Heaven". Tiantan refers not to one building but to the whole complex.

Marble Platform

Three tiers of marble form a circle 90-m (300-ft) in diameter and 6-m (20-ft) high. The balusters on the upper tier are carved with dragons to signify the imperial nature of the structure.

THE SHINTO RELIGION

Shinto is Japan's oldest religion, the "way of the gods". Its core concept is that deities, *kami*, preside over all things in nature, be they living, dead or inanimate. The Sun Goddess Amaterasu is considered to be Shinto's most important *kami*. From ancient times the emperor's rule was sanctioned by the authority of the greatest of gods, said to be his ancestors. Religious rituals in Shintoism are centred around the offering of gifts and food, and the saying of prayers. Although Shinto was the state religion from the 1870s to 1940s, few Japanese today are purely Shintoists, but most will observe Shinto rituals alongside Buddhist practices.

Extravagant carving by the Yomeimon Gate

FEATURES OF THE TOSHU-GU SHRINE

The magnificent design of the Toshu-gu shrine is not at all in keeping with the sense of duty and simplicity that is normally central to Shintoism. This incongruity highlights the transformation that Shintoism has undergone, following the introduction of Buddhism to Japan in the 6th century. Many of the buildings in the shrine share elements from Buddhist architecture. The 5-storey temple (▷ *Pagoda*) and the gate guarded by the Nio figures (▷ *The Niomon*) are just two examples of how both Buddhism and Shintoism co-exist at Tosho-gu Shrine. The shrine is famous for its ornate carvings that decorate entire buildings both inside and out. The most exquisite is the Twilight Gate (▷ *Yomeimon Gate*) whose name implies that it can take all day to view the carvings.

Tosho-gu Shrine, Nikko

Nikko was a renowned Buddhist-Shinto religious centre, and the warlord Tokugawa Ieyasu chose this area specifically for his mausoleum. Tokugawa Iemitsu set out to dazzle with this mausoleum-shrine for his grandfather, and his elaborately decorated result is magnificent. Some 15,000 artisans worked on the shrine, building, carving, gilding, painting, and lacquering. Although designated a shrine in the late 17th century, it retains many Buddhist elements. The *sugi-namiki* (Japanese cedar avenue) leading to the shrine was planted by a 17th-century lord, in lieu of a more opulent offering.

Honden (inner sanctuary)

Haiden (sanctuary)

The Karamon gate is the smallest at Tosho-gu.

The Honji-do's ceiling is painted with the "crying dragon," which echoes resoundingly if you clap your hands beneath it.

Sleeping Cat Carving
Over an entrance in the east corridor, this tiny, exquisite carving of a sleeping cat is attributed to Hidari Jingoro (Hidari the Left-handed).

Bell tower

Drum tower

The Rinzo contains a sutra library of Buddhist scriptures in a revolving structure.

★ **Yomeimon Gate**
Lavishly decorated with beasts and flowers, this gate has one of its 12 columns carved upside-down, a deliberate imperfection to avoid angering jealous spirits. Statues of imperial ministers occupy the niches.

STAR FEATURES

★ **Yomeimon Gate**

★ **Pagoda**

★ **Sacred Stable**

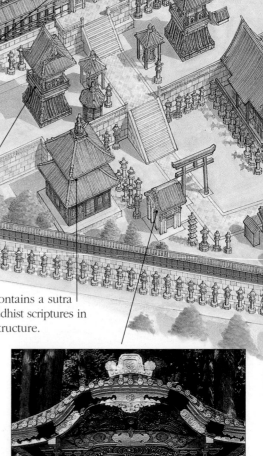

Sacred Fountain
The granite basin (1618), for ritual purification, is covered with an ornate Chinese-style roof.

TOKUGAWA IEYASU

Ieyasu (1543–1616) was a wily strategist and master politician who founded the dynasty that would rule Japan for over 260 years. Born the son of a minor lord, Ieyasu spent his life accumulating power, not becoming shogun until 1603, when he was 60. He built his capital at the swampy village of Edo (now Tokyo), and his rule saw the start of the flowering of Edo culture. He ensured that, after his death, he would be enshrined as a god and *gongen* (incarnation of the Buddha). His posthumous name was Tosho-Daigongen (the great incarnation illuminating the East).

CELEBRATIONS

Tosho-gu Festivals are held on 17 and 18 May and on 17 October. Over 1,200 participants, dressed in clothes from the Edo period, take part in processions in which relics from the shrine are displayed.

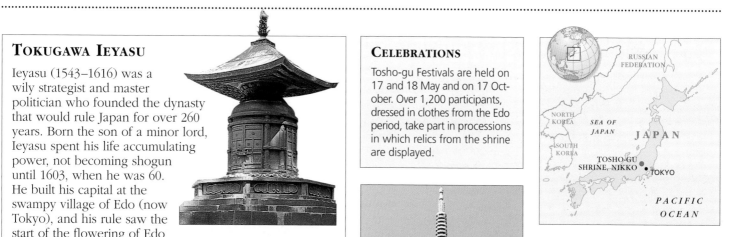

KEY DATES

1603–1867 The Tokugawa Shogunate brings about a prolonged period of peace.

1616 Death of Tokugawa Ieyasu.

1617 Construction begins on the Tosho-gu Shrine as a mausoleum for Tokugawa Ieyasu.

1636 The mausoleum and shrine are completed.

1999 The shrines and temples in Nikko are designated a World Heritage Site.

THREE WISE MONKEYS

Introduced to Japan by a Buddhist monk from China in the 8th century AD, the proverb of the Three Wise Monkeys represents the three truths of Tendai Buddhism. The names of the monkeys are *Mizaru* meaning "see no evil", *Kikazaru* meaning "hear no evil" and *Iwazaru* meaning "speak no evil". In Japan, monkeys are traditionally thought to keep horses healthy. At Tosho-gu, these monkeys are the guardians of the sacred horse, an animal long dedicated to the Shinto gods (▷ *Sacred Stable*). Their well-known gestures of covering their eyes, ears and mouth are a dramatic representation of the commands of the blue-faced deity Vadjra: if we do not see, hear or speak evil, we will be spared from all evil. As their names not only express their gestures but also the three truths, anyone referring to them will also proclaim their message.

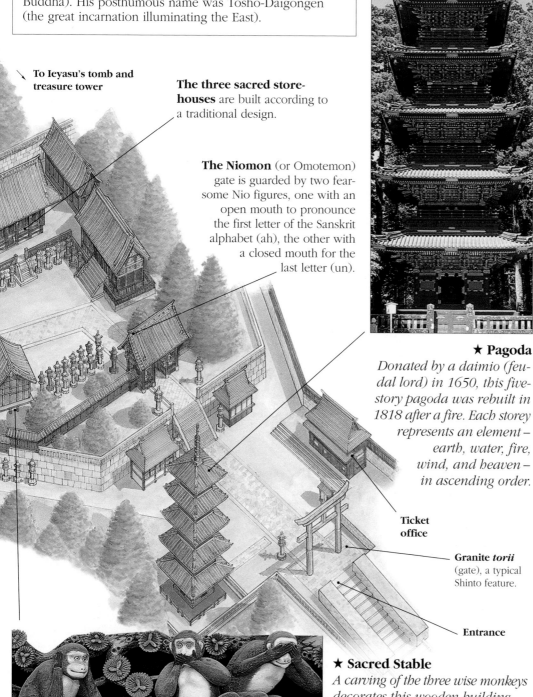

To Ieyasu's tomb and treasure tower

The three sacred storehouses are built according to a traditional design.

The Niomon (or Omotemon) gate is guarded by two fearsome Nio figures, one with an open mouth to pronounce the first letter of the Sanskrit alphabet (ah), the other with a closed mouth for the last letter (un).

★ **Pagoda**
Donated by a daimio (feudal lord) in 1650, this five-story pagoda was rebuilt in 1818 after a fire. Each storey represents an element – earth, water, fire, wind, and heaven – in ascending order.

Ticket office

Granite *torii* (gate), a typical Shinto feature.

Entrance

★ **Sacred Stable**
A carving of the three wise monkeys decorates this wooden building. A horse given by the New Zealand government is kept here a few hours a day.

Tosho-gu Shrine

Todai-ji Temple, Nara

EMPEROR SHOMYO

The imperial court at Nara embraced Buddhism in the 8th century, during the reign of Emperor Shomyo (r.724–49). Shomyo (or Shomu) built temples in every province, and used this vast network to strengthen the administration and to consolidate control of his empire. He is, however, best known for commissioning the Todai-ji Temple and its ▷ *Great Buddha Vairocana* statue in 743. This phenomenal endeavour took seven years to complete and was so expensive it almost drained Japan's economy as well as its reserves of precious metals. When the temple finally opened in 752, Shomyo personally painted the statue's eyes and declared himself the Buddha's servant. By this time his daughter Koken (r.749–758) had been declared the new ruler of Japan. Shomyo died in 756.

Temple of Kofuku-ji, one of the many temples built by Shomyo

THE CONSTRUCTION OF TODAI-JI TEMPLE

Wood has long been the basis of Japanese architecture, particularly temples, mainly because of its ability to endure weathering in winter. It has, however, also meant that such structures are highly susceptible to devastating fires. Todai-ji's ▷ *Great Buddha Hall* is constructed in the traditional post-and-lintel style. The base of the hall has posts anchored along a rectangular perimeter. This rigid geometric shape marks the boundary between the material and divine world. There are 62 pillars supporting the grand sloping roof. A unique roof construction (▷ *Wooden Hall*) is effective in resisting minor earthquakes.

Stone lantern at Todai-ji Temple

T HERE ARE MANY REASONS to visit the impressive Todai-ji Temple in Nara but sheer size must be its main attraction. After alterations and fires over the centuries, the huge wooden structure, finished in the 18th century, is only two-thirds of the original yet it is still the largest wooden building in the world. An enormous and costly project, the temple was ordered by Emperor Shomyo in the mid-8th century to highlight the position of the city as a powerful Buddhist site and Japan's capital. Inside, the magnificent seated figure at 16 m (53 ft) is Japan's largest bronze image of the Buddha.

The 19-m (62-ft) high Nandaimon (great southern gate) of Todai-ji

Koumokuten, a heavenly guardian, dates from the mid-Edo period (1603–1868).

Kokuzo Bosatsu
This bosatsu, *or* bodhisattva, *"Enlightened Being" was completed in 1709.*

Entrance

★ Great Buddha Vairocana
The casting of this vast statue required hundreds of tons of molten bronze, mercury, and vegetable wax. Fires and earthquakes have destroyed the head several times; the current head dates from 1692.

GREAT BUDDHA HALL

The main hall of Todai-ji was rebuilt several times after natural disasters in the 12th and 16th centuries. The enormous figure inside is a jaw-dropping sight. Occasionally it is possible to see several monks standing in the upturned palm — dusting.

Sacred Site
Above Nara, the ancient city that was once Japan's capital, sits Todai-ji Temple. The curved roof is almost hidden by surrounding trees.

OMIZU-TORI FESTIVAL

The Omizu-tori or water-drawing festival has been celebrated at Todai-ji Temple since the 8th century to signal the arrival of spring. During the festival, held from March 1–14, water is ritually drawn from a sacred well to the sound of music in the early hours on the 13th day. Enormous torches are used to purify the water.

KEY DATES

752 The temple is completed.

1180, 1567 Great Buddha's head melts in raging fires.

1998 The Todai-ji complex at Nara is declared a UNESCO World Heritage Site.

BUDDHISM IN JAPAN

Buddhism was founded in India and arrived in Japan via China and Korea in the 6th century AD. Prince Shotoku (573–621) promoted Buddhism in its early days. Initially, despite incorporating parts of the native belief system, Buddhism had an uneasy relationship with Japan's oldest religion, Shinto. Buddhism lost official support after Shinto was declared Japan's national religion in 1868, but it flowered again after World War II. Today, the beliefs and morality of Buddhism permeate modern Japanese life, especially the Zen Buddhist emphasis on simplicity and mental control. The religion's cornerstone is meditation, which is also believed to be the road to Enlightenment. Pilgrimages to sacred sites are still popular, and devotees, dressed in white, sometimes make journeys lasting several weeks. Festivals take place to honour events in the Buddha's life and the return of spirits *(bon)* to Earth, and often incorporate Shinto elements. Buddhist temples in Japan include a main hall *(hondo)*, with its stark interior, a cemetery, and often a tiered pagoda, housing a relic of the Buddha, and a small Shinto shrine.

Ornamental roof decoration

★ **Wooden Hall**
The unusual bracketing and beam-frame construction of this vast wooden hall, built in 1688–1709, were possibly the work of craftsmen from southern China.

Interior of Daibutsuden (Buddha hall)

Roofline
The striking roofline, with its golden "horns" and curved lintel, was an 18th-century embellishment.

Tamonten, another heavenly guardian, dates from the same period as Koumokuten on the other side of the hall.

Niyorin Kannon Bosatsu, like the Kokuzo Bosatsu to the left of the Great Buddha, is an Enlightened Being and dates from 1709.

Behind the Buddha is a small hole bored into a large wooden pillar. A popular belief holds that those who can squeeze through the hole will attain Nirvana.

Covered walkway in compound

STAR FEATURES

★ **Great Buddha Vairocana**

★ **Wooden Hall**

Todai-ji Temple, Nara, containing Japan's largest bronze Buddha ▷

THE HOLIEST SHRINE

The Sikh community's holiest shrine, the Golden Temple complex is actually a city within a city, with a maze of lanes protected by 18 fortified gates. The main entrance is through the northern gateway, the Darshani Darwaza, which also houses the Central Sikh Museum and its collections of paintings, manuscripts and weapons. From here, steps lead down to the Parikrama (marble pathway), encircling the ▷ *Amrit Sarovar* ("Pool of Nectar", after which Amritsar is named) and ▷ *Hari Mandir* ("Temple of God"), the golden-domed main shrine. Several holy sites line the Parikrama, including the Dukh Bhanjani Ber, a tree shrine said to have healing powers, and the Athsath Tirath, representing 68 pilgrim shrines. The Parikrama continues to the ▷ *Akal Takht*. The complex includes the Guru ka Langar, a free kitchen symbolizing the caste-free, egalitarian society the Sikh gurus sought to create.

MAHARAJA RANJIT SINGH

One of North India's most remarkable rulers, Maharaja Ranjit Singh (r.1790–1839) established Punjab's first Sikh kingdom by persuading rival chieftains to unite. A military genius, his strong army kept both the British forces and Afghan invaders at bay, by making Punjab a prosperous centre of trade and industry. A devout Sikh, the one-eyed Ranjit Singh was an enlightened ruler who liked to say "God intended me to look at all religions with one eye".

The Golden Temple, with its central shrine and main entrance

The Golden Temple, Amritsar

Pietra dura detail

THE SPIRITUAL CENTRE of the Sikh religion, the Golden Temple was built between 1589 and 1601, and is a superb synthesis of Islamic and Hindu styles of architecture. In keeping with the syncretic tradition of those times, its foundation stone was laid by a Muslim saint, Mian Mir. The temple was virtually destroyed in 1761 by an Afghan invader, Ahmed Shah Abdali, but was rebuilt some years later. Maharaja Ranjit Singh, ruler of Punjab, covered the dome in gold and embellished its interiors with lavish decoration during his reign.

First Floor
The marble walls have pietra dura *inlay and decorative plasterwork, bearing animal and flower motifs covered in gold leaf.*

Hari Mandir
The holiest site for Sikhs, the three-storeyed temple, decorated with superb pietra dura, *is where the Holy Book is kept during the day.*

★ **Sheesh Mahal**
The Hall of Mirrors on the top floor has a curved bangaldar *roof, and its floors are swept with a special broom made of peacock feathers.*

The dome, shaped like an inverted lotus, is covered in 100 kg (220 lbs) of gold donated by Ranjit Singh in 1830.

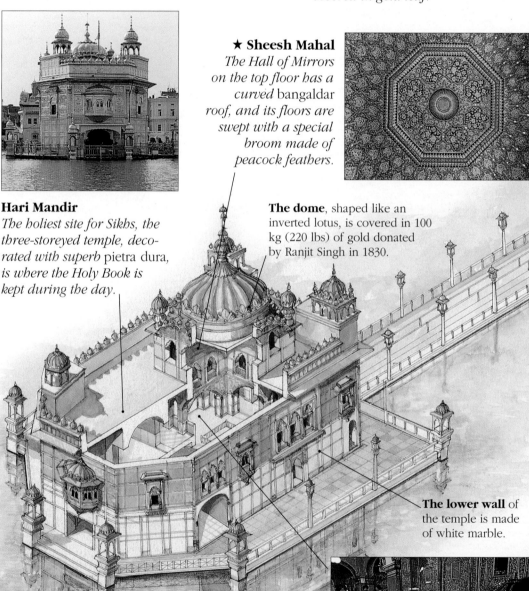

The lower wall of the temple is made of white marble.

STAR FEATURES
★ Sheesh Mahal
★ Guru Granth Sahib

★ **Guru Granth Sahib**
Covered by a jewelled canopy, the Holy Book lies in the Durbar Sahib ("Court of the Lord").

Darshani Deorhi
This gateway provides the first glimpse of the temple's inner sanctum. It has two splendid silver doors and sacred verses carved on its walls.

GURU PARAB

The festival of Guru Parab celebrates Guru Nanak's birthday on a full moon night in late Oct–early Nov (date varies). It is particularly spectacular at the Golden Temple, which is illuminated by thousands of lamps.

Akal Takht
The seat of the supreme governing body of the Sikhs, it houses the gurus' swords and flagstaffs, as well as the Holy Book at night.

Akal Takht

Amrit Sarovar, the pool where Sikhs are baptized, was built in 1577 by Ram Das, the fourth guru.

The Causeway
The 60-m (197-ft) long marble causeway is flanked by nine gilded lamps on each side, and leads to the temple across the Amrit Sarovar.

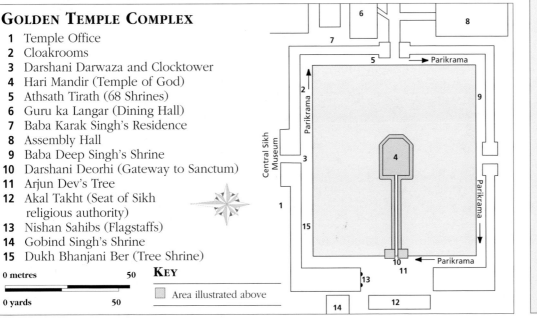

KEY DATES

1589–1601 Golden Temple is constructed.

1757, 1761, 1762 Afghans demolish Golden Temple.

1776 Golden Temple rebuilt.

1830 Maharaja Ranjit Singh adorns the dome with gold.

1984 Golden Temple damaged during Operation Blue Star, undertaken by the army to flush out extremists.

2003 Punjabi government funds an extensive beautification project of the area surrounding the Golden Temple.

SIKHISM

With their characteristic turbans and full beards, the Sikhs are easy to identify. Sikhism is a reformist faith, founded in the 15th century by Guru Nanak. It believes in a formless God. It is also called the Gurmat or the "Guru's Doctrine", and Sikh temples are known as *gurdwaras*, literally "doors to the guru". Nanak, the first of a series of 10 gurus, chose his most devout disciple as his successor. The tenth and last guru, Guru Gobind Singh (1666–1708) reorganized the community as a military order, the Khalsa, to combat religious persecution by the Mughals. He gave the Sikhs their distinctive identity as well as the Khalsa's five symbols – *kesh* (long hair), *kachha* (underwear), *kirpan* (small sword), *kangha* (comb) and *kara* (bracelet) – that all Sikhs are obligated to wear.

GOLDEN TEMPLE COMPLEX

1 Temple Office
2 Cloakrooms
3 Darshani Darwaza and Clocktower
4 Hari Mandir (Temple of God)
5 Athsath Tirath (68 Shrines)
6 Guru ka Langar (Dining Hall)
7 Baba Karak Singh's Residence
8 Assembly Hall
9 Baba Deep Singh's Shrine
10 Darshani Deorhi (Gateway to Sanctum)
11 Arjun Dev's Tree
12 Akal Takht (Seat of Sikh religious authority)
13 Nishan Sahibs (Flagstaffs)
14 Gobind Singh's Shrine
15 Dukh Bhanjani Ber (Tree Shrine)

0 metres   50

0 yards   50

KEY

Area illustrated above

MUGHAL STYLE

Mughal buildings, whether built of red sandstone or marble, assert their exalted, imperial status. The emperors were great patrons of the arts, literature and architecture and their rule established a rich pluralistic culture, blending the best of Islamic and Hindu traditions. Their greatest contribution was the garden tomb, raised on a high plinth in the centre of a ▷ *charbagh*. Decorative elements such as perforated *jalis* or screens, used extensively for privacy and ventilation, refined inlay work, and cusped arches gave Mughal buildings an ethereal grace that offset their massive size. Other features include *chhatris* (domed rooftop pavilions) that were adapted from Rajput architecture, and minarets that gave symmetry to the buildings.

Marble inlay above the mosque's central arch, Taj Mahal

THE PARADISE GARDEN

The hallmark of Mughal landscape design, the Paradise Garden was introduced by Babur (1483–1530), the first Great Mughal, who yearned for the beauty of Ferghana, his homeland in Central Asia. Based on Islamic geometric and metaphysical concepts of design, the ▷ *charbagh* was an enclosed garden divided by raised walkways, water channels and sunken groves, into four quarters, representing the four quarters of life. Water, the source of life in Central Asian desert kingdoms, was the central element and the intersecting channels met at a focal point which contained a pavilion for the emperor, seen as a representative of God on Earth.

Taj Mahal, Agra

Carved dado on outer niches

Oᴺᴱ ᴏꜰ ᴛʜᴇ ᴡᴏʀʟᴅ'ꜱ most famous buildings, the Taj Mahal was built by the Mughal emperor Shah Jahan in memory of his favourite wife, Mumtaz Mahal, who died in 1631. Its perfect proportions and exquisite craftsmanship have been described as "a vision, a dream, a poem, a wonder". This sublime garden-tomb, an image of the Islamic garden of paradise, cost nearly 41 million rupees and 500 kg (1,102 lb) of gold. About 20,000 workers laboured for 12 years to complete it in 1643.

★ Marble Screen
The filigree screen, daintily carved from a single block of marble, was meant to veil the area around the royal tombs.

Four minarets, each 40 m (131 ft) high and crowned by an open octagonal pavilion or *chhatri*, frame the tomb, highlighting the perfect symmetry of the complex.

Plinth

The Dome
The 44-m (144-ft) double dome is capped with a finial.

Yamuna river

★ Tomb Chamber
Mumtaz Mahal's cenotaph, raised on a platform, is placed next to Shah Jahan's. The actual graves, in a dark crypt below, are closed to the public.

STAR FEATURES

★ **Marble Screen**

★ **Tomb Chamber**

★ **Pietra Dura**

The *charbagh*
was irrigated with
water from the
Yamuna river.

**Main
entrance**

MUMTAZ MAHAL

Arjumand Banu (later Mumtaz Mahal) was the emperor's favourite wife. She accompanied him on all his campaigns and died in 1631, while giving birth to their 14th child. They were married 19 years.

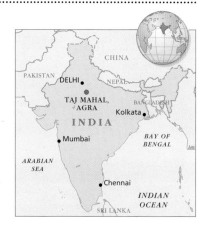

The Lotus Pool
Named after its lotus-shaped fountain spouts, the pool reflects the tomb. Almost every visitor is photographed sitting on the marble bench here.

Pishtaq
Recessed arches provide depth while their inlaid panels reflect the changing light to give the tomb a mystical aura.

★ Pietra Dura
Inspired by the paradise garden, intricately carved floral designs inlaid with precious stones embellish the austere white marble surface to give it the look of a bejewelled casket.

Calligraphic Panels
The size of the Koranic verses increases as the arch gets higher, creating the subtle optical illusion of a uniformly flowing script.

TAJ MAHAL

1 Main Tomb
2 *Masjid* (mosque)
3 *Mehmankhana* (guesthouse)
4 *Charbagh* (quadrified garden)
5 Gateway

KEY

☐ Area illustrated

☐ *Charbagh*

KEY DATES

1632 Following the death of Mumtaz Mahal in 1631, construction of the Taj Mahal begins.

1643 Taj Mahal completed.

1666 Shah Jahan dies and is laid to rest beside his queen.

1983 Taj Mahal declared a UNESCO World Heritage Site.

2001 Taj Mahal Conservation Collaborative begins restoration of Taj grounds, and improvement of visitors' facilities.

DECORATIVE ELEMENTS OF THE TAJ MAHAL

It is widely believed that the Taj Mahal was designed to be an earthly replica of one of the houses of paradise. Its impeccable marble facing, embellished by a remarkable use of surface design, is a showcase for the refined aesthetic that reached its zenith during Shah Jahan's reign (r.1627–1658). The Taj manifests the wealth of Mughal art as seen in architecture, garden design, painting, jewellery, calligraphy and textiles. Decorative elements include ornamental *jalis* (screens), carved panels of flowering plants, inlaid calligraphy, as well as floral motifs in ▷ *pietra dura*. The Florentine technique of *pietra dura* is said to have been imported by Emperor Jahangir. Even today, artisans in Agra's old quarter maintain pattern books on the fine motifs used on the Taj to recreate 17th-century designs in contemporary pieces.

Taj Mahal

THE JAMI MASJID & SALIM CHISHTI

Towering over Fatehpur Sikri is the grand open mosque ▷ *Jami Masjid*. Its vast congregational area has monumental gateways to the east and south. The 54 m (177 ft) high Buland Darwaza, a triumphal arch, was erected by Akbar to mark his 1573 conquest of Gujarat. The spiritual focus of the complex is the tomb of Sufi mystic Salim Chishti. Ever since Akbar's childlessness was ended after the saint's prediction in 1568, his tomb has attracted thousands, particularly childless women in search of a miracle. Visitors make a wish, tie a thread on the screen around the tomb, and return home confident that their wish will come true.

The exquisite, white marble tomb of Salim Chishti

AKBAR THE GREAT

The greatest Mughal emperor, Akbar (r.1556–1605) was a brilliant administrator and enlightened ruler. He was only 14 years old when he ascended the throne and his first task was to consolidate and expand his fledgling empire. His most significant moves were the political and matrimonial alliances he formed with the neighbouring Rajput king of Amber (now Jaipur). However, it was his policy of religious tolerance that truly set him apart. Akbar was fascinated by the study of comparative religion and built a special "House of Worship" in Fatehpur Sikri where he often met leaders of all faiths. The outcome was *Din-i-Ilahi* (Religion of God), that tried to bring together all religions.

Fatehpur Sikri

Fretwork *jali*

BUILT BY EMPEROR AKBAR between 1571 and 1585 in honour of Salim Chishti, a famous Sufi saint of the Chishti order, Fatehpur Sikri was the capital of the Mughal empire for 14 years. One of the best examples of a Mughal walled city with defined areas and imposing gateways, its architecture, a blend of Hindu and Islamic styles (▷ *Mughal Style p204*), reflects Akbar's secular vision as well as his type of governance. After the city was abandoned, some say for lack of water, many of its treasures were plundered. It owes its present state of preservation to the efforts of the viceroy, Lord Curzon, a legendary conservationist.

Pillar in the Diwan-i-Khas
The central axis of Akbar's court, supported by carved brackets, was inspired by Gujarati buildings.

Haram S
comp
\ Jami Masjid

Khwabgah
The emperor's private sleeping quarters, with an ingenious ventilating shaft near his bed, lie within this lavishly decorated "Chamber of Dreams".

Anoop Talao is a pool associated with Akbar's renowned court musician Tansen, who as legend says, could light oil lamps with his magical singing.

Abdar Khana

Entrance

★ Turkish Sultana's House
The fine dado panels and delicately sculpted walls of this ornate sandstone pavilion make the stone seem like wood. It is topped with an unusual stone roof of imitation clay tiles.

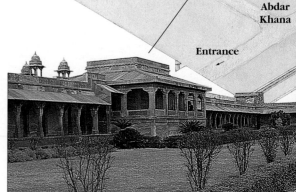

Diwan-i-Aam
This large courtyard with an elaborate pavilion was originally draped with rich tapestries and was used for public hearings and celebrations.

★ Panch Mahal

This five-storeyed open sandstone pavilion, overlooking the Pachisi Court, is where Akbar's queens and their attendants savoured the cool evening breezes. Its decorative screens were probably stolen after the city was abandoned.

TANSEN

A musical genius, the legendary Tansen was Emperor Akbar's Master of Music and one of the "nine jewels" in his court. He developed an exciting new range of *ragas* or melodic modes.

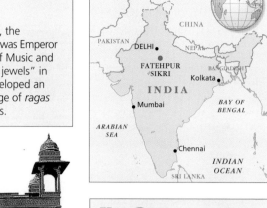

★ Diwan-i-Khas

This hall for private audience and debate is a unique fusion of different architectural styles and religious motifs.

Jodha Bai's Palace

Sunehra Makan

Birbal's House

Ankh Michauli

Sometimes identified as the treasury, this building has mythical guardian beasts carved on its stone struts. Its name means "blind man's buff".

Pachisi Court is named after a ludo-like game played here by the ladies of the court.

STAR FEATURES

★ **Turkish Sultana's House**

★ **Panch Mahal**

★ **Diwan-i-Khas**

PLAN OF FATEHPUR SIKRI

Fatehpur Sikri's royal complex contains the private and public spaces of Akbar's court, which included the harem and the treasury. The adjoining sacred area with the Jami Masjid (great mosque), Salim Chishti's Tomb and the Buland Darwaza, are separated from the royal quarters by the Badshahi Darwaza, an exclusive royal gateway.

KEY

- Area illustrated
- Other buildings
- Sacred complex (Jami Masjid)

KEY DATES

1571 Construction begins on Akbar's new capital at Fatehpur Sikri.

1576 Buland Darwaza is erected by Akbar.

1585 Fatehpur Sikri is abandoned by Akbar.

1986 Fatehpur Sikri becomes a UNESCO World Heritage Site.

LORD CURZON, VICEROY & CONSERVATIONIST

One of British India's most flamboyant viceroys, Lord Curzon (1859–1925), believed British rule was necessary to civilize "backward" India. He introduced sweeping changes in the education system. Paradoxically, the western-style institutions set up helped make Indians more aware of the injustices of colonial rule. Remembered for his role as conservator of Indian monuments, Curzon was responsible for the restoration of a vast number of Hindu, Islamic and Mughal buildings. Among them are the gateway to Akbar's tomb at Sikandra, Agra Fort, buildings at Fatehpur Sikri, the Jain temples at Mount Abu and the Taj Mahal. In 1905, due to differences with the British military commander-in-chief, Lord Kitchener, Curzon returned to England. By the time he left, he had achieved sufficient legislation to protect historic buildings, and set up an organization to conserve them.

THE ORIGIN & PHILO-SOPHY OF BUDDHISM

The Buddha was born in 566 BC as Siddhartha Gautama, prince of Kapilavastu. Renouncing his princely life, he left his palace at the age of 30 to search for answers to the meaning of human existence and suffering. He spent six years living with hermits, undertaking severe fasts and penances, only to find that self-mortification gave him no answers. Enlightenment finally came at Bodh Gaya where, after meditating for 49 days under the Bodhi Tree, he discovered that the cause of suffering is desire; and that desire can be conquered by following the Eightfold Path of Righteousness: Right Thought, Understanding, Speech, Action, Livelihood, Effort, Concentration and Contemplation. The essence of his teachings is non-violence and peace.

BUDDHIST STYLE

India's earliest Buddhist monuments were stupas, large reliquaries in which the ashes of the Buddha and other great teachers were interred. Solid throughout, the stupa itself is undecorated, designed to stimulate prayer and represent the path to divine understanding. As Indian traditions spread throughout southeast Asia, the Buddhist stupa reached new heights of complex Buddhist symbolism. Borobodur Temple in Java, with its design and sculpture of the highest order, is probably the greatest monument of this architectural style.

Buddhist tope (sculpture) on the East Gateway, Sanchi

The Great Stupa, Sanchi

Animals on the torana (gateway)

DOMINATING THE HILL at Sanchi, one of India's best preserved and most extensive Buddhist sites, is the Great Stupa. Its hemispherical shape is believed to symbolize the upturned alms bowl of a Buddhist monk, or an umbrella of protection for followers of the Buddhist dharma. The stupa's main glory lies in its four stone *toranas* (gateways), added in the 1st century BC. Their superb sculptures replicate the techniques of wood and ivory carving, and cover a rich variety of Buddhist themes.

West Gateway
This animated scene from the Jataka Tales *shows monkeys scrambling across a bridge to escape from soldiers.*

Circumambulatory Paths
The paths have balustrades carved with medallions of flowers, birds and animals, and the names of donors who funded them.

South Gateway
The Wheel of Law, being worshipped by devotees, symbolizes the Buddha.

The four gateways show scenes from the Buddha's life, and episodes from the *Jataka Tales*. The Buddha is not depicted in human form, but only through symbols such as a Bodhi Tree, footprints or a wheel.

Detail of Architrave
The intricate carving on the architraves is the work of wood and ivory craftsmen hired to carve the stone.

★ North Gateway
Sujata, the village chief's daughter, offers the Buddha (represented by the Bodhi Tree) kheer *(rice pudding), as the demon Mara sends the temptress to seduce him.*

The *vedika* (railings) are an impressive recreation in stone of a typical wooden railing design. They were the inspiration for the stone railings around Sansad Bhavan or the Parliament House in New Delhi.

THE JATAKA TALES
The Buddha's past lives are retold in this large collection of fables, where an animal or bird often took the part of the Buddha.These tales had great religious, moral, social and cultural significance.

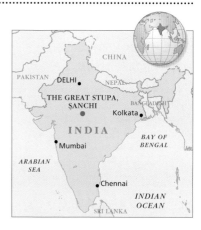

The Great Stupa and its West Gateway
Enclosing a smaller brick stupa built by Emperor Ashoka in the 3rd century BC, the Great Stupa is capped by a three-tiered stone umbrella, symbolizing the layers of heaven.

Statues of the Buddha meditating, added in the 5th century AD, face each of the gateways.

East Gateway
This scene shows a royal retinue at the palace of Kapilavastu, the Buddha's home before he renounced his princely life.

★ Salabhanjika
Supporting the lowest architrave of the East Gateway is this sensuous, voluptuous tree nymph, gracefully positioned under a mango tree.

STAR FEATURES
★ North Gateway

★ Salabhanjika

KEY DATES
2nd century BC The Great Stupa is built at Sanchi.

14th century AD The Great Stupa is deserted.

1818 General Taylor of the Bengal Cavalry "rediscovers" the Great Stupa.

1912–19 Director General of Archaeology in India, Sir John Marshall, excavates and restores the site.

1989 The Great Stupa is declared a UNESCO World Heritage Site.

EMPEROR ASHOKA
One of India's greatest rulers, Ashoka (r.269–232 BC) was the grandson of Chandragupta Maurya, who founded the country's first empire. The carnage and misery brought about by Ashoka's bloody conquest of Kalinga (now Orissa) in 260 BC filled him with remorse. He gave up *digvijaya* (military conquest) for *dharmavijaya* (spiritual conquest), and became a great patron of Buddhism instead, building many stupas including the original brick stupa at Sanchi. Ashoka was a humane ruler, whose edicts on rocks and pillars all over his vast empire record his ethical code of righteousness and non-violence *(ahimsa)*. His decree at Dhauli (site of the Kalinga battle) declares, "All men are my children". He asked his officials to be impartial, just and compassionate, and his subjects to respect others' religions, give to charity and avoid the killing of animals.

THE LEGEND OF THE EMERALD BUDDHA

In 1434, lightning struck Wat Phra Kaeo in Chiang Rai, revealing a simple stucco image, encasing a jadeite image, the ▷ *Emerald Buddha*. Chiang Mai's king sent an army of elephants to bring the image to him, but as the animal bearing it refused to take the road to Chiang Mai, it was enshrined at Lampang. After several moves, the image was taken to Laos in 1552, where it remained until Rama I brought the Buddha back to Thailand in 1778. For several years it was kept in Wat Arun, until it was brought to its current resting place in 1785.

Ramakien figure outside the Phra Si Rattana Chedi

THE RAMAKIEN

The *Ramakien* is an allegory of the triumph of good over evil. Rama, heir to the throne of Ayodhya, is sent into a 14-year exile with his wife Sita and brother Lakshman. Tosakan, the demon-king of Longka, abducts Sita from the forest. Hanuman, the monkey god, helps rescue Sita and defeat Tosakan, and Rama returns triumphantly to Ayodhya. This epic tale was probably established after the Thais occupied Angkor in the 15th century. All the Chakri kings adopted Rama as one of their names, and the 14th-century kingdom of Ayutthaya was named after the fictional Ayodhya. The legend has also been a great inspiration for Thai painting, classical drama and puppetry.

Grand Palace and Wat Phra Kaeo, Bangkok

Detail on Phra Mondop Library

CONSTRUCTION OF this remarkable site began in the late 18th century to mark the founding of the new capital and to provided a resting place for the sacred Emerald Buddha (Phra Kaeo), and a residence for the king. Surrounded by walls stretching for 1.9 km (1.18 miles), the complex was once a self-sufficient city within a city. The Royal Family now lives in Dusit, but Wat Phra Kaeo is still Thailand's holiest temple and a stunning piece of Buddhist architecture (▷ *Buddhist Style p208*).

Wat Phra Kaeo's skyline, as seen from Sanam Luang

The Emerald Buddha, displayed in the temple, is carved from a single piece of jade.

The Chapel of the Gandharara Buddha, adorned with glazed ceramic tiles, was constructed in the 19th century.

Hor Phra Rajphongsanusorn

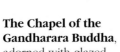

★ **Bot of the Emerald Buddha**
Devotees make offerings to the Emerald Buddha at the entrance to the bot, *the most important building in the* wat.

Eight *prangs* border the east side of the *wat*.

★ **Ramakien Gallery**
Extending clockwise all the way around the cloisters are 178 panels depicting the complete story of the Ramakien.

STAR FEATURES

★ **Bot of the Emerald Buddha**

★ **Ramakien Gallery**

Decorative Gilt Figures

Encircling the exterior of the bot are 112 garudas (mythical beasts that are half-man, half-bird). They are shown holding nagas (serpents) and are typical of the wat's dazzling decorative details.

HIS MAJESTY THE KING'S BIRTHDAY

On 5 December, Thais venerate their king. Buildings all over Thailand are decorated, including the Grand Palace and Wat Phra Kaeo. In the evening, there are fireworks and celebrations.

Apsonsi

A mythical creature (half-woman, half-lion), Apsonsi is one of the beautiful gilded figures on the upper terrace of Wat Phra Kaeo.

Phra Mondop (library)

The Phra Si Rattana Chedi contains a piece of the Buddha's breastbone.

Upper Terrace

Ho Phra Nak (royal mausoleum)

Northern Terrace

Wihan Yot

WAT PHRA KAEO

Wat Phra Kaeo (shown here) is a sub-complex within the greater Grand Palace complex. The temple is Thailand's most important shrine, but unlike other Thai *wats*, has no resident monks.

Model of Cambodia's Angkor Wat

The Hor Phra

Prasat Phra Thep (Royal Pantheon) was built by King Rama IV to house the Emerald Buddha, but the building was considered too small.

GRAND PALACE AND WAT PHRA KAEO

1 Entrance
2 Wat Phra Kaeo complex
3 Dusit Throne Hall
4 Aphonphimok Pavilion
5 Chakri Throne Hall
6 Inner Palace
7 Phra Maha Monthien Buildings
8 Siwalai Gardens
9 Rama IV Chapel
10 Boromphiman Mansion
11 Audience Chamber

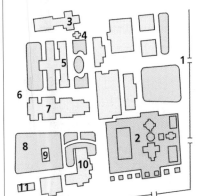

KEY

Wat Phra Kaeo complex

Buildings

Lawns

KEY DATES

1783 Work begins on Wat Phra Kaeo, Dusit Throne Hall and Phra Maha Monthien.

1809 Rama II remodels the building and introduces new Chinese details.

1932 The Chakri Dynasty's 150th year in power is celebrated at the palace.

1982 The Grand Palace and Wat Phra Kaeo is restored.

EXPLORING WAT PHRA KAEO

When Rama I established his new capital, he envisioned a temple that would surpass its Sukhothai and Ayutthaya predecessors. The result was the splendid Wat Phra Kaeo. The ▷ *bot* houses the surprisingly small image of the Emerald Buddha, seated in a glass case high above a gilded altar. Opposite, the ▷ *Upper Terrace* has several structures; the most striking is the ▷ *Phra Si Rattana Chedi*, built by King Mongkut (Rama IV) in 1855 to house sacred Buddha relics. The adjacent ▷ *Phra Mondop* was initially used as a library. Its exterior has Javanese Buddha images on the four outer corners. To its north is a ▷ *model of Cambodia's Angkor Wat*, commissioned by Rama I. On the ▷ *Northern Terrace*, the ▷ *Ho Phra Nak* or royal mausoleum enshrines the ashes of minor royals, while the ▷ *Wihan Yot* contains the Nak Buddha (an alloy of gold, silver and copper) rescued from Ayutthaya.

Grand Palace and Wat Phra Kaeo

Wat Arun

THE CHAKRI DYNASTY

In 1782, Chao Phraya Chakri (later King Rama I) established the Chakri dynasty in Krung Thep (Bangkok). The reigns of Rama I, II and III signalled an era of stability. Rama II was a literary man, while Rama III was a staunch traditionalist. King Mongkut (Rama IV) modernized Siam (Thailand), and opened it up to foreign trade and influence. His son, King Chulalongkorn or Rama V (r.1868–1910), perhaps the greatest Chakri king, furthered modernization by introducing financial reforms and abolishing slavery. He was idealized by his subjects, and his cremation was a grand state affair. Even today, his death is commemorated on Chulalongkorn Day (23 October).

KHMER ARCHITECTURE

Thailand's stone temple complexes, or *prasats*, were built by the Khmers, who ruled much of modern Cambodia and northeast Thailand in the 9th–13th centuries. Khmer *prasats* were built to symbolize kingship and the universe. Most have staircases or bridges lined with *nagas* (a seven-headed serpent thought to be the keeper of life's force), leading to a ▷ *central monument*. This is usually decorated with carved stone reliefs, and topped by a *prang* (tower). *Prangs* symbolize Mount Meru, the mythical abode of the gods. Lintels and pediments over the sanctuary entrances depict Hindu and Buddhist deities.

Gold leaf honouring the Buddha

Wat Arun, Bangkok

Ceramic flower on main *prang*

NAMED AFTER ARUNA, the Indian god of dawn, Wat Arun temple is one of Bangkok's best-known landmarks. Legend says that King Taksin arrived here from the sacked capital, Ayutthaya, in 1767. He then enlarged the temple that stood on the site into a Royal Chapel to house the most revered image of the Buddha in Thailand, the Emerald Buddha. Rama I and Rama II were responsible for the size of the current temple: the main *prang* is 79 m (260 ft) high and the circumference of its base is 234 m (768 ft). In the late 19th century, Rama IV added ornamentation created with broken pieces of porcelain. The style of the monument derives mainly from Khmer architecture.

★ River View of Temple
This popular image of Wat Arun, seen from the Chao Phraya river, appears on the 10-baht coin and in the Tourism Authority of Thailand (TAT) logo.

Minor *prangs* at each corner of the *wat*

Chinese Guards
These figures, at the entrances to the terrace, complement the Chinese-style porcelain decorating the prangs.

STAR FEATURES

★ River View of Temple

★ Ceramic Details

Multicoloured Tiers
Rows of demons, decorated with pieces of porcelain, line the exterior walls of the main prang.

CENTRAL MONUMENT OF WAT ARUN
The monument's design symbolizes Hindu-Buddhist cosmology. The central *prang* (tower) is the mythical Mount Meru, and its ornamental tiers are worlds within worlds. The layout of four minor *prangs* around a central one is a symbolic mandala shape.

Top terrace

One of the eight entrances

Gallery of the Bot
Elsewhere in the temple complex are the usual buildings found in a wat. This image of the Buddha in the main ordination hall or bot sits above the ashes of devotees.

Indra's weapon, the *vjra* or thunderbolt, at the crest

SYMBOLIC LEVELS

The Devaphum (top) is the peak of Mount Meru, rising above four subsidiary peaks. It denotes six heavens within seven realms of happiness.

The Tavatimsa Heaven (central section), where all desires are fulfilled, is guarded at the four cardinal points by the Hindu god Indra.

The Traiphum (base) represents 31 realms of existence across the three worlds (Desire, Form, and Formless) of the Buddhist universe.

ROYAL BARGE PROCESSION

Every 5 or 10 years, the King of Thailand takes robes and gifts to the monks at Wat Arun inside a splendid royal barge on the Chao Phraya River.

Stairs on the Central Prang
The steep steps represent the difficulties of reaching higher levels of existence.

Small Cove
On the second level of the central prang *are many small coves, inside which are* kinnari, *mythological creatures, half-bird, half-human.*

Decoration of the Four Minor Prangs
Inside the niches of each minor prang *are statues of Nayu, the god of wind, on horseback.*

Square-based structures topped by spires, *mondops*, at the cardinal points

★ **Ceramic Details**
Much of the colourful porcelain used to decorate the prangs was donated by local people. The flowers depicted are said to evoke the vegetation of Mount Meru, home of the gods.

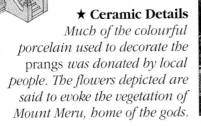

MYANMAR (BURMA)
LAOS
Chiang Mai
Khon Kaen
THAILAND
WAT ARUN, BANGKOK
CAMBODIA
VIETNAM
ANDAMAN SEA
GULF OF THAILAND
MALAYSIA

KEY DATES

18th century King Taksin remodels the Wat Arun temple.

Early 19th century Rama II restores the temple and extends the central *prang's* height.

1971 Wat Arun undergoes minor repairs after lightning splits a section of the spire.

ARUNA, INDRA & NAYU

Worshipped in India from the early Vedic age (1500 BC), the Hindu deities Aruna, Indra and Nayu personify nature and the elements. Aruna, the beautiful god of dawn, is the charioteer of Surya, the sun god. Red-skinned, he stands on the chariot in front of the sun, sheltering the world with his body from the sun's fury. Indra, the god of the sky and the heavens, rides a golden chariot drawn by horses and is armed with a *vajra* or thunderbolt. Indra sends the rain and rules the weather, and is often depicted sitting on Airavatta, the four-trunked white elephant who represents a rain-cloud. Nayu (or Vayu) is the god of the winds and messenger of the gods. He is also the regent of the northwest quarter of the heavens and is depicted as white-skinned sitting on an antelope. His other names are "Pavana" (the purifier), "Gandha-vaha" (carrier of perfumes) and "Satata-ga" (always moving). Illustrations from the *Ramayana* (an ancient Indian epic text dating from 500 BC) portray him carrying his baby son Hanuman, the monkey god.

Wat Arun

BAS-RELIEFS

Angkor Wat is covered with 1,200 sq m (12,917 sq ft) of intricately carved scenes depicting Khmer myths, Angkorian warfare and tales from the great Hindu epics the *Ramayana* and the *Mahabharata*. Divided into eight sections, some of the most celebrated panels include the *Battle of Kuruk-setra* in the ▷ *West Gallery*, the *Churning of the Ocean of Milk* in the east gallery, and the *Heavens and Hells* in the ▷ *South Gallery*. Angkor Wat is also covered with 1,850 carved ▷ *apsaras*, Sanskrit for celestial dancers. These sensuous goddesses, naked except for ornate jewellery and elaborate head-dresses, have enigmatic smiles, known as the "Khmer Smile", and are the glory of Angkor.

Battle of Kuruksetra from the Hindu epic the *Mahabharata*

THE FALL OF ANGKOR

The last great king of Angkor was Jayavarman VII (1181–1220) who built the temple of the Bayon at Angkor Thom amongst many others. His ambitious temple building programmes probably dep-leted the kingdom's coffers, as did wars with neighbouring Siam (present-day Thailand) and Champa (Vietnam). Succeeding kings are little known but in 1432, the Siamese sacked Angkor and the last king, Ponhea Yat, was forced to move south towards Phnom Penh, the present capital of Cambodia. Although Angkor Wat remained a holy place, the empire subsequently went into decline and most of the tem-ples were deserted, gradually becoming covered in jungle.

Angkor Wat

ONE OF THE LARGEST RELIGIOUS monuments in the world, the 12th-century temple of Angkor Wat is covered with exquisite carvings, forming the longest bas-relief in existence. Part of a vast complex of sacred monuments spread over 400 sq km (154 sq miles), it was constructed between the 9th and 14th centuries, when the Khmer Empire spanned half of Southeast Asia. The temple is an earthly representation of the Hindu cosmos. Its five towers, shaped like lotus buds, form a pyramidal structure symbolizing the mythical Mount Meru, home of the gods. The outer walls represent the edge of the world, and the moat the cosmic ocean. Dedicated to Vishnu, it was built for the god-king Suryavarman II (r.1113–50), probably as a funerary monument. It faces west, towards the setting sun, a symbol of death.

Meditating Buddhist Monk
Angkor was originally Hindu but subsequently became a Buddhist site. Today, the monks live in a pagoda by the side of the temple.

★ **Central Sanctuary**
Rising 65 m (213 ft) from the centre of Angkor Wat, the Central Sanctuary has four entrances, each facing one of the cardinal directions. Originally dedicated to Vishnu, the sanctuary now houses Buddhist images.

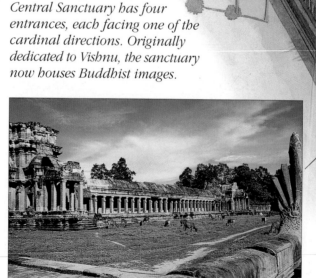

★ **Gallery of the Bas-Reliefs**
The walkway is framed by balustrades terminating with the body of the naga, *the seven-headed serpent. Beyond is the Gallery of the Bas-Reliefs – the outer side comprising 60 columns, while the inner wall is carved with beautiful bas-reliefs of epic events.*

◁ **Vast expanse of the Angkor Wat temple complex**

View of Towers

The well-preserved monument of Angkor Wat rises on a series of colonnaded platforms and is surrounded by a moat. The view of the five towers of the temple when reflected in water makes for a stunning spectacle.

South Gallery

★ Apsaras
Numerous celestial dancers are carved onto the walls, each slightly different in gesture and detail. The variety of hairstyles and headdresses is extraordinary.

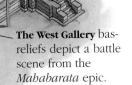

The West Gallery bas-reliefs depict a battle scene from the *Mahabarata* epic.

The Causeway
Angkor Wat's majestic façade can be seen from the causeway at its west entrance. Balustrades in the form of nagas *border the causeway on either side and extend all around the temple.*

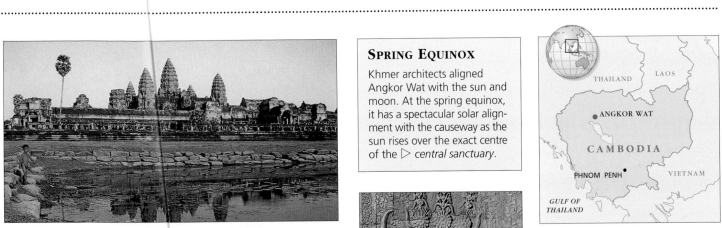

STAR FEATURES

★ **Central Sanctuary**

★ **Gallery of the Bas-Reliefs**

★ **Apsaras**

KEY DATES

1113–50 Construction of Angkor Wat during the rule of the Khmer Empire.

1432 The Siamese sack Angkor Wat.

1860 Angkor Wat is rediscovered by Henri Mouhot.

1898 The French *École Française d'Extrême Orient* starts to clear the site.

1992 Angkor Wat is declared a UNESCO World Heritage Site.

1993 International conservation project begins to preserve the temples of Angkor Wat.

REDISCOVERY OF ANGKOR

Although the ruins of Angkor Wat had been chronicled by a number of foreigners, it was the Frenchman Henri Mouhot, travelling under the auspices of the Royal Geographical Society in 1860, who is attributed with the rediscovery of Angkor Wat. A naturalist and botanist, he spent three weeks among the ruins, drawing and surveying the temples and writing a detailed and lyrical account in his diaries. They were published after his death in Laos a year later from malaria. His descriptions inspired numerous travellers, including the Scottish photographer John Thomson who took the first black and white photos of Angkor in 1866.

Angkor Wat

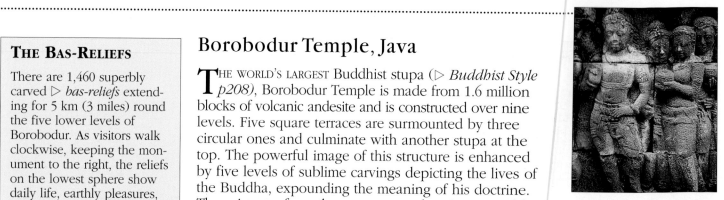

THE BAS-RELIEFS

There are 1,460 superbly carved ▷ bas-reliefs extending for 5 km (3 miles) round the five lower levels of Borobodur. As visitors walk clockwise, keeping the monument to the right, the reliefs on the lowest sphere show daily life, earthly pleasures, the punishments of hell and the laws of cause and effect, *karma*. This vivid evocation of daily life in ancient Javanese society was later covered with stone to support the temple's weight. The second level depicts the Buddha, Siddhartha Gautama and his life, showing him leaving his father's palace and going out into the world. These reliefs feature graceful figures with serene expressions wearing jewels and head-dresses. Images on the other levels follow texts such as the *Lalitavistara*, and the *Jataka* tales, Buddha's earlier incarnations, and search for enlightenment.

A graceful, bejewelled king and queen holding court at Borobodur

THE SAILENDRA DYNASTY

Between AD 730–930, the Sailendra dynasty ruled most of Java in Indonesia. Their name is Sanskrit for "Lords of the Mountain" and they were heavily influenced by Indian culture through the maritime trade routes of the region. Java was one of the world's leading civilizations during this period, enriched by trade and the sale of rice, and the Sailendras created the greatest monuments in Asia at the time. Borobodur Temple, arguably their finest accomplishment, took 75 years to complete. The balance of power shifted in the late 9th century, and the Sailendras were forced to leave Java.

Borobodur Temple, Java

THE WORLD'S LARGEST Buddhist stupa (▷ *Buddhist Style p208*), Borobodur Temple is made from 1.6 million blocks of volcanic andesite and is constructed over nine levels. Five square terraces are surmounted by three circular ones and culminate with another stupa at the top. The powerful image of this structure is enhanced by five levels of sublime carvings depicting the lives of the Buddha, expounding the meaning of his doctrine. These images form the most comprehensive ensemble of Buddhist reliefs ever carved. As pilgrims circumambulate, praying before each image, they ascend from the terrestrial to the divine world. Abandoned in the 10th century, and later buried under ash from a volcanic eruption, the temple was not discovered again until 1815.

View of Borobodur Temple
The name of this colossal structure probably came from the Sanskrit Vihara Buddha Uhr, meaning High Buddhist monastery. It is the earthly manifestion of the Buddhist vision of the universe.

Temple Roof
The view from the top of Borobudur Temple shows the volcanic plain with its palm trees and groves.

STAR FEATURES

★ **Rupadatu Bas-Reliefs**

★ **Meditating Buddhas**

★ **Kamadhatu Bas-Reliefs**

★ **Rupadatu Bas-Reliefs**
These carvings depict the life of Siddhartha Gautama, the Buddha.

CONSTRUCTION

Borobodur is square in plan, rising to 34.5 m (113.19 ft). Originally, five square diminishing terraces were built, leading to a sixth terrace from which three circular terraces arose, with a stupa at the summit. The original intention seems to have been to construct a pyramid but the weight was so immense that a stone buttress was constructed around the base to prevent it collapsing. The geometrical precision and complex imagery of Borobodur continue to fascinate scholars.

★ Meditating Buddhas

Most of the Buddhas on the temple roof are enclosed in individual stupas but several are exposed. They are remarkable for their serenity and poise.

RESTORATION

In 1973, a $21 million restoration project began. The terraces were dismantled, catalogued, cleaned and reconstructed on a concrete foundation. This Buddhist site is now a national monument in a Muslim country.

Carved Gateway

This archway leading to the roof is guarded by Kala, a protective deity and a mythical monster who swallowed his own body.

KEY DATES

AD 770 Construction begins on Borobodur Temple.

AD 845 Borobodur Temple is completed.

c.900 The balance of power shifts to East Java and the temple is abandoned.

c.900 Heavy volcanic activity submerges the temple in ash.

1815 Borobodur is rediscovered by Sir Stamford Raffles.

1991 Borobodur is declared a UNESCO World Heritage Site.

THE MEANING OF BOROBODUR

Initially built as a Hindu temple, Borobodur is a recreation of Mount Meru, the mythical mountain abode of Hindu gods. Symbolically the temple is a *mandala*, an aid to meditation, and a meeting place of heaven and earth. It represents the transition from the lowest manifestations of reality through to the highest spiritual awareness at the summit. The base represents the lowest sphere of consciousness, (▷ *Kamadhatu Bas-Reliefs*). The next level (▷ *Rupadatu Bas-Reliefs*), is the intermediate period of consciousness. The upper levels, with 72 small, perforated stupas, each containing a seated ▷ *meditating Buddha*, represent the sphere of formlessness, *Arupadhatu*. At the top, the empty central stupa suggests *nirvana* (Sanskrit for extinction), and symbolizes enlightenment, the ultimate spiritual realm or nothingness.

Seated Buddha

Sitting within an arched niche in the temple, this Buddha is thought to represent a hermit in a mountain cave.

★ Kamadhatu Bas-Reliefs

Illustrating ancient Javanese society, the finesse and quality of the carvings on the first level of the temple are superb. This bas-relief depicts a group of musicians.

TRADITIONAL BELIEFS

Animism, ancestor worship and a sense of the supernatural permeate Balinese life. The term *sekala niskala* (visible-invisible) sums up the idea that the physical world is permeated by a spirit world. Loosely described as "gods" and "demons", the spirits are believed to dwell in natural objects such as stones or trees. Shrines are built for them and they are honoured with offerings of flowers and other materials. The invisible world is represented in many vivid symbols. Ancestors are deified in complex rituals and venerated at temples. Guardian effigies such as the dragon-like Barong and his demonic counterpart Rangda are periodically awakened to restore a village's spiritual balance.

Canang or daily flower offerings made to the spirits

THE BALE GONG & THE GAMELAN ORCHESTRA

In Bali and Lombok, traditional music is performed by a *gamelan* orchestra, a percussion ensemble consisting largely of bronze metallophones (instruments with tuned metal keys), led by drums *(kendang)*. Bronze gongs of various sizes form the heart of the orchestra. Struck with mallets, they produce resonant sounds which punctuate the keyed instruments' melodies. There are a few wind and stringed instruments, including bamboo flutes *(suling)*. Most villages own a set of *gamelan* instruments for ritual occasions; some are sacred and played only at religious ceremonies. Temples have pavilions known as ▷ *bale gong* to house the instruments.

Pura Ulun Danu Batur, Bali

Stone sculpture

ONE OF BALI'S MOST popular and spiritually significant temples, the Pura Ulun Danu Batur has a vital association with Lake *(danu)* Batur, however it is uncertain when the temple was built. It is the country's guardian temple of water supplies as it controls the irrigation system of much of the island. From a distance the temple's silhouette can be seen on the rim of the vast Batur caldera.

Temple Flags
Deities and mythical beasts are often depicted in rich colours on temple flags and sculptures.

Inner Courtyard
The inner courtyard is the most sacred. Three gateways lead from one courtyard to the next.

Garuda
The figure of Garuda, a bird from Hindu mythology, is depicted in this stone relief on the courtyard wall.

★ **Central Courtyard**
The great quadrangle, shown here occupied by a festive structure of bamboo and straw, is the occasional setting for ritual dances.

OFFERINGS TO THE LAKE GODDESS

Offerings of fruits and flowers

Devotees from all over Bali present elaborate offerings at this temple, which is dedicated to Ida Betari Dewi Ulun Danu, the goddess of Lake Batur. The respect accorded to the goddess is reinforced by events in the temple's history. At its former location closer to the lake, the temple was miraculously saved from destruction in the volcanic eruption of 1917, when the lava flow stopped just short of its walls. Another eruption, in 1926, prompted the villagers to move the temple to its present location.

TEMPLE FESTIVALS

Odalan (temple festivals) are anniversary ceremonies where deities are honoured with offerings, prayers and entertainment, creating a carnival atmosphere that generally lasts for three days.

KEY DATES

1917 Pura Ulun Danu Batur is miraculously unharmed during a volcanic eruption.

1926 Another eruption almost entirely covers the temple.

1927 The temple is rebuilt at its current location.

BALINESE TEMPLE ARCHITECTURE

A Balinese *pura* (public temple) is a holy enclosure where Hindu deities are periodically invited to descend into *pratima* (effigies) kept in shrines. The arrangement of Balinese temples follows a consistent pattern, with individual structures oriented along a mountain-sea axis. Degrees of sacredness are reflected in proximity to the mountain. Of the three temple courtyards, the outer and ▷ *central courtyards* have a variety of secondary shrines and pavilions including the *kulkul* (watchtower), which houses a drum that is sounded when deities are thought to descend. It also traditionally serves as a general alarm bell. The *jeroan* (▷ *inner courtyard*) contains shrines to the temple's core deities and often to deities of the mountains, lakes and sea. The *padmasana,* or lotus throne shrine, in the temple's most sacred corner, has an empty seat on top signifying the Supreme God. The *meru* shrine with a number of tiers, depending on its deity's importance, symbolizes the mythical Hindu peak, Mount Meru.

★ Gold-painted Doors

The great timber doors of the main temple gateway are reserved for the use of priests on important occasions.

Side Gate

This tall, slender gate, built in a combination of brickwork and paras *stone decoration, leads to another temple.*

The *bale gong* is a pavilion housing the temple's set of *gamelan* instruments, including a great gong believed to have a magical history.

Entrance

STAR FEATURES

★ Central Courtyard

★ Gold-painted Doors

THE WORLD'S MUST-SEE PLACES

AUSTRALASIA

PAGES 224-227

Sydney Opera House

Advertising poster

No other building on earth looks like the Sydney Opera House. Popularly known as the "Opera House" long before the building was complete, it is, in fact, a complex of theatres and halls linked beneath its famous shells. Its birth was long and complicated. Many of the construction problems had not been faced before, resulting in an architectural adventure which lasted 14 years. An appeal fund was set up, eventually raising A$900,000, while the Opera House Lottery raised the balance of the A$102 million final cost. Today it is the city's most popular tourist attraction, as well as one of the world's busiest performing arts centres.

★ **Opera Theatre**
Mainly used for opera and ballet, this 1,547-seat theatre is big enough to stage grand operas such as Verdi's Aïda.

DESIGN AND CONSTRUCTION

In 1957, the Danish architect Jørn Utzon won the international competition to design the Sydney Opera House. He envisaged a living sculpture that could be viewed from any angle, land, air or sea. It was boldly conceived, posing architectural and engineering problems that Utzon's first compendium of sketches did not initially solve. When construction began in 1959, the intricate design proved impossible to execute and had to be greatly modified. The project remained so controversial that Utzon resigned in 1966 and an Australian design team completed the building's interior. However, he was reappointed as a consultant, to develop a set of guiding principles for any future alterations to the building.

ROLE AND SIGNIFICANCE

The astounding Sydney Opera House is instantly recognizable around the world. It is managed by the Sydney Opera House Trust, who are responsible for maintaining its high status as Australia's cultural landmark and performing arts centre. The building has been credited as one of the world's renowned architectural marvels and it has won numerous awards, including the prestigious international Top Ten Construction Achievements of the 20th Century award in 1999. Since its opening, the Opera House has become a symbol of Australia. An estimated 4.4 million people visit the Opera House every year, 75 percent of whom go just to look around the magnificent structure.

Aerial view of the Opera House

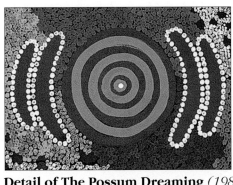

Detail of The Possum Dreaming *(1988)*
The mural in the Opera Theatre foyer is by Michael Tjakamarra Nelson, an artist from the central Australian desert.

The Opera Theatre's ceiling and walls are painted black to focus attention on the stage.

Opera House Walkway
Extensive public walkways around the building offer the visitor views from many different vantage points.

STAR FEATURES

★ **Opera Theatre**

★ **Concert Hall**

★ **Roofs**

Northern Foyers
The Reception Hall and the large northern foyers of the Opera Theatre and Concert Hall have spectacular views over Sydney harbour.

◁ **Sydney Opera House, with a unique arched roof design**

★ Concert Hall

This is the largest hall, with seating for 2,690. It is used for symphony, choral, jazz, folk and pop concerts, chamber music, opera, dance and everything from body building to fashion parades.

BACKSTAGE

Artists performing at the Opera House have the use of five rehearsal studios, 60 dressing rooms, suites and a green room complete with restaurant, bar and lounge. The scene-changing machinery works on well-oiled wheels; crucially in the Opera Theatre where there is regularly a nightly change of performances.

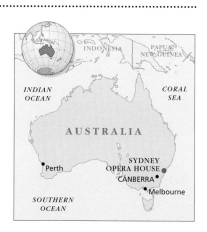

The Monumental Steps and forecourt are used for outdoor films and free entertainment.

Bennelong Restaurant

This is one of the finest restaurants in Sydney.

The Playhouse, seating almost 400, is ideal for intimate productions, while also able to present plays with larger casts.

★ Roofs

Although apocryphal, the theory that Jørn Utzon's arched roof design came to him while peeling an orange is enchanting. The highest point is 67 m (221 ft) above sea level.

KEY DATES

1957 Jørn Utzon wins the Opera House design competition.

1959–73 The Sydney Opera House is constructed.

1973 Prokofiev's opera *War and Peace* is the first public performance in the Opera House.

THE THEATRE AND HALLS

Underneath the ten spectacular ▷ *roofs* of varying planes and textures lies a complex maze of more than 1,000 rooms of all shapes and sizes showcasing different events. The ▷ *Concert Hall* is decked out in native white birch and brush box (hardwood timber). A Grand Organ, built by Ronald Sharp from 1969–79, is the centrepiece of the hall. The Drama Theatre stage is 15 m (49 ft) square, and can be clearly viewed from every seat in the auditorium. Refrigerated aluminium panels in the ceiling control the temperature. Fine Australian art hangs in the ▷ *Playhouse* foyer, notably Sidney Nolan's *Little Shark* (1973) and a fresco by Salvatore Zofrea (1992–3). The ▷ *Opera Theatre* is the second largest venue in the building. It hosts both spectacular opera and dance performances. The proscenium opening is 12 m (39 ft) wide, and the stage extends back 21 m (69 ft), while the orchestra pit accommodates up to 70–80 musicians.

Curtain of the Moon (1972)

Designed by John Coburn, this and its fellow Curtain of the Sun *were originally used in the Drama and Opera theatres. Both have been removed for preservation.*

Sydney Opera House

BEGINNING OF DUNEDIN'S RAILWAY

In the early 1860s gold was discovered in Dunedin and gold-miners from other parts of the country poured into the region. The money gold brought into the area ensured, for a time, that Dunedin became the commercial capital of New Zealand. Railways were therefore constructed to transport the growing population. The first journey, with the new "Josephine" trains, was from Dunedin to Port Chalmers, on 10 September 1872. In 1875 a second station was built in Dunedin to ease the busy station; a third followed four years later. As the number of passengers on the railway increased further, Dunedin Railway Station was commissioned.

Front view of Dunedin Railway Station

AN ARCHITECTURAL CHALLENGE

For its day, the construction of Dunedin Railway Station was an engineering challenge. Built on the foundations of the old harbour, iron-bark piles had to be driven deep into the reclaimed land to prevent flooding. George Troup used a number of railway staff, who he had trained in the art of stonemasonry, to help build the station. Machinery, including cranes, was also loaned by New Zealand Railways for use during building works to reduce cost. It is believed that New Zealand's first electrically driven concrete mixer was used in the station's construction. Costing £120,500, the station is seven times larger than its predecessor, Dunedin's third station, built in the late 1800s.

Dunedin Railway Station

Frieze with cherub and foliage

O NE OF NEW ZEALAND'S finest historic buildings, Dunedin Railway Station is also one of the best examples of railway architecture in the southern hemisphere. Although not large by international standards, the station's delightful proportions lend it an air of grandeur. It was designed in the Flemish Renaissance style (▷ *Renaissance Style p131*) by New Zealand Railways architect George Troup, whose detailing on the outside of the building earned him the nickname "Gingerbread George".

★ Exterior Stonework
Beige Oamaru limestone detailing provides a striking contrast to the darker Central Otago bluestone on the walls and the finely polished Aberdeen granite of the columns.

The turret provides a visual counter-balance to the main clock tower.

The roof is covered with clay Marseille tiles from France.

Dormer windows projecting from the sloping gable roof are typical Flemish architectural features.

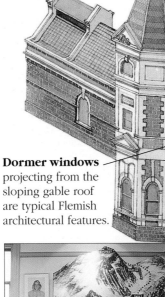

New Zealand Sports Hall of Fame
This features imaginative displays recounting the exploits and achievements of famous New Zealanders.

A frieze of cherubs and foliage from the Royal Doulton factory in England encircles the ticket hall below the wrought-iron bordered balcony.

Main entrance

Ticket Windows
The ticket windows are ornately decorated with white tiles and a crest featuring the old New Zealand Railways logo.

STAR FEATURES

★ **Exterior Stonework**

★ **Stained-glass Windows**

★ **Mosaic Floor**

★ Stained-glass Windows

Two imposing stained-glass windows on the mezzanine balcony depict approaching steam engines, lights blazing, facing each other across the ticket hall.

FLOOR RESTORATION

By 1956 the original floor had subsided dramatically. Exact replica mosaics had to be laid on a new concrete foundation in order to alleviate the problem.

Finely carved sandstone lions on each corner of the clock tower guard the cupola behind them.

The clock tower rises 37 m (120 ft) above street level.

Staircase

Complete with wrought-iron balustrades and mosaic tiled steps, a staircase sweeps up from the ticket hall to the balcony above.

The platform behind the station is still a departure and arrival point for travellers.

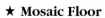

★ Mosaic Floor

More than 725,000 Royal Doulton porcelain squares form images of steam engines, rolling stock and the New Zealand Railways logo.

KEY DATES

1906 Dunedin Station is opened.

1956 The clock tower is restored.

1994 The station is sold to Dunedin City Council for a nominal sum.

1996–98 The exterior stonework is cleaned.

TROUP & THE DESIGN OF DUNEDIN STATION

In 1884 the 20-year-old George Troup (1863–1941) arrived in New Zealand, after emigrating from his home in Scotland with an apprentice-ship in architectural design. He quickly secured a job with New Zealand Railways in Dunedin, where he was employed to design bridges and stations all over the country. He was soon pro-moted to Head of the Archi-tectural branch and while working in this new role he designed the renowned Dunedin Railway Station. No expense was spared to create this magnificent station. The ▷ *roof* was adorned with red Marseille tiles, while the ▷ *exterior stonework* featured lavish ornate detailing – referred to as "Gingerbread style". Inside, Troup covered the floor with rich mosaic tiles (▷ *mosaic floor*), some embellished with images of railway engines, wheels, sig-nals and wagons. After retir-ing from the railway, Troup became a patron of the arts and Mayor of Wellington. He was knighted in 1937.

Dunedin Railway Station

THE WORLD'S MUST-SEE PLACES

NORTH, CENTRAL & SOUTH AMERICA

PAGES 230-261

Sacred vessels in the museum attest to the pilgrims' devotion

St Anne Museum

Many works of art that describe earlier pilgrims' devotion to St Anne are on view in the museum at the shrine. There are also displays dedicated to the heritage of French Canada, from the 17th century to the present, with wax figures, paintings and educational artifacts illustrating the life of St Anne. One of the most important pieces is an 18th-century ▷ *sailor painting*, which depicts the story of shipwrecked sailors.

In and Around the Basilica

The lower level has two chapels: the ▷ *Immaculate Conception Chapel* and the Blessed Sacrament Chapel. Also on the lower level is a copy of Michelangelo's ▷ *Pietà* and the tomb of Venerable Father Alfred Pampalon (1867–96), patron saint of alcoholics and drug addicts. The main church is on the upper level, where hundreds of crutches, braces and artificial limbs attest to miraculous cures. The earliest healing here, in 1658, is said to have been that of Louis Guimond, a crippled man who insisted on carrying stones for the construction of the first church despite his affliction, and who was cured before the other workers' eyes. Pilgrims gather on the hillside to follow the Way of the Cross and to go up the Holy Stairs, representing Christ's climb to meet Pontius Pilate. A model of the original church stands next to the Holy Stairs. Nearby, a building showcases the world's largest cyclorama depicting Jerusalem at the time of the Crucifixion.

Sainte-Anne-de-Beaupré

Sainte-Anne-de-Beaupré

THE SHRINE TO ST ANNE, mother of the Virgin Mary, is the oldest pilgrimage site in North America. In 1620 a group of sailors who had survived a shipwreck established the shrine and dedicated it to St Anne. In 1658 a chapel was erected and since then several churches have been built on this site. The fifth and present one, dating from the 1920s, receives 1.5 million visitors every year, including those who come for the annual pilgrimage on St Anne's Feastday on 26 July. The collection of crutches in the entrance bears witness to the basilica's reputation for miraculous cures. Inside, the dome-vaulted ceiling is decorated with gold mosaics portraying the life of St Anne. She is represented in a large gilt statue in the transept, cradling the Virgin Mary.

PLAN OF THE SHRINE

1 Basilica   4 Museum
2 Monastery   5 Blessing Office
3 Church store

THE BASILICA

In 1876, St Anne was proclaimed patron saint of Quebec, and in 1887 the existing church was granted basilica status. The Redemptorist order became the guardians of the shrine in 1878.

Façade
The present basilica was built by the Canadian architect Napoleon Bourassa. He based the design on a mix of Gothic and Romanesque ideals.

★ **The Great Rose Window**
This beautiful stained-glass window was designed by the French artist Auguste Labouret (1950).

The spire

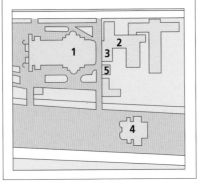

Entrance to the basilica's upper floor

◁ **Golden Gate Bridge, San Francisco, the third-largest single span bridge ever built**

Interior
Lit by sun streaming through the stained-glass windows, the cream and gold interior is divided into a nave and four aisles by large pillars topped with sculpted capitals.

BASILICAS
Originally, a basilica was simply any public building modelled on Roman structures with a nave, aisles and an apse. The Roman Catholic church has given special, honorary significance to the term. A basilica is entitled to display certain papal emblems, and it is also expected to celebrate the liturgy solemnly and maintain choirs whose repertory includes great church music of the past.

Sainte-Anne-de-Beaupré

KEY DATES

1876–1922 The first basilica, built in honour of St Anne, is used for worship.

1922 A fire on 29 March destroys the basilica.

1923 Work on the present basilica begins.

1976 The basilica is consecrated by Cardinal Maurice Roy.

THE LIFE OF ST ANNE
Although the Bible makes no mention of the mother of the Virgin Mary, Christians from the earliest times had an interest in knowing more about Jesus' family, especially his mother and grandmother. A 3rd-century Greek manuscript called the *Revelation of James* tells the story of Jesus' grandparents, naming them Anne (from Hannah) and Joachim. According to this account, Anne of Bethlehem and Joachim of Nazareth, a shepherd, were childless after 20 years of marriage. Each cried out separately to God, asking why they were childless, and vowing to dedicate any offspring to His work. An angel came to Joachim and Anne, and they learned that they were to have a child, Mary, who became the mother of Christ. There is no mention of Anne and Joachim's death in this record, but a later one claims that Jesus was with his grandparents when they died. In Canada, Anne is the patron saint of Quebec and her feast day is celebrated on 26 July.

The Statue of St Anne is on the upper floor. It sits in front of the relic of St Anne, presented to the shrine by Pope John XXII in 1960.

★ Pietà
A faithful copy of Michelangelo's original in St Peter's, Rome, this shows Christ at his death being held by a seated Madonna.

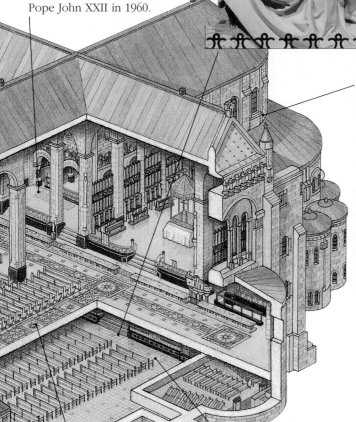

Immaculate Conception Chapel

Bright mosaic floor tiles echo the ceiling patterns.

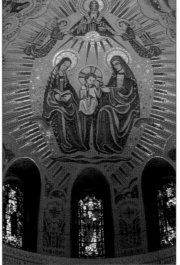

Sanctuary Mosaic
This splendid mosaic was created by the artists Auguste Labouret and Jean Gaudin (1940–41). God is shown overlooking an infant Jesus, flanked by Mary and St Anne.

STAR FEATURES

★ **The Great Rose Window**

★ **Pietà**

Sailor Painting
The Ex-voto of the Three Shipwrecked Sailors from Lévis (1754) *is an oil on wood painting. It is on display in the St Anne Museum.*

CN Tower, Toronto

CN Tower

At NO LESS THAN 553 m (1,815 ft) high, the CN Tower is the world's tallest building, acclaimed as one of the wonders of the modern world. In the 1970s Canadian National Railway (CN), the railroad conglomerate, in consultation with local broadcasters, decided to build a new transmission mast in Toronto on its land, to meet the telecommunications needs of the growing city and to demonstrate its pride in Toronto. Upon opening, it so overwhelmed the city's visitors that it soon became one of Canada's prime tourist attractions. Its revolving restaurant is also renowned for both its food and wine.

View of the CN Tower from Centre Island's gardens

OBSERVATION DECKS

The ▷ *Lookout Level* enables visitors to look out and over Toronto. Actually built over several levels, the upper tier has a café and a photo shop. Below, visitors can feel the wind at 113 storeys up, peer straight down through the ▷ *glass floor* or dine in the revolving ▷ *restaurant*. Thirty-three storeys above the Lookout Level, the ▷ *Sky Pod* is higher than most of the world's tallest skyscrapers, even though it is not at the top of the Tower. With an impressive 360-degree view of Toronto and Lake Ontario, on a clear day visitors can see as far as Niagara Falls.

FASCINATING FACTS

Construction of the CN Tower began in 1973, took about 40 months and cost around $63 million to build. A 6,968 sq m (75,000 sq ft) entertainment expansion and renovation was completed in 1998 at a further cost of $26 million. The tower has six ▷ *lifts*, which travel at 24 km/h (15 mph) and reach the ▷ *Lookout Level* at 346 m (1,136 ft) in 58 seconds; a separate lift takes visitors 101 m (329 ft) higher to the ▷ *Sky Pod*. The tower is flexible, and in winds of 195 km/h (120 mph), the Sky Pod can sway as much as 0.48 m (1.5 ft) from the centre. Every year, about 2 million people visit the tower.

Foundations for the single-shaft structure were sunk 17 m (55 ft) and required the removal of over 56,000 tonnes of earth and shale.

★ **The Sky Pod**
The world's highest observation platform at 447 m (1,465 ft), the Sky Pod offers fantastic views in every direction. It is reached by its own lift.

★ **Exterior Lookout**
Open to the elements, this outdoor terrace is secured with steel safety grills. Air temperatures at this height can be up to 10°C (50°F) cooler than at ground level.

The interior staircase is the longest metal staircase in the world with 1,776 steps. The stairwell is only open to the public twice a year for fundraising stair climbs which attract almost 20,000 climbers.

The exterior lifts are high-speed and glass-fronted, shooting visitors up the outside of the building to the upper levels. Travelling at high speeds, they reach the Lookout Level in under a minute.

The CN Tower from Lake Ontario
The tower's height is highlighted by the comparison with the SkyDome stadium (left) and the buildings of the Harbourfront.

The CN Tower at Night
Lit up against the night-time skyline, the majestic and elegant CN Tower soars above the city. Toronto is home to about 2,000 high-rise buildings but they are all at least 250 m (820 ft) lower than the CN Tower.

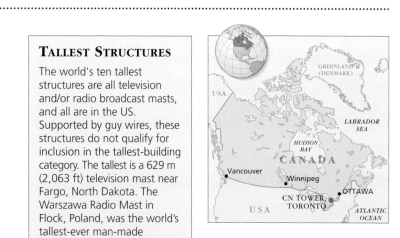

KEY DATES
1973 Construction begins.

1976 The CN Tower opens to the public.

1977 The first annual stair-climb is held for charity.

1995 The CN Tower is declared a Wonder of the Modern World by the American Society of Civil Engineers.

TALL BUILDINGS
The CN Tower's claim as "World's Tallest Building" at 553 m (1,815 ft) does not go undisputed. To sort out these claims, it is helpful to define three categories: tallest *supported* structure (such as radio masts), tallest *freestanding* structure and tallest *habitable* building. By these criteria, the CN Tower is clearly the tallest free-standing structure, even since the 2004 completion of Taipei's 101 skyscraper (509 m/1,669 ft). Other tall structures include the Ostankino Tower in Moscow (537 m/1,762 ft); the Shanghai World Financial Centre (460 m/1,509 ft); Petronas Towers in Kuala Lumpur (452 m/1,483 ft); Sears Tower in Chicago (442 m/1450 ft); and the Menara Kuala Lumpur Tower (421 m/1,381 ft). The Oriental Pearl Tower in Shanghai, at 468m/1,535 ft, yields fifth place to Union Square Phase 7 in Hong Kong at 474 m/1,555 ft completed in 2004. The new World Trade Center in New York will have a tower with an antenna reaching 541 m/1,776 ft, just under the CN Tower height.

360 The Restaurant at the CN Tower
At a height of 350 m (1,148 ft), the revolving restaurant turns a full circle every 72 minutes, and boasts the world's highest wine cellar with more than 500 labels.

A bar and disco
are located on the rotating restaurant level.

View of the City from the Lookout Level
At 346 m (1,136 ft) above the city, the Lookout Level provides panoramas of Toronto, Lake Ontario and the surrounding area. Visibility can stretch to just under 160 km (100 miles).

★ Glass Floor
The ground is over 342 m (1,122 ft) below this thick layer of reinforced glass. It is made from 24 sq m (256 sq ft) of solid glass that is five times stronger than the weight-bearing standard for commercial floors.

STAR FEATURES
★ Sky Pod

★ Exterior Lookout

★ Glass Floor

CN Tower

EARLY HISTORY

Old State House spire

Constructed in 1713 to replace the original Town House, the Old State House is Boston's oldest surviving public building. During its period as the seat of the colonial government, it was also the Boston centre for the political activity that led up to the American Revolution (1775–81). From the first-floor gallery (1766), Boston's citizens could – for the first time in the English-speaking world – watch their elected legislators debate the issues of the day. The west end housed the county and colony law courts. Wealthy merchant and patriot John Hancock, active opponent of the Stamp Act (1765) which imposed a tax on all paper goods and the first signer of the Declaration of Independence, had warehouse space in the basement.

THE BOSTONIAN SOCIETY

The Bostonian Society, which maintains the Old State House, also runs the museum in the State House and a library across the street. Changing and permanent exhibitions depict the history of the city from the settlement of the town through the American Revolution to the 21st century. Permanent exhibitions also include a sound-and-light show on the Boston Massacre of 1770, "From Colony to Commonwealth," interpreting the role of Boston in the Revolution, "Treasures from the Bostonian Society's Collections" in the ▷ *Council Chamber*, which includes Revolutionary icons and militia equipment, and "Preservation of the Old State House," tracing progress from 1881–1981.

Old State House, Boston

DWARFED BY THE TOWERS of the Financial District, this historic building is typical of the modest and unique architectural style of New England in the 18th century. It was the seat of British colonial government between 1713 and 1776. A replica royal lion and unicorn decorate each corner of the eastern façade. After independence, the Massachusetts legislature took possession of the building, and it has since had many uses, including being a produce market, merchants' exchange, Masonic lodge and Boston City Hall. Its wine cellars now function as a downtown subway station, and it also houses Bostonian Society memorabilia.

Old State House amid the sky-scrapers of the Financial District

A gold sculpture of an eagle, symbol of America, can be seen on the west façade.

West Façade
A Latin inscription, relating to the first Massachusetts Bay colony, runs around the outside of this crest. The relief in the centre depicts a local Native American.

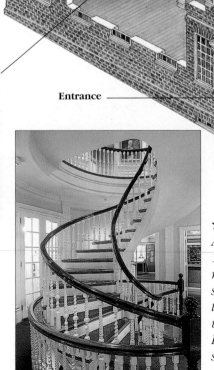

Entrance

Keayne Hall
This is named after Robert Keayne who, in 1658, gave £300 to the city so that the Town House, predating the Old State House, could be built. Exhibits in the room depict events from the Revolution.

★ Central Staircase
A fine example of 18th-century workmanship, the central spiral staircase has two beautifully crafted wooden handrails. It is one of the few such staircases still in existence in the US.

SITE OF THE BOSTON MASSACRE

Cobbled circle: site of the Boston Massacre

A circle of cobblestones below the balcony on the eastern façade marks the site of the Boston Massacre. After the Boston Tea Party (where Boston patriots, in protest at taxation, boarded three British East India Company ships and threw their cargoes of tea into Boston Harbor), this was one of the most inflammatory events leading up to the American Revolution. On 5 March 1770, an unruly mob of colonists taunted British guardsmen with insults, rocks and snow-balls. The soldiers opened fire, killing five colonists. A number of articles relating to the Boston Massacre are exhibited inside the Old State House.

The tower is a classic example of Colonial style. In 18th-century paintings and engravings it can be seen clearly above the Boston skyline.

British Lion and Unicorn
A royal symbol of Britain, the original lion and unicorn were pulled down when news of the Declaration of Independence reached Boston in 1776.

The Declaration of Independence was read from this balcony in 1776. In the 1830s, when the building was the City Hall, the balcony was enlarged to two tiers.

THE FREEDOM TRAIL

Boston's sites relating to the Revolution have been linked together as "The Freedom Trail". This 4-km (2.5-m) walking route, marked in red on the pavement, begins at the Boston Common.

★ East Façade
This façade has seen many changes. An earlier clock from the 1820s was removed in 1957 and re-placed with an 18th-century replica of the sundial that once hung here. The clock has now been reinstated.

Council Chamber
Once the chambers for the royal governors, and from 1780 chambers for the first governor of Massachusetts (John Hancock), this room has hosted many key events. Among them were numer-ous impassioned speeches made by Boston patriots.

STAR FEATURES

★ East Façade

★ Central Staircase

Old State House

KEY DATES

1667 Boston Town House is constructed of wood.

1711 Fire destroys the build-ing which is rebuilt in 1713.

1780–98 Serves as Massachusetts State House.

1798 Renovated for private retail tenants.

1830–40 Becomes the Boston City Hall.

1840–80 The building falls into disrepair.

1881 The Old State House is completely restored by the city.

1976 Queen Elizabeth II addresses Bostonians from the balcony.

LIFE IN COLONIAL BOSTON

First settled by Puritans in 1630, Boston became one of North America's leading colonial cities. Its life and its wealth centred around its role as a busy seaport, but its streets were crooked, dirty and crowded with people and livestock. Other prob-lems included waste dis-posal, fire fighting and caring for the numerous poor. Unlike the other major Amer-ican cities outside of New England, Boston had a "town meeting" form of govern-ment. This was unusually democratic for the times and helps to explain why Boston became such a centre of colonial resistance prior to the American Revolution.

The Solomon R Guggenheim museum floodlit at dusk

GUGGENHEIM AND WRIGHT

Guggenheim amassed his wealth through his family's mining and metal businesses, which he ran from New York. He collected modernist paintings and in 1942, Frank Lloyd Wright was asked to design a permanent home for the collection. Wright disagreed with the choice of New York for the project. He felt the city was overbuilt, overpopulated and lacking in architectural merit, but he acquiesced and designed a structure to challenge these shortcomings. He wished to disregard Manhattan's rectilinear grid system and to bring a fresh notion of exhibition areas to the city using curving, continuous spaces.

THE OTHER MUSEUMS

The Guggenheim Foundation runs three other museums. In Bilbao, Spain, a building designed by US architect Frank O Gehry houses a permanent collection of modern art with exhibitions from ancient China to Jasper Johns. Solomon's niece, Peggy Guggenheim, donated her collection of post-1910 masterpieces of surrealist and abstract painting and sculpture to the Foundation. Opened in 1951, this collection is housed in her villa on the Grand Canal in Venice. In cooperation with Deutsche Bank, the Deutsche Guggenheim Berlin has four exhibitions a year, including performance art and music. The Foundation is also considering plans for new museums in Rio de Janeiro, Vienna and St Petersburg.

Solomon R Guggenheim Museum, New York

HOME TO ONE of the world's finest collections of modern and contemporary art, the building itself is perhaps the museum's greatest masterpiece. Designed by architect Frank Lloyd Wright, the shell-like façade is a New York landmark. It takes its inspiration from nature, attempting to render the fluidity of organic forms. The spiral ramp curves down and inward from the dome, passing works by major 19th- and 20th-century artists. The imaginative layout of the Great Rotunda affords visitors the opportunity of simultaneously viewing works located on different levels.

Fifth Avenue façade

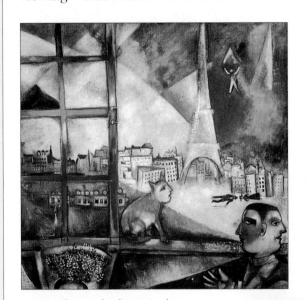

Paris Through the Window
The vibrant colours of Marc Chagall's 1913 masterpiece illuminate the canvas, conjuring up images of a magical and mysterious city where nothing is quite what it appears to be.

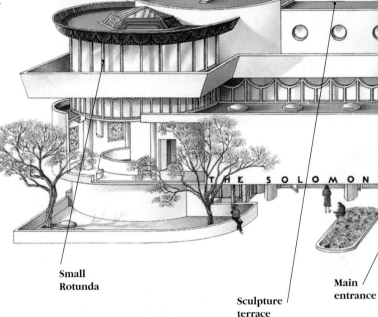

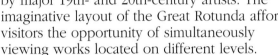

Small Rotunda

Sculpture terrace

Main entrance

Woman Ironing (*1904*)
A work from Pablo Picasso's Blue Period, this painting is his quintessential image of hard work and fatigue.

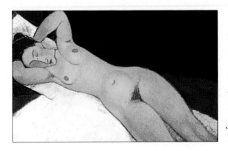

Nude (*1917*)
This sleeping figure is typical of Amedeo Modigliani's stylized work. His simplified faces are reminiscent of African masks.

Solomon R Guggenheim Museum

MUSEUM GUIDE

The Great Rotunda puts on special exhibitions. The Small Rotunda shows some of the museum's celebrated Impressionist and Post-Impressionist holdings. The Tower galleries feature exhibitions of work from the permanent collection as well as contemporary pieces. A sculpture terrace on the fifth floor overlooks Central Park.

Tower galleries

Great Rotunda

Before the Mirror (1876)

In trying to capture the flavour of 19th-century society, Edouard Manet often used the image of the courtesan.

GUGGENHEIM ONLINE

Encompassing highlights from the Guggenheim holdings worldwide, the excellent online site (www.guggenheimcollection.org) includes conceptual definitions, artist biographies, and suggested further reading.

Woman Holding a Vase

Fernand Léger incorporated elements of Cubism into this work from 1927.

Black Lines (1913) *This is one of Vasily Kandinsky's earliest examples of his work in "non-objective" art.*

KEY DATES

1946 Construction begins.

1949 Solomon Guggenheim dies.

1959 Guggenheim Museum opens on Fifth Avenue.

1992 The Frank Wright building is restored and supplemented by a new tower.

THE COLLECTION

At first a collector of mediocre Old Masters, Guggenheim began, after meeting artist Hilla Rebay, to amass a superb stock of works by modernists such as Delaunay, Léger and Kandinsky. The Guggenheim Foundation was founded in 1937 and established the Museum of Non-Objective Art, as it was known until 1959, in a temporary residence. Design of the new building began in 1943, but it was not until after Guggenheim's death in 1949 that the collection was expanded, through purchases and bequests, to include such artists as Picasso, Cézanne, Klee and Mangold. Other highlights include works by Modigliani, Chagall, Braque and Rousseau. Thannhauser's collection of Impressionist, Post-Impressionist and early Modern art, donated from 1978 to 1991 by collector Justin Thannhauser and his widow, is hung in the ▷ *Tower galleries.* This collection includes masterpieces by innovators such as Cézanne, Degas, Manet, Pissarro, van Gogh and an exceptional number of works by Picasso. The Guggenheim's exhibits change on a regular basis.

Woman with Yellow Hair

(1931) Marie-Thérèse Walter, Picasso's mistress, is shown as a gentle, voluptuous figure.

FRANK LLOYD WRIGHT

During his lifetime, Wright was considered the great innovator of American architecture. Characteristic of his work are Prairie-style homes and office buildings of concrete slabs, glass bricks and tubing. Wright received the Guggenheim commission in 1942 and it was completed after his death in 1959, his only New York building.

Interior of the Guggenheim's Great Rotunda

THE SKYSCRAPER RACE

With the construction of the Eiffel Tower in 1889, American architects were challenged to build ever higher, so at the beginning of the 20th century the skyscraper race began. By 1929, New York's Bank of Manhattan Building, at 283 m (972 ft), was the tallest skyscraper but Walter Chrysler, the famous car manufacturer, was planning to top that height. John Jakob Raskob, of rival General Motors, decided to join the race and, with Pierre S Du Pont, was a major investor in the Empire State project. Since Chrysler was keeping the height of his building a secret, Raskob had to be flexible in his planning. He first aimed at building 85 floors but, unsure of Chrysler's goal, he kept going until the building reached 102 floors, and by adding a spire beat Chrysler by 62 m (204 ft).

WHO DESIGNED IT?

The Shreve, Lamb & Harmon company has designed some of the most notable skyscrapers in Manhattan. By the time work on the Empire State Building began, they had designed seven buildings, including 40 Wall Street (now the Trump Building), at 70 floors, which was completed in only 11 months. With a team of top engineers and contractors, using up to 3,000 workers, the Empire State Building, too, was completed under budget and in record time.

Al Smith, former governor of NY State, with a model of the ESB

Empire State Building, New York

Empire State Building

Oᴺᴇ ᴏꜰ ᴛʜᴇ ᴡᴏʀʟᴅ's most famous buildings, the Empire State broke all height records when it was finished. Construction began in March 1930, not long after the Wall Street Crash but by the time it opened in 1931, it was so hard to find anyone to fill it that it was nicknamed "the Empty State Building". Only the popularity of its observatories saved it from bankruptcy. However, the building was soon seen as a symbol of New York throughout the world.

Art Deco Medallions
Displayed throughout the lobby, these depict symbols of the modern age.

CONSTRUCTION
The building was designed to be erected easily and speedily with everything possible prefabricated and slotted into place at a rate of about four storeys per week.

The framework is made from 60,000 tons of steel and was built in 23 weeks.

Aluminium panels were used instead of stone around the 6,500 windows. The steel trim masks rough edges on the facing.

Ten million bricks were used to line the whole building.

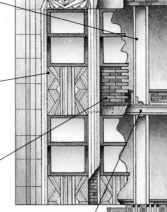

Sandwich space between the floors houses the wiring, pipes and cables.

Over 200 steel and concrete piles support the 365,000-ton building.

STAR FEATURES

★ **Views from the Observatories**

★ **Fifth Avenue Entrance Lobby**

102nd-floor observatory

The Empire State has 102 floors, but only 85 have office space. A 46 m (150 ft) mooring mast for Zeppelins was added. Now 62 m (204 ft), the mast transmits TV and radio to the city and four states.

Coloured floodlighting of the top 30 floors marks special and seasonal events.

High-speed lifts travel at up to 366 m (1,200 ft) a minute.

Ten minutes is all it takes for fit runners to race up the 1,576 steps from the lobby to the 86th floor, in the annual Empire State Run-Up.

★ Views from the Observatories
The 86th floor has outdoor observation decks for bird's-eye views of Manhattan. On a clear day, visitors can see more than 80 miles (125 km) in all directions. The observatory on the 102nd floor closed in 1994.

ART DECO DESIGN
The Empire State Building is considered New York City's last Art Deco masterpiece. The movement flourished from the 1920s to the 1940s and was noted for its use of crisp, graphic lines, geometric shapes, and vertical setbacks evocative of Aztec ziggurats.

KEY DATES

1930 Building work begins.

1931 Empire State Building is tallest building in the world.

1977 The first annual Empire State Run-Up takes place.

2002 Donald Trump sells the Empire State Building to a real estate consortium.

BUILDING SKYSCRAPERS

The modern skyscraper would not have been possible without several building developments. Lifts had been in use for some time, but it was not until Elisha Otis's 1854 demonstration of his safety brake that the public began to trust them. The second necessary innovation was the use of the structural steel skeleton, seen in the world's first skyscraper in 1885. With this kind of construction, the walls became merely a sheathing, not a load-bearing element, and enormously tall, heavy buildings could now rise ever higher. Building in the heart of Manhattan presented a further problem; large amounts of essential construction materials could not be kept in the street. To solve this, the aluminium elements were prefabricated and only three days' worth of structural steel was kept on site, creating an extremely complicated organization job. Although no longer the world's tallest, the Empire State Building is arguably still the most famous.

Sky Builder
Suspended high above Fifth Avenue, this steel worker was one of many men whose bravery was well documented in a series of photographs, during the 1930s construction of the building.

Empire State 443 m (1454 ft) with mast

Eiffel Tower 324 m (1,063 ft)

Great Pyramid 147 m (482 ft)

Big Ben 97.5 m (320 ft)

Lightning Strikes
A natural lightning conductor, the building is struck up to 100 times a year. The observation decks are closed during inclement weather.

Pecking Order
New Yorkers are justly proud of their city's symbol, which towers above the icons of other countries.

★ Fifth Avenue Entrance Lobby
A relief image of the skyscraper is superimposed on a map of New York State in the marble-lined lobby.

STARRING ROLE

The Empire State Building has been seen in many films. However, the finale from the 1933 classic *King Kong* is easily its most famous guest appearance, as the giant ape straddles the spire to do battle with army aircraft. In 1945 a real bomber flew too low over Manhattan in fog and struck the building just above the 78th floor. The luckiest escape was that of a young lift operator whose cabin plunged 79 floors. The emergency brakes saved her life.

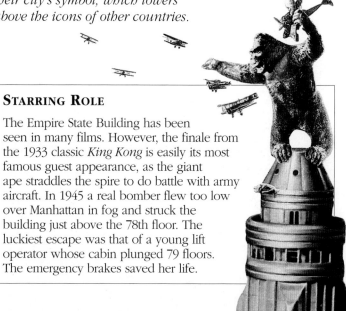

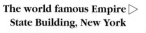
The world famous Empire ▷ State Building, New York

Empire State Building

BUILDING THE LADY

In his Parisian workshop, the sculptor Bartholdi began by creating four scale models, the largest at one-fourth the actual size. This was divided into 300 plaster sections, and each section was then enlarged to full size. A mould of laminated wood was made from each of these sections, and sheets of copper were pounded into the moulds to a thickness of only 2.5 mm (0.1 in). In all, 350 sheets were connected with 50 mm- (2 in-) wide iron straps. The straps acted like springs, which allowed the surface to flex in high winds or extremes of temperature. The statue arrived in New York packed in over 200 crates and was attached to the frame using some 300,000 copper rivets.

Statue construction workshop in France, c.1882

FUND-RAISING

Although the French contributed to the cost of the statue, early on in the plan it was decided that funds for the pedestal would come from the US. As fund-raising was going slowly, media baron Joseph Pulitzer used the editorial clout of his newspaper *The World* to criticize the wealthy for withholding their financial support and the middle class for relying on the wealthy. He pointed out that the statue was a gift to the entire US and attacked those who were not supporting it on the grounds that it was a New York project. Soon the whole nation was involved. When the crated statue arrived on 19 June 1885, fund-raising rose to fever pitch. It reached its target in just two months.

Statue of Liberty, New York

A GIFT FROM THE FRENCH to the American people, the statue was a celebration of a century of independence. The brainchild of French politician Edouard-René Lefebvre de Laboulaye, it has become a symbol of freedom to many since it was unveiled by President Grover Cleveland on 28 October 1886. Its spirit is encapsulated in the poem engraved on the base "Give me your tired, your poor, /Your huddled masses yearning to breathe free." After decades of wear and tear, the statue needed restoration work and was given an expensive facelift in time for its 100th anniversary in 1986.

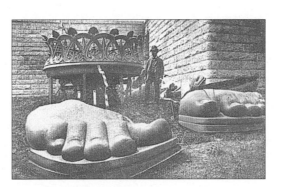

From Her Toes to Her Torch
Three hundred moulded copper sheets riveted together make up Lady Liberty.

★ **Statue of Liberty Museum**
Posters featuring the statue are among the items on display.

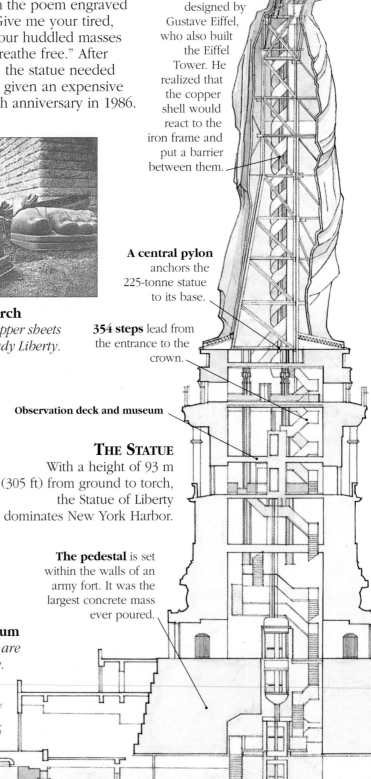

The Golden Torch is a 1986 replacement for the original, which became corroded over the years. The replica's flame is coated in 24-carat gold leaf.

The frame was designed by Gustave Eiffel, who also built the Eiffel Tower. He realized that the copper shell would react to the iron frame and put a barrier between them.

A central pylon anchors the 225-tonne statue to its base.

354 steps lead from the entrance to the crown.

Observation deck and museum

THE STATUE
With a height of 93 m (305 ft) from ground to torch, the Statue of Liberty dominates New York Harbor.

The pedestal is set within the walls of an army fort. It was the largest concrete mass ever poured.

The original torch now stands in the main lobby.

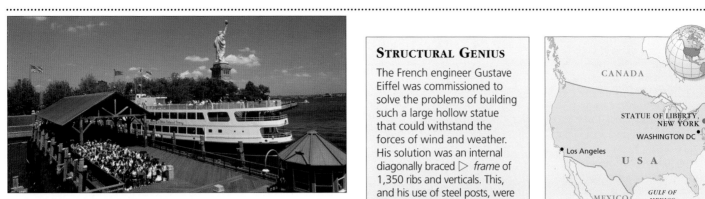

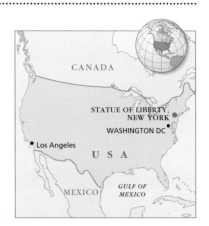

★ **Ferries to Liberty Island**
Ferries cross New York Harbor to Liberty Island, which was originally known as Bedloe's Island.

STRUCTURAL GENIUS

The French engineer Gustave Eiffel was commissioned to solve the problems of building such a large hollow statue that could withstand the forces of wind and weather. His solution was an internal diagonally braced ▷ *frame* of 1,350 ribs and verticals. This, and his use of steel posts, were seen as structural innovations.

KEY DATES

1865 Bartholdi has the idea of building a tribute to Liberty in America.

1876 Bartholdi is given the commission to create the Statue of Liberty.

1886 The Statue of Liberty is unveiled.

1986 The Statue of Liberty is reopened after extensive restoration.

THE MUSEUM

The ▷ *Statue of Liberty Museum* is located in the base of the structure. The Torch Exhibit in the lobby holds the much-altered flame and the ▷ *original 1886 torch*. Overlooking the lobby is a display covering the history of the torch and flame. The Statue of Liberty Exhibit, on the pedestal's second level, is a biography of Lady Liberty and an examination of the ideals for which she stands. Through artifacts, prints, photographs, videos and oral histories, seven sections with topics such as "From Image to Ideal" and "Stretching Technology" focus on her history. Another area has five sections on her symbolism, exploring ideas such as "Mother of Exiles," and "The Statue in Popular Culture." There is also a display of full-scale models of Liberty's face and left foot (▷ *A Model Figure*). A plaque dedicated to Emma Lazarus's famous sonnet *The New Colossus* was added to the pedestal in the early 1900s.

Face of Liberty
The sculptor's mother was the model for Liberty's face. The seven rays of her crown represent the seven seas and seven continents.

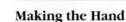

Making the Hand
To make the copper shell, the hand was made first in plaster, then in wood. The scale of the project can be seen by the figures around it.

A Model Figure
A series of graduated scale models enabled Bartholdi to build the largest metal statue ever constructed.

FRÉDÉRIC-AUGUSTE BARTHOLDI (1834–1904)

Initially called "Liberty Enlightening the World", the Statue of Liberty was intended by its designer the French sculptor Bartholdi as a monument to the freedom he thought was lacking in his own country. He said "I will try to glorify the Republic and Liberty over there, in the hope that some day I will find it again here." He devoted 21 years of his life to the project, travelling to the US in 1871 to persuade President Ulysses S Grant and others to help to fund the pedestal.

STAR FEATURES

★ **Statue of Liberty Museum**

★ **Ferries to Liberty Island**

Restoration Celebration
On 4 July 1986, after a $100 million clean-up, the statue was revealed. The $2 million fireworks display was the largest ever seen in America.

THE WAR OF 1812

Tensions with Britain over restrictions on trade and freedom of the seas began to escalate during James Madison's administration. On 18 June 1812, the US declared war on Britain. In August 1814, British troops reached Washington and officers of the Capitol fled, taking the Declaration of Independence and the Constitution with them. On 24 August, the British defeated the Americans at Bladensburg, a suburb of Washington. They set fire to the War Department, the Treasury, the Capitol and the White House, but a night of heavy rain prevented the city's destruction. The Treaty of Ghent, which finally ended the war, was signed on 17 February 1815.

Façade of the White House Visitor Center

THE WEST WING

In 1902, the West Wing of the White House was built by the architectural firm McKim, Mead, and White for a total cost of $65,196. This wing (▷ *The West Terrace*), houses the Cabinet Room, where government officials convene with the president, and the Oval Office where the president meets visiting heads of state. Many presidents have personalized this room in some way: President Clinton chose as his desk a table given to President Rutherford B Hayes by Queen Victoria in 1880.

The White House, Washington DC

THE OFFICIAL RESIDENCE of United States presidents for over 200 years, the White House is one of the most distinguished buildings in America and was built on a location chosen by George Washington in 1790. Irish-born architect James Hoban designed the original building in a Palladian style (▷ *Neo-Classical Style p56*) and when it was nearing completion, President and Mrs John Adams became the first occupants. It has survived two fires, in 1814 and 1929, and the interior was completely gutted and renovated throughout President Harry S Truman's presidency, 1945–53. In 1901, President Theodore Roosevelt officially gave the White House its current name.

★ State Dining Room
Able to seat as many as 140 people, the State Dining Room was enlarged in 1902. A portrait of President Abraham Lincoln, by George P A Healy, hangs above the mantel.

The West Terrace
leads to the West Wing, the Cabinet Room and the Oval Office, the President's official office.

STAR ROOMS

★ State Dining Room

★ Red Room

★ Vermeil Room

The North Façade
The Palladian-style façade of the White House is familiar to millions of people around the world.

The stonework
has been painted over and over to maintain the building's white façade.

★ Red Room
One of four reception rooms, the Red Room is furnished in red in the Empire style (1810–30). The fabrics were woven in the US from French designs.

Lincoln Bedroom

President Lincoln used this room as his Cabinet Room, and it was turned into a bedroom by President Truman who filled it with furnishings from the Lincoln era.

THE WHITE HOUSE VISITOR CENTER

Interesting exhibits about the history of the White House, its décor and its inhabitants are on display in the White House Visitor Center. Guided tours of the presidential official residence are extremely limited and can only be booked by special arrangement through a Member of Congress or an embassy.

The White House

The East Terrace leads to the East Wing.

The East Room is used for large gatherings, such as dances and concerts.

Treaty Room

The Green Room was first used as a guest room before Thomas Jefferson turned it into a dining room.

Blue Room

★ Vermeil Room
This yellow room houses seven paintings of first ladies, including this portrait of Eleanor Roosevelt by Douglas Chandor.

KEY DATES

1792 Construction begins on the Executive Mansion (renamed the White House in 1901).

1800 President Adams and his wife are the first to move into the White House.

1814 The British set fire to the White House during the war of 1812–15.

1902 The West Wing, including the Oval Office, is built.

1942 The East Wing of the White House is added, on the instructions of Franklin D Roosevelt, completing the final structure.

THE WHITE HOUSE INTERIOR

The rooms in the White House are decorated in period styles and filled with valuable antique furniture, china and silverware. Hanging on its walls are some of America's most treasured paintings including portraits of past presidents and first ladies. The room that served as the Cabinet Room from 1865 for ten presidential administrations (▷ *Treaty Room*), was restored in 1961 and contains Victorian pieces bought by President Grant. The most central room on the State Floor (▷ *Blue Room*) was decorated in 1817 in the French Empire style by President Monroe. The same style was later used by First Lady Jackie Kennedy to redecorate one of the reception rooms (▷ *Red Room*) in 1962.

Diplomatic Reception
This room is used to welcome friends and ambassadors. It is elegantly furnished in the Federal Period style (1790–1820).

WHITE HOUSE ARCHITECTS

After selecting the site, George Washington held a design competition to find an architect to build the residence where the US president would live. In 1792 James Hoban, an Irish-born architect, was chosen for the task. It is from Hoban's original drawings that the White House was initially built and all subsequent changes grew. In 1902 President Theodore Roosevelt hired the New York architectural firm of McKim, Mead, and White to check the structural condition of the building and refurbish areas as necessary. The White House underwent further renovations and refurbishments during the administrations of Truman and Kennedy.

James Hoban, architect of the White House

THE DOME

By the 1850s, the original Charles Bulfinch ▷ *Dome* was too small for the enlarged Capitol. Moreover, it leaked and was deemed a fire hazard. In 1854, the first $100,000 was appropriated for Thomas U Walter's new dome to be constructed of cast iron. Walter's double-dome design recalls the Panthéon in Paris. Thomas Crawford designed and executed a 6-m (19.5-ft) sculpture to crown the dome, and in 1863, during the American Civil War (1861–5), the Statue of Freedom was raised atop the 87.5-m (287-ft) high dome – a Classical female figure standing on a globe with the national motto, *E Pluribus Unum* (Out of many, one). The statue was restored in 1993.

View of the US Capitol in Washington DC

THE ROTUNDA FRIEZE

Thomas U Walter's 1859 drawings showed a recessed, bas-relief sculpture in the ▷ *Rotunda*. Plans changed, and by 1877, a fresco 2.5 m (8.3 ft) high and 91 m (300 ft) in circumference was being painted. The *Frieze of American History* has 19 panels. The first contains the only allegorical figures in the frieze: America, an American Indian maiden, History and an American eagle. The second panel represents Columbus's landing, and the next six show well-known events from early New World history. Panel ten represents the founding of Georgia and is followed by familiar military and political scenes from US history. The first flight in 1903 is featured in the final panel, *The Birth of Aviation,* completed in 1953.

United States Capitol, Washington DC

THE US CAPITOL IS ONE of the world's best-known symbols of democracy. The centre of America's legislative process for 200 years, its Neo-Classical architecture reflects the principles of Ancient Greece and Rome that developed America's political system. The cornerstone was laid by George Washington in 1793 and by 1800, although unfinished, the Capitol was occupied. With more funding, construction resumed under architect Benjamin Latrobe, however the British burned the Capitol in the War of 1812. Restoration began in 1815. Many features, such as the Statue of Freedom and Brumidi's murals, were added later.

Dome
Originally ma of wood and copper, the dome was designed by Thomas Walter.

★ **Rotunda**
Completed in 1865, the 55-m (180-ft) high Rotunda is capped by The Apotheosis of Washington, *a fresco by Constantino Brumidi.*

The Hall of Columns is lined with statues of notable Americans.

The Rotunda Frieze

The House Chamber

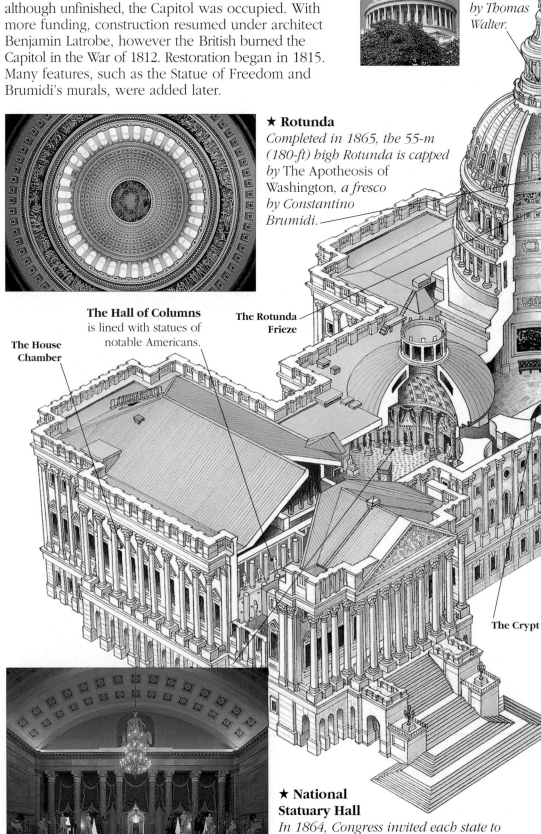

The Crypt

★ **National Statuary Hall**
In 1864, Congress invited each state to contribute two statues of prominent citizens to stand in this hall.

★ Old Senate Chamber

Occupied by the Senate until 1859, this chamber was then home to the Supreme Court for 75 years. Today it is used mainly as museum space.

The Senate Chamber has been the home of the US Senate since 1859.

The Columbus Doors, created by Randolph Rogers (1825–92), are made of solid bronze and depict Christopher Columbus's life and his discovery of America – a theme echoed throughout the works of art in the Capitol.

US Capitol

Not only representative of the legislative heart of Washington, the Capitol marks the precise centre of the city. The city's four quadrants radiate out from the middle of the building.

East Entrance

Carved on the pediment are striking Classical female representations of America. These are flanked by figures of Justice and Hope.

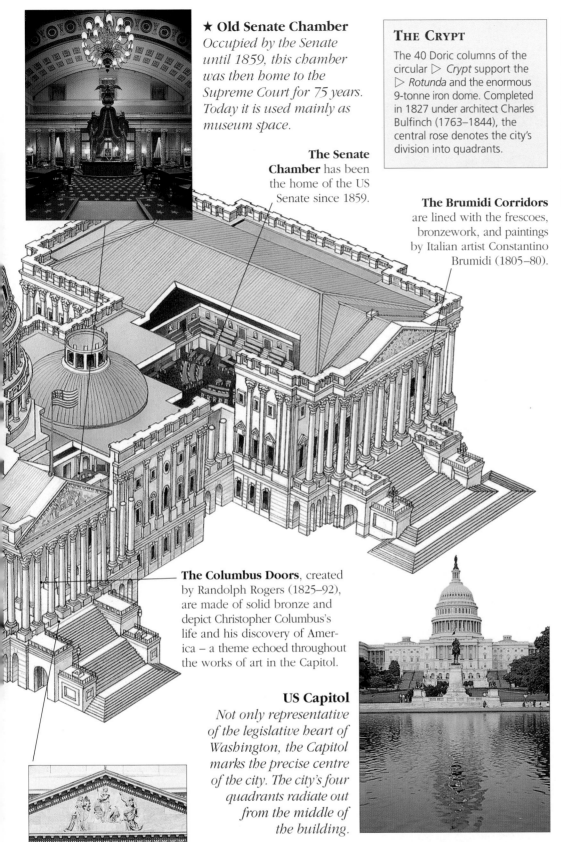

THE CRYPT

The 40 Doric columns of the circular ▷ *Crypt* support the ▷ *Rotunda* and the enormous 9-tonne iron dome. Completed in 1827 under architect Charles Bulfinch (1763–1844), the central rose denotes the city's division into quadrants.

The Brumidi Corridors are lined with the frescoes, bronzework, and paintings by Italian artist Constantino Brumidi (1805–80).

KEY DATES

1791–92 Site is chosen for new national capital; city of Washington DC is designed and mapped.

1829 Original Capitol building is completed.

1851 Cornerstones are laid for new wings.

1983–93 West front and terrace are restored.

STATUARY

In 1864, Congress invited each state to contribute two statues of notable citizens to stand in the ▷ *National Statuary Hall*. Soon the collection grew too large, and much of it can now be seen in the ▷ *Hall of Columns* and the various corridors of the Capitol. Four statues of former US Presidents Washington, Jackson, Garfield and Eisenhower can be found in the ▷ *Rotunda*. Also here is a statue of Sacajawea, Native American translator for the Lewis and Clark Expedition (1803–1806) into the new Lousiana Territory, pending selection of a permanent location. In the Statuary Hall itself, visitors can see Confederate General Robert E Lee and President Jefferson Davis; King Kamehameha I, unifier of Hawaii; Robert Fulton, inventor of the first commercially successful steamboat; Huey P Long, Depression-era demagogue from Louisiana; Sam Houston, president of the Republic of Texas; and Sequoyah, inventor of the Cherokee alphabet.

STAR FEATURES

★ **Rotunda**

★ **National Statuary Hall**

★ **Old Senate Chamber**

United States Capitol

BUILDING THE BRIDGE

The Golden Gate Bridge is a classic suspension bridge of the kind first built in the mid-19th century. Its main elements are the anchorages, towers (pylons), cables and road. Enormous concrete anchorages were poured at either end to hold the cables. The steel for the towers was fabricated in Pennsylvania and shipped through the Panama Canal. Engineer Joseph B Strauss chose John A Roebling and Sons, builders of the Brooklyn Bridge, to make the cables. Since no derrick of the time could lift cables as heavy as these would be, they were spun in place, the machines passing back and forth continuously for six months. Rejecting steel grey, architect Irving Morrow chose "International Orange" for the bridge's paint colour, believing it better suited the natural light of the area.

BRIDGE PARTY

The Golden Gate Bridge opened to pedestrian traffic on 27 May 1937, on schedule and under budget. On a typically foggy and windy day, over 18,000 people took part in the grand opening by walking its total length (including the approaches) of 2,737 m (8,981 ft). The next day, President Franklin D Roosevelt pressed a telegraph key in the White House which opened the bridge to vehicular traffic. Every siren and church bell in San Francisco and Marin County sounded simultaneously. A week-long celebration followed the event.

The Golden Gate in "International Orange" paint

Golden Gate Bridge, San Francisco

SUPERLATIVES FLOW WHEN describing this world-famous landmark. It is the third-largest single-span bridge ever built and, when it was erected, was the longest and tallest suspension structure. Named after the part of San Francisco Bay dubbed "Golden Gate" in the mid-19th century, the bridge opened in 1937. There are breathtaking views of the bay from this spectacular structure, which has six lanes for vehicles as well as a free pedestrian walkway.

One of the builders in a protective mask

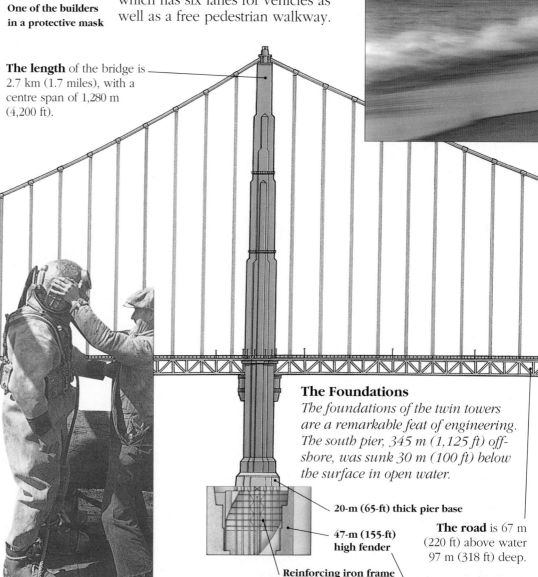

The length of the bridge is 2.7 km (1.7 miles), with a centre span of 1,280 m (4,200 ft).

Divers
To reach the bedrock, divers were employed to dynamite 6-m (20-ft) deep holes in the ocean floor.

The Foundations
The foundations of the twin towers are a remarkable feat of engineering. The south pier, 345 m (1,125 ft) off-shore, was sunk 30 m (100 ft) below the surface in open water.

20-m (65-ft) thick pier base

47-m (155-ft) high fender

Reinforcing iron frame

The road is 67 m (220 ft) above water 97 m (318 ft) deep.

The Concrete Fender
During construction, the south pier base was protected from the force of the tides by a fender of concrete. Water was pumped out to create a vast watertight locker.

THE GOLDEN GATE BRIDGE

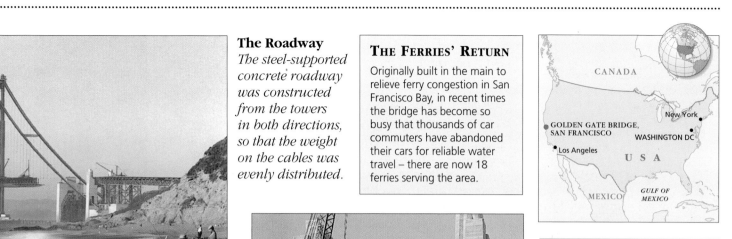

The Roadway
The steel-supported concrete roadway was constructed from the towers in both directions, so that the weight on the cables was evenly distributed.

THE FERRIES' RETURN
Originally built in the main to relieve ferry congestion in San Francisco Bay, in recent times the bridge has become so busy that thousands of car commuters have abandoned their cars for reliable water travel – there are now 18 ferries serving the area.

Construction of the Towers
The twin steel towers rise to a height of 227 m (746 ft) above the water. The towers are hollow.

KEY DATES

c.1872 Earliest discussion of building a bridge across the entrance of San Francisco Bay.

1923 California legislature passes a bill to explore the feasibility of building the bridge.

1933 Construction begins in January.

1937 Bridge opens on time to great celebrations.

1985 The one-billionth car passes over the bridge.

DESIGNER SQUABBLES

Conceived as early as 1872 by railway tycoon Charles Crocker, building a bridge across the Golden Gate was not considered feasible until architect Joseph B Strauss stepped forward with a plan in 1921. Nine years of bureaucratic wrangling passed before Strauss was named chief engineer, but it was assistant chief engineer Clifford Paine and architect Irving Morrow who actually deserve credit for the design and construction of the bridge that stands today. By all accounts, Strauss seems to have been a difficult individual; he fired his first assistant chief engineer, Charles Ellis, for attracting too much publicity. Strauss even kept Ellis's name from appearing on any official documents. Ellis had his supporters however, who blocked a proposal to erect a statue of Strauss on the bridge until 1941.

Man with a Plan
Chicago engineering titan Joseph Strauss is officially credited as the bridge's designer. He was assisted by Leon Moisseiff, Charles Ellis and Clifford Paine. Irving F Morrow acted as consulting architect.

THE BRIDGE IN FIGURES

• Every day about 118,000 vehicles cross the bridge; this means that every year more than 40 million cars use it.
• The original coat of orange paint lasted for 27 years, needing only touch-ups. But since 1965, a crew has been stripping off the old paint and applying a more durable coating.
• The two great 2,332-m (7,650-ft) cables are more than 1 m (3 ft) thick, and contain 128,744 km (80,000 miles) of steel wire, enough to circle the earth at the equator three times.
• The volume of concrete poured into the piers and anchorages during the bridge's construction would be enough to lay a 1.5-m (5-ft) wide pavement from New York to San Francisco, a distance of more than 4,000 km (2,500 miles).
• The bridge can stand firm in the face of 160 km/h (100 mph) winds.
• Each pier has to withstand a tidal flow of more than 97 km/h (60 mph), while supporting a 44,000-ton steel tower above.

View towards Marin County

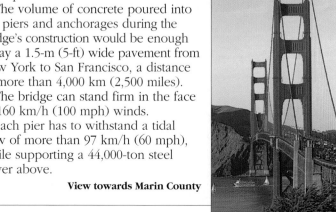

THE KIVAS

Usually a pueblo had a number of adjoining ▷ *kivas* (pit-houses), as well as one great *kiva*. Early smaller *kivas* seem to have been dwellings, but most scholars today agree that the great *kivas* were ceremonial places, barred to women and children, not merely community gathering sites. The first Chaco Canyon *kivas* appeared around AD 700 and while most were round, some were D-shaped. *Kivas* were entered through a hole in the roof and there was also a hole in the floor called a *sipapu*, which possibly symbolized the people's connection from birth with Mother Earth. Near the centre was a fireplace and air shafts on the sides of the *kivas* made them more livable.

Elaborate cliff dwellings built into the walls of Mesa Verde

OTHER ANASAZI SITES

The Aztec Ruins National Monument was built by Puebloans in the 12th century. This important archaeological site is situated 111 km (69 miles) north of Chaco Canyon. There is a reconstructed great *kiva* here, as well as a pueblo consisting of 450 interconnecting rooms built of stone and mud. Further to the north is Mesa Verde, Spanish for "green table", which was inhabited by Puebloan people between AD 550 and 1300. The Navajo National Monument, located 358 km (223 miles) northwest of Chaco Canyon, was also occupied by the Puebloan people in the late 13th century. Three of their best preserved cliff dwellings, including the splendid Keet Steel, are located here.

Chaco Culture National Historical Park

Arrowhead at Chaco Museum

ONE OF THE MOST IMPRESSIVE cultural sites in the American Southwest, Chaco Culture National Historical Park at Chaco Canyon reflects the sophistication of the Ancestral Puebloan civilization (also known as the Anasazi) that existed here. With its six "great houses" (pueblos containing hundreds of rooms) and many lesser sites, the canyon was once the political, religious and cultural centre for this people. Despite the size of the pueblos, it is thought that Chaco's population was small because the land could not have supported a larger community. Archaeologists believe that the city was mainly used as a ceremonial gathering place, with a year-round population of less than 3,000. The inhabitants sustained themselves largely by growing their own crops and trading.

Kivas are round pit-like rooms dug into the ground and roofed with beams and earth.

PUEBLO BONITO
Pueblo Bonito is an example of a "great house". Begun around AD 850, it was built in stages over the course of 300 years. This reconstruction shows how it might have looked, with its D-shaped four-storey structure that contained more than 650 rooms.

Chetro Ketl
A short trail from Pueblo Bonito leads to another great house, Chetro Ketl. Almost as large as Pueblo Bonito, Chetro Ketl has more than 500 rooms. The masonry used to build the later portions of this structure is among the most sophisticated found in any Puebloan site.

Stone Doorway
Chaco's skilled builders had only stone tools to work with to create this finely wrought stonework.

Casa Rinconada
The great kiva of Casa Rinconada is the largest religious chamber at Chaco, measuring 19 m (62 ft) in diameter. It was used for spiritual gatherings.

Pueblo Alto
Located on top of the mesa at the junction of several Chacoan roads is Pueblo Alto. In the 1860s W H Jackson discovered an ancient stairway carved into the cliff wall.

CHACO POTTERY

Archaeologists believe that the inhabitants of Chaco Canyon replaced baskets with ceramics for culinary usage between AD 400 and AD 750. Pieces of ceramics found so far are decorated with geometric designs and painted with minerals and carbons.

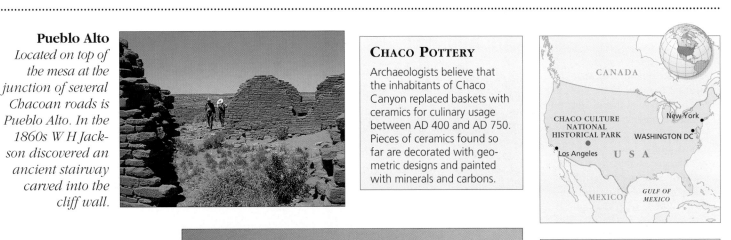

Chaco Culture National Historical Park

This great house was four storeys high.

Early Astronomers at Fajada Butte
Measurement of time was vital to the Puebloans for crop planting and the timing of ceremonies. A spiral petroglyph, carved on Fajada Butte, is designed to indicate the changing seasons through the shadows it casts on the rock.

KEY DATES

AD 700–900 Domestic and ceremonial *kivas* are built in Chaco Canyon.

AD 850–1250 Chaco Canyon serves as a religious, trade and administration centre for the Anasazi people.

1896–1900 Archaeologist George H Pepper and his team excavates Pueblo Bonito.

1920 Edgar L Hewitt excavates Chetro Ketl.

1987 Chaco Culture National Historical Park is named a UNESCO World Heritage Site.

THE ANASAZI

Around AD 400, the Chaco Canyon people began to settle in well-defined groups with a common culture known as "Anasazi", a Navajo name said to mean "Ancient Enemy Ancestor". For centuries their villages stayed small, but a population explosion beginning in the 11th century led to the construction of elaborate cliff dwellings and the building of a road system connecting some 400 settlements. Agriculture thrived with the building of dams and irrigation systems. Better strains of corn (maize) that could reach deep into the ground for scarce water were also planted to support the growing population. However, by AD 1130, the towns began to empty, perhaps because of drought. People migrated east, south and west, and by the 13th century the canyon was completely deserted.

EXPLORING CHACO

The area around Chaco Canyon is full of hauntingly beautiful ruins left behind by the Ancestral Puebloan people. As well as the sites described here, they include Una Vida, the fifth largest great house with intriguing petroglyphs, Wijiji, Pueblo del Arroyo and Kin Kletso, a two-storey pueblo.

KEY

═	Highway
═	Unpaved road
--	Hiking route
△	Campground/RV
⛺	Picnic area
ⓘ	Visitor information

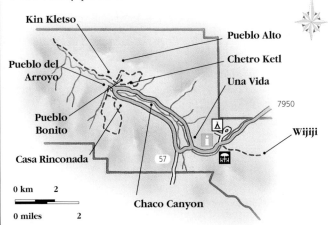

Kin Kletso

Pueblo Alto

Chetro Ketl

Pueblo del Arroyo

Una Vida

7950

Pueblo Bonito

Wijiji

Casa Rinconada

57

0 km 2

0 miles 2

Chaco Canyon

Hundreds of rooms within Pueblo Bonito show little sign of use and are thought to have been kept for storage or for guests arriving to take part in ceremonial events.

MAYAN DEITIES

A vast array of gods and goddesses were worshipped by the Maya. Some of them related to celestial bodies, such as the stars, sun and moon. Some had calendrical significance, while others held sway over creation, death and aspects of daily life. Deities were feared as much as revered so it was essential to appease them as much as possible, often through human sacrifice. Kukulcan, a feathered serpent, was an important deity. Chac, the Mayan god of rain and lightning, was venerated as abundant rainfall was vital to farming communities. Also worshipped was Kinich Ahau, the "great sun" or "sun-eyed" lord. This deity was associated with the jaguar, an animal that evoked the vigour and power of the rising sun.

EL CASTILLO PYRAMID

Built around AD 800, the incredible ▷ *El Castillo* pyramid has a perfect astronomical design. The four staircases face the cardinal points, with various features corresponding to aspects of the Mayan calendar. At the two yearly equinoxes a fascinating optical illusion occurs whereby a serpent appears to crawl down the north staircase due to the play of light and shadow. The temple at the top of the inner pyramid contains a *chacmool*, a carved reclining figure, with a stone dish on its stomach thought to have held sacrificial offerings. There is also a beautiful, bright-red throne carved as a jaguar and encrusted with jade. The entrance to the temple is divided by snake-shaped columns.

A serpent's head representing the god Kukulcan, El Castillo

Chichén Itzá

Carved figure, Temple of the Warriors

THE BEST PRESERVED Mayan site on the Yucatán peninsula, Chichén Itzá continues to confound archaeologists. The date of first settlement in the older, southern part of the site is uncertain, but the northern section was built during a Mayan renaissance in the 11th century AD. Similarities with Tula, the ancient capital of the Toltec empire, and myths of exiled Toltec god-king Quetzalcoatl (Kukulcan) settling at Chichén Itzá, suggest that the renaissance was due to a Toltec invasion. However, other theories hold that Tula was influenced by the Maya, not vice versa. In its heyday as a commercial, religious and military centre, which lasted until about the 13th century, Chichén Itzá supported over 35,000 people.

★ Ballcourt
At 168 m (550 ft) in length, this is the largest ballcourt in Mesoamerica. Still in place are the two engraved rings that the ball had to pass through.

★ Observatory
Also called El Caracol (The Snail) for its spiral staircase, this building was an astronomical observatory. The various slits in the walls correspond to the positions of certain celestial bodies on key dates in the Mayan calendar.

Main entrance

Tomb of the High Priest

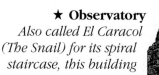

Nunnery
So named because its small rooms reminded the Spaniards of nuns' cells, this large structure, built in three stages, was probably a palace. This façade of the east annexe has particularly beautiful stone fretwork and carvings.

Chichén Viejo

The building known as "La Iglesia" is decorated with fretwork, masks of the rain god Chac, and the *bacabs* – four animals who, in Mayan myth, held up the sky.

0 metres 150

0 yards 150

The Tzompantli is a low platform whose perimeter is carved with grinning skulls. Archaeologists believe that it was used to display the heads of victims of human sacrifice, practised during Chichén Itzá's late period.

OFFERINGS

Incense, statues, jade, metal discs and humans were cast into the ▷ *Sacred Cenote* in offering. Surviving sacrificial victims supposedly emerged with the power of prophesy, having conversed with deities.

Sacred Cenote

A sacbe (Mayan road) leads to this huge natural well, thought to have been revered as the home of rain god Chac, and used for human sacrifice.

Platform of the Jaguars and Eagles

★ El Castillo
Built on top of an older structure that can also be visited, this 24-m (79-ft) high pyramid was dedicated to Kukulcan, the Mayan representation of the god Quetzalcoatl. Its height and striking geometric design dominate the whole site.

The Group of a Thousand Columns, made up of carved stone colonnades on two sides of a huge plaza, may have been used as a market.

Entrance

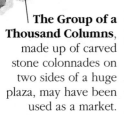

STAR FEATURES

★ **Ballcourt**

★ **Observatory**

★ **El Castillo**

Temple of the Warriors
Set on a small pyramid, this temple is decorated with sculptures of the rain god Chac and the plumed serpent Kukulcan. A chacmool *and two columns, carved to represent snakes, guard the entrance.*

KEY DATES

c.750 The Sacred Cenote is used for ritual offering.

c.900 Chichén Itzá becomes the centre of Mayan culture.

1960–1 The Sacred Cenote is thoroughly dredged.

1988 Chichén Itzá is added to UNESCO's World Heritage Site list.

MAYAN CULTURE

Unlike the other peoples of Mesoamerica, the Maya did not develop a large, centralized empire. Instead they lived in independent city-states. Once thought to have been a peaceful people, the Maya are now known to have shared the lust for war and human sacrifice of other ancient civilizations. Immensely talented, they also cultivated a remarkable understanding of astronomy and developed sophisticated systems of writing, counting, and recording the passing of time (▷ *Observatory*). They observed and predicted the phases of the moon, equinoxes and solstices, and solar and lunar eclipses. They knew that the Morning and Evening Star were the same planet, Venus, and calculated its "year" to 584 days, within a fraction of the true figure (583.92 days). It is almost certain that they calculated the orbit of Mars as well. Remarkably, they achieved all this without the use of lenses for observing distant objects, instruments for calculating angles, or clocks to measure the passing of seconds, minutes and hours.

Chichén Itzá

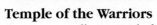

View toward El Castillo pyramid, dominating the Mayan site of Chichén Itzá ▷

THE INTERIOR

Like the exterior, the interior decoration reflects a blend of the prevalent colonial period styles. Its Baroque altars and side chapels are particularly ornate. A highlight is the richly carved ▷ *Altar de los Reyes*. A statue of Christ, the *Señor del Cacao*, probably dating from the 16th century, is worshipped in the ▷ *Capilla de San José*. Its name derives from the donations made in cocoa beans by the indigenous people towards the construction of the cathedral – a common currency during the pre-colonial era. An urn containing the remains of Emperor Agustín de Iturbide (1783–1824), the champion of Mexican Independence, is located in the chapel of San Felipe de Jesús.

The southern façade of the Metropolitan Cathedral

THE CONQUISTADORS AND CHRISTIANITY

When the Spanish conquistadors arrived in the New World in the 1500s, they encountered flourishing indigenous settlements. In addition to their desire for conquest and greed for gold, silver, copper and land, the conquistadors also saw themselves as missionaries, attempting to convert the established civilizations from paganism to Christianity. Franciscan and Dominican friars tirelessly preached to, converted and baptized the Mesoamericans. Although the New World was ultimately conquered, elements of the indigenous cultures survived and were absorbed into the developing Christian society.

Metropolitan Cathedral, Mexico City

Hymn book on view in the choir

THE BIGGEST CHURCH in Latin America, Mexico City's cathedral is also at the heart of the world's largest Catholic diocese. Its towers rise 67 m (220 ft) above one of the largest public squares in the world, and it took almost three centuries – from 1525 to 1813 – to complete. This long period is reflected in the multiple styles of its architecture, ranging from Classical through Baroque (▷ *Baroque Style p81*) to Neo-Classical (▷ *Neo-Classical Style p57*). It has five principal altars and 16 side chapels containing a valuable collection of paintings, sculpture and church furniture.

Sacristy
The sacristy contains 17th-century paintings and items of carved furniture such as this decorated cabinet.

Kings and Queens
The sculptures adorning the Altar de los Reyes are of kings and queens who have been canonized.

The high altar is a block of white marble carved with images of saints.

Side entrance

★ Altar de los Reyes
The two oil paintings on this Baroque masterpiece are the Adoration of the Kings *and the* Assumption of the Virgin, *both by Juan Rodríguez Juárez.*

Capilla de San José
This side chapel is one of 16 dedicated to saints and manifestations of the Virgin, all exquisitely decorated with statues and oil paintings.

STAR FEATURES

★ **Altar de los Reyes**

★ **Choir**

The Sinking Cathedral
The cathedral is sinking into the soft clay of what was once the bed of Lake Texcoco. Scaffolding has been installed in the interior in an attempt to stabilize the building.

Sagrario Metropolitano
Built in the mid-18th century as the parish church attached to the cathedral, the Sagrario has a sumptuous high Baroque façade adorned with sculpted saints.

ALTAR OF PARDON
A figure of the Virgin, by Simón Pereyns, was replaced after the 1967 fire with a black Christ which, legend says, absorbed the poison from a devout man who kissed it on his deathbed.

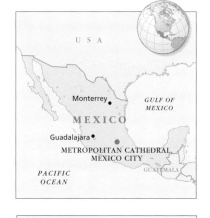

KEY DATES

1521 Construction starts on the cathedral.

1667 The cathedral is consecrated.

1967 Fire causes damage to parts of the cathedral.

1985 A powerful earthquake damages the cathedral.

1987 The Historic Centre of Mexico City is inscribed UNESCO's World Heritage Site.

THE SINKING OF MEXICO CITY

When Spanish conquistador Hernán Cortés led his army into the Aztec capital of Tenochtitlán in 1521, it stood on an island in Lake Texcoco. After conquering the city the Spanish razed it to the ground, reusing much of the stonework in their own constructions and gradually filling in the lake. The cathedral was built on the ruins of the main Aztec temple of worship whose stones were used in the building's walls. Like so many of Mexico City's buildings, the cathedral has been sinking, almost since its initial construction, into the ground beneath – the slant is quite visible despite extensive work to stabilize the structure in recent years (▷ *The Sinking Cathedral*). This is due to the large amount of water pumped from the aquifer beneath the city which supplies the needs of the rapidly-growing city.

The clocktower is decorated with statues of Faith, Hope, and Charity.

The façade is divided into three parts and flanked by monumental bell towers.

Main entrance

★ Choir
With its gold-alloy choir-rail imported from Macao, superbly carved stalls and two magnificent organs, the choir is a highlight of the cathedral.

Metropolitan Cathedral

Inca terraces and irrigation channels preventing soil erosion

INCA ARCHITECTURE

The people who built this most famous of Inca sites displayed incredibly advanced construction methods. Despite some of the building blocks weighing more than 50 tons, they are meticulously designed and fit together so exactly that the thinnest knife cannot be inserted between the mortarless joints. The ruins are roughly divided into two areas: the agricultural sector, consisting of terraces for cultivation; and the urban sector, with different sized structures, canals and steps. The design of the site emphasizes the aesthetic creativity of the builders. The enormous walls, delicate terracing and steep ramps could almost have been sculpted by the elements into the rock.

HIRAM BINGHAM

When this major Inca site buried in undergrowth was discovered, it was one of the most significant archaeological discoveries of the 20th century. American explorer Hiram Bingham had set out to find Vilcabamba, the legendary last refuge of the defeated Inca Empire, but instead he came across Machu Picchu. It took Bingham and his team several years to clear the massive growth of jungle that had covered the ruins. Underneath were houses, temples, canals and thousands of steps and terraces. What made his discovery so exciting was not only the fact that the Spanish Conquistadors had never discovered Machu Picchu, but also that the site had been completely untouched by treasure hunters.

Machu Picchu

THIS LOST CITY of the Incas is one of the most spectacular archaeological sites in the world. Perched high on a saddle between two peaks, surrounded by thick jungle and often shrouded in clouds, it is almost invisible from below. A compact site of just 13 sq km (5 sq miles), it was built in AD 1460 by the Inca ruler Pachacuti Inca Yupanqui. Although frequently referred to as a city, it was more of a royal retreat for the Inca aristocracy. About 1,000 people inhabited the area and they were completely self-sufficient, being surrounded by agricultural terraces and watered by natural springs. Even at the time, few people outside the closed Inca community were even aware of Machu Picchu's existence.

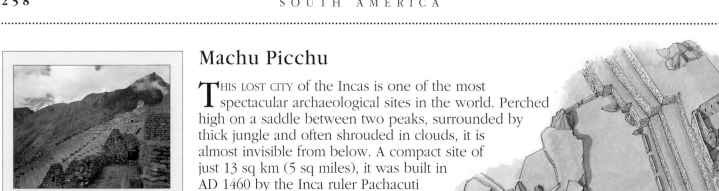

★ Intihuatana
This sundial, the size of a grand piano, was extremely sacred and one of the most important features of the whole site. Winter solstice festivals would take place here.

★ Sacred Plaza
With huge windows, the Temple of the Three Windows adjoins the Sacred Plaza, along with the Main Temple, which contains a wall almost flawlessly constructed.

STAR FEATURES

★ **Intihuatana**

★ **Sacred Plaza**

★ **Temple of the Sun**

0 metres   25

0 yards   25

The Sacred Rock is a large rock which is believed to have been used by the Incas for their sacrificial rituals.

MACHU PICCHU TRAIN

A train for the site leaves the town of Cusco on a regular basis. It makes the scenic 5-hour journey through the valley to Aguas Calientes, a town just below Machu Picchu. From here a local bus zig-zags up the mountain to this historical Inca site.

View of Machu Picchu
Made up of around 200 buildings and connected by more than 100 stairways, the ruined palaces, temples and residences were built around large central squares.

Preserved Brick Work
The Incas are admired today for their stone constructions, although it is unknown how they managed to make the blocks fit so closely together.

Residential and industrial areas within the urban sector

★ Temple of the Sun
The only circular building on the site, this temple contains two windows positioned precisely to catch the first rays of the winter and summer solstices.

KEY DATES

c.1200 Rise of the Inca Empire.

1460 Machu Picchu is constructed by the Incas.

Mid-1500s Machu Picchu is abandoned, possibly due to civil war over succession.

1911 Site is discovered by Hiram Bingham.

1983 Declared a World Heritage Site by UNESCO.

INCA CULTURE

Although at its peak the Inca Empire only lasted a century, it ruled around 12 million people and reached from Chile to Colombia. This incredibly organized civilization had a sophisticated economy and social system and an efficient road network of nearly 32,200 km (20,000 miles). The Incas ruled with fierce military might and had a strict social hierarchy, yet also managed to learn from the cultures they conquered. Worshipping the natural world, they saw the sun as the ultimate giver of life, believing their leader to be its direct descendant and that the mountain peaks, where they made human sacrifices, were the home of spirits. Celestial events were monitored so they knew when to plant and harvest crops and when to hold religious ceremonies. Machu Picchu stands as testimony to the sophistication of the Inca society, demonstrating what the New World had already achieved prior to Spanish arrival.

THE INCA TRAIL

The legendary Inca Trail climbs and descends a number of steep valleys and crosses three mountain passes of more than 3,658 m (12,000 ft). The breathtaking scenery includes snow-capped mountains, dense cloud forest and delicate flowers. Cobblestones laid by the Incas, as well as the tunnels that they constructed, can still be seen. It takes about four or five days before hikers are rewarded with the unforgettable sight of Machu Picchu through the sun gate (Intipunku).

Majestic view of Machu Picchu at the end of the Inca Trail

Agricultural terraces

THE LAYOUT OF THE CITY

The city's unique design is referred to as the ▷ *Pilot Plan*. Urban planner Lucio Costa said he simply used a shape that followed the lie of the land. He wanted to form a centralized, geometric city plan to create an ideal city and therefore an ideal society. The design is based on two axes (▷ *Monumental Axis* and ▷ *Residential Axis*). Six wide avenues were intended to provide the grandeur of a capital city, with the ▷ *Supreme Court*, ▷ *Congress Complex* and Presidential Palace (▷ *Planalto Palace*) representing the balance of the three powers. The residential area is made up of large six-storey "super-blocks", each grouped to form a neighbourhood.

Statues of apostles by Alfredo Ceschiatti, Brasília Cathedral

THE COMPETITION

In 1957 Lucio Costa and Oscar Niemeyer were announced as the winners of the competition launched to choose the urban design of Brasília. Costa was responsible for the general design of Brasília, but Niemeyer created the main buildings. Both were students of the modernist Le Corbusier, the father of functional, box-like buildings. Costa has been criticized for not providing for public transport and for designing a city for 500,000 people which today accommodates two million residents, many living in slums. However, it is generally agreed that Niemeyer achieved his aim of creating a city with "harmony and a sense of occasion" with his powerful public buildings.

Brasília

A 20TH-CENTURY CITY of pure invention, Brasília is the realization of a seemingly impossible dream. President Juscelino Kubitschek de Oliveira (1956–60) was elected partly on the basis of his highly ambitious pledge to move the capital of Brazil 1,200 km (746 miles) inland, from Rio de Janeiro into the country's empty centre, before the end of his first term. This was miraculously achieved by tens of thousands of workers who created the purpose-built city from an area of scrubland. The principal public buildings, which include the cathedral, are each strikingly designed. Brasília fulfilled Kubitschek's ambition to develop the interior and to create a monument both to modern architecture and the country's economic potential.

The Baptistry is an unusual egg-shaped building said to be a representation of the Host. It is connected to the cathedral by a tunnel.

← **The cathedral's entrance**

Interior of the Cathedral

Through coloured panes designed by Antonia Marianne Peretti, daylight falls on the seating area for hundreds of worshippers. Suspended from the ceiling are three floating angels made by the Brazilian sculptor Alfredo Ceschiatti.

JK Memorial

Inaugurated in 1981, this monument was built to honour the former Brazilian President Juscelino Kubitschek, whose tomb is housed here.

Monumental Axis

Light gilds the row of rectangular buildings standing sentry-like along the Esplanade of the Ministries. Each one is home to a different government department. In the distance is the Congress Complex.

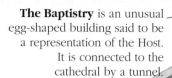

BRASÍLIA CATHEDRAL

The striking yet simplistic form of the cathedral provides Brasília with an instant and recognizable identity. An illusion of space is created in the interior by the circular floor being set below ground level and therefore lower than the entrance.

A PRIESTLY VISION

In 1883 an Italian priest called Dom Bosco had a vision about the future site of Brazil's new capital. Each year on the last Sunday in August, a procession in Brasília celebrates the anniversary of his dream.

The design by Oscar Niemeyer symbolizes a crown of thorns, and consists of 16 40-m (131-ft) high concrete columns which appear as arms reaching to the sky.

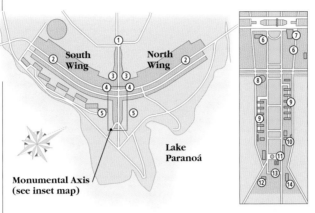

THE PILOT PLAN

Brasília's design, the Pilot Plan, is based on the shape of an aeroplane: the Monumental Axis (the fuselage) intersects with the Residential Axis (the wings). Two main traffic arteries divide the city while the infrastructure is strictly divided into sectors.

Monumental Axis (see inset map)

South Wing

North Wing

Lake Paranoá

KEY

① JK Memorial
② Residential Axis
③ Hotel sectors
④ Commercial sectors
⑤ Embassy sectors
⑥ Cultural sectors
⑦ National Theatre
⑧ Brasília Cathedral
⑨ Esplanade of the Ministries
⑩ Palace of Justice
⑪ Congress Complex
⑫ Supreme Court
⑬ Plaza of the Three Powers
⑭ Planalto Palace

Water is a recurring theme in Brasília. Here it surrounds the cathedral.

KEY DATES

1956 Kubitschek is inaugurated as President of Brazil. A competition is launched for the design of the city.

1957 Construction of the city based on the Pilot Plan begins.

1959 Building work starts on the cathedral.

1960 Brasília is inaugurated on 21 April and becomes the capital city of Brazil.

1987 Brasília is designated a World Heritage Site by UNESCO.

OSCAR NIEMEYER

The vision of Oscar Niemeyer has become synonymous with the rise of modern Brazil. Born in Brazil in 1907, Niemeyer graduated from Rio de Janeiro's National School of Fine Arts in 1934 and collaborated with Lucio Costa and Le Corbusier on the new Ministry of Education and Health in Rio. In 1947 he designed the Brazilian pavilion at the New York World's Fair. His architectural style became more daring as he adapted reinforced concrete into a modern style of architecture. He is probably best known for his designs for the main public buildings in Brasília such as the concave and convex domes of the ▷ *National Congress*, the spectacular ▷ *Palace of Justice* and the simple yet evocative ▷ *Cathedral*. Recognized as a pioneer of modern architecture, he has won numerous prizes for his work.

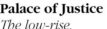

Palace of Justice
The low-rise, unimposing Palace of Justice features water cascading between its delicate white arches. Nearby is a stone sculpture of the head of President Juscelino Kubitschek.

National Congress
The juxtaposition of the dishes and twin towers provides a dramatic, space-age silhouette that is a symbol of the city.

GENERAL INDEX

A

Abd al-Jabbar 184
Abd el-Malik, Caliph 178
Abu Simbel 7, 162–3
Acropolis (Athens) 136–7
Adalbert, St 92
Adams, John 244, 245
Agra 204–5
Akbar the Great, Emperor 206, 207
Albert, Archduke 44
Alexander II, Tsar 96, 97
Alhambra (Granada) 9, 114–15
Amadour, St 66, 67
Amiens Cathedral 48–9
Amritsar 202–3
Anasazi people 250, 251
Androklos 151
Angkor Wat 216–17
Anne, St 230, 231
Antwerp 9, 44–5
Apeldoorn 46–7
Arc de Triomphe (Paris) 9, 56–7
Arnolfo di Cambio 124, 125, 131
Art Deco 239
Ashoka, Emperor 209
Assisi 126–7
Athens 136–7
Attila, József 95
Aubert, St 50, 51
Augustine, St 43
Austerlitz, Battle of (1805) 56
Australia 224–5
Austria 82–5
Aztecs 257

B

Babur, Emperor 204
Bali 220–1
Bangkok 210–13
Bannockburn, Battle of (1314) 22
Barcelona 110–11
Baroque style 81
  Château de Versailles 58–9
  Metropolitan Cathedral (Mexico City) 256
  Royal Castle (Warsaw) 86–7
  Rubens' House (Antwerp) 44–5
  Santiago Cathedral 104–5
  Schönbrunn Palace (Vienna) 84–5
  St Gallen Monastery 80–1
  St Paul's Cathedral (London) 32–3
  Winter Palace (St Petersburg) 96–7
  Würzburg Residence 72–3
Bartholdi, Frédéric-Auguste 242, 243
Basil, St 98
Basilica of Euphrasius (Poreč) 134–5
Basilica of St Francis (Assisi) 126–7
Beaker people 38
Becket, St Thomas 42, 43
Beckett, Samuel 18
Beer, Johann Michael 80
Beijing 192–5
Belgium 44–5
Bentheim, Lüder von 68, 69
Bernini, Gianlorenzo 130
Bilbao 106–7, 236
Bingham, Hiram 258
Book of Kells 18
Borgund Stave Church 12–13
Boston 234–5
Boston Massacre (1770) 235
Bostonian Society 234
Brasilia 9, 260–1
Braun, Matthias 92, 93
Brazil 260–1
Bremen Town Hall 68–9
Bridge of Sighs (Venice) 120
Brokoff family 92, 93
Brunelleschi, Filippo 124, 125
Bryullov, Aleksandr 97
Budapest 94–5
Buddha 198, 208, 209, 218–19
Buddhist style 208
  Borobodur Temple (Java) 218–19

Buddhist architecture (cont.)
  Great Stupa (Sanchi) 208–9
  Todai-ji Temple (Nara) 198–9
  Tosho-gu Shrine (Nikko) 196–7
  Wat Phra Kaeo (Bangkok) 210–11
Bulfinch, Charles 246, 247
Burckhardt, Joann l 162, 183
Byzantine style 149
  Basilica of Euphrasius (Poreč) 134–5
  Dome of the Rock (Jerusalem) 178–9
  Haghia Sophia (Istanbul) 148–9
  St Mark's Basilica (Venice) 116–17

C

Cai Kai, General 189
Cambodia 216–17
Campo dei Miracoli (Pisa) 122–3
Canada 230–3
Canterbury Cathedral 42–3
Cape Town 168–9
Capistrano, Johannes 83
Carrara marble 122
Casablanca 154–5
Cashel, Rock of 20–1
Castelli, Matteo 86
El Castillo pyramid (Chichén Itzá) 252, 253
Castle of Good Hope (Cape Town) 168–9
Cathedral and Baptistry (Florence)124-5
Catherine de' Medici 62, 63
Catherine II the Great, Empress of Russia 87, 96, 97
Cellini, Benvenuto 112, 113
Chaco Culture National Historical Park 250–1
Chakri dynasty 212
Chalgrin, Jean 56, 57
Charlemagne, Emperor 68
Charles Bridge (Prague) 92–3
Charles IV, Emperor 92, 93
Charles V, Emperor 112, 113
Chartres Cathedral 60–1
Château de Chenonceau 62–3
Château de Versailles 58–9
Chaucer, Geoffrey 42
Cheikou Amadou, King of Djenné 166, 167
Chichén Itzá 252–3
China 188–95
Christ 174–5
Christodoulos, Blessed 140, 141
Chrysler, Walter 238
Chulalongkorn, King of Thailand 212
Church of the Holy Sepulchre (Jerusalem) 174–5
Classical style 137
  Acropolis (Athens) 136–7
  Colosseum (Rome) 128–9
  Dome of the Rock (Jerusalem) 178–9
  Ephesus 150–1
  Leptis Magna 158–9
  Metropolitan Cathedral (Mexico City) 256–7
  Petra 182–3
  Pompeii 132–3
  see also Neo-Classical style
CN Tower (Toronto) 232–3
Cologne Cathedral 8, 70–1
Colosseum (Rome) 128–9
Conquistadors 256, 257
Constantine I, Emperor 130, 131, 149, 174, 175
Constantine Monomachus, Emperor 174
Cormac MacCarthy, King of Munster 20, 21
Cormont, Thomas de 49
Costa, Lucio 260, 261
Cranmer, Thomas, Archbishop of Canterbury 42
Crawford, Thomas 246
Croatia 134–5
Crusaders 172–3
Curzon, Lord 206, 207
Czech Republic 88–93

D

Dalai Lama 186–7
De L'Orme, Philibert 63
Diane de Poitiers 62, 63

Djenné Mosque (Mali) 166–7
Doge's Palace (Venice) 120–1
Dome of the Rock (Jerusalem) 178–9
Douglas, Earl of 23
Druids 38, 39
Dublin 18–19
Dunedin Railway Station 226–7
Dutch East India Company 168, 169

E

Edinburgh Castle 24–5
Edward, The Black Prince 43
Edward I, King of England 22, 23, 173
Edward IV, King of England 34, 35
Egypt 160–5
Elgin Marbles 137
Elizabeth, Tsarina 96, 97
Elizabeth I, Queen of England 18, 30, 34
Elizabeth II, Queen of England 22, 30, 31
Ellis, Charles 249
Empire State Building (New York) 238–9
Ephesus 150–1
Eschwege, Baron von 102
Euphrasius, Bishop 135

F

Fatehpur Sikri 206–7
Fehr, Dr William 168
Felipe II, King of Spain 112–13
Ferenc Rákoczi II, Prince 95
Firmin, St 49
Fischer von Erlach, J B 84
Florence 7, 124–5
Forbidden City (Beijing) 192–3, 194
France 48–67
Francis, St 126, 127
François I, King of France 63
François II, King of France 55, 63
Franz Joseph I, Emperor 85

G

Gall, St 81
Gamelan orchestras 220
Gaudí, Antoni 110, 111
Gehry, Frank O 106, 236
Germany 68–79
Ghiberti, Lorenzo 124, 125
Giotto 124, 125, 126, 127, 131
Giza 7, 9, 160–1
Gobind Singh, Guru 203
Golden Gate Bridge (San Francisco) 8, 248–9
Golden Temple (Amritsar) 202–3
Gothic style 55
  Amiens Cathedral 48–9
  Basilica of St Francis Assisi 126–7
  Borgund Stave Church 12–13
  Bremen Town Hall 68–9
  Canterbury Cathedral 42–3
  Charles Bridge (Prague) 92–3
  Chartres Cathedral 60–1
  Cologne Cathedral 70–1
  Doge's Palace (Venice) 120–1
  Heidelberg Castle 74–5
  Krak des Chevaliers 172–3
  Mont-St-Michel 50–1
  Notre-Dame (Paris) 54–5
  Old-New Synagogue (Prague) 88–9
  Palace of Pena (Sintra) 102–3
  Parliament (Budapest) 94–5
  Sagrada Familia (Barcelona) 110–11
  St Stephen's Cathedral (Vienna) 82–3
  Westminster Abbey (London) 30–1
  York Minster 28–9
Granada 9, 114–15
Grand Palace (Bangkok) 210–11
Great Britain 22–43
Great Mosque (Kairouan) 156–7
Great Pyramid (Giza) 7, 9, 160–1
Great Stupa (Sanchi) 208–9
Great Wall of China 9, 188–9
Greece 136–43
Greek Orthodox Church 140–1
Guggenheim, Solomon 236, 237
Guggenheim Museum (Bilbao) 9, 106–7, 236

Guggenheim Museum (New York) 9, 236–7
Gustav II Adolf, King of Sweden 14, 15

H

Habsburg dynasty 82, 84
Haghia Sophia (Istanbul) 148–9
Hampton Court Palace 36–7
Hancock, John 234, 235
Haram ash-Sharif (Jerusalem) 178
Hassan II, King of Morocco 154
Heidelberg Castle 74–5
Helena, St 174, 175
Henri II, King of France 62, 63
Henry II, King of England 42, 66
Henry VI, King of England 30, 34, 35
Henry VII, King of England 30
Henry VIII, King of England 31, 34, 35, 36, 37, 42, 43
Herod the Great 180, 181
Herrera, Juan de 112, 113
Het Loo Palace (Apeldoorn) 46–7
Hinduism
  deities 213, 221
  symbolism 219
Hoban, James 244, 245
Hugo, Victor 54
Hungary 94–5

I

Ieyasu, Tokugawa 196, 197
Incas 258–9
India 202–9
Indonesia 218–21
Ireland 16–21
Isabella, Infanta 44
Islam 155
  Djenné Mosque (Mali) 166–7
  Dome of the Rock (Jerusalem) 178–9
  Great Mosque (Kairouan) 156–7
  Mosque of Hassan II (Casablanca) 154–5
Israel 174–81
Istanbul 144–9
Italy 116–33
Ivan the Terrible, Tsar 98, 99

J

James IV, King of Scotland 22, 23
James the Great, St 104, 105
Jank, Christian 76, 77
Japan 196–201
Java 218–19
Jayavarman VII, King of Angkor 216
Jerusalem 174–9
John Nepomuk, St 93
John the Divine, St 140
Jordan 182–3
Josef II, Emperor 88
Justinian, Emperor 159

K

Kairouan 156–7
Károlyi, Mihály 95
Khmer architecture 212
  Angkor Wat 216–17
  Wat Arun (Bangkok) 212–13
Khufu, Pharaoh 160, 161
Kiwas (pithouses) 250
Knights of St John (Knights Hospitallers) 142, 143, 172, 173
Koi Konboro, King of Djenné 166
Koran 178
Kos 142
Kossuth, Lajos 95
Krak des Chevaliers 172–3
Kubitschek de Oliveira, Juscelino 260, 261

L

Latrobe, Benjamin 246
Lawrence, St 112, 113
Le Brun, Charles 58, 59
Le Nôtre, André 58
Le Vau, Louis 58, 59
Leaning Tower of Pisa 122–3
Leptis Magna 158–9
Lhasa 186–7

Libya 158–9
Lincoln, Abraham 244, 245
London 42–7
Louis-Philippe, King of France 58, 59
Louis XIV, King of France 58–9
Louis XV, King of France 58
Louis XVI, King of France 58, 59
Löw, Rabbi 88, 89
Ludwig II, King of Bavaria 9, 76
Luzarches, Robert de 49
Lysimachus 150, 151

M

Machu Picchu 8, 258–9
McKim, Mead and White 244, 245
Mali 166–7
Mansart, Jules Hardouin 58, 59
Maria II, Queen of Portugal 102, 103
Maria Theresa, Empress 84, 85
Marie-Antoinette, Queen 59, 84
Mark, St 116, 117
Marot, Daniel 46, 47
Martini, Simone 126, 127
Mary, Virgin 150
Mary II, Queen of England 36, 46, 47
Mary Stuart 25, 55, 63
Masada 180–1
Mateo, Maestro 104, 105
Maurus, St 134
Maya 252–3
Mehmet II, Sultan 244, 245
Mesa Verde 250
Metropolitan Cathedral (Mexico City) 256–7
Mexico 252–7
Mexico City 256–7
Michelangelo 122, 124, 130, 131, 230, 231
Ming dynasty 188, 194–5
Modern architecture 261
Modernisme 110
    Sagrada Familia (Barcelona) 110–11
Mohammed, The Prophet 145, 155, 178, 179
Monastery of St John (Pátmos) 140–1
Mont-St-Michel 50–1
Moorish style 115
    Alhambra (Granada) 114–15
Morocco 154–5
Morrow, Irving 249
Mosaics, Byzantine 135
Moscow 164–5
Mosque of Hassan II (Casablanca) 154–5
Mouhot, Henri 217
Mughal style 204
    Fatehpur Sikri 206–7
    Taj Mahal (Agra) 204–5
Mumtaz Mahal 204, 205
Murat III, Sultan 144, 145, 149
Muslim beliefs and practices 155 see also Islam

N

Nabataeans 182, 183
Nanak, Guru 203
Napoleon I, Emperor 55, 56–7, 99, 116, 120
Nara 198–9
Nasrid dynasty 114, 115
Nefertari 154, 162, 163
Neo-Classical style 57
    Arc de Triomphe (Paris) 56–7
    Metropolitan Cathedral (Mexico City) 256–7
    United States Capitol (Washington DC) 246–7
    White House (Washington DC) 244–5
    see also Classical style
The Netherlands 46–7
Neumann, Balthasar 72, 73
Neuschwanstein Castle 9, 76–7
New York City 9, 236–43
New Zealand 226–7
Newgrange 16–17
Nicholas II, Tsar 97
Niemeyer, Oscar 260, 261

Norway 12–13
Notre-Dame (Paris) 54–5

O

Olav the Holy, King of Norway 13
Old-New Synagogue (Prague) 88–9
Old State House (Boston) 234–5
Orange-Nassau, House of 46
Oswald, King of Northumbria 28

P

Pacassi, Nikolaus 84, 85
Pachacuti Inca Yupanqui 258
Paine, Clifford 249
Palace of Pena (Sintra) 102–3
Palace of the Grand Masters (Rhodes) 142–3
Paradise Garden 204
Paris 9, 54–9
Parliament (Budapest) 9, 94–5
Parthenon (Athens) 136, 137
Pátmos 140–1
Patrick, St 20, 21
Peretti, Antonia Marianne 260
Perikles 136, 137
Peru 258–9
Peter, St 130, 131
Peter I the Great, Tsar 96
Petra 182–3
Pilgram, Anton 82, 83
Pinseau, Michel 154
Pisa 122–3
Pisano, Giovanni 122, 123
Pisano, Nicola 204
Poland 86–7
Pompeii 132–3
Poniatowski, Stanislaw August, King of Poland 87
Poreč 134–5
Portugal 102–3
Potala Palace (Lhasa) 186–7
Poulenc, Francis 67
Prague 88–93
Puebloan civilization 250–1
Pugin, A W 94
Pura Ulun Danu Batur (Bali) 220–1
Puyi, Emperor of China 192, 193
Pyramids 160–1

Q

Quetzalcoatl 252, 253

R

Rama, Kings of Thailand 210, 211, 212, 213
Ramakien 210
Ramayana 216
Ramses II, Pharaoh 9, 154, 162, 163
Raskob, John Jakob 238
Rastrelli, Bartolomeo 96
Ravy, Jean 54, 55
Red Palace (Lhasa) 186
Reformation 42
The Registan (Samarkand) 184–5
Renaissance style 131
    Bremen Town Hall 68–9
    Cathedral and Baptistry (Florence) 124–5
    Château de Chenonceau 62–3
    Dunedin Railway Station 226–7
    Heidelberg Castle 74–5
    Palace of Pena (Sintra) 102–3
    Parliament (Budapest) 94–5
    Rubens' House (Antwerp) 44–5
    St Peter's (Rome) 130–1
    Stirling Castle 22–3
Rhodes 142–3
Riebeeck, Jan van 168, 169
Robert the Bruce 22, 23
Rocamadour 66–7
Rock of Cashel 20–1
Rococo style 72
    Neuschwanstein Castle 76–7
    Schönbrunn Palace (Vienna) 84–5
    St Gallen Monastery 80–1
    Würzburg Residence 72–3
Rodondo, Giacomo 86
Roland 68

Roman, Jacob 46
Romanesque style 122
    Campo dei Miracoli (Pisa) 122–3
    Chartres Cathedral 60–1
    Cormac's Chapel, Rock of Cashel 20–1
    Mont-St-Michel 50–1
    Rocamadour 66–7
    St Stephen's Cathedral (Vienna) 82–3
    Pórtico da Gloria (Santiago Cathedral) 105
Romans 122
    Colosseum (Rome) 128–9
    Ephesus 150–1
    Leptis Magna 158–9
    Masada 180–1
    Pompeii 132–3
Romanticism 74, 103
Rome 128–31
Roosevelt, Theodore 244, 245
Rubens, Pieter Paul 44–5, 97
Rubens' House (Antwerp) 9, 44–5
Rudolf the Founder, Duke 82
Ruprecht III, Elector Palatine 74, 75
Russia 96–101

S

Sagrada Família (Barcelona) 110–11
Sailendra dynasty 218
Sainte-Anne-de-Beaupré 230–1
St Basil's Cathedral (Moscow) 7, 98–9
St Gallen Monastery 80–1
St Mark's Basilica (Venice) 116–17
St Paul's Cathedral (London) 32–3
St Peter's (Rome) 9, 130–1
St Petersburg 8, 96–7
St Stephen's Cathedral (Vienna) 82–3
Samarkand 184–5
San Francisco 8, 248–9
Sanchi 208–9
Santiago Cathedral 104–5
Saxe-Coburg-Gotha, Ferdinand of 102, 103
Schönbrunn Palace (Vienna) 84–5
Scotland 22–5
Second World War 88
Severus, Septimius, Emperor 158, 159
Shah Jahan, Emperor 204, 205
Shintoism 196, 199
Shomyo, Emperor 198
Shreve, Lamb & Harmon 238
Sikhism 202, 203
Sintra 102–3
Solomon R Guggenheim Museum (New York) 236–7
Songtsen Gampo 187
South Africa 168–9
Spain 104–15
Sphinx (Giza) 160, 161
Statue of Liberty (New York) 9, 242–3
Steindl, Imre 94, 95
Stephen I, St, King of Hungary 94
Stirling Castle 22–3
Stockholm 14–15
Stone of Destiny 24, 25, 31
Stonehenge 38–9
Strauss, Joseph B 248, 249
Subirachs, Josep Maria 110
Suryavarman II, King 216
Sweden 14–15
Switzerland 80–1
Sydney Opera House 9, 224–5
Synagogues 89
Syria 172–3

T

Taj Mahal (Agra) 6, 8, 9, 204–5
Taksin, King 212, 213
Tamerlane 184, 185
Tancred, Prince of Antioch 173
Tansen 206, 207
Tara (Ireland) 16
Temple of Heaven (Beijing) 194–5
Thailand 210–15
Thumb, Peter 80
Tibaldi, Pellegrino 112, 113
Tibet 186–7
Tiepolo, Giovanni Battista 72, 73

Todai-ji Temple (Nara) 7, 198–9
Toledo, Juan Bautista de 113
Topkapi Palace (Istanbul) 144–5
Toronto 232–3
Tosho-gu Shrine (Nikko) 196–7
Tourism 8
Tower of London 34–5
Trevano, Giovanni 86
Trinity College (Dublin) 18–19
Troup, Sir George 226, 227
Truman, Harry S 244, 245
Tunisia 156–7
Turkey 144–51

U

Unesco World Heritage Sites 7–8
United States Capitol (Washington DC) 246–7
United States of America 234–51
Uqba ibn Nafi 156, 157
Utzon, Jørn 224, 225
Uzbekistan 184–5

V

Vasa Museum (Stockholm) 14–15
Vauban, Sébastien Le Prestre de 169
Velten, Yuriy 96, 97
Venice 116–21
Versailles, Château de 58–9
Vespasian, Emperor 128, 129
Vesuvius, Mount 132, 133
Victoria, Queen 34, 244
Vienna 82–5
Vikings 13
Villa of the Mysteries (Pompeii) 132
Villar i Lozano, Francesc de Paula 111
Villaret, Foulkes de 143
Viollet-le-Duc, E E 48, 49, 55

W

Wagner, Richard 77
Wallace, William 22, 23
Walter, Thomas U 246
War of 1812 244
Warsaw 86–7
Washington, George 244, 245, 246
Washington DC 244–7
Wat Arun (Bangkok) 212–13
Wat Phra Kaeo (Bangkok) 210–11
Wencheng, Princess 186, 187
Weser Renaissance architecture 68
Westminster Abbey (London) 30–1
White House (Washington DC) 244–5
Wilhelmina, Queen of the Netherlands 47
William III, King of England 36, 46, 47
William of Sens 42
William the Conqueror, King 34, 35
Winter Palace (St Petersburg) 8, 96–7
Wolsey, Cardinal Thomas 36, 37
Wren, Sir Christopher 32–3, 36, 37
Wright, Frank Lloyd 236, 237
Würzburg Residence 72–3

Y

Yakovlev, Postnik 98
Yongle, Emperor of China 195
York Minster 28–9
Yuan Shikai, General 195

Z

Zealots 180
Zygmunt III Vasa, King of Poland 86

ACKNOWLEDGMENTS

The Publishers would like to thank the following people whose contributions and assistance have made the preparation of this book possible:

Additional Contributors: Jane Egginton, Frances Linzee Gordon, Denise Heywood, Andrew Humphries, Roger Williams.

Editorial Assistance: Peter Bently, Stephanie Driver, Jane Hutchings, Jacky Jackson, Jane Hutchings, Marianne Petrou, Mary Sutherland, Karen Villabona, Fiona Wild.

Illustrators: Richard Almazan, Studios Arcana, Modi Artistici, Robert Ashby, William Band, Gilles Beauchemin, Dipankar Bhattacarga, Anuar Bin Abdul Rahim, Richard Bonson, François Brosse, Michal Burkiewicz, Cabezas/Acanto Arquitectura y Urbanismo S.L., Jo Cameron, Danny Cherian, Yeapkok Chien, ChrisOrr.com, Stephen Conlin, Garry Cross, Bruno de Robillard, Brian Delf, Donati Giudici Associati srl, Richard Draper, Dean Entwhistle, Steven Felmore, Marta Fincato, Eugene Fleury, Chris Forsey, Martin Gagnon, Vincent Gagnon, Nick Gibbard, Isidoro González-Adalid, Kevin Goold, Paul Guest, Stephen Gyapay, Toni Hargreaves, Trevor Hill, Chang Huai-Yan, Roger Hutchins, Kamalahasan R, Kevin Jones Assocs., John Lawrence, Wai Leong Koon, Yoke Ling Lee, Nick Lipscombe, Ian Lusted, Andrew MacDonald, Maltings Partnership, Lena Maminajszwili, Kumar Mantoo Stuart, Pawel Marczak, Lee Ming Poo, Pawel Mistewicz, John Mullaney, Jill Mumford, Gillie Newman, Luc Normandin, Arun P, Lee Peters, Otakar Pok, Robbie Polley, David Pulvermacher, Avinash Ramscurrun, Kevin Robinson, Peter Ross, Simon Roulstone, Suman Saha, Fook San Choong, Ajay Sethi, Derrick Slone, Jaroslav Stanêk, Thomas Sui, Ashok Sukumaran, Peggy Tan, Pat Thorne, Gautam Trivedi, Frank Urban, Mark Warner, Paul Weston, Andrzej Wielgosz, Ann Winterbotham, Martin Woodward, Bohdan Wróblewski, Hong Yew Tan, Kah Yune Denis Chai, Magdalena Zmadzinska, Piotr Zubrzycki.

Proofreader and Researcher: Stewart J Wild.

Indexers: Hilary Bird, Jane Henley.

Special Assistance
Maire ní Bhain at Trinity College, Dublin; Chartres Cathedral, Procurate di San Marco (Basilica San Marco); Campo Dei Miracoli, Pisa; Hayley Smith and Romaine Werblow from DK Picture Library; Mrs Marjorie Weeke at St. Peter's; Le Soprintendenze Archeologiche di Agrigento di Pompei; Topkapi Palace, Istanbul; M. Oulhaj (Mosque of Hassan II); The Castle of Good Hope.

Additional Photography
Shaen Adey, Max Alexander, Fredrik & Laurence Arvidsson, Gábor Barka, Philip Blenkinsop, Maciej Bronarski, Demetrio Carrasco, Tina Chambers, Joe Cornish, Andy Crawford, Ian Cumming, Tim Daly, Geoff Dann, Robert O'Dea, Barbara Deer, Vladimír Dobrovodský, Jiři Doležal, Alistair Duncan, Heidi Grassley, Paul Harris, Adam Hajder, John Heseltine, Nigel Hicks, Ed Ironside, Stuart Isett, Dorota & Mariusz Jarymowicz, Alan Keohane, Dinesh Khanna, Dave King, Paul Kenward, Andrew McKinney, Jiří Kopřiva, Neil Lukas, Paweł Marczac, Eric Meacher, Wojciech Mędrzak, Michael Moran, Roger Moss, Tomasz Myśluk, Stephen Oliver, Vincent Oliver, Lloyd Park, John Parker, Amit Pasricha, Aditya Patankar, Artur Pawłowski, František **Přeučil**, Ram Rahman, Bharath Ramamrutham, Rob Reichenfeld, Magnes Rew, Lucio Rossi, Jean-Michel Ruiz, Kim Sayer, Jürgen Scheunemann, Colin Sinclair, Toby Sinclair, Frits Solvang, Tony Souter, Jon Spaull, Eric Svensson, Cécile Tréal, Lübbe Verlag, BPS Walia, Mathew Ward, Richard Watson, Stephen Whitehorn, Linda Whitwam, Jeppe Wikström, Alan Williams, Peter Wilson, **Paweł Wójcik**, Stephen Wooster, Francesca Yorke.

Photography Permissions
Dorling Kindersley would like to thank all the churches, temples, mosques, castles, museums, and other sights too numerous to list individually for their assistance and kind permission to photograph their establishments.

Picture Credits
t=top; tl=top left; tlc=top left centre; tc=top centre; trc=top right centre; tr=top right; cla=centre left above; ca=centre above; cra=centre right above; cl=centre left; c=centre; cr=centre right; clb=centre left below; cb=centre below; crb=centre right below; bl=bottom left; b=bottom; bc=bottom centre; bcl=bottom centre left; bcr=bottom centre right; br=bottom right; d=detail.

Every effort has been made to trace the copyright holders and we apologize in advance for any unintentional omissions. We would be pleased to insert the appropriate acknowledgments in any subsequent edition of this publication.

Dorling Kindersley would like to thank the following for their assistance: National Archaeological Museum, Naples: 133bcr; © Patrimonio Nacional 112-3; Private Collection 28bl, 36cl, 44clb, 48tl, 54tl, 58cl, 88cl, 126tl, 130tl, 168bl, 208bl; Etablissement public du musée et du domaine nationale de Versailles 58tl/58tr/58b/59t/ 59cra/59cla/59b.

Works of art have been reproduced with the permission of the following copyright holders: *Paris through the Window* (1913), Marc Chagall © ADAGP, Paris, 2003 236c; *Black Lines* (1913) Vasily Kandinsky © ADAGP, Paris, 2003 237crb; *Woman Holding a Vase* (1927), Fernand Léger © ADAGP, Paris, 2003 237cra; *Woman Ironing* (1904) Pablo Picasso © Succession Picasso/DACS 2004 236clb; *Woman with Yellow Hair* (1931) Pablo Picasso © Succession Picasso/DACS 2004 237bl; *The Snake* (1996) Richard Serra © ARS, NY and DACS London 2004 106br.

The Publishers thank the following individuals, companies, and picture libraries for permission to reproduce their photographs:

A1 Pix: Mati 184cb.

Accademia Italiana: Sue Bond 133c.

Archivo Iconografico S.A. (AISA) : 145bl.

AKG: 88c, 89crb, 173t, 174cla.

Alamy Images: Walter Bibikow 118 -9; Robert Harding World Imagery 185c; Dallas and John Heaton 176-7; David Jones 166-7; Steve Murray 254-5.

Ancient Art & Architecture Collection: 160br.

Arcaid: Paul Rafferty 106bcl.

Archivio dell'Arte: Luciano Pedicini 132cl.

Fabrizio Ardito: 182tr.

The Art Archive: 163cra; Devizes Musem/Eileen Tweedy 39c.

Art Directors: Eric Smith 185t.

Austrian Tourist Board: 85bc.

Axiom: Heidi Grassley 163bcl; James Morris 163tc.

Tahsin Aydogmus: 148tr.

Osvaldo Böhm:117tc.

Bord Fáilte/Irish Tourist Board: Brian Lynch 16tc, 16tr.

Gerard Boullay: 55bl; 55cra.

Brazil Stock Photos: Fabio Pili 260tr.

Bridgeman Art Library, London/New York: Private Collection 42bc; Royal Holloway & Bedford New College, *The Princes Edward and Richard in the Tower* by Sir John Everett Millais 35bc; Basilica San Francesco, Assisi 215br; Smith Art Gallery and Museum, Stirling 22bc; Stapleton Collection 160cb, 162tr.

Camera Press: Cecil Beaton 30clb.

Demetrio Carrasco: 97cra, 97bc.

Chinapix: Zhang Chaoyin 186c, 186b.

Photos Editions Combier, Macon: 49tc.

Corbis: Archivo Iconografico, S.A. 210b; Yann Arthus-Bertrand 260cr; Bettmann Archive 22cl, 238bl, 239cl, 242c; Dave Bartruff 69c, 151tc; Marilyn Bridges 38c; Chromo Sohm Inc./Jospeh Sohm 188b; Elio Ciol 4br, 173cra; Dean Conger 192cr; Eye Ubiquitous/Thelma Sanders 167b; Owen Franken 64-5; Todd Gipstein 243t; Lowell Georgia 192cr; Farrell Grehan 90 -1; John and Dallas Heaton 9b, 9t; John Heseltine 52-3, Angelo Hornak 35tl, 42tr; Wolfgang Kaehler 166tl, 185bl; Kelly-Mooney Photography 195t; Charles Lenars 188cl; Craig Lovell 187br; David Samuel Robbins 187tl; Galen Rowell 6; Sakamoto Photo Research Lab 199ca; Kevin Schafer 39b; James Sparshatt 1; Paul A Souders 5c; Sandro Vannini 167c; Vanni Archive 140tl; Nik Wheeler 166c; Adam Woolfitt 146-7;

Corbis Sygma: Thierry Prat 66c.

Crescent Press Agency: David Henley 211ca.

Gerald Cubitt: 211tl.

Culver Pictures Inc.: 239cr, 242cb, 243cra, 243crb.

Das Fotoarchiv: Henning Christoph 166tr.

Deutsche Apothekenmuseum: 74tr.

Diatotale: Château de Chenonceau 62tr.

Ashok Dilwali: 206tc.

Dombauverwaltung des Metropolitankapitels Köln: Brigit Lambert 70tc, 70c, 70bc, 71tl, 71cra, 71cb, 71bc, 71bl.

D.N. Dube: 204ca, 205cr, 206tr, 207tl.

Ekdotike Athenon S.A.: 140bc, 143b.

Mary Evans Picture Library: 38bl, 42ca, 56br, 103bc, 128bc.

Eye Ubiquitous: Julia Waterlow 260b.

Fortidsminneforeningen: Kjersheim/Lindstad, NIKU 13b.

Michael Freeman: 246bc, 247tl.

Christina Gambaro: 175bc.

Gehry Partners LLP: 106tl.

Eva Gerum: 72c, 73tl, 73cra, 73c, 73bc, 75tr, 76cla, 76clb, 76bc.

Getty Images: Altrendo Images 138-9; Robert Harding World Imagery/Gavin Heller 214-5; Hulton-Deutsch 18bc, 193b; Image Bank /Anthony Edwards 40-1, Mitchell Funk 240-1; /Peter Hendrie 210tr, Frans Lemmens 170-1, /A. Setterwhite 243bc; National Geographic/Raymond K Gehman 190-1; Photodisc/Life File/david Kampfner 100-1; Photographer's Choice/John Warden 189t; Stone/Jerry Alexander 259cb, /Stephen Studd 152 -3; Taxi/Gary Randall 228-9, /Chris Rawlings 10–1, 222-3.

Eva Gleason: 256tr, 256tc, 256bc, 256br, 257bc.

La Goélette: *The Three Graces* Charles-André Van Loo photo JJ Derennes 62br.

Golden Gate Bridge, Highway & Transportation District (GGBHTD): 248tc, 248-9tc, 248br, 249clb, 249cra, 248cl.

Golden Gate National Recreational Area: 249bl, 249c.

Guggenheim Bilbao Museo: 106tr, 106br, 107tc, 107bc.

Sonia Halliday: Laura Lushington 61ca.

Robert Harding Picture Library: 67cr, 131bc, R.Francis 54clb; R. Frerck 259b; Sylvain Grandadam 260cl; Michael Jenner 145bc; Christopher Rennie 200-1; Eitan Simanor 173bc; James Strachan 184ca; Explorer/P. Tetrel 59crb.

Denise Heywood: 216cl, 216cr, 216b, 216t, 217tl, 217tr, 217b, 218tl, 218car, 218cl, 218cbr, 219tr, 219bl, 219br.

Juliet Highet: 219tl.

Historic Royal Palaces (Crown Copyright): 36tc, 36tr, 36c, 36bc, 37bc, 37tl, 37ca, 37cb.

Historic Scotland (Crown Copyright): 23cra, 24tr, 24c, 25bl.

Angelo Hornak Library: 28tlc, 28bc.

Images of Africa: Shaen Adey 168cb; Hein von Horsten 168ca; Lanz von Horsten 169tl.

Imaginechina: 193cr, 195c.

Impact Photos: Y Goldstein 184tl.

Insight Guides: APA/Jim Holmes 157tl.

Hanan Isachar: 151bc, 174clb, 175cra, 180tr.

Israel Museum: 181c

Paul Jackson: 183br.

Jarrold Colour Publications: 18br.

Michael Jenner Photography: 172ca.

Kea Publishing Services Ltd.: Francesco Venturi 96cla, 96bc, 96br.

Kostos Kontos: 140cla.

Kunsthistorisches Museum, Vienna: *Italienische Berglandschaft mit Hirt und Herde* (GG 7465) (Italian Landscape with Shepherd and Herd), Joseph Rosa 85cra.

Bernd Lasdin: 68cla, 68c, 68cra.

Håkon Li: 12c, 12bc, 13c.

Jürgen Liepe: 160tc.

Lübbe Verlag: 84tl.

Magnum: Topkapı Palace Museum/Ara Guler 145tl.

National Park Service (Chaco Culture National Historical Park): Dave Six 250tc.

National Park Service (Statue of Liberty National Monument): 242cl, 243clb.

Jürgen Nogai: 68tr, 68bc.

Norwegian Tourist Board: Per Eide 12tl.

Richard Nowitz: 174bc, 175tc, 175cr, 179cr, 180br, 181bl, 181bc, 183bl.

© The Office of Public Works, Ireland: 16c, 17tl, 17c.

Orleta Agency: Jerzy Bronarski 86ca, 86cb, 87c, 87bl, 87br.

Paleis Het Loo: 46tr, 46ca, 46cb, 46bc, 47tl.

Panos Pictures: Christien Jaspars 167t.

Photos 12: Panorama Stock 188cr.

Photobank: Peter Baker 150c, 150bc.

Andrea Pistolesi: 246c.

Powerstock: Superstock 78 -9.

Prague City Archives (Archiv Hlavniko Mesta Praha): 92cr.

Rocamadour: 67ca.

The Royal Collection © 2004, Her Majesty Queen Elizabeth II:34br, 34bc, 35tl, 36br.

Royal Geographical Society Picture Library: Chris Caldicott 166b, 258tl; Eric Lawrie 5t, 259t; Sassoom 258cb.

Shalini Saran: 208tr, 208cla, 208clb, 209tl, 209crb, 209bl.

Scala Group SpA: 122bc, 123tc, 124cla, 126ca, 126cb, 127bl, 129b, 130br, 131tl

Schloss Schönbrunn: 84tr, 84ca, 84c, 84bc, 85tc.

Shrine of Sainte-Anne-de Beaupré: 230tl, 230tr, 231cb, 231ca, 231b.

Skyscan: 39t.

Solomon R Guggenheim Museum: photo by D Heald 236c, 236bcl, 236bc, 237tc, 237ca, 237crb, 237bl.

South American Pictures: Tony Morrison 261br.

State Russian Museum: 96bl.

Superstock Ltd.: 212ca.

Sydney Opera House Trust: 224tr, 224ca, 225bc, 225bl, 225tc.

Suzie Thomas Publicity: 224bc.

Travel Ink: Allan Hatley 213tc; Pauline Thorton 212cb.

Trizechahn Tower Limited Partnership: 232c, 233bl, 2337tl.

Trinity College, Dublin: 19cr.

Turner Entertainment Co.: 239bc

University Museum of Cultural Heritage - University of Oslo, Norway: 13t.

Vasamuseet: Hans Hammarskiöld 14tr, 14cla, 14clb, 14br, 15tc, 15cra, 15crb, 15bc.

Mireille Vautier: 258ca, 259ca, 261bl.

Roger Viollet: 57tl.

Visions of the Land: Garo Nalbandian 182bc, 182cla; Basilio Rodella 174tr, 180cl, 180bc, 181tl, 181cra.

B.P.S. Walia: 202tc, 202tr, 202cla, 202cra, 202br, 203tl, 203ca, 203clb.

Reproduced by kind permission of the Dean & Chapter, Westminster: 31bl.

White House Historical Association: 244cla, 244bc, 245tl, 245c, 245bl, 245bc.

Peter Wilson: 136ca.

Woodmansterne: Jeremy Marks 32tr, 33ca.

World Pictures: 185br.

Reproduced by kind permission of the Dean and Chapter of York: Alan Curtis 29tr; Jim Korshaw 28tr; Newbury Smith Photography 28c.

ZEFA: age fotostock 108-9; Masterfile/Gail Mooney 10-1.

Front Jacket: Alamy Images: Geoff du Feu (main); Corbis: Phil Schermeister tl; Getty Images: Stone/Dale Boyer clb; Taxi VCL cla.

Back Jacket: Alamy Images: Christopher Wyatt br; Corbis: Tibor Bognar cr; Aaron Horowitz cra; John and Lisa Merrill crb; Getty Images: Stone/Gary Yeowell tr.

Spine: Corbis: Royalty Free

All other images © Dorling Kindersley. For further information see: www.dkimages.com

The World's Must-see Places

USA
(ALASKA)

Greenland
(to Denmark)

Baffin Island

ICELAND
Reykjavik

See Europe Map on

REPUBLIC OF IRELAND
UNITED KINGDOM
London
NET

Paris

FRANCE

SPAIN
PORTUGAL
Madrid
Algiers
Kai

Rabat
Casablanca
Mosque of Hassan II ▲ ● Marrakech

MOROCCO
ALGER

C A N A D A

Vancouver ●

Winnipeg ●

Seattle ●

Sainte-Anne-de-Beaupré ▲
CN Tower ▲ Montréal ●
● Ottawa

Toronto ●
UNITED STATES
OF AMERICA
Chicago ●

Boston ●
New York
● Old State House

Golden Gate Bridge ▲

Denver ●

Washington DC ●

▲ The White House
▲ United States
Capitol

▲ Solomon R Guggenheim Museum
▲ Empire State Building
▲ Statue of Liberty

San Francisco ●

Los Angeles ●

▲ Chaco Culture
National Historical Park

Atlanta ●

Bermuda

Houston ●

*Guadelupe
(to Mexico)*

Monterrey ●

Miami ●
BAHAMAS

WESTERN
SAHARA

MAURITANIA

MALI

M E X I C O

Havana ●

Chichén Itzá ▲

CUBA
● Santiago de Cuba

*Hawaii
(to US)*

Mexico City ●
Metropolitan Cathedral ▲

JAMAICA HAITI DOM. REP.

*A T L A N T I C
O C E A N*

SENEGAL
Dakar ●
GAMBIA
GUINEA-BISSAU

● Djenné Mosc
● Bamako
BURKINA
FASO
GUINEA

Tegucigalpa ●
HONDURAS

*West
Indies*

CÔTE
D'IVOIRE

SIERRA LEONE

GUATEMALA
EL SALVADOR
NICARAGUA
COSTA RICA
PANAMA

Panama
City ●
VENEZUELA

● Caracas

Monrovia ●
LIBERIA GHANA
TOGO
BEN

P A C I F I C

Bogota ●
COLOMBIA

GUYANA SURINAME
FRENCH
GUIANA

EQUATORIA
GUINE

O C E A N

*Galapagos Islands
(to Ecuador)*

Quito ●
ECUADOR

*French Polynesia
(to France)*

PERU

B R A Z I L

*Ascension Island
(to UK)*

Lima ●

Machu Picchu ▲

*Pitcairn Islands
(to UK)*

*San Felix Island
(to Chile)*

● La Paz
BOLIVIA

▲ Brasília

*St Helena
(to UK)*

Rio de Janeiro ●

*Easter Island
(to Chile)*

*Sala y Gomez
(to Chile)*

PARAGUAY

São Paulo ●

CHILE

Asunción ●

A T L A N T I C

Santiago ●
● Córdoba

*Juan Fernandez Island
(to Chile)*

Buenos Aires ●
URUGUAY
● Montevideo

O C E A N

*Tristan da Cunha
(to UK)*

ARGENTINA

P A C I F I C

O C E A N

*Falkland Islands
(to UK)*

*South Georgia &
South Sandwich Islands
(to UK)*

KEY

- Europe *see pp10–151*
- Africa *see pp152–169*
- Asia *see pp170–221*
- Australasia *see pp222–227*
- North, Central and
  South America *see pp228–261*
- ▲ Must-see Place